Reconsidering The Role of P
Childhood

Reconsidering The Role of Play in Early Childhood: Towards Social Justice and Equity—a compilation of current play research in early childhood education and care—challenges, disrupts, and reexamines conventional perspectives on play. By highlighting powerful and provocative studies from around the world that attend to the complexities and diverse contexts of children's play, the issues of social justice and equity related to play are made visible. This body of work is framed by the phenomenological viewpoint that presumes equity is best confronted and improved through developing an expanded understanding of play in its multiple variations and dimensions. The play studies explore the potential and troubles of play in teaching and learning, children's agency in play, the actual spaces where children play, and different perspectives of play based on identity and culture. The editors invite readers to use the research as an inspiration to reconsider their conceptions of play and to take action to work for a world where all children have access to play.

This book was originally published as a special issue of *Early Child Development and Care.*

Julie Nicholson is an Associate Professor of Practice at Mills College, Oakland, USA and the Director of the Center for Play Research. She is also the Deputy Director for WestEd's Center for Child and Family Studies.

Debora B. Wisneski is the John T. Langan Community Chair in Early Childhood Education at the University of Nebraska Omaha, USA and the Director of the Early Childhood Inclusive Program.

Reconsidering The Role of Play in Early Childhood

Towards Social Justice and Equity

Edited by
Julie Nicholson and Debora B. Wisneski

LONDON AND NEW YORK

First published 2019
by Routledge
2 Park Square, Milton Park, Abingdon, Oxon, OX14 4RN, UK

and by Routledge
52 Vanderbilt Avenue, New York, NY 10017, USA

First issued in paperback 2020

Routledge is an imprint of the Taylor & Francis Group, an informa business

British Library Cataloguing-in-Publication Data
A catalogue record for this book is available from the British Library

ISBN 13: 978-0-367-58379-8 (pbk)
ISBN 13: 978-1-138-36794-4 (hbk)

Typeset in Myriad Pro
by codeMantra

Publisher's Note
The publisher accepts responsibility for any inconsistencies that may have arisen during the conversion of this book from journal articles to book chapters, namely the possible inclusion of journal terminology.

Contents

PART IV
Expanding play perspectives

Citation Information

The chapters in this book were originally published in *Early Child Development and Care*, volume 187, issues 5–6 (May 2017). When citing this material, please use the original page numbering for each article, as follows:

Foreword

Is play a privilege or a right? And what's our responsibility? On the role of play for equity in early childhood education
Mariana Souto-Manning
Early Child Development and Care, volume 187, issues 5–6 (May 2017) pp. 785–787

Introduction

Julie Nicholson and Debora B. Wisneski
Early Child Development and Care, volume 187, issues 5–6 (May 2017) pp. 788–797

Chapter 1

Block play: spatial language with preschool and school-aged children
Lynn E. Cohen and Janet Emmons
Early Child Development and Care, volume 187, issues 5–6 (May 2017) pp. 967–977

Chapter 2

Early childhood curriculum development: the role of play in building self-regulatory capacity in young children
Linda R. Kroll
Early Child Development and Care, volume 187, issues 5–6 (May 2017) pp. 854–868

Chapter 3

Understanding and supporting block play: Video observation research on preschoolers' block play to identify features associated with the development of abstract thinking
Kaoru Otsuka and Tim Jay
Early Child Development and Care, volume 187, issues 5–6 (May 2017) pp. 990–1003

Chapter 4

The relative emphasis of play rules between experienced and trainee caregivers of toddlers
Kinga Gyöngy
Early Child Development and Care, volume 187, issues 5–6 (May 2017) pp. 840–853

Chapter 5

Influencing factors on professional attitudes towards risk-taking in children's play: a narrative review
Martin van Rooijen and Shelly Newstead
Early Child Development and Care, volume 187, issues 5–6 (May 2017) pp. 946–957

Chapter 6

Follow the leader: attending to the curriculum making potential of preschoolers
Monica Miller Marsh and Ilfa Zhulamanova
Early Child Development and Care, volume 187, issues 5–6 (May 2017) pp. 1004–1014

Chapter 7

Playing at violence: lock-down drills, 'bad guys' and the construction of 'acceptable' play in early childhood
Katherine K. Delaney
Early Child Development and Care, volume 187, issues 5–6 (May 2017) pp. 878–895

Chapter 8

Where is my stuff? Conceptualizing Hip Hop as 'play'
Anthony Broughton
Early Child Development and Care, volume 187, issues 5–6 (May 2017) pp. 869–877

Chapter 9

They're lovin' it: how preschool children mediated their funds of knowledge into dramatic play
Anne Karabon
Early Child Development and Care, volume 187, issues 5–6 (May 2017) pp. 896–909

Chapter 10

Civic action and play: examples from Maori, Aboriginal Australian and Latino communities
Jennifer Keys Adair, Louise Phillips, Jenny Ritchie and Shubhi Sachdeva
Early Child Development and Care, volume 187, issues 5–6 (May 2017) pp. 798–811

Chapter 11

Rethinking young children's digital game play outside of the home as a means of coping with modern life
Youn Jung Huh
Early Child Development and Care, volume 187, issues 5–6 (May 2017) pp. 1042–1054

Chapter 12

Playing with power: an outdoor classroom exploration
Eden Haywood-Bird
Early Child Development and Care, volume 187, issues 5–6 (May 2017) pp. 1015–1027

Chapter 13
Where do the children play?: An investigation of the intersection of nature, early childhood education and play
Jeanne M. Brown and Candace Kaye
Early Child Development and Care, volume 187, issues 5–6 (May 2017) pp. 1028–1041

Chapter 14
Sandboxes, loose parts, and playground equipment: a descriptive exploration of outdoor play environments
Heather Olsen and Brandy Smith
Early Child Development and Care, volume 187, issues 5–6 (May 2017) pp. 1055–1068

Chapter 15
'They get enough of play at home': a Bakhtinian interpretation of the dialogic space of public school preschool
Jamie Huff Sisson and Janice Kroeger
Early Child Development and Care, volume 187, issues 5–6 (May 2017) pp. 812–826

Chapter16
Rooms with gender: physical environment and play culture in kindergarten
Hege Eggen Børve and Elin Børve
Early Child Development and Care, volume 187, issues 5–6 (May 2017) pp. 1069–1081

Chapter 17
Children's engagement in play at home: a parent's role in supporting play opportunities during early childhood
Doré R. LaForett and Julia L. Mendez
Early Child Development and Care, volume 187, issues 5–6 (May 2017) pp. 910–923

Chapter 18
Parents' perceptions of play: a comparative study of spousal perspectives
Barbara G. Warash, Amy E. Root and Meghan Devito Doris
Early Child Development and Care, volume 187, issues 5–6 (May 2017) pp. 958–966

Chapter 19
The social kindergartener: comparing children's perspectives of full- and half-day kindergarten
Kaitlyn Heagle, Kristy Timmons, Fabienne Hargreaves and Janette Pelletier
Early Child Development and Care, volume 187, issues 5–6 (May 2017) pp. 978–989

Chapter 20
Interpersonal fields of play
Sophie Jane Alcock
Early Child Development and Care, volume 187, issues 5–6 (May 2017) pp. 924–934

Chapter 21

The Black baby doll doesn't fit the disconnect between early childhood diversity policy, early childhood educator practice, and children's play
Maggie MacNevin and Rachel Berman
Early Child Development and Care, volume 187, issues 5–6 (May 2017) pp. 827–839

Chapter 22

Using cross-cultural conversations to contextualize understandings of play: a multinational study
Zoyah Kinkead-Clark and Charlotte Hardacre
Early Child Development and Care, volume 187, issues 5–6 (May 2017) pp. 935–945

Notes on Contributors

Jennifer Keys Adair is an Associate Professor of Early Childhood Education at The University of Texas at Austin, USA. Her areas of expertise include early childhood education, immigrant parent engagement, project-based learning, and the importance of young children exploring racial and cultural differences.

Sophie Jane Alcock is a Senior Lecturer in Early Childhood at Victoria University of Wellington, New Zealand. She has previously researched play and playfulness in young children's communication using ethnographic methods and sociocultural theory. She is interested in children's play from relational, creative, complex, and equitable social-justice perspectives.

Rachel Berman works at the School of Early Childhood Studies at Ryerson University, Toronto, Canada. She teaches courses on social research with children, theoretical frameworks for early childhood studies, and research methods. She is currently the Graduate Program Director for the MA in Early Childhood Studies.

Elin Børve has a master's degree in Special Education and experience as a Head Teacher and Pedagogical Leader in kindergartens. She works as a Lecturer at Nord University, Bodø, Norway and teaches on topics such as toddlers' pedagogy, early intervention, diversity, and younger children's learning environments.

Hege Eggen Børve has a PhD in Sociology and works as an Associate Professor at Nord University, Bodø, Norway. She is currently teaching and doing research on topics such as organization and work, gender, equality, work and family, welfare policy, and globalization.

Anthony Broughton is an Assistant Professor of Early Childhood Education at Claflin University, Orangeburg, USA. His scholarly interests include hip-hop play, hip-hop pedagogy, and culturally relevant pedagogy.

Jeanne M. Brown is a Preschool Teacher and Adjunct Instructor in the Department of Curriculum and Instruction at New Mexico State University, Las Cruces, USA. Her research interests include nature, risk-taking, and fantasy play.

Lynn E. Cohen is a Professor at Long Island University at Post, Brookville, USA, where she teaches courses at both the master's and doctoral levels. Before this, she was a preschool, kindergarten, and literacy teacher. Her passions span all aspects of teaching and learning including early childhood education, play and creativity, classroom environment, and assessment and evaluation.

Katherine K. Delaney is an Assistant Professor of Early Childhood Education whose research examines intersections of policy, practice, children, families, and communities in early childhood settings.

Meghan Devito Doris is a graduate of the Child Development and Family Studies Program at West Virginia University, Morgantown, USA. She teaches courses on the role of the family in lifespan development.

Janet Emmons is the Founder of Blockspot®. Her early childhood education background, school district leadership, and business background all culminated in the creation of Blockspot®, the first organization of its kind to marry education and block play within a retail concept. It operates in Southampton, USA.

Kinga Gyöngy earned her PhD from the Doctoral School of Psychology at Eötvös Loránd University, Budapest, Hungary. Her research interests focus on nursery nurse training and behavior management of toddlers. Between 2010 and 2015, she coordinated the development of a new under-threes arts curriculum for infant and early childhood educator bachelors courses in Hungary.

Charlotte Hardacre is a Lecturer in the Department of Health, Psychology and Social Science at the University of Cumbria, UK, where she has been a faculty member since 2014. She teaches a range of undergraduate modules on the 'Working with Children and Families' degree program, with a focus on early childhood education and intergenerational learning.

Fabienne Hargreaves is a certified teacher and completed her Master of Arts in Child Study and Education at the Dr. Eric Jackman Institute for Child Study at the Ontario Institute for Studies in Education at the University of Toronto, Canada. Her research interests lie in early literacy learning and methods for accessing the perspectives of young children.

Eden Haywood-Bird is a qualified teacher and an Assistant Professor of Early Childhood Studies at California State Polytechnic University, Pomona, USA. Her research interests include nature in education, social aspects of learning and development within preschool, expression of power and agency of young children, and teacher intersectional identities.

Kaitlyn Heagle is a Registered Early Childhood Educator and a certified teacher. She has conducted research at the University of Ottawa, Canada and the University of Toronto, Canada. Her research interests lie in children's perspectives in play and their experiences in social situations. She is currently an education consultant at a national education technology firm based in Toronto, Canada.

Youn Jung Huh is an Assistant Professor in the Department of Childhood Education and Care at Salem State University, USA. She has published articles on young children's digital game play and culture. Her work focuses on digital technology in early childhood education, ethnography, critical theory, and popular culture.

Tim Jay is a Professor of Psychology of Education at Sheffield Hallam University, UK. His research concerns individual differences in the ways that children learn and the ways that social and cognitive aspects of learning interact.

Anne Karabon is an Assistant Professor of Teacher Education at the University of Nebraska Omaha, USA, specializing in Early Childhood and Elementary STEM Education. Her research and publications focus on culturally responsive and socially just teaching practices for young children and families. She teaches and supervises preservice teachers and leads professional development for teachers.

Candace Kaye is a retired Associate Professor of Curriculum and Instruction at New Mexico State University, Las Cruces, USA. She continues as an Affiliated Graduate Faculty and also as a Visiting Scholar at the Mongolian National University of Education, Ulaanbaatar, Mongolia. Her areas of specialization include multicultural policy issues in early childhood education and action research methodology and application.

Zoyah Kinkead-Clark is an Early Childhood Lecturer at The University of the West Indies, Mona, Jamaica. She had been a kindergarten teacher for several years, and her current research focus is aimed at exploring how young children can be provided with greater opportunities during the crucial first five years of life, especially considering the significant challenges many of them face.

Janice Kroeger is an Associate Professor in the School of Teaching, Learning and Curriculum Studies at Kent State University, USA. Her research interests include homeschool community relationships, ethnographic method, discourse processes, school change, identity, and Bakhtinian applications.

Linda R. Kroll is the Holland Professor of Early Childhood Education in the School of Education at Mills College, Oakland, USA.

Doré R. LaForett is an Advanced Research Scientist at The University of North Carolina at Chapel Hill, USA, whose research on young children's school readiness and mental health spans the promotion, prevention, and treatment continuum. She is also interested in how family and school contexts shape children's development and mental health.

Maggie MacNevin has been working as an Early Child Educator since 2008. She has worked in preschool education, in family resources, and as a toddler teacher. She earned her Master of Arts in Early Childhood Studies from Ryerson University, Toronto, Canada, in 2014. She currently lives in Toronto and works as a part-time instructor in the School of Early Childhood Studies at Ryerson University, Toronto, Canada.

Monica Miller Marsh is an Associate Professor of Early Childhood Education and the Director of the Child Development Center at Kent State University, USA. Her areas of interest include family diversity, the formation of teacher and student identities, and curriculum development. She is co-founder of the Family Diversity Education Council and the *Journal of Family Diversity in Education*.

Julia L. Mendez is a Professor of Psychology at The University of North Carolina at Greensboro, USA. She has research and teaching interests related to the impact of poverty on the development of young children, parent engagement in children's education, risk and resilience, and clinical interventions for ethnic minority children and families.

Shelly Newstead is a PhD Candidate at the UCL Institute of Education, London, UK. She is the Managing Editor of the *International Journal of Playwork Practice* and President of the International Council for Children's Play. She is also the Series Editor for the Routledge 'Advances in Playwork Research' series.

Julie Nicholson is an Associate Professor of Practice at Mills College, Oakland, USA and the Director of the Center for Play Research. She is also the Deputy Director for WestEd's Center for Child and Family Studies.

Heather Olsen is an Associate Professor and serves as the Executive Director of the National Program for Playground Safety, USA. Her work includes providing education, outreach, and advocacy to, for example, early childcare programs and schools. She researches the safety and environmental components of children's outdoor spaces to enhance the health and safety of children.

Kaoru Otsuka teaches English to adult students in Japan. She studied Educational Research at the University of Bristol, UK. Her main interest is in the development of critical thinking in educational settings and instructional methods in which this may be enhanced for students from different cultural and linguistic backgrounds.

Janette Pelletier is a Professor of Applied Psychology and Human Development at the Dr. Eric Jackman Institute of Child Study at the Ontario Institute for Studies in Education at the University of Toronto, Canada. She carries out research in early education and development, seeking to understand the connections among research, practice, and policy.

Louise Phillips is an Academic in Arts and Early Years Education at The University of Queensland, Brisbane, Australia. Her areas of expertise include storytelling; children's rights and citizenship; and creative, perceptual, and place-based pedagogies.

Jenny Ritchie lectures at Victoria University of Wellington, New Zealand. Her research and teaching focus on early childhood care and education policy and pedagogies and social, cultural, and environmental justice issues.

Martin van Rooijen is a PhD Candidate at the University of Humanistic Studies, Utrecht, the Netherlands. His primary research focuses on children's risk-taking in play, the resilience of children in outdoor environments, and normative professionalism of pedagogues with children in their care. He is involved in international networks on nature play and children's play rights.

Amy E. Root is an Associate Professor of Child Development and Family Studies at West Virginia University, Morgantown, USA. Her primary research interests include the examination of the role of parents in young children's socio-emotional development.

Shubhi Sachdeva is a PhD Candidate in Early Childhood Education at The University of Texas at Austin, USA. Her research interests include global perspectives on childhood, sociocultural processes in early education, and equity and social justice issues in early education.

Jamie Huff Sisson is a Senior Lecturer in the School of Education at the University of South Australia, Adelaide, Australia. Her research interests include teachers' professional identities, children's voices and participation as citizens, and early childhood curriculum and pedagogy. She is interested in engaging in collaborative relationships to reimagine learning communities.

Brandy Smith is a Doctoral Candidate in Early Childhood Education. Currently, she serves as the Program Coordinator for the National Program for Playground Safety, USA. She has developed and implemented numerous trainings supporting physical, cognitive, and social-emotional domains of childhood.

Mariana Souto-Manning is an Associate Professor of Early Childhood Education and the Director of the Doctoral Program in Curriculum and Teaching at Teachers College at Columbia University, New York, USA. She is a former preschool and primary grades teacher and now teaches courses related to early literacy, multicultural education, and critical pedagogy.

Kristy Timmons is an Assistant Professor in the Faculty of Education at Queen's University, Kingston, Canada. Her teaching experience spans the early years, elementary, undergraduate, and graduate levels. Her research interests center on the processes that influence young children's learning, engagement, and self-regulation.

Barbara G. Warash is a Professor of Child Development and Family Studies at West Virginia University, Morgantown, USA. She is the Director of the West Virginia University Nursery School and is an expert in early childhood education.

Debora B. Wisneski is the John T. Langan Community Chair in Early Childhood Education at the University of Nebraska Omaha, USA and the Director of the Early Childhood Inclusive Program.

Ilfa Zhulamanova is a Doctoral Candidate in Curriculum and Instruction at Kent State University, USA. Her research focuses on play and learning in early childhood. She has studied the foundations of Waldorf/Steiner pedagogy and was a founder of a Waldorf kindergarten in her home country, Kyrgyzstan.

FOREWORD

Is play a privilege or a right? And what's our responsibility? On the role of play for equity in early childhood education

Mariana Souto-Manning

'It's just play;' we hear this often in a way to diminish its importance. In the name of rigor and adult measures of educational success, play has been nearly extinguished from educational research and practice. While the history of research in play is rich, recently play has nearly disappeared – not only from preschool classrooms, but also from studies of young children. Thus, this special issue.

Although the United States remains one of the only countries which has not ratified the *United Nations Rights of the Child* (United Nations, 1989), Article 31 declares that play is the right of all children. Not a privilege, but a right. As adults and as educators, it is our responsibility to ensure children's right to play. Otherwise, we deny them the right to be children. But – what is the difference between a privilege and a right? Although they are all nouns, they have markedly different meanings.

(1) Privilege (n): An immunity or benefit enjoyed only by a person beyond the advantage of most.
(2) Right (n): That which is due to anyone by just claims, legal guarantees, or moral principles.
(3) Responsibility (n): Being answerable or accountable for something within one's power, control, or management. (Searcy, 2011)

Here, I posit that although play has traditionally been positioned as a privilege, it must be (re)positioned as a right, as outlined by the *United Nations Rights of the Child*, Article 31.

Play as a right: rejecting play as a privilege, a matter of equity

Play must be the right of every child. Not a privilege. After all, when regarded as a privilege, it is granted to some and denied to others, creating further inequities. Play as a right is what is fair and just. Although children will engage in play differently, play is a child's right. It is currently being denied in the name of rigor and academics, both of which have been used as racist ways of keeping the status quo in place. That is, in low-income preschools and schools, we see mandates, which seek to standardize and manage. In wealthier preschools, we witness the possibilities of play unleashed.

When positioned as a privilege, play is granted to children who are in the dominant group while those in non-dominant groups are denied the right to play. This is because children and their families are blamed for opportunity gaps as if they were achievement gaps – even in spite of Delpit's research review (2012), which found that 'there is no achievement gap at birth' (p. 3). Instead of blaming children and their families for the supposed gaps they have, we must embrace the responsibility for a history of debt to minoritized children and their families (Ladson-Billings, 2006). Instead of seeking to fix young children from minoritized backgrounds, we must strive to 're-mediate' (Gutiérrez, Morales, & Martinez, 2009) our teaching and their learning environments. We must reject the 'ideology of pathology linked with most approaches to remediation. Instead of emphasizing basic skills – problems of the individual – re-mediation involves a reorganization of the entire ecology for learning' (p. 227).

Decades ago, educator Paulo Freire (1970) explained the impoverished nature of the banking approach to education – whereas knowledge is supposedly deposited in brains as money in banks. This is simply a narrow definition of teaching that does not apply to young children, who learn by exploring, interacting, and doing. Play is valuable in itself, but can also provide children opportunities to develop sophisticated understandings of academic knowledge and concepts – through authentic, engaging, participative, and agentive ways.

On our responsibility: upholding the ethics of our profession

The National Association for the Education of Young Children (NAEYC, 2005) Code of Ethics states that early childhood education has ethical responsibilities to young children. It affirms that childhood 'is a unique and valuable stage in the human life cycle,' and that we must commit 'to supporting children's development and learning; respecting individual differences; and helping children learn to live, play, and work cooperatively' (p. 2). How, then, can we be ethical professionals if we do not embrace our responsibility to foster time and space for play? Its first principle states:

> 'Above all, we shall not harm children. We shall not participate in practices that are emotionally damaging, physically harmful, disrespectful, degrading, dangerous, exploitative, or intimidating to children. This principle has precedence over all others in this Code' (NAEYC, 2005).

Here, I posit that expecting children to learn passively and denying them the right to play inflicts harm. I urge our profession to claim the responsibility to defend play. But this seems a lot easier than is the case.

The right to play is highly racialized within a society that denies African American children their childhoods. Ladson-Bilings (2011) underscored that we must embrace the responsibility of restoring 'Black boys' childhood' (p. 7). She goes on to explain that (pre)schools are 'the source of the problem' (p. 12) by 'creating' infractions that will apply primarily to Black boys' (p. 13) and withholding the privilege of playing. We must reject the framing of play as a privilege and must reclaim it as the right of every child.

Yet, some boys cannot play. They are immediately constructed as problems. The practices of their communities may be diminished and rejected altogether due to what teachers deem appropriate (such is the case of Hip Hop). For example, when boys of colour play, they are often criminalized. Playing may cost their very lives. This is evident in the murder of Tamir Rice, an African American boy killed by a White police officer while playing at a park with a toy gun and by Clint Smith's TED Talk *How to Raise a Black Son in America* (Smith, 2015), in which he explains how terrified his father was when he was playing with water guns in a parking lot. It could have cost his life, as he explains.

We must recognize our responsibility to all children, by making sure that they have the right to play. After all, play is powerful. As Plato proposed: 'You can discover more about a person in an hour of play than in a year of conversation.'

On the power of play: an invitation to unleash children's infinite potential

Play is a powerful medium for learning. In play, children enact the three Fs of childhood – friendship, fantasy, and fairness (Paley, 2010), they learn about diversities, engage with familiar and unfamiliar materials, and share their own perspectives and experiences while considering others. In play, children are agents. They are doers. As Albert Einstein posited: 'Play is the highest form of research.' Children collaborate and make discoveries through play. They author stories. They take risks. They engage in resistance and plot subversive actions. They learn.

If we are to unleash children's infinite potential, not only do we have the responsibility to position play as a right, we must also understand the agency children need to have during play. Their play will likely come to life in ways that are unfamiliar – and at times uncomfortable – to adults. May we blur the roles of teacher and learner and learn alongside them. Mr. (Fred) Rogers explained: 'Play gives children a chance to practice what they are learning.' I posit that play allows children to rehearse and enact change, by asking questions, developing community, and standing up for fairness – which will later be (re)named justice.

I invite you to learn from the distributed expertise in this publication … after all, there is more expertise across studies and articles than in any one study or finding. In doing so, I invite you to (re)position play as a right and take on this responsibility for the sake of educational equity. By ensuring that children have the right to play, we ensure that they engage in learning that unleashes their infinite potential and capacity – to learn, to grow, to get along, and to strive for fairness and justice.

References

Delpit, L. (2012). *"Multiplication is for white people": Raising the expectations for other people's children*. New York, NY: The New Press.

Freire, P. (1970). Pedagogy *of the oppressed*. New York, NY: Continuum.

Gutiérrez, K. D., Morales, P. Z., & Martinez, D. C. (2009). Re-mediating literacy: Culture, difference, and learning for students. *Review of Research in Education, 33*, 212–245.

Ladson-Bilings, G. (2011). Boyz to men? Teaching to restore Black boys' childhood. *Race Ethnicity and Education, 14*(1), 7–15.

Ladson-Billings, G. (2006). From the achievement gap to the education debt: Understanding achievement in U.S. schools. *Educational Researcher, 35*(7), 3–12.

National Association for the Education of Young Children. (2005). *Code of Ethics. Code of ethical conduct and statement of commitment: A position statement of the National Association for the Education of Young Children*. Retrieved from http://www.naeyc.org/files/naeyc/file/positions/PSETH05.pdf

Paley, V. (2010). *An interview with Vivian Paley*. Retrieved from http://illinoisearlylearning.org/interviews/paley.htm

Searcy, D. (2011). *Voting: A right, a privilege, or a responsibility?* Retrieved from http://www.fairvote.org/voting-a-right-a-privilege-or-a-responsibility

Smith, C. (2015). How to raise a Black son in America. *TED Talk*. Retrieved from https://www.ted.com/talks/clint_smith_how_to_raise_a_black_son_in_america

United Nations. (1989). *Convention on the rights of the child*. Retrieved from http://www.ohchr.org/Documents/ProfessionalInterest/crc.pdf

Introduction

Julie Nicholson and Debora B. Wisneski

Throughout the western history of research and understanding of early child development, care, and education, children's play is often at the centre of our inquiry. Childhood play has provided the context for understanding development and learning (Piaget, 1945; Vygotsky, 1978) and has provided insight into cultural and social understanding of childhood itself (Rogoff, 2003; Sutton-Smith, 1995). Play has also been the centre of the curriculum for young children in many societies (Van Hoorn, Nourot, Scales, & Alward, 2015; Wisneski & Reifel, 2012). Furthermore, play remains central for many local, national, and worldwide advocacy organizations (i.e. International Play Association, US Play Coalition, Defending the Early Years, Alliance for Childhood, Play England, Association for Childhood Education International) inspired by decades of child development research highlighting the benefits of play for children's learning, development and overall well-being (Ginsburg, 2007) and Article 31 of the Convention on the Rights of the Child promoting a child's right to play and their right to enjoy a full cultural and artistic life (United Nations, 1989). Thus, play in the early years of life has been framed as an optimal foundation for children's learning and construction of meaning in the world, an intervention to redress the negative consequences of poverty and other inequities, a form of therapy to support healing and resilience from childhood stress and traumas, and an effective means to strengthen children's educational and developmental outcomes.

Yet, many world events and social and institutional policies inhibit and threaten children's access to, and involvement in, play. Further, children's play is not an innocent endeavour and many scholars have documented how children make sense of the world through play in ways that mirror and/or reinforce inequities in the societies in which they live (e.g. racism, sexism, classism). Therefore, play is a contested, complex, and contradictory human experience that offers researchers a rich opportunity to explore the ruptures in our current knowing and understanding of childhood development, care, and education (Grieshaber & McArdle, 2010; Nicholson, Kurnik, Jevgjovikj, & Ufoegbune, 2015; Sutton-Smith, 1997/2001).

Reconsidering the Role of Play in Early Childhood: Towards Social Justice and Equity is a collection of current research and theorizing about play that challenges, disrupts, and reexamines our current 'contexts, perspectives and meanings' (Fromberg & Bergen, 2015) of play in early care and education. Highlighted are pressing issues involving play for children living in diverse contexts around the world. Specifically, the issues of social justice and equity related to children's play today are made visible and expand our theorizing and educational practices for supporting play while also recognizing the complexity of its expression and role in children's lives.

Our interest in this topic springs from our shared experience as professors charged with the responsibility of guiding early childhood students to learn about the complex construct of young children's play. Our students range from young twenty-something millennials to seasoned grandmothers returning to school after decades of raising children into adulthood. One of us teaches a primarily white population, the other a population that is racially and ethnically diverse with childhoods that took place in various socioeconomic and sociocultural contexts internationally. We are passionate about helping our students to gain a deep understanding about the many cognitive, social, emotional, and physical benefits afforded to children through play. We ardently communicate that through play, children communicate important information about their life stories; they share with adults how they are organizing and making sense of their world and reveal what has happened to them, how they feel about it, and what they need and want from the adults around them. We believe it is a professional obligation that early childhood professionals learn how to mindfully observe children's play and listen to the stories they convey and disclose to us while they are playing. We stress in our coursework that play is a right of all children and deeply connected to how democracy functions. And we often find our students' understanding of play's association with larger societal issues – liberation, voice, equality, justice – is elusive without persistence in unfurling the layers of discovery that characterize deep learning in college classrooms. Issues of equity and social justice are central to children's play. It is our job to make this visible.

Given the alarming rates of trauma impacting children's lives globally – whether the increasing rates of extreme poverty in the United States, the unaccompanied minors fleeing gangs and violence in Central and South America, or the countless children losing their lives in conflict areas including Syria and Afghanistan – it is essential that we protect and defend children's right to play. Without play, we are taking away their most natural and therapeutic context to endure (and resist, subvert, and reassemble) the injustices we expose them to. The global zeitgeist is shifting fast as evidenced in recent elections across Europe and the United States where we have witnessed shifts from 'we' to essentialized and marginalized 'other'. Our children are going to grapple with the messages they see swirling around them about divided red and blue nations, and hate, oppression and bigotry and they will reflect our best and worst sensibilities in their play. As early childhood professionals, we are charged with not pretending not to notice but instead, developing our own, and our students' and colleagues' skills, knowledge and capacities in learning how to respond both sensitively and intentionally in a manner that disrupts cycles of injustice.

The manuscripts in this collection can each be viewed as powerful and provocative on their own. However, when read together we found four strong themes that help us understand play through a lens of equity, social justice, and complexity. The first theme explores the potential and troubles of play in teaching and learning. The next theme reminds us to reconsider the agency and power that children bring to play experiences that challenge the adult interpretations or attempts to control play. In a third theme, readers are asked to re-focus their attention on the physical and virtual spaces of play that are often overlooked or taken for granted. A final theme helps us consider different perspectives of play, from parents, to children, to cross-cultural conversations about play – reminding us that children's play occurs in a complicated web of relationships and contexts. The following sections will provide an introduction to each of the manuscripts in the context of these themes.

Potential and troubles of play in teaching and learning

While play has been situated as part of early education and care settings for young children, the role of play in learning has been complex. Too often children's play is not understood or visible as part of the process of teaching and learning. Some have troubled the notion of having play as an integral part of learning when play itself is seen as incongruent with formal teaching and learning. Furthermore, policies and practices of schools can create barriers to play and educators, based on their knowledge, skills, and dispositions towards utilizing play as a pedagogical tool, hold much power over when, where, and how children play. The following research studies illuminate such struggles.

Cohen and Emmons' article, *Block play: Spatial language with preschool and school-aged children*, is a response to the decline of unit block play due to current educational reforms and policies. The authors situate their study in this context of the lack of play in preschool as well as elementary schools, despite the strong research evidence that children learn through play. The purpose of this study is to describe and examine the use of spatial words in a playful venue and document children's development of spatial language supported by adult-guided play with blocks. Their findings lead us to see how block play with adult guidance in using spatial language does enhance children's use of spatial language, not only for preschool age children, but older children, as well. Hence, the authors advocate for use of unit block play across childhood.

Kroll's study, *Early childhood curriculum development: The role of play in building self-regulatory capacity in young children*, takes a similar approach as Cohen and Emmons in showing the benefits of play for learning by highlighting the positive enhancement of children's self-regulation through play. The study takes place in a lab school kindergarten where teachers regarded play as central to their curriculum and to the development of self-regulation in their students. In discussing the findings, Kroll considers the educational context in which these children will enter once leaving the lab school environment. She argues that current educational standards are 'detrimental, miseducative, and unrealistic for 5 year olds, but, nevertheless, as early childhood educators, we have to think about how we can prepare our young children to weather these conditions as healthily as possible.' Kroll speculates, if children are in play-less educational settings without teacher support, as play experiences are the optimal context in which to learn self-regulation, how will children learn self-regulation?

Otsuka and Jay's study, *Understanding and supporting block play: Video observation* was completed with preschool children in England in which the researchers closely observed and listened to the play interactions to explore the process in which the children's self-directed block play supported their development of abstract thinking. Through observing play behaviours, the authors are able to follow children's connections between symbolic representations leading to abstract thinking. Three main features of this process are described as (i) child/child sharing of thinking and adult and child sharing of thinking; (ii) pause for reflection; and (iii) satisfaction; and these aspects are identified as signs of learning. Once again, our authors lead us to a place in which educators are urged to understand the value of play and provide adequate time, space, and a thoughtful environment for children to play. From the perspective of these three studies which illustrate how learning occurs through play, the conclusion can also be drawn that access to play in educational settings for children leads to access to learning opportunities. While these research studies are not directly framed in the context of social justice or equity, they challenge the current policy trends towards removing play from education and the current assumptions that only through direct instruction can low-income children or children of colour learn. Furthermore, in each study the educator has an integral role in providing access to play for children and for enhancing the process of learning through play for children.

The following two studies illustrate how educators' perceptions and understanding about play can also be a barrier for children's access to play. These studies seem to illustrate what has been suggested before by Rogers (2011): while there has been a consensus about the importance and benefits of play in Western discourse, there are great difficulties in realizing this in practice and conceptualization of play.

The difficulty in play arises in Gyöngy's study, *Play rules: Experienced and trainee caregivers of toddlers nursery practitioners in Hungary*, as the author recognizes that within the context of free play in nurseries in Hungary, caregivers create different rules for children while playing. The study exposes rules adults impose during free play as social, health and safety, and environment-related rules. While experienced and novice caregivers seemed to agree upon safety and health rules, there were disagreements on the environment-related rules, which controlled space utilisation in toddler groups. Interestingly, they find that there has been little research on this type of rule-making that heavily shapes children's play, but this seems to be part of the practical knowledge of the profession. As one can imagine, many rules are imposed on children's play based on the assessment and fear of risk. Yet, risk has been documented as an important aspect of play. Educators are often torn between their desire to encourage play and their reluctance to accept the risk inherent in play.

In van Rooijen and Newstead's paper, *Influencing factors on professional attitudes towards risk-taking in children's play: A narrative review*, the authors propose an alternative approach to supporting practitioners in allowing risk by exploring the complexity of these influencing factors. This narrative literature review reveals five inter-related factors which affect professionals' attitudes to risk from which the authors create a model which illustrates the complexity faced by practitioners when carrying out risk assessments. The authors argue that children's opportunities to benefit from risk in play may increase if these influencing factors could be explored within professional development. These studies on rules and risk (or we could also frame them as control and freedom) emphasize again the power of adult educators' influences on play and the tension between play and the context of learning in educational contexts.

How does one begin to reconcile these tensions between the goals of educators and the context of controlled learning environments and the seeming contradictory nature of play that includes risk and the unknown? Rogers (2011) suggests that the process of teaching and learning be expanded to include the free and intrinsic aspects of play and for educators to consider teaching through play as a process of co-construction and negotiation. The study by Miller- Marsh and Zhulamanova, *Follow the leader: Attending to the curriculum making potential of preschoolers' funds of identity* perhaps allows us to imagine what Rogers asks us to do in rethinking play and education. The authors of this study use a new concept based on the 'funds of knowledge' approach called 'funds of identity' which positions children as capable of contributing to creating the class curriculum and learning experiences. The setting for the study is in an 'inquiry-oriented, play-based, preschool curriculum' in which the participants (researchers, preschool-age children and their families) take part in a collaborative action research to discover what learning looks like when children are positioned as co-creators of curriculum based on their personal stories. The first phase of the study included the visual narratives and conversations guided by the children so that the adults could learn about the children's interests and the knowledge they bring with them from home into school. The next phase included the teachers enhancing the play environment in preschool based on the children's interests and observing children's play to learn what children knew and valued. The findings were that the children engaged more with learning and the class became a more inclusive. This study concludes, 'We came to recognize that our perspectives of the children's interests and knowledge were limited by our inability to see their curriculum-making potential and by our hesitation to offer the curriculum the children desire.'

Children's agency in play

Several authors consider the role of children's agency – their opportunity to insert their voices and self-determined choices – in shaping their play experiences. The question for these scholars is not whether children are able to engage in play, but additionally, how much power children have to bring their own interests, questions, and concerns into their play and the degree to which the play they engage in can affirm their cultural and community contexts. Through this collection of studies, we see how children use play to participate in the world around them, including their choices to resist adult actions that aim to control and constrain them intellectually and physically.

Delaney's study, *Playing at violence: Lock down drills, 'bad guys' and the construction of 'acceptable' play in early childhood,* critically reflects on children's experiences 'playing at violence', in a pre-k classroom. Documenting how teachers and children engage with, pretend at, and play around violent themes, Delaney juxtaposes the inherent inequity between our current zero tolerance policies that prevent children from exploring certain themes in their play, including death, violence, loss and fear – even with the research evidence we have showing this play to be beneficial for children's development – while another version of play at violence is being actively supported and endorsed in schools across the United States (US) in the form of Code Red drills (also known as Lock-Down or Active Shooter drills). She reports on her role as a participant observer in a PreK classroom for a year where she documented the incongruity between the classroom rules against children's imaginative 'bad guy' play and the mandatory safety drills that required the same children to imagine and then play out pretend scenarios of reacting to violent intruders. Delaney reminds readers that zero-tolerance policies are most likely to exist and be enforced in schools serving low-income children of colour. She critiques the injustice of these policies and practices and calls for the importance of supporting all children to have agency to safely explore violent themes through imaginary play.

Broughton's contribution titled, *Where is my stuff? Conceptualizing Hip Hop as 'play'*, challenges the definitions of play as culturally exclusionary and reminds us to make all children visible and to challenge the biases we have that leave out children's cultural competencies in our early childhood classrooms. This text explores the possibilities of Hip Hop culture as 'play' as an approach for nurturing children's cultural competence, cultural identities, and individual identities while supporting the development of children. Additionally, Broughton explores the power dynamics of teachers choosing to allow, sustain, and support Hip Hop play. A main argument in this paper is that children should be encouraged to engage in play in ways that are culturally affirming and for many children, Hip Hop is deeply connected to their identities. However, many teachers reject Hip Hop from inclusion in their classrooms which denies children of the culturally responsive environment that would help them to thrive. In this way, Broughton concludes that early childhood classrooms are too often denying children the integration of their 'stuff' into the environment, curriculum, pedagogy. He argues that more consideration be given to the intersections of culture and children's play if we want to increase equity in our early childhood programmes.

Karabon's study titled, *They're lovin' it: How preschool children mediated their funds of knowledge into dramatic play*, points out that although teachers often determine the knowledge sources to emphasize in their classroom curricula, the authors suggest young children should have agency to integrate their own funds of knowledge, or the historical, social, and cultural knowledge they gain from their families and communities, into their play. Grounded in critical sociocultural theory, this study explores how children mediate their cultural knowledge, and specifically, their interests in popular culture (e.g. TV show characters) into their dramatic play. The findings reveal that supporting children to integrate their own funds of knowledge, including popular culture, into their play provides them with power and agency to act as experts in their learning experiences and interactions with others. Karabon suggests that it is teachers' responsibility to become learners of children's lifeworlds and importantly, that children must have agency to identify their own cultural knowledge in addition to having opportunities to insert this knowledge into the classroom through their play.

Adair, Phillips, Richie, and Sachdeva, provocatively challenge and expand traditional conceptions of play in *Civic action and play: Examples from Maori, Aboriginal Australian and Mexican-American communities*. In this study, play is positioned as a common yet endangered political time and space that makes civic action possible in the everyday lives of children. Using data from an international, comparative study in preschools in New Zealand, Australia, and the United States, the authors apply the work of Rancière and Arendt to consider the types of civic action that are possible when time and space are offered for children to use their agency to initiate, work together, and collectively pursue ideas and things that are important to the group. Findings of the study reveal that in New Zealand, the term 'play' was not frequently used; however, children were free to move inside or outside, enjoy whatever materials they wished and move around throughout the space with their classmates; a sense of agency and movement that extended to the educators as well. In Australia, the preschool structure had a lot of open time labelled as 'play' where educators observed or engaged with the children. The US site was the most structured space in the study. The authors conclude that when children have time and space to lead their own actions, they are better able to pursue civic action. They urge all early childhood educators to create opportunities for young children to engage in civic action through a range of classroom activities including child-initiated play.

Huh describes agency in the context of digital play. In *Rethinking young children's digital game play outside of the home as a means of coping with modern life*, we learn how young children transform public spaces into their own play spaces by navigating boundaries and rules imposed by adults in these spaces for engaging in digital game play. This study emphasizes children as capable of resistance and subversion in their expressions of power. The author asks whether young children use digital game play to survive and thrive in public spaces that limit their participation through four studies highlight how sociohistorical and sociocultural contexts influence children's play and in this case, how a growing integration with digital devices has impacted children and their play and relationships with others. Through this study we are inspired to ask how we can design environments in a manner that support children to have more agency and participation.

Troubling spaces for play

Several authors raised questions about equity and social justice in relationship to the geography and physical environments associated with children's play. These studies challenge play's shrinking landscape in children's lives, that is, the increasingly limited environments we allow children to utilize for their playful activities. We are called to consider questions of agency, power, safety, control, and resistance and reminded that for children, the spaces for play are often contested and political arenas where the desires of children often must bend to the changing tides of adults' accord.

Hayward-Bird's, *Playing with power: An outdoor classroom exploration*, is inspired by concerns that children today are not being allowed to play outdoors as much as children in the past. She reports on an ethnography she completed within a preschool classroom where outdoor play was a centrepiece of their daily schedule. She observed children as they played and took risks together in a forest climbing trees and as they engaged in dramatic play with their peers. Although there are studies that examine what teachers and parents believe children gain from being outdoors, Hayward-Bird documented children's worlds of play in the forest and describes how the children communicated the value of outdoor play as documented through their experiences of agency and powerful moments.

Taking readers through a historical journey, Brown and Kaye's, *Where do the children play?: An investigation of the intersection of nature, early childhood education and play,* examines how children's access to and experiences with outdoor play have changed significantly in England and Wales over time. We learn about how children could roam, forage, gather, and create their own wild spaces during feudal times; times when children could establish sub-societies of unsupervised and child-governed play. We then read about how the Enclosures Acts between 1604 and 1914 led to wide spread privatization where forests and pastureland were fenced off and punishable for any child who attempted to trespass. The authors describe how philosophers (including Locke, Rousseau, Pestalozzi, Fröbel, and Sir Robert Owen) influenced how children and childhoods were perceived by adults and the shifting conceptions of children's play that accompanied their ideas. The authors conclude by describing the contemporary reform movements focused on bringing nature back to children in the form of forest kindergartens and other similar approaches. The historical lens the authors showcase in this text reminds us that the current state of children's play – and specifically their loss of access to outdoor environments for play – is a pattern resonant throughout history.

Olsen and Smith's text, *Sandboxes, loose parts, and playground equipment: A descriptive exploration of outdoor play environments*, examines children's play by zooming in on playground safety. Using a playground safety checklist informed by injury data from the Center for Disease Control and Injury Prevention and safety guidelines from the Consumer Product Safety Commission and the American Society for Standards and Materials, the authors visited 61 child-care programmes in one state to rate their outdoor play environments. They found that although the majority of the programmes had a variety of opportunities for children to engage in safe outdoor play, primarily on play structures, very little explicit planning took place in relation to children's use of the outdoor environment. Their study inspires questions about how early childhood educators can be more intentional in utilizing outdoor play environments as part of their curriculum planning in the manner in which they do for children's experiences inside classrooms.

Sisson and Kroeger examine preschool children's experiences of play when their classrooms are co-located on a public-school campus in their paper titled, *'They get enough of play at home': a Bakhtinian interpretation of dialogic space of public preschool.* They situate their study in a body of research showing that as preschools become more associated with public schools, they often shift away from play-based approaches and begin to emphasize more teacher-directed and academic pedagogy. Studying the professional identities of five public preschool teachers from a major metropolitan school district in the United States, Sisson and Kroeger describe a dialogic space where discourses of play-based pedagogies and academic readiness were in competition. The authors draw on Bakhtin's notion of dialogism to examine how the preschool teachers juxtaposed their own inner dialogue about play with the polyphonic environment in the district where competing discourses of readiness and academics required that they navigate pedagogical tensions on a daily basis. The authors highlight how the teachers drew upon their own internally persuasive discourses to contest and reject the official discourses about play that circulated in their public schools. They also describe how the need to manage competing discourses had a significant impact on their sense of professional identity and the actions they took in the classroom.

Borve and Borve, in *Rooms with gender: physical environment and play culture in kindergarden* examine how the physical environment of two Norwegian kindergartens affect the culture of play in the classrooms. Noting that despite the Norwegian Ministry of Education and Research expects that kindergartens will promote democracy and equality, many early childhood staff perceive play and play materials as gendered and often perpetuate gender stereotypes within the classroom. Borve and Borve note that female staff members take a prominent role in designing kindergarten spaces, but suggest that if children have a more active role in design decisions perhaps the children may offer solutions to create a more gender-neutral environment.

Expanding play perspectives

Many play scholars have drawn attention to the tenuous and incomplete understandings of children's play due to the limited perspectives applied to research in children's play. Often play research has been limited to the study of Western children and contexts or interpreted through a Western lens, not taking into consideration cultural interpretations to play or to the perspectives of children or adults who fall 'outside' the mainstream societies (Gaskins & Miller, 2009; Rogers, 2011; Roopnarine, Johnson, & Hooper, 1994). The following studies are included in an effort to illuminate different perspectives about play and deepen our understanding of play.

Parents' perspectives can offer much insight into understanding children's play, but their input is not always considered in planning of programmes. LaForett and Mendez's study *Children's engagement in play at home: A parent's perspective* recognizes the need for educators to gain a better understanding of adults' beliefs about young children's play, particularly of low-income parents of colour with children in Head Start programmes. These beliefs are shaped by culture and can influence children's play opportunities and potential play competence. These perspectives may also allow educators a more complete picture of children's development. In this study, parents' beliefs about the importance of play for children's development were reported, along with children's actual play experiences at home and in neighbourhoods. Findings suggest that there are differences in how parents from different cultural backgrounds view play as part of education and of how they assess their own children's play abilities. These various perspectives were also not always congruent with the values and expectations around play by educators.

Warash, Root, and Doris' study *Parents' perceptions of play: A comparative study of spousal perspectives* also helps shed light on parental perspectives about play with children. The findings from this study showed that mothers rated play support higher than fathers. Also, as children grew older, parents' ratings of the importance of play support lessened. The relation between child age and academic focus differed by child gender, as well. The findings suggest that parents in this study perceive play as valuable, but these perceptions change as children approach formal schooling.

The study titled *The social kindergartener: Comparing children's perspectives of full- and half-day kindergarten* by Heagle, Timmons, Hargreaves, and Peletier give us insights into children's own perspectives about what is for some, their first school experience. The researchers explored and compared children's responses to questions regarding their own evaluation of the kindergarten experience. Their responses revealed that children in half-day kindergarten considered academic activities as being important significantly more often with their full-day counterparts. However, there was no significant differences between the children's reports of their favourite thing about school – play and social activities. Perhaps, a perspective not often asked within educational settings, but a very important one nonetheless, is the children's preferences and desires. Once again, these findings also support the importance of including play in early educational settings, especially for children who attend for long part of the day.

Alcock's study *Interpersonal fields of play* uses ethnographic methods to investigate infant–toddlers' relationships in a bicultural early childhood setting and thus, offers a different perspective beyond Western interpretations of early childhood. This text raises important questions about definitions of 'best practices' in relation to infant and toddler caregiving, including play that are based in Western beliefs and values regarding child rearing. Contrasting the western based idea of 'primary caregiving', the author introduces the indigenous Maori world-views and values that emphasize the interconnectedness of all phenomena and the importance of sustainability-beliefs that strongly contrast with a dyadic and individualistic nature of primary caregiving. We learn about caregiving in a centre in New Zealand that has a commitment to Aotearoa's bicultural heritage, particularly the responsibility to exercise kaitiakitanga or guardianship of the environment. In this context, the focus on sustainability provides a rationale for teachers to reject the view of primary caregiving as a best practice. The author also suggests that Western beliefs about children's play as innocent and happy are not culturally aligned with the Maorian beliefs that recognize the wide range of emotions children bring into their play at the centre. This study concludes with a recommendation that research in early childhood (including studies of children's play) be informed by the relevant cultural values for the community being served and in this case, the importance of interconnectedness and sustainability.

MacNevin and Berman's study *The black baby doll doesn't fit: The disconnect between early childhood diversity policy, early childhood educator practice, and children's play* challenges Ontario's early childhood policy to have culturally diverse artefacts and toys available for children's play without addressing the power relations exhibited through personal interactions during play between teachers and children or considering how race and other positionalities influence how curriculum is created. Using data collected through participant observation of children's play in a preschool/kindergarten classroom, interviews with early childhood professionals, and document analysis of a particular early years policy, the authors highlight the shortcomings of the focus on materials as the main way to address 'race' and other differences in early childhood education. Assumptions about children's play are examined and critiqued, with examples of children's play episodes provided to emphasize how play can and does reproduce systems of power and oppression present in the broader social context.

In Kinkaid-Clark and Hardacre's study *Using cross cultural conversation to contextualise understandings of play: A multinational study,* the authors use the research tool of reflexivity – a reflective practice in which a researcher examines her own positionality and personal experiences that may influence her interpretation and understanding of the research topic. In this study, two researchers examine their own perspectives on play in the lives of children from diverse cultural contexts and from different disciplinary backgrounds. Two questions guided this study: (1) how do researchers conceptualize children's play and (2) what shapes their understanding of play. The two authors had each completed ethnographic studies of play in the UK and Jamaica and each challenged the other's thinking about play through a critical discourse. This discursive method allowed concepts of play to be grounded, not in theoretical concepts, but rather in national contexts. In this case, the authors remind all adults making meaning of play – researchers, as well as educators – that all our interpretations are situated, contextualized, and problematic.

Social justice, equity, and children's play: inviting a critical dialogue

As noted by social justice scholars, the term social justice is hard to define as it is associated with a range of constructs, including, 'equity, equality, inequality, equal opportunity, affirmative action, and most recently diversity' and each of these ideas 'takes on different meanings in different national contexts' (Blackmore, 2009, p. 7). Despite this complex variation, social justice scholarship aims to make visible the experiences of marginalized groups and inequities associated with educational opportunities and outcomes. The scholarship we highlight examines social justice in relationship to children's play by attending to both of these considerations. We spotlight several theoretical perspectives and descriptions of children children's play that are too often silenced and/or marginalized in the privileged discourses represented in early childhood literature and research. We also highlight scholarship that aims to critique children's diminishing access to and experiences with play, especially child-initiated and self-determined play.

Spanning across the texts are courageous questions about distributive, cultural, and associational aspects of social justice (Gewirtz & Cribb, 2002) as related to children's play. For example, we are asked to collectively examine how distributive justice is being achieved by considering the inequitable allocation of resources that impact children's differential access to play within early learning programmes, public schools, and communities. We are also called to scrutinize aspects of cultural justice by engaging in a critical audit of our early childhood pedagogies to consider how, if at all, we respect, recognize, and allow for diverse cultural perspectives and expressions to be made visible in children's play. Additionally, we are called to make an honest account of how we are limiting the topics and themes children are allowed to make sense of and organize through play and recognize the types of play we support and those we interrupt and discourage. Scholars attending to cultural justice in this collection of texts leave us pondering how the decisions we make as early childhood professionals are disrupting or perpetuating cultural domination that privileges certain cultural beliefs and knowledge over others. Their fortitude to reveal our biases is matched with urgent calls to become more culturally responsive and culturally sustaining in our practices (Paris, 2012). Still other scholars focus our attention in the direction of associational justice, querying how children have agency to participate in the decisions that impact their lives, including choices about where, what, how, and if they can play in a world that frequently seeks to subjugate their voices and power into compliance with adults' desires and preferences.

Complementing this tripartite emphasis on social justice, this body of work attends to equity as apposite with complexity – a phenomenological viewpoint that presumes equity is best confronted and improved through developing a deepened understanding of human variation, idiosyncrasy and variegated contexts (El-Haj, 2003; Himley, 2000; Shimpi & Nicholson, 2013). As childhood play is a mirror into the diverse contexts in which children live, differing across multiple dimensions, including geography, sociocultural beliefs and values, political environment, and historical milieu, the work we highlight attempts to capture these multiplicities instead of muting play's complex expressions in children's lives around the world. By highlighting different relationships of power and toggling our attention to different discourses and perspectives about children's play, we aim to highlight the complexities and tensions inherent to any honest scholarly discussion that considers the role of play in the development and learning of young children. Attending to social justice and equity means focusing our attention towards keeping the most marginalized, silenced, and under-resourced as the inspiration guiding our professional work and steering the actions we take towards equalizing opportunities and resources in order to interrupt disparities for young children and families.

We invite you to draw inspiration from these collective texts by allowing the authors' questions and empirical evidence to disrupt your intellectual efficiencies, to break open your cultural conceptions and theorizing about children's play, and to goad you into action in working for a world where children have a right to play in diverse and culturally responsive ways. Our invitation is fuelled by our belief that it is through play that children dream, build relationships, create, connect, belong, heal, take risks, and love. We owe our children nothing less.

References

Blackmore, J. (2009). Leadership for social justice: A transnational dialogue. *Journal of Research on Leadership Education, 4* (1), Article 5. Retrieved from http://www.ucea.org/jrle

El-Haj, T. (2003). Practicing for equity from the standpoint of the particular: Exploring the work of one urban teacher network. *Teachers College Record, 105*(5), 817–845.

Fromberg, D. P., & Bergen, D. (Eds.). (2015). *Play from birth to twelve: Contexts, perspectives, and meanings.* New York, NY: Routledge.

Gaskins, S., & Miller, P.J. (2009). The cultural roles of emotions in pretend play. In C. Dell Clark (Ed.), *Transactions at play: Play and cultural studies* (pp. 5–21). Lanham, MD: University Press of America.

Gewirtz, S., & Cribb, A. (2002). Plural conceptions of social justice: Implications for policy sociology. *Journal of Education Policy, 17*, 499–509.

Ginsburg, K., & The Committee on Communications and the Committee on Psychosocial Aspects of Child and Family Health. (2007). The importance of play in promoting healthy child development and maintaining strong parent-child bonds. *Pediatrics, 119*(1), 182–191. doi:10.1542/peds.2006-2697

Grieshaber, S., & McArdle, F. (2010). *The trouble with play.* Milton Keynes: Open University Press.

Himley, M. (2000). The value/s of oral inquiry, or 'you just had to be there!' In M. Himley (Ed.), with P. Carini, *From another angle: Children's strengths and school standards: Prospect Center's descriptive review of the child* (pp. 199–211). New York, NY: Teachers College Press.

Nicholson, J., Kurnik, J., Jevgjovikj, M., & Ufoegbune, V. (2015). Deconstructing adults' and children's discourse on children's play: Inserting children's voices to destabilize deficit narratives. *Early Child Development and Care 185*(10), 1569–1586.

Paris, D. (2012). Culturally sustaining pedagogy: A needed change in stance, terminology, and practice. *Educational Researcher, 41*(3), 93–97. doi:10.3102/0013189X12441244

Piaget, J. (1945). *Play, dreams and imitation in childhood.* London: Heinemann.

Rogers, S. (Ed.). (2011). *Rethinking play and pedagogy in early childhood education: Concepts, contexts, and cultures.* New York, NY: Routledge.

Rogoff, B. (2003). *The cultural nature of human development.* New York, NY: Oxford University Press.

Roopnarine, J., Johnson, J., & Hooper, F. (1994). *Children's play in diverse cultures.* Albany, NY: State University of New York Press.

Shimpi, P., & Nicholson, J. (2013). Using cross-cultural, intergenerational play narratives to explore issues of social justice and equity in discourse on children's play. *Early Child Development and Care.* doi:10.1080/03004430.2013.813847

Sutton-Smith, B. (Ed.). (1995). *Children's folklore: A source book* (Vol. 647). New York, NY: Routledge.

Sutton-Smith, B. (1997/2001). *The ambiguity of play.* Boston, MA: Harvard University Press.

United Nations. (1989). *Convention on the rights of the child.* Retrieved from http://www.ohchr.org/EN/ProfessionalInterest/Pages/CRC.aspx

Van Hoorn, J., Nourot, P., Scales, B., & Alward, K. (2015). *Play at the center of the curriculum* (6th ed.). New York, NY: Pearson.

Vygotsky, L. (1978). The role of play in development. In *Mind in society* (M. Cole, Trans., pp. 92–104). Cambridge, MA: Harvard University Press.

Wisneski, D., & Reifel, S. (2012). The place of play in early childhood curriculum. In N. File, J. J. Mueller, & D. B. Wisneski (Eds.), *Curriculum in early childhood education: Re-examined, rediscovered, renewed* (pp. 175–187). New York, NY: Routledge.

Block play: spatial language with preschool and school-aged children

Lynn E. Cohen and Janet Emmons

ABSTRACT
Implementing a play-based curriculum presents challenges for pre-service and in-service teachers given the current climate of standards and didactic pedagogies. This study highlights the value of playful learning and its rightful place in early childhood classrooms for children of all ages. The purpose of the present study was to investigate the use of spatial words with children aged between three and nine years. The benefits of the use of spatial words in a playful venue to advocate block play for not only preschool children, but elementary-school-age children were examined. This article suggest that industry and academia need to collaborate to provide play venues for children, and unit blocks need to be brought back into early childhood programmes.

Throughout the decades, the area of childhood education has grown by leaps and bounds. A classroom 50 years ago would be barely recognizable to parents and pre-service teachers today. Many states are removing blocks and block play from their programmes to provide more drill and didactic instruction. Educators struggle to maintain the accelerated pace associated with application of Common Core Standards, standardized tests, scripted reading programmes, and new technologies. This research provides an alternative form of assessment by demonstrating the value of block play and spatial language with preschool and school-aged children. Children's block play naturally enhances skills of observation, communication, experimentation, as well as the development of construction skills. While playing, children develop social, language, math, artistic, creative, and academic skills (Hanline, Milton, & Phelps, 2009). Research (Bairaktarova, Evangelov, Bagiati, & Brophy, 2011) also attests to block building as a starting point for architecture and civil engineering skills.

From a theoretical perspective, Vygotsky's (1978) sociocultural theory can be applied to the current study. For Vygotsky, the social context includes social, as well as cultural levels that influence a child's language and learning. Vygotsky (1978) argued that there are a number of acquired and shared tools, 'cultural tools' that aid in human thinking and behaviour. These skills help us think more clearly and better understand our own thinking processes. Vygotsky's (1978) sociocultural theory rejects an individualistic view of the developing child in favour of a socially formed mind. Bodrova and Leong (2015) clearly state that Vygotsky's theory about play describes 'only one kind of play, namely socio-dramatic or make-believe play typical for preschoolers and children of primary age' (p. 205). Although Vygotsky (1978) did not specifically include block play, it can be argued that additional principles of Vygotsky's cultural-historical theory can be applied to block play (Rogoff, 1995; Wertsch, 1991, 1998). A principle illustrating the importance of the social context in children's block play is Vygotsky's ideas of *internalization* and the *zone of proximal development* (ZPD).

According to Vygotsky (1978) internalization occurs when knowledge moves from a social level (external) to an individual plane (mental), from a state of knowing with assistance with others to a state of knowing for oneself. Vygotsky coined the term the ZPD to refer to the conditions under which children's understanding is furthered as a result of social interaction and language. A child will display a particular level of performance when building a structure alone as opposed to a higher level when building with a peer or given direction by a teacher. In a block play context, children's efforts are supported not by deliberate instruction, but through language, perspective taking, and problem-solving skills. Vygotsky's (1978) sociocultural theories are conceptualized as they relate to block play in the present research. The purpose of this research is to describe and examine the use of spatial words in a playful venue to advocate block play for all ages.

The present study

An investigation was implemented at Blockspot® (www.blockspotlearning.com), a retail business that invites children to visit, play, and learn outside of the classroom. At Blockspot® opportunities are provided that put the children (age: 2–12) in charge of their own block-building outcomes. Previous research has investigated spatial language and block play with preschool and kindergarten children (Caldera et al., 1999; Casey et al., 2008) and parent–child dyads (Ferrara, Hirsh-Pasek, Newcombe, Golinkoff, & Lam, 2011; Pruden, Levine, & Huttenlocher, 2011), but there is little research that examines wooden unit block play with school-age children. Two research questions were examined in the present study:

(1) In what ways do children (4–12-year-old) use spatial words in guided block play? Specifically, do they use spatial words when teachers verbally scaffold block play?
(2) Is there evidence that older children will use more spatial words than younger children in block play?

Thus, we begin with the literature related to the notion of guided play in the context of block play. Vygotskian theories believe that teachers' observations and verbal scaffolding in a child's ZPD can create learning experiences that build upon the child's existing understanding. Next, the literature related to spatial skills, language and blocks is discussed. Finally, age differences between younger and older block builders are presented.

Guided play with blocks

Two pedagogical methods of play that are often contrasted are free play and guided play. Free play is child-initiated and child-directed; children decide what to play and how. Several researchers have provided evidence of the value of free play for children's development (Hirsh-Pasek, Golinkoff, Berk, & Singer, 2008; Singer, Golinkoff, & Hirsch-Pasek, 2006). There is evidence that free play support's children's social development (Hyson, 2004), cognitive development (Bergen, 2002), and imagination and creativity (Brown, 2009). Guided play is a blend of adult-scaffolded learning objectives but is child-directed. In guided play, adults initiate the learning process, constrain the learning goals and maintain focus on these goals as the child guides his or her discovery (Weisberg, Hirsh-Pasek, & Golinkoff, 2013). This perspective embodies a sociocultural view on play that supports scaffolding and guidance in discovery learning (Honomichl & Chen, 2012). The adult's role is to follow the child's lead and guide the child in the context of the environment by suggesting, not directing important learning goals. Honomichl and Chen (2012) summarized three approaches to facilitate discovery learning that have proven to be effective: (1) strategic presentation of materials, (2) sequential feedback, and (3) probing questions and self-explanation. Several researchers have used guided play in the context of block-building activities (Ferrara et al., 2011); Gregory, Kim, & Whiren, 2003; Ramani, Zippert, Schweitzer, & Pan, 2014) For example, Vygotsky's theories of scaffolding and guided block play is illustrated in a study by Gregory et al. (2003), who trained adults to recognize degrees of complexity in block constructions and then had them observe children at block play and offer verbal support for creating increasingly complex structures. While the adults did not interfere in the play and took a supportive rather than a directive role, they engaged in verbal scaffolding such as asking open-ended questions, posing problems (e.g. What would happen if ..., How could ...), making leading statements (e.g. sometimes people use a block to join a structure ...), and thinking of possibilities out loud (e.g. I wonder if ...). The result was an increase in the complexity of the children's block structures. Symbolic play recreated an experience in which knowledge and skills were transmitted to children to help him or her better understand reality. In that sense, play lead to the development of complex block structures (Vygotsky, 1978).

Similarly, in the present study, adults scaffolded block play for both prekindergarten and school-age children by presenting challenges, posing problems, and asking open-ended questions. A few examples of open-ended questions were: How are you planning to make your airport? How's your house coming? Examples of problems posed: With these blocks what can you build? Would some small blocks like this one (holding up a unit block) help to complete your structure? Which blocks are you thinking about to enhance your idea?

In sum, from a cultural-historical tradition, play does not develop spontaneously in all children once they reach preschool age. For play to be a leading activity, adult mediation or having older children acting as play mentors for younger children can facilitate the quality of block-building skills (Bodrova & Leong, 2015). Although, we do not want adults to take over children's play and turn it into educational lessons that destroy children's freedom, joy, and passions. Children need to be able to initiate their own learning and adults need to know when to intervene and pose questions and problems to support new skills.

Spatial skills, language, and play

There is some evidence that constructive play is related to spatial skills (Caldera et al., 1999; Ness & Farenga, 2007). According to the scientific literature, constructive play activities such as Legos and blocks exert the most influence on children's spatial skills. Most of the studies with older children (Brosnan, 1998; Nath & Szücs, 2014; Pirrone, Nicolosi, Passanisi, & Di Nuovo, 2015) have focused on the relationship between Lego building blocks, mathematics, and spatial skills (Nath & Szücs, 2014; Pirrone et al., 2015). Brosnan (1998) asked mixed-gendered nine-year-olds to follow instructions to build a bridge with Lego blocks. Results found that those that completed the Lego model scored significantly higher in spatial ability than those who did not. There were no significant sex differences as both sexes played with Lego blocks. Caldera et al. (1999) examined 51 preschoolers' play preferences, performance on standardized measures, and skills building with blocks. Structured and unstructured block play was videotaped and coded. They found no preference between structured or unstructured play. Play with art materials and reproduction of complex block structures were interrelated to tests of spatial visualization.

Fewer studies have examined communication skills during block building with preschool children. Cohen and Uhry (2007) observed individuals, dyads, and small groups of children in the block area in a preschool classroom. The dyads and small groups talked more than children building by themselves. Sluss and Stremmel (2004) observed preschool dyads and found that girls communicated more when paired with an experienced partner. The girls' block building, communication skills, and understanding were further developed by socially interacting with another peer.

In view of findings that show spatial thinking is an important predictor of Science, Technology, Engineering, and Mathematics (Wai, Lubinksi, & Benbow, 2009), it is important to explore how language in a context of constructive play is related to spatial thinking. Spatial words that refer to spatial features and block-building properties (e.g. big, little, tall, fat), or the shapes of blocks (e.g. circle, rectangle, octagon, triangle,), and the spatial properties of blocks (e.g. bent, curvy, flat, edge, pointy) are commonly used as children build and talk about their structures. Although communication among peers during play could support spatial skills as well as spatial language skills, the majority of the research on play and spatial language has focused on preschool (Casey et al., 2008; Ramani et al., 2014) and parent–child dyads (Ferrara et al., 2011; Pruden et al., 2011). Casey et al. (2008) used a guided play intervention using unifix cubes and storytelling with kindergarten children. They found teaching block building improved spatial abilities and the story telling provided a context for teaching spatial language. Ramani et al. (2014) used guided play to investigate four- and five-year old's communication and building behaviours using cardboard blocks. They found the dyads engaged in spatial talk about math-related concepts, such as number and spatial relations, and matching the size and relations between blocks.

Parental spatial language input has been compared to children's use of spatial language when playing with blocks (Ferrara et al., 2011; Pruden et al., 2011) using the same spatial language coding system, *A System for Analysing Children and Caregivers' Language about Space in Structured and Unstructured Contexts* (Cannon, Levine, & Huttenlocher, 2007), used in the present research. Ferrara et al. (2011) investigated MegaBloks with preschool, kindergarten, and parents in three conditions: (a) guided play, (b) free play, and (c) play with preassembled structures. Parents in the guided play condition produced significantly higher proportions of spatial talk than those in the free play condition. Similarly, Pruden et al. (2011) found that the amount of parental spatial language input predicted the amount of spatial language preschool children used as parents played alongside their child. The work by Pruden et al. (2011) was an experimental study with children aged 14 to 46 months in a sample of 52 parent–child dyads as they engaged in everyday activities in the context of the home. Three categories of spatial terms were coded: (a) shape terms (e.g. circle, triangle, octagon), (b) dimensional adjectives (e.g. big, little, tall), and (c) spatial features (e.g. bent, curvy, side). The amount of spatial words used by children and parents was assessed when children were 46 months. There was variability in the amount of children and parents' spatial words but overall the results found when parents produced a lot of spatial words, children also used large percentages of spatial words.

Age differences

As indicated earlier, a goal of the study was to examine the differences in spatial language between younger and older block builders. This question is of interest because although the literature has not examined the differences in the use of spatial language and unit block play between preschool and elementary students, early research has described how spatial relations within children's block-building structures become more complex with age. Toddlers and young preschoolers are limited in their language and spatial dimensionality, building structures with one or two blocks in rows or towers. Later, preschool children start to arrange structures in arches or build bridge structures. Ness and Farenga (2007) found differences between four-year-old and five-year-old structures. They analysed videotapes of children's block play to observe and record cognitive abilities of the relationship between space and architectural relationships. Thirteen codes were associated with 90 young children's engagement in spatial, geometric, and architectural thinking based on *The Assessment for Measuring Spatial, Geometric, and Architectural Thinking of Young Children*. The buildings for five-year-old children included more symmetry and patterns. Reifel (1984) suggests that child's block constructions, age's four years and younger, result in the vertical structures by placing blocks on top of one another or creating horizontal structures by placing blocks next to one another. This early framework by Reifel (1984) shed important information for examining block complexity with four–seven-year-old children. Reifel (1981) and Reifel and Greenfield (1982, 1983) examined block play complexity with children aged between four and seven years. Reifel and Greenfield (1982) found that construction becomes more structurally complex with age. Seven-year-olds were able to label and discuss finished block structures at a higher rate than four-year-old children.

Review of the literature highlights the point that preschool and kindergarten children in guided play produce more spatial words when parents are playing and talking about block building alongside their children. Additionally, the literature has reported significant findings related to Lego play, mathematics, and spatial skills with elementary children, but the findings do not necessarily capture children's spatial language during their building interactions with peers. Although early research found children's block structures became more complex and they talked more about their structures with increased age, these studies did not investigate the use of spatial language with unit blocks. Thus, the goal of the present study was to examine the use of spatial words in guided block play and if older children would use more spatial words than younger children.

Methods

Setting

Data were collected at Blockspot® a retail business in Southampton, New York for children of all ages to play with unit blocks. It was developed by a certified teacher, the founder (co-author), and run by certified teachers. The goal is to get unit blocks back in the hands of children of all ages. The founder (co-author) believes that as children mature their play will become more complex. Block play classes are held mornings for preschool children and after school for elementary children. Multiage drop-in play is offered every Saturday morning. Recently, local public school districts serving Pre-K to fifth grade leave the classroom and take field trips to Blockspot®. It is in this setting that classroom curricula are transformed into block-building experiences and play for children of all ages. The children and teacher work together to create block-building plans before the trip; so learning has been scaffolded and guided by an adult or a peer. Onsite, children use their block-building plans to build structures related to a curricula theme. For most classes, these experiences are tied to an English Language Arts or Social Studies concept. Many are linked to the children's writing either through their writers' workshop selections, linked to a book read in class or a unit of study such as Colonial Times. For example: some classes may select to build structures related to their reading writing workshop stories by showcasing the characters and setting. Other classes may demonstrate their full understanding of an urban/suburban/rural unit of study and replicate characteristics of each. While others may select between three significant stories read in class and have to choose the one they wish to represent through their block structure. For all of the options mentioned ... the details both in structure and material selection are purposeful and powerful indicators of thought and understanding. The transference of the experience comes full circle in the return to the classroom where images of student work are used in a variety of ways to bring the experience to fruition. The teachers in this study supported the children's work by observing the way the children interacted, planned, engineered, and selected materials. Comments would be observational 'I see you are planning to build a large structure' 'I see you are building the interior. Are you planning to do a second story or a roof? How will you support that?' This type of observational scaffolding is dually important as it validates the process in place and encourages thoughtful next steps. For optimal student-driven block building, it is crucial that the teachers scaffold and pull back with the correct balance. Thus allowing the children to drive the process and result in the completed structure as intended by their minds' eye.

Participants

Blockspot® serves children who are predominately from upper-middle income families with the exception of school field trips. All participants of this study were upper-middle income and monolingual English speakers. Participants were 8 beginning builders aged 4–5 years (4 girls and 4 boys) and 6 after-school builders aged 8–12 years (2 girls and 4 boys). The classes for beginning builders are designed to support children's emerging block-building stages: stacking, making rows, bridges, pathways, and enclosures, while constructing stories with block accessories. The after-school builders' club provides children the freedom to learn and work on weekly activities planned on rotating topics created with blocks. Children learn physics, study architecture, solve math questions, and read and build story elements from classroom-independent reading.

Materials

Children's block building and conversations were videotaped by the researchers who quietly stayed in the corner during the play session. The video camera was placed unobtrusively in a corner where the block building took place, with full view of the children, the blocks, and the structures. An external microphone was attached to the video camera. A digital camera was used to photograph completed block structures.

Blocks were standard Caroline Pratt unit blocks (unit = 1⅜″× 2¾″ × 5½″) made of hard rock maple. The recommended number of blocks is 100 per child and space for construction is a minimum of 25 square feet per child (Phelps, 2006). Blockspot® has over 10,000 ++ unit blocks in a 2500 space designed for block play (See Figure 1). The number of unit blocks and space Blockspot® provides was more than adequate for children participating in the present study.

Procedure

Videotape sessions of guided play were recorded for three weeks that culminated in three hours of video data. The preschool children were videotaped in the morning and the after-school builders were taped in the afternoon. Each session was approximately 30 minutes in length. The building sessions included introductions, building time, share sessions, and cleanup time. Teachers began the beginning builders (four- to five-year-olds) sessions by discussing what children were to build and some things that their structures should include. The after-school builders were given a weekly challenge. For example, a challenge might be to build something 100″ wide but less than 36″ high using 5 different types of blocks or to build something that flies. The activity was a guided play activity because the children were given a goal, but could complete the goal in multiple ways with the

Figure 1. Blockspot® provides children with 10,000 + + unit blocks in a variety of different geometric shapes for children in elementary and preschool classrooms. Ample shelving is available to allow children to classify and organize the blocks during clean-up, an important learning experience.

teacher minimally involved. Usually, the teacher(s) used strategies similar to Gregory et al. (2003)'s verbal scaffolding of asking open-ended questions, posing problems, or making leading statements to support children's building process. At the end of the session children talked about their block-building structures.

Transcription and coding

All videotape block play sessions were transcribed for children's use of spatial words. Reliability in transcription was achieved by having a second research assistant independently transcribe 20% of the videotapes. The reliability criterion was set at 95%. Both transcribers were in agreement on 95% of the utterances, $r > .95$. For each participant, the total number of utterances in all transcripts was calculated. To arrive at this measure, the flow of talk into utterances during block-building sessions was based on conversational turn taking (Cohen & Uhry, 2007). An utterance consisted of a single international contour within a conversational turn. This included declaratives and questions in which there was a pause preceding and following it. An utterance could also include a single word (e.g. bigger), a phrase (e.g. a little table) or a single or multiword sentence.

These transcriptions were then coded using the eight spatial categories of the University of Chicago spatial language coding system, *A system for analyzing children and caregivers' language about space in structured and unstructured contexts* (Cannon et al., 2007). The coders identified terms that included the following spatial categories: (1) spatial dimensions are words that describe the size of objects, people, and spaces (e.g. big, little, wide, narrow, size, length), (2) shapes are words that describe mathematical names of two- and three-dimensional objects and spaces (e.g. rectangle, square, triangle, circle), (3) location/direction are words that describe the position of objects, people, and points in space (e.g. up, down, in, under, high, row), (4) spatial orientations or transformations are words the relative orientation or transformation of objects and people in space (e.g. turn it around, right side up, upside down, upright, rotate), (5) continuous amount are words that describe amount of continuous quantities (e.g. part, a lot, all, same, more, equal, half, inch, foot), (6) deictic terms identify spatial location and rely on the context or participants to understand their referent (e.g. here, there, where, anywhere), (7) spatial features or properties are words that describe the features and properties of two- and three-dimensional objects, people, and spaces (e.g. side, curvy, straight, flat, corner, horizontal, vertical), and (8) pattern are words that indicate a person may be talking about a spatial pattern (e.g. pattern, order, next, first, last, before, increase, decrease). Reliability was also investigated on 50% of the spatial word coding. Again, the reliability criterion was set at 95%. Research assistant one and two both were in agreement, yielding reliability for the spatial word codes, $r > .95$.

Results

To address the first research question related to the use of spatial words in guided block play, the total numbers of utterances were calculated. There were 851 utterances in the three hours of videotape data. Fifty-seven per cent of the utterances were elicited by the beginning builders and 43% were spoken by the after-school builders. Next, descriptive statistics indicated both groups as a whole used spatial words while playing with unit blocks. The category of patterning was eliminated from the data set because the beginning builders and after-school builders did not produce a single spatial word in this category. On average both groups produced a total of 376 spatial words during the three hours of guided play. Both groups used spatial words but there was variability in the production of spatial words (Table 1). In the category of location/direction the children produced an average of 13.07 (SD = 17.70) spatial words and in the continuous amount category an average of 5.30 (SD = 5.15) words were produced. In comparison, children produced very low averages for categories of shapes ($M = .36$, SD = .74) and orientation words ($M = .64$, SD = 2.13).

Table 1. Mean and standard deviations of spatial word categories.

Spatial word category	*M*	SD
Dimension	2.79	3.33
Shape	0.36	0.74
Location	13.07	17.70
Orientation/transformation	0.64	2.13
Continuous amount	5.30	0.15
Deictic	2.79	3.30
Feature/property	0.71	1.59

The categories of location/direction were words that described the relative position of the blocks and their location in space. It also was the largest category of words and included terms that function in numerous parts of speech. Frequently used words were above, top, in, and behind. The category of continuous amount was words that describe the amount of continuous quantities. Frequently used words were standard spatial measurement units such as inch and foot, as well as words that describe a comparison of continuous amounts such as more, less, same, equal.

To assess differences between groups' (beginning builders and after-school builders) use of spatial words a *t*-test was used. There was no significant difference ($p > .05$) between the beginning builders ($M = 404.37$, $SD = 421$) and after-school builders ($M = 338.5$, $SD = 350$) on all spatial word categories. Thus, the after-school builders did not produce more spatial words than the beginning builders.

Discussion

This study investigated the use of spatial words in the context of unit block play with preschool children and elementary children. Two research questions were examined: (a) to examine the use of spatial words with children 4 years to 12 years in guided block play (Caldera et al., 1999; Casey et al., 2008) and (b) to assess if spatial language would differ with age level and older children would use more spatial words in block play (Reifel & Greenfield, 1982). First is a discussion of children's use of spatial words with unit blocks during guided block play followed by an examination of the age differences in the use of spatial words while building structures with unit blocks.

Children's use of spatial words varied widely in the present study. Some children used many spatial words as they were building their structures; others did very little talking and used a minimal number of spatial words. The children were able to communicate with peers during all videotaped sessions. While some conversed with peers, many were engaged in the process of building and both the beginning builders and after-school builders mainly discussed the task of building (e.g. what they were going to do, what blocks they needed). This possibly suggests that children's talk was related to the quality of the structures. This type of communication is consistent with previous research examining discourse strategies and meaning-making among young children in the block centre (Cohen & Uhry, 2007).

Additionally, all guided play-building sessions were indirectly scaffolded by the teachers. The findings may suggest that more direct scaffolding of spatial words may increase the frequency of spatial language children hear and use on their own to support the use of spatial words. Ferrara et al. (2011) examined parental scaffolding in three play conditions and found that when parents played less of an assertive role in talking to their child, the child became more absorbed with the activity of the building and did not elicit as much conversation about spatial configurations. Perhaps teachers could provide older builders with spatial vocabulary words; beginning builders may benefit from the use of parents building and talking alongside their children.

The second was to examine the use of spatial words in both groups of block builders, beginning builders, and after-school builders. Again, a review of the video transcripts and interactions indicated that older builders appeared to be demonstrating goal-oriented design, problem-solving skills, and engineering thinking. Older builders were more focused on language to share the initial construction goal, give input regarding the solution, or consult with a peer than the preschool builders. Additionally, the use of spatial words by the after-school builders varied widely. Sutton-Smith's (1997) defined different types of play from different disciplines and discussed the play rhetoric of *progress*. Block play cannot be examined from a lens of stages and ages, but rather examined through a lens of children's meaning-making and understanding of how things should be constructed and how they work.

There were differences in spatial talk between the girls ($M = 28.7$) and boys ($M = 22.7$). Two girls used many spatial words while building and after-school boys rarely engaged in any spatial talk. In an examination of one videotape, the girls used 58 spatial words and the boys spoke 18 spatial words. Gender differences and spatial talk needs further investigation.

An interesting discovery was that the current literature related to block play and spatial language highlights the different kinds of blocks used in constructive play. Studies have used mega blocks (Ferrara et al., 2011); pattern blocks (Casey et al., 2008); cardboard blocks (Ramani et al., 2014), and an assortment of blocks in a box (Caldera et al., 1999). Research with elementary students (Brosnan, 1998; Nath & Szücs, 2014; Pirrone et al., 2015) has primarily investigated Lego construction abilities with mathematical performance, not spatial language. The use of Lego blocks is very different from unit wooden blocks. Lego blocks require children to construct a specific three-dimensional model. Lego blocks come with pictorial instructions that indicate which piece should be added where, without the use of any written material. It appears that current empirical studies with wooden unit blocks is limited and it could be argued that this lack of empirical research of the value of unit block play and spatial language might be attributed to the disappearance of wooden unit blocks in many prekindergarten and kindergarten classrooms.

Conclusion

Play, once a daily activity in all early childhood classrooms, has been pushed out of most elementary public schools, and presently the trend is to also eliminate it from preschool settings (Nicolopoulou, 2010). The idea that research on early brain development implies that low-income children need direct instruction to overcome the achievement gap, as well as Race to the Top Common Core Standards have led to more standardized tests and less play in early childhood classrooms. Teachers need to understand the standards in place and use those standards to enhance children's play opportunities. There are no standards written that cannot be supported through play, and especially scaffolded play with blocks. Blockspot® has taken that challenge of using the standards and curricula to allow children opportunities to play and create within disciplines of language arts, mathematics, science, art, and literature.

Overall, observations of children's unit block play suggested guided play allowed children to develop linguistic skills. Finally, the study of spatial words is an area of inquiry with the potential to help us better understand ways block play might promote further inquiries related to spatial skills in mathematics and science that use unit blocks, not Legos, as a material for future investigations.

References

Bairaktarova, D., Evangelov, D., Bagiati, A., & Brophy, S. (2011). Engineering in young children's exploratory play with tangible materials. *Children, Youth, and Environments, 21*(2), 212–235.

Bergen, D. (2002). The role of pretend play in children's cognitive development. *Early childhood research and practive, 4*(1), 2–15. Retrieved from http://ecrp.uiiuc.edu/v4n1/bergen.html

Bodrova, E., & Leong, D. J. (2015). Standing "a head taller than himself. Vygotskian and post-Vygotskian views on children's play (Vol. 1). In J. E. Johnson, S. G. Eberle, & T. S. Henricks (Eds.), *The handbook of the study of play* (pp. 215–227). Lanham, MD: Rowman & Littlefield.

Brosnan, M. J. (1998). Spatial ability in children's play with Lego blocks. *Perceptual and Motor Skills, 87*, 19–28.

Brown, S. (2009). *Play: How it shapes the brain, opens the imagination, and invigorates the soul.* New York, NY: Penguin Group.

Caldera, Y. M., Culp, A. M., O'Brian, M., Truglio, R. T., Alvarez, M., & Huston, A. (1999). Children's play preferences, construction play with blocks and visual spatial skills: Are they related? *International Journal of Behavioral Development, 23*, 855–872.

Cannon, J., Levine, S., & Huttenlocher, J. (2007). *A system for analyzing children and caregivers' language about space in structured and unstructured contexts.* Spatial Intelligence and Learning Center (SILC) technical report.

Casey, M. B., Andrews, N., Schindler, H., Kersh, J. E., Sampler, A., & Copley, J. (2008). The development of spatial skills through interventions involving block building activities. *Cognition and Instruction, 26*, 269–309.

Cohen, L., & Uhry, J. (2007). Young children's discourse strategies during block play: A Bakhtinian approach. *Journal of Research in Childhood Education, 21*, 302–315.

Ferrara, K., Hirsh-Pasek, K., Newcombe, N. S., Golinkoff, R. M., & Lam, W. S. (2011). Block talk: Spatial language during block play. *Mind, Brain, and Education, 5*, 143–151.

Gregory, K. M., Kim, A. S., & Whiren, A. (2003). The effect of verbal scaffolding on the complexity of preschool children's block constructions. In D. E. Lytle (Ed.), *Play and educational theory and practice* (pp. 117–133). Westport, CT: Praeger.

Hanline, M. F., Milton, S., & Phelps, P. C. (2009). The relationship between preschool block play and reading and math abilities in early elementary school. *A longitudinal study of children with and without disabilities. Early Childhood Development and Care, 180*(8), 1005–1017.

Hirsh-Pasek, K., Golinkoff, R. M., Berk, L. E., & Singer, D. G. (2008). *A mandate for playful learning in preschool: Applying the scientific evidence.* New York, NY: Oxford University Press.

Honomichl, R. D., & Chen, Z. (2012). The role of guidance in chidren's discovery learning. *WIREs Cognitive Science, 3*, 615–622.

Hyson, M. (2004). *The emotional development of young children.* New York, NY: Teacher's College Press.

Nath, S., & Szücs, D. (2014). Constructive play and cognitive skills associated with the development of mathematical abilities in 7-year-old children. *Learning and Instruction, 32*, 73–80.

Ness, D., & Farenga, S. J. (2007). *Knowledge under construction: The importance of play in developing children's spatial and geometric thinking.* Lanham, MD: Rowman & Littlefield.

Nicolopoulou, A. (2010). The alarming disappearance of play from early childhood education. *Human Development, 53*(1), 1–4.

Phelps, P. C. (2006). *Beyond centers and circle time: Scaffolding and assessing the play of young children.* Lewisville, NC: Kaplan Early Learning.

Pirrone, C., Nicolosi, A., Passanisi, A., Di Nuovo, S. (2015). Learning potential in mathematics through imagination and manipulation of building blocks. *Mediterranean Journal of Social Sciences, 6*, (4 S 3), 152–159.

Pruden, S. M., Levine, S. C., & Huttenlocher, J. (2011). Children's spatial thinking: Does talk about the spatial world matter? *Developmental Science, 14*, 1417–1430.

Ramani, G. B., Zippert, E., Schweitzer, S., & Pan, S. (2014). Preschool children's joint block building during a guided play activity. *Journal of Applied Developmental Psychology, 35*, 326–336.

Reifel, S. (1981). An exploration of block play as symbolic representation. *Dissertations Abstracts International, 42*(4), (UMI No.8121040).

Reifel, S. (1984). Block construction. Children's developmental landmarks in representation of space. *Young Children, 40*, 61–67.

Reifel, S., & Greenfield, P. M. (1982). Structural development in a symbolic medium: The representational use of block constructions. In G. Forman (Ed.), *Action and thought: From sensorimotor schemes to symbolic operations* (pp. 203–232). New York, NY: Academic Press.

Reifel, S., & Greenfield, P. M. (1983). *Part-whole relations: Some structural features of children's representational block play. Child Care Quarterly, 12*(1), 144–151.

Rogoff, B. (1995). Observing sociocultural activity on three planes: Participatory appropriation, guided participation, and apprenticeship. In J. V. Wertsch, P. Del Rio, & A. Alvarez (Eds.), *Sociocultural studies of mind* (pp. 139–184). New York, NY: Cambridge University Press.

Singer, D. G., Golinkoff, R. M., & Hirsch-Pasek, K. (Eds.). (2006). *Play = learning: How play motivates and enhances children's cognitive and social-emotional growth.* New York, NY: Oxford University Press.

Sluss, D. J., & Stremmel, A. J. (2004). A sociocultural investigation of the effects of peer interaction on play. *Journal of Research in Childhood Education, 18*(4), 293–305.

Sutton-Smith, B. (1997). *The ambiguity of play*. Cambridge, MA: Harvard University Press.

Vygotsky, L. S. (1978). The role of play in development. In M. Cole, V. John-Steiner, S. Scribner, & E. Soubermann (Eds.), *Mind in Society: The development of higher psychological processes* (pp. 92–104). Cambridge, MA: Harvard University Press.

Wai, J., Lubinksi, D., & Benbow, C. P. (2009). Spatial ability for STEM domains: Aligning over 50 years of cumulative psychological knowledge solidifies its importance. *Journal of Educational Psychology, 101*, 817–835.

Weisberg, D., Hirsh-Pasek, K., & Golinkoff, R. (2013). Guided play: Where curricular goals meet a playful pedagogy. *Mind, Brain, and Education, 7*(2), 104–112.

Wertsch, J. (1991). *Voices of the mind: A sociocultural approach to mediated action*. Cambridge, MA: Harvard University Press.

Wertsch, J. (1998). *Minds in action*. New York, NY: Oxford University Press.

Early childhood curriculum development: the role of play in building self-regulatory capacity in young children†

Linda R. Kroll

ABSTRACT

This case study examines the development of self-regulation, socially, cognitively and emotionally, through the use of play in the curriculum in five preschool classrooms for children ages 2–5 years old at a university laboratory school. Five teachers were interviewed about their deliberate use of play to support the development of self-regulation in their students, and subsequently, each classroom was observed for a total of 2 hours over a period of 2 months. Data included interview transcripts, observational notes and photographs and videos of the classrooms and children's play. Findings showed that the teachers regarded play as central to their curriculum and to the development of self-regulation in their students. Observations demonstrate strong interaction between the curriculum, environment, routines and the development of self-regulation. Supporting the development of self-regulatory capacities is a social justice and equity issue most effectively addressed through the inclusion of play in the early childhood curriculum.

Introduction

With the advent of the new model standards for kindergarten through the 12th grade, the expectations for children's abilities to pay attention, get along with others, focus independently for long periods of time, follow fairly regimented schedules and maintain a strong energy level have greatly increased. We can (and do) argue that these standards are detrimental, miseducative and unrealistic for 5-year-olds, but, nevertheless, as early childhood educators, we have to think about how we can prepare our young children to weather these conditions as healthily as possible. One of the goals of kindergarten used to be to help children learn to be 'in school', which means, among other things, learning to get along in a group, learning to wait one's turn, learning to listen within the group for directions and then follow directions and developing fine motor skills in handling crayons, pencils, scissors and so forth. Now, when children come to kindergarten, they are often expected to already know the letters of the alphabet, to be able to read their name and to be ready to be taught what was once essentially a first-grade curriculum. Kindergarten used to include many opportunities for play, to try out the more grown-up roles that children were not yet ready to take on 'for real'. Kindergarten now includes very little time for play and imagination (Bodrova & Leong, 2007).

Further complicating this situation is the diversity of the preschool population and the accompanying diverse experiences that children bring to school. Such expectations are particularly unfair and

---

†An early version of this study (interview data only) was presented at the Annual Meeting of the Jean Piaget Society, June 2010. A more complete version (interviews, observations and review of the two) of this study was presented at the Annual Meeting of the American Educational Research Association, April 2011.

miseducative for children whose earlier experiences have not included cultural expectations or experiences that are characteristic of 'mainstream' middle-class American culture (if such a thing exists). Play and the development of self-regulating behaviours within the context of play can provide children with an opportunity to exercise agency in their own education, even children as young as 2 years old. Thus, early childhood curriculum that affords the exercise of agency supports the aims of social justice and equity in providing each child with the opportunity and support to fully develop their potential and interests, both for now in the preschool classroom and for the future in the K-12 context.

In early childhood classrooms, we have the opportunity to help children develop the resilience and basis for learning that they will need to succeed in later years of schooling. Monitoring one's behaviour, understanding one's feelings, pursuing one's interests and curiosity, and acting in a way that is conducive to successful group learning are all related to the ability to self-regulate physically, emotionally, socially and cognitively. Early childhood teachers think hard about how to provide contexts in which children can learn to self-regulate, and develop those skills in the variety of contexts that the school provides and demands. They are focused on seeing that the children they teach have both the opportunity and the support to find joy in learning together, developing the skills they need now in the preschool classroom and that they can further develop in K-12 classrooms. Early Childhood Education teachers must think and plan for the child as she or he is now, recognizing her or his strengths and capabilities. A curriculum focused on play provides this opportunity.

In this study, I document the relationship between play and self-regulation in five preschool classrooms, by observing children's pretend play, art work, building and construction play and outdoor play. To begin this study, I interviewed the teachers who are the head teachers in these classrooms to see how they were thinking about the relationship between play, curriculum and the development of self-regulation in children aged 2½–5 years, before attempting to observe the actual development of these behaviours. Subsequently, I observed and documented the development of self-regulatory behaviour through play in their classrooms.

Conceptual framework

For the purposes of this paper, we need to be specific about our definitions of both play and self-regulation, and to understand how the relationship between the two can promote both social justice and equitable opportunities for all children. While we may all agree on what they are, being specific will help us to understand the data and the purposes of the teachers' work.

Self-regulation 'involves the regulation of both cognitive processes and social-emotional ones' (Blair, 2002 quoted from Bodrova & Leong, 2007, p. 128). Although they are all related, and part of the whole child, physical, emotional, social and cognitive self-regulation do not all happen at once, but rather develop throughout the child's life. 'Children first learn to regulate their physical behaviours, then their emotional ones' (Bodrova & Leong, 2007, p. 128). Social and cognitive self-regulation follows, although the development of self-regulation in all these areas continues throughout both childhood and adulthood.

Self-regulation is not about compliance. While children who are self-regulated may also appear to be 'well-behaved', there is a difference between internal regulation (that is, self-regulation) and external regulation (where someone else is determining the child's behaviour). Children bring to the classroom their diverse experiences, many more troubling or difficult than we would wish. Children who live in poverty or experience trauma will have found ways to adapt to these circumstances that are sometimes not conducive to learning in a group or being in a group setting for many hours at a time. And going to school for the first time can prove stressful for all children, no matter how secure or safe their family circumstances. Developing a curriculum that supports children's agency (rather than seeking compliant behaviour) is an act of social justice and will support the development of a more equitable education system for our youngest children. The purposeful inclusion of play in the curriculum can support children's agency as well as their development of self-regulation.

In the foreword to *Rethinking Readiness in Early Childhood Education* (Ayers, 2015), Bill Ayers talks about the choices teachers must make to 'unbolt the vitality of the world, or to hide and repress it ... Every school and each teacher must decide whether – and then *how*, in the hard-edged spaces we often inhabit – to keep the questions and the passions alive ... ' (p. xiii). In using play to support children's learning, teachers can enact the insight that 'learning is to all intents and purposes living' (p. xiii), trusting children's native enthusiasm, imagination, curiosity and purpose, as well as their essential social and caring natures. Self-regulation as opposed to *other* regulation is both natural and essential to this process.

Play, particularly make-believe or imaginary play, enables children to work on regulation in a 'safe' environment, promoting the development of both cognitive and social abilities, as well as the regulation of oneself physically and emotionally. Play allows children to practice behaviours that they are not ready to take on 'for real', in the context of a supportive environment, from the tools they use, their teachers and their peers (Dewey, 1913/1975; Piaget, 1951; Vygotsky, 1978). Play allows children to develop and pursue interests, to be fully engaged in trying to figure out how the world works. DeVries (2002) reminds us that play is full of purpose and intention. While there are educators who have defined free play as aimless and without substance, for the most part, well-structured educational contexts support play that encourages children to develop and pursue their interests, learning to learn and to regulate themselves so that they can get along in the world and contribute to it. For children who come from non-mainstream contexts (i.e. not white, not middle class, not English only and not heteronormative), the inclusion of play in/as the curriculum and the encouragement of their individual agency and power is particularly important. In addition, providing equitable opportunities for children does not mean that we can or should provide the same curriculum for them. Play as a central feature of the curriculum allows for context-specific activities that respond to the interests and expertise of the children involved. Play allows children to take a lead in developing a curriculum for their own learning.

Methods

My question for this study is 'What do the teachers at the Mills College Laboratory School do and think about to support the development of self-regulation in their young students? How do they use play to support this development?' I developed a short interview and interviewed each of the five teachers for about 30 minutes. The questions are presented in the appendix. These questions focused on the use of play throughout the programme, the intentional support throughout the programme of the development of self-regulatory capacity in all areas of development and the connections the teachers saw between play and the development of self-regulation.

I tape-recorded each interview and analysed the responses for themes and ideas. Following the interviews, each of the three classrooms was observed for 3 hours, with the morning and afternoon programmes being observed also for 3 hours each, resulting in a total of 15 hours of data. Observational data were collected with observational notes and photography.

Analysis of the interviews revealed several consistent themes. The categories included play, environment, routines, curriculum and self-regulation. I will discuss the findings by these categories, using the teachers' own words and my interpretations to help us understand the relationship between play and the development of self-regulation. For each category, I demonstrate how what the teachers reported was actually observed.

The context for this investigation is the laboratory school at Mills College. There are three classrooms with a total of five head teachers who serve children 2–5 years old. (Infants and toddlers are in a separate classroom, with two head teachers, and were not included in this study.) Two of the three classrooms have morning and afternoon programmes. The third classroom is a morning programme only, with children who stay into the afternoon joining one of the other classrooms. Thus, in one classroom the children are in a mixed-age setting all day. In the other two classrooms, children are in younger and older groupings in the morning and in a mixed-age setting in the afternoon. Each classroom has from 15 to 18 children in it at any one time (although there can be as many as 20 children in the afternoon combined programme). Children come from the surrounding local community and from the Mills College faculty, staff and student community. They represent much of the diversity of this community, although there are limited scholarships, so most families are middle-class economically. Each classroom also has several student teachers, often as many as six different student teachers during the week. Student teachers may change classrooms at the end of the semester, so that each classroom has a changing staff, on a daily basis throughout the semester and on a semester basis as well. Thus, the children have many adults to get to know, as well as numerous transitions between classroom settings. Each classroom has its own indoor and outdoor space, allowing children to be inside and outside as they wish and the weather permits.

A caveat for these findings that follow is that I did the interviews and coded them, initially. I also related the observational findings to the interview results. I did member checks with the teachers with regard to my inferences, and also reviewed the findings with two student research assistants.

Findings

To discuss the findings, I begin with the categories identified in the interviews. As I discuss the interview findings, I include observations that support or enhance the categories. In addition, at the end I add other observations about the development of self-regulation that the teachers may not have mentioned.

In each of the interviews each teacher made comments, statements and observations in the following categories: play, environment, routines, curriculum and self-regulation. Many comments linked these categories, particularly to self-regulation, which is understandable, since the interviews focused on asking the teachers to comment on how they thought about self-regulation in their classrooms.

Play

All the teachers said that play underlays all aspects of their classrooms, as 'the core of the curriculum' (JS),[1] as related to everything that happens in the classroom (NC), as the root of almost everything you do in the classroom (SS). Within this overarching view of play, the teachers had very definite connections between play and the goals they had for the children, for their student teachers and for the classroom community.

Using play to learn about the world

Play is how children learn about the world and learn to interact in and with the world, with materials, with people, in various contexts. Teachers use play as an opportunity to observe, guide and teach children and to learn about what children are thinking, feeling and learning about. '(Play) helps us to see how they think about their world, how they're thinking about their current role in the world and how they approach problems' (SS). Play in the classroom addresses the developmental needs of the whole child and all the different domains of growth and learning. It happens naturally and it can happen in a more directed way through how teachers plan, thinking about how to emphasize, strengthen or highlight children's learning and experiences (JS).

CK explained how gardening and learning about planting are an extension of playing in the dirt, learning what dirt is like, pushing trucks around in the dirt, to learning how dirt interacts with plants, seeds, water and sunlight. So, in this description, play supports the development of the understanding of how the world works, a scientific understanding.

In SS's afternoon classroom, the children were investigating the nature of ramps, and were constructing ramps from a variety of materials. I observed a series of complicated interactions between children and the materials, between children, teachers and the materials, where the children were figuring out how to make balls run through tubes more or less quickly. One child developed this investigation into a game or competition where he and SS each held one end of a flexible tube into which he placed a small ball. Then they would take turns lifting the end of the tube, so that sometimes the ball came out at his end and sometimes it appeared at the teacher's end. He was determined that it would come out even, so that they would have comparable 'scores'. Within this observation are several instances of self-regulation. First, to adjust the height of the ramp to see how fast or if the ball would come out the predicted end requires some preliminary control of variables, a cognitive regulation of experimentation. Second, demonstrating concern for his teacher, this student showed a sense of collaboration and community in determining that they should both 'win'. Third, this collaboration represents in many ways a co-regulation between the teacher and the student, to problem-solve a student-initiated problem with teacher help, but not guidance. This is a delightful example of the support of a student's agency with regard to problem-solving and the physical world in these three areas of regulation: cognitive, social and physical (Figure 1).

Play as problem-solving

Children use play to problem-solve in many different ways. For example, self-talk, and then, later, dialogue, contributes to children's developing understanding and language development.

> As they become verbal and maybe when they have dolls or building blocks.., they'll begin talking to themselves as they get language as they play, and they are problem-solving and thinking and imagining scenarios ... Vygotsky tells us that talk scaffolds the thinking that's developing around the play. (PB)

Play provides opportunities for problem-solving, language development, the development of scientific observation and, socially, opportunities for negotiation in terms of taking other people's perspectives and negotiating the sharing of toys and play equipment. It provides a transition from experience with a medium to learning about and extending the medium.

In CK's classroom, a parent brought a hula hoop for every child. She puts several hoops out in the yard and the children struggle to move with the hoops. One child (A) begins to build an obstacle course, using a saw horse, some large activity mats and the hula hoops. She works on this for a very long time, involving one of the student teachers in helping her support this structure she is building. Other children come over and are interested to try her structure. She ignores them, continuing to experiment with the process by moving the hoops from one area of the course to another, making them things to crawl through, jump through or simply adorn the structure. This is a lovely example of equity in terms of meeting the needs of an individual child. A is totally focused on her goal of building the obstacle course and pursues this goal independently and alone. The student

Figure 1. Ramps and Balls negotiation.

teacher who is observing her focus and concentration neither interferes nor abandons her, but rather provides support when A asks for it. The other children understand (and are regulating themselves) that this is something A is doing by herself. They can also work with the hoops, but they do not disturb her concentration. The context supports the different needs of the children, allowing them to pursue their own investigations and play (Figure 2).

Play as a way of working out issues you are struggling with

Play has long been seen as a vehicle for working through issues that are too hard to deal with in reality, or for practising conflict resolution and negotiation. CK had a wonderful example of children who are interested in cats. The stuffed cats have become part of the classroom, and children have had to learn to negotiate around pretend play with the cats, around sharing the cats and around dealing with disappointment if their favourite cat is already in someone else's basket. Each teacher had several examples of children learning to negotiate turn-taking, learning to care for one another and their 'babies' and 'animals', through dramatic play.

I observed numerous occasions when children used play to regulate their emotions, particularly when they were upset. In one instance, S was really upset that her mother had left without being able to say the usual long goodbye that she was accustomed to. She stood in the middle of the play yard shrieking. Several children surrounded her and were concerned. Finally, her friend D led her over to the hammock area in the far corner of the yard. She and S sat down on the large pillow beneath the hammock and D helped S take her shoes off. Then they both got into the hammock. They played in the hammock for nearly 30 minutes. Eventually, other children came to join them. Later, when I discussed this incident with the teacher, CK, she explained that S likes to wave goodbye to her mother from the hammock. D had remembered that and guided her over there to help her feel less upset. All this activity was initiated by D, for her friend S, without teacher intervention. Here, D and S are co-regulating S's upset through a comforting play ritual. Thus, there is both the opportunity and expectation in the classroom that children will care for one another. Children take note of one another's needs and respond to each other with respect and care. Learning to care and respect their classmates is a reflection of how social justice and equity are enacted in the classroom.

Play as the curriculum

Play in the curriculum (JS)

> Play is the core of the curriculum. It's totally central. It's what the curriculum is, but it's not that the children just play. ..It's really a balance between the intentional, about what we want the children to experience and how we want to shape that play. And also just in terms of observing and seeing what … naturally emerges. It's a balance.

Figure 2. Obstacle course construction.

She elaborates, saying that children have an intrinsic motivation to play, and that one of her goals is that children be intrinsically motivated to participate in an activity, to play, and that the curriculum will capitalize on that intrinsic motivation, by extending or elaborating the play in ways that the children might not have thought of. Building on children's play in this way provides an opportunity for individual and small group interests. Children can act and take initiative in their own learning and education, which supports their agency as learners – an important social justice and equity goal.

In NC's classroom, where the children are the oldest in the school, part of the day is devoted to 'studying' a particular content. At this time, children commit to an activity that is focused around the current content. When I observed, the children had just completed a study of *Anansi* and *Coyote* stories. They were about to begin a study of outer space. To begin that study, the teachers had added many new materials to the dramatic play area. When the children discovered the new materials, they were entranced and began some elaborate cooperative pretend play, with several stories happening simultaneously. While there were some disagreements, for the most part children were able to solve them on their own. When they were not, when a teacher intervened, it was always to help the children explain their points of view and to figure out how to solve the problem.

Environment

The environment is seen as an essential part of classroom curriculum and teaching. According to Gandini (2012), it is the 'third educator' along with a team of two teachers (p. 339). How the environment is arranged is seen to affect children's learning, children's interactions and the development of self-regulation in children.

CK in thinking about play mentioned the environment first. She teaches the youngest children. In thinking about the role of play, she said she distinguishes between the set-up of the inside and the outside, because there are some children who will play outside all day. She wants to make sure that they have a variety of areas for interaction, so she sets up this variety outside. For example, if she wants to make sure that children have the opportunity to listen to stories, look at books or play board games, she will set up an area outside where these activities are available. Likewise, water play is available both inside and outside, as is pretend play, with appropriate props and equipment.

When I observed in CK's classroom, I saw her take *In the Night Kitchen* (by Maurice Sendak) outside and gather children together to hear the story. She wanted children to be able to take a short break in the middle of the morning to listen to a story if they wanted to, without having to come back inside. She set up a couple of benches right near the play structure; about seven children came over to hear the story.

JS, too, spoke about constructing the environment to provide children with different opportunities, and in conjunction with thinking about when and how teachers intervene in children's play. She noted that in outside play, where children could experience physical freedom and exploration, she is much less likely to intervene, because she sees the play as supporting the goals she has for the children without her intervention. On the other hand, she does sometimes intervene in gentle ways to extend the children's play or offer them some extension opportunities for the play.

All the teachers spoke about the role of the environment in supporting the development of self-regulation. Children from 2 to 5 years old, who spend long periods of time in school, often all day, need opportunities to play alone and to play together. CK talked about the difficulties children experience when they have to be in sync with the large group all day long, with no opportunities for alone time, down time or playing with just one friend. While all the children who are at school all day have a sleeping or resting time, those times are seen as different from allowing the child to figure out (or self-regulate) when he or she needs to be alone or to be with the group.

Hence, the classrooms are set up with a variety of spaces available. There are inside and outside spaces, and inside and outside there are set-ups that allow children to be with a large group, a small group, one friend or alone. All the classrooms have spaces where children can contain themselves in a small comfy space, with a pillow, or even a translucent blanket to provide a bit of privacy. Teachers set up tables with specific numbers of chairs for some activities, indicating to the children that this is an activity for one, two or maybe four or five people. In this way, the environment is teaching the children about turn-taking, negotiating space and finding appropriate space for oneself. Likewise, there are spaces for the children to be all together at certain times of the day (like circle time); although with the youngest children, sometimes this circle time is for three or four children and a teacher to listen to a story.

The classroom is set up with environments for children of different ages and temperaments, with consideration for individual different energy levels throughout the day, taking account of energy level and the need for different ways to express that is part of setting up the environment, whether it is to provide a space and opportunity for a child to run around the play structure several times before coming in, or to jump on the trampoline before joining the circle. JS says to the children before circle, 'If your body's feeling like jumping, come on over *(to the trampoline)*. If your body's feeling like sitting you can go over to the couch'. The teachers create many things within the situation that the children can learn to 'read' and thus, learn to decide for themselves if this is a situation they can join and how to join it, whether it be the number of chairs at the table, or a waiting area for using the trampoline.

Routines and structures

Routines and knowing what to expect are very important for children being able to regulate themselves during the school day. All the teachers think carefully, particularly about the transitions in the day when children are emotionally vulnerable, making sure that they occur in regularly expected ways and that they allow for children to regulate themselves as they move from one part of the day to another. PB said, 'young children get anxious when the future seems really unpredictable. So we have assigned seats, we have the same children sitting together to have lunch together'.

PB talked about moving from playtime to clean-up time to circle time. To move very abruptly from playing to cleaning up with no warning does not allow the children to make adjustment themselves.

> We don't go out there and ring a bell and say it's clean up time, come inside. Because it's too hard for them to make that transition. Again this is respect for how deeply involved they are and how important it is.

So teachers start clean up gradually, warning the children that soon it will be clean-up time and cleaning up from the 'outside to the inside', so that the outside areas are gradually closed and children are urged to begin the transition to inside. For some children, a quiet alone activity after playing outside, but before joining the circle, is helpful in organizing themselves for the large group activity. PB says, 'I have children when we make that transition from outside to inside, every day we go to the easel'. She goes on to say that traditionally we would have insisted that everyone begin the circle together, but she says she is learning that children do not need to be in lockstep with one another at that time, that if she allows them a few minutes to finish their paintings, they are able to come to the circle themselves, having organized themselves to do this gradually. This is a great example of equity in action: PB shows respect for individual differences, trusting children to learn to organize themselves and to participate appropriately in community activities.

SS describes her clean-up time. In her classroom recently there has been great interest in building with blocks. However, the classroom is small, so there is no space to leave the constructions up for the next day. So, she says

> we make a plan about clean up. It is going to happen, I'm going to come over and help you. We do a counting activity, we do shape matching. There's different machines that come into play – cranes, bulldozers, shapesorter. And so it's interesting, they're actually problem-solving (while cleaning up).

Here she has taken an issue (like clean-up) and turned it into a rich exploration. In addition, this interaction between the children's needs and desires and the classroom environment shows respect (once again) for children's agency in their own education.

Other kinds of routines include how the day is structured. NC who teaches the oldest children in the morning commented that her day is structured somewhat differently from the mixed-age and younger children's classrooms. She found that her students found a day of all free play overwhelming and that they welcomed a period of focused structured 'work' time in which they are deliberately 'studying' a particular topic through a variety of activities. She cited two reasons for this decision. First, with children turning 4 and 5 years, she felt they needed more cognitive challenges; so she uses the word 'studying' about something to convey that she and they will take this work very seriously. Second, and she described it almost as the flip side of the coin, the main thing that 4- and 5-year-olds are working on is learning how to get along with other people. She said, 'as the social stuff becomes really the main thing that it's about, it's almost like it's too much' to have 3½ hours of free play where they are working so hard on negotiating with one another. The 20–40 minutes of structured activities in the middle of the morning give them a break, as the structure of the activity provides parameters for things like sharing materials and deciding what will be happening in the activity.

Another aspect of routines and structures that is helpful to the development of children's self-regulation is the purposeful grouping of children, both in terms of size of the group and in terms of individual interactions. For example, frequently small groups of children (2–4) go on walks around the campus. Sometimes the teachers may choose the groups based on who is going to get along the best, but sometimes the children are chosen because they need some support in learning how to get along. NC said,

> there were 3 boys who are really struggling learning to play as a threesome. So yesterday we picked the three of them to go together on the walk where they could have time away from the classroom in a more (private setting).

Also, sometimes children are chosen for a work group because some of them are strong in that skill or area and some need some support. In this way, the children can both be recognized for their competence and also learn from one another. But the groupings are purposeful. While these purposeful groupings may seem contrived, in fact they address issues of social justice and equity. Providing opportunities for children to learn to get along in a setting that is both freer than the classroom (going on a walk on campus) and less 'crowded' (only three children) gives them the emotional space to discover common interests, address differences and to do so in a context where they can manage their own emotions. Again, recognizing children's agency also promotes social justice and equity within the classroom and the school.

JS described the schedule and how they think about their day as creating the culture in the classroom and the community ... 'what the routine of the day looks like, the expectations of the children, how we speak to them, how we relate to the parents, how we model'. She went on to describe how important it is to build an infrastructure. The more children know what is expected of them, the more able they are to be independent and autonomous in routine activities, such as snack, handwashing and clearing the table after snack.

The afternoons can be particularly challenging, since children experience many transitions during this time. At the end of the morning, some children go home and some go to lunch (one transition). After lunch, some go to nap and some are 'resters' in the classroom (a second transition). The two afternoon classrooms use this resting time differently. In one classroom, where the children who are there have been in this classroom all morning, the afternoon resters generally have special projects they are working on, and a writing time. For those who need some alone time, there are activities set up where they can work alone, with their back to the room, focused on a soothing and engaging activity. On the day I observed, however, the children had discovered rainbows in the classroom. They were chasing and documenting the path of the rainbows.

In the other afternoon classroom, two groups of children come together who have not been together in the morning. Many of these children nap, but those who do not have a change of both children and teaching personnel to adapt to. PB, the teacher, has the resters rest alone at an individual activity for about 20–30 minutes. The day I observed was Valentine's day and all of the older children in the classroom were very involved in drawing, colouring and cutting out hearts.

The younger children (only one or two, most of them sleep) were busily involved in a train-building activity at a table, where they stayed focused for a good 45 minutes.

Thus, in each classroom where children have a number of transitions, the teachers think carefully about how to structure the environment so that children can rest effectively to be prepared for more activity later in the afternoon.

Curriculum

Curriculum in the lab school is very much based on the interests of the children. While the teachers have different ways of planning for curriculum, all of them draw on the children to decide what to do. For most of the teachers, curriculum is almost in the moment. As teachers observe what children do and talk about, they provide props and activities to meet those interests. Sometimes there will be something that children show a compelling interest in, and sometimes a very social child will express an interest, and as PB said, 'that child will suck the group into their interest'. Interests can be as mundane as cats, babies or as esoteric as dinosaurs, frogs and outer space. Depending on the classroom and the age of the children, activities will be planned and offered around these interests. The dramatic play corner is a good place for these interests to be supported; but there are also opportunities for building, sand play, water play, art and writing around interests.

In one classroom, the teacher had introduced a variety of materials to explore ramps and pathways. Many children were experimenting with building ramps and seeing how they interacted with sand, balls, water and so forth. In another classroom, children were exploring sculpture with various found and recyclable objects (like egg cartons, milk cartons, strawberry baskets, paper tubes, etc.). They were working with balance, relationships between objects aesthetically and structurally, and commenting on one another's work as they worked.

In addition to the curriculum around children's interests, all the teachers talked about the curriculum or focus of learning being about learning to have friends and be a friend, hence, the set up of different opportunities for engaging with different size groups. CK said that you have to 'structure it so that children will naturally move toward being more social, being more in the midst of a lot of action. But they (the children) also have to know that there is always a possibility to move back'.

Student teacher investigations form a large part of the curriculum. These investigations offer reciprocity between children and teacher interests, where the student teachers base their development of an investigation on something *they* are interested in seeing how children respond to it. But they also have to build these investigations around what they observe. The opportunity to have six or seven different adults thinking about what might be interesting and engaging to children, and what might teach them something, is a rich resource for the lab school.

There are a variety of curricular areas that the teachers see as a way of helping children develop self-regulation in cognitive, social and emotional ways, and that they use to support this development. PB talked about sensory motor integration as an important area of curricular development, citing an obstacle course that one of her student teachers developed that was very useful to the mixed-age group of children she teaches. CK added an interesting insight into the use of the balance beam and other balance activities for children, some of whom were experts and some of whom learned to be brave and adventurous, despite initial timidity. The example of A building the obstacle course with the balance beam is a nice example of providing a context for children to develop their own challenges in this area (see Figure 2).

SS says that one of her goals for children is that they behave as scientists in their world, learning what things are used for, how things work and observing closely the world around them. Cooking and gardening provide great opportunities for these observations, as well as the use of a variety of materials for a variety of purposes. Choosing materials and props for play has a great effect on the efficacy and results of that play, so teachers are continually observing and experimenting with different possibilities, recognizing that each group of children is unique, and that one child or one group of children may not respond in the same way as another had earlier. In addition, curriculum can be used to encourage children to try new things, to go to a less comfortable cognitive place, while feeling comfortable enough to be in disequilibrium. One example that SS gave was of three little boys who wanted nothing more than to play outside in the sand box, and who were very averse to ever trying painting. A student teacher introduced 'dinosaur bones' into the sand box, and the children got very involved in being archaeologists. She then suggested painting a replica of the bones so other folks could know about what they found. These three boys, who had never touched a paintbrush, enthusiastically created a record of their dinosaur bones!

One of the main goals for the children is that they be supported in regulating themselves throughout the day. Curriculum is an important aspect of this support and this learning. For example, water play and play dough are soothing to many children. There may be children who will spend a lot of time doing these activities initially as they watch to see what else is going on and possible. As they get themselves focused and organized, they become able to move away from these activities to other activities that may challenge them in different ways. In addition, these soothing activities can allow for all kinds of imaginary play and self-talk, also an avenue to self-regulation.

Self-regulation

The focus of the conversations that I had with the teachers was play and self-regulation, so it is not surprising that these categories appeared to be the most complex and many-layered in our interviews. What became clear is that all the categories, play, environment, routines and curriculum, contribute to creating classroom settings where children can be supported in developing their abilities to self-regulate across different domains and in many contexts. What is particularly clear is how purposeful and intentional the teachers are in thinking about how to support children's self-regulation.

They all get to know their children very well and think about what is regulating for them (each child) and how to help each child know him- or herself what will help them when they are disregulated. Recognizing the unique characteristics and needs of each child contributes to an equitable and socially just classroom, providing children the opportunities to learn to regulate themselves and take control of their own lives. SS spoke about one child who gets very disregulated at certain times of the day. She realized that in these circumstances, close-ended activities, like working with pattern blocks, were very calming for him and made him feel successful as well. So when she notices him becoming disregulated, she steers him in that direction. She also helps him to notice it himself so that at this point in the year (April), it is enough for her to say to him, 'looks like you might find working with the pattern blocks helpful right now' and he'll agree with her and move to that activity.

All the teachers noted the challenge of being in school for a long day, being around people all day and being away from your family all day when you are only 2 or 3 or 4 or 5 years old. Particularly for the children in the afternoon, when they are tired and have already been in school for a while, the need for opportunities to be alone, be in a soothing activity or have family reminders around them is paramount. SS talks frankly with the children about it being 'really hard work to be with other people all day long', encouraging them and guiding them to one person activities, or particular activities that help them. One goal she has for the children is that they develop coping strategies for when they are disregulated, while a goal she has for her student teachers and herself is to recognize that disregulation in each child, knowing that it can manifest itself differently for individuals and that each individual may need something else to be self-regulated.

Anticipating changes and transitions in the classroom, like coming up to clean-up time, is an example of helping children anticipate what they can do to keep themselves together and focused during those transitions and into the next activity. For example, SS talked about clean-up.

> Part of the major process in supporting the children being regulated is that we have to deal with a major problem of clean up *(in this case cleaning up the blocks after the children have built major structures)*. Cause it's no fun to clean up. And it's also very disregulating, because it's very loud, we have a lot of blocks. It's very overwhelming. All the blocks are on the ground *(and they have to be put away)*. So it's been really interesting to try out different ways of supporting their regulation.

JS talked about ways to support children who are disregulated.

> If they're disregulated then they're distracted, they're agitated, they're all over the place. And that's really hard when you have kids who are like that, to get them to hook in; it's really hard .... The trick is supporting their strengths, and finding what their intrinsic motivation is. How can you interest them? How can you reach them and really connect to them? That's the thing with young children; you either do or you don't .... Well, you do it through play.

She goes on to say that when she and the child find a way for him or her to feel comfortable, she will point it out not only to that child, but also to the other children, to be something that everyone can learn from and move to understanding themselves better. Again, this perspective demonstrates respect for children both individually and socially, as children learn to support one another in their ways of operating in the world. Such respect contributes to an atmosphere of social justice and a concern for equity within the classroom, on the part of teachers *and children*.

Teachers set up areas that children can go to themselves when they are feeling upset. For example, in CK/PB's classroom, there are cubbies for children to go into if they are unhappy about something. While I was observing one morning, one little boy, X, was not able to go ride bikes with the others, because too many children had already requested to go. He was extremely upset about missing out on this turn right at that moment. Instead of having a tantrum, however, he headed for the cubbies to crawl in, pull up a chair to create a 4th wall and sat there calming down. Within several minutes he was able to come out and find something else to do, having calmed himself down. He did all this without any teacher input, although there were other children supporting him as he moved into the cubby. Later, when the next group went to ride bikes, he joined them, thus demonstrating a strong sense of his own interests and purpose. Teachers had developed *with him* ways to confront disappointment and to postpone but maintain achieving his desires (Figure 3).

Through the conversations with these teachers, it became clear that helping children to be self-regulated throughout the day and helping them develop coping strategies so that they can self-regulate when they are disregulated are main goals of the preschool. This self-regulation includes developing the ability to cope when their parents leave, or when they are unhappy about an altercation with another child, or when they are physically uncomfortable or hungry (emotional self-regulation); developing the ability to negotiate with one another, to be a friend and to have a friend, and to eventually have more than one friend, so that by the time they leave to go to kindergarten they know how to be in a group and how to get along, to solve problems, to negotiate with each other and to have fun together. NC said that 'being four is about understanding how to get along with other people!' (social self-regulation). Without social and emotional self-regulation, it is difficult to have cognitive self-regulation, but cognitive self-regulation can contribute to the development of other aspects of self-regulation. Thus, children need to learn to concentrate and focus on an activity, to be engaged, to find joy in their learning. The curriculum and the individualization of that curriculum foster the development of this aspect of learning and self-regulation.

The development of self-regulation is supported by the use of play. There were many, many examples that the teachers described, some of which I have already discussed. One particularly poignant example was one mentioned by PB about a little boy in her classroom who was very interested in going around and kissing everyone.

> He was trying to kiss the other children a lot. And we said, we can't allow it, germs get spread that way and we're not going to kiss in school. Well, the next day or two he was over at the little playhouse, he has the two little dolls and the dolls are kissing each other. So the opportunity for this imaginary play gave him the opportunity to think about and work through whatever it is that's so fascinating and compelling. He needs to figure out about the kiss and in terms of socially it's a lot better for all of us that he's making the dolls kiss rather than going around and trying to kiss everybody. The children, most of them, really were not interested in all this kissing, and certainly the adults weren't very comfortable about it. So that was a socially much more acceptable way for him to try and figure it out.

Here's an example of a child self-regulating this interest and compulsion appropriately, and eventually working it out, so that he will learn to kiss when it is appropriate.

Figure 3. X calming down in a private space.

Finally, children develop play that helps them work on self-regulation. PB and NC both described an activity or game that was clearly focused on this interaction. In PB's classroom, children play the 'help' game where they are helping one another as they 'fall' down the slide and try to climb up it. In her classroom, the children are of mixed age, so that the game is focused on helping one another get up the slide. 'They go over to the slide and the whole game is they're trying to help each other get up the slide.' However, in NC's classroom, where all of the children are 4 or 5 years of age, they play this 'help' game much more roughly.

> Someone is falling down the slide and they're pulling them up and trying to save them, and pulling them up. And there's a lot of crashing down the slide and crashing into each other. And in order to play this game without anybody actually getting hurt, the self-regulation that has to happen ... three ways really, three things. To control their actual bodies, so that although they might be crashing into somebody, they're crashing into them with a certain amount of gentleness, but there's also a certain amount of self-regulation, somebody just smashed their foot into my face, but this is a game and this is part of the game and I'm not gonna fall apart because of it. I'm thinking about this, because the kids have been playing this for the last couple of days and there was a little girl who was playing this game who normally is such a delicate little thing, but she was there and it was really rough. It was perfectly controlled, but it was really rough and she was just brushing it off, and for her that was a really lot of self-regulation. And I guess the other side of it is the same thing, that the kids who would slip into anger really easily who have to stop themselves when somebody smashes into them ... and it's especially really clear in this game. When I was watching them, you could see them take that moment to think about whether they were going to have their usual response *(having a tantrum, falling apart)* and then actually make a conscious decision not to because they wanted to be able to stay in the game ... And there was one little boy playing the game who periodically would step aside and take a few moments, and then he'd come back in. (See Figure 4)

Here the children have created a scenario where they can practise what they might do if someone hurts them, or interferes with what they are doing, but in the context that they have all agreed upon. They get to *feel* emotions in a safe setting and practise handling them. They also have the opportunity to leave the game periodically if it gets to be too much, and that, too, is self-regulation. Some of the same children play this game in the morning, in the older classroom and more roughly, and in the afternoon, in the mixed-age grouping, where there are younger children involved in the game. We see here very explicitly children's consciousness of care for one another – an important part of implementing social justice and equity in a classroom.

NC made another observation and generalization that relate to this intersection of play and self-regulation. She observed that because being four is about understanding how to get along with

Figure 4. The Help Game.

other people, then play becomes the vehicle for working that out, for learning to do that, rather than that because they play, they will be confronted with conflicts and negotiations. She said,

> It's almost as if we (the four year olds) have to figure out how to get along with each other because that's what being 4 years old is all about. So what are we going to do, well let's play, and then we'll see what happens while we play and we'll get into a conflict and we'll solve it!

She said of course nothing like that really happens, but that it certainly seems as if the drive to play comes out of the need to learn to be together.

Conclusion

The teachers at the Mills College laboratory school think all the time about the relationship between play and self-regulation. Their work is purposefully and intentionally designed to support children's learning emotionally, socially and cognitively. When they leave for the K-12 context, these children have a good foundation in learning how to learn, in being able to self-regulate so that they can take advantage of, take joy in and be productive in a context that is not necessarily as supportive of them as preschool has been. One last comment and observation is that here in the preschool, learning to manage oneself physically, emotionally, socially and cognitively is a major part of the curriculum. Once children get to elementary school, they are expected to know how to do this. While elementary teachers do focus on building community and helping children to become independent learners, the methods for doing so are not the result of differentiated instruction that you see in this preschool setting. Children come into kindergarten with self-regulation developed along a continuum; some children are very well regulated and manage themselves well, while others are still working on learning to do this. For those children, differentiated instruction in learning to manage one's feeling, social relations and ability to learn is probably no longer available. Hence, as NC observed, children who have difficulty self-regulating in kindergarten continue to have that difficulty as they get to the 5th grade. This is a critical issue in creating socially just and equitable learning spaces for all children. In elementary school, good behaviour often becomes compliance rather than self-regulation, preventing children from developing the tools they need to learn and contribute to their classrooms and their schools. The difference between compliant behaviour and self-regulated behaviour is something teachers focused on issues of equity must recognize, and they need to figure out how to continue to support self-regulation. The use of play as a vehicle for helping this process could be a resource for elementary school teachers, their students and their families, if we could figure out how to include it as an essential part of the curriculum.

Note

1. Initials in parentheses indicate which of the teachers is being quoted. CK teaches the youngest children in the morning (2–3.5). NC teaches the older children in the morning (3.5–5). PB teaches these children in a mixed-age group in the afternoon. These children come 5 days/week. JS and SS teach a different mixed-age group (2–5) morning and afternoon, respectively. In this class, children come 2, 3 or 5 days/week.

Acknowledgements

This study and article could not have been completed without the generosity and support of the teachers in the Mills College Children's School (MCCS). Paula Buel, Nanu Clark, Christine Kaes, Jane Simon and Sara Sutherland gave generously of their time in speaking with me, in allowing me to spend many hours in their classrooms, sharing their photographs with me and commenting on this study as it progressed. In addition, I would like to thank the children and the families of the MCCS who allowed me to photograph their play.

Disclosure statement

No potential conflict of interest was reported by the author.

References

Ayers, W. C. (2015). Ready or not: Learning and living. In J. M. Iorio & W. Parnell (eds.), *Rethinking readiness in early childhood education: Implications for policy and practice* (pp. xi–xv). New York, NY: Palgrave/Macmillan.

Bodrova, E. & Leong, D. J. (2007). *Tools of the mind: The Vygotskian approach to early childhood education* (2nd ed.). Upper Saddle River, NJ: Pearson.

DeVries, R. (2002). Understanding constructivist education. In R. DeVries, B. Zan, C. Hildebrandt, R. Edmiaston, & C. Sales (Eds.), *Developing constructivist early childhood curriculum: Practical principles and activities* (pp. 3–11). New York, NY: Teachers College Press.

Dewey, J. (1975/1913). *Interest and effort in education*. Edwardsville: Southern Illinois University Press.

Gandini, L. (2012). Connecting through caring and learning spaces. In C. Edwards, L. Gandini, & G. Forman (Eds.), *The hundred languages of children: The Reggio Emilia experience in transformation* (pp. 317–342). Santa Barbara, CA: Praeger.

Piaget, J. (1951). *Play, dreams and imitation in childhood*. New York, NY: Norton.

Vygotsky, L. S. (1978). *Mind and society: The development of higher mental process*. Cambridge, MA: Harvard University Press.

Appendix
Interview questions for Early Childhood Curriculum building self-regulation.

1. The use of play as a building block for curriculum in early childhood education is of long-standing use. How do you think about play as part of your curriculum?
   - What goals or purposes do you see play serving for your students?
   - How do you plan for play that will meet those goals and purposes?
   - What about the curriculum is preplanned and what about it is emergent, based on student interests?
2. One of the developmental goals for preschoolers is the development of emotional and social self-regulation such that children can participate happily and productively in social settings such as school and friendships. What aspects of your curriculum are planned with the goal of the development of self-regulation?
   - What goals do you have for your students with regard to self-regulation?
   - How does your curriculum help them to develop self-regulation?
   - What is the role of imaginary play and curriculum that encourages imaginary play in developing self-regulation?
   - How do you know when your students have met your goals for them?

4

Understanding and supporting block play: Video observation research on preschoolers' block play to identify features associated with the development of abstract thinking

Kaoru Otsuka and Tim Jay

ABSTRACT
This article reports on a study conducted to investigate the development of abstract thinking in preschool children (ages from three years to four years old) in a nursery school in England. Adopting a social influence approach, the researcher engaged in 'close listening' to document children's ideas expressed in various representations through video observation. The aim was to identify behaviours connected with features of the functional dependency relationship – a cognitive function that connects symbolic representations with abstract thinking. The article presents three episodes to demonstrate three dominating features, which are (i) *child/child sharing of thinking* and *adult and child sharing of thinking*; (ii) *pause for reflection*; and (iii) *satisfaction* as a result of self-directed play. These features were identified as signs of learning, and were highlighted as phenomena that can help practitioners to understand the value of quality play and so provide adequate time and space for young children and plan for a meaningful learning environment. The study has also revealed the importance of block play in promoting abstract thinking.

Introduction

This article reports a video study conducted to identify behaviours of preschool children (ages from three to four years old) connected to the development of abstract thinking during block play. Block play involves the use of unit blocks made from hardwood, which are cut into mathematically proportionate dimensions. For this study, the blocks used in this research were manufactured by Community Playthings in the UK. Given the open-ended nature of the wooden blocks, children were able to use them in any way they liked to fit their play, including stacking, piling, sorting, and lining up (see Figures 1 and 2).

The purpose of the study was to explore some of the ways in which children's learning is visible in play. Play is often overlooked in early years settings in favour of teaching approaches that lend themselves more obviously to assessment and accountability policies. A recent study in the UK found that the best settings did not see teaching as separate from play, but that this ran counter to the prevailing view in the sector that teaching and play are 'separate, disconnected endeavours in the early years' (Ofsted, 2015, p. 1). This same study concludes that one of the reasons that many early years practitioners fail to see the value of play is that it can be difficult to 'see' the learning that results. The study reported here addresses this issue, by describing features of children's play that may be considered as markers of learning.

Figure 1. A series of screen captures from video documentation illustrating the transformation in David's construction.

Figure 2. A screen capture from the video documentation illustrating Olivia's play of sorting food onto each cylinder – a moment when Olivia is extending the play by adding more cylinders.

The specific aspect of children's learning that we focus on here is the functional dependency relationship (Athey, 1990). 'Functional dependency' is a type of schema – 'schema' being defined by Piaget as a pattern of repeatable behaviour taking place as children learn about the world around them. Schema has been used by a number of researchers to describe the different kinds of actions that precede and lead to symbolic or abstract thought. The functional dependency schema refers to a child's playing out of the fact that some action depends on some other action, or that the action depends on some state of the world being the case. For example, from Atherton and Nutbrown (2013, p. 52),

> Henry demonstrated an understanding of functional dependency relationships: in order for him to use the car, it would have to be pulled out and the big bike moved, i.e.: his use of the car was functionally dependent on obstacles being moved out of the way.

In this article, we focus on functional dependency as a promising locus for markers of children's transition from concrete to symbolic thought.

The study took a sociocultural approach (Angelillo, Rogoff, & Chavajay, 2007) to study individual children's thinking as they interacted with the immediate learning context including friends, the researcher, and the environment. The research placed emphasis on children's representations and ideas by engaging in 'close listening' (Confrey, 1995), which will be discussed in detail in this article.

The research question guiding the study was thus:

What are the features that constitute the functional dependency relationship, associated with the development of abstract thinking, in preschool children (3–4 years old) during block play in English nursery school environments?

Theoretical foundation

Piagetian theory (Inhelder, Sinclair, & Bovet, 1974; Piaget, 1953, 1962, 1964, 1977) has played an important role in establishing a strong foundation for researching cognitive development. In the context of this article, two aspects of Piagetian theory are key. Firstly, there is the idea that children move through stages of development, beginning with the sensorimotor stage where children begin to make connections between sensory experience and their own actions in the world, through to the formal operational stage where children are capable of abstract logical thought. While some of the details regarding the ages at which transitions take place, and the idea that progress through stages occurs at the same rate across domains, has not stood the test of time, the idea that children's learning involves transitions from action, through symbolic mediation, to abstract thought, continues to represent a foundation of understanding of children's cognitive development. A second aspect of Piagetian theory that is important for this article is the concept of the 'schema'. A schema is a pattern of actions carried out in a particular context, and so represents the simplest building block of children's thinking. Athey (1990) extended the idea of the schema, following systematic observations of three- and four-year-old children in a nursery setting, and described several kinds of schema that were visible in early years children's behaviours. One particular schema, functional dependency, will be discussed in more detail below.

Bringing in the social

The Piagetian, cognitive, model provides a useful account of children's learning, but leaves some questions unanswered. A key issue relates to the way in which transitions between forms of thinking actually take place; young children's understandings of the world that begin in the form of sensorimotor, and then concrete, representations are *somehow* transformed into abstract representations (Gopnit et al., 2004). The mechanism of this *somehow* part that would describe the process of transformation is still under-researched (Bjorklund, 2014; Siegler, 2000; Taggart & Ridley, 2005). The study presented in this article attempted to investigate the behaviours of young children that support such a transformation between concrete and abstract thinking in order to provide early years practitioners with more effective guidelines for practice to support the development of thinking. To investigate such behaviour, it is also important to understand social constructivist theory and its influence on learning, since the attitude of modern constructivist theory acknowledges the importance of the social influence on learning. For instance, the sociocultural theory of Vygotsky (1978) and Wertsch and Stone (1985) has become increasingly more prominent. Essentially, Vygotsky places learning on the social plane, occurring through interaction with peers and with more knowledgeable others. Knowledge on the social plane is then internalised by individual children. Employing such theory, researchers have come to understand more about the complex interrelationship between cognitive, social, and emotional development (Aubrey, Ghent, & Kanira, 2012; Pascal, Bertram, Mould, & Hall, 1998). A particular challenge of contemporary child development research consists in the need to develop ways to take account of both cognitive and sociocultural perspectives on learning. Studies inspired by sociocultural theory tend to place focus on aspects of the social and cultural sphere such as words, objects, and technologies used during interactions (Sfard, 2007).

Rogoff (1998) developed a dynamic sociocultural approach, which complements both traditional sociocultural theory and Piagetian theories (Fleer & Robbinsons, 2003), emphasising the 'sharedness' and 'mutually constituting contribution' of children's learning (Angelillo et al., 2007, p. 190), by considering cognitive development as taking place within the full social context in which it occurs. It is Rogoff's approach that has informed the design of the present study. In acknowledging and attending to the social influence on the individual's learning, this study attempted to present results that were as child-centred as possible.

Functional dependency relationship

The functional dependency relationship is a cognitive schema identified by Athey (1990) as she conducted systematic observations of young children at different stages of thinking. Athey's work was influenced by Piaget (1953), who explained that sensorimotor experience provides the foundation for the development of abstract thinking, whereby young children transform real-life experience into mental schemata and representations. This occurs via states of cognitive conflict and disequilibration that are resolved through processes of assimilation and accommodation. Assimilation refers to the employment of existing knowledge to solve new problems, whereas accommodation is when the knowing subject must alter or construct knowledge in order to tackle a new challenge. Based on this idea, Athey (1990) conducted systematic observations of children's development of thinking, and categorised them into four progressive stages: (i) motor, (ii) symbolic representation, (iii) functional dependency relationship, and (iv) thought. At the symbolic representation stage, children symbolically represent figurative features of objects existing in their immediate environment or in their memory. For instance, children may pretend a piece of unit block is a piece of cake. At the thought stage, a child is able to describe this piece of cake and explain that it can be cut in half to share with friends without looking at the object. Before this thought stage, a child would have to observe and understand that slicing a cake in the middle will split it in half to produce two smaller pieces, which was identified as functional dependency relationship. In other words, young children at this transitional stage are practising making connections between concrete reality and abstract representation. In Athey's study, a total of 4854 observations of children's behaviour were collected. Of these, 22.8% observations were categorised as instances of motor action, 66% as symbolic representation, and 11.1% as belonging to the thought category. Motor action was most prominent among children aged around three years and one month, symbolic representation at four years and one month old, and the thought level was most common at four years and five months old (Athey, 1990). The functional dependency relationship category was created as a sub-category of thought level in her study, as she discovered all children manifesting thought level demonstrated conservation of their previous schematic activities. In Athey's study, there were 225 instances of explicit functional dependency relationship. While this is not a large proportion of the total number of observations, the detailed analysis of observations of these events has shown how each child experimented and internalised what Nutbrown (2011) described as the cause and effect of their actions. Athey (1990) defined the functional dependency relationship as:

> ... [b]efore thought becomes reversible the child's thinking proceeds by 'functions' in the modern sense of 'mappings' [...] when children observe the effects of action on objects or material" to understand that, for instance, "the distance of a ball depends on the power of the throw. (Athey, 1990, p. 70)

It is this stage that this article focuses on to investigate how the practitioners can support such practice in early years settings.

Implications for early years practice: supporting the development of abstract thinking

Young children seek for patterns that help to generalise their experience when constructing knowledge (Gopnik, Meltzoff, & Kuhl, 1999), and they output the understanding, which is expressed in different forms of representations (Carruthers & Worthington, 2005; Gifford, 2004). Such patterns occur in interactive play, especially when this is carried out with sensitive response and reinforcement from a more knowledgeable partner. Frequent exposure to such play is crucial in the early years. This was further emphasised by van Oers and Poland (2007) who argued that to tackle the problem of formal learning, early years education should focus on bridging the gap between concrete and abstract through play.

With regard to abstract thinking, van Oers and Poland (2007, p. 14) explained that abstraction is 'a dialectical process between the concretely given objects and the abstract representations of them', where symbolic representations are constructed as mental objects, which sustain 'inner relationship' with the concrete world (van Oers, 2001, p. 287). In Donaldson's (1986) terms, abstract thinking was described as 'modes of thought [...] "disembedded" from the vicissitudes of immediate context' (Grieve & Hughes, 1990, p. 5). Both definitions signify that the development of abstract thinking is linked with its detachment from the concrete world, while maintaining connection with it through representations.

So, how should early years practitioners support children's development of abstract thinking? Donaldson (1986, pp. 94–108) hypothesised that there are five elements required in children's play that supports the development of abstract thinking. They are (a) to allow time for reflection, (b) to have a feeling of being in control, (c) structure, (d) to have opportunity to make errors, and (e) intrinsic motivation. Yet, observational studies that focused on the development of thinking such as Athey (1990) are rare. Employing the social influence approach and Athey's (1990) theory of the functional dependency relationship, this article presents three episodes collected through the study to identify behaviours of young children that suggest transition between concrete and abstract thinking in order to provide practitioners with guidelines for more effective practice.

Methodology

The study presented in this article adopted a qualitative methodology that acknowledged the researcher's position within the process of knowledge production (Guba & Lincoln, 2005). To interpret the data, and determine as closely as possible what participating children are thinking, the researcher is required to be as close to children's natural environment as possible. This is a function of the 'close listening' approach used here (Confrey, 1995), where the researcher's role was to understand each child's intention, and to follow and support such intentions without disturbing their flow of play. What was important in taking such an approach was a positive attitude towards respecting young children's voices, ideas, and thinking expressed in various forms such as gestures, actions, narrations, constructions, and behaviour (Gifford, 2004; Ginsburg, 2009), and avoiding directing their play.

Such understanding was further expanded to support the children in their decision on how they wanted to participate in the research. Some children silently indicated a desire to not participate in the research, through their body language. Another child directed where to place the voice recorder. Before participating in the study, all children were shown a small picture book showing the purpose of the video recording and how it will be used to 'write a story about them'. At the end of the story, they were asked if it was alright for the researcher to do so. While formal informed consent was sought and received from participating children's parents, the children's right to express their intention was respected throughout the research process. After the study, all children and their parents had an opportunity to watch the video and listen to how the data were analysed.

Data collection

The study was conducted in one classroom in an English nursery school, where 30 children from mixed cultural backgrounds attended three-hour morning sessions for five days a week. The children followed a routine of starting a day with a 30-minute adult-led activity, followed by two hours of free play. The video observation took place during this free-play time when children were accessing the block area freely to start their own play or were invited to join an activity initiated by the researcher.

With technological advancement, video cameras have become more familiar in life, allowing more natural integration of video observation into preschool classrooms (Knoblauch & Tuma, 2011). The video camera and audio recording devices were set up in such a way that they were documenting children's behaviour, gestures, facial expressions, words, intonations, concentration, persistence, and any other signs of cognitive transformation in the light of the functional dependency relationship (Angelillo et al., 2007; Barron, 2007). In qualitative research with interpretive analysis, maximum effort has to be exhausted in producing video documentation to allow a genuine reproduction of 'semiotic space' between the data and the researcher during the analysis process where meaning can be renegotiated (Fosnot & Perry, 2005; Guba & Lincoln, 2005; Wertsch, 1991). With this approach, the statement by Blumer (1969) below still holds significant relevance in this particular study, which helped to set the protocol during the fieldwork.

> it signifies immediately that if the scholar wishes to understand the action of people it is necessary for him to see their objects as they see them. Failure to see their objects as they see them, or a substitution of his meanings of the objects for their meanings, is the gravest kind of error that the social scientist can commit. (1969, p. 51)

Ethical considerations

Gaining access to nursery schools can be a complex process. This particular study involved thorough preparation and coordination with multiple layers of gatekeepers, using emails and meetings to explain the purpose of the study, while allowing sufficient time to develop trust and connections with teachers of the setting. Such negotiation constitutes a key to the success of the research (Lofland, Snow, Anderson, & Lofland, 2006). The second stage of gaining access involved gaining informed consent from participating children's parents and guardians, in line with British Educational Research Association ethical guidelines (2011). To ensure the confidentiality and anonymity of participating children, all names in this article are reported using pseudonyms. The Graduate School of Education, University of Bristol, actively promotes ethical mindfulness, which was also adopted throughout the fieldwork by sensitively listening out for unheard voices of young children in their decision towards participation in the research (Alderson, 1995; Aubrey, David, Godfrey & Thomson, 2000; Bourke & Loveridge, 2014; Dockett, Einarsdottir, & Perry, 2011; Dockett & Perry, 2011). Furthermore, ethical procedures, including approval by the lead author's home institution ethics committee, were completed prior to the fieldwork taking place.

Findings and discussion

In the study, 640 minutes of video-recorded data were edited down to 199 minutes for further analysis. A total of 26 events were analysed and organised into three categories as follows:

16 concrete thinking,
7 concrete to abstract thinking, and
3 abstract thinking.

Three episodes from the concrete to abstract category were chosen to be presented in this article in order to demonstrate the behaviours suggesting transitions between concrete and abstract thinking. Reasons for selecting such episodes were for their clear documentation of behavioural features, facial expressions, and verbal representations that suggested the moment of concrete functioning and moment of abstract thinking stage, and the transition in the mode of thinking during the block play. The length of the recording ranged from 3 minutes to 9 minutes, and they demonstrate insights into what children do in their play when their cognitive stage exhibits functional dependency relationship.

The interpretive analysis was conducted using NVivo, which assisted in organising and highlighting sections of video recordings with the researcher's interpretation of the child's representations. The analysis leads to eight types of behaviour and six types of social interactions. A further six categories were created to isolate moments in play that identified either motor action, symbolic functioning, or functional dependency relationship.

The context of play was also taken into consideration during the analysis by applying 'rich interpretation', which Ginsburg (1997, p. 79) described as 'assign[ing] meaning to words or actions on the basis of how they fit into the entire context of the session and what we know about the interviewer and child'. This includes speech on the basis of what he or she understands about the environment, the child, and what the researcher was thinking and the reasons for the ways the researcher interacted with the child during the event.

Findings: episodes

Episode 1: David's Transformation of Construction

David (age: 3 years 10 months) is building a 2D plain surface using wide slopes, 1/2 and 1/4 blocks. His friend William (age: 4 years 2 months) joins in the construction using different size blocks, but David removes them swiftly and replaces with 1/4 block. It appears that David has a 'design' in his mind which is not affected by his friend's intervention. Four minutes into the play, William lifts one of the slopes and stands it up vertically. David repeats this and begins lifting all other slopes until their construction is transformed into 2D horizontal enclosure (see Figure 1).

Researcher: Look, what you building, David.
David: I building this thing Daniel built.
Researcher: Oh! Daniel built yesterday.
David: [nods]
Researcher: Do you know what this does? [pointing at slopes standing vertically]
David: I don't know [as he tries to fix one of the slope which is not lined up with the rest because its right angle is not facing the same direction.]
Researcher: You don't know. [Pause] Try turning this around [twirling the finger to suggest turning the slope around so that the right angle is lined up with the rest of the slopes] turn it around, that's it.
David: [begins to place 1/2 and 1/4 blocks on the opposite side of vertical slopes, transforming the plain surface construction to 2D horizontal enclosure.]
William: [places an orange truck inside the enclosure and nudges the vertical slope with the truck]
David: [begins to lower down one of the slope but pauses briefly, then continues to lower two more slopes, and William drives the truck down the slope.]
Researcher: Ah!
David: If he goes out to get some food ... [pause]
Researcher: He's going out to get some food.
Researcher: Did it just open to let the truck out?
David: Yeah, and they close again, and when he (an orange truck) comes back they open again.
Researcher: They open again, do they?

This section presents transcripts of the three episodes followed by the researcher's commentary on the episodes and detailed discussions focussing on the features identified.

Summary of Episode 1

In this episode, David is building a construction, which is the same as what his friend was building on the previous day. He uses his memory to reconstruct the building until it begins to look like the same structure, until his friend William joins in and alters the structure by lifting up the slopes. Upon the observation of William's action, David begins to imitate the action. Yet, David is still not sure of the function of the structure, and his thinking still remains concretely embedded within what he is experiencing in front of him. However, David's transition in thinking begins as William places an orange truck inside the structure, which David could relate to, allowing David to change his thinking towards the function of the structure. As David watches William using the orange truck to nudge the 'wall' of the structure as if to say 'let me out', David began thinking 'what if I lower this ... ', which triggered his action to slowly lower the slope piece to transform the function of the 'wall' into a 'ramp' for the truck to drive out. As William continues on to drive the truck out, David begins to

Episode 2: Olivia is Sorting Caterpillar's Food
The block area is quiet, and cylinders have been left out from previous play. Olivia (age: 3 years 9 months) is playing with Eric Carle (1969)'s Hungry Caterpillar display table, which has small pieces of food and a caterpillar. Olivia brings caterpillar's food into block area and hands them to the researcher (see Figure 2).

OLIVIA:	Olivia passes the pictures of caterpillar food to the researcher, who is sat next to the cluster of vertical cylinders.
Researcher:	An apple, a plum, a candy, a cupcake, a watermelon, a strawberry, and an ice cream [placing each piece of fruit onto each cylinder. Two cylinders are left without food].
OLIVIA:	We need some more,
Researcher:	We need some more? Okay, go get it.
OLIVIA:	We need two left.
Researcher:	We've got two left.
Researcher:	Let's have a look. Oh, and then you've got a pear, and an orange. Is that enough now?
OLIVIA:	Yeah.
Researcher:	Yes. We've got everything.
OLIVIA:	[8 second pauses] We need some more.
Researcher:	We need some more? Okay, go on then.
OLIVIA:	[Goes to get one cylinder from block shelf, and places it next to the rest of the cylinders. Olivia then gets one piece of food from the Hungry Caterpillar display table, and gives it to the researcher]
Researcher:	And, that's a cherry pie.
OLIVIA:	We did it! [Jumps up, takes off her sunglasses and looks at the collection.]
OLIVIA:	We need to grab the plate. [Grabs a plate and places all the food onto the plate]

tell his story about what his construction can do, at which point his thinking had reached the abstract state.

Summary of Episode 2

Episode 2 was initiated by the researcher based on an observation from the previous day in which Olivia was enjoying placing cylinders on a square platform constructed by ¼ blocks. Each cylinder was placed neatly onto each piece of ¼ block, suggesting one-to-one sorting behaviour. In this episode, the researcher begins placing one piece of food onto each cylinder. There are two cylinders left after all the food has been placed, and Olivia announces that she needs two more food to complete the game. The game was started without a set rule, but as Olivia observes the researcher's action, she perceives the sorting as what seems to be a rule, and uses it to extend the activity.

Episode 3: Poppy's Parking Space

Researcher:	Ah right, what were you building?
POPPY:	I building it, around the circle one. [gestures a large circle with her arm]
Researcher:	Around the circle?
POPPY:	I'm gonna make it very big.
Researcher:	You gonna make it very very big.
THOMAS:	beep beep.
POPPY:	That could be your broken down truck. [continue to play with loading and unloading trucks, and transporting blocks]
POPPY:	[to Thomas] Excuse me, could I borrow a brick, please?
THOMAS:	No.
POPPY:	These bricks, please.
Researcher:	Did you just borrow the bricks?
POPPY:	I need the bricks to ... I think I need another ... [looking for blocks to construct parking]
POPPY:	Truck has to go in first [drives the truck into the half enclosed space and places 1/2 sticks around the truck to surround it] and then the truck goes out that way. [pointing at a small gap made between the blocks, which is not big enough for the truck]
Researcher:	Ah, I see. That's the entrance.
POPPY:	[pauses and looks at her construction] But I take it off because I don't need it. [removes one block to open enough space for the truck to drive out]
Researcher:	You take it off because you don't need it.
POPPY:	Just put it here. [places the removed block out of the way, then drives the truck out]
Researcher:	So what does this space do? What is this?
POPPY:	It's a parking place.

She begins to take on the lead and extends furthermore by adding more cylinders. She shows her satisfaction for completion by jumping up.

Summary of Episode 3

In episode 3, Poppy (age: 4 years 8 months) is constructing a 'parking' space for a truck, which she has been playing with. She begins by describing her design as 'a circle' thing excitedly. She uses a truck to guide her with the construction to build an enclosure around it. At this point, her play is described as concrete thinking as her verbal representation is figurative, which is embedded within the experience. Poppy's thinking begins to advance further towards abstract thinking when she pauses for a reflection and notices that the gap was not big enough for the truck to go through. Her thinking has demonstrated functional dependency relationship as she acquires the concept that a complete circle will obstruct the truck from driving out; therefore, she needs to remove a piece a block to open up a space required for the truck to go through. This episode is illustrating the early development of abstract thinking with an assistance from concrete experience as Poppy begins to apply her understanding of her acquired concept to alter her construction to meet the function of the 'parking place'.

General discussion of the three episodes

The interpretive analysis revealed three dominant features, depicted in the presented episodes. They are (i) *sharing of thinking between child and child*, and *sharing of thinking between adult and child*; (ii) intrinsically driven *pause for reflection*; and (iii) the demonstration of *satisfaction* as a result of their self-directed play. This section discusses each feature in detail.

(1) Sharing of thinking – child/child sharing of thinking

In episode 1, David had completed constructing an enclosed space. His friend William placed a truck inside and nudged the wall. In this particular sequence of play, William saw the feature of the construction, that is, the enclosed space created by upright slopes and other surrounding blocks. Placing the truck inside this space demonstrated that William had internalised the containing schema, which focuses on the *in and out* state of an object (Athey, 1990). Although David was the one who built this construction, it was only after observing William's behaviour and letting the truck out by lowering the slope that it could be concluded that David had internalised the containing schema. Here, the outcome of this sequence of play is a sharing of thinking which led to David's learning.

Child/child sharing of thinking involved unintentional sharing of thinking. The focus is the *unintentional* nature of the event, which is distinguished from 'tutoring' as seen in scaffolding (Wood, Bruner, & Ross, 1976) or active delivery of problem-solving strategies as seen in the zone of proximal development (Gifford, 2004). Rather, the sharing is regarded as the outcome of the action when a child observes an incidence or operation that interests him or her, internalises it, and turns it into his or her own knowledge (Edwards, 2014).

Sharing of thinking – adult/child sharing of thinking

In contrast to Child/Child Sharing of Thinking, Adult/Child Sharing of Thinking is where an adult takes on an active role to pose a relevant question to extend a child's thinking. For instance, in episode 1, the researcher asked David 'did it just open to let the truck out?' David then explained that it can open and close, demonstrating David's thinking represented the functional dependency relationship. It indicated that his understanding on the functional capability of his block construction had developed during this block play by observing his friend placing a truck inside the enclosure to pretend that it was trapped.

Adult/child sharing of thinking involved the researcher's active involvement in their play to extend the child's thinking through the use of appropriate observations and judgements on what the child might be interested in. Adopting such pedagogical approach stimulates the implementation of a curriculum of thinking. It demonstrates that teaching thinking can be employed at young ages with appropriate approach. The style of such curriculum is described as 'infusion' style (Aubrey et al., 2012), where development of thinking skills are embedded within spontaneous play. Asking appropriate questions involves practitioners to engage in the play and gain a deeper understanding of what the child is focused on.

Social implications observed in the episodes include child/child observations and 'sustained shared thinking' between the adult and the child. Siraj-Blatchford (2009) derived the term sustained shared thinking through the Effective Provision of Pre-School Education Project as 'sharing of thinking, and [...] sustained nature of some of the interactions'. The emphasis is placed upon the extended period of activity intentionally prolonged by the supporting adults through participation in the activity and sharing their interests, and organising a timely provision of suitable learning environment in order to develop their critical thinking. Similar notions include scaffolding (Wood et al., 1976) and the zone of proximal development (Vygotsky, 1978). However, unlike scaffolding or the zone of proximal development, the intention is not to deliver knowledge or strategies to the child. The intention of sustained shared thinking assumes the child as a powerful learner who is capable of constructing knowledge him- or herself, with relevant social support. Holding such assumptions at the heart of the early years practice leads to the formation of a pedagogical structure that incorporates 'interactionist' approach. The interactionist approach, as described by Gura and Bruce (1992), constantly searches for a child's interests that can be used to extend learning opportunities. Especially for children as young as preschool age, skills to think abstractly are still developing, which makes teaching of mathematical concepts, skills, and strategies through direct method difficult. In such cases, mathematical concepts can be conveyed indirectly through play, where the concepts are concretely embedded. The demonstration of such procedure can be seen through this research, where the researcher actively sought for learning opportunity as a child played with unit blocks, and either initiated, extended, or asked open-ended questions that would extend critical thinking. Such an approach coincides with Claxton and Carr's (2004) arguments that teaching in early years should be about supporting the development of learning disposition.

(2) Pause for reflection

In episode 1, David was lowering the slope to let William's truck out. He lowered the slope halfway and paused briefly as if to think whether what he was doing was the right thing. Then he continued to lower two more slopes. In episode 2, Olivia had an 8 second pause between the moment she said that she has enough caterpillar food and the moment she decided to get some more. Poppy in episode 3 also had a brief pause after she had constructed her 'parking space', when she looked at the construction and made an alteration by taking a piece of block out to make enough space for the truck to drive out.

These preschool children's behaviour of pausing for reflection resonated with the development of awareness. Donaldson (1986) described that such development occurs when ' something gives us pause and when consequently, instead of just acting, we stop to consider the possibilities of acting which are before us' (Donaldson, 1986, p. 94). This is also another feature identified to be emerging in this functional dependency relationship where children's thinking transformed between concrete and abstract. These children in the presented episodes demonstrated their abilities to reflect on their actions, while eliminating irrelevant factors around them and giving considerations towards the product of their actions. Such behaviour is the process of 'turn[ing] language and thought in upon themselves' (Hughes, 1990, p. 123), and continuous practice of such behaviour will help children to develop abstract thinking.

These episodes also demonstrated that reflective pauses occurred intrinsically. While a further investigation is required to determine what triggers effective reflection in young children, it is suggested that the ability to reflect is linked to possessing a feeling of being in control (Donaldson, 1986; Hughes, 1990). It is argued that the act of stopping and pausing to think about one's own thinking and to actively 'choose to direct our thinking' is 'relevant to the development of intellectual self-control, with incalculable consequences for the development of the kinds of thinking which are characteristic of logic, mathematics and the sciences' (Donaldson, 1986, pp. 94–95). Although the children referred to in Donaldson's (1986) text are at school age and capable of writing (i.e. turning their thought into visual form), it is also evident in these episodes that young children are beginning to apply a form of reflection when they witness their achievement concretely. Since this reflective action has to be initiated intrinsically, the practitioners should understand the value of time and space required by children to complete their play and assist them to look back on their action by using the products of their play. This will support the children to practice the process of running through their cognitive process.

It is uncertain if the child held any explicit theory or a plan in mind before the reflection that linked with what their block construction can do. It may be that the young children whose form of thinking is at this functional dependency relationship stage have the ability to remain open-ended, allowing them to scan through the world for relevant and interesting information.

(3) Satisfaction

The third sign of learning at this transitional stage of functional dependency relationship is satisfaction, which is connected with reflection. Olivia in episode 2 jumped up with joy, took off her sunglasses to take a closer look, and said 'we did it!' Satisfaction from David in episode 1 was very clear when his energy in speech changed as he began explaining his achievement and what his construction can do.

While not all children display satisfaction in such an obvious manner, each activity that is completed fully will have an end point. Bennett, Wood, and Rogers (1997, p. 13) described that 'children's self-directed activities often reveal powerful evidence of children effectively directing their own learning, particularly if supported in the process by an adult'. Yet the argument goes that the degree of child-centred approach which ensures children's rights to choose can sometimes cause conflicts with the curriculum objectives, where teachers attempt to facilitate for children to 'experience breadth, balance and progression' (Bennett et al., 1997, p. 13).

Some nursery schools in England appear to have introduced literacy hours for 0–5-year-olds since the revision of the Early Years Foundation Stages (EYFS) in 2014 with the aim for young children to enter school with pre-equipped literacy skills. The practitioners' interpretation of Communication and Language in certain settings was to teach vocabulary through repeating and reciting. Since these activities were far from children's interests, signs of learning as seen in this research were not observed. Similarly, a recent report from the UK's All Party Parliamentary Group for Maths and Numeracy criticised Early Years settings for an excessive focus on rote learning of number facts at the expense of approaches that help children develop number sense through play (APPG for Maths and Numeracy, 2014). For early years curricula such as the EYFS, which dictates learning areas, practitioners are required to understand how young children learn and have practical skills to apply topics of teaching agenda appropriately. Appropriate methods of teaching will incorporate a holistic approach that fully engages children's play as directed by themselves. The teachers' job is to introduce any relevant academic concepts into their play without interrupting the flow of their play. In such an approach, these three signs of learning as identified in this study will become useful in guiding the teachers about children's learning.

Conclusion

The study presented in this article was driven by its aim to identify behaviours of preschool children that would indicate a transformation between concrete and abstract thinking in order to allow early years practitioners to better understand the importance of effective scaffolds. The main focus was on Athey's functional dependency relationship, and it was crucial not to guide children in this study other than to support their intentions through effective communication. For this reason, the data collection stage was underpinned by the act of 'close listening', which allowed children to express their ideas in various forms of representations. It was important to establish such a methodology, since this was a study of young children's thinking and learning in their natural context (Angelillo et al., 2007; Ginsburg, 1997; Schoenfeld, 2002).

For the purpose of this paper, the number of reported episodes was reduced down from 26 to 3, focusing on the ones in which the young children had demonstrated transformation from concrete to abstract thinking. The analysis of these 'concrete to abstract' episodes demonstrated that children's thinking was continuously transforming back and forth between concrete and abstract. Furthermore, the transformation was supported by a complex interplay of young children's cognitive development and their social interaction. When young children observe other children, they memorise and imitate any features that interest them. Through the act of imitation, children internalise various concepts that help them to understand the world around them. It is difficult to judge when such sharing of thinking occurs between children, and what features are presented to them. The best support the practitioners can give to allow the development of concepts through child/child sharing of thinking is by organising varieties of activities over a long period of time, observing their play from a distance, and allowing space for the children to negotiate their play without having the practitioners to intervene. This requires practitioners' sensitivity and knowledge and understanding of what children are doing in their play, in order to know when *NOT* to step in.

The research has also identified the importance of a pause for reflection in young children, as a feature that may suggest the development of abstract thinking. After the young children paused to think about their action, their block construction became more complex and more refined, suggesting that their spontaneous reflection is connected with the development of abstract thinking (Aubrey et al., 2012; Chatzipanteli, Grammatikopoulos, & Gregoriadis, 2014; Taggart & Ridley, 2005). As in the case of these young children, they require time and space to complete their play, and to feel that they have been in control of their own play. To support the development of abstract thinking, practitioners need to plan adequate space and time for such activities, and understand what reflective questions or props to use to support such development. For this, the practitioners should be prepared to be with the children during the play to understand their intentions, and understand what reflective questions or props to use if required. It important to reiterate that playing together with young children is not about guiding them with a curriculum, but it is about organising various environments in which their exposure to various concepts is maximised for them to experience and discover.

While more early years settings are feeling a pressure to conduct formal teaching to young children, it is important for practitioners to understand that young children are able to retain such a concept more effectively once their abstract thinking has developed. Until their abstract thinking skill is fully developed, early years practitioners can provide the best environment that young children can have to practise thinking skills by exposing them to different types of play using open-ended equipment, and allow opportunities to physically experience the concepts before giving didactic instructions.

Disclosure statement

No potential conflict of interest was reported by the authors.

References

Alderson, P. (1995). *Listening to children: Ethics and social research.* London: Barnardo's.

Angelillo, C., Rogoff, B., & Chavajay, P. (2007). Examining shared endeavors by abstracting video coding schemes with fidelity to cases. In R. Goldman, R. Pea, B. Barron, & J. Derry (Eds.), *Video research in the learning sciences* (pp. 189–206). Mahway, NJ: Erlbaum.

Atherton, F., & Nutbrown, C. (2013). *Understanding schemas and young children: From birth to three*. London: Sage.
Athey, C. (1990). *Extending thought in young children: A parent-teacher partnership*. London: Paul Chapman.
Aubrey, C., David, T., Godfrey, R., & Thompson, L. (2000). *Early childhood educational research: Issues in methodology and ethics: Debates and issues in methodology and ethics*. Oxon: Routledge.
Aubrey, C., Ghent, K., & Kanira, E. (2012). Enhancing thinking skills in early childhood. *International Journal of Early Years Education, 20*(4), 332–348.
Barron, B. (2007). Video as a tool to advance understanding of learning and development in peer, family, and other informal learning contexts. In R. Goldman, R. Pea, B. Barron, & S. Derry (Eds.), *Video research in the learning sciences* (pp. 159–187). Mahway, NJ: Erlbaum.
Bennett, N., Wood, L., & Rogers, S. (1997). *Teaching through play: Teachers' thinking and classroom practice*. Buckingham: Open University Press.
Bjorklund, C. (2014). Powerful teaching in preschool – a study of goal-oriented activities for conceptual learning. *International Journal of Early Years Education, 22*(4), 380–394.
Blumer, H. (1969). *Symbolic interactionism: Perspective and method*. Englewood Cliffs, NJ: Prentice Hall.
Bourke, R., & Loveridge, J. (2014). Exploring informed consent and dissent through children's participation in educational research. *International Journal of Research and Method in Education, 37*(2), 151–165.
British Educational Research Association. (2011). *Ethical guidelines for educational research*. London: BERA.
Carle, E. (1969). *The very hungry caterpillar*. London: Puffin.
Carruthers, E., & Worthington, M. (2005). Making sense of mathematical graphics: The development of understanding abstract symbolism. *European Early Childhood Education Research Journal, 13*(1), 57–79.
Chatzipanteli, A., Grammatikopoulos, V., & Gregoriadis, A. (2014). Development and evaluation of metacognition in early childhood education. *Early Child Development and Care, 184*(8), 1223–1232.
Claxton, G., & Carr, M. (2004). A framework for teaching learning: the dynamics of disposition. *Early Years, 24*(1), 87–97.
Confrey, J. (1995). How compatible are radical constructivism, social-cultural approaches and social constructivism? In L. Steffe (Ed.), *Constructivism in education* (pp. 185–225). Hillsdale, NJ: Lawrence Erlbaum.
Dockett, S. Einarsdottir, J., & Perry, B. (2011). Balancing methodologies and methods in research with young children. In D. Harcourt, B. Perry, & T. Waller (Eds.), *Researching young children's perspectives: Debating the ethics and dilemmas of educational research with children* (pp. 68–82). London: Routledge.
Dockett, S., & Perry, B. (2011). Researching with young children: Seeking assent. *Child Indicators Research, 4*(2), 231–247.
Donaldson, M. (1986). *Children's minds*. London: Fontana Press.
Edwards, K. (2014). *Video observation of preschool children at block play in english nursery school: Identifying elements which constitute development of abstract thinking* (MSc Educational Research diss.). Bristol University.
Fleer, M., & Robbinsons, J. (2003). 'Hit and run research' with 'Hit and miss': Results in early childhood science education. *Research in Science Education, 33*(4), 405–431.
Fosnot, C., & Perry, R. (2005). Constructivism: A psychological theory of learning. In C. Fosnot (Ed.), *Constructivism: Theory, perspectives and practice* (pp. 8–38). New York, NY: Teachers College Press.
Gifford, S. (2004). A new mathematics pedagogy for the early years: In search of principles for practice. *International Journal of Early Years Education, 12*(2), 99–115.
Ginsburg, H. (1997). *Entering the child's mind: The clinical interview in psychological research and practice*. Cambridge: Cambridge University Press.
Ginsburg, H. (2009). The challenge of formative assessment in mathematics education: Children's minds, teachers' minds. *Human Development, 52*(2), 109–128.
Gopnik, A., Glymour, C., Sobel, D., Schulz, L., Kushnir, T., & Danks, D. (2004). A theory of causal learning in children: Causal maps and bayes nets. *Psychological Review, 111*(1), 3–32.
Gopnik, A., Meltzoff, A., & Kuhl, P. (1999). *How babies think*. London: Weidenfeld and Nicolson.
Grieve, R., & Hughes, M. (1990). An introduction to understanding children. In R. Grieve & M. Hughes (Eds.), *Understanding children* (pp. 1–10). Oxford: Basil Blackwell.
Guba, E., & Lincoln, Y. (2005). Paradigmatic controversies, contradictions and emerging confluences. In N. Denzin & Y. Lincoln (Eds.), *The SAGE handbook of qualitative research* (pp. 191–216). Thousand Oaks, CA: Sage.
Gura, P., & Bruce, T. (1992). *Exploring learning: Young children and blockplay*. London: Paul Chapman.
Hughes, M. (1990). Children's computation. In M. Hughes & R. Grieve (Eds.), *Understanding children* (pp. 121–139). Oxford: Basil Blackwell.
Inhelder, B., Sinclair, H., & Bovet. (1974). *Learning and the development of cognition*. London: Routledge & Kegan Paul.
Knoblauch, H., & Tuma, R. (2011). Videography: An interpretative approach to video-recorded micro-social interaction. In E. Margolls & L. Pauwels (Eds.), *The SAGE handbook of visual research methods* (pp. 414–430). Los Angeles, CA: Sage.
Kuhn, D. (2010). What is scientific thinking and how does it develop? In U. Goswami (Ed.), *Blackwell handbook of child cognitive development* (pp. 497–524). Oxford: Wiley- Blackwell.
Lofland, J., Snow, D., Anderson, L., & Lofland, L. (2006). *Analyzing social settings: A guide to qualitative observation and analysis* (4th ed.). Belmont, CA: Wadsworth.
Nutbrown, C. (2011). *Threads of thinking: Schemas and young children's thinking*. London: Sage.
van Oers, B. (2001). Contextualisation for abstraction. *Cognitive Science Quarterly, 1*(3), 279–305.

van Oers, B., & Poland, M. (2007). Schematising activities as a means for encouraging young children to think abstractly. *Mathematics Education Research Journal, 19*(2), 10–22.
Ofsted. (2015). *Teaching and play in the early years – a balancing act? A good practice survey to explore perceptions of teaching and play in the early years.* London: Office for Standards in Education.
Pascal, C., Bertram, T., Mould, C., & Hall, R. (1998). Exploring the relationship between process and outcome in young children's learning: Stage one of a longitudinal study. *International Journal of Educational Research, 29*(1), 51–67.
Piaget, J. (1953). *The origins of intelligence in the child.* London: Routledge & Kegan Paul.
Piaget, J. (1962). *Play, dreams and imitation in childhood.* Oxon: Routledge.
Piaget, J. (1964). Development and learning. In R. Ripple & V. Rockcastle (Eds.), *Piaget rediscovered* (pp. 7–20). Ithaca, NY: Cornell University Press.
Piaget, J. (1977). *The development of thought: Equilibration of cognitive structures.* Oxford: Viking Press.
Rogoff, B. (1998). Cognition as a collaborative process. In W. Damon, D. Kuhn, & R. Siegler (Eds.), *Cognition, perceptions and language* (Volume Eds.), Handbook of child psychology (5th ed., pp. 679–744). New York, NY: Wiley.
Schoenfeld, A. (2002). Research methods in (mathematics) education. In L. English (Ed.), *Handbook of international research in mathematics education* (pp. 435–488). Mahwah, NJ: Lawrence Erlbaum.
Sfard, A. (2007). When the rules of discourse change, but nobody tells you: Making sense of mathematics learning from a commognitive standpoint. *Journal of the Learning Sciences, 16*(4), 565–613.
Siegler, R. (2000). The rebirth of children's learning. *Child Development, 71*(1), 26–35.
Siraj-Blatchford, I. (2009). Conceptualising progression in the pedagogy of play and sustained shared thinking in early childhood education: Vygotskian perspective. *Educational and Child Psychology, 26*(2), 77–89.
Taggart, G., & Ridley, K. (2005). *Thinking skills in the early years: A literature review.* Slough: NFER.
Vygotsky, L. (1978). *Mind and society.* Cambridge, MA: Harvard University Press.
Wertsch, J. (1991). *Voices of the mind: A sociocultural approach to mediated action.* Cambridge, MA: Harvard University Press.
Wertsch, J., & Stone, C. (1985). The concept of internalization in vygotsky's account of the genesis of higher mental functions. In V. Wertsch (Ed.), *Culture, communication and cognition: Vygotskian perspectives* (pp. 162–182). Cambridge: Cambridge University Press.
Wood, D., Bruner, J., & Ross, G. (1976). The role of tutoring in problem solving. *Journal of Child Psychology and Psychiatry, and Allied Disciplines, 17*(2), 89–100.

4. # The relative emphasis of play rules between experienced and trainee caregivers of toddlers

Kinga Gyöngy

ABSTRACT
Content analysis of a large-scale ($N = 920$) qualitative data set with MAXQDA12 from a nationwide questionnaire of nursery practitioners in Hungary was able to demonstrate various types of rules during free play: social, health and safety, and environment-related rules. Environment-related rules, which govern space utilisation in toddler groups, have not been previously described in the literature but seem to be part of the practical know-how of the profession. Whereas there was a general agreement among respondents for social and health and safety rules, some disagreements in the presentation of environment-related rules were detected. Responses of a subsample ($N = 255$) consisting of three groups ($N = 85$) were analysed quantitatively: frequencies of environmental-rule-contents were statistically compared between a trainee group and two matched (a colleague and an independent) experienced nursery nurses' groups (chi-squared test, one-way ANOVA). For trainee nursery practitioners, rules have a greater importance ($p < .05$) than for experienced caregivers.

Introduction

Free play is an important part of nursery life. The author's own work in nurseries and contact with nursery practitioners suggested that there are many implicit rules that practitioners apply during free play. There is little literature that connects behaviour management and free play. In the following, a literature review of the relationship between free play and rules is given; then, the Hungarian nursery system is described for cultural context. These will give the setting of the current work, which sought to examine the behavioural expectations towards toddlers during free play using content analysis.

Free play and rules

Free play forms the heart of the Hungarian nursery curriculum for under threes (Korintus, Nyitrai, & Rózsa, 1997). The notion of free play implies that it is *free from* adult-imposed developmental goals and the child is *free to* choose the content of play. Throughout the 165-year history of Hungarian nursery pedagogy, the adult's role in children's play has been debated for decades (Gyöngy, 2014a). On the one hand, the importance of child-initiated play for the self-governed development of children was emphasised; on the other hand, it was feared that the adult's impact on children's development would be lost without animated play or adult input in the form of ideas, assistance or taking part in children's play. Of all of the trends in Hungarian nursery pedagogy, the Pikler approach has been the most committed to the notion and realisation of free play for infants and toddlers (Kálló & Balogh, 2005). The Pikler pedagogy has had a great and long-lasting impact on the Hungarian mainstream nursery pedagogy from the 1970s, but in its original way, it was gradually sidelined after the fall of the Iron Curtain (Révész, 2013).

The notion of free play means that children can chose the content of their play. However, this 'does not imply an absence of boundaries. It does imply that these boundaries are managed within a primary consideration of the child's need to choose its own play' (Santer, Griffiths, & Goodall, 2007, p. xi). Even in the Pikler pedagogy, there are boundaries present for children, but there is an aim to eliminate any unnecessary rules that would lead to conflict between the adult and the child or would not support the children's autonomy (Tardos, 1975).

The question is how to draw a line between reasonable and restrictive rules. Even reasonable boundaries clash with young children's limitless ideas for play and creative use of equipment, whereas boundaries that serve the adults' convenience (e.g. putting away toys earlier than the end of the play session and forbidding children to use them prior to closing time) can undermine children's opportunities to play freely.

Environmental shortcomings (e.g. not child-safe environment) can be a source of unnecessary rules. Without childproofing, toddlers' behaviour has to be managed instead of the management of the environment. Johnson (1987) explored actions Canadian caregivers prohibited children in their care. The environment played a significant role in rules. Adults worried that children's play would harm the state of their homes where they cared for these children; conversely, children could get hurt from playing without boundaries. In nurseries, the environment should be designed to be child-safe. Nevertheless, hazardous situations can still present themselves during children's play, so supervision is needed at all times (The California Child Care Health Program, 2007). It is known that out of all age groups, toddlers are most prone to suffer injuries in a day-care centre, and most of the injuries are self-induced (Elardo, Solomons, & Snider, 1987).

Supervision and continuous risk assessment of children's play is a task of the nursery practitioners, depending on their personal judgement of what is allowed and what is prohibited during play. Health and safety rules seemingly oppose the notion of free play. Children have a right to free play unless they are stopping other people from enjoying their own rights or endangering their own safety, meaning that children do not only have rights to free play, but also responsibilities to keep themselves and others safe during their play. Restrictive rules, however, could curtail children's rights to free play if out of fear for something bad happening, caregivers are inhibiting children's play.

An example of cultural differences in judgement over health and safety risks between pedagogues in the United States of America and Sweden is reported by Baker and Ross-Bernstein (2014). The American authors observed a Swedish preschool where children were playing 'catching fish': one of them was the fish and the others caught him with a rope in a rough-and-tumble play. The authors were astonished and shocked at the scene, while the Swedish educator smilingly acknowledged the play. Educators perceive risk differently depending on the given culture and the pedagogy they are practising.

Research typically does not focus on the content of classroom rules. Concerning rules and behavioural expectations, researchers agree that boundaries are necessary (Baumrind, 1996). Previous observational studies typically focused on the process of rule enforcement or caregiver control strategies. Studies in childcare were concerned with the disciplinary process (Howes & Olenich, 1986) and factors influencing child compliance (Wachs, Gurkas, & Kontos, 2004).

Given the above discussion, the following question arises: Is the content of rules irrelevant to rule enforcement or otherwise culturally or locally so varied that it is not worth examining? A Head Start[1] training video (Sandall, 2014) on classroom rules encourages educators to generate their own rules for their own classroom (i.e. local variation) and describes rules in general (being small in number, short, simple and positively formulated), but does not suggest any pre-formulated rules (i.e. irrelevance of specific content). However, it is admitted in the video that rules in different classrooms might seem similar from the outside, so it seems that there could be an agreement between caregivers in terms of the most important rules for childcare.

This study is new in two respects. Firstly, rules are studied in the context of free play. Studies on compliance and rule breaking are typically not done during free play, rather during structured tasks, for example, clearing up toys or circle time. Although free play is not a typical setting for rule enforcement, behavioural expectations are still present, just not frequent enough for researchers to be able to study them effectively. Secondly, this study focusses on the content of rules in the context of free play.

Cultural context of the study: characteristics of Hungarian nurseries

Rules are part of behaviour management. Behaviour management (regulating children's behaviour from the outside) is embedded in the structure of care in the nursery. It has been demonstrated that environmental chaos, that is, the lack of physical and temporal structure, as well as high levels of noise and crowding, is negatively associated with child compliance as well as with childcare quality (Wachs et al., 2004). Therefore, it is worth examining the structural characteristics of the Hungarian nursery care and education to be able to understand the context of rules.

The first nurseries for under threes were founded in the second half of the nineteenth century in Hungary. After the Second World War, institutions were nationalised, and all nurseries became part of the state sector. Many nurseries were created but the quality of care was questionable. From the late 1970s, the Pikler approach offered solutions to the needs of the Hungarian nursery system and permeated the thinking of early childhood care in Hungary (Gyöngy, 2014a). Several structural changes occurred during the 1970s and 1980s, partially thanks to the influence of the Pikler approach. The practice of looping, sequential care, individual adaptation periods, delegation of non-caring duties and the room-group system are seen as guarantees for high-quality provision.

Looping

The concept of stability in key person relationships means that children stay with their own caregivers for the entire time in the nursery (called 'looping' in English by Hedge & Cassidy, 2004). If spatial transition is to happen (such as moving from an infant to a toddler room), it always happens with the children changing rooms with their key person (a similar approach was later described by Essa, Favre, Thweatt, & Sherry, 1999). Thanks to the common practice of looping, rules are not changing, because the adults are constant who set up the rule system. Rules can be better defined and enforced because adults and children form a long-term relationship that includes longer term educational goals.

Sequential care

At routine care situations, children are not cared for simultaneously: instead, they follow each other in a given sequence, thereby allowing the caregiver to focus her attention on the individual needs of the children. Children learn their place in the sequence, individually playing while other children are being cared for by the adult (Stróbl, 1981). This is an important piece in the puzzle as to why free play is of great importance in Hungarian nurseries also in terms of behaviour management. To eliminate idle waiting time for children, some children are still playing while others are being cared for. This practice requires the children to be able to play on their own without adult guidance. If the children play peacefully, the practitioners can dedicate their attention to the children they feed or help in toileting. So, it is an aim of the nursery nurses to support children's autonomy in their play; otherwise, the practice of sequential care will not work.

Individual adaptation periods

From the early 1980s, a two-week adaptation period – in the presence of a parent – was introduced to every child entering nursery (Németh, Polónyi, & Dobszay, 1979). Three-year-old children leave nursery and enter kindergarten on the 1st September. From the time empty spaces open up in the nursery, new children can start their adaptation period in the presence of their main attachment figure. One key person should welcome one new child during the two weeks of the adaptation period. Two nursery practitioners work together in a room, so two new children start nursery every two weeks per room during the first couple of weeks of the school year. According to current legislation, a room can accommodate 12 children if they are under two, and 14 children if all children in the room are over two years of age (Ministry of Welfare, 1998). If a group is starting with no children at the beginning of September, then the group will reach its full size at the end of November or at the beginning of December. The sequential adaptation periods make it possible for nursery nurses to get to know the individual children, and to teach them the rules of the nursery. Because the parent is present in the group for a substantial time during the adaptation period, the nursery nurses have a chance to observe the parent's way of setting limits to their own children. These observations will help them to foresee the children's possible reactions to limits in the nursery and the potential challenging behaviours.

Delegation of non-caring duties

The work of nursery practitioners is supported by an untrained support worker, who does all kinds of tasks not directly related to the children, for example, fetching the food from the kitchen, cleaning, laying out the beds and so on. Two rooms make up one group, which is allocated one support worker. The delegation of non-caring duties enables nursery nurses to focus their attention on children's care and education. This also means that the people who get in contact with the children are limited to those who are trained, and who have already built a relationship with the child. The limited number of caregivers makes it possible to have consistent/consequent teaching and enforcement of a set of rules. Because teaching rules in a consequent fashion requires a lot of patience and individual attention, lightening the workload of the nursery nurses in terms of household chores helps the pedagogical work to be more sensitive.

Room-group system

The purpose-built nurseries have a common planning principle: two rooms make up one group. These rooms can be opened together. Every group has its own bathroom that is connected to the two rooms of the group. A changing room is connected to the group where every child has a changing cabinet for his or her coat, indoor clothes and change of shoes. According to current standards, the size of the room should be at least 3 m^2 per child; from 10 children up it should be at least 40 m^2 (Balogh et al., 2012). The nursery practitioners work in different shifts, with all of them being present from 9:30 to 13:00. Nursery practitioners in adjacent rooms work together in the early hours and in the afternoons. Occasionally it happens that a nursery practitioner is alone with a room full of children. If the children can play freely without adult guidance and if they know the boundaries, then according to Hungarian practice, being alone with a room full of toddlers is manageable. Without clear rules, this periodic high child:adult ratio would lead to chaos.

In summary, Hungarian nursery care and education has a higher child:adult ratio than is recommended in other developed countries, but it lays a great emphasis on personal stability, long-term relationships and individual care. Rules are taught to children individually. Free play complements the behaviour management in three respects. Firstly, it is accompanied by rules, and secondly, encouraging free play works as a pre-emptive behaviour management strategy, that is, a proactive style of pre-empting opportunities for misbehaviour (Dowling, Smith Slep, & O'Leary, 2009); and thirdly, it is a necessary component for sequential care.

Research questions

Four research questions were formulated in relation to play, paying particular attention to the topic of rules:

Research Question 1: What are the rule types for free play on a nationwide sample?

Research Question 2: Is there disagreement in the content of responses concerning rules in toddler rooms? One could hypothesise that there is no general code of conduct that would hold for all nurseries. Disagreement in the content of responses concerning rules in toddler rooms would support this hypothesis.

Research Question 3: Are there any rules that restrict children's rights to free play? From the introduction, we have seen examples where children's rights to free play have been curtailed. Can we see consistent examples from the current nationwide sample?

Research Question 4: Is there a statistically significant difference in the relative emphasis trainees and experienced nursery nurses place on different rules?

Methods

Participants

In February 2011, a database of Hungarian day-care centres was put together. Out of a total of 654 addresses, 317 centres had a public email address and were contacted about this study. Firstly, the directors were contacted via email. We explained the aims of the research and asked them for permission to conduct a study among their workforce. Then, the participants were recruited with a covering letter that they received at their work place. They were asked to describe their practical knowledge and voice their opinion about current and ideal early education and care practice. The participants were not compensated for the completion of the questionnaire. A total of 725 printed questionnaires were returned by post and 195 questionnaires via email, thus the sample consisted of 920 early childhood practitioners, all of whom were female.

According to the Hungarian Central Statistical Office's data, 6631 infant and early childhood educators were working at the time of this study (Tokaji, 2012). This makes the sample size 13.9% of the entire Hungarian infant and early childhood educator population. All seven regions of Hungary are represented in the sample, albeit unevenly (when calculating the average number of questionnaires returned per day-care centre, the statistics for the seven regions were $M = 1.49$, SD = 0.91).

In terms of vocational training, 30% of the respondents went to vocational school and 54% of the respondents held an associate degree. At the time of the study, an associate degree was the highest level of training obtainable for infant and early childhood educators. The first infant and early childhood educator BA courses started in 2009 and students had not yet received their diplomas by spring 2011. Therefore, respondents holding a higher level diploma than associate degree (6.4%) would have received it from a different field of study.

The sample age distribution was negatively skewed, with 63.2% being over 41 years. The overrepresentation of older age groups in the sample was also found in other regional (Szele, 2000) and national studies (Szűcs, 2012).

Children's groups consisted of 13.3 children on average (SD = 2.7). The age of the youngest child in the group was 23.1 months on average (SD = 6.3 months), and the oldest child in the group was 36.7 months old on average (SD = 6.6 months). The largest age difference between children in a group was on average 13.6 months (SD = 7.4 months).

Questionnaire

Three open-ended questions were formulated to enquire behaviour management techniques in the context of free play:

(1) What are the adult's duties during free play?
(2) What is the key to keeping things under control during free play?

(3) What are the rules children have to accept in your room?

Apart from the eight demographic questions, the rest of the questionnaire were not used in the current work. These included 3 questions on nursery practitioners' views on ideal qualities and traits of childcare professionals; 3 questions about challenges of the childcare profession to the individual; 17 questions about art education practices, for example, songs, rhymes, stories and creative activities/ art explorations (results published in Hungarian: Gyöngy, 2014b).

Qualitative methods: coding

Coding process with MAXQDA12

To ease the coding process and produce reliable coding, MAXQDA12 with MAXDictio module (VERBI Software GmbH, Germany) was employed. Handwritten questionnaires were typed in. Digitally returned questionnaires were pre-processed for document import to the content analysis software: each questionnaire was saved as a separate .rtf document; only responses were kept, all other text (e.g. questions, instructions) was erased. Responses quoted in this article were translated into English from Hungarian.

After document import, word frequencies were calculated for the text corpus. During the partially automated content analysis, we were looking for verbal markers of certain topics. Contents were already familiar from an initial manual coding process that was declared unreliable. The challenge was to locate all different word forms that conveyed the same meaning. Different phrasing was collected from the text corpus in two ways. Firstly, after identifying a good search word for a content, all search results were listed and the co-occurrences of different word forms around the initial search word were written down. These co-occurrences were later tested as to whether they returned any new search results for a given code. Secondly, synonyms were found in a thesaurus dictionary and new searches were conducted to test whether they were present in the text corpus.

For each code, a dictionary was created with words that returned the most accurate and comprehensive search results. The lexical search returned some content bearing a different meaning than the given code, expressed by the same words as the search terms. These were removed from the text manually. Coding reliability over time was tested over three weeks and the discrepancies in coding helped to refine code contents. The final coding was done by two coders, inter-rater reliability was computed (overall Cohen's Kappa = 0.835) and discrepancies in coding were resolved.

Guidelines for coding relevant content

Throughout the coding process, an important aspect was to consider whether the nursery practitioners reported rules directed towards the toddlers (i.e. not an expectation towards themselves or other nursery practitioners). Only clear behavioural expectations towards the children were coded as rules.

The second aspect to keep in mind was that rules had to be related to free play. Other rules were omitted from coding, for example, expectations about civilised behaviour during eating or toilet-use.

Lastly, it was also important to remember that the same rules could have been formulated either positively or negatively, while still bearing the same meaning.

Validation of the code set

Validation of the code set via member check was not possible because the respondents were anonymous in the research. Other experienced nursery practitioners and directors were interviewed about the code set. The questions to elicit feedback were: Have you encountered such rules during your work, set either by yourself or by others? Can you give an explanation for these rules?

Quantitative methods: subsampling and statistical analysis

A subsample of 255 respondents was created in the following manner. Newly qualified nursery nurses with a maximum work experience of 2.5 years were selected ($N = 85$) in a subsample ($M = 1.35$ years, SD = 0.08 years). The dividing line was drawn because according to current legislation, a nursery nurse is considered a trainee in the first two or three years, depending on the level of qualification she holds (Barbainé Bérci, 2014).

Matched subsamples were created: an 'experienced colleague to trainee' subsample ($N = 85$) and an 'experienced nursery nurse from a different centre' subsample ($N = 85$). Firstly, the sample was sorted according to postcode, respondent ID number and years of work experience. (To be able to trace back which nurseries took part in the study but at the same time keep respondents' identity anonymous, respondents were asked to reveal the postcode of their workplace. ID numbers were assigned one by one when questionnaires came in. Questionnaires returned by post came in batches from nurseries, so ID numbers in close proximity sharing the same postcode meant that questionnaires were most likely from the same centre.) To each trainee, two other nursery practitioners were selected, with at least 10 years of experience, one with the same postcode and one with the next postcode. This way, one matched subsample was created from the work colleagues of each trainee, and another matched subsample was created from nursery practitioners from a different day-care centre but in a balanced way from the same region. By selecting a related and an independent matched subsample, it could be tested whether colleagues from the same centres have influenced each other when answering the questions.

In both matched subsamples, the minimum work experience was 10 years and the maximum 40 years (experienced colleague to trainee subsample: $M = 19.6$ years, SD = 8.8 years; experienced nursery nurse from a different centre: $M = 23.4$ years, SD = 8.1 years). One-way ANOVA was run to compare the means of subsamples' work experience. Because the assumption of homogeneity of variances has been violated, Welch's ANOVA was calculated ($F_{(2,\ 114.02)} = 484.06, p < .001$), which showed differences within all three groups. Nevertheless, as we do not expect much difference between having almost 20 years of experience and having 3.8 years more on average, we continued the analysis with these subsamples. Statistical analyses of one-way ANOVA and chi-squared test were deployed to compare distributions of the three subsamples.

Results

Research Question 1: Rule types for free play

The coding of responses ($N = 920$) eventually resulted in three main play-related rule types: social rules, health and safety rules, and environment-related rules.

I. *Social rules* were mentioned by 34.0% of respondents ($N = 313$). Children are required to adapt to the group in some ways: they have to accept their key person and the way of subsequent caregiving, as well as to other children's presence, needs and rights (e.g. 'Adaptation to community: he/she is not alone'). Social rules also reflected in the limited ability of toddlers to follow rules of social conduct. They signal the development of understanding the notion of ownership and ways of sharing (e.g. 'Children should respect each other's play things, they should not destroy each other's creations, and are not allowed to take away toys from each other.'). They also reflect children's lacking skills in civilised conflict resolution (e.g. 'Children should ask for a toy, not just take it away; they are not allowed to hurt each other.').

II. *Health and safety rules* were mentioned by 43.8% of respondents ($N = 403$). Health and safety is mainly a concern for nursery practitioners but is also conveyed towards the children in the form of behavioural rules. These rules were about keeping children physically safe (e.g. 'Children are not allowed to climb on furniture') and preserving the good condition of equipment and toys (e.g. 'Children are to follow the normal use of toys i.e. they are not allowed to throw them').

III. *Environment-related rules* were mentioned by 33.1% of the respondents (*N* = 305). These are rules in the context of play, in which the environment plays a considerable role. The responses referred either to certain room locations by naming the place for a certain activity (e.g. 'Certain parts of the room can be used for certain types of play') or to a space utilisation technique during play (e.g. 'clearing the floor from toys for great movement play').

It should be noted that there is some overlap between these rule types. For example, not being able to follow civilised ways of social conduct in a conflict (e.g. biting) could end in a health safety hazard for another child (being bitten). Therefore, we can think about these rule types as overlapping sets.

Research Question 2: Disagreement in content of play-related rules

For social and health and safety rules, there was virtually no disagreement in how content was presented by respondents.

The contents of environment-related rules, however, seemed to partially contradict each other (e.g. 'Running is forbidden indoors.' vs. 'They are not allowed to run around the tables.') or seemed non-universal across respondents (e.g. a typical statement concerning book viewing was: 'They should look at books at the table.' whereas some responses were more allowing: 'Picture books and leporello books can be looked at on the couch.').

Research Question 3: Rules restricting children's rights to free play

Social rules mentioned by respondents generally expressed an explicit need for all children to have equal access to free play and forbid children to curtail others' rights to it (e.g. 'Community code of conduct: respect for each other and others' play, patience for each other, adaptation and tolerance').

Health and safety rules did not provide enough detail to explore individual differences in restrictiveness. Most respondents only provided general guidelines (e.g. 'Children cannot risk their own physical integrity').

Environment-related rules were hypothesised to curtail children's rights to free play, so they were further analysed. In the following, individual codes are listed and their occurrence rate is given as well as percentage in relation to the whole sample (*N* = 920).

1. *Specified location for certain play forms*
   - 1.a. *Non-specific location* (*N* = 30; 3.3%). Nursery practitioners refer to a rule that defines a constant place for toys where children can find them or they refer to spaces where play can take place, but do not specify further.
   - 1.b. *Table-top toys* (*N* = 110; 12.0%). Certain toys (manipulatives having small pieces or tools for creative or messy play) should be used at the table in a sitting position.
   - 1.c. *Space for book viewing* (*N* = 54; 5.9%). Typically, children are asked to look at books at the table. Some responses allow children to look at books in a sitting position on a rug or even allow children to build a castle from (foldable) leporellos, but these are rather atypical responses.
   - 1.d. *Construction and car play mat* (*N* = 35; 3.8%). Building blocks and toy cars should be used on a large play mat (sometimes with a road pattern). Oppositely formulated content e.g. 'toy cars should be played on the car mat' and 'it is not allowed to play with cars on the table' or

'on the radiator cover' both indicate that there is a certain place designated for playing with toy cars.

1.e. *Pretend play area: doll kitchen* (*N* = 16; 1.7%). Children should keep utensils in the doll kitchen.

2. *Regulating indoor gross-motor movement*

2.a. *Running in the room forbidden* (*N* = 114; 12.4%). Fast movement such as running and chasing is not allowed in the room. If formulated positively: running belongs to the outdoor play area.

2.b. *Conditional allowance for running in the room* (*N* = 25; 2%). The nursery practitioner makes allowances for the children to be able to run in the room under certain conditions: there should be enough space for it (e.g. 'not between or around tables and chairs'); it should happen within a structured play session (e.g. 'among playful exercises' or 'dancing').

2.c. *Space for large movement toys* (*N* = 52; 5.7%). Strollers, riding toys, bouncers should only be used within certain boundaries in the room. Balance toys, rocking horse, seesaw, baby slide should be used in a sitting position, with no toys in the child's hands. Large movement toys are not allowed when the tea-trolley enters the room before meals.

3. *Putting away toys* (*N* = 87; 9.5%) Unused toys should go back to the open shelves.

After coding, validating of environment-related rules commenced. All of the questioned nursery nurses confirmed the existence of these rules (they have heard of them). The validation process added some explanation to the environment-related rules:

1. *Specified location for certain play forms*

1.a. *Non-specific location*: During parallel play, the protection of children is ensured by spatial separation.

1.b. *Table-top toys*: Nursery nurses store certain toys (manipulatives, having many small pieces or tools for creative or messy play) out of reach of children. These toys are only available to toddlers when educators can provide close supervision. This means that these toys will only be presented to children when both nursery practitioners are in the room, so that one of them can stay at the table with the playing children. The table sets the boundaries to the activity and makes it easier for the adult to keep track of the small parts. When children ask for these toys, the nursery practitioner helps to remind them to sit at the table whereby she lays the toy on the table and assists the toddler with sitting down.

1.c. *Space for book viewing*: The main motivation for regulating children's independent usage of books is to preserve them, especially picture books made of normal paper. Children learn how to turn the pages. Determining the position for book viewing lowers the likelihood of books being torn or stepped on.

1.d. *Construction and car play mat*: Delegating play with toy cars and building blocks on a carpet helps to lower noise levels in the room. The soft surface absorbs the sound of the toy cars. The carpet is big enough to contain building blocks even if a tower falls over.

1.e. *Pretend play area: doll kitchen*: ---

2. *Regulating indoor gross-motor movement*

2.a. *Running in the room forbidden*: Running indoors is forbidden in fear of accidents.

2.b. *Conditional allowance for running in the room*: Whether indoor running is allowed or not depends greatly on the individual's and the specific centre's pedagogical views as well on the facilities (e.g. utilisation of great entrance halls in case of rainy weather).

2.c. *Space for large movement toys*: When using balancing toys, jumping toys, push along toys, riding toys, slide, tunnel or balls indoors, nursery practitioners control the space available for the activity as well as the intensity to protect children from accidents.

3. *Putting away toys*: To maintain the available space in the room and not to allow chaos to reign, unused toys should go back to their designated place. The nursery nurses ask children to help them with clearing up the toys. The aim of the educators is for older children to be able to put back toys alone, but the adult can help them in this process.

Experienced nursery practitioners and nursery directors held different views about the necessity of these rules. Some of them perceived environment-related rules as old-fashioned and over-controlling, pointing out that, for example, not allowing children to use kitchen utensils outside the doll kitchen seems to serve the adult's convenience by reducing the workload of putting away toys. Others regarded environment-related rules as reasonable and necessary: an efficient way of proactive behaviour management strategy. The question of running indoors especially evoked discussions.

Research Question 4: Rules and work experience

Chi-square test was run on the subsamples ($N = 255$) to see whether there was a significant association between work experience and the number of environment-related rules mentioned by respondents. Some codes (*Construction- and car play mat, Pretend play area: doll kitchen, Conditional allowance for running in the room*) did not occur frequently enough to allow for Chi-square testing. The rest of the codes were tested with the Chi-square statistic. Significant difference between the beginners and the two other groups was found in one occasion, namely *Running in the room forbidden* (Table 1). Trainee nursery practitioners mention it twice as many times as experienced caregivers that toddlers should not run around indoors. According to Cramer's *V*, the effect size is relatively weak (see Table 1).

There is a significant difference ($p = .01$) between experienced and trainee subsamples and no significant difference between the response rates of the two experienced subsamples, which suggests that colleagues have not influenced each other significantly when filling out the questionnaire.

Respondents used environmental codes relatively frequently (33.1% in the whole sample), but the frequency of the individual code categories was relatively low. To make up for the small occurrence rates of the individual code categories, codes with similar contents were merged.

Specified location for certain play forms ($N = 179$; 19.5%). All codes were merged into this supercode that specifies where a type of play is supposed to take place. This code received a coding of 1 (and only 1) if any of the following codes were bigger than 0: 'Non-specific location' + 'Table-top toys' + 'Space for book viewing' + 'Construction- and car play mat' + 'Pretend play area: doll kitchen'.

Regulating indoor gross-motor movement ($N = 173$; 18.8%). All codes about indoor gross-motor movement were combined into this supercode. This supercode reflects the dilemma that the children have a need for large movement but the rooms are not well suited for this type of play. This code received a coding of 1 (and only 1) if any of the following codes were bigger than 0: 'Running in the room forbidden', 'Conditional allowance for running in the room', 'Space for large movement toys'.

Chi-square analysis of the newly created supercodes returns significant results only for 'Regulating indoor gross-motor movement' with moderate effect size (Table 2).

Table 1. Crosstab for 'Running in the room forbidden' and Experience: $\chi^2_{(2)} = 9.12$, $p = .01$, Cramer's $V = 0.189$.

			Experience			
			Trainee	Experienced colleague	Independent experienced	Total
Running forbidden	No mention	Count	63	76	75	214
		Expected count	71.3	71.3	71.3	214.0
	Mention	Count	22	9	10	41
		Expected count	13.7	13.7	13.7	41.0
Total		Count	85	85	85	255
		Expected count	85.0	85.0	85.0	255.0

Table 2. Crosstab for Regulating indoor gross-motor movement and Experience $\chi^2_{(2)} = 9.12$, $p = .003$, Cramer's $V = 0.21$.

			Experience			
			Trainee	Experienced colleague	Independent experienced	Total
Regulating indoor gross-motor movement	No mention	Count	53	69	70	192
		Expected count	64.0	64.0	64.0	192.0
	Mention	Count	32	16	15	63
		Expected count	21.0	21.0	21.0	63.0
Total		Count	85	85	85	255
		Expected count	85.0	85.0	85.0	255.0

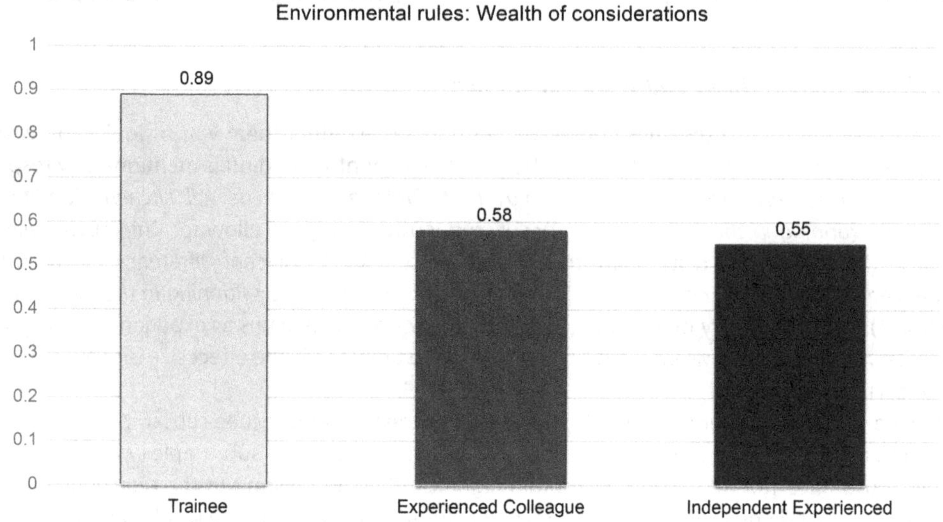

Figure 1. Trainees mention more rules on average than either other experienced groups.

To answer how many different aspects of environmental rules were mentioned by respondents, another new supercode was created: 'Wealth of considerations' by counting all the different environment-related codes a person mentioned. We compared the three groups (Trainees, Experienced Colleagues and Independent Experienced nursery practitioners) with one-way ANOVA. We found significant differences between the trainees and the other two groups ($F_{(2)} = 3.298$, $p = .039$). Trainees mention more rules than either other groups (Figure 1). The mean difference to experienced colleagues is significant at $p = .033$, and also to randomly selected experienced caregivers at $p = .022$. For the inexperienced trainees, rules seem to be of greater importance than to experienced nursery nurses.

Exploring the effect of any other variable (children's group size, children's age) on the 'Wealth of considerations' supercode does not return any significant results.

Discussion and conclusions

Research Question 1: Rule types for free play

On a nationwide sample, three partially overlapping rule types were found in relation to free play. One could argue that environment-related rules are a subtype of health and safety rules, because partially, they are there to prevent accidents. An independent rule type was created for them because they describe how children should utilise indoor space during free play. Environment-related rules seemed to be part of the practical know-how of the profession that has received little attention until now albeit being prevalent. The purpose of environment-related rules is not only to prevent accidents but also to enhance the experience of free play from the perspective of the children by allowing peaceful parallel play. It has got a behaviour management function as well. Nevertheless, a different categorisation would be possible as well.

Research Question 2: Disagreement in content of play-related rules

A general code of conduct was found describing that toddlers should play in a socially acceptable way, not risking their safety. Disagreement in the content was found in environment-related rules that suggests that environment-related rules are either not uniform or not generally accepted.

Research Question 3: Rules restricting children's rights to free play

Contradictory results were found in terms of whether environment-related rules are restrictive to children's rights to free play. Environmental rules convey a spatial partitioning practice of toddler rooms during free play. It is not clear from the written answers how restrictive these rules are from the toddlers' perspective. Environment-related rules prevent local crowding during free play and thereby minimise conflict. However, if the use of space is rigidly predetermined by the adults, then flexible multifunctional space utilisation where the educator supports children's play with space alterations throughout the day (a recommendation by Tardos, 1975) will not happen. Without seeing the application of an actual rule in real life, it is hard to draw conclusions on the content of a rule curtailing children's rights to free play. Observation studies are needed to explore how flexible nursery educators are about the use of space.

Research Question 4: Rules and work experience

Statistically significant differences were detected in the relative importance of environment-related rules to trainees and experienced nursery nurses. The differences were significant between the inexperienced subsample and both experienced subsamples. It seems that the environmental rules are of greater importance to the trainees. From this study, it is not clear why this is the case. Several explanations present themselves. On the one hand, inexperienced nursery nurses may rely heavily on environmental-related rules because these seem to be able to compensate for their lack of experience. On the other hand, trainees could mention these rules more often, thereby signalling that they are of greater importance to them, because enforcing these rules poses a greater challenge to them than to experienced nursery nurses. It could well be that trainees are less successful in providing boundaries for free play. Further observational studies are needed to explore these questions.

Rules in regard to indoor large-movement play are the mostly debated topic of this study. As it was shown in this study, risky play (involving speed, height or dizziness) among four walls evokes adult restrictiveness or control of the activity due to health and safety concerns. Further studies need to find answers for the dilemma of how to provide enough opportunities for toddlers' need for intensive physical exercise.

In conclusion, a mixed-methods study could show that there is a nationwide rule system that accompanies the free play of toddlers. This study also highlighted the need to understand nursery practice in the smallest detail, for example, the content of rules for toddlers.

Note

1. An early childhood education programme to disadvantaged families in the United States of America.

Acknowledgements

The author wishes to thank Anna Galambos, Nikolett Horváth, Magdolna Péceli, Noémi Stumpf, Rita Emese Tóth for their contribution to the coding process. Thanks to Stephen Christie, Miklós Gyöngy and Katalin Kollár for their proofreading.

Disclosure statement

No potential conflict of interest was reported by the author.

Funding

This research was supported by the Eötvös Loránd University Doctoral School of Psychology graduate scholarship.

ORCiD

Kinga Gyöngy http://orcid.org/0000-0001-6416-8548

References

Baker, M., & Ross-Bernstein, J. (2014). No bad weather, only bad clothing: lessons on resiliency from Nordic early childhood programs. In L. P. Kuh (Ed.), *Thinking critically about environments for young children. Bridging theory and practice* (pp. 49–68). New York, NY: Teachers College Press.

Balogh, L., Barbainé Bérci, K., Kovácsné Bárány, I., Nyitrai, Á., Rózsa, J., Tolnayné Falusi, M., & Vokony, É. (2012). *A bölcsődei nevelés-gondozás szakmai szabályai* [Professional standards of nursery education and care]. Budapest: Nemzeti Család- és Szociálpolitikai Intézet.

Barbainé Bérci, K. (2014). Gyakornok a bölcsődében [Trainee in the nursery]. In G. Jávorka (Ed.), *Bölcsődevezetők kézikönyve* (pp. 1–35). Budapest: Raabe Klett.

Baumrind, D. (1996). The discipline controversy revisited. *Family Relations, 45*(4), 405–414. doi:10.2307/585170

Dowling, C. B., Smith Slep, A. M., & O'Leary, S. G. (2009). Understanding preemptive parenting: relations with toddlers' misbehavior, overreactive and lax discipline and praise. *Journal of Clinical Child & Adolescent Psychology, 38*(6), 850–857. doi:10.1080/15374410903258983

Elardo, R., Solomons, H. C., & Snider, B. C. (1987). An analysis of accidents at a day care center. *American Journal of Orthopsychiatry, 57*(1), 60–65. doi:10.1111/j.1939-0025.1987.tb03509.x

Essa, E. L., Favre, K., Thweatt, G., & Sherry, W. (1999). Continuity of care for infants and toddlers. *Early Child Development and Care, 148*(1), 11–19.

Gyöngy, K. (2014a). A bölcsődepedagógia története a játékirányítási elvek és a művészeti nevelés szempontjából [The history of nursery pedagogy with a special emphasis on play and art curriculum]. In K. Gyöngy (Ed.), *A bölcsődei művészeti nevelés előzményei és jelen gyakorlata* (pp. 9–56). Budapest: ELTE-Eötvös.

Gyöngy, K. (2014b). Egy országos kutatás tanulságai a bölcsődei művészeti nevelésről. [Lessons from a national survey on arts education in nurseries]. In K. Gyöngy (Ed.), *A bölcsődei művészeti nevelés előzményei és jelen gyakorlata* (pp. 57–151). Budapest: ELTE-Eötvös.

Hedge, A. V., & Cassidy, D. J. (2004). Teachers and parents perspectives on looping. *Early Childhood Educational Journal, 32* (2), 133–138. doi:10.1007/s10643-004-1080-x

Howes, C., & Olenick, M. (1986). Family and child care influences on toddler's compliance. *Child development, 57*(1), 202–216. doi:10.2307/1130652

Johnson, L. C. (1987). The developmental implications of home environments. In C. S. Weinstein, & T. G. David (Eds.), *Spaces for children – The built environment and child development* (pp. 139–157). New York, NY: Plenum Press.

Kálló, É., & Balogh, G. (2005). *The origins of free play*. Budapest: Pikler-Lóczy Társaság.

Korintus, M., Nyitrai, Á., & Rózsa, J. (1997). *Játék a bölcsődében. Módszertani levél* [Play in the nursery. Methodological letter]. Budapest: BOMI.

Ministry of Welfare. (1998). *Jogszabálykereső*. Retrieved from 15/1998. (IV. 30.) NM rendelet a személyes gondoskodást nyújtó gyermekjóléti, gyermekvédelmi intézmények, valamint személyek szakmai feladatairól és működésük feltételeiről (15/1998. (April 30.) Ministry of Welfare decree). Retrieved from http://net.jogtar.hu/jr/gen/hjegy_doc.cgi?docid=99800015.NM

Németh, M., Polónyi, E., & Dobszay, L. (1979). A bölcsődei adaptáció ("beszoktatás") [Adaptation to nursery]. *Gyermekgyógyászat, 30*(3), 376–381.

Révész, S. (2013). Szabad élet, szabad baba. Interjú Tardos Annával [Free life, free baby. Interview with Anna Tardos]. *Népszabadság online*. Retrieved from http://nol.hu/kultura/20131224-szabad_elet__szabad_baba-1434397

Sandall, S. (2014). *Creating classroom rules*. Washington, DC: NCQTL Media Team. Retrieved from https://eclkc.ohs.acf.hhs.gov/hslc/tta-system/teaching/practice/engage/iss/classroom-rules.html

Santer, J., Griffiths, C., & Goodall, D. (2007). *Free play in early childhood. A literature review*. London: National Children's Bureau.

Stróbl, M. (1981). *Folyamatos napirend a bölcsődében* [Consecutive daily routine in the nursery]. Budapest: Bölcsődék Országos Módszertani Intézete.

Szele, B. (2000). Bölcsődei gondozónők, szakgondozónők, vezető-gondozónők helyzete, jelene, jövője [Position, present and future of nursery nurses, qualified nursery nurses and head nursery nurses]. In *III. Bölcsődei Kongresszus szakmai anyaga* (pp. 61–67). Szombathely: Szombathely Megyei Jogú Város Önkormányzata, Egyesített Bölcsődei Intézmény.

Szűcs, V. (2012). *Felmérés a bölcsődei szak- és egyéb dolgozókról képzettség, szolgálati idő és bér szerint. (2012. október 31-i állapot szerint)* [Survey on nursery nurses and other workforce according to education, lenght of service and salary]. Budapest: Bölcsődei Dolgozók Demokratikus Szakszervezete. Retrieved from http://regi.bddsz.hu/download2.php?filename=hirek_szakmai/bolcsodei_dolgozok_helyzete_vegso_fejleces_2012_.pdf

Tardos, A. (1975). *Neveléstan III Csecsemő- és gyermekgodnozónő, gyermekápolónőképző egészségügyi szakiskolák hallgatói részére* [Care and education for vocational schools of infant and early childhood educators]. Budapest: Egészségügyi Minisztérium.

The California Child Care Health Program. (2007). *Health and Safety in the Child Care Setting: Prevention of Injuries*. Berkeley: The California Child Care Health Program. Retrieved from http://cchp.ucsf.edu/sites/cchp.ucsf.edu/files/Prev_Injuries_052407.pdf

Tokaji, K. (2012). *Kisgyermekek napközbeni ellátása* [Day care for children]. Budapest: Központi Statisztikai Hivatal.

Wachs, T. D., Gurkas, P., & Kontos, S. (2004). Predictors of preschool children's compliance behavior in early childhood classroom settings. *Journal of Applied Developmental Psychology, 25*(4), 439–457. doi:10.1016/j.appdev.2004.06.003

5. # Influencing factors on professional attitudes towards risk-taking in children's play: a narrative review

Martin van Rooijen and Shelly Newstead

ABSTRACT

There is a growing concern that adults who supervise children's play may restrict opportunities for children to engage in risky activities. Risk-benefit assessment is commonly advocated as a way of allowing children to take managed risks within settings. However 'risk-benefit' adopts a limited strategy of convincing professionals of the developmental benefits of risk, disregarding other factors which may also influence professionals when making risk assessments in their settings. This paper proposes an alternative approach to supporting practitioners in allowing risk by exploring the complexity of these influencing factors. A narrative literature review identifies five inter-related factors which affect professionals' attitudes to risk. The relationships between these factors are discussed and presented as a model which illustrates the complexity faced by practitioners when carrying out risk assessments. The authors argue that children's opportunities to benefit from risk in play may increase if these influencing factors could be explored within professional development.

1. Introduction

In recent years there has been a growing concern about what has been regarded as the changing nature of children's play, and particularly the trend for children to spend more of their free time in institutionalized settings (Meire, 2013; Valentine & McKendrick, 1997). One of the objections raised to children spending more time in supervised settings is the potential impact of supervisory adults on children's abilities to engage in challenging situations and risk activities in their play. Risk-taking is an important part of childhood development which builds confidence, resilience and creativity in children whilst allowing them to test their own limits (Gill, 2007; Staempfli, 2009; Stephenson, 2003; Tovey, 2007), and by taking developmentally appropriate risks in their play children gain experiences which will benefit their future lives as independent and capable adults (Ball, 2002; Ungar, 2007/2008). However, adult-imposed restrictions on risk-taking in play is often justified on the grounds of 'safety', with children being banned from a variety of experiences such as running on school playgrounds, playing outside in the snow and accessing areas of forbidden territory (Thomson, 2014). In many Western countries child safety and prominent injury prevention strategies are commonly employed as a justification for increasing playground safety standards and levels of adult supervision (Brussoni et al., 2015).

One of the reasons behind heightened sensitivity to risk in children's play is a fundamental professional dilemma experienced by practitioners on a day-to-day basis. Descriptions of the role of supervisory adults are often expressed in terms of 'keeping children safe', whilst also requiring these professionals to be responsible for the future development of the children in their care. Daily practice is therefore fraught with conflicting priorities, with the 'safety' and 'development' imperatives creating two different narratives of what constitutes 'good practice'. Professionals experience a dilemma between ensuring 'safety' which may result in children being prevented from taking risks in their play, thereby curtailing the desired developmental benefits which such play opportunities afford. In an attempt to address this contradiction in professional practice, the risk-benefit approach encourages practitioners to allow children to experience more risk in their play by evaluating the developmental benefits of risk-taking (Ball, Gill, & Spiegal, 2012). In contrast to risk assessment, which focuses attention on potential harm by identifying hazards and making judgements about how much harm these hazards are likely to cause, 'risk-benefit' attempts to re-frame risk in a positive light by encouraging practitioners to focus on the advantages of risk-taking in children's play, as well as the potential harm which may occur. The underlying assumption of the risk-benefit model is that some adults are inherently 'risk-averse' and an increased awareness of the value of risk will result in these adults allowing children to take more risks in their play (Sandseter, 2014; Smith, 1998).

However this approach to convincing adults of the benefits of risk for children disregards several complex factors in daily professional practice, as it ignores the wider context in which professionals who work with children operate. Childcare and educational settings involve a complex web of relationships, theories, practices, cultural norms and legalization. Well-intentioned practitioners, who want to do 'the right thing' and support children's development through allowing risk in play, can be caught up in this conflicting mesh of personal, professional, regulatory and cultural priorities which obscure what 'the right thing' is when it comes to allowing children to take risks. Arriving at such judgements involves a complex assessment of not only the physical risk to the child within an institutional context, but also the risk to the teacher themselves in the event of an accident. For example, one of the authors of this paper was informed by a teacher that 'Children are not allowed to climb on top of the playhouse, but your daughter may do so during break playtime because I know you think that it's good for her.' In allowing one child to engage in such an activity the teacher risks complaints from other children who are excluded from the same activity, and perhaps also their parents. There may also be consequences for the teacher if colleagues complain about an exception being made for one particular child in the face of guidelines, which explicitly forbid this particularly activity. In coming to such a decision, this professional must carry out multiple layers of risk assessment over and above simply appreciating the developmental benefits of such an activity, which may also include an assessment of risk to themselves on several fronts.

Supporting adults to allow children to experience risk in their play may therefore require a more nuanced approach than simple 'risk-benefit' in order to address the fundamental tensions for professionals in arriving at decisions about risk in play. This paper proposes that one such approach could be the exploration of the underlying influences on professionals' perceptions of risk as a route to understanding the potential causes of so-called risk-aversion in professional practice.

1.1. Methodology

A narrative review synthesizes different primary studies and discusses existing theory and context using the reviewer's own background knowledge and emerging concepts (Collins & Fauser, 2005; Green, Johnson, & Adams, 2006). Our intention in this paper is not to provide an overview of all recent research on risk in children's play, but rather to interrogate the literature for relevant factors that influence professionals in either supporting or constraining children in engaging in risk in their play. This paper therefore focusses on literature published in English in peer-reviewed journals between 2005 and 2015 listed in the Scopus databases. The following keywords were used as search terms: 'risky play' and 'risk-rich', and these terms identified 93 potentially relevant articles. All abstracts were read in order to exclude articles which did not contain material on the role of professionals in relation to risk in play. As a result, 17 articles were selected as relevant for analysis, which included empirical studies, theoretical articles and one literature review. As age or setting were not defined in the search method, the articles incorporated children's play up to 12 years and settings including preschool, child care and primary school play environments.

At this stage a thematic analysis (Braun & Clarke, 2006) was applied to gain insight into re-occurring themes regarding the influences on professional's attitudes to risk-taking in children's play. After coding, the themes were reviewed and the next stage involved defining and naming these themes. Five themes which influence professionals in their attitude towards children's risk-taking in play were identified, and these themes were developed into a model drawing on Bronfenbrenner's (1979) ecological model which illustrates the interconnected and complex relationships between the different types of influencing factors. The following sections describe the separate influencing factors in a hierarchical order of closeness to the professional in the model; constructs of children and their impact on professional objectives; how professionals' attitude to risk in play may be affected by personality and gender; the professional–parent relationship; regulatory and legal factors; the societal context and cultural factors.

2. Influencing factors

2.1. Constructs of children and their impact on professional objectives

A variety of constructs of children and childhood underpin professional practice (Petrie, Egharevba, Oliver, & Poland, 2000). Two particular dichotomous constructs of children, either as fundamentally vulnerable or as resilient in nature, may create dilemmas for professionals in deciding appropriate responses to risk in play. Professionals who conceptualize children as essentially vulnerable may overcompensate for their perceived need for care and protection, whilst children conceptualized as resilient may be afforded more opportunities for risk over and above their actual competencies. However these two seemingly diametrically opposed constructs of children are not mutually exclusive. Risky situations can offer children an opportunity to increase their resilience by developing their risk-management strategies. In this context resilience means that children are capable of understanding their competencies, moderating their risky play and accepting other child's different internal boundaries in carrying out risk-taking behaviour (Brussoni, Olsen, Pike, & Sleet, 2012). Seen in this light, the vulnerability of the child is not something which should be denied at all costs. Instead professionals can acknowledge the child's vulnerability and at the same time enable the child to deal with this by focussing on coping strategies, leading to the strengthening of their self-esteem (Hewitt-Taylor & Heaslip, 2012).

Adult constructs of children may also have an influence on children's opportunities to assess risk for themselves. In situations where play takes place unsupervised, it is children who must identify hazards (things which are likely to cause harm) by themselves and make their own judgements about the levels of risk with which they feel comfortable. In other words, when there are no adults around, children are responsible for making their own risk assessments. However, in supervised settings where the adults are responsible for the well-being of the children in their care, those practitioners often have a duty to perform risk assessments on children's play activities. This professional responsibility may detract from children's opportunities to practise risk assessment for themselves, particularly if the adult construct of children does not allow for children being potentially capable of making such judgements. Children's perceptions of risk can be different from that of an adult, because adult and child perceptions of affordances (Gibson, 1977) are different as they relate to individual capabilities, physical characteristics and motivation (Little & Sweller, 2015). As a result children's risk assessments may in some situations be more relevant than that of the adult observer. For example, one study described staff restrictions on 'climbing very high up in trees' (Sandseter, 2009), even though the adults did not know whether children were capable of engaging in this form of play safely.

Constructs of children as vulnerable and in need of protection are unlikely to involve notions of risk-competence (defined as children's skills to recognize, engage and evaluate risks in play in order to protect themselves). In some cases this may result in professionals underestimating children's risk-assessment capabilities and overriding children's legitimate decisions about appropriate levels of risk in their play, thus undermining children's own efforts to make decisions for themselves. Furthermore, in supervised settings, where responsibility for 'safety' lies with the professional, it is the – potentially uninformed – adult risk assessment which must hold sway. With the support of the legal and regulatory framework, adults who already construct children as vulnerable may assume that their own risk assessment is the only valid one, and are unlikely to incorporate children's own evaluations of risk into their finite decisions on acceptable levels of risk in children's play.

MacQuarrie et al.'s (2015) study on nature-based learning settings in Norway and Scotland demonstrates how this privileging of adult perspectives on risk was avoided through mutual trust and negotiation between adults and children. Children were appreciated as competent partners in learning, which led to adult–child consultation and supported collaboration in risk-taking situations. In this way professionals are influenced by children's view on risk in their daily practice, and such an approach appears to enhance the potential for children to engage in risk in their play. This could be of importance in terms of children's development as the professional's changing view on risk can also have substantial effect on the ways that children construct risk (Niehues et al., 2013).

In settings which involve some form of curriculum for children, this very existence of a curriculum may also create further dilemmas for professionals in dealing with risk assessments in play. Scientific theories embedded into curricula have an impact on professionals' beliefs and practices relating to children's risk-taking in play (Sandseter, Little, & Wyver, 2012). Such pedagogical foundations often remain unexamined by professionals, and risk is therefore evaluated by adults using tacit or 'unwritten' rules (Sandseter, 2012). Influences on belief and practice regarding risk from these embedded philosophical and theoretical approaches seem to result in different outcomes in supporting or restricting risk in play (Little, Sandseter, & Wyver, 2012).

The potential of a 'risk-rich' curriculum resides in adults and children exploring new topics and unfamiliar terrains, as children are capable and wanting to test their capabilities and understandings (New, Mardell, & Robinson, 2005). New et al. state that views on childhood environments vary on beliefs and goals and therefore it could be meaningful introducing beyond reach of children activities, allowing and also encouraging risk in play even if culture or professionals would not see it as well-arranged or appropriate.

Given that the potential benefit and harm of each situation involving risk is highly individual (Hewitt-Taylor & Heaslip, 2012), practitioners are often encouraged to use their professional judgement to arrive at decisions about the individual needs of children. Devising a uniform curriculum around risk, where, for example, certain activities or areas are banned to all children at all times, disables professionals from weighing up the benefits of certain play situations against the potential risks according to individual children's developmental needs.

2.2. Professional's personal attitudes to risk

A further set of influences on professionals' approach to risk stems from an individual's personal values and experiences. Professionals' own attitudes and beliefs around risk may be brought into their practice, which may then reflect their own boundaries, causing the practitioner to either constrain or enable children's risk-taking. Interventions are then explained by ensuring children's safety 'within reason', meaning they inquire their own limits for risk in order to consider what is suitable for children under their supervision (Sandseter, 2012). In some cases practitioners override their own personal hesitations around risk in order to enable children to take risks in their play, whereas other professionals act 'in a manner that suits them' as they more attend to their own needs around risk-management rather than to the developmental needs of the children they supervise. Professionals can take control over children's activities, putting themselves in a 'position of power' over children (Stan & Humberstone, 2011) and disempowering children in the important developmental area of risk assessment.

Interestingly, adult attitudes to risk may be influenced by gender. Sandseter (2014) found that male practitioners score higher than female practitioners on a scale which measured whether adults were willing to take more risk and seek for new experiences themselves. Male practitioners have a more liberal attitude towards children's risk-taking play and they allow children to engage in greater risky play than women (Sandseter, 2014). Individual high scores on the excitement-seeking scale were positively correlated to a more broad-minded attitude on risk in play, suggesting a connection between personality and professional attitudes to risk. The same study indicated that age does not seem to influence the perception of risk in individuals.

To gain an alternative insight in the difference between professionals who are more or less risk-tolerant, Hill and Bundy (2014) introduced a tool for measuring risky play tolerance. The instrument, called TRiPS (Tolerance of Risk in Play Scale), reflects Sandseter's (2007) six categories of risky play and can provide a basis for measuring interventions with the purpose to transform professionals' attitude to risk in play. Measuring changes in the beliefs of adults about risky play can contribute to gaining insight in the added value or effectivity of interventions. Beneficial effects were also reported on changing the professionals' beliefs as result of an intervention course which caused a greater understanding of children's playful risky behaviours (Cevher-Kalburan, 2015). The six-week course provided in pedagogical readings, assignments in observing children's play, interviewing teachers and parents and drawing an imaginary playground. Participant's understanding changed from the negative term 'hazard' into understanding the distinction with the positive notion of risk, complementing the outcomes that the concept of risk is socially constructed and often has negative connotations in a theoretical treatise on defining risk (Little & Eager, 2010).

2.3. The professional–parent relationship

The relationship between professionals and parents is a significant factor in practitioners' attitudes to risk in play. A collaborative relationship between professionals and parents could lead to a collective effort on including risk and challenge into the organization policy as developmentally worthwhile. In investigating the possibilities of a 'risk-rich' curriculum both parents and children can discover new challenging topics and unknown areas of play, conventionally recognized as out of reach of children (New et al., 2005). The conclusion drawn from this study is that a transfer can be made from 'playing it safe to being collaboratively courageous' (New et al., 2005, p. 13) where parents are invited into a collaborative relationship with professionals who accompany the child, resulting in well-informed decisions on the curriculum.

Professionals have been found to engage with parents in various ways, proactively as well as reactively (MacQuarrie, Nugent, & Warden, 2015). In the proactive approach professionals take the initiative to discuss risk with parents, and the reactive approach occurs when professionals and parents retained different opinions about supporting children's challenging experiences. In sharing viewpoints practitioners aim to align the parents' views with their own in order to gain support for their approach to risk-taking in the setting (MacQuarrie et al., 2015, p. 8). Hewitt-Taylor and Heaslip (2012) regard practitioners as designated professionals to engage parents in discussions about achieving a balance between degrees of risk-aversion and protection. They call it partnership; a relationship in which parents and professionals are conscious of the fact that perceptions of risk can differ and are capable of reasoned discussion and sharing understanding. They also draw attention to the impact such a dialogue can have on professionals working in a risk-adverse society. On the one hand, professionals who stimulate risk-taking which results in harm to children may be fearful of litigation. On the other hand parents who follow professional advice and allow their children to engage in risk in their play may fear being called negligent. This may in turn have an effect on the professional standing of the practitioner in the eyes of those parents, in that the professional's future advice is devalued due to the adverse consequences suffered by the parents.

The ways in which professionals address parental concerns about risk seems to be important and requires a degree of confidence in the professional–parent relationship. Exploring beliefs and attitudes in discussions between professionals and parents has been found to be valuable in influencing parents' beliefs around risk-taking. Niehues et al. (2013) introduced collective group interventions called 'risk-reframing sessions' which included parents, educators, staff and volunteers. One of the objectives was to elucidate the process in which parents and educators were enabled to jointly reconstruct healthy risk-taking for children. The findings suggested that both professionals and parents benefitted from sharing their perceptions of risk, as the adults could achieve trusting relationships amongst each other as well as with children. Successful results were reported in considering alternative responses to risk in play; in modelling a process which allowed participants to critique responses and supported them in making considered decisions; and in changing the conceptualization of risk to uncertainty and opportunity. The distinction between danger and risk is also an interesting area of discussion between professionals and parents.

One of the challenges for professionals in discussing risk with parents appears to be the difference between real and imagined risk, and high or marginal risk (Hewitt-Taylor & Heaslip, 2012). This is not an easy task as play context differs and the individual child's actions are not foreseeable, parents and professionals should therefore focus on relative risks and benefits of children's challenges in play. Hewitt-Taylor and Heaslip stress the necessity of professionals exploring their attitude towards risk-taking behaviour as well as enabling parents to address fears over acceptable risk-taking of their children. However it should be noted that even if professionals and parents share an understanding about the value of risk in play, there could still be a hesitation in the practitioner's freedom to act in practice. Little et al. (2012) found that professionals did not allow other peoples' children the same amount of risk as they allow their own children. In this Norwegian context accountability issues were not the case as a culture of litigation from parents is uncommon, but professionals were very aware of their responsibility in having other people children in their care and were therefore more cautious in their approach to risk when working with other peoples' children.

2.4. Regulatory factors

The fourth theme to emerge from the analysis of the literature was that professionals can feel both constrained and enabled by regulatory factors when they want to enhance possibilities for risk in play. In Australian early childhood education centres almost half of the organizations studied experienced regulatory restrictions (Little & Sweller, 2015). Specifically height restrictions of playground equipment limit the possibilities of risk-taking (Coleman & Dyment, 2013; Dyment & Coleman, 2012; Little & Sweller, 2015). Professionals are therefore reluctant to let children play on natural elements such as rocks and trees. General safety issues regarding supervision and child/staff ratios also prevented professionals from enabling children to take risks in their play. Top-down regulations, in many situations a requirement of licencing organizations to provide care, could therefore inhibit settings developing their own policies in the area of risk in play.

However regulations are also sometimes regarded by professionals as enabling, which is noteworthy as regulations are experienced negatively in most studies in this review. Australian practitioners felt that regulations could also support their practice (Little, Wyver, & Gibson, 2011). The explanation for this was that professionals found regulations necessary in order to ensure minimum standards of playground equipment. This implies that professionals may find some regulations helpful in setting clear boundaries around risk, as well as welcoming the possibility to use their own expertise and experience in assessing children's risky activities.

One possible unintended consequence of the regulation of safety is that it creates accountability and liabilities for the adults responsible for supervising children's play. Possibilities of accountability therefore have an impact on professionals facilitating risk in play (Little et al., 2012). External regulations which can constrain professionals in their risk-management practices may also contribute to a broader culture of risk-aversion and litigation in society. Professionals demonstrate their awareness of potential health and safety responsibilities by depriving children of risk-taking experiences, and even if they criticize safety policies as over-protective they do not feel able to use their common sense and abilities in carrying out risk assessment (Stan & Humberstone, 2011).

2.5. Cultural factors

The thematic analysis revealed that the cultural interpretations of 'safety' consists of a diverse set of factors which interact with one another, making the subject of risk in play culturally embedded and complex. For New et al. (2005) the socio-cultural context in which children live and are prepared for the demands of the social and physical environment must be considered in relation to adult attitudes to play. These authors offer enlightening discussions of Italian, Scandinavian, Japanese and U.S. approaches to risk in childhood in relation to cultural practices and settings. Different countries appear to have different approaches to risk in play, which can be seen particularly with regard to outdoor play in the literature. New et al. give prominent examples of nations' play cultures; American professionals are amazed at how Scandinavian children are allowed to roam outside for extended periods in all kinds of weather, as they would fear child molesters and liability suits. As an explanation for Nordic educational practices, New et al. state it is important to recognize that an appreciation of the outdoors is considered an important value to propagate among children, as pride in the countryside is prevalent throughout these countries. Children and teachers' beliefs therefore automatically encourage outdoor adventure, despite the weather, as otherwise children would stay indoors during the cold winter months. This enhanced positive approach to risky play in Scandinavian countries, where professionals stimulate children to engage in challenging activities are further explored in interviews with Australian and Norwegian professionals. In a comparative analysis of their beliefs, professionals in both countries appear to acknowledge the importance of risk-taking for the development of children, but they have different ways of applying this in practice (Little et al., 2012). Australian professionals feel restricted by external factors: legal environment, regulatory requirements and the quality of the outdoor environment. Norwegian practitioners feel less obligated to consider these barriers and are therefore freer to apply their own professional judgement in supervising children's risk-taking in outdoor play. This could be interpreted to mean that they are more at liberty to heed their own principles and hence to attach more importance to evaluating the play context than to obeying rules or considering potential liability. This corresponds with Sandseter's (2014) description of Norwegian professionals as having 'few worries' when children engage in risky activities.

3. Developing a more sophisticated approach to supporting practitioner risk assessment

So far this paper has explored the five themes identified from the literature review which have an influence on professional attitudes towards risk in children's play. However, the presentation of these five factors as separate is a constructed one, as in practice these influences cannot be seen as distinct from one other. Socio-cultural differences in perceptions on risk in play have an influence on institutional practices and hence on individual professional practices. In a similar trickle-down effect, legal and regulatory frameworks can affect professionals' trust in their own ability to allow play which involves risk, as they fear legal repercussions from parents. Constructs of children which regard children as competent risk-assessors which are not shared by parents and professionals require careful negotiation in order to arrive at an agreed tolerance level of risk, although institutional and regulatory frameworks may still conspire against shared liberal risk-management strategies. Furthermore, there is of course no guarantee that, even if parents and setting take a 'pro-risk' approach to children's play, that all the individual practitioners in that setting will adopt the same position, given that individual approaches to risk seem to be influenced by a variety of different and highly personalized factors.

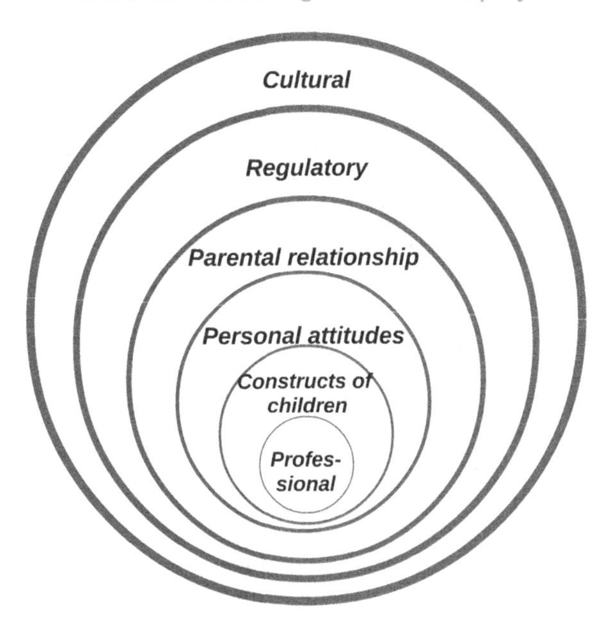

Figure 1. Model.

The inter-relatedness of these five influencing factors may be more usefully conceptualized as a model which draws on Bronfenbrenner's (1979) ecological model of development (see Figure 1). This model depicts the different layers of influences, and also acknowledges the connections in between those layers which may in themselves create different sorts of influences. Based on the five themes identified from the literature review, the diverse factors are represented by circles which create a scheme wherein the professional is surrounded by influences. As in Bronfenbrenner's original model, the influencing factors which may have a more immediate impact on the practitioner's attitudes to risk in play are placed closer to the professional in the centre of the model. Wider regulatory and cultural factors, although no less important, are depicted as the broader context in which the more immediate personal and professional attitudes and relationships must operate.

1. Constructs of children
2. Professional's personal attitudes to risk
3. Professional–parent relationship
4. Regulatory factors
5. Cultural factors

It is perhaps unsurprising that professionals who supervise children's play feel conflicted in the area of risk (Delahoy, 2012). Practitioners must weigh up all of the influencing elements, taking into account the various practical, personal, ideological and cultural implications for themselves, the children and their setting, and then assess and prioritize them before deciding what might be an appropriate response to risk in play. However, these influencing factors are often unseen: embedded in organizational policies or pedagogical curricula, professional perceptions of parental beliefs, the unwritten implications of regulatory good practice, and cultural and society expectations of 'normal' levels of risk for children. At a fundamental level, professionals must balance the need to protect children from harm with the need to help children to achieve their developmental potential, which creates a central dilemma in deciding which risks could contribute to development and which risks might result in serious harm. Having worked in play settings with children, we recognize this fundamental dilemma: offering freedom and challenge to the child in general, whilst at the same time responding to parental and societal need for protection and security. Professionals have the dual responsibility to provide for a safe play environment and to stimulate children's development to independence, which includes the ability to deal with risk and challenge in their play.

However in practice, the risk-benefit assessment process involves a much bigger and vastly more complex set of personal and professional factors. Even in small settings, practitioners must take account of the opinions of diverse actors: the parents, the manager and other colleagues, and are often unsure whether their course of action is supported by regulations and organization policy. Furthermore, personal and professional judgements must often be taken quickly without time to consult colleagues, placing more pressure on the individual practitioner to do 'the right thing' with any specific protocols to follow. Far from being a simple causal relational between an individual's attitude to risk in play and professional confidence in terms of risk, as the risk-benefit process suggests, practitioners frequently find themselves in the middle of a professional blizzard of contradictory opinions, guidelines and legislation related to risk. Practitioners must navigate their way through the tensions which these influencing factors create, often at some considerable risk to themselves when it comes to allowing risk in play. Perhaps it is therefore unsurprising when professionals adopt the default 'no risk' strategy, saving themselves time and energy in weighing up all the various influencing factors and potentially avoiding a law suit into the bargain. Often regarded as a personal affliction of 'risk-aversion', professional's reluctance to allow risk in play may in fact be a symptom of a tangled web of influencing factors which are relative to not only individual play situations but also to individual settings, as different factors exert more or less influence on different types of provision and the users of individual settings. Practitioners may not be suffering from personal risk-aversion as much as professional risk confusion, as their views and approaches to risk are shaped by their changing professional experiences in different settings with different influencing factors coming to the fore.

We therefore suggest that the influencing factors on professionals' attitudes to risk-taking in children's play should be further explored by play advocates and researchers. Whilst the 'risk-benefit' approach may encourage some professionals to adopt more positive attitudes to risk-taking in children's play, what this literature review has demonstrated is that professionals working in supervised settings are under significant pressure to juggle potentially conflicting priorities in this area. Even those who are willing and able to address the fundamental contradiction between 'risk' and 'development' in their work may struggle with other influencing factors such as cultural, regulatory, institutional or parental imperatives to limit risk-taking in play. A more sophisticated approach to enabling professionals to support risk-taking in children's play could also support practitioners in recognizing and balancing the various influencing factors in their specific situations of practice. Continuous professional development programmes should first of all acknowledge professionals' everyday dilemma of practice: that their dual responsibility requires them to both provide protection from harm and to facilitate the development of children. By further exploring the underlying influencing factors which create the conflicting situations of daily practice, practitioners could be enabled to address for themselves their own individual and institutional limitations to risk in play. In responding authentically to children's needs, professionals are often required to take risks themselves, frequently finding themselves in situations where they must make choices without being able to predict or even control the results of their interactions. Understanding the multi-faceted influencing factors at play in supervised settings may empower professionals to make their own risk assessments about the benefits of supporting risk-taking in play. Whilst such a process may involve more effort on behalf of professionals themselves and those who support them, the responses of individual adults can have an impact on the way that risk is perceived by others (Bundy et al., 2009), and professionals who are confident about their own parameters in responding to risk may act as 'change agents' in influencing other professionals, parents and society at large.

4. Conclusion

This analysis of the literature revealed that professionals working with children in supervised settings are influenced by a variety of diverse and complex factors. The current risk-benefit approach to supporting practitioners to allow children to take risks in their play may be helpful in drawing attention to the developmental benefits of risk. However risk-benefit may fail to convince practitioners to allow more risk in their settings due to a whole host of other inter-related factors which they must take into account when performing risk assessments. These five factors (professional constructs of children, professionals' individual approaches to risk, the professional–parent relationship, regulatory and cultural factors) create dilemmas for professional practice with regard to offering children the necessary opportunities to experience challenge and risk in their play, and can have a significant impact on an individual practitioner's abilities to make clear and supported judgements about the benefits of risk in children's play. By further examining these influencing factors and how they relate to individual practitioners in their specific situations of practice, more may be learnt about how to support professionals to enable children to take risks in their play. Further empirical research is therefore required to investigate whether and how these five inter-related influencing factors impact professional practice in the area of risk in play.

Disclosure statement

No potential conflict of interest was reported by the authors.

ORCiD

Martin van Rooijen http://orcid.org/0000-0002-7544-8358
Shelly Newstead http://orcid.org/0000-0001-7398-1135

References

*Selected articles for review.

Ball, D., Gill, T., & Spiegal, B. (2012). *Managing risk in play provision: Implementation guide*. London: National Children's Bureau.

Ball, D. J. (2002). *Playgrounds – Risks, benefits and choices: HSE contract research report 426/2002*. Sudbury: HSE Books.

Braun, V., & Clarke, V. (2006). Using thematic analysis in psychology. *Qualitative Research in Psychology, 3*(2), 77–101. doi:10.1191/1478088706qp063oa

Bronfenbrenner, U. (1979). *The ecology of human development: Experiments by nature and design*. Cambridge, MA: Harvard University Press.

Brussoni, M., Gibbons, R., Gray, C., Ishikawa, T., Sandseter, E. B. S., Bienenstock, A., … Tremblay, M. S. (2015). What is the relationship between risky outdoor play and health in children? A systematic review. *International Journal of Environmental Research and Public Health, 12*(6), 6423–6454. doi:10.3390/ijerph120606423

*Brussoni, M., Olsen, L. L., Pike, I., & Sleet, D. A. (2012). Risky play and children's safety: Balancing priorities for optimal child development. *International Journal of Environmental Research and Public Health, 9*(9), 3134–3148. doi:10.3390/ijerph9093134

Bundy, A. C., Luckett, T., Tranter, P., Naughton, G., Wyver, S., Ragen, J., & Spies, G. (2009). The risk is that there is 'no risk': A simple, innovative intervention to increase children's activity levels. *International Journal of Early Years Education, 17* (1), 33–45. doi:10.1080/09669760802699878

*Cevher-Kalburan, N. (2015). Developing pre-service teachers' understanding of children's risky play. *Journal of Adventure Education and Outdoor Learning, 15*(3), 239–260. doi:10.1080/14729679.2014.950976

*Coleman, B., & Dyment, J. E. (2013). Factors that limit and enable preschool-aged children's physical activity on child care centre playgrounds. *Journal of Early Childhood Research, 11*(3), 203–221. doi:10.1177/1476718X12456250

Collins, J. A., & Fauser, B. C. J. M. (2005). Balancing the strengths of systematic and narrative reviews. *Human Reproduction Update, 11*(2), 103–104. doi:10.1093/humupd/dmh058

Delahoy, A. (2012). *A culture of fear in playwork?* (Unpublished master's thesis). Leeds Metropolitan University, Leeds.

*Dyment, J., & Coleman, B. (2012). The intersection of physical activity opportunities and the role of early childhood educators during outdoor play: Perceptions and reality. *Australian Journal of Early Childhood, 37*(1), 90–98. Retrieved from http://www.earlychildhoodaustralia.org.au

Gibson, J. J. (1977). The theory of affordances. In R. Shaw, & J. Bransford (Eds.), *Perceiving, acting and knowing* (pp. 67–82). Hillsdale, NJ: Lawrence Erlbaum Associates.

Gill, T. (2007). *No fear, growing up in a risk averse society*. London: Calouste Gulbenkian Foundation.

Green, B. N., Johnson, C. D., & Adams, A. (2006). Writing narrative literature reviews for peer-reviewed journals: Secrets of the trade. *Journal of Chiropractic Medicine, 5*(3), 101–117. doi:10.1016/S0899–3467(07)60142-6

*Hewitt-Taylor, J., & Heaslip, V. (2012). Protecting children or creating vulnerability? *Community Practitioner, 85*(12), 31–33. Retrieved from PubMed, ID: 23304892.

*Hill, A., & Bundy, A. C. (2014). Reliability and validity of a new instrument to measure tolerance of everyday risk for children. *Child: Care, Health and Development, 40*(1), 68–76. doi:10.1111/j.1365-2214.2012.01414.x

Little, H., & Eager, D. (2010). Risk, challenge and safety: Implications for play quality and playground design. *European Early Childhood Education Research Journal, 18*(4), 497–513. doi:10.180/1350293X,2010.525949

*Little, H., Sandseter, E. B. H., & Wyver, S. (2012). Early childhood teachers' beliefs about children's risky play in Australia and Norway. *Contemporary Issues in Early Childhood, 13*(4), 300–316. doi:10.2304/ciec.2012.13.4.300

*Little, H., & Sweller, N. (2015). Affordances for risk-taking and physical activity in Australian early childhood education settings. *Early Childhood Education Journal, 43*(4), 337–345. doi:10.1007/s10643-014-0667-0

*Little, H., Wyver, S., & Gibson, F. (2011). The influence of play context and adult attitudes on young children's physical risk-taking during outdoor play. *European Early Childhood Education Research Journal, 19*(1), 113–131. doi:10.1080/1350293X.2011.548959

*MacQuarrie, S., Nugent, C., & Warden, C. (2015). Learning with nature and learning from others: Nature as setting and resource for early childhood education. *Journal of Adventure Education and Outdoor Learning, 15*(1), 1–23. doi:10.1080/14729679.2013.841095

Meire, J. (2013). *Over vrijbuiters en ankertijd: De tijdsbeleving van kinderen onderzocht* [About freebooters and anchortime: Exploring time perception of children]. Brussel: Kind en Samenleving.

*New, R. S., Mardell, B., & Robinson, D. (2005). Early childhood education as risky business: Going beyond what's 'safe' to discovering what's possible. *Early Childhood Research and Practice, 7*(2), 1–21. Retrieved from http://ecrp.illinois.edu

*Niehues, A. N., Bundy, A., Broom, A., Tranter, P., Ragen, J., & Engelen, L. (2013). Everyday uncertainties: Reframing perceptions of risk in outdoor free play. *Journal of Adventure Education and Outdoor Learning, 13*(3), 223–237. doi:10.1080/14729679.2013.798588

Petrie, P., Egharevba, I., Oliver, C., & Poland, G. (2000). *Out-of-school lives, out-of-school services*. Norwich: The Stationery Office.

Sandseter, E. B. H. (2007). Categorizing risky play – How can we identify risk-taking in children's play? *European Early Childhood Education Research Journal, 15*(2), 237–252. doi:10.1080/13502930701321733

*Sandseter, E. B. H. (2009). Affordances for risky play in preschool: The importance of features in the play environment. *Early Childhood Education Journal, 36*(5), 439–446. doi:10.1007/s10643-009-0307-2

*Sandseter, E. B. H. (2012). Restrictive safety or unsafe freedom? Norwegian ECEC practitioners' perceptions and practices concerning children's risky play. *Child Care in Practice, 18*(1), 83–101. doi:10.1080/13575279.2011.621889

*Sandseter, E. B. H. (2014). Early childhood education and care practitioners' perceptions of children's risky play; examining the influence of personality and gender. *Early Child Development and Care, 184*(3), 434–449. doi:10.1080/03004430.2013.794797

*Sandseter, E. B. H., Little, H., & Wyver, S. (2012). Do theory and pedagogy have an impact on provisions for outdoor learning? A comparison of approaches in Australia and Norway. *Journal of Adventure Education and Outdoor Learning, 12*(3), 167–182. doi:10.1080/14729679.2012.699800

Smith, S. J. (1998). *Risk and our pedagogical relation to children: On the playground and beyond.* New York: State University of New York Press.

Staempfli, M. B. (2009). Reintroducing adventure into children's outdoor play environments. *Environment and Behavior, 41* (2), 268–280. doi:10.1177/0013916508315000

*Stan, I., & Humberstone, B. (2011). An ethnography of the outdoor classroom – How teachers manage risk in the outdoors. *Ethnography and Education, 6*(2), 213–228. doi:10.1080/17457823.2011.587360

Stephenson, A. (2003). Physical risk-taking: Dangerous or endangered? *Early Years: An International Research Journal, 23* (1), 35–43. doi:10.1080/0957514032000045573

Thomson, S. (2014). Adulterated play: An empirical discussion surrounding adults' involvement with children's play in the primary school playground. *Journal of Playwork Practice, 1*(1), 5–21. doi:10.1332/205316214X13944535662152

Tovey, H. (2007). *Playing outdoors: Spaces and places, risk and challenge*. Maidenhead: Open University Press.

Ungar, M. (2007/2008). Too safe schools, too safe families: Denying children the risk-takers advantage. *Education Canada, 48*, 6–10. Retrieved from http://www.cea-ace.ca/education-canada.

Valentine, G., & McKendrick, J. (1997). Children's outdoor play: Exploring parental concerns about children's safety and the changing nature of childhood. *Geoforum, 28*(2), 219–235. doi:10.1016/S0016-7185(97)00010-9

6 # Follow the leader: attending to the curriculum making potential of preschoolers

Monica Miller Marsh and Ilfa Zhulamanova

ABSTRACT

This research focused on making visible children's funds of identity [Esteban-Guitart, M., & Moll, L. (2014). Funds of identity: A new concept based on the funds of knowledge approach. *Culture & Psychology*, *20*(1), 31–48] and incorporating these resources into an inquiry-oriented, play-based, preschool curriculum. Participants in this collaborative action research included 4 co-investigators, 36 children aged 3–5 from diverse backgrounds, and 8 focal children and their parents/guardians. Data were gathered through observations, digital photographs, and photo-elicitation interviews. Through visual narratives and conversations guided by the children, the research team gained greater insight into children's interests and the knowledge they bring with them from home into school. We came to recognize that our perspectives of the children's interests and knowledge were limited by our inability to see their curriculum making potential and by our hesitation to offer the curriculum the children desire.

Introduction

While much effort is currently focused on designing preschool curricula based on developmental norms and standards, few studies focus on developing curricula that seek to consult with families to understand the home and community resources that young children bring with them to school (Dantas & Manyak, 2010; Greene, 2013; Pushor, 2010; Souto-Manning, 2013). Even fewer studies take into account the role of young children in curriculum development (Hedges, Cullen, & Jordan, 2011; Huber, Murphy, & Clandinin, 2011). This study positions the voices and images of young children at the forefront of the preschool curriculum and views curriculum development as a collection of stories of everyday 'human practices open to ongoing modifications' (Ryan, 2011, p. 39, in Henderson et al. 2015, p. 91), where each child's experiences, including those beyond the school walls, are considered knowledge.

Theoretical framework

When young children enter school they bring their families, neighbourhoods, and communities with them in the form of the multiple identities they are living (Pushor, 2010). These identities include daughter or son, sister or brother, adoptee, ward of the state, members of various cultural, racial, and economic groups, as well as identities that are situated in specific geographical locations. As Pushor explains, 'When they come to school, they come with this multiplicity and contextuality, not independent of it' (2010, p. 7). It is especially important for those who are teaching children in the early years to take into account the multiple storylines that each child brings from home into school, since this is where the crafting of student identities begins.

If we think about identities as a collection of stories or narratives about persons (Sfard & Prusak, 2005) then creating spaces for all children to enter into storylines that provide them with opportunities to participate in the preschool curriculum should become a top priority. In order to understand and make visible the stories children bring with them from their homes and communities into the preschool classroom, we adopted a *funds of identity* approach (Esteban-Guitart & Moll, 2014). The work of Esteban-Guitart and Moll (2014) builds on the notion of *funds of knowledge* (FoK) (Moll, Amanti, Neff, & Gonzales, 1992). FoK constitute living experiences of children learned at home and in their communities. These include information, skills, and strategies, which underlie a household's functioning and well-being (Moll et al., 1992). Drawing on the work of Vygotsky, Esteban-Guitart and Moll contend, '*Funds of knowledge* become *funds of identity* when people actively internalize family and community resources to make meaning and to describe themselves' (2014, p. 33). From this perspective the crafting of identities is both social and individual. 'People define themselves through other people and through the artifacts and resources – visible and invisible – of their social and cultural worlds' (2014, p. 36). This is especially important to consider when undertaking research with children. Children, like adults, create their own social worlds and FoK, which may be independent from the social lives of the adults with whom they live (Rios-Aguilar, Kiyama, Gravitt, & Moll, 2011). Funds of identity provide researchers with a way to explore how children are crafting their identities through the ways in which they express the historical, cultural, and social resources that circulate in and through their lives.

Once children's FoI are identified, teachers' can create curriculum that bridges home, school, and community. This is especially important because while some children's identities are interwoven with storylines that resonate with their teachers and the majority of their peers, other children's stories are not as visible or as easily accessible. Huber et al. ask educators to attend very carefully to the negotiation of lives that takes place in these more hidden spaces so that we are able to make visible the 'gaps and silences children experience' as they move from their homes and communities into school (2011, p. 108). Our hope is that making the gaps in the preschool curriculum visible will lead to the crafting of curriculum that is engaging to all of the children who attend our school.

Methodology and data sources

The data shared in this paper are derived from a participatory action research study involving four co-investigators: a university researcher, a female preschool teacher, a male preschool teacher, and a graduate assistant who is also a parent of a child enrolled in the preschool classroom. Participatory action research is a collaborative approach to research that is driven by a group of people who intend that their work will result in some action, change, or improvement on the issue being researched (Kindon, Pain, & Kesby, 2007). Our team engaged in this research because we wanted to make certain that each child had the opportunity to shape a positive social identity in the early childhood curriculum. We wanted the children to lead our curriculum making and were prepared to take action to shift the curriculum based on the data we gathered. Our research question is: How can we make visible the home and community resources that young children bring with them to preschool in order to create a curriculum that is accessible to all children?

The Child Development Center is a nationally known laboratory school located in the United States of America. The program is inquiry-oriented, social constructivist, and inspired by the Reggio Emilia approach to teaching. The center serves 154 children 18 months through age 6 in mixed age classrooms. The center also serves undergraduate and graduate students seeking degrees in early childhood education as well as other related degrees and university faculty and doctoral students who are engage in a variety of research studies.

The study comprised three phases. During Phase I, the lead researcher and graduate student observed two classrooms comprising 36 children, ages 3–5 from culturally, linguistically, and economically diverse backgrounds. Each observer was in the classroom for two hours per week over the course of a three-month period. During this time, the research team met weekly and discussed how children were responding to the preschool curriculum. Eight children who were identified as *not being as engaged in the curriculum* as their peers became the focal children for the study.

During Phase 2, in order to make visible the funds of identity the children were bringing with them from home into school, we invited the children to take digital photographs of things that were meaningful to them in their homes and communities. All 36 of the preschool children were invited to take a digital camera home over a period of two or more days to capture images of 'things you do when you are not at school.' All children had prior experience in the classroom with the digital cameras as Mrs P and Mr H ask children to document their work regularly through photography.

We specifically chose photography as a vehicle to use in our research with children because it 'provides them with the power to make their own choices (what and when to photograph something) and visualise their ideas' (Loizou, 2011, p. 149). As Loizou noted further in her study on young children using photographs to document instances of humour, as researchers we are not even aware of the possibilities children might generate for the research project. Einarsdottir tells us, 'the data gathering is in part in the hands of the children, and they provide evidence of their own rather than being directed by adults' (2005, p. 527, in Loizou, 2011, p. 149). Loizou (2011) also noted that the use of cameras may help children who have difficulty expressing themselves verbally or, as is the case in our school, when their primary language is not the dominant language spoken in their classroom.

Using photography with children has many advantages, yet, because we have a fairly large Saudi Arabian population, we wanted to be respectful of the restrictions that some of our Saudi families, and others who practice the Islamic religion, place on images of women. We consulted with a small group of our Muslim families to ask about their thoughts on the project. All of the parents who were asked indicated that the project would be beneficial for their children.

Each child had an opportunity to share three to five of their images and discuss them with the preschool class during morning meeting. In addition to sharing their photos with the class, the four focal children were invited to meet with pairs of co-investigators to participate in photo-elicitation interviews (Rose, 2012). In the photo-elicitation interviews the children, accompanied by their parents/guardians, were asked to share any or all of the 25 images they captured in their photographs. They chose the order in which they discussed the photographs and in all cases led the telling of the stories. The power of choice was the intention of this project, as we wanted children to choose the images and stories that were the most meaningful to them so that they could share their knowledge. Parents and the research team added to the effort by either asking probing questions or by extending the information that the children had shared.

Photo-elicitation was chosen as a method for this phase of the research because it required collaboration between the co-investigators, the children, and their families and it allowed the children to make visible things that are important and meaningful to them (Rose, 2012). The co-investigators conducted a content analysis of the photo-elicitation interviews and worked collaboratively to create curriculum incorporating the codes and themes embedded in the FoK that were made visible through the content analysis.

In Phase 3, co-investigators worked together to shape curriculum that incorporated themes from the FoK that emerged from the photo-elicitation interviews. Observations were then made to gather data on how children responded to the shifts that were made in the curriculum.

Focal children

For the purposes of this paper we focus on data analysis from two focal children, Noor and Ananda. Noor is a three-and-a-half-year-old Arabic female who was born in the United States. Her father migrated to the United States from the Middle East five years ago but is originally from Uzbekistan. He is pursuing his Ph.D. in physiology. Her mother has recently finished an English as Second Language programme at the university and will start her undergraduate degree in molecular biology this fall. Noor and her five-year-old brother, Asir, are both in Mr H's preschool classroom. Arabic is their primary language and it is the only language that is spoken at home. Noor's father said, 'I do not want my children to lose their language as I lost my language when I left Uzbekistan' (interview 17 March 2015). Noor's family will return to Saudi Arabia in three years when her father finishes his Ph.D. and takes on a guaranteed position as a university lecturer.

Noor was chosen as a focal child because during the course of our three-month observation period in the fall of 2014 she interacted very little with her peers and often sat on the periphery of the classroom crying. Mr H and his associate teacher would attempt to get her involved in classroom activities but once she was without the support of an adult, she would often disengage and sit by herself. Even though her five-year-old brother was in the same class and one other male child who spoke Arabic, she rarely interacted with them.

Noor took 28 photographs and shared all of those images during our photo-elicitation discussion. These photographs and the conversation surrounding them were analysed through a funds of identity approach. Like Esteban-Guitart and Moll (2014), we paid careful attention to the social, cultural, and geographical funds of identity as well as daily practices. Noor's photo-elicitation interview helped us to understand that she defines her mother, father, and brother as significant others in her life (social funds of identity). While there were no images of her mother included in this collection as dictated by her religion, the very first photograph she shared was of a Barbie doll that she used as a representation of her mother. Consider the following excerpt taken from the photo-elicitation interview on 17 March 2015:

Lead Researcher (LR):	Tell me about your pictures.
Noor (N):	picks up the first picture and points to the Barbie 'Barbie ... '
LR:	Tell me about the Barbies. What do you do with the Barbies?
N:	I play with them ... It's like my Mom. It's like my Mom.
L:	You play Barbies with your Mom?
N shakes her head and points more firmly at the picture:	'It's just like my Mom.' ... 'It's like my Mom ... ' She points at the photo of the princess house in the picture and says, 'This is like home. Daddy fix it up.' She then points to a chair in front of her child-sized princess themed vanity and says, 'This is a seat he is fixing.'

Noor referred to the Barbie doll as her mother in the photo-elicitation interview as well as when she was sharing the images with her classmates on 17 March 2015. She shared that her Mom bought her princess books, played with her on Noor's iPad, and that she made a behaviour chart for Noor, which she 'puts stars on all day.' The last image Noor shared with her friends was of a sandwich cutter shaped like a crown. She ended her comments by saying, 'Today, Mommy is like a princess ... this is my favorite princess.'

Noor's geographical identity is evident in the pictures she shares of riding her bicycle in her neighbourhood and of her brother and father sitting on the hood of the car in front of their home. While she shares many photographs of artefacts inside of her home such as her bed, couch, dishes, books, and toys, the most salient theme in all of the photographs is the emphasis on popular culture, especially Disney princesses. She has a princess couch, a princess bicycle, a princess songbook, a princess workbook, princess plates and cups, and a princess sandwich cutter that transforms all of her sandwiches into the shape of a crown. When she shares the image of the sandwich cutter during the photo-elicitation interview she puts it on her head and says, 'I'm a princess!' and she and Dad both laugh. At one point during the interview she sings, 'Rapunzel, Rapunzel, let down your hair!' (17 March 2015).

When Noor shares a photograph of her iPad during the photo-elicitation interview Dad says, 'she has a game on this that she makes make-up for girls. She watches video clips on how to do that. If she is good during the week she is able to use this game on the weekends.' Dad also shares that 'she watches Youtube, kids movies, and sometimes listens to songs.'

Noor's funds of identity are shaped by her prior knowledge and experiences with a family who has migrated from the Middle East, speaks the Arabic language, practises the Muslim religion, and heavily consumes items of popular culture, especially, Disney princesses. Yet, there is little connection between home and school for Noor. Her home language and religion, while acknowledged and accepted, are rarely visible in the classroom. In addition, artefacts based on popular culture are typically banned from dramatic play. The artefacts and tools that appear to be most important to her identity are almost non-existent at school.

Ananda, a three-and-a-half-year-old African-American female, became a second focal child. Ananda, an only child living with a single mother pursuing her undergraduate degree in Family Studies at the University, spent much of her time with her grandmother who lived in the same apartment complex and worked at the campus Student Center cafeteria. Ananda arrived at school after the conclusion of the morning meeting almost every day. This meant that she missed time to check in with her teachers and peers in a more informal manner at the beginning of the day and entered into the classroom when children were already engaged in activities. Perhaps because of the lateness of her arrival, it was difficult for her to enter into activities with other children and she, like Noor, was often seen moving around the periphery of the activities in which other children were engaged.

Data from Ananda's 36 photos and photo-elicitation interview helped us to understand that her mother, grandmother, and some of the individuals with whom her grandmother works heavily influence her social funds of identity. The first photograph she shared during the interview was of her 'cousin.' Consider the following excerpt:

Ananda:	'This is my cousin. He's at Granny's work. He's a cooker and he cooks everything.'
Mom (explains he is a family friend):	'That's not really a family member ... We know him from way back.'

Later in the interview Ananda says quite proudly of her grandmother, 'She makes all the food for the football players.' (1 April 2015)

Ananda's geographical identity is evident in the pictures she shares of riding her bicycle on the sidewalk in her apartment complex and images of places she frequents in her community such as the park, laundromat, grocery store, and Wal-mart. She also shares a series of images that include Ananda inside the laundromat and at home washing dishes. She also talks about baking pies with her grandmother. She says as she explains the latter photo (1 April 2015):

Ananda:	In this picture I'm going to make dinner for Granny and the water is froze.
Mom:	No, it wasn't – it just looks like it in the picture. She was helping with the dishes.
LR:	Do you help with a lot of chores at home?
Mom:	Do you like to put your own clothes in the washer? Do you like to put your quarters in the machine?
Ananda (smiling):	Yes, I do.

It is evident through images and conversations that Ananda is included in many of the activities in which her mother and grandmother are engaged as a part of their daily lives. She spends her time in the community and at home interacting with adults, helping with household tasks, and contributing to the greater good of her family.

Ananda also shares photographs taken inside of her home and the home of her grandmother that portray beauty products, her hair, and her sparkly toenails. At one point she curves a photograph of a Christmas tree around her face and hides behind it, 'Come into my home – I want to tell you about Christmas.' She then opens the photograph and the following conversation ensues (1 April 2015):

Ananda:	I got a new bike and a new tablet and a Princess Sophia doll for Christmas.
Mom:	You forgot about your favorite toy – you got a Frozen karaoke machine.
LR:	What is your favorite song to sing?
Ananda:	Frozen, Rapunzel, and Mulan!

Mom asks Ananda to sing Mulan for us, but she chooses not to do so.

As is evident from the above exchange, popular culture is also a part of Ananda's life. She talks about her Barbie bicycle and Rapunzel toothbrush. She shares that she watches a number of movies and cartoons including *Little Einstein, Doc McStuffins, Mickey Mouse,* and the *Disney* princess movies.

Ananda's funds of identity are shaped by her prior knowledge and experiences with family and friends, especially her mother and grandmother. Much of the focus in her photographs is on helping Mom and grandma with daily chores in the home and around the university and greater community. When examining home and school connections for Ananda, there are opportunities for her to help with clean up in the classroom as the children are responsible for cleaning up after themselves, but there is no other designated housekeeping area in this classroom specified for dramatic play. As stated before, artefacts based on Disney princesses or popular culture are discouraged in all classrooms and in dramatic play. Like Noor, artefacts and experiences that appear to be important in Ananda's daily life are almost non-existent in her preschool classroom.

Integrating funds of identity into the existing classroom curriculum

As the research team entered Phase 2 of the research project, they took on the task of integrating aspects of the girls' funds of identity into the preschool curriculum. Princesses, household tasks, and an emphasis on physical beauty emerged as the most salient themes in these two focal children's photo-elicitation interviews. Mr H was hesitant to integrate themes of princesses and beauty into the classroom curriculum due to the ways in which racism, classism, and sexism have been perpetuated through the Disney princesses (Condis, 2015; England, Descartes, & Collier-Meek, 2011) as well as reports of how popular culture may negatively impact children (Palmer, 2006, in Marsh, 2014). Even one of our own research team members questioned the focus on princesses and princess play. Yet, collectively we believed that if Ananda, Noor, and others would be able to enter into the preschool curriculum through these familiar princess storylines they would have increased opportunities to interact and collaborate with their peers, which would lead to the development of social and emotional relationships in the classroom (Wright, Diener, & Kemp, 2013).

Once Mr H embraced the theme of princesses, he did so with intentionality.

He was committed to following the lead of the children, but also made the decision that he would expand upon the emphasis on Disney princesses by introducing other stories of princesses if and when the opportunity arose. He also decided that he would provide the children with materials so that they could create their own princess clothing and props. In addition, he organized an informal housekeeping area in one corner of the classroom.

Mr H introduced the shift in curriculum by placing some tulle fabric and fairy wings in the housekeeping area. He shared that he had purchased these materials because he noticed some of the children, especially Ananda and Noor, were interested in princesses. During this initial discussion, he asked the children what other types of materials they thought princesses would need. The children generated a list that included: 'ponies and unicorns to ride on, tutus, dresses, castles, crowns, doors, thrones, princes, wings, and carpets' (3 April 2015). Mr H made additional materials available to the children, so that they could create their own props for dramatic play such as wands and crowns. As Wohlwend (2015) found in her research on princess doll play with girls, making props and costumes is a 'key way of demonstrating in a tangible way to children that commercial media products and their messages are open and available for children to revise' (p. 104).

'I Love My Hair!' – Tanisha

Both focal children were immediately drawn into the princess play and were observed playing together and in small groups. For example, on 8 April 2015, Noor and Ananda were observed playing princesses with wooden dolls in the block area. On 10 April 2015, Noor, Ananda, and Anna were acting out the story of Rapunzel. Ananda pretended to be Rapunzel at the top of a tower made from cardboard. She wore a golden, felt wig made by Anna. When Anna called out, 'Rapunzel,

Rapunzel, Let Down Your Hair' Ananda let her hair down and Anna pretended to climb up. Noor sat off to the side watching the interaction waiting for her turn to wear the wig and let down her hair.

At the time the research was being conducted much of the talk in this classroom was focused on hair. Tanisha, an African-American female and one of the more sought-after peers in the classroom, always came to school with beautiful elaborately beaded hairstyles. When the children in the class wanted to know more about Tanisha's hairstyles, Mr H gave the children and Tanisha space to talk about her hair. During the course of the conversation Tanisha shared that her mother styled her hair and the hair of other family members and friends in their home. The children expressed that they wanted to get their hair done by Tanisha's mother so Mr Hodges extended an invitation for her to come into the classroom to talk about natural black hair and to share some beading techniques. He also read some children's literature in anticipation of the visit including *I love my hair* by Natasha Anastasia Tarpley. Children from all races, ethnicities, and genders got their hair done by Tanisha's mother as did Mr H. This discussion on hair led to the Associate Teacher organizing a trip to the University Pan African building on 23 April 2015 to view a photo exhibit entitled, *Good Hair: Celebrating the Diversity of Beauty and Black Hair*. The curator of the exhibit was the mother of two children who attended the school. She led the children through the exhibit, shared information with them, and answered their questions.

Hair was used as a vehicle to talk about princesses cross-culturally. In order to reinforce the notion that there are multiple variations of beauty, Mr H introduced the children to the story of *Rapunzel* written by Rachel Isadora. In this version of the familiar princess story, Rapunzel is an African princess who has beautiful long dreadlocks interwoven with flowers. Consider the following exchange at the conclusion of the story:

Tanisha: Rapunzel can have black hair with beads and braids.
Ananda: She can have curly hair.
Anna: She's not really like *Tangled*, but still beautiful with stuff in her hair.

This type of conversation and the subsequent play that ensued illustrates that this particular group of children acknowledges varied cultural representations of beauty. For example, Ananda, Noor, and Anna all wore the traditional Rapunzel wig during princess play and all chose to have their hair braided and take on the African version of Rapunzel when the opportunity arose.

'Princesses don't need a lot of money' – Robin

While Ananda enjoyed playing Rapunzel and taking on the role of other princesses, such as Mulan and Elsa, in her most extended play sessions she took on the role of Tiana the African-American protagonist princess in *The Princess and the Frog*. Consider the following interaction in which Ananda is playing with Emma, an English Language Learner from China, who spoke very little English:

> Ananda and Emma were lining stuffed animals up in the corner of the housekeeping area. Emma sits near the animals and Ananda says, 'Get off that bed – this is your bed and points to another bed across the room. Emma moves to the spot that Ananda points out.
>
> Ananda: 'I want to be a princess … I want to be *Tiana,* like Rapunzel, so I can go to the ball with a prince.' She grabs Emma's hands and says, 'We are both going to the ball with princes, some handsome princes!' She wraps herself in some of the fabric in the housekeeping area and says to Emma: 'I changed my dress, now you're a prince! Can I dance with you? I am Tiana!' She grabs Emma's hands and begins to dance. Emma smiling and giggling mimics Ananda's steps as they move around the room.
>
> When it is time to leave the ball, Tiana tells Emma that they came in a carriage, but they are leaving the ball in her car, a structure that the girls made out of blocks. She tells Emma, 'Get in!' as she pretends to drive. 'We're home!' Ananda shouts as she takes off her dress. Emma following her lead takes off her dress as well.
>
> Ananda: 'I have to go to work – princess work.' Looking at Emma she says, 'Princesses do everything so they can buy things for you, they make us soup, like chicken noodle soup. I have to go to work! Have a good day!' She

heads toward the car, but runs back into the housekeeping area, grabs her handmade crown and throws it on the car seat. 'Let's go!' She shouts as she drives away.

While Ananda does take up aspects of the storyline from *The Princess and the Frog,* when she attends the ball and talks about cooking food for others, she makes this princess story her own as she dances at the ball with a prince and then drives away in her own car. Ananda is exercising her own agency and creative production as she shifts the Disney princess storylines of Rapunzel and Tiana to meet her desires through play (Wohlwend, 2015). It is interesting to note how often a grandmother is threaded throughout Ananda's play or that Ananda is often engaged in household chores as a princess. While some scholars might argue that Ananda, when taking on the role of Tiana, is excluded from the white world of princesses because she is working so hard, which firmly positions her as a member of the working class (Condis, 2015), we theorize this a bit differently. Ananda's funds of identity are partially shaped by two strong, motivated, working-class, African-American female role models who work hard on a daily basis to realize their goals. This is a space Ananda can enter into because the story is consistent with what she lives on a daily basis. Experiences in everyday life determine and frame how children play. Observing their parents' and significant adults' daily activities such as cooking, cleaning, washing, or driving a car generates a powerful motive for children to do these tasks when at play. These adult activities are attractive to children, but they cannot fulfil their desire directly in a real life. Instead, they enter into the world of adults by imitating and exploring social roles and relations in the course of their pretend play.

In the above play scenario, Ananda is not only an active play participant she is leading the play. Both girls are observed smiling, laughing, and physically interacting with one another even though Emma speaks very little due to her primary language being Chinese. In scenarios such as these we observed how 'princess play practices offer children opportunities for pleasure and cooperation, a means of transforming social relationships, and a source of empowerment in peer culture' (Wohlwend, 2015, p. 94).

'Princesses can do anything!' – Eugene

As Mr H shifted the curriculum to invite princess play into the classroom, the concept of gender also became a topic of class discussion. On 6 April 2015 Princesses Dan and Tommy were dressed in tulle fabric, wielding handmade magic wands, and playing together near the block area. When they went to join the other princesses who all identified as female at this time, some questions emerged from the children: 'Can boys wear dresses? Can boys be princesses?' Mr H asked the children these questions during a class meeting the following day when he addressed these questions and further supported the boys' princess play through the reading of the book, *My princess boy* by Cheryl Kilodavis. During a discussion after the reading the children decided that 'if they see a boy dresses as a princess they will not laugh at him or call him names but will play with him and like him for who he is' (Daily Reflection, 7 April 2015). Consider the following exchange:

Tommy: Boys can be princesses if they want.
Dan: Boys can dress pretty.
Emma: Dan is a princess!!

While Tommy moved in and out of the princess play as did most of the other children who identified as boys in the classroom, Dan became a consistent princess play partner. On 29 April 2015, a group of six children extended their indoor play into the outdoor meadow area. During the play planning session Dan suggested, 'Let's have a picnic like we did in the morning with the fabric.' Zander, who was most often seen dressed as a knight wearing a suit of armour and brandishing a sword and shield, took on the role of a princess and suggested that they include instruments to make music for the party. When the children got outdoors, they put on their princess costumes and set out a picnic blanket for lunch. Maggie played the role of granny and Noor and Ananda were the princess granddaughters. Dan was the fairy princess. Consider the following excerpt taken from the Daily Reflection on 29 April 2015:

Ananda (turning around so Grandma can see her tutu and wings):	Grandma, Grandma aren't I beautiful? Look at my dress and hair!
Maggie (smiling and moving over towards Ananda):	You are so pretty there! I want to help you with the tutu.
Noor (smiling at Ananda):	I am the Cinderella princess. Ananda is my friend.
Dan (twirling around in the middle of the group clutching his magic wand):	I am the fairy of all of you. My wings are magic.

The children had their picnic, danced together to Zander's 'fairy princess' music, and explored areas in the meadow in which to build their houses.

Like Ehrensaft (2011), this research team believes that 'A child's gender development is always a work in progress' (p. 133). In this play scenario we see children who identify as both boys and girls taking on a princess role. Much of the critique against princess play for girls is focused on the gender stereotyping and gender conformity that is found in many of the Disney princess movies (Condis, 2015; England et al., 2011), although stronger female characters such as Mulan, Merida, and Elsa have emerged in the last several years (Condis, 2015). A simplistic view of learning gender by absorbing the social environment (watching or listening) fails to explain the complexities evident in children's play and denies children's abilities as agents in their own learning. There are many contradictory messages in children's worlds and they negotiate their way through dialogue and interaction, by hearing and being heard. Describing and analysing 15 preschooler's princess and pirate play through a rhizomatic approach, Pacini-Katchabaw, Nxumo, Kocher, Elliot, and Sanches (2015) suggest that children are not just marked by gender discourses; they do gender (p. 150). Through the princess-focused curriculum, Mr H created a gender-expansive classroom where all children were encouraged to be their gender-creative selves.

Throughout the research project, Noor's verbal communication in English is limited and she often chooses to take on a more passive role in princess play. Yet, there were moments when she chose to take on a more active, assertive role. Consider this observation recorded on 4 May 2015:

Noor joins her brother, 2 other boys and Ananda in the block area where the children have put 'the dragon' (a painted box) on top of a block structure. Ananda, dressed as a princess wielding a plastic tube around in the air says, 'This is a sword of legendary!' All the children except for Noor and Ben run to another part of the room. It is Noor who steps up and 'knocks out' the dragon with her sword two more times before the other children run back over some of them arguing, 'let's hit the dragon' While others say, 'the dragon is our friend. Ananda tries to defend the dragon and starts hitting other children with her sword. Mr. H. takes the sword away and Ananda starts to cry.

As Ananda cries Maggie shifts the play scenario.

Maggie:	OK, everyone get on the ship! We are pirates!
Maggie and another girl start to sing:	We are the pirates ... going to the fairy castle.
Noor says to Ananda as she rubs her back:	'Princess, princess, quit crying.' Soon they are playing together as Noor pretends to feed Ananda her crying baby.

In this play scenario, Noor is definitely not relegated to the role of a princess waiting for the prince to save her from the dragon. She steps up and slays the dragon on her own. This may have been related to Mr H's reading of *The paper bag princess* by Robert Munsch, in which the princess is the heroine of the story, but we also believe it is related to the fact that she is a more confident play partner who can follow the storyline. Even more importantly the strong bond that is developing between Noor and Ananda is exhibited again in this scenario as Noor soothes the visibly upset Princess Ananda by rubbing her back and pretend feeding her.

Discussion and conclusions

Through the photographs and photo-elicitation interviews this research team was able to view a slice of the world through the eyes of the focal children. We came to recognize that there was a mismatch between the focal children's funds of identity and the existing curriculum. We also came to realize that our perspectives of the children's interest and knowledge were limited by our inability to see their curriculum making potential beyond the classroom walls and by our hesitation to offer the curriculum the children desire. The children's input led to a stronger, more inclusive classroom environment in which children were engaged in the curricular experiences offered by Mr H.

The types of interactions between and among Noor and Ananda and the other children were not happening prior to Mr H's intentional creation of curriculum that included the girls' funds of identity. As Quintero's (2015) research has illustrated when the curriculum respects the life of the child and the children are able to dramatize their personal stories and interests through pretend play, 'topics become layered with complex issues regarding development and learning that must be discussed and addressed in education' (p. 149). In this preschool curriculum issues of race, beauty, and gender emerged and were addressed through dialogue and acted out in the children's play scenarios. Children from diverse cultural and linguistic backgrounds played together, advocated for one another, and provided comfort during times of distress.

The power of Disney princesses to bring the children together in this classroom cannot be underestimated. The Disney princess culture provided initial entry spaces into the curriculum for Ananda, Noor, and other children. They entered into pretend play by accessing familiar storylines, and based on their own identities and the children's literature they were reading, created new storylines along the way. The children had opportunities to articulate their thoughts and ideas about various issues and refused to have their social identities limited by stereotypes in the royal world they were negotiating within their preschool community.

Disclosure statement

No potential conflict of interest was reported by the authors.

References

Condis, M. (2015). Applying for the position of princess: Race, labor, and privilege in the Disney princess line. In M. Forman-Brunell & R. Haines (Eds.), *Princess cultures: Mediating girls' imaginations and identities* (pp. 25–44). New York, NY: Peter Lang.

Dantas, M., & Manyak, P. (Eds.). (2010). *Home-school connections in a multicultural society: Learning from and with culturally and linguistically diverse families*. New York, NY: Routledge.

Ehrensaft, D. (2011). *Gender born, gender made: Raising healthy gender-nonconforming children*. New York, NY: The Experiment, LLC.

England, D. A., Descartes, L., & Collier-Meek, M. A. (2011). Gender role portrayal and the Disney princesses. *Sex Roles, 64*, 555–567. doi:10.1007/s11199-011-9930-7

Esteban-Guitart, M., & Moll, L. (2014). Funds of identity: A new concept based on the funds of knowledge approach. *Culture & Psychology, 20*(1), 31–48. doi:10.1177/1354067X13515934

Greene, S. (2013). *Race, community, and urban schools: Partnering with African American families.* New York, NY: Teachers College Press.

Hedges, H., Cullen, J., & Jordan, B. (2011). Early years curriculum: Funds of knowledge as a conceptual framework for children's interests. *Journal of Curriculum Studies, 43*(2), 185–205. doi:10.1080/00220272.2010.511275

Henderson et al. (2015). *Reconceptualizing curriculum development: Inspiring and informing action.* New York, NY: Routledge.

Huber, J., Murphy, M. S., & Clandinin, D. J. (2011). *Places of curriculum making: Narrative inquiries into children's lives in motion* (1st ed.). Bingley: Emerald.

Kindon, S., Pain, R., & Kesby, M. (2007). *Participatory action research approaches and methods: Connecting people, participation and place.* New York, NY: Routledge.

Loizou, E. (2011). Disposable cameras, humor and children's abilities. *Contemporary Issues in Early Childhood, 12*(2), 148–162. Retrieved June 3, 2014, from http://dx.doi.org/10.2304/ciec.2011.12.2.148

Marsh, J. (2014). Media, popular culture and play. In L. Brooker, M. Blaise, & S. Edwards (Eds.), *The Sage handbook of play and learning in early childhood* (pp. 403–414). London: Sage publications.

Moll, L. C., Amanti, C., Neff, D., & Gonzales, N. (1992). Funds of knowledge for teaching: Using a qualitative approach to connect homes and classrooms. *Theory into Practice, 31*(2), 132–141.

Pacini-Katchabaw, V., Nxumo, F., Kocher, L., Elliot, E., & Sanches, A. (2015). *Journeys: Reconceptualizing early childhood practices through pedagogical narration.* Toronto: University of Toronto Press.

Pushor, D. (2010). Are schools doing enough to learn about families? In M. Miller Marsh & T. Turner-Vorbeck (Eds.), *(Mis) understanding families: Learning from real families in our schools* (pp. 4–16). New York, NY: Teachers College Press.

Quintero, E. P. (2015). *Storying learning in early childhood: When children lead participatory curriculum design, implementation, and assessment.* New York, NY: Peter Lang.

Rios-Aguilar, C., Kiyama, J., Gravitt, M., & Moll, L. (2011). Funds of knowledge for the poor and forms of capital for the rich? A capital approach to examining funds of knowledge. *Theory and Research in Education, 9*(2), 163–184.

Rose, G. (2012). *Visual methodologies: An introduction to researching with visual materials.* London: Sage publications.

Sfard, A., & Prusak, A. (2005). Telling identities: In search of an analytic tool for investigating learning as a culturally shaped activity. *Educational Researcher, 34*(4), 14–22.

Souto-Manning, M. (2013). *Multicultural teaching in the early childhood classroom: Strategies, tools, and approaches, prek-2nd grade.* New York, NY: Teachers College Press.

Wohlwend, K. (2015). Playing to belong: Princesses and peer cultures in preschool. In M. Forman-Brunell & R. C. Hains (Eds.), *Princess cultures: Mediating girls' imaginations and identities* (pp. 89–112). New York, NY: Peter Lang.

Wright, C., Diener, M. L., & Kemp, J. L. (2013). Storytelling dramas as a community building activity in an early childhood classroom. *Early Childhood Education Journal, 41*, 197–210. doi:10.1007/s10643-012-0544-7

Playing at violence: lock-down drills, 'bad guys' and the construction of 'acceptable' play in early childhood

Katherine K. Delaney

ABSTRACT
This study examines how acceptable play was framed for a class of pre-Kindergarten children by their teacher and classroom aide. Using comic subjectivity theory [Zupančič, A. (2008). *The odd one in: On comedy*. Cambridge: MIT Press], the author explores how children's playing at pretend violence (bad guy and pretend gun play) is forbidden, but playing at real violence (in the form of active-shooter lock-down drills) positioned the children in the classroom as victims of violence, rather than agentic powerful players. As gun violence in the United States continues to invade school spaces, this paper crtitically examines how 'acceptable' play for young children is being framed and defined by outside forces rather than pedagogical and professional knowledge.

Simon: 'Shhh ... I'm the bad guy. Ok? And you – you've got the guns. But don't let anyone see ... we are sneaking into the school ... pretend we are the bad guys, right?!'
Kazadi: 'I've got my gun. Have you got yours?' (Observation, Afternoon Class)

As teachers and researchers working within the field of early childhood, we know that young children use play to make sense of the world around them (Holland, 2003; Levin & Carlsson-Paige, 2006; Paley, 1988; 2004). After a trip to the doctor, for example, a child might turn the housekeeping corner into an examination room. Similarly, the death of a loved one may result in a funeral procession weaving around the classroom (Paley, 1988). Other experiences too, such as overheard adult conversations, cartoons, an interesting story or book, may filter into and influence the play of children as they take up themes and ideas that capture their imaginations (Edmiston, 2008). As in the exchange at the opening of this paper, these play themes often extend to the realm of violence and bad guy play.

'Playing at violence' is a phrase that I use throughout this paper to conceptualize the ways in which teachers and children engage with, pretend at and play around violent themes. The phrase plays on the idea that both children's imagined scenarios, and the imagined scenarios that we ask children to pretend/play during school drills (such as Code Red) are reflective embodiments of one another, an idea I will discuss at length later in this paper. This 'playing at violence' represents a type of play that many adults, teachers and school districts are not comfortable with (Holland, 2003; Katch, 2001; Levin & Carlsson-Paige, 2006). While adults may not want children to play at themes such as death, violence, loss and fear, there is evidence that this type of play is an important part of children's sense-making processes (Levin, 2003). Research indicates that these play scenarios give children opportunities to be simultaneously safe and powerful (Rich, 2003), to examine and understand traumatic events on their own terms (Berson & Baggerly, 2009; Gil, 2006), and to develop language and strategies for dealing with bullying and stressful experiences (Bacigalupa & Wright, 2009; Logue & Shelton, 2008). While research indicates that this kind of play is important, many schools maintain zero-tolerance policies around children playing or pretending at violent themes (Katch, 2001; Rich, 2003). Additionally, research indicates that these zero-tolerance policies are more likely to exist and be enforced in schools serving low-income and non-white students (Arcia, 2007; Skiba et al., 2011). From a social justice perspective, therefore, it is important to consider how the play of children (particularly children of color and low-income children) is framed by policies and practices that aim to control the play of children (Shimpi & Nicholson, 2014).

As schools restrict children's 'playing at violence', another version is being endorsed in schools in the United States (U.S.) in the form of Code Red drills (also known as Lock-Down or Active-Shooter drills). As a year-long participant observer in a pre-K classroom, I have participated in these drills and quieted children as we waited for the 'all clear' announcement over the loud speaker. At the time, I was struck by the ways in which this sanctioned form of 'playing at violence' existed, incongruously, with rules against children's imaginative 'bad guy' play. While the perceptions of teachers, parents and school leaders might not be that Code Red drills are playful, the pretending aspect of school safety drills requires children to be complicit to and pretend along with imagined scenarios. According to a recent study by the U.S. Department of Education, more than 70% of surveyed U.S. schools report that they drill students and teachers in how to respond to active-shooter situations (IES, 2014). These drills require teachers to shut and lock classroom doors, pull window shades, and huddle quietly with their students until the drill is completed.

In this paper, I examine the ways in which acceptable forms of 'playing at violence' were constructed for a group of four-year olds by their teacher (Wanda) and other school staff as they participated in newly implemented Code Red drills. Additionally, I explore how the children responded to these notions of acceptable play. To do this, I ask the following questions: How were notions of 'playing at violence' constructed in one pre-K classroom and the larger school? How did Wanda frame notions of acceptable play for her students? How did a small group of children in the class use play to make sense of and/or resist varied versions of acceptable 'playing at violence?'

Framing play

Play is powerful

Conceptions of 'play as children's work', or the activity through which children learn and develop, are central to the ways in which we frame curriculum, practice and the natural development of young children in Western early childhood educational spaces (Grieshaber & McArdle, 2010; Paley, 2004; Samuelsson & Carlsson, 2008). In this way, play is promoted as good practice in early childhood education classrooms, and the growing loss of time and attention given to play in early primary school (and even some preschools) is a growing concern for many in our field (Copple & Bredekamp, 2009; Russell, 2010). We know that imaginative play helps children to make sense of the world around them, to unpack and re-examine events that shift their realities and lived experiences, to try on new selves, and to understand experiences of othering/being othered (Hirsh-Pasek, Michnik Golinkoff, Berk & Singer, 2008; Paley, 1988). Play is so powerful that it pushes children to ask questions and pursue ideas that may provoke uncomfortable feelings in the adults around them (Holland, 2003; Katch, 2001).

Play as a site of compliance and resistance

When adults are made uncomfortable by children's imaginative play, this play can become a site of compliance and resistance. Teachers and family members may set the parameters of acceptable play, and children may actively struggle against these restrictions (Corsaro, 2003). As the adults seek compliance, the children may use play to resist. For example, children may be told that for the sake of 'safety' or 'scaring other children', that they are not allowed to play 'bad guys' or superheroes. The result is these kinds of play often go underground where children continue to assert their right to play (Moore, 2015; Skånfors, Löfdahl, & Hägglund, 2009). This creates spaces where there is no knowledgeable peer or scaffolding adult who can help support children's sense-making through play.

When teachers dictate what can and cannot be played, the value of play as the basis for early childhood curriculum is greatly diminished. By this I mean that once play is restricted, so too is the range of what children can learn from a play-based curriculum. The elimination of certain kinds of play in early childhood classrooms, while seemingly simple and straightforward, may in fact further inform the imbalance of power between children and teachers/adults and limit democratic approaches and opportunities for discussion and meaning-making (Millei, 2012).

From a social justice perspective, play can also be envisioned as a site where children enact agency and power, making opportunities for imaginative play an important right for all children (MacNaughton, 2005). As children resist adult expectations and regulation of their play, they can be seen to be asserting their right to make sense of the world around them. However, too often resistance to teachers' and schools' rules is framed very differently for different groups of children (Arcia, 2007; Peguero, Shekarkhar, Popp, & Koo, 2015; Skiba et al., 2011). Particularly for children who live in low-income, non-white and/or immigrant communities, opportunities to make sense of lived experiences through play are even more limited (Stirrup, Evans, & Davies, 2016). Instead, when these children assert their play rights, they are more likely to be framed as difficult, unable, or problematic and to be subjected to higher rates of discipline (CRDC, 2014).

This may be particularly true in early childhood settings where accountability-driven regulations and fears of children being harmed at school result in banning certain kinds of play. In these situations, children's play interests run up against regulations that prioritize imagined risks and/or 'accountability under regulations' (Little, Hansen Sandsetter, & Wyver, 2012, p. 307). As a result, the kinds of play that are valued in the curriculum are shaped by external forces rather than the pedagogical and developmental knowledge of teachers, and the needs and interests of children. Though children use play to make sense of the world around them, an adult fear of what the play of children means, or could mean, frame what is acceptable and allowable. Instead of seeking to understand the play, often the adult response is to seek to contain or control.

'Playing at violence'

Within the U.S., school districts are responding to gun violence by having teachers and children engage in practice drills in preparation for a violent event at their school (Gereluk, Donlevy, & Thompson, 2015). These Code Red (or Lock-Down) drills, which are occurring in over 70% of U.S. public schools (IES, 2014), frame 'playing at violence' as a part of learning at school. I use this phrase, 'playing at violence' to broadly conceptualize play and pretending involving violent themes. As such 'playing at violence' can be reflected in children's imaginative play about 'bad guys', as well as the acts of compliance that we require of children and teachers when we ask them to pretend to be the potential victims of violence during school drills.

In this paper, I examine two versions of 'playing at violence'. 'Playing at pretend violence', are moments when children engage in an imaginative play that includes or is based around violent themes (such as 'bad guys') and often includes pretend weaponry. The other version is 'playing at real violence', which indicates activities where children and teachers pretend to be enduring a violent act at school (such as a Code Red/Lock-Down drill).

'Playing pretend violence' represents child-initiated, imaginative play around themes like 'bad guys', often using toys or other classroom materials to create weapons and guns as a part of their play. This is an act initiated by children. In these play scenarios, children are powerful because they can both enact powerful roles and because they choose the roles that they play (bad guys, heroes, victims, etc.) (MacNaughton, 2005). In contrast, 'playing real violence' represents play or pretending in which children and teachers are asked to simulate being potential victims of violent acts (the killing of children and teachers in schools). In these roles during Code Red drills, the children are subject to, and objectified by, the violent narratives of the world around them (Foucault, 1982). They do not choose these roles and are required to comply. These pretend scenarios embody real violence and real 'bad guys', and children and teachers are positioned as victims/subjects of violence.

To understand these contrasting versions of 'playing at violence', I use two theoretical frameworks: Foucault's (1979, 1982) power theory and comic subjectivity theory (Zupančič, 2008). Foucault's power theory is a lens for better understanding the ways in which power dynamics and political discourses can position child and play (Blaise & Ryan, 2012). Using this theory, I examine the ways in which the children in this classroom were both positioned as victims through 'playing real violence' in the form of Code Red drills, and simultaneously exerted their power and resistance by 'playing pretend violence' in their imaginative play, despite rules against that kind of play.

The second theory is comic subjectivity theory (Zupančič, 2008), which I use to examine the incongruities of the two constructs of 'playing at violence' and how the children engaged with and made sense of the contrast. Comic subjectivity theory is grounded in the works of Lacan, Kant and Schopenhauer (Morreall, 1983; Watson, 2015). Comic incongruity examines how some moments in life are like a Mobius, wherein '[there is] only one surface .... yet at every point there is also the other side ... this endless movement of contradiction, [which can] be recognized as the essence of tragedy ... and tragic comedy' (Zupančič, 2008, pp. 54–55). In this case, the incongruities and contradictions of acceptable/unacceptable forms of 'playing at violence' reflect one another, informing and mutually constructing notions of sanctioned play for young children, as well as notions of children as powerful (enactors of play) and powerless (victims of violence).

Both theories aim to highlight stories from the margins, and to bring those hidden narratives into the broader, sociocultural dialogue. Instead of focusing on the sanctioned forms of play, these theories allow a researcher to understand how acts of power and agency within play are an assertion of rights by children. For example, the right to use play to make sense of the world around them, and the right to teachers and schools that meaningfully support, rather than constraint, their sense-making. As such, these theories are tied to understandings of social justice for children, and play as a means of asserting agency through resistance and subversion of adults' constraints on play (Grieshaber & McArdle, 2010).

Using these theories, I have constructed three vignettes of 'playing at violence' through which I present my findings from this case study. Vignettes allow an interpretive researcher to bring together a broad cross-section of data and fold those into narrative structures that reflect many data points in one rich example (Richardson & Lockridge, 1998). The vignettes from Wanda's classroom represent distilled examples of the three main themes that emerged in my analyses of how she and the children in her classroom negotiated playing at violence, both pretend and real. These themes were: (1) how Wanda frame and negotiated boundaries for acceptable playing at violence, (2) how the children made sense of the role of Code Red drills in Wanda's rules about playing at violence and (3) how the four players negotiated acceptable play after the implementation of the Code Red drills.

Methods

This study is a qualitative, interpretive case study (Stake, 1995) of one class of 15 pre-schoolers and their teacher, Wanda.[1] This study took place during the first year of implementation of a district-wide, play-based, public pre-Kindergarten (pre-K) initiative. This work is part of a larger study known as the *4-year-old Kindergarten Professional Development Project* (or 4K-PD), funded by the National Science Foundation. The pre-K teachers who enrolled in the 4K-PD study participated in 4, 3-credit professional development courses offered over four semesters. These classes focused on engaging the teachers in developing developmentally, culturally and individually responsive practices and mathematics teaching in pre-K settings. Using Funds of Knowledge as a framework for this work (Moll, Amanti, Neff, & Gonzalez, 1992), the study foregrounded the knowledge and lived experiences of the children in preschool classrooms as the site for designing and implementing curriculum. Coursework contributed towards graduate degree credit. All participating teachers were teaching in community-based or public school-based district pre-K classrooms and had state licensure. The PD classes met one evening a week during the school year, across two years. I was a graduate research assistant on this project, responsible for fieldwork and course instruction.

When I met Wanda, I hoped that she would be willing to work with me because she was making a transition that I was curious about: moving from 10 years as a Kindergarten teacher into a pre-K classroom. Early in our discussions, Wanda identified the motivation for this move as her hope that she might finally be able to use the developmentally responsive practices she had learned about in her teacher education coursework nearly 12 years prior. Wanda's transition, and her goal to make sense of the different practices she had used in Kindergarten and envisioned for pre-K, made her a prime example of a borderland between Early Childhood and Elementary approaches to curriculum and practice that I wanted to better understand from a research perspective. Using a purposive sampling approach (Creswell, 1998), I chose to study Wanda's first-year experiences in teaching pre-K, as well as those of her students. The case study was bounded (Stake, 1995) by Wanda's teaching practice at Fuji Elementary and her participation in the 4K-PD programme during her first year of teaching pre-K. I was a participant observer in her classroom during the 2011–2012 school year. The case was largely informed by my participation in her classroom practices and her work with her students.

Data collection and analysis

I gathered extensive data from October 2011 to June 2012 in Wanda's classroom (see Table 1). These data included weekly observations in Wanda's classroom, where I wrote thickly detailed, ethnographic fieldnotes and personal reflections of the Afternoon preschool session; three semi-structured interviews with Wanda (Spradley, 1979); notes from discussions and reflections with Wanda following each observation; email correspondence with Wanda; and photographs of the classroom and children at play during each visit. In addition, I used transcriptions of Wanda's participation in the 4K-PD coursework, as well as intermittent observations of her participation in the courses across four semesters, as part of my data set.

I analysed these data via NVIVO 8 (Bazeley & Jackson, 2013), using both the frameworks of power theory (Foucault, 1979) and comic subjectivity/incongruity theory (Zupančič, 2008), as the initial coding structures for my analyses. In a second round of coding I used a deductive approach, identifying themes across the initial codes. I used memo writing as a key analytic strategy (Saldana, 2009) to identify emerging themes and findings. I then included these memos in NVIVO as I recoded and revisited data in a recursive manner (Patton, 2002), using triangulation across data sources (observations, interviews, my own reflections and transcriptions of PD coursework) to better understand, challenge and evaluate my interpretations (Stake, 1995; Yin, 2003). This paper focuses on one set of findings from this larger case study: how Wanda and the children made sense of incongruous practices about 'playing at violence' in school.

Table 1. Data collection.

Source	Setting	Time period	Number
Interviews	Classroom	September, April, June	3
Fieldnotes	Classroom/school observation	Once a week, October through June	31
	PD course	Intermittently throughout fall/spring/summer semesters	12
Transcriptions of small and whole group discussions	PsD course	Weekly, September through June	209
Photos	Classroom	Each visit	123
Reflections	Classroom/PD	Once a week, October through June	32
Child memos	Classroom	Intermittent	5
General memos	Classroom/PD	Intermittent	7
Email with Wanda		Intermittent throughout school year	43

The Afternoon Class

Since pre-K programming in the District was half-day, there was a Morning Class and an Afternoon Class at each elementary school. The Morning Class opened with breakfast, and the Afternoon Class opened with lunch. In the year that I was a participant observer in Wanda's classroom, I was a biweekly figure in her Afternoon Class.

Wanda, as mentioned earlier, had been teaching Kindergarten for 10 years, 8 of those at Fuji Elementary. In her mid thirties, Wanda had an elementary-school-aged son, and had grown up in a suburban community about 30 miles from Fuji. At the time of the study, her son attended a different elementary school in the same school district, one that Wanda characterized as having 'fewer challenges ... most of the families are much wealthier than we are, and have a lot more resources than my families at Fuji do'. As a teacher, she was deeply committed to working with children with what she termed as having 'fewer opportunities and resources' than her own family. According to Wanda,

> I want to work with children and families who need me. I grew up in this family – we were all adopted, all from different countries. And there weren't a lot of families like ours. So I feel like I understand diversity and what kids from different backgrounds need. And I want to teach someplace where I really am needed.

Wanda's journey had led her to Fuji Elementary, a school that served a predominantly low-income community of non-white students within a large district in a mid-sized, Midwestern University town. The school served large refugee communities of both Hmong and West African families, and a majority of the students qualified for free/reduced lunch.

Wanda's reputation at Fuji was as a strong, committed Kindergarten teacher. Before and after school she could be found on the playground surrounded by children and family members. For many families, Wanda had taught all of their children as they passed through Kindergarten.

Wanda's Afternoon Class consisted of 15 students at the start of the school year, and 14 at the close, with one student returning with his family to China midway through the school year. In this paper, I zoom in on the experiences of four children who, throughout the year, were deeply involved in imaginative 'bad guy' play. Their fascination with vivid and engaging 'bad guy' scenarios fuelled much of the discussion that Wanda, her classroom aide (Mrs B), and I had around what made for acceptable playing at violence.

These four players were the main participants in the negotiation of playing at violence that took place in Wanda's classroom that year. The two lead players, Kazadi and Simon, were both boys and youngest brothers. Simon was the youngest child of a teacher at Fuji. He was a white and middle class. His older sister was in 3rd grade that year at Fuji. Kazadi was the youngest of three sons of a family who had fled violence in western Africa, nearly a decade before. Kazadi was born in the U.S., and spoke both French and English at home. Both of his elder brothers were at Fuji, and both had had Wanda as their Kindergarten teacher. The third player was Kwame, an African-American boy, who often augmented the original play plans with more details and difficulty. Kwame was an only child and came each day to the Afternoon Class on the day-care bus with several other children. Kwame's focus was to fill all the games with daring acts of speed and agility, as well as complicating and exciting details. The fourth player, Virginia, was a tall, blonde girl who was always eager to carry 'weapons', usually a stick or a converted wooden block. Midway through the school year, her mother had a baby, and suddenly 'protecting babies' as became a central trope of the group's play.

As a participant observer in Wanda's classroom, my own background and experiences are also at play in this research (Labaree, 2002). Prior to graduate school, I was a preschool teacher: for three years in a university preschool, and then for three years in an inner-city preschool. At both sites, I was interested in the ways in which children used play to be powerful, and often crafted their play in response to lived experiences in which they had been or felt powerless. A central theme in my own work as a teacher was finding ways to support and have conversations with young children about the difficult or sometimes even controversial themes that arose in their play. Given this focus in my teaching, I was highly attentive to how the children and Wanda responded as difficult themes (such as death, violence and weapons) came up in play and conversation. Having never had to implement a Code Red drill, a school practice that has only emerged in the last few years, I was particularly struck by the ways in which this drill was positioned for and experienced by the children in this class.

In addition, I was a member of the instructional and research team for the professional development project in which Wanda was a participant. This informed our relationship, sometimes positioning me as an 'expert' and Wanda as a 'novice'. This power dynamic is visible in the vignettes presented in this paper, and was something that Wanda and I discussed in our work together. In these conversations, my goal was for her to see me as a supporter of her work and the work of her students. By mid-year, we both viewed our relationship as more of a partnership and space for sense-making, rather than as an observer and subject.

The children, after several weeks of ignoring me, came to view me as a silent watcher and occasional player, but never a teacher. I first realized that I was seen this way early in November 2011. In my fieldnotes, I noted it this way, "Today, Kazadi walked past my computer, eyeing my typing. He walked over to Simon and said, 'She's working again. But I bet we can get her to play later.'" This struck me as being quite telling about how the children envisioned my role in their classroom. I never heard the children speak of Wanda or Mrs B in this way. Perhaps in their minds, as teachers, Wanda and Mrs B were always working and did not have much time to drop everything and play. With me they knew that when asked to join play, I would set aside my computer and do so. In this way, the children seemed to view me as a player rather than a teacher, and so would let me observe their imaginative play, rarely amending their themes and roles when I came closer or listened and questioned.

When I joined Wanda's classroom as a participant observer in October 2011, these four players were a well-established play grouping, with well-defined roles, weapons, and modes of hiding their play from Wanda and Mrs B. The first vignette presented in the next section is from my first few weeks of observation in Wanda's classroom, and reflects these organized roles and play themes.

Vignette 1: Setting the boundaries of 'acceptable' playing at violence

Through the month of October, I watch Simon, Kazadi, Kwame and Virginia, as they spend each outdoor recess deeply engaged in detailed bad guy games. In what Wanda describes as a 'long running game', the bad guys are invisible, and the children are powerful in their roles as 'mommy', 'daddy' and 'brothers' as they run around the wood chip covered play space quietly shooting 'webs' from their 'arms'. These 'webs' and 'arms' are concessions made by Wanda and Mrs B to the constraints of Fuji's zero-tolerance policy towards violence and violent themes. When I ask about the webs, Wanda laughs,

> I know that they will turn it into something. At least this way, I am sort of in control of what they are doing and if the Principal walks by I might be able to get away with Spider Man play.

All around, acceptable play is being negotiated.

The four children use the somewhat hidden spaces under the climbers to reassure each other that they are, however, 'really using guns', and not webs 'cause webs can't really stop bad guys'. Often, when they make these reassuring remarks to one another, they look over and see me, and nod. They know I am just there to observe and would not give them away. 'When those bad guys come' Kazadi says, 'I'm gonna kill them all.'

During each outdoor playtime, the children can gain distance from the hearing of Wanda and the games escalate. At some point the 'webs' are forgotten and one of the players points his or her hand in a gun shape and makes shooting noises. This is when Wanda stops the play. 'We talk about this everyday. You can do webs. But no guns – they are just too scary for our friends and our school', Wanda repeats for the hundredth time. Invariably, Simon reminds Wanda that the guns are 'just pretend', to which she responds, 'I don't even like pretend guns. And we don't play that way at school. It's too scary.'

As the winter sets in, we spend less time on the playground, and the small classroom makes it difficult for the four players to continue their games in the same way. As a result, they step up their deception of Wanda and Mrs B around the extent of their 'bad guy' play. One day, Kazadi is crouched in the housekeeping area launching unifix cubes from the end of what looks like a unifix gun into the block area. When queried by Wanda, he holds up the unifix object, flipping its orientation, 'It's a 7, see?' The class has been studying numbers and Wanda immediately smiles. Simon joins Kazadi and shows Wanda his unifix '4', which moments before was a machine gun, rapidly firing unifix cubes at the bad guys. 'Alright', Wanda says, 'I just don't want any guns.' The boys nod and run back to their game. Virginia welcomes them home to the housekeeping corner, and hands them each a cooking pan filled with unifix ammunition, 'They are coming to hurt the babies!' she tells them.

Day after day, Wanda worked to set boundaries for acceptable imaginative play. As seen in the above vignette, when Wanda would set the boundaries of acceptable play, the four players would push against them. They were only willing to go along with her (and the school's) rules for so long. Then their violent play would burst out, forcing Wanda to either shut down the play, or remind them of the rules. In private conversations after the children went home, Wanda would tell me she was uncertain how to proceed.

> I hate guns, and all this gun play. My son has never played that way, but Simon's mom (a teacher at Fuji) is ok with that kind of play. But the kids need to know that they just can't play that way here at school. There is a zero tolerance policy. And next year, they can be suspended for playing like that.

In my observations and through my analyses, I came to understand Wanda's framing of 'acceptable' play in the classroom as centring around four main elements.

First, at the start of the school year, what Wanda attributed to the children's play, and how the children conceptualized their play, was at odds. When Simon asserted 'guns are pretend', he was pointing out to Wanda that their play was just play, and not whatever 'scary' things Wanda brought to it. However, Wanda's own values and beliefs framed her understanding of the bad guy play in her classroom. Research has shown that teachers' often frame what kinds of play are 'acceptable' through their own values (Sherwood & Reifel, 2010b) and avoid allowing play that may highlight their own fears (Henricks, 2010).

As Wanda told me on multiple occasions, her own son had never been interested in playing violent themes. Per Wanda, 'Maybe it's because I didn't let him. But he never did super hero play, or play guns. And he didn't try to sneak it in like these guys do when I say no.' In Wanda's conversations with the children in her classroom, she would assert, 'I don't like guns – even pretend guns. They hurt people … '. Wanda's perception of the children's playing at pretend violence was that it represented real violent acts, rather than children working to make sense or to feel powerful in a world where they are rarely in control. Her personal discomfort was clear, and manifested itself in the limits she placed on the children's imaginative play.

The second way that Wanda framed the children's playing at pretend violence was as a Pandora's box for conversations she was not prepared, nor supported, to have. In our discussions about the children's playing at violence, Wanda was surprised by my perspective that the children might be using the play to feel powerful and/or to process themes, topics or events they were witnessing. Given my own background as a preschool teacher, I tried to encourage her to *use* the play as a way to start a dialogue about guns, violence and fear. To Wanda, however, this was like opening Pandora's box, 'Even if I got them talking, I'm not sure what I would say, and then what?'

Instead of having the difficult conversations, Wanda worked to restrict what kinds of imaginative play were acceptable. As seen in the above vignette, the children pushed these boundaries, turning webs in to bullets and unifix cubes into handguns. As the four players persisted in their 'bad guy' play,

I began to push Wanda to consider why the children might be playing that way, even if she was not ready to use it as a starting point for classroom dialogue. When pressed to consider *why* the children might be playing that way, Wanda noted 'maybe they feel strong when they do it. I mean their moms and dads protect them, right?'

Even though she came to recognize how the children might be asserting their agency and power in this kind of play (MacNaughton, 2005), her discomfort continued to set the parameters for play. How the children played became something Wanda felt she both strongly needed to control and yet also began to recognize as something they needed to be allowed to do.

Wanda's dual understanding of imaginative play, as important for children's sense-making and agency but also out of the teachers' control and therefore possibly dangerous, made her responses to the children's playing at pretend violence both unclear and permissive. This was evidenced in the children's nimble responses to Wanda's inquiries about their play. When Kazadi showed Wanda his '7' instead of his gun, he did not bat an eye. He and the other players had clearly figured out that they could keep playing at violence, as long as it was hidden.

The third element influencing Wanda's emerging sense of what playing at violence might mean for the children was her new role as a pre-K teacher during the school district's first year implementing a play-based pre-K programme. Understanding how playing (at violent themes or otherwise) might be simultaneously important (for the children's sense-making of the world around them *and* as part of what informed teacher planning and responding to inform the daily curriculum) was a new pedagogical space for Wanda.

According to Wanda, in Kindergarten, play was a tightly controlled experience in which the children moved through academically focused centres for a two-hour block in the morning and afternoon. As Wanda noted,

> It wasn't play in the sense that children were making choices, or setting the game. There would be a board game, or a sheet, or something and they would be sent to play at that center, and then they would go to the next center, and so on – so it was playful.

This version of play was structured and rigid, aimed at learning outcomes and readiness. From this perspective, what constituted acceptable play was play that could be tied to standards, an increasingly common way in which curriculum in the early years is framed as play (Brooker, 2010). In contrast, the play in Wanda's pre-K classroom represented something that could not be easily controlled and directed. While Wanda could join or direct the play of one small group of children, in doing so, the other children in the room could be involved in play and learning in which she was not a central actor (Grieshaber & McArdle, 2010). This reduction of control around what play was happening (and how and why), was a new way of teaching that was deeply contradictory to Wanda's past approaches to teaching and her experiences of the role of the teacher in Kindergarten (Delaney, 2015).

Finally, Wanda's boundaries for what constituted acceptable play was the district's zero-tolerance policy around playing pretend violence. In this vignette the ways in which the repercussions of the school's zero-tolerance policy weighed upon Wanda is highlighted in her statements about how she would justify the children's Spiderman play to her principal. Wanda was clearly afraid that allowing the children to play violent themes would put them at risk of punishment under the zero-tolerance policy. As Wanda told me, in prior years, Kindergartener and first-grade students sent home for 'rough' or 'bad guy' play. The message from the school principal was clear: school was no place for playing at pretend violence. The policy, and the fear of possible negative outcomes for the children, pushed Wanda to restrict play in ways that restricted dialogue and joint sense-making for her and the children. The zero-tolerance policy objectified the children, making them no longer players and learners, but instead subjects to a higher authority that sought to control their behaviour without valuing their need for agency (Foucault, 1982). Ironically, there is growing evidence that if children can play out their fears and make sense of the world around them, they may be less likely to engage in actual violence (Berson & Baggerly, 2009).

However, just as the children understood that if they were away from Wanda's gaze, they could play at violence, Wanda too allowed the children some leeway in adhering to Fuji's zero-tolerance policy both on the playground and during free play in her classroom. Perhaps this reflected Wanda's emerging understandings of why the children might be playing that way, and why some level of playing at pretend violence might be important in children's sense-making processes and sense of agency. As noted in the vignette, Wanda sought ways to bend the rules of the zero-tolerance policy, allowing webs and Spiderman play, but drew a firm line at pretend guns. Even so, the powerful force of the zero-tolerance policy informed Wanda's approaches to pedagogy, and tempered her willingness to engage with the children to understand *why* they were choosing that play and what she might learn from asking them about their playing at violence.

Vignette 2: 'Code Red' and acceptable playing at violence

It is early February and we have just returned to the classroom from recess in the gym, a concession to the relentless snowstorm outside. As the children settle onto the carpet for sharing, the loudspeaker comes on: 'This is a drill. Code Red. Code Red.' The children look up at the speaker and then at Wanda and Mrs B. I can see them trying to understand. Is this a fire drill? A tornado drill? The term 'Code Red' was new to all of us, except Wanda and Mrs B, who later tell me that they have been waiting for this moment for several weeks. Like the children, I am caught off guard.

Wanda and Mrs B both jump up. Wanda runs across the room and locks the door. Mrs B pulls the shades on the three, ceiling height windows in the basement classroom. They both return to the corner of the room where we are waiting on the rug. Wanda tells the children, 'Everyone stand up and move over here to the corner. Scrunch together real tight. I am putting my body in front of your bodies.' The children look confused, but comply. One child, Will, who always struggles with strong emotions and fear during fire and tornado drills, begins to whimper. 'It's ok, Will. We are just pretending. We are going to be very quiet. We are hiding so no one can find us.' Wanda pulls Will into her lap and puts one arm around him, using her other arm to pull other children gently towards her. She repeats, 'Everyone "shhhh" – we need to be very quiet.' As Wanda says this, Virginia, the powerful player and protector on the playground, climbs into my lap, and several other children press against me. They seem to be somewhere between fear and confusion. Kazadi is sitting in front of me, and puts his thumb into his mouth. We hear footsteps outside of the classroom and someone in the hall jiggles the door handle, rattling the door. Will whimpers again. 'Shhhhh', Wanda tells him. 'It's just pretend.'

After about three minutes, the voice comes over the loudspeaker again. 'Thank you students for your help today. You did a great job keeping each other safe.' Wanda and Mrs B help the children out of the corner and turn on the lights. While Mrs B opens the shades, Wanda encourages everyone to return to the carpet. She tries to continue with sharing time, but the children are all subdued. 'That was just pretend, right?' Will asks. 'Yes, just pretend. We do that to be safe at school.' Simon, whose mother is a teacher at the school says, 'Cause people wanna hurt kids in schools sometimes'. Wanda's face shows her surprise at his statement, and she quickly shifts the conversation to the centres that are open for that day. Few children seem to notice Simon's comment, and as soon as Wanda tells them to, they run off to play. Will, however, hangs around Wanda for the rest of the afternoon.

As this vignette captures, playing at violence became a real part of the children's lives via the Code Red drills. This is the second theme I identified in my data analysis: how through the Code Red drills an acceptable form of playing at violence was introduced to the children, one that both reflected and contradicted (Zupančič, 2008) school rules about imaginative play. The Code Red drills in Wanda's classroom occurred multiple times over the second half of the school year. According to Wanda, the training that she and Mrs B had received around the drills had been minimal, consisting of a brief announcement at the end of a staff meeting: turn out the light, lock the door, close the shades, put the children in a corner away from windows, and wait for the 'all clear' over the loudspeakers. The missing piece, according to Wanda, was how to talk about it with the kids. As Wanda noted,

'I think they think we can just treat it like a fire drill.' When I pointed out that the kids might come up with their own scary scenarios for why we are having Code Red drills if teachers and children did not discuss it, Wanda agreed and told me, 'a note did go home, so I am hoping parents will have that conversation'. This hope that parents would handle discussion of why they were having a Code Red drill was reflected in Wanda's overall discomfort with discussing violence, or allowing playing at violence. In the vignette, Wanda's response to Simon during sharing time reflects this discomfort. Simon had clearly talked about the Code Red drill with his mother (a Fuji teacher), and wanted to talk about it at school as well. Wanda, however, did not feel prepared to talk about why we were having Code Red drills at school. Her response was to simply move on.

Across the next few months, however, Simon persisted. During sharing time, he would occasionally mention snippets of information relating to violence against schools and children. For example, in late February he brought up a shooting at a high school in Ohio stating, 'My mom said there was a shooting at a big kid school.' Wanda nodded, made eye contact with me, and said to Simon, 'Oh wow, I bet they were all ok though' and moved on. Three students died in that shooting, and three more were injured. We do not know what Simon knew of that event.

After a few similar instances, Wanda became reluctant to call on Simon to share. This was particularly true on the days immediately following a Code Red drill, when Simon seemed to want to talk about *why* they were doing the drills. Perhaps Simon realized this too, as I noticed that he began to share less and less about violence-related topics over the course of the spring. Instead, he began to share this information when he and the other players were planning their play away from Wanda's hearing.

Wanda was willing to explain to the children why she did not want them playing at pretend violence ('guns scare me and hurt people'). However, this second vignette reflects her discomfort in talking with the children about why they were practising Code Red drills. According to Wanda, 'I'm worried that they will get really scared that someone will come and really hurt us. I don't want to open that door ... I mean, how can I explain that to the kids. I don't even get it'. Once again, the fear of opening Pandora's box pushed Wanda to respond with avoidance. In both cases, Wanda's own values and beliefs were at the root of her discomfort and unwillingness to discuss these difficult topics (Little et al., 2012). However, not talking about 'the why' of the Code Red drills did not stop the children from using play to make sense of what they were experiencing during Code Red drills (Levin, 2003).

According to Wanda, no parents asked her about the drills, or reported about kids being overly concerned. In my observations, aside from Will, it did not appear that any of the children did fear the Code Red drills. Even Simon, who clearly was aware of and discussing (or over-hearing) information at home, did not seem to be afraid of the drills. The violence that the children were pretending at during the Code Red drills seemed abstract to them, as opposed to how real it was to me, Wanda and Mrs B.

After the first Code Red in February, the drills simply became another act of compliance, and were ostensibly treated just like a tornado or fire drill by Wanda, Mrs B and the children. While the children's compliance with this simulated real violence was expected in order to ensure their safety, it also positioned the children, teachers and staff as victims and subjected bodies (Foucault, 1982). When Wanda and Mrs B drew the shades and shushed the children, telling them 'shhhh, it's just pretend', the inherent contradiction and incongruity between children's and adult's versions of 'playing at violence' was stark. More striking, however, was how this incongruous positioning of playing at violence began to bubble up in the children's play through in the months following the advent of Code Red drills.

Vignette 3: Negotiating incongruities in playing at violence

Spring has arrived and we are finally on the playground again nearly every day. Clouds and rain bursts do not dampen the children's spirits, and they love being back outside on a consistent basis. In part, this may be because, for the four players, it is much easier to play in ways that can remain hidden from Wanda and Mrs B. Though the field beyond the playground is muddy, the four players head there almost immediately each day. The play has taken on a new pattern: the four run out to the field, meet up for a few moments and then return to the perimeter of the playground, walking along the wooden beams, shouting and running under the structures, and then back out to the field to regroup. This pattern is repeated throughout recess.

'You watch that guy!' Simon shouts to Kazadi, 'I got him. He can't get us friends!'. They run under the play structure crouching, their right arms, held out a little ways from their bodies. Virginia and Kwame are the wood-beamed perimeter of the play structure, ducking and spinning, shouting 'Look out' 'Do you see that guy?!', looking in many directions. Up on the structure, Simon and Kazadi are walking around on the upper most platform. When I asked what the game is, Kazadi tells me, 'We's police, you know, making sure all the kids is safe.'

The children's right arms, held slightly away from their bodies, their hands flat, occasionally take aim and make a shooting noise. Given Wanda's clear prohibition of pretend guns, this action seems risky. As their time on the playground persists, the players seem to forget about the no guns policy and dash from the structure making firing noises, pointing their hands flat, but outstretched like guns. This flat hand way of making a gun has resulted from not being able to use wood chips anymore as pretend weapons. Several weeks earlier, Wanda decided that she had to ban woodchips from outside games, 'They are always turning them into guns. I mean they turn everything into guns. But really, they just can't play that way at school'. As with their other playing at violence, however, this just drives the game to hidden spaces: high above teachers' heads and out in the field just beyond the playground.

Several times, when the play gets especially frantic, Wanda and Mrs B turn towards the field or up towards the top of the structure. After one particularly frenzied sprint by the four players, I wander out to the field and ask about the game. 'What's happening in your game?' Virginia and Kwame run towards me, an ally adult who never seems to tell Wanda or Mrs B what I see and hear. 'We are making sure we are all safe. If those guys come up in here and hurt our friends, we are gonna get them!' Kwame tells me, out of breath. 'Which guys?' I ask. 'The guys who come on the days we hide', he tells me. 'Yeah, they are gonna pay if they hurt any of us guys!' Virginia shouts, her fists clenched at her sides. They run off again, and I wander back towards the playground where Wanda and Mrs B have turned their attention back to the rest of the class who have stayed on the playground.

Following the implementation of the Code Red drills, the children's play began to shift. This shift seemed to reflect the children's recognition of the inherent incongruity (Zupančič, 2008) that existed in the school's simultaneous suppression and introduction of playing at violence. At first the subtle change was not apparent. However, in looking across my observational data for the spring, I began to notice that following the implementation of the Code Red drills, the four players shifted their 'bad guy' play from protecting imaginary babies and families to protecting their classmates and teachers.

In this vignette, Simon and Kazadi patrol the fields surrounding the playground with Virginia and Kwame, seemingly protecting their other classmates who remain on the climbing structure near Wanda and Mrs B. Perhaps the children perceived that taking on the roles of protectors of teachers and classmates aligned more closely with the school-sanctioned version of playing and violence than the games that they were not allowed to play. What was clear was that the children were adopting this new version of playing at violence; the one that was both sanctioned by the school via Code Red drills, but also reflected the children's reimagined, powerful response to a 'bad guy' trying to hurt their friends and teachers. This new version of 'bad guy' play seemed to be framed by the children in two ways: (1) as a means of making sense of the Code Red drills and the incongruity between sanctioned and forbidden forms of playing at violence (Zupančič, 2008), and (2) as a way to flip their positioning (Foucault, 1982) from subjects of potential violence to powerful protectors of their teachers and classmates.

As noted in this vignette, this new protecting game was primarily played a distance from Wanda and Mrs B, out in the fields well beyond their hearing. In the first vignette, the four players would at some point let go of the pretence that they were using webs rather than guns. This never happened in the new game, no matter how frantic their playing became. By the spring, it was as if a wall had gone up, and adults who might stop their play were shut out entirely. It was only when they returned to the field that they would start telling each other what they were doing or had seen in relation to the 'bad guys'.

Another example of the shift in the play was that the children never brought this new version of playing at violence into the classroom. Perhaps there was simply not enough room to patrol without being noticed or questioned. Perhaps the children sensed that this new version of playing at pretend violence, where they protected their friends and teachers from a real and recognized kind of violence, was too close to the real violence that Wanda was unwilling to talk about. Though the reason was never made clear to me by the children, Kwame's statement that this new game was about protecting their classmates and teachers from 'the guys who come on the days we hide', made it clear that the four players were resisting their positioning as potential victims of violence, reclaiming their agency through powerful play (Levin, 2003; Rich, 2003).

Aside from Simon, I do not know whether the other children had talked with their parents or family members about the reasons for the Code Red drills. I did often overhear Simon, however, providing information to the other players about school shootings and other violent acts that he had either overheard on the news or discussed with his parents. Also important to consider here is how Simon's position, as the child of a Fuji teacher, as a white, middle-class student, perhaps allowed him more leeway when it came to the zero-tolerance policy. Quite often that year, Simon's mother would visit the classroom, coming and sitting and playing with the children while her students were at gym or art. This protective quality, of a mother who was an insider within the system, and of a child who knew the ins and outs of expected school behaviours that aligned with his own middle-class whiteness, should not be discounted. We know that children who align with school practices and cultural norms often experience greater leeway and support from teachers when it comes to imaginative play (Stirrup et al., 2016).

Simon's position as the leader of the playing at violence reflects his position and privilege. So too does the positioning of Kwame and Kazadi, both African-American, as implementers of the playing at violence, rather than instigators. The literature certainly indicates that the ramifications of violating school rules and zero-tolerance policies are much more severe for non-white, non-middle-class and non-primary English-speaking children (Arcia, 2007; Skiba et al., 2011). Playing at violence may have very different consequences for different groups of children, and yet play is a centrally important part of how all children make sense of the world around them.

The incongruity of these two versions of playing at violence, one embodied in the acceptable position of children and teachers as helpless victims via Code Red drills, and one framed as unacceptable via the zero-tolerance policy and Wanda's own discomfort and yet allowing the children to act powerful agents, seemed to provoke the children's need to play more. When they could not engage in dialogue about *why* they were playing at those themes, or *why* certain forms of playing at violence were sanctioned and others forbidden, or *why* they were participating in Code Red drills, the fervour and intensity that the children brought to their playing at violence seemed to increase. This is evidenced in the more hidden and frantic nature of the post-Code Red version of playing at violence as described in the above vignette. It is also evidenced in the much more hidden nature of this version of playing at violence.

In the end, no measures taken by Wanda or the school could squelch the play. The school's zero-tolerance policy and Wanda's own discomfort did not stop the children. Rather, these policies only halted meaningful and democratic dialogue. The Code Red drills added another layer of incongruity and control that the children seemed to be compelled to both make sense of and resist (MacNaughton, 2005). Not only could the children not play at pretend violence, but they were subject to pretending to be potential victims of real violence. And in neither case was there a space or support to talk about why.

For the children in Wanda's class, the combination of Code Red drills, their teachers' unpreparedness and/or unwillingness to discuss the reasons for the drills, and their interpretations of acts of violence perpetrated against students, seemed to crystalize. The play that emerged embodied their need to enact power when powerless (Foucault, 1982) and to make sense of the two versions of playing at violence that were framed in opposition to one another (Zupančič, 2008). Taking their play out into the field and up to the top of the structure (Moore, 2015), the children subverted the control of Wanda and Mrs B, once again asserting their own power and ability to reframe the most unacceptable versions of play as the most agentic. In the months after the Code Red drills began, the hidden, frenzied, and compulsive qualities of the children's play reflected the intensity with which they were insisting upon and asserting their right to make sense of their lived experiences. Virginia's clenched fists, Kwame's insistent tone ('We's police, you know, making sure all the kids is safe.'), Simon's statements to his peers ('I got him. He can't get us friends!'), and the player's justifications to me for *why* they were playing that way were all new manifestations in their playing at violence.

Discussion and conclusion

In this paper, my goal is to explore the ways in which the notions of playing at violence were constructed by a classroom teacher, Wanda, a school's zero-tolerance policy and the implementation of Code Red drills. My findings indicate child-initiated playing at violence, involving bad guy scenarios and pretend weapons, was largely framed as unacceptable. This reflected Wanda's own personal discomfort with children playing at violence, her concerns over penalties her students might experience due to the zero-tolerance policy at school, and a lack of professional support for how to have difficult conversations with children and use their play as a site for dialogue and joint sense-making.

In addition, I found that the children used play to make sense of violent events and the Code Red drills, playing out scenarios that reflected their experiences (Levin, 2003). Positioned as helpless victims during the Code Red drills, the children reacted with play scenarios in which they had power and the agency. They took on the same power that the faceless 'bad guys' in the Code Red drill held over them when they were huddled in the corner of their dark classroom. The four players became the powerful defenders of their classmates and teachers, disrupting the narrative that they were helpless victims. The consistent ways in which these four children resisted both teacher gaze and reshaping of their play into 'productive' or 'good' play, foregrounds how school rules around play can restrict the agency of young children, and yet their subversive play can be a means of reasserting their power (Foucault, 1982; Blaise & Ryan, 2012).

In an ironic twist, the Code Red drills, as the school-sanctioned version of playing at violence, became the new game of the children. In this way, the children pushed back against the incongruity of the zero-tolerance policy towards playing at pretend violence and the sanctioned playing at real violence embodied in the Code Red drills. The absurdity of these two positions, representing 'only one surface … [but also] the endless movement of contradiction' (Zupančič, 2008, pp. 54–55) was manifested in the shifting nature of the play scenarios imagined and enacted by the four players. Their expression of agency and power in the face of feeling helpless or compromised fits with what we know from research about how children utilize imaginative play to make sense and process new information and experiences (Paley, 2004). Children can actively challenge feelings of powerlessness and fear by enacting agency in places where they do have control, in this case in hidden imaginative play (Corsaro, 2003; James & Prout, 2008). In addition, when children have teachers who are well prepared to support this kind of play through discussion and shared meaning-making, it can help them to build resilience in the face of lived or imagined traumas (Berson & Baggerly, 2009). In contrast, when this play is driven underground, the opportunity to support resilience disappears.

While early childhood educators largely accept that play is a central site of sense-making for young children (Wisneski & Reifel, 2012), how schools and individual teachers frame acceptable play is important. At Fuji, there was a doubling down on framing acceptable play: first with the school-wide zero-tolerance policy towards playing at pretend violence, and second through Wanda's own discomfort and uncertainty around how to support playing at violence. In addition, Wanda's hesitation to discuss the Code Red drills, even when the children in her classroom raised questions, concerns or ideas, compounded the need for the children to make sense of this new lived experience through play that was hidden from her view (Moore, 2015). As a result, Wanda's classroom policy towards playing at pretend violence was both restrictive and 'out-of-sight' permissive. The four players could only play out their sense-making in secret, distant spaces. As Wanda noted repeatedly, there was no support, either in her professional education or via her school administration, for how to discuss the Code Red drills with the children or support their sense-making through play. The existence of the zero-tolerance policy made clear that this kind of play, regardless of what we know of children's uses of play to make sense of the world around them (MacNaughton, 2005), was simply unacceptable. As a single teacher, with little support, it is not surprising that Wanda's approach was to ignore and restrict the children's imaginative playing at violence, as well as dismiss their bids to discuss the 'why' of the Code Red drills.

While the assumption of many school and district leaders seems to be that zero-tolerance policies will help reduce unwanted behaviours, in fact these policies simply exacerbate existing inequalities around school discipline and result in higher suspension rates for African-American and Latino children (Arcia, 2007; Skiba et al., 2011). As of 2014, a federal report notes that while African-American children make up only 18% of the preschool population, they account for 48% of children receiving one or more suspensions (CRDC, 2014). In addition, if we consider play to be a central right of childhood then policies that restrict children's play without opportunities for dialogue and discourse (Millei, 2012), represent an important social justice issue in the field of early childhood education.

At Fuji, the zero-tolerance policy prevented opportunities for meaningful dialogue and for helping the children make sense of the world around them. This points to a central concern that emerged from this study: when play is restricted, rather than used as a site for joint-sense-making and dialogue, have we abandoned a central tenet of early childhood pedagogy? For this and numerous other reasons, zero-tolerance policies are ill-suited for young children, if not all children and schools. Zero-tolerance policies move the power of decision-making away from teachers who know children and their limits and abilities, and organises and controls both teachers' and children's actions to be in line with a top-down consensus of how children *should* be. This imagined child, complicit and complacent at every turn, is powerless (Foucault, 1982).

These policies stifle the subtle, democratic discourses that can empower children, teachers and other actors to play and learn in ways that are meaningful and rich, rather than strictly controlled and contrived (MacNaughton, 2005). For Wanda and the four players, their tentative agreement that playing at violence was acceptable as long as it was out of earshot (or masked in webs and unifix counting cubes, rather than pretend bullets and guns) existed incongruously with Code Red drills, where compliance and victimhood was a requirement. When the children complied with the acceptable versions of playing at violence (Spiderman and Code Red drills), their play was not questioned or forbidden. As Foucault (1982) notes, '[Power] is a total structure of actions brought to bear upon possible actions; it incites, it induces, it seduces, it makes easier or more difficult' (p. 789). The assertion of adult power over children's play, through zero-tolerance policies, adult unwillingness to discuss violence or violent themes, and adult uncertainty about how to respond to children's playing at violence are all 'brought to bear' on the rights of children to make sense of their lived experiences through play.

Perhaps what is so scary to so many adults about children playing at violence is that we cannot predict where children will take this play or what meanings they ascribe to the violent themes they choose. Unless, of course, we ask them (Millei, 2012). However, this shifts the balance of power to children. If we accept that children have an inherent right to make sense of their lives through play, we must consider how contradictory practices and perspectives within schools, communities, and broader cultural dynamics and fields of power may be blocking this right (Shimpi & Nicholson, 2014).

Giving early childhood teachers leeway to create meaningful guidelines for playing at pretend violence in their own classrooms would help teachers to understand how children are making sense of Code Red drills, as well as the real violent acts that permeate American news cycles and the conversations of parents and family members (Katch, 2001). However, these dialogues around play are not likely to occur without teacher education and professional development about how to make sense of difficult ideas and experiences with children (Grieshaber & McArdle, 2010).

While critical theorizing helps us to recognize top-down practices within school structures around play, and to push for more child-centred practices, enacting more nuanced and child-driven practices towards allowing 'playing at pretend violence' in school sites may be more difficult. In addition, early childhood teachers (and school leaders) need professional development that supports their engagement in the difficult, democratic conversations that children need and want to have about the world around them (Sherwood & Reifel, 2010a). Similarly, school communities can and should create opportunities for parents to learn how to support meaningful home conversations about safety and violence perpetrated against schools, and how to meet children's needs and concerns at home.

This paper raises questions about the costs of 'playing at real violence' in school lock-down drills, while simultaneously preventing children from 'playing at pretend violence' in order to feel powerful and in control of events that are beyond their control. Drawing attention to this incongruity allows the early childhood community to more carefully examine how we create and/or deny opportunities for children to make sense (Grieshaber & McArdle, 2010; MacNaughton, 2005) of what may continue to be a central theme in their lives: acts of violence from real 'bad guys'. If we stop the play, we drive it underground (Moore, 2015), and as a result, lose the opportunity for discussion (Millei, 2012), for identifying and processing teachers' and children's fears (Hirsh-Pasek, Michnick Golinkoff, Berk, & Singer, 2008) about their own safety within their school communities. Instead, we must support teachers and school leaders, families and children, to find ways to both productively discuss and play out the realities of young children's lives (Holland, 2003; Katch, 2001), even when we may wish to ignore these realities.

Note

1. All names in this article are pseudonyms.

Disclosure statement

No potential conflict of interest was reported by the author.

Funding

This work was supported by National Science Foundation (NSF) under Grant [1019431].

References

Arcia, E. (2007). A comparison of elementary/K-8 and middle schools' suspension rates. *Urban Education*, *42*, 456–469. doi:10.1177/0042085907304879

Bacigalupa, C., & Wright, C. (2009). And then a huge, huge giant grabbed me!" aggression in children's stories. *Early Childhood Research Practice, 11*(2), 1–16.
Bazeley, P., & Jackson, K. (Eds.). (2013). *Qualitative data analysis with NVivo*. Thousand Oaks, CA: Sage.
Berson, I. R., & Baggerly, J. (2009). Building resilience to trauma: Creating a safe and supportive early childhood classroom. *Childhood Education, 85*(6), 375–379. doi:10.1080/00094056.2009.10521404
Blaise, M., & Ryan, S. (2012). Using critical theory to trouble the early childhood curriculum. In N. File, J. J. Mueller, & D. B. Wisneski (Eds.), *Curriculum in early childhood education: Re-examined, rediscovered, renewed* (pp. 80–92). London: Routledge.
Brooker, L. (2010). *Engaging play*. New York, NY: McGraw Hill.
Copple, C., & Bredekamp, S. (2009). *Developmentally appropriate practice in early childhood programs serving children from birth through age 8*. Washington, DC: NAEYC.
Corsaro, W. A. (2003). *We're friends right?* Washington, DC: Joseph Henry Press.
CRDC. (2014). *U.S. Department of education office for civil rights: Data snapshot (Early Childhood)* Retrieved March 21, 2014 from https://www2.ed.gov/about/offices/list/ocr/docs/crdc-early-learning-snapshot.pdf
Creswell, J. W. (1998). *Qualitative inquiry and research design: Choosing among the five traditions*. Thousand Oak, CA: Sage.
Delaney, K. K. (2015). Dissonance for understanding: Exploring a new theoretical lens for understanding teacher identity formation in borderlands of practice. *Contemporary Issues in Early Childhood, 16*(4), 374–389. doi:10.1177/1463949115616326
Edmiston, B. (2008). *Forming ethical identities in early childhood play*. London: Routledge.
Foucault, M. (1979). *Discipline and punish: The birth of the prison*. New York, NY: Vintage Books.
Foucault, M. (1982). The subject and power. *Critical Inquiry, 8*(4), 777–795.
Gil, E. (2006). *Helping abused and traumatized children: Integrating directive and nondirective approaches*. New York, NY: Guilford Press.
Grieshaber, S., & McArdle, F (2010). *The trouble with play*. Maidenhead: Open University Press.
Gereluk, D. T., Donlevy, K., & Thompson, M. B. (2015). Normative considerations in the aftermath of gun violence in schools. *Educational Theory, 65*(4), 459–474. doi:10.1111/edth.12127
Henricks, T. S. (2010). Play as ascending meaning revisited: Four types of assertive play. In E. Nwokah (Ed.), *Play as engagement and communication* (pp. 189–216). Play and cultural studies (Vol. 10). Lanham, MD: University Press of America.
Hirsh-Pasek, K., Michnick Golinkoff, R., Berk, L. E., & Singer, D. (2008). A mandate for playful learning in preschool. doi:10.1093/acprof:oso/9780195382716.001.0001
Holland, P. (2003). *We don't play with guns here: War, weapon and superhero play in the early years*. Maidenhead: Open University Press.
IES. (2014). Public school safety and discipline: 2013–2014. U.S. Department of Education: National Center for Education Statistics.
James, A., & Prout, A. (Eds.). (2008). *Constructing and reconstructing childhood: Contemporary issues in the sociological study of childhood* (2nd ed.). New York, NY: Routledge.
Katch, J. (2001). *Under a deadman's skin: Discovering the meaning of children's violent play*. Boston, MA: Beacon Press.
Labaree, R. V. (2002). The risk of 'going observationalist': Negotiating the hidden dilemmas of being an insider participant observer. *Qualitative Research, 2*(1), 97–122.
Levin, D. E. (2003). Beyond banning war and superhero play: Meeting children's needs in violent times. *Young Children, 58* (May), 60–63.
Levin, D. E., & Carlsson-Paige, N. (2006). *The war play dilemma* (2nd ed). New York, NY: Teachers College Press.
Little, H., Hansen Sandsetter, E. B., & Wyver, S. (2012). Early childhood teachers' beliefs about children's risky play in Australia and Norway. *Contemporary Issues in Early Childhood, 13*(4), 300–316. doi:10.2304/ciec.2012.13.4.300
Logue, M. E., & Shelton, H. (2008). The stories bad guys tell: Promoting literacy and social awareness in preschool. *The Constructivist, 19*(1). Retrieved March 23, 2016, from http://www.odu.edu/educ/act/journal/vol19no1/FinalLogue.doc
MacNaughton, W. (2005). *Doing Foucault in early childhood studies*. London: Routledge/Falmer.
Millei, Z. (2012). Thinking differently about guidance: Power, children's autonomy and democratic environments. *Journal of Early Childhood Research, 10*(1), 88–99. doi:10.1177/1476718X11406243
Moll, L. C., Amanti, C., Neff, D., & Gonzalez, N. (1992). Funds of knowledge for teaching: Using a qualitative approach to connect homes and classrooms. *Theory into Practice, 31*(2), 132–141.
Moore, D. (2015). 'The teacher doesn't know what it is, but she knows where we are': Young children's secret places in early childhood outdoor environments. *International Journal of Play, 4*(1), 20–31. doi:10.1080/21594937.2014.925292
Morreall, J. (1983). *Taking laughter seriously*. Albany: State University of New York Press.
Paley, V. G. (1988). *Bad guys don't have birthdays: Fantasy play at four*. Chicago, IL: University of Chicago Press.
Paley, V. G. (2004). *A child's work: The importance of fantasy play*. Chicago, IL: University of Chicago Press.
Patton, M. Q. (2002). Two decades of developments in qualitative inquiry a personal, experiential perspective. *Qualitative Social Work, 1*(3), 261–283.
Peguero, A. A., Shekarkhar, Z., Popp, A. M., & Koo, D. J. (2015) Punishing the children of immigrants: race, ethnicity, generational status, student misbehavior, and school discipline. *Journal of Immigrant & Refugee Studies, 13*(2), 200–220. doi:10.1080/15562948.2014.951136

Rich, D. (2003). Bang, bang! Gun play, and why children need it. *Early Education*, (Summer), 1–6. Retrieved from http://www.richlearningopportunities.co.uk

Richardson, L., & Lockridge, E. (1998). Fiction and ethnography: A conversation. *Qualitative Inquiry*, *4*(3), 328–336.

Russell, J. L. (2010). From child's garden to academic press: The role of shifting institutional logics in redefining kindergarten education. *American Educational Research Journal*. doi:10.3102/0002831210372135

Saldana, J. (2009). *The coding manual for qualitative researchers*. New York, NY: Sage.

Samuelsson, I. P., & Carlsson, M. A. (2008). The playing learning child: Towards a pedagogy of early childhood. *Scandinavian Journal of Educational Research*, *52*(6), 623–641. doi:10.1080/00313830802497265

Sherwood, S. A., & Reifel, S. (2010a). The multiple meanings of play: Exploring preservice teachers' beliefs about a central element of early childhood education. *Journal of Early Childhood Teacher Education*, *31*(4), 322–343.

Sherwood, S. A., & Reifel, S. (2010b). Valuable and unessential: The paradox of preservice teachers' beliefs about the role of play in learning. *Journal of Research in Childhood Education*, *27*(3), 267–282.

Shimpi, P. M., & Nicholson, J. (2014). Using cross-cultural, intergenerational play narratives to explore issues of social justice and equity in discourse on children's play. *Early Child Development and Care*, *184*(5), 719–732. doi:10.1080/03004430.2013.813847

Skånfors, L., Löfdahl, A., & Hägglund, S. (2009). Hidden spaces and places in the preschool: Withdrawal strategies in preschool children's peer cultures. *Journal of Early Childhood Research*, *7*(1), 94–109. doi:10.1177/1476718X08098356

Skiba, R. J., Horner, R. H., Chung, C. G., Rausch, M. K., May, S. L., & Tobin, T. (2011). Race is not neutral: A national investigation of African American and Latino disproportionality in school discipline. *School Psychology Review*, *40*(1), 85. doi:10.1007/978-1-4939-0863-9_7

Spradley, J. P. (1979). *The ethnographic interview*. Belmont, CA: Wadsworth.

Stake, R. E. (1995). *The art of case study research*. Thousand Oaks, CA: Sage.

Stirrup, J., Evans, J., & Davies, B. (2016). Early years learning, play pedagogy and social class. *British Journal of Sociology of Education*, 1–12. doi:10.1080/01425692.2016.1182010

Watson, C. (2015). A sociologist walks into a bar (and other academic challenges): Towards a methodology of humor. *Sociology*, *49*(3), 407–421.

Wisneski, D. B., & Reifel, S. (2012). The place of play in early childhood curriculum. In N. File, J. J. Mueller, & D. B. Wisneski (Eds.), *Curriculum in early childhood education: Re-examined, rediscovered, renewed* (pp. 175–187). London: Routledge.

Yin, R. K. (2003). *Case study research: Design and methods*. Thousand Oaks, CA: Sage.

Zupančič, A. (2008). *The odd one in: On comedy*. Cambridge: MIT Press.

Where is my stuff? Conceptualizing Hip Hop as 'play'

Anthony Broughton

ABSTRACT
Cultural continuity between home and school has been emphasized in a range of research concerning diversity and multicultural education (Colombo, M. (2005). Reflections from teachers of culturally diverse children. *Young Children, Beyond the Journal, 60*(6). Retrieved from http://www.journal.naeyc.org/btj/200511/ColomboBTJ1105.asp). However, research that examines ways Hip Hop culture can be conceptualized as 'play' in early childhood contexts is dismal. This dearth of literature regarding Hip Hop play suggests that Hip Hop play may not be regularly occurring or documented in early childhood classroom/learning settings. However, we do know that when culture is bridged from the home of some children to their schools, and when children experience positive outcomes academically and personally. This paper explores the possibilities of Hip Hop culture as 'play' as an approach for nurturing children's development, cultural competence, cultural identities, and individual identities; and the power dynamics of teaches choosing to 'allow', sustain, and 'support' Hip Hop play.

Introduction

As natural inquisitors, children are very inquisitive about the world around them – especially about themselves and others, how things operate, why things operate the way they do, where babies come from, why skin tones and hair texture differ, and a vast array of other topics and concepts. Though children engage in inquiry, learning, and exploration (e.g. life experiences) as natural inquisitors, it should be noted that children are also astute, conscientious, and competent in skills, concepts, subjects, and content in which they may have not yet mastered the development competencies to communicate to adults (Boutte, 1999, 2015). However, adults can identify the cultural identities, knowledge, emotions, perspectives, special needs, and developmental competencies (e.g. developing phonological awareness, mastering self-regulation, social–emotional skills) and expressions of children through play (Hoorn, Nourot, Scales, & Alward, 2011). 'Play is an expression of the child's developing personality, sense of self, intellect, social capacity, and physicality. At the same time, through their play, children direct their energy towards activities of their own choice. These activities stimulate further development' (Hoorn et al., 2011, p. 4).

Unfortunately, many children of colour are and have been historically negatively impacted by the mainstream experience in formal school/child-care settings, where many teachers and administrators undervalue, invalidate, and underappreciate differences (e.g. cultural play, customs, and communication modes) or cultures other than European/European American (Au, 1993; Boutte, 1999; Colombo, 2005; Gay, 2013, 2002; Hilliard, 1991; Woodson, 1933). Such experiences may lead to some children of colour feeling uncomfortable, alienated, marginalized, and inferior to their white counterparts (Boutte, 2015; Gay, 2002), which has impacted the academic performance and personal development of some children of colour (Ladson-Billings, 2006; Noguera, 2014; Perry, Steele, & Hilliard, 2003; Woodson, 1933). Sadly, children may fall victim to culturally insensitive learning settings and encounter feelings of alienation and marginalization when they are not culturally affirmed (Derman-Sparks & Edwards, 2010; Emdin, 2011). In early learning settings, children should be encouraged to engage in 'play' in ways that are culturally affirming (Dodge, Colker, & Heroman, 2002; Hoorn et al., 2011). However, play can be subjective. What constitutes as 'play' for one teacher or caregiver may vary for another teacher (NAEYC, 2014).

What happens when the 'expression' of some children's 'personality, sense of self, intellect, social capacity, and physicality' (Hoorn et al., 2011, p. 4), manifests as Hip Hop during play? With an awareness of dismal research conceptually exploring Hip Hop culture as play, this article explores Hip Hop as 'play' in early childhood curriculums where some teachers embrace the 'stuff' (i.e. cultural values, cultural customs, individuality, etc.) that children bring with them to early learning settings. First, I begin by identifying foundational issues to contextualize Hip Hop play. Second, since Hip Hop is multidimensional and very complex to define within the confinement of an article, I provide a brief backdrop of Hip Hop. Third, I theoretically frame Hip Hop as 'play' for young children. Fourth, I provide recommendations for teachers and administrators who desire to consider the 'voices' (perspectives, ideas, beliefs, culture, interests) of children through Hip Hop play.

Exploring foundational issues

Considering the premise that play is essential to nurturing the development of the 'Whole child' (e.g. culturally, physically, intellectually, individually, etc.; ASCD, 2014), I contend that if conceptualizations of cultural play are not extended beyond tokenism approaches and deficit thinking (Cannella, 2002) children of colour may become invariably marginalized, especially developmentally, because they are not supported in ways that are culturally affirming or culturally relevant (Boutte, 2015; Kincheloe, 2008; Kunjufu, 2002, 2005; Ladson-Billings, 2006; Noguera, 2008; Woodson, 1933) in early learning settings (Derman-Sparks & Ramsey, 2011). For instance, research regarding rap in early childhood is moderately increasing which frames rap as something to be 'used' to teach children from a direct instructional standpoint (Rando, O'Connor, Steuerwalt, & Bloom, 2014) while, in contrast there is a dearth of research that comprehensively explores Hip Hop pedagogy (which encompasses 'rap') as something to be fostered, embodied, cultivated and primarily student generated in the context of early childhood classrooms and learning settings (Love, 2015). Knowing that many children of colour engage in Hip Hop in their communities (Love, 2015) and research literature that explores or conceptualizes how early childhood teachers or caregivers support Hip Hop in their early learning settings is scant, Hip Hop as 'play' in early learning settings should be explored and investigated.

Although Hoorn et al. (2011) suggested that children make 'their own choice' (p. 4) regarding activities and play, researchers such as Cannella (2002) who examines critical issues in early childhood suggested otherwise. Whether or not Hip Hop as 'play' is valued in early childhood settings/classrooms, Kincheloe (2008) contended that teachers hold the power to make decisions. Such decisions which are informed by the worldviews and perspectives of teachers may positively or negatively impact the trajectory of children into adulthood (Gay, 2002; Kunjufu, 2005). Thus, it is essential for research literature regarding culture, such as Hip Hop, to contribute to the cultural competence development of teachers to support them in understanding the divergent children in which they are charged to care for.

For many children, Hip Hop is connected to identity and we need to create classrooms that includes, respects and celebrates children, their families and their identities. However, we have many teachers who may outright reject Hip Hop (Love, 2015; Simmons et al., 2013) which therefore denies children of the culturally responsive environment that would help them to thrive. Baring the multifaceted history of Hip Hop in mind, the notion of defining Hip Hop is complex. Thus, the following background represents a brief historical overview of Hip Hop, acknowledging the multifaceted attribute of Hip Hop.

Brief background on Hip Hop

> The death of civil rights; the militarization of urban space; the infiltration of political movements (Black Panthers, Brown Berets, Young Lords); massive joblessness; urban blight the dozens; the digital age; declining parks, schools, and youth programs; and innovation, creativity and play – all have collectively converged to make Hip Hop's origins multifaceted, politically conflicting, consistently debated, and highly complicated. (Akom, 2009, p. 53)

For many people of colour, the social climate of the United States posed economic and social justice challenges (Chang, 2005). With racial tension still steaming from several devastating events from the Civil rights era as the United States transitioned from industrialization to new and advancing technologies, many Americans, particularly Black American and people of colour experienced increasing unemployment, poverty, as many White business or upper class Americans migrated to suburbs, consequently abandoning cities which became poor (Chang, 2005; Rose, 1994). Amid poverty, and social ills that stemmed thereof was several budget cuts in education in which truncated art programmes from several urban schools (Rose, 1994). Further complicating this social climate, the urban renewal platform of engineer, Robert Moses led him to spearhead the construction of the Cross Bronx Expressway in New York, which destroyed many ethnic neighbourhoods; consequently, displacing poor community members to areas like east Brooklyn and South Bronx (Chang, 2005; Tanz, 2007). Youth, amid these social conditions, streamlined their talents, marginal resources, cultural arts and self-expression to manifest an 'underground', or non-mainstream culture, Hip Hop. Hip Hop evolved over time from African/Black expression aesthetics such as call-and-response, improvization, syncopated rhythm and beats (Perkins, 1996).

Aspects of Hip Hop can be traced from the 1920s with dance moves from African-American performers like Earl 'Snake Hips' Tucker in the Cotton Club, to the pioneering style of jazz rhyming called the 'jive scat' of Cab Calloway; whom is referred to as the grandfather of rap music (Perkins, 1996). While the exact birth date is challenging to pinpoint, Hip Hop scholars and pioneers such as Grandmaster Flash, Kool Herc, and Afrika Bambaataa (African-American male youth at the time who engaged in Hip Hop) have formed a consensus that rap originated in the South Bronx in 1974 (Perkins, 1996).

The youth at the time of the 'origination' of Hip Hop in the 1970s sought Hip Hop as a viable coping mechanism to the social ills prevalent in middle-lower class Americans in the urban area (Chang, 2005; Rose, 1994; Tanz, 2007). Hip Hop served as a social outlet to openly express many of their thoughts and perspectives, while enjoying the 'fun' they socially constructed in the midst of chaos. Many of the youth would congregate in the park, on the block (block party) or outside housing apartments to socialize and to dance to music from turn tables and exchange rhymes (rap). Highly expressive, energetic, charismatic, and outspoken youth, who often led 'call-and-response' chants, acting as the master/mistress of ceremonies – which was the block party, were known as the MC's. As technology evolved, urban youth artists became disc jockey's like, DJ Kool Herc (the 'father' of Hip Hop), a who advantageously began to manipulate music technology such as turntables to mix records and create 'breaks', or instrumental, rhythmic portions of songs. During these 'breaks', youth typically created complex dance moves, which later became a competitive form of dance called break-dancing or b-boy/bgirl dance. Even without music, many artists innovatively used their mouth as an instrument to make beats, which is called beat boxing. As the social ills of society continued, the urban youth evolved Hip Hop and aspects such as graffiti writing/art, a type of street literacy which served as the visual aspect of Hip Hop to amplify their marginalized voices; since many felt voiceless or helpless in a social climate (Chang, 2005; Rose, 1994; Tanz, 2007). The urban youth began to draw from spoken word art forms styles such as that of Gil Scott-Heron, an African-American poet, music, and author; and braggadocios rhyming styles like that of Muhammad Ali (Perkins, 1996).

Urban youth Hip Hop artists manifested rap, an amalgamation of spoken word, braggadocios rhyming, over rhythmic beats. Hip Hop pioneers, such as DJ (Disc Jockey) Afrika Bambattaa a Black male youth at the time, who promoted peace amongst gangs, began to streamline knowledge of self and traditional African cultural perspectives into Hip Hop; thus inspiring 'conscious rap' (Perkins, 1996). Break-dancing, rap, graffiti writing/art, MCing, beat boxing, and self-knowledge all comprise up Hip Hop culture (Chang, 2005; Hill, 2009; Love, 2015; Rose, 1994). Hip Hop, with a very complex, and multi-dimensional form and history collectively serves as the identity of many people who have been historically marginalized. For some, Hip Hop culture was and is a vehicle to cope with the social ills of society and/or to express themselves without creative restriction. For instance, a person may use various aspects of Hip Hop to cope or express themselves; such as through rap with rhythmic words and rhymes; through graffiti writing with visual artistic expressions of their thoughts and identities; and through break-dancing which may be a physical method of self-expression (Chang, 2005; Rose, 1994). While social ills still exist (Kozol, 2005) Hip Hop is a global phenomenon, which enhances the likelihood that children will encounter people (e.g. family members, community members, local artists) in Hip Hop communities of practice who engage in Hip Hop; and begin to create Hip Hop themselves (Love, 2015), which may emerge as 'play' for some young children.

Hip Hop in early childhood education as 'play'

According to Kemple, Batey, and Hartle (2004) 'Because young children engage in music as play, it makes sense to offer musical activities during choice time' (p. 32). If teachers fail to sacrifice 'teacher-controlled activities' for musical play, the creativity and autonomy of children can be constrained (Kemple et al., 2004). This may require teachers to position themselves as 'learners' so the children can 'teach' them what they can do and what they know. As children engage in music as play, they can become the more knowledgeable other, sharing a wealth of information (that teachers may not be aware of) about themselves, which can inform teachers in constructing holistic views about children. The Association for Supervision and Curriculum Development (ASCD & CDC, 2014), refers to this view as the *Whole Child*, which is an integration and collaboration between health and education to support the social–emotional, cognitive, and physical development of all children.

'Play is a human phenomenon that occurs across the life span, as well as cultures' (Hoorn et al., 2011, p. 4). The notion of play spanning across life span suggests the complexity and multidimensionality of play. Play looks differently in various contexts with different people. The activities children engage in during play may be informed by their culture, personal interests, location, experiences, and perceptions (Hoorn et al., 2011). Thus, children's play may be informed by Hip Hop because it is a culture (Derman-Sparks & Edwards, 2010). According to Love (2015), children are typically informed their 'Hip Hop communities of practice' (Love, 2015, p. 110). That is, essentially a context in which people engage in Hip Hop in ways that can be analysed to understand how and why people engage in Hip Hop. Analysing Hip Hop play from a 'Hip Hop community of practice' perspective, may support scholars (including teachers) in understanding some of the children in their class who come from these communities (Love, 2015).

According to Love (2015), 'Children raised in a Hip Hop community of practice are developing cognitive skills by participating, observing, and being in physical and digital proximity to Hip Hop cultural practitioners and influencers' (p. 112). By digital proximity, Love (2015) referred to the notion that many children may encounter Hip Hop culture through books, music and children's television programmes. Streamlining songs and musical styles from the communities of children can foster continuity between home and the childcare setting; and possibly validate the culture of children while nurturing their sense of safety and security (Parlakian & Lerner, 2010). What are experiences like for children who come from Hip Hop communities of practice into early childcare settings where Hip Hop is not visible; thus consequently lack of continuity from their homes? Where is their 'stuff?' Fasting forward into the adulthood of Hip Hop scholar, Dr Christopher Emdin recollects 'feeling invisible' in his biology class as an older student until the moments in which he felt validated by his friends when he was in a 'space' in which he could engage in Hip Hop (Emdin, 2011, p. 11).

Validating the cultural identity of children by reflecting some home/community practices through play such as cooperative learning heightens the likelihood of promoting success for children (Boutte, 2015; Richards, Brown, & Forde, 2004). In such settings, children are able to play and interact with others using their cultural practices (e.g. rapping) to communicate in ways that are reflective of their identity, because teachers honour the home cultural values and norms of children (Derman-Sparks & Edwards, 2010). As young children are dancing and generating moves, they can develop social–emotional skills, such as making friends and resolving conflicts (Lobo & Winsler, 2006). This may be the same for children who engage in Hip Hop play. Further research is needed to explore this notion.

Play is described by features such as spontaneous, guided, and teacher directed (Van Hoorn, Nourot, Scales, & Alward, 2011). 'Spontaneous play refers to behaviours that arise from intrinsic motivation, that are self-directed, and that represent expressions of children's own interest and desires' (Van Hoorn et al., 2011, p. 10). This type of play may allow children to naturally manifest their culture in the context of their childcare setting. It is during this type of play that teachers may learn about the culture (perspectives, ideas, history, interests) of their children (Van Hoorn et al., 2011). Like Hip Hop, play is also linked to divergent thinking and coping ability (Christiano & Russ, 1996; Fiorelli & Russ, 2012). Hip Hop as play may manifest as spontaneous play, guided play, or teacher directed play in scenarios such as the following:

Type of play	Example	Areas of development
Spontaneous play	Four-year-old Stasha and Chase are break-dancing to the beats of some instrumental Hip Hop music. Sarah, John, and Shawn join them and decide that they wanted to make it a 'dance battle competition'. In another area of the class, in Dramatic Play centre two four-year-olds, Malcom and Jake are performing a 'concert'	*Social–emotional*: Children were collaborating and working together to create dances or music *Physical*: Children were moving working their small and large muscles *Language*: A child introduced new vocabulary 'dance battle completion' and 'concert' to peers
Guided play	Mrs Wigfall places a large bulletin board paper in a designated area in the classroom. She places markers, paints, die cut letters, pencils, crayons, and pens in a bin and adds them to the area. She then draws her name using her favourite colours and draws bear claws around it. Her graffiti writing conveys information about her favourite colours and her favourite football team's mascot. She models for the children how they can express themselves with the graffiti art/writing wall	*Social–emotional*: Mrs Wigfall models for children how to express one's self *Physical*: Children will use small motor skills in their hands to grip the art/writing tools *Cognitive*: Children will think of what to draw/write and others will interpret what they draw/write
Teacher directed play	Mr Parker creates a rap to help children learn about patterns. Seven kindergarteners gather around Mr Parker and begin to repeat the rhymes. Mr Parker recites one rap verse and the children repeat after him	*Social–emotional*: Mr Parker welcomes all children to come together to rap. Children learn how to work together through song *Language*: The children learn mathematical terms for different shapes. They practice pronunciation of the words while learning rhyming words in the rap *Cognitive*: Children mentally process the lyrics of the rap song. They interpret the lyrics for understanding

The worldviews, experiences, and perceptions that teachers bring with them to their classrooms oftentimes influences the decision-making (Kincheloe, 2008). This means that their personal perception and understandings may shape their curriculum and classroom environment. Teachers and administrators must be conscious of this inevitable personal bias and work towards ensuring that their bias does not impede the personal and academic growth and development of children. Professional development opportunities that welcome 'funds of knowledge' of people from various cultures (Moll, Amanti, Neff, & Gonzalez, 1992) may support teachers in unpacking their biases and assumptions with 'new' divergent knowledge (Boutte, 2015; Freire, 1970; Gay, 2002; Kincheloe, 2008). That is, teachers value the wealth of cultural knowledge that children and their families possess and begin to learn from that knowledge. Kincheloe (2008) suggested that teachers can engage in ongoing critical reflection to evaluate their approaches and decision-making. Through such reflection, teachers may be able to self-critique themselves and each other to address the negative perceptions or conceptions that they hold. Through such an ongoing, collaborative process, teachers may uncover new ideas, perspectives, and understandings that may support them in re-conceptualizing their thinking. Armed with new, divergent knowledge, teachers may uncover for themselves that some of their knowledge is deficit, incomplete, or distorted (Adichie, 2009; Kincheloe, 2008). It is through this self-discovery that teachers develop a premise that all ways of being and cultural identities should be reflected, sustained, and cultivated in classrooms because children have rights as human beings to be supported developmentally with equity and social justice in mind (Derman-Sparks & Edwards, 2010).

The reality is that many teachers may unintentionally employ a tokenism approach to 'addressing' culture by simply playing and dancing to rap music or state that they 'don't like Hip Hop or don't know how to foster Hip Hop Play' as a deflective mechanism. Thus, I recommend the following to share knowledge with teachers who already value Hip Hop as 'play'; and to support teachers who are willing to consider, conceptualize, or re-conceptualize cultivating Hip Hop as 'play'.

Recommendations for teachers

1. Teachers should recognize and acknowledge the impact of their power as teachers. Teachers must critically engage in ongoing introspection to examine how their personal biases, personal beliefs and worldviews impact their decision-making and change their thinking and instructional approaches (King, 1991). According to Kincheloe (2008) education is inherently political. Meaning the very nature and structure of schooling is composed of politics. School districts, some teachers and administration decide upon curriculum, assessments, policy, funding, etc. Teachers make curricular decisions on a daily basis. These decisions may be based on scholarly work, school/district policy, theory, personal preferences, and bias. Teachers must first recognize and acknowledge the impact their worldviews have on their decision-making, before they are able to reflect upon how and if they will modify their practices (King, 1991). To change, we must first acknowledge the need to change. Otherwise, teachers may take on colourblind stances diminishing the prevalent issues of race and diversity (King, 1991). Therefore, teachers must reflect upon their dispositions and how they have unintentionally perpetuated some of these issues. If a teacher dislikes Hip Hop, has subscribed to limited, distorted, and deficient information regarding Hip Hop and does not have desire to learn about Hip Hop knowing that Hip Hop interests children, what are their actions inconspicuously conveying dysconscious racism?
2. Teachers must develop cultural competence (Gay, 2002) and expand their conceptualizations of Hip Hop (Chang, 2005; Dyson, 2007; Edwards, 2009; Emdin, 2010; Rose, 1994) and other cultures different (Boutte, 1999) than their own by becoming an active scholar (Kincheloe, 2008). This may support teachers in building and sustaining relationships with their students. Research has shown the benefits of positive, meaningful, and authentic teacher–student relationships (Foster, 1997). Such relationships are based upon teachers' ability to understand, nurture, and support students holistically which supports the countering of cultural mismatch between teachers and students. Teachers must be open to exploring the cultures and the subcultures of their students. This may require that teachers use various methods that will allow the students opportunities to teach their teachers about their cultures. In terms of Hip Hop play, this may entail a teacher asking students questions about their performances or experiences during Hip Hop play. Teachers should also consider attending and sustaining visibility at student's events in the community.
3. *Teachers must engage in ongoing professional development to continue to evolve personally and professionally.* This endeavour may be achieved through individual research, study groups, observation, small groups, coaching, teacher mentorship, collaboration, team planning, meetings, online collaboration, college courses, workshops, conferences (Mizell, 2010), and live performances. Teachers must engage in personal and professional development because they desire to learn more and evolve as a teacher; rather than desiring to meet school required professional

development expectations. Professional development for Hip Hop play could involve teacher assistants, instructional coaches, administrators, paraprofessionals, community members and others. Community members could consist of families, local Hip Hop scholars or local Hip Hop artists would could demonstrate, engage, and reciprocally educate and learn during professional development process. Hip Hop artists, Hip Hop pedagogical scholars, Hip Hop scholars or older students who engage in Hip Hop could assist teachers in ongoing assistance and feedback. To support the effective usage of data, I suggest that instructional coaches and Hip Hop scholars (which can be a student who is a Hip Hop artist) to provide ongoing support and assist teachers in analysing their data and applying their data to curriculum and instructional planning. Additionally, teachers should also engage in action research to improve their instructional practices (Kincheloe, 2008) and supplement the dearth of research regarding Hip Hop pedagogy and Hip Hop play.

4. *Teachers must develop authentic and meaningful relationships with children, families, and community members.* Teachers must unpack, analyse, interrogate and overcome negative stereotypical perceptions of low-income Latino/a American, Black American, and Native Americans such as a belief that those families undervalue education (Boutte, 1999). Contrastingly, I purport that instead many Latino/a, Black, and Native Americans have been historically miseducated (Hilliard, 1991; Woodson, 1933), and negatively impacted by the 'schooling' process (Boutte, 1999; Kincheloe, 2008; Kunjufu, 2002, 2005; Ladson-Billings, 2006; Noguera, 2008). In fact, rappers such as Tupac Shakur (McQuillar & Johnson, 2010) and DMX (Fontaine, 2002) have unveiled how their negative experiences with schooling negatively impacted their lives. Fontaine (2002) shared a glimpse into DMX's schooling experiences, 'As the third grade went on, I started getting bored… Nothing in school inspired me and after I learned all of the material and finished all of the assignments the gave me, I didn't have anything else to do' (p. 28). This experience reminds us that building relationships with students will require more than teachers who are 'nice' or make students 'feel good' (Ladson-Billings, 1995a, 1995b) but also teachers who demand the best from their students in many ways such as challenging them and having high expectations (Boutte, 2015; Ladson-Billings, 1995a, 1995b; Lynn, 2006) through, 'tough love' (Boutte, 2015, p. 114).

Conclusion

In order to provide environment in which children are able to freely express themselves through, much consideration must be made to culture and the role of culture in play. As the populations of students continue to become increasingly diverse, educators must be willing to grow as scholars to expand notions of culture and notions of play. This will require the teachers, administrators, and all stake holders continue to grow as life-long learners. We can learn much from how children make meaning of their learning through Hip Hop play.

Disclosure statement

No potential conflict of interest was reported by the author.

References

Adichie, C. (2009). *The danger of a single story*. TED: Ideas worth spreading. Retrieved February 6, 2015, from http://www.ted.com/talks/chimamanda_adichie_the_danger_of_a_single_story.html

Akom, A. (2009). Critical hip hop pedagogy as a form of liberatory praxis. *Equity and Excellence in Education*, *42*(1), 52–66.

ASCD & CDC. (2014). *Whole school whole community whole child: A collaborative approach to learning and health*. Retrieved from http://www.ascd.org/ASCD/pdf/siteASCD/publications/wholechild/wscc-a-collaborative-approach.pdf

Au, K. H. (1993). *Literacy instruction in multicultural settings*. New York, NY: Harcourt-Brace.

Boutte, G. (1999). *Multicultural education: Raising consciousness*. Belmont, CA: Wadsworth.

Boutte, G. S. (2015). *Educating African American students: And how are the children?* New York, NY: Routledge.

Cannella, G. (2002). *Deconstructing early childhood education: Social justice and revolution*. New York, NY: Peter Lang.

Chang, J. (2005). *Can't stop, won't stop: A history of the hip hop generation*. New York, NY: Basic Civitas.

Christiano, B., & Russ, S. (1996). Play as a predictor of coping and distress in children during an invasive dental procedure. *Journal of Clinical Child Psychology, 25*, 130–138.

Colombo, M. (2005). Reflections from teachers of culturally diverse children. *Young Children, Beyond the Journal, 60*(6). Retrieved from http://www.journal.naeyc.org/btj/200511/ColomboBTJ1105.asp

Derman-Sparks, L., & Edwards, J. O. (2010). *Anti-bias education for young children and ourselves*. Washington, DC: National Association for the Education of Young Children.

Derman-Sparks, L., & Ramsey, P. (2011). *What if all the kids are white? Anti-bias/multicultural teaching strategies* (2nd ed.). New York, NY: Teachers College Press.

Dodge, D. T., Colker, L., & Heroman, C. (2002). *The creative curriculum for preschool* (4th ed.). Washington, DC: Teaching Strategies.

Dyson, M. E. (2007). *Know what I mean? Reflections on hip-hop*. New York, NY: Basic Civitas Books.

Edwards, P. (2009). *How to rap: The art and Science of the hip-hop MC*. Chicago, IL: Chicago Review Press.

Emdin, C. (2010). Affiliation and alienation: Hip-hop, rap and urban science education. *Journal of Curriculum Studies, 42*(1), 1–25.

Emdin, C. (2011). Moving beyond the boat without a paddle: Reality pedagogy, black youth, and urban science education. *The Journal of Negro Education, 80*(3), 284–295.

Fiorelli, J., & Russ, S. (2012). Pretend play, coping, and subjective well-being in children: A follow-up study. *American Journal of Play, 5*(1), 81–103.

Fontaine, S. D. (2002). *E.A.R.L.: The autobiography of DMX*. New York, NY: Harper Collins.

Foster, M. (1997). *Black teachers on teaching*. New York, NY: The New Press.

Freire, P. (1970). *Pedagogy of the oppressed*. New York, NY: Continuum.

Gay, G. (2002). Preparing for culturally responsive teaching. *Journal of Teacher Education, 53*(2), 106–116.

Gay, G. (2013). Teaching to and through cultural diversity. *Curriculum Inquiry, 43*(1), 48–70.

Hill, M. L. (2009). *Beats, rhymes, and classroom life: Hip-hop pedagogy and the politics of identity*. New York, NY: Teachers College Press.

Hilliard, A. G., III. (1991). Do we have the will to educate all children? *Educational Leadership, 49*(1), 31–36.

Hoorn, J., Nourot, P., Scales, B., & Alward, K. (2011). *Play at the center of the curriculum*. Upper Saddle River, NJ: Pearson.

Kemple, K. M., Batey, J. J., & Hartle, L. C. (2004). Music play: Creating centers for musical play and exploration. *Young Children, 59*(4), 30–37. Retrieved from www.naeyc.org/files/tyc/file/MusicPlay.pdf

Kincheloe, J. L. (2008). *Critical pedagogy: Primer*. New York, NY: Peter Lang.

King, J. (1991). *Dysconscious racism: Ideology, identity, and the miseducation of teachers. The Journal of Negro Education, 60* (2), 133–146.

Kozol, J. (2005). *The shame of the nation: The restoration of apartheid schooling in America*. New York, NY: Crown Publishers.

Kunjufu, J. (2002). *Black students middle class teachers*. Chicago, IL: African American Images.

Kunjufu, J. (2005). *Keeping Black boys out of special education*. Chicago, IL: African American Images.

Ladson-Billings, G. (1995a). But that's just good teaching! The case for culturally relevant pedagogy. *Theory Into Practice, 34*(3), 159–165.

Ladson-Billings, G. (1995b). Toward a theory of culturally relevant pedagogy. *American Educational Research Journal, 32*(3), 465–491.

Ladson-Billings, G. (2006). From the achievement gap to the education debt: Understanding achievement in U.S. schools. *Educational Researcher, 35*(7), 3–12.

Lobo, Y. B., & Winsler, A. (2006). The effects of a creative dance and movement program on the social competence of head start preschoolers. *Social Development, 15*(3), 501–519.

Love, B. L. (2015). What is hip hop-based education doing in nice fields like early childhood and elementary education? *Urban Education, 50*(1), 106–131.

Lynn, M. (2006). Education for the community: Exploring the culturally relevant practices of Black male teachers. *Teachers College Record*, 108, 2497–2522.

McQuillar, T. L., & Johnson, F. (2010). *Tupac Shakur*. Cambridge, MA: Dacapo Press.

Mizell, H. (2010). *Why professional development matters*. Oxford, OH: Learning Forward.

Moll, L., Amanti, C., Neff, D., & Gonzalez, N. (1992). Funds of knowledge for teaching: Using a qualitative approach to connect homes and classrooms. *Theory Into Practice, 31*(2), 132–141.

NAEYC. (2014, May). *Defining and advocating for play. Young Children*. Washington, DC: Author.

Noguera, P. (2008). *The trouble with black boys and other reflections on race, equity, and the future of public education*. San Francisco, CA: Wiley & Sons.
Noguera, P. (2014). Urban schools and the Black male 'challenge'. In H. R. Milner IV & K. Lomotey (Eds.), *Handbook of urban education* (pp. 114–128). New York, NY: Routledge.
Parlakian, R., & Lerner, C. (2010). Beyond twinkle, twinkle: Using music with infants and toddlers. *Young Children, 65*(2), 14–19.
Perkins, W. E. (1996). *Droppin' science: Critical essays on rap music and hip hop culture*. Philadelphia, PA: Temple University Press.
Perry, T., Steele, C., & Hilliard, A., III. (2003). *Young, gifted, and Black: Promoting high achievement among African American students*. Boston, MA: Beacon Press.
Rando, B., O'Connor, E. A., Steuerwalt, K., & Bloom, M. (2014). Raps and young children: Encouraging emergent literacy. *Young Children, 69*(3), 28–33.
Richards, H., Brown, A., & Forde, T. (2004). *Addressing diversity in schools: Culturally responsive pedagogy*. Denver, CO: National Center for Culturally Responsive Educational Systems (Practitioner Brief Series).
Rose, T. (1994). *Black noise: Rap music and black culture in contemporary America*. Hanover, NH: Wesleyan University Press.
Simmons, R., Carpenter, R., Ricks, J., Walker, D., Parks, M., & Davis, M. (2013). African American male teachers and African American students: Working subversively through Hip Hop in three urban schools. *International Journal of Critical Pedagogy, 4*(2), 69–86.
Tanz, J. (2007). *Other people's property: A shadow history of hip-hop in White America*. New York, NY: Bloomsbury.
Van Hoorn, J., Nourot, P., Scales, B., & Alward, K. (2011). *Play at the center of the curriculum* (5 th ed.). New York: Prentice-Hall.
Woodson, C. G. (1933). *The mis-education of the Negro*. New York, NY: Wilder Publications.

They're lovin' it: how preschool children mediated their funds of knowledge into dramatic play†

Anne Karabon

ABSTRACT
The funds of knowledge framework promotes connecting community contexts with curriculum aimed to activate children's prior knowledge. Typically, teachers determine what knowledge sources harmonise best with their existing programming, potentially omitting particular resources that may not align. Young children, on the other hand, can act as agents when integrating knowledge for themselves into play. This article explores how children mediated their cultural knowledge into dramatic play and what factors were key to empowering children to naturally incorporate funds of knowledge across contexts. Grounded in critical sociocultural theory, findings reveal that children use mediation as a form of power and agency to act as experts in their learning experiences and interactions with others. Early childhood educators must design a classroom space that is consistent and promotes social interactions, establish relationships with and amongst children, support the co-construction of new understandings of the world, and recognise and honour all sources of knowledge.

Introduction

A central tenet of the *fund of knowledge* [FoK] framework in education is for teachers to design learning experiences that draw from children's historical, social, and cultural knowledge. From the earliest writings, scholars linked Vygotsky's theoretical approaches of learning and development to the transformative power of drawing on children's cultural ways of knowing for curriculum planning (Moll, Amanti, Neff, & González, 1992). The emphasis was to understand the rich social and linguistic resources present in all children's daily lives and communities. In early childhood classrooms where play continues to be the centre of curriculum, this means providing a context for young children to negotiate and co-construct new understandings that are connected to their cultural resources (Wisneski & Reifel, 2012).

Funds of knowledge methodology places the teacher as a learner in students' lifeworlds with the onus on the teacher to determine what cultural knowledge and content is of value to transfer across contexts. In an attempt to know their students holistically as children rather than just in the context of schooling, teachers can use a number of tools, such as neighbourhood observations, home visitations, attending extracurricular events, games, and performances, to move toward an asset-based perspective. Challenges exit as a tendency is to identify daily home practices and skills that best align with the existing curriculum and are positive (Zipin, 2009). In addition to this romanticised

---

†The opinions expressed in this paper do not necessarily reflect the position, policy, or endorsement of the National Science Foundation.

view of FoK, teachers must navigate power roles and boundaries with families (Rodriguez, 2013; Whyte & Karabon, 2016) and recognise that their own professional and personal FoK that influences what they improvisationally draw on in play (Graue, Whyte, & Karabon, 2015).

Teachers have responded to these concerns by encouraging students to determine their own FoK and actively design lessons and curriculum around their self-selected resources and skills (Thomson & Hall, 2008). Children study and share family traditions, histories, and activities with classmates to further understandings of differing perspectives and unpack biases. More informally, young children incorporate these elements into play. For instance, in the dramatic play area, children reproduce real-life scenarios in their own imaginative way. Given the incredible influence mass media has on their lives, this may mean that young children will opt for FoK based on popular culture (Hedges, 2011). Early educators may grapple with identifying this knowledge as valuable to learning at school because it may not align with the disciplinary focus of the existing curricula.

The research presented here focuses on the dramatic play area of a preschool classroom to examine factors were key to empowering children to naturally incorporate FoK in learning. More specifically, this study focuses on children's recreation of McDonald's™ to learn how children mediate their cultural knowledge across contexts.

Review of literature

Play

Play remains a cornerstone of curriculum for young children (Van Hoorn, Nourot, Scales, & Alward, 2014). It places learning and development within children's social and cultural contexts (Vygotsky, 1978). Play is an opportunity for children to connect various elements of their lives together to replicate what they know and socially construct new understandings as they engage with others, materials, and the environment. Often referred to as their 'work', when children play they have the opportunity to creatively and imaginatively imitate previous experiences they participated in or observed (Rogoff, 2003).

The dramatic play area is one such space in early childhood settings that lends itself for children to demonstrate culturally and socially learned practices, such as cooking or family interactions. The space typically includes a combination of realistic objects (e.g. phone, utensils, clothes) that direct the play as well as open-ended materials (blocks, boxes) to promote imaginative manipulation. Children make a narrative by sharing knowledge through plot lines of play, character role play, and reenactments (McDonnell, 2000).

A teacher can observe the play for children's FoK and discover their way of life (Riojas-Cortez, 2001). Teachers keen to designing spaces that are culturally responsive provide artefacts that demonstrate a value of children's culture in the classroom. Even further, teachers can join children inside their imaginative play not only to extend the play but also to genuinely learn about children's expertise (Fleer, 2015). However not all socially replicated play is accepted in educative spaces. Labelling children's popular culture interests as rich resources is a challenge (Hedges, 2011).

Mediation

A key principle of the sociocultural perspective places value on building from children's prior knowledge to co-construct new understandings. Children benefit from the integration of cultural resources into learning experiences through cultural mediation (Vygotsky, 1978). In cultural mediation, the individual uses representational (e.g. computers, maps), semiotic (e.g. language), or mental (e.g. memory strategies) tools to problem solve, inform actions and make meaning in various contexts (Bodrova & Leong, 2006). The cyclical notion of mediation situates knowledge in historical and cultural contexts in order to carry out existing cultural activities, interactions with the social world, and in the construction of new knowledge.

Teachers can enhance a social, cultural, and historical perspective by incorporating students' social and cultural histories and ways of knowing into learning experiences (Souto-Manning, 2013). Educators use cultural mediation in an attempt to link everyday traditions, behaviours, and communication styles (outside of school) with more scientific knowledge (in school). From a Vygotsky (1978) perspective, the teacher's role is to assist within children's zone of proximal development to contextualise resources and connect interests. This plays a crucial role in the development of deeper understanding. Through adult guidance or collaboration with peers, young children can advance their abilities beyond their individual capabilities.

Drawing from the same principles, the FoK framework engages teachers in fostering the mediation of students' cultural ways of knowing between the structures of home and school and attributing a value to their cultural resources (González, Moll, & Amanti, 2005). This is not to be understood as a direct transfer of information. Instead, it is a continuous, context-based reorganisation of information. Adults play a vital role in assisting young children in mediating their cultural and historical connections by designing curriculum and learning experiences that build on children's resources and expertise. The ownership of curriculum transformation then lies with the teacher (Zipin, 2009). What is troublesome in early education is that what is prioritised or deemed 'appropriate' for play may not be the same for children and adults (Henward, 2015).

Popular culture

Children are situated in a world of commercial cultural influences that begins as early as gestation (Kincheloe, 2002). It makes sense that as children age and develop understandings of the world that their interests and activities would reflect social and cultural impacts. Early childhood literature about popular culture in play often is focused on media forms, such as TV shows (Hedges, 2011), characters (Henward, 2015), or music (Axelrod, 2014), and how children take up roles as actors in an attempt to recreate what they have heard and/or seen.

Whilst the term popular culture is commonly associated with media forms, it is important to not overlook cultural institutions (e.g. fast-food restaurants, big box companies). People mutually engage with these social places and influence the practices and traditions of these community institutions. It may be easier to recognise the ways adults participate in cultural institutions; however, young children are active participants too. Take for example McDonald's™, a globally visible and prominent entity. Like other fast-food chains, it's intention is to produce food for consumption, yet as Kincheloe (2002) writes the symbol of McDonald's is marketed in such a feverish way that it has become an experience and an anecdote of Western lifestyle. Aside from physically visiting McDonald's, children are constantly inundated with subliminal messages through cross-promoted marking, leaving a cultural influence from toys, food products, and promotional offers. It is only natural for these observations and their participation at this franchise to have an influence in shaping their interests, curiosities, and identities.

Naturally, one would expect to see these influences present in children's play scenarios in home and schooling contexts. However, as early childhood curriculum continues to be dominated by notions of standardisation (Sleeter, 2005), accountability (Brown, 2009), and child development (Hatch, 2010), planning for educative experiences tends to exclude popular and commercial culture trends. But academic content does not have to be given up in lieu of interest-based activities. In fact, research focused on content knowledge, such as science, suggests that value in engaging children's multiple resources (including popular culture interests) can support academic achievement while honouring students' voices (Calabrese Barton & Tan, 2009). Bringing these two together offers the chance for young children to possess power in their learning and incorporate interests that are important to them to connect their lifeworlds to schooling.

A dominant discourse in early childhood curriculum literature is of popular culture being a 'problem' or 'inappropriate' for school most notably because the content knowledge within popular culture play may not be obvious to teachers (Edwards et al., 2016). Popular culture items in play are considered a distraction from more typically accepted early childhood items such as play-dough or blocks. Teachers may be concerned with the hegemonic narratives associated with popular culture media products (Henward, 2015) and the over-marketisation to young children (Linn, 2004). In response, early educators may limit commercial products in preschool classrooms; however, children 'learn how to navigate, negotiate, and subvert teachers' expectations about cultural objects and texts' (Henward, 2015, p. 221). As young children do so, they learn ways to mediate their cultural interests into play and curriculum.

For children, popular culture interest 'is one of the few places where they can speak for themselves, produce alternative public spheres, and represent their own interests' (Giroux, 2000, p. 13). In Simmons (2014) study of how elementary-aged children shared popular culture knowledge during drama, she concludes that 'popular culture and drama allows children a momentary power balance within a realm, the school curriculum, where they are predominantly positioned as powerless' (p. 281). Children utilised their shared knowledge of popular culture to construct sophisticated, mature play scenarios, deepen social interactions, extend language use, and strengthen their identities through developing peer cultural understandings. With even younger children, the same behaviours and acts are present in their free play and learning (Edwards et al., 2016; Hedges, 2011).

If young children are considered active agents in understanding their world and their learning (Hedges, 2014), then adults must recognise rather than be in competition with their perspectives (Nicholson, Kurnik, Jevgjovikj, & Ufoegbune, 2015). Children being viewed as experts when it comes to their own lives can shift by whom, how, and what is mediated across contexts. This article aims to examine the question: What happens when children are given a space for their voice and interests to influence the direction of learning?

The study

This article is based on part of a larger investigation into how early childhood educators take up and enact the FoK framework. The broader research design involved two in-depth case studies that examined how prekindergarten teachers conceptualised the FoK framework within three contexts: a professional development (PD) setting, in students' homes, and in the classroom. Early educators ($n = 23$) studied the framework in a two-year PD programme focused on developmentally and culturally responsive mathematics. Over four graduate level courses, teachers met weekly to (re)think about the learning opportunities, delivery of instruction, and resources available for young children and to reconstruct them bearing in mind children's cultural experiences and resources from outside school. The PD programme wove in discussions of what high-quality mathematics looked like in early childhood.

The PD was offered concurrently with the Summerville[1] School District's first year of a state-funded, tuition-free, play-based preschool programme. This initiative provided over 2000 four-year-olds access to public prekindergarten programmes that are play-based, developmentally appropriate, and align with state early learning standards. To serve the large racially, ethnically, and economically diverse community, Summerville housed four-year-old kindergarten classes in elementary schools and early childcare and education sites. This preserved the already established prekindergarten programmes present in the Summerville community.

Two case study participants were purposefully selected from this PD programme who demonstrated understandings of children's cultural resources through pedagogical decisions, specifically environment design, curriculum, and verbal interactions. Participants for this study were identified based on Classroom Assessment Scoring System (CLASS) (Pianta & Hamre, 2009) classroom quality scores, specifically looking at Instructional Support[2] scores which assess concept development, quality of feedback, and language modelling. The intention was to study teachers who demonstrated social learning pedagogy and practices.

Sadie, the focal teacher for this article, was teaching a publicly funded prekindergarten class at London Bridges Child Care Center located in a working class area of Summerville. The centre offered a 3-hour morning session 4 days per week with optional wrap-around care, a fee-based service for families before and/or after prekindergarten, for enrolled students. For the 2012–2013 school year, 19 students were enrolled. Sadie and Sylvia, the educational assistant, were present daily in the classroom.

This study drew on ethnographic foundations to learn about the social phenomenon of how children incorporate popular culture interests or FoK into play and importantly, how this is honoured and supported by adults in the early childhood setting. In many ways, Sadie and her class at London Bridges serve as an instrumental case study (Stake, 1995) to understand what happens in instances when children's resources and interests clash with hegemonic cultures of schooling. four- and five-year-old children at London Bridges were often observed discussing video games and television shows, singing hip hop songs, and brought popular culture toys for show and tell. Sadie welcomed these references to their lifeworlds and in most cases expanded on them.

Method and analysis

Examining children's cultural knowledge in play meant that research had to include multiple methods and points of analysis to understand the role of the physical space and the social interactions. In spring of 2013, a total of 36 hours was spent as a participant observer in Sadie's classroom. I wrote detailed ethnographic field notes, including dialogue and context, took photographs, and wrote post-observation reflections. As an unfamiliar adult and observer, I recognise that my presence may have affected the behaviours of the children and the classroom setting (Patton, 2002). Additionally, I conducted neighbourhood observations within a two-mile radius of the site taking photographs of areas, such as parks, homes, businesses, and restaurants to enrich my understanding of the community and residents' cultural patterns. To understand pedagogical decisions and classroom design, I conducted open-ended interviews, with Sadie asking her about her personal and professional learning experiences, the curriculum, and the application of FoK and early math into her practice.

Data were analysed in order to understand what factors and how children are empowered to mediate their own FoK across contexts. Initial analysis included open coding yet was structured with external codes that drew from sociocultural-historical theory, specifically the concept of mediation, to look for themes and explanations in the data. The dramatic play area was of particular interest because it was a space where children consistently incorporating popular culture references and cultural knowledge (e.g. playing Spiderman™, Frozen™, or singing radio hit songs). Patterns in popular culture play, such as cultural congruence, were pulled apart and recombined to develop a more robust description of the how children mediated knowledge with others across contexts. The interviews were coded for teacher pedagogical beliefs and for confirming and disconfirming evidence of what was observed. Analytic tools in the NVivo software were utilised to run queries and matrices of the data.

Findings

The results discussed below shed light. Sadie and the classroom space supported young children in mediating their knowledge of McDonald's across contexts and with one another. The construct of funds of knowledge was well-suited to make sense and appreciate the extensive understanding these children have of the rules and roles of this cultural institution. As the play scenario was negotiated and carried out, three themes were consistent in the data: (1) the designed classroom environment, (2) establish relationships with and amongst children, and (3) interactions amongst children play significant roles in empowerment of young children's voices in learning experiences.

Consistent materials and promotion of social interactions

As young children engaged in free play, they socially co-construct meaning with others and the classroom environment (Bodrova & Leong, 2006). Often, they drew on their social and cultural knowledge

Figure 1. A child-created replica of a McDonald's drive thru.

to replicate what they observe and experience in life. What began as one child's idea evolved into sophisticated and reoccurring play. At the beginning of April in Sadie's classroom, Omar decided to use large wooden blocks to build a McDonald's Drive thru. He recruited other children in the area to help him construct the structure (Figure 1).

Within minutes there are blocks set up. Omar is sitting in the middle of the blocks and Oscar is behind him playing with blocks on the shelf. Mike is at a Lego table with a red bin tipped on its side and a long Lincoln log. On the block structure, a hollow box is the cash register and beanbags are used as Happy Meal toys.

Chris: We are **busy** on Friday.
Omar: One hundred million bucks.
Sylvia: What are you doing?
Omar: Making McDonald's!

Mike goes over to the red bin and sits behind it. He picks up the Lincoln Log. He is talking into it about toys.

Omar: I need more toys!
Oscar: I need more food!

Mike holds up a block to his eye. He is looking at something.

Mike: (yells) The toys are coming! The toys are coming!

Mike goes over to the shelf with bins. He spends some time looking at the bins. He takes a bin of plastic animals and dumps it behind Oscar. Oscar is holding up a long rectangular block.

Oscar: You guys! Customers are coming!
Omar: Talk to the customers.
Oscar: I can't I am looking through the binoculars. I can't talk on the phone.

Omar talks into a block.

Omar: I need more toys and chicken nuggets.

Across the room, Sadie is filling up water at the sink for the sensory table. Mike, Omar and Chris go over to her.

Mike: I am the boss of McDonald's.
Sadie: Oh you're the manager.

The children in this play experience used a variety of materials in imaginative play to represent real-life objects from McDonald's. All of the items (wooden blocks, bean bags, toy cars, and animals) used in this play were consistent classroom materials that were available every day. Not only did children use these familiar items in mature play to represent real things (Bodrova, 2008), such as a block to be a phone to see customers, they also demonstrated their social and cultural experiences and resources from their lifeworlds. At some point, these children must have, in some way, observed staff at McDonald's perform the actions of taking orders and know the significance of toys.

Verbal interactions were also used in addition to the resources in the classroom to contribute to children mediating their FoK. In the scene above, the communication between the children in the block area was seamless and quick. They all appeared to have background knowledge of observing staff at a McDonald's restaurant and knew there were multiple roles to getting an order to a customer. The children shared their play with Sadie, who at that time was facilitating a small group activity, and she provided them with vocabulary to extend their knowledge.

The combination of symbolic representation while taking on and sustaining specific roles are characteristics of what Bodrova (2008) describes as mature play. In this particular scenario, children were able to mediate their knowledge into the dramatic, make-believe play with little adult interaction. Though Sadie was only directly involved when the children shared their play with her, her pedagogical decisions were indirectly present in the scene. She made decisions about classroom environment design and to have consistent materials available that supported social engagement amongst student peers.

Cultural connections occurred at other times than just free play. Established routines also allowed for moments in which children demonstrated historically and culturally accumulated knowledge. When children could anticipate what would happen next, they were able to draw connections between the current experience and prior lifeworld knowledge (Copple & Bredekamp, 2009). Sometimes the connections were obvious and other times the teacher asked furthering questions to uncover how the child was making the associations.

Establish relationships with and amongst children

The emphasis of the FoK framework is on understanding the rich social and linguistic resources present in all children's daily lives and communities (González et al., 2005). In many ways, Sadie modelled a desire to accept all knowledge and experiences as valuable. Other adults and children in Sadie's classroom also demonstrated this disposition by welcoming one another's ideas during play and other routine times.

Meal times in Sadie's classroom were family-style, which meant the children helped set the table and serve themselves. Sadie and Sylvia, the educational assistant, sat and ate with the children. Discussions were informal and lighthearted in nature.

During a breakfast conversation on a very cold temperature week in April, Sadie is serving sliced pear to the red table where Sylvia and seven children sit.

Kyle: Guess who I saw at McDonald's?
Sadie: Who?
Kyle: Natasha.
Sadie: No way!
Kyle: Yes Way!
Sylvia: (to Corrina) What did you do last night?
Corrina: Nothing, because my mom forgot.
Nikki: We went to McDonald's but we didn't eat anything.
Shamya: Did you play?
Nikki: Yeah. We just played.

It is important to add that this restaurant was a powerful aspect of many children's lifeworlds because their families frequented this fast-food place. A McDonald's restaurant was one block from London

Bridges and accessible by many of those who live in the area and for families and staff to stop at on their way to and from the centre. McDonald's was not only a place for people to eat but a social space to gather. For these children, McDonald's was a cultural community place that played an important part of their lives (Kincheloe, 2002). Families went there in the bitter cold winter months to socialise with other adults and it served as a place for children to play on the playland structure.

At the end of April, Omar and Chris rebuilt the wooden McDonald's structure. The children still played a variety of roles and the materials from the block area were once again used for imaginative play.

When the 'cashier' was asked for a bag to take the big mac and fries home, he handed the 'customer' a large hollow box and took the invisible money. (Figure 2)

Omar: Chris, this is your cash register and this is my cash register. This is my money.
Omar: I would like chicken nuggets, a happy meal and a drink.
Chris: That will be $.25.

Sylvia comes over to the block area.

Sylvia: You guys made McDonald's?
Chris: That will be $500 million dollars. Here is your order. He put blocks inside of the hollow block.
Sylvia: Do you have a bag or something? How am I gonna carry all this home? Oh wait. I have an idea.

She puts the small wood blocks into a hollow block. As she does she says what each item is.

Sylvia: I got a big mac and some fries, some more fries, and a coffee and this ... I don't know what this is. I didn't order this.
Chad: Nuggets.
Sylvia: That is exactly what it is!

Figure 2. Omar hands a pretend bag of food to a customer.

Sylvia enhanced this play experience by incorporating the restaurant food names and authentic reactions with the imaginative play scenario the children started. Sylvia provided scaffolding of language and social competencies to mature the play and create a zone of proximal development (Bodrova, 2008) instead of academicising the play or correcting the extravagantly fanciful $500 million dollars,

Relationships amongst adults and children were established in this classroom. Sadie and Sylvia recognised the role of McDonald's in the lives of their students. Families carried disposable coffee cups and paper bags from McDonald's. Weekly, Sylvia brought her breakfast from there to eat with the children during meal time. The interactive and communicative approach present during meals as well as a shared understanding of terminology and behaviours of going to the fast-food restaurant transferred into play scenarios. This is due in part to their established relationships and connections with one another.

Co-construct new understandings

Two weeks later in the beginning of May, TJ extended Omar's original structure by using blocks in a different way to build his own interpretation of a drive thru.

TJ vertically stacks large block, places a thin cylinder at the top of the stack, and sings, 'bada bum bum bum' (the McDonald's theme song). TJ sits down on the step and looks through the hollow block. TJ picks up a rectangle block and holds it to his ear to represent a fast-food drive thru headset. He passes blocks through the hollow block (Figures 3 and 4).

TJ: (to himself) McDonald's. [Pause] Give me a soda.

Sadie comes over and stands next to the block structure.

Sadie: I will take a number 3.

TJ hands her a block.

Sadie: What about my drink?
TJ: Here's a soda.
Sadie: I want a milkshake.
TJ: Here you go.
Sadie: You didn't ask me what kind I want.
TJ: What kind do you want?
Sadie: Strawberry banana.

TJ turns around and pretends to push buttons.
TJ:(to himself) Hook up strawberry banana.
TJ hands Sadie a block.

Sadie: My little person would like a mini happy meal.

TJ gives her more blocks and tells her this is the toy.

Omar: I would like a happy meal ... [pause] ... with a chocolate shake.

TJ gives him blocks.

Jason: May I have um ... a root beer and Toy Story cake?
TJ: Your food will be done in a few seconds. Here is your ticket.

Omar comes back over to TJ with his block. He hands TJ the block.

Omar: Where is my chocolate shake?

TJ hands him a block. TJ calls to Sadie. He points at the Lincoln Log bin that he is sitting on.

Figure 3. TJ stands on blocks to work as the cashier of the drive thru.

TJ: I am sitting on money, Mr. Crab.

TJ sings 'SpongeBob Square Pants. SpongeBob Square Pants.'

Through verbal interaction, teachers and children co-constructed shared meaning of objects and ideas that meld cultural resources of school and home. TJ conveyed his idea to Sadie, who responded to him to continue to play and reproduce an authentic customer reaction. This was an example of a feedback loop in which Sadie used questioning and statements to continue the conversation (Pianta & Hamre, 2009). Omar enters the play and places a realistic order. Jason, on the other hand,

Figure 4. TJ uses a block to represent a drive thru headset to take customer orders.

understands that he can order food, however his order is not representative of menu food at McDonald's. TJ accepts this idea and continues the play by offering him a receipt. Interestingly, TJ further connected this play scenario of McDonald's to his interest FoK of the TV show Sponge Bob Square Pants. In the TV show, Mr. Crab is the manager of a burger shop and Sponge Bob works as a cashier.

The children in Sadie's class continued to recreate and play McDonald's through the end of the school year. In June during an exit interview, Sadie brought up the McDonald's play when asked about children's FoK in play. She discussed her students' recent interest in creating Dunkin Donuts in the block area and connected it to the McDonald's play.

Sadie: McDonald's is still cranking. Especially when Omar's here. Sometimes it doesn't happen when Omar's not here.
Anne: It's very intense.
Sadie: It is! But so is McDonald's, I guess [laughs].
Anne: And delicious. They're lovin' it, right?

Sadie recognised that Omar is a leader in this play scene and understood his direct family connection to the restaurant. Sadie explained that his mother uses McDonald's as an incentive for 'good' behaviour and it has a lot of power with him. Sadie saw these as instances to 'incorporate a small bit of FoK. It doesn't necessarily have to be a big old theme. It can be little things here or there, like something they do on the weekends like go to Dunkin Donuts'. She acknowledged that this was a step away from the traditional FoK approach of designing curriculum and saw how the cultural practice of visiting particular restaurants could be present in play.

Discussion

Sadie took a sociocultural approach in the classroom. This rejects the typical learning situations where skills are transmitted from adults to children and students are perceived as passive learners who sit quietly and reproduce information. Instead, it focuses on the construction of authentic spaces where children can try and manipulate ideas as they make sense of the world. Children in these spaces are active in their own academic and cultural development and learn content through various social relationships facilitated by the teacher.

Most notably, the children in Sadie's classroom innovatively created the cultural place, McDonald's, in the block area. Through this play scenario, the children demonstrated their understanding of the restaurant: the roles of employees and patrons, the commercial jingle, the cultural materials, the transactions, and the fast-paced nature of the eatery. Unlike a conventional approach to child-directed, popular culture scenarios in play, Sadie did not inundate the play with academic content. A discussion about money and the role of a 'manager' occurred, though I argue the mature play stayed alive over months because she provided consistent materials, participated in their cultural experience by ordering McDonald's specific foods and using vocabulary heard in that real-life space, and encouraged children to mediate and co-construct knowledge with one another.

The silent actor in empowering young children to mediate their own FoK was the classroom context. Sadie designed the physical space of the classroom to encourage social interactions and learning. Together, the group co-constructed a class culture that fostered children's sharing of their FoK with other children and adults. Because this space existed, children naturally integrated their cultural experiences, interests, and expertise into their play.

Researchers continue to recommend honouring and incorporating children's cultural resources and popular culture knowledge in learning tasks (Henward, 2015). Furthermore, teachers continue to seek ways to view children from an asset-based perspective, bridge connections between home and school, and integrate children's popular culture interests into play. This is beautifully idealistic and remains quite a challenge (Edwards et al., 2016). With the growth of universal prekindergarten programmes and growing diversity of student populations, many teachers acknowledge the importance of addressing individual needs of young children yet may struggle with the idea of allowing play that is FoK rich yet is not directly connected to the thematic unit or have apparent academic content.

Often, teachers view favourite popular culture characters or games as non-academic and of little to no value in the classroom. Hedges, Cullen, and Jordan (2011) argued that from a sociocultural perspective, popular culture interests influence young children's language, play, relationships, and behaviours in ways consistent with the FoK framework. Teachers who welcome children's interest-based FoK are demonstrating an acceptance of social norms and rules, values, behaviours, humour, and playfulness that are important for building social-emotional and cognitive skills at a young age. Further, child-mediated conversations about popular culture can lead to critical conversations about gender roles, identity, and other social justice topics.

The role of the teacher is to co-construct and mediate this space to foster child control to eventually do so independent of their assistance. This is especially true for teachers situated in an academically driven climate of schooling culture. González and her colleagues (2005) recognised that the emancipatory FoK approach contends with the push for standardisation and can actually isolate teachers. Practitioners may find themselves in the crux of an incredible dilemma of how to retain play in prekindergarten classrooms that allows children's FoK in the current context of early childhood education. As Sadie reflected about McDonald's and Dunkin Donuts, stepping away from the thematic unit to incorporate little instances of FoK can work.

Teachers also require support in understanding that in a hybrid space that welcomes children's lifeworld knowledge and empowers them to use it in the school context has incredible effects on learning. Helping pre- and in-service teachers experience being inside the play with young children (Fleer, 2015) has potential to develop children's play and characteristics of teacher pedagogy. Teacher education and PD programmes need to emphasise ethnographic methods and other ways to incorporate and honour children's cultural ways of knowing into school activities. Taken together, these approaches move early educators to reshape deficit perspectives.

Conclusion

This study draws attention to the importance of children mediating their popular culture interest into learning activities (play) at school and demonstrates that a lack of emphasis on cultural knowledge and resources can no longer be 'accepted' or 'justified' in early childhood education. Recent literature emphasises the need for teachers to design learning experiences that honour and respond to children's cultural interests outside school (Henward, 2015; Souto-Manning, 2013). While popular culture interests, such as TV-show characters or McDonald's, may be difficult to view as a resource acceptable for an educational space, other forms of interest, such as holidays or construction vehicles, often are accepted and at times become themes of study. This is not to say that learning about diggers and bulldozers are bad or that understanding another's festivities is wrong. Rather, attention should be raised of why particular interests are deemed as of value to learning over others. The idea that we need to change in the way educators perceive their students' experiences outside of school is not new (Moll et al., 1992). This approach assists teachers in reframing their professional dispositions to view all children as capable and active agents in their learning.

Children need support and social interactions during play to mediate social and cultural knowledge across contexts. This can be from the environment, adults, and peers. Drawing on Vygotskian view of play, scholars such as Bodrova (2008) raise the question of the degree and quality of the adult mediation to propel learning and development of higher mental functions. Considering this spectrum of adult involvement is wide, variable and non-linear, additional research is necessary to truly understand teachers' spontaneous choices to connect children's interest FoK into activities, routines, and play. A study that included reflective interviews or written and oral reflection following instruction would allow access to the momentary decision-making process (Loughran, 2002). This research would be twofold. It would provide the researcher insight into the teachers' thinking and potentially influence practice. A research study of this nature would also benefit from examining how connections to children's FoK were purposefully avoided and/or unintentionally unseen. What influences teachers' decisions to include or ignore particular FoK? Or popular culture? How do teachers determine what is 'appropriate' for the classroom context?

Most importantly and widely overlooked in FoK and popular cultural interest research is the child's experience. The cultural experiences and expertise for children may differ from that of adults and other siblings in the household (Esteban-Guitart & Moll, 2014). Literature investigating the child's involvement in the household and cultural institutions such as McDonald's would provide insights into what children identify as their cultural knowledge. Doing this type of research with young children may be more of a challenge, yet it is completely possible. Exploring the child's role at home from their perspective would offer a view into *their* FoK in addition to the families.

Notes

1. All names including city and school site have been changed to protect the identities of teachers, staff, children, and families in this study.
2. The three main domains of focus in CLASS are emotional support, classroom organization, and instructional support. Each of these domains includes multiple dimensions, rated on a 1–7 scale, that are later used to calculate a quality rating score. See Pianta and Hamre (2009) for detailed information about the scoring system.

Disclosure statement

No potential conflict of interest was reported by the author.

Funding

This work was supported by the National Science Foundation [grant number 1019431].

References

Axelrod, Y. (2014). 'Todos vamos a jugar, even the teachers' – everyone playing together. *Young Children, May*, 24–31.

Bodrova, E. (2008). Make-believe play versus academic skills: A Vygotskian approach to today's dilemma of early childhood education. *European Early Childhood Education Research Journal, 16*(3), 357–369.

Bodrova, E., & Leong, D. J. (2006). Tools of the mind: The Vygotskian approach to early childhood education (2nd ed.). Boston, MA: Pearson.

Brown, C. P. (2009). Being accountable for one's own governing: A case study of early educators responding to standards-based EC education reform. *Contemporary Issues in EC, 10*(1), 3–23.

Calabrese Barton, A., & Tan, E. (2009). Funds of knowledge and discourses and hybrid space. *Journal of Research in Science Teaching, 46*(1), 50–83.

Copple, C., & Bredekamp, S. (2009). *Developmentally appropriate practice in early childhood programs serving children from birth through age 8*. Washington, DC: National Association for the Education of Young Children.

Edwards, S., Skouteris, H., Cutter-Mackenzie, A., Rutherford, L., O'Conner, M., Mantilla, A., … Elliot, S. (2016). Young children learning about well-being and environmental education in the early years: A funds of knowledge approach. *Early Years, 36*(1), 33–50. doi:10.1080/09575146.2015.1064099

Esteban-Guitart, M., & Moll, L. C. (2014). Funds of Identity: A new concept based on the funds of knowledge approach. *Culture & Psychology, 20*(1), 31–48.

Fleer, M. (2015). Pedagogical positioning in play-teachers being inside and outside of children's imaginative play. *Early Child Development and Care*. doi:10.1080/03004430.2015.1028393

Giroux, H. A. (2000). *Stealing innocence.* New York, NY: St. Martin's Press.

González, N., Moll, L., & Amanti, C. (2005). *Funds of knowledge: Theorizing practices in households, communities, and classrooms.* Mahwah, NJ: Lawrence Erlbaum.

Graue, M. E., Whyte, K. L., & Karabon, A. E. (2015). The power of improvisational teaching. *Journal of Teaching and Teacher Education, 48,* 13–21.

Hatch, J. A. (2010). Rethinking the relationship between learning and development: teaching for learning in early childhood classrooms. *The Educational Forum, 74*(3), 258–268.

Hedges, H. (2011). Rethinking Spongebob and Ninja Turtles: Popular culture as funds of knowledge for curriculum co-construction. *Australasian Journal of Early Childhood, 36*(1), 25–29.

Hedges, H. (2014). Children's content learning in play provisions: Competing tensions and future possibilities. In L. Booker, M. Blaise, & S. Edwards (Eds.), *The SAGE handbook of play and learning in early childhood* (pp. 192–203). Thousand Oaks, CA: Sage.

Hedges, H., Cullen, J., & Jordan, B. (2011). Early years curriculum: Funds of knowledge as a conceptual framework for children's interests. *Journal of Curriculum Studies, 43*(2), 185–205.

Henward, A. S. (2015). 'She don't know I got it. You ain't gonna tell her, are you?' popular culture as resistance in American preschools. *Anthropology & Education Quarterly, 46*(3), 208–223.

Kincheloe, J. L. (2002). *The sign of the burger: McDonald's and the culture of power.* Philadelphia, PA: Temple University Press.

Linn, S. (2004). *Consuming kids: The hostile takeover of children.* New York, NY: New York Press.

Loughran, J. (2002). Understanding self-study of teacher education practices. In J. Loughran, & T. Russell (Eds.), *Improving teacher education practices through self-study* (pp. 239–248). London: Routledge/Falmer.

McDonnell, K. (2000). *Kid culture: Children and adults and popular culture.* Melbourne: Pluto Press.

Moll, L., Amanti, C., Neff, D., & González, N. (1992). Funds of knowledge for teaching: Using a qualitative approach to connect homes and classrooms. *Theory Into Practice, XXXI*(2), 132–141.

Nicholson, J., Kurnik, J., Jevgjovikj, M., & Ufoegbune, V. (2015). Deconstructing adults' and children's discourse on children's play: Listening to children's voices to destabilize deficit narratives. *Early Development and Care, 185*(10), 1569–1586.

Patton, M. Q. (2002). Variety in qualitative inquiry: Theoretical orientations. In *Qualitative research & evaluation methods* (3rd ed., pp. 75–137). Thousand Oaks, CA: Sage.

Pianta, R. C., & Hamre, B. K. (2009). Conceptualization, measurement, and improvement of classroom processes: Standardized observation can leverage capacity. *Educational Researcher, 38*(2), 109–119.

Riojas-Cortez, M. (2001). Preschoolers' funds of knowledge displayed through sociodramatic play episodes in a bilingual classroom. *Early Childhood Education Journal, 29*(1), 35–40.

Rodriguez, G. M. (2013). Power and agency in education: Exploring the pedagogical dimensions of funds of knowledge. *Review of Research in Education, 37*(March), 87–120.

Rogoff, B. (2003). *The cultural nature of human development.* New York, NY: Oxford University Press.

Simmons, C. A. (2014). Playing with popular culture – an ethnography of children's sociodramatic play in the classroom. *Ethnography and Education, 9*(3), 270–283.

Sleeter, C. E. (2005). *Un-standardizing curriculum: Multicultural teaching in the standards-based classroom.* New York, NY: Teachers College Press.

Souto-Manning, M. (2013). *Multicultural teaching in the early childhood classroom.* New York, NY: Teachers College Press.

Stake, R. (1995). *The art of case study.* Thousand Oakes, CA: Sage.

Thomson, P., & Hall, C. (2008). Opportunities missed and/or thwarted? 'Funds of knowledge' meet the English national curriculum. *The Curriculum Journal, 19*(2), 87–103.

Van Hoorn, J., Nourot, P. M., Scales, B., & Alward, K. R. (2014). *Play at the center of the curriculum* (6th ed.). Upper Saddle River, NJ: Merrill/Prentice Hall.

Vygotsky, L. (1978). *Mind in society: The development of higher psychological processes.* Cambridge, MA: Harvard University Press.

Whyte, K. W., & Karabon, A. (2016). Transforming teacher-family relationships: Shifting roles and perceptions of home visits through the funds of knowledge approach. *Early Years.* doi:10.1080/09575146.2016.1139546

Wisneski, D. B., & Reifel, S. (2012). The place of play. In N. File, J. Mueller, & D. Wisneski (Eds.), *Curriculum in early childhood education: Re-examined, rediscovered, renewed* (pp.175–187). New York, NY: Routledge.

Zipin, L. (2009). Dark funds of knowledge, deep funds of pedagogy: Exploring boundaries between lifeworlds and schools. *Discourse: Studies in the Cultural Politics of Education, 30*(3), 317–331.

Civic action and play: examples from Maori, Aboriginal Australian and Latino communities

Jennifer Keys Adair, Louise Phillips, Jenny Ritchie and Shubhi Sachdeva

ABSTRACT
Using data from an international, comparative study of civic action in preschools in New Zealand, Australia and the US, we consider some of the types of civic action that are possible when time and space are offered for children to use their agency to initiate, work together and collectively pursue ideas and things that are important to the group. We use an example from each country and apply the work of Rancière and Arendt to think about collectivity as civic action in young children's schooling lives. Play, rather than an act itself, is positioned here as political time and space that make such civic action possible in the everyday lives of children. We argue here that play is the most common (and endangered) time and space in which children act for the collective.

Introduction

While play is often associated with a type of action children do or a concept worth advocating for because of increasingly rigid early childhood educational programmes (Brown, 2010; Nicholson, Shimpi, & Rabin, 2014), this article focuses on play as a political space that is free and unstructured. Play is seen here as a time and space in which children can initiate collective action (Pacini-Ketchabaw & Nxumalo, 2015). Using data from an international, comparative project on civic action in preschools, we consider some of the types of civic action that are possible when time and space are offered for children to use their agency to initiate, work together and collectively pursue ideas and things that are important to the group. These acts, what we refer to as civic action, are collective acts. Play, rather than an act itself, is positioned here as merely making such a civic action possible in the everyday lives of children. Consider the following example that took place in Katoa Kindergarten in New Zealand.

A four-year-old boy, Manu, often initiates complex dramatic play scenarios, in which he usually plays the character of a dog named 'Toby'. One day (as was usual) several other children joined in, each determining their own roles. Keanu, Rōpata and Wiremu were all dogs. Charles decided he was a pussy-cat and Nikau was a puppy. Donald decided he would be a boy rather than an animal. A younger boy, Mikey, imitated the play at the periphery, without fully joining in. The boys initiated a fetching game, taking turns to retrieve small beanbags. Donald and Jenny (author) were assigned the role of being the throwers.

Soon, 'Toby' mimed that he had an injury, and suggested that there were Band-Aids in the imaginary cupboard. The game changed and the 'animals' now began supplying imaginary plasters (Band-Aids) and bringing them to Toby to restore his wounds. The game continued for some time, with activities often initiated by Manu (Toby), as the dogs and cats met their various needs for exercise and for food and water, which needed to be supplied from the imaginary kitchen.

Manu (Toby) initiated what became a collective enterprise. Children were welcome to enter the play even if they were not a dog or a cat. All of the children who wanted to participate, even at varying degrees, joined in without too much effort. In this game, children exercised their *rangatiratanga* (self-determination) and civic identity, acting as a group for the benefit of the group's overall health. All of the participants were able to contribute to the collective enterprise. They made decisions about who needed exercise first and who needed Band-Aids and how the fetching game would work. The dual honouring of both agency and participation is evident in this vignette. These elements of civic action – civic identity, civic deliberation, collective enterprise and shared concern – are part of everyday living of young children when they are able to use their agency to influence and even control how and what they are learning.

The collective action of the children being animals and then entertaining and caring for one another is not the development of civic action, but the actual *doing* of civic action. They are caring for one another. They are compromising, making collective decisions, identifying as a group, welcoming diversity and sharing concern. Using examples from children across the sites of our international, comparative ethnographic project – Civic Action and Learning with Young Children – we hope to demonstrate that seeing play as a political time and space rather than as an act of development allows us to recognize and value children's doing of civic action. Rather than seeing young children as developing civic action attributes, we will argue with examples and theory that children are doing civic action, that they are concerned and committed (right now) to collectivity. Play is the most common (and endangered) time and space in which children act for the collective.

Play as a political space that supports the serious work of civic action

Ethnographic research across the world describes how children organize play agendas, find play partners, resolve disputes, source and construct their own materials, and socialize younger children into the rules, goals and agendas, while adults are on the periphery or even out of sight (Hayashi & Tobin, 2011; Bock, Gaskins, & Lancy, 2008). We argue that it is in this free unstructured time (with reduced teacher direction) that children have agency to demonstrate and enact their civic capabilities and to respond to what is happening in a collective, rather than an individualistic, way.

The allocation of time and space where children have free choice is often labelled as play. When children govern themselves during this time and space, their acts are often seen as apolitical. And yet, children are actors within structures, institutions and communities that shape and are shaped by politics. Indeed, through the philosophical lens of Rancière (1991), even the exercise of an infant learning to express herself through language demonstrates her political agency, her intersubjective assertiveness, in articulating her intentions and communicating her feelings, desires, intentions and needs within the space she shares with others (Rancière, 2010b). A young child's early experimentation with communicating is viewed as reflecting a liberatory intent, described as 'stepping into language with all the force that is entailed in any political encounter of the emancipatory sort' (Bingham & Biesta, 2010, p. 59).

Often children advocate for themselves and others in contexts labelled as 'play'. We suggest that the free choice times often known as 'play' can be seen as sites of political engagement. In accordance with Rancière's (2010a) definition, politics is about counting 'a part of those without a part' (p. 36). In the origins of citizenship and democracy in Ancient Greece, only wealthy men counted. Women, children and slaves were not included as citizens. And so, Rancière defines politics as the claims made to count those who are not counted, as witnessed through, for example, women's rights, race rights, working-class rights, children's rights, disability rights, asylum-seeker rights and lesbian, gay, bisexual, trans or intersex rights movements. Young children are typically not recognized as political beings, nor as bearers of politicalness. They are rarely (if ever) heard in public debate. Parents and early childhood educators listen to children, but it is unclear whether young children are engaged with as political beings. This study documented many examples of children acting as political beings, as those who actively seek to count 'a part of those without part', who may be excluded through ruling demarcations instated by educators, state or national policies, or by children who devise and assert their self-made rules. For example, we see children welcoming others into their play regardless of what animal or human form they entered in as and adapting games for newcomer participation as enacting civic agency and as acts of collective concern.

Also, part of being political is being able to initiate concern, change and collectivity as a citizen who can initiate action in the polis – a place of coexistence with others, many who may be unknown. Arendt's (1958, 1998) theory of human action offers a useful definition that is workable for young children. To Arendt, action is beginning something new in the world, public realm or *polis*, outside of our internal and personal spaces. Early childhood settings are, for many children, their first entry into the *polis* (a community of unknown others) (MacNaughton, 2007), thereby offering space for children to do civic action. The impulse for action comes from wanting to begin something new and emerges unexpectedly from what has happened before. Action differs from routine actions (such as eating, washing and cleaning), which consume most of our day as these are either work or labour. Actions do not exist in isolation: instead, 'they fall into an already existing web where their immediate consequences can be felt' (p. 184). In Arendt's theory, actions are recognized as affecting others, yet the effect is invariably not what the initiator intended because of conflicting wills and intentions in the web of human relationships in the polis. If an initiator tries to control how others respond to his or her action, or if individuals block others' opportunities to begin, agency is denied (Arendt, 1998; see also Biesta, 2010). Arendt advocated for worldly care for the public realm, where initiated actions are enacted with consideration for others. This understanding of action seemed workable in possibilities for young children's civic action through the recognition that young children would be motivated to begin something new in response to what they see, feel and hear in the early childhood setting.

By seeing play as a space for civic action, children are viewed as political through their capacity to initiate and respond to others in ways that support the initiatives of each other. Actions then involve responsive interaction with others through the interplay of doing, saying, listening and waiting. Such interactions welcome plurality and difference in that children's initiated actions 'are taken up by others in unprecedented, unpredictable and uncontrollable ways', as noted by Biesta (2010, p. 9) in his proposal of Arendt's theory of action for political coexistence in democratic education.

In this article, we combine Rancière and Arendt's ideas of political agency to notice children's influence, decisions and acts in the public sphere of their early childhood education and care settings. We see children's collective efforts to count those who are not always counted as civic action and we used this understanding to make sense of what children often do during play, particularly the initiation of acts for the common good. We recognize that it is the context of child-directed play that provides the greatest opportunity for young children to exercise civic action as political agency.

Play, civic action and collectivity

Our ideas about civic action stem from a communitarianism approach (Delanty, 2002) to defining and framing what civic action capabilities might be for young children. As a citizenship theory, communitarianism is focused on families, communities and cultural groups (rather than the state and economy), which form the polis that children have access to and are included in. Of particular interest in communitarianism is how people act in groups – group action. In our study of civic action and young children in different national, cultural and linguistic spaces, we sought to examine child-initiated group action in early childhood settings.

There are two specific principles of communitarianism (e.g. see Delanty, 2002; Etzioni, 1993; Monro, 2005) that guided our approach to civic action as a collective act by children. First, social cohesion and interrelatedness are developed through compassion, care and concern for fellow community members and responsibility to the community. For example, on numerous occasions we witnessed at all three sites young children comforting or helping another child so that they could rejoin the community activities. Second, *social practices and values only have meaning within the historically developed social fabric of societies and cultures* and are not isolated in just one moment. As witnessed at the Aboriginal Australian site, the cultural value and practice of 'looking out for your mob' are known and enacted by young children through getting extras (e.g. lolly (candy) or even a handful of sand) for your kin. This act of collectivity is as political as it is historical because young children are acting against decades, centuries even, of oppressive acts that try to destroy their affection and care for one another. *Often in our work in all three countries, we saw practices of children's acts as responses to not just what was in their immediate classrooms or outdoor preschool spaces, but as responses to serious collective concerns that burden their families and communities.*

The civic action and learning study

The Civic Action and Learning with Young Children study is a video-cued, comparative ethnographic project in three countries: New Zealand, Australia and the US. In each country, research teams have been working within an educational setting that serves communities who are politically underrepresented. In New Zealand, we are working with an early childhood education and care setting that serves Maori and Pacific Islander families. New Zealand is unique in our study because they have the least restricted space for children and they have the only bilingual/bicultural curriculum that attempts to privilege the values and language of Maori communities. In Australia, we are working with an Aboriginal Australian community formed a century ago through the government and missionaries' horrific forced relocation of 35 tribes and removal of children from their families, decimating dozens of languages and communities. In the US, we are working with a large city preschool that primarily serves Latina/o and African-American communities. The preschool teaches in both Spanish and English. Each of the three sites is explored in greater detail before each country's discussion of civic action and play. Included in these descriptions are the national/local understandings of play as well as the political standing of play in each country.

Data collection in three countries

Our study began with developing relationships with respected community members and educators at each site. We met with administrators, teachers and families to get to know them and their needs from us as researchers. We explained the study and sought their input on our data collection plan as well as how permission might be sought for observing and filming children. After the sites agreed to participate, we met with educators and families to seek permission, explain our study and answer questions.

After permission was granted, we spent eight to twelve months in each site collecting data through participant-observation and taking consistent field notes. All of the researchers participated in daily classroom life with children's activities and were available much like a teacher's assistant to help with whatever children or educators needed. Usually we watched children until invited to participate by them in a game, art project, dramatic activity or shared concern. We were eventually treated as part of the community and blended in easily to everyday life. When children and educators were familiar and comfortable enough with us in their space, we began to film and take pictures of daily civic action examples. We looked for children working together, including one another, having conflict, excluding others and caring for one another as well as caring for plants and animals. This resulted in substantial field notes, video recordings and photographic examples of children doing civic action.

While participating, observing and recording civic action in each site, we also interviewed the educators, community members and children using the video as a cue for discussion. For example, we showed the children video footage of themselves working together to get their responses. Children enjoyed watching films of themselves and their classmates. They also enjoyed watching films of children in other sites. We also showed educators scenes we filmed in their own classrooms for their feedback and suggestions, and to reassure them of what we were looking for. Educators in each country sought reassurance in different ways that we were getting what we hoped to. Showing them the films not only yielded a great deal of insight into practices, but also deepened relationships between the research team and the educator community in each space.

Comparing approaches to play

Towards the end of data collection in the US (the last site scheduled in the study), we noticed that all three sites in our study approached children and childhood somewhat differently and there were varying amounts of control and agency at each site for the children. These ideas connected to how much play was used as a term for children's actions as well as to label a specific time that was less structured. In New Zealand, for example, the term 'play' was not used nearly as much as in the other two sites. Katoa Kindergarten has only approximately 20 minutes of structured time in a 6-hour school day. Children are free to move inside or outside, enjoy whatever materials they wished and move around with classmates in any part of the space. The only exception is a small adult-sized kitchen on one side where teachers can freely go and eat food, get tea and socialize, and the teachers' office room. The sense of agency and movement extended to the educators as well. When educators described to us what children were doing, they hardly used the word play as if it was too general a term. They described children as doing art, work, caring, advocacy, resistance, developing empathy, working out problems and so forth.

In Australia, the preschool structure had a lot of open time labelled as 'play' where educators observed or engaged with the children. The educators viewed and advocated for play as a space for children to freely choose and direct activity. There were some structured times when children were asked to sit and pay attention, which engaged some children. Outside time happened multiple times a day, with the whole group required to relocate outside for adult supervision ratios to be maintained. Each age group had a separate, fenced outside space. Children's acts were often labelled as play in the children's presence, with teachers complimenting children on their play or letting children know that their play was too harsh.

The US site was the most structured space in our study. Children often gathered on 'the carpet' to listen to books read aloud by teachers, get instructions, learn about the day's schedule or practice letters and numbers. Children danced each day on the carpet. Children went outside as a class 1 or sometimes 2 times a day for a scheduled portion of time, as they shared the playground with 21 other classrooms and only a few classes could use the playground at a time. They had scheduled 'work time' each day in which children could move around the room and choose groups with ease. There were areas labelled as dramatic play, block area and computer area and there was also a book reading corner and an art area with lots of supplies. Teachers in the US used the word 'play' to talk in advocating ways about the need for play and for children to just explore and discover. When children were present, they used the word work to describe acts. For example, children would be complemented on how they were working, not on how they were playing. But all of the US teachers spoke to researchers about how important it was for children to play, describing acts they labelled to children as work.

Although there were many differences across the three sites, we did notice that during less or unstructured time when children could use their agency, there were acts children did every day at each site. Many of these acts were in pursuit of the common good. For the remainder of this article, we will describe children's efforts during unstructured time to initiate for the common good and try to make sense of their pursuits within the larger political and educational frameworks of each country and community.

Play as constructed in the New Zealand early childhood context

Play has historically been the predominant pedagogical approach in New Zealand early childhood care and education settings (May, 2009, 2013; Somerset, 1976). The New Zealand early childhood curriculum, *Te Whāriki*, recognizes that children 'learn through play' (New Zealand Ministry of Education, 1996, p. 82). The strand of 'exploration' states that children should experience an environment where 'their play is valued as meaningful learning and the importance of spontaneous play is recognized' (p. 15). By means of a focus on the curriculum principle of 'empowerment', children are encouraged to explore their environment, creating and acting on the own ideas, thereby developing their interests, knowledge and skills. In this context, 'Play activities in early childhood education invite rather than compel participation' (p. 40). *Te Whāriki* also states that 'There should be a recognition of Māori ways of knowing and making sense of the world and of respecting and appreciating the natural environment' (p. 82).

At Katoa Kindergarten, in Titahi Bay near Wellington, the capital city of New Zealand, the philosophy of the teachers is to allow children, ages 2–5 years, a great deal of freedom to determine their own agendas both indoors and in the large outside area. The outdoor spaces include some picnic-style tables, a sandpit, raised vegetable gardens, swings and flexible cubes, ladders and ramps that can be shifted in formation and operate as a climbing apparatus. Inside the kindergarten there are two food tables, several activity tables, books, puzzles and a large open space for block and dramatic play. Aside from two brief mat or circle times, one near the start of the day, and the other just before children leave to go home, children are free to move inside or out, to eat whenever they feel the need and to interact with whom or whatever they choose.

There are up to 40 kindergarten children attending on any 1 day, many of whom have Māori and/or Pacific Islands' ancestry and affiliations. Currently, there are 10 pairs of siblings in attendance, as well as numerous others who are cousins. Research has shown that inviting under-two-year-olds to participate in kindergartens, traditionally oriented to three- and four-year-olds, has raised some challenges, and that having older siblings present can ameliorate some of these issues (Duncan & Dalli, 2006). This is also consistent with Māori whānau practices of tuakana (older siblings) being expected to care for teina (younger siblings). On two days a week, additional younger children and parents are also present as part of a playgroup for the association's home-based programme that runs a morning session in conjunction with the kindergarten, this integrated service being part of the Whānau Manaaki kindergarten association's broader social equity initiatives (Whānau Manaaki, 2016). The six teachers, three women and three men, support the children in their endeavours, ensuring that they are observing the full spectrum of children's engagement as much as possible.

During our time of regular observations at Katoa, the teachers had a consistent and conscious focus on supporting children's social competence, scaffolding children to negotiate their social interactions. The current planning focus of the teachers is leadership, or *rangatiratanga* (self-determination). The morning mat-time is known as 'Kotahitanga time' (Kotahitanga means unity, solidarity, or collectivity). It is signalled by children acting as the *kaikaranga* (caller), standing at the edge of the doorway, calling out in *te reo* Māori (the Māori language) to the other children to come to the mat. The mat-time begins with a collective recital of the kindergarten *whakatauki* (proverb) which reflects the wisdom of Te Rauparaha, an ancestor of the local Māori tribe, Ngāti Toa. On a recent visit (January 2016), the teacher (Jared) who was leading Kotahitanga time asked the children 'Who will be the *rangatira* (chief/leader) to start off our *whakatauki* today?' Several children indicated that they were keen to take on this leadership role. One of these children, Miriama, was chosen by Jared, and she duly led the group into recitation of the *whakatauki*. Later in the mat-time, Jared encouraged the children to reflect on how they can let others know how they feel about something that is upsetting to them, and then to practise saying 'Stop it, I don't like it!' This pedagogical approach of freedom, accompanied by guidance and modelling, is consistent with Rancière's discussion of the role of teachers in 'making visible' the 'unequal equality' of our 'democratic' societies (Rancière, 2010b, pp. 8–9).

Learning to be *Tuakana* in New Zealand (collective caring)

In relation to the civic action of social responsibility, children at this centre demonstrated caring for others on a daily basis during their engagement in the play-based programme. Because children ages 2–6 years were welcomed and shared the entire space at Katoa, the older and younger children (tuakana and teina), particularly siblings, spent a lot of time together. Teachers are very conscious of the role of the older siblings (tuakana) in offering secure attachment which regulates the sense of security of the younger sibling (teina). One two-year-old child named Anika greatly relied on her brother Donald for support and could usually be found in the vicinity of her brother, trailing behind him as he moved from one area to another. One afternoon Anika had hurt her toe and it was bleeding quite badly. Donald was summoned from where he had been playing outside, but after briefly checking on Anika, he returned to his outdoor preoccupation. One of the teachers continued to try and comfort her, but she was still crying inconsolably. A four-year-old girl Maria noticed Anika's distress and went to the child-height fridge/freezer that was available for children's use. She took out one of the ice-packs and brought it to the very upset Anika. Maria then sat alongside the teacher who was still holding Anika, and for quite some period of time leaned over towards Anika, talking softly to her, demonstrating care and *aroha* (love, concern).

More recently, Donald moved on from Katoa to start school. Several teachers explained to us that several other children at Katoa had taken over Donald's former role and were supporting Anika. Miriama, a three-year-old girl, along with several other girls had taken Anika under her wing, including her in their daily activities. This was having a reciprocal effect on Anika, helping her to learn to be a contributing part of the community. One morning Miriama and Anika were playing together outside. As they ran to the climbing frame, Miriama tripped and scraped her knee. The supervising teacher Jared suggested to Anika that she could go and get Miriama an icepack. Anika and Miriama then walked quietly inside and Anika retrieved an icepack from the fridge/freezer without any assistance, just as months earlier Maria had done for her. She gave the icepack to Merenia and then went and got a paper towel from the dispenser and handed it to Merenia. She bent over to help Merenia hold the paper-towel-wrapped icepack on her injured knee. This action lasted less than a minute before they tidied up together, putting the paper towel in the bin and ice pack back in the fridge/freezer. The only conversation took place at the end, when Anika asked Merenia 'You okay now?' The two girls then ran back outside to the climbing frame.

Anika, who previously had been cast as the *teina* and on the receiving end of care, has now assumed the role of *tuakana*, in caring for her friend. With no need for verbal agreements, the community helped Anika be a civic participant. There was trust and shared understanding that existed among the teachers and children to help Anika not just by doing things for her or comforting her, but giving her opportunities to do the comforting. Rancière's political agency ideals highlight the community value of 'being counted in' and what children can do and teach to others when they have agency to influence what they do as well as the space to move about freely and access useful materials. Anika is now part-taking in the political space of the early childhood play-based programme, able to initiate for the common good as many other children have done previously. The modelling of care by her brother, by Maria and Miriama, and the teachers has 'made visible' this aspect of social responsibility and agency in the service of others.

Play as constructed in Australian early childhood education

Play as a context for learning in Australia is generally well supported with play-based learning explicitly emphasized in the national early childhood curricula for 0–5-year-olds – Belonging, being and becoming: The Early Years Learning Framework for Australia (DEEWR, 2009). The introduction of a national standards school curriculum from 2010, and the growing attention to national (e.g. National Assessment Program – Literacy and Numeracy) and international (e.g. Program for International Student Assessment) standardized testing comparisons have produced a growing 'push down' effect foregrounding pressure to produce measurable academic achievement at younger and younger ages through didactic curriculum and pedagogy. Increased attention to standardized curriculum and assessment has meant that more early years teachers are moving away from play-based pedagogies to didactically address standardized content (Queensland Government Department of Education and Training and Griffith University, 2015). To campaign against these trends, play activism has also emerged among parents and educators wanting less structured experiences for children (e.g. see https://www.facebook.com/protectingchildhoodAER/).

In the Aboriginal community where we became part of the educational community of Buranba child care centre, play is understood as children freely exploring the environment and learning cultural values and practices. It is accepted community practice for children three years and older to independently wander the community. By 9–12 years of age, children have a home range of independent mobility of 7.8 sq km (Kreutz, 2014). The community is an entirely Aboriginal community of just under 2000, in which everyone knows each other. A central cultural value is shared care responsibility. Community members look out for each other, especially the young and the elders (Maddison, 2009). Children are expected to participate in this shared care. *Veronica Ecenarro (a Bardi woman) explains that Aboriginal Australian adults trust older children to look after younger children and freely permit children to act out real-life situations that involve risks (*Fasoli, Wunungmurra, Ecenarro, & Fleet, 2010*).*

As a licensed child care centre, however, educators have to follow Australian child care regulations, standards and building codes to operate and receive government funding. Under these regulations, children's protection is foregrounded to the disservice of children's participation and agency. Children are confined to rooms and yards per year of age, separating family members for most of the day. Most of the educators do not interfere with children's play; rather, they stand back and are there when needed to comfort an injury and remind children of the imposed 'whitefella' boundaries and rules.

Catching bees in Australia (collective venture)

Outside one afternoon, all the children from toddlers to four-year-olds and visiting older school-age siblings/cousins were gathered in the same yard. Ezra and Talia noticed bees[1] buzzing around a flowering shrub close to the boundary fence with the aged care facility. Ezra found a small plastic container and lid at the craft trolley outside one of the classrooms. He brought it back to the shrub with the intent to catch a bee. Talia stood beside him honouring interest in his initiative. Her younger sister Nelly and another two-year-old girl Mary (who had been crying for some time) also moved towards the shrub. Nelly offered lip gloss to Mary and she stopped crying. As the more experienced older sister, Talia supported and guided the application. Suddenly, this was interrupted by Ezra's highly animated excited leaps and yelps of 'I've got it' as he ran to tap Talia on the back to ensure she was part of the bee catching. The whole group followed around to the other side of the shrub, with Ezra and Talia saying 'my babybob' [bumblebee] and then squabbling 'no my babybob'. Then Ezra whacked Talia and she slightly cried. Ezra screamed vehemently 'my babybob'. Jarrah (a visiting school-aged cousin) lightly pushed Nelly from behind, and she whimpered. Jarrah tapped Ezra, who did not flinch as he and Talia were stealthily focused on following the bee as it moved around the shrub. Nelly started kicking the shrub and Mary started hitting the bush with a plastic wand. Talia stopped them by saying: 'No it's a bumblebee flower'. She returned to bee tracking.

Soon Ezra's eyes were fixed on a bee. He slowly leaned into the bush with the jar and the lid poised apart in opposing hands. Talia encouraged him with 'catch it'. At just the right moment he brought the jar and lid together and caught the bee. Talia exclaimed: 'Ezra got it!' Ezra then proudly admired his catch from all angles. Nelly looked in and Aiden came over to look too. He showed the bee in the jar to the others, then threaded his hand holding the jar through the fence so he could have a look without interruption. He told the others 'Don't touch', putting his other hand up to them. Then Ezra walked off with the bee in the jar, yelling 'Hey I got a bee' as he found his younger brother. He sat down on the grass to admire and observe the bee in the jar. Andrew and Talia looked for other bees in the bush. After some time, Ezra took the lid off the jar, emptying the bee onto the ground. Talia witnessed this. They both looked around to follow the bee and eventually moved back to the bush to locate another bee.

Ezra initiated bee catching in the community of children. Talia supported his venture; she did not block Ezra's bee-catching action. Ezra welcomed Talia into the action – a political conception of agency (Biesta, 2010). The supporting of each other's agency happens fluidly and frequently throughout the encounter. When Nelly applies lip gloss on crying Mary, Talia assists. And when Ezra catches the bee, others come to admire the catch.

Of course, everyone's agency was not welcomed and supported every time. For example, Ezra tried to control how others responded to his initiated action (bee catching) by whacking Talia when she claimed it was her bumblebee and stopping others from touching the jar. And Jarrah tried to interrupt the group action by pushing Nelly and Ezra. Yet these moments of blocking another's civic agency were brief interruptions. Welcoming one another into the action was a political act and this movement of agency between the children was fluid. The collective pursuit of the bee seemed to be more important than squabbles here and there. When Ezra and Talia squabbled over ownership of the bee, energy for this conflict was soon lost as attention to the cause (bee catching) overrode. In the end, Ezra even considered the agency of the bee and released it. The release of the bee passed by unremarkably as they promptly returned to the joint interest of bee catching.

Reading the encounter with Rancière's (2010a) understandings of politics, Ezra could be seen as the ruling in this context as the initiator of the action. He determined who was counted in and what actions were acceptable. He readily welcomed Talia (they share the same great grandmother) in as an accomplice who supported and encouraged, but her efforts to claim ownership of the bee were not acceptable and she was blocked with a whack. Ezra willingly showed his catch to others of all ages (especially seeking out his younger brother), while firmly setting the rule of no touching. Nelly and Talia advocated for the inclusion of Mary through offering the appeasement of the desirable lip gloss. And Jarrah sought to be included through attention-grabbing whacking, but stopped when he received no response from Ezra.

The cultural value of looking out for younger children and your kin shapes the enactment of who is counted in (the politics in play). From a very young age, these children know to look after anyone younger and their kin. For Aboriginal Australians, kinship commitments are wide, including a broad extended family of nans and pops, aunts, uncles, cousins and cousin's cousins. By learning from a very young age that you care for each other and you work together as a large extended family, community Elder, Sylvia, explains that 'you go together with your people and you'll win or you'll finish it that day and sort it out, 'cos you're not being a proper black fella unless you go in together'.

Play as constructed in the US' preschool context

At the start of institutional early childhood programmes in the US, play was conceptualized as a tool to help children develop skills and knowledge across physical, social, cognitive and emotional domains (Frost, Wortham, & Reifel, 2008). Play was not necessarily for the pleasure of children, but more for the opportunity to learn through child-centred activities (Tobin, 2008). Play can be labelled and assessed as 'high-quality play' (Kessler & Hauser, 2000; Meier, Engle, & Taylor, 2010). Children are often taught how to play correctly (Paley, 2004). Teachers, to justify play in their classrooms, often have to learn how to assess play for learning and development (Subramanian, 2015). Regardless of diverse approaches and struggles with the concept of play, early education programmes are changing in the light of neo-liberal policies such as No Child Left Behind (Brown, 2009; Kane, 2015).

Approaches, access and ideas about play in the US are also cultural (Gaskins, 2014; Gupta, 2009), generational (Nicholson, Shimpi, Kurnik, Carducci, & Jevgjovikj, 2014), gendered and sexualized (Blaise & Taylor, 2012). Play intersects with racial, cultural and linguistic discrimination (Adair & Doucet, 2014). This continues to be the case in the US as children have different levels of access to play inside and outside of classrooms, in the larger community and in their neighbourhoods (Copeland, Sherman, Kendeigh, Kalkwarf, & Saelens, 2012; Miller & Almon, 2009), increasingly dependent on the racial and economic characteristics of their families (Adair, 2014).

Lead by a Latina principal, Cielo Early Childhood Center serves primarily Mexican immigrant, African-American and Hispanic families centrally living in a large city. Children attend from ages three to five years. Children are assigned to age-differentiated classrooms of 12–16 children, so siblings are not usually in the same classroom. Each classroom has one lead teacher and one assistant teacher, except for the classroom serving special needs where there are two assistant teachers. Children attend school from 7:30 am to 2:30 pm and follow a daily routine of activities rotating from small group, outside time, work time, breakfast and lunch. Children are usually gathered together with a short book, song or set of instructions before moving on to the next activity. Days can include a visit to the garden, inside gym, science room or library. Worktime is the terminology used for the 45-minute period of time when children can move around the room and use the materials without much teacher direction. In other US classrooms, this time might be labelled as 'play' or 'free-time' or 'centres'. Educators at Garcia speak often about the importance of play for young children's development and learning.

Fishing for letters in the US (collective governance)

During centre time, Brittany picked up some wooden fishing poles from a bookcase. She brought the pole and a box of magnetic fish with letters painted on them to a nearby table. She spread the fish out on the table and began to catch them using the pole. Alvin saw this and got interested, picking up another fishing pole. He and another child, Diamond, joined in with Brittany trying to connect the magnet of the pole to the magnet on the lettered fish. Brittany tried to attach her pole to two fish and showed her efforts to us as well as to children around her. Alvin watched and then tried to pick up two as well. Noticing Alvin's attempts, Brittany quickly gathered all the fish and put them closer to her. Diamond saw this and said, 'Brittany, give some fish to Alvin, he doesn't have any!' Brittany looked at Diamond through the corner of her eye, pretending that she did not listen. She kept collecting the fish and pulling them towards her. Diamond again looked at her and said, 'Brittany, give Alvin some fish, it's not nice!' Brittany kept eyeing Diamond and Alvin but did not move the fish back to the centre part of the table.

Frustrated, Diamond started moving slowly towards the teacher all the while keeping an eye on Brittany. Brittany continued fishing but kept an eye on Diamond, who slowly inched towards the teacher, taking one step at a time. As soon as Diamond reached half way towards her teacher, Brittany, who was following her with her eyes, quickly moved all the fish that she had accumulated towards the centre of the table, where Alvin and Diamond could share. Diamond saw this and came back to the table.

Diamond noticed the injustice and unfairness in one person holding on to all the community resources. She spoke out against it and stood up for Alvin, arguing that all at the table should be counted as participants. When Brittany did not respond to her concern, she used nearby adults as leverage. Diamond could have run over to the teacher and encouraged the teacher to solve the problem. Alvin could have yelled out or followed Diamond to the teacher. Instead, Diamond walked slowly and purposely, giving Brittany time and space to influence what would happen. And Alvin watched and went along with the girls' responses. With Diamond and Alvin's support, Brittany had the opportunity to change the course of things without adult intervention. Diamond initiated action to create opportunity for Alvin and gave space for Brittany to make a decision that recognized others in the space. This all happened within a time and space that were not controlled by others (Arendt, 1998). The ability to solve communal problems without outsiders is an important skill for children of colour, who are often part of communities overly managed and controlled by outsiders in educational institutions (Delpit, 2006; Goldstein, 2008; Howard, 2006; Stipek, 2006) and beyond.

Theorizing civic action led by children

In each of the three examples, there was attention and care of the collective. In many child development models, young children are described as acting in their self-interest rather than a collective good (See Corsaro, 2005 for a longer explanation of how children can be seen in social collectives, particularly peer cultures). In our examples, however, and through our two years of data collection, we have seen children routinely leave their activities, sacrifice something precious and share time and space in the pursuit of collective interest, not just an individual one. This included those who fought, hit, snatched and made trouble. When offered time and space to use their agency, children gave one another time and space to make decisions in the best interest of the collective. In all three countries, we saw countless examples of this phenomenon. Instead of doing whatever they wanted to with the space and time of play, young children in all three countries many times each day made decisions based on welcoming all to be counted and in support of a continuing sense of collectivity over individuality. Children, we are finding, have enormous potential for civic action and political will that is focused on the collective, rather than the individual. We see children use their agency towards civic action as an offer into the polis with consideration for others (Arendt, 1958, 1998).

As is the case with civic action and political agency, it does not mean children did not have conflict. In fact, conflict was often an opportunity to demonstrate the ability to do civic action, not just merely be in the process of developing civic action. As researchers, it was how we could see the collective direction of children's efforts. Play can be an opportunity to place ideals of the community in the pathway of the ideas of individual children, where children have to make decisions about inclusion and teachers have to make decisions about control and their role as a guide or authority figure (see Wisneski, 2011 for a classroom example of how play can challenge community ideals in early grade classrooms). Instead of giving in to individual agency, children in our three country studies seemed to give space and time to one another to make decisions that maintained the collective when they were given time and space to act. Preliminary data from our study suggest that adult intervention has a significant effect on the type and quantity of civic action children can do on a regular basis. There were many more examples of civic action in New Zealand and Australia, for example, than in the US because time and space directed by children are much less. Educators at Katoa (NZ) did not enter children's conflict or games unless invited and they usually did not enter conflict directly, but rather made suggestions to individual children who took them back into the conflict. They explained that children learn by trying to solve their problems themselves and through repeated failures to get what they want.

Adult intervention was different at Buranba and Cielo. Educators at Buranba (AU) offered specific directives and complements to children, as reminders of being caring community members. Educators often referred to the larger community or to kin when reminding children to share, be kind, not whack or help other children. They advocate for young children to be safe, to have good food, to be loved and to care for each other. The educators especially argue for these rights, because of the legacy of the intergenerational trauma of genocide and institutionalized racist abusive policies and practices. Educators at Cielo (US) helped children through conflict and disagreements, often moving from one side of the room to the other if they noticed a problem. Educators gave children words and phrases they could use in the conflict and then coached children through sharing what bothered them and making changes to avoid future conflict. They explained that children often need help solving problems and that young children who are victims or marginalized need support from them as adults. Educators in the US also explained that parents get really upset when children are hit, bit or pushed by other children, so they have to watch conflict closely.

While these differences require much more time and thought, it is important to share these differences in the context of civic action as children in different schools had different amounts of opportunities for young children to act collectively depending on how what educators thought was best for their learning experience as well as outside influences such as regulation or community values. As with previous studies, ideas about how much agency children should use in their learning and play was different at each site and these ideas seemed to impact the amount and type of civic action children could do more than say, developmental levels, school readiness measurements or children's backgrounds (see also Adair & Colegrove, 2014). As Arendt (1958, 1998) explains, if an initiator tries to control how others respond to his or her action, or if individuals block others' opportunities to begin, agency is denied.

Supporting civic action in and outside of play

Children did civic action even in the most structured spaces, though often in smaller amounts and frequency. In the most structured of the three environments, we saw daily examples of children doing civic action, primarily acting towards the collective and counting all those who are not always counted. Play secured time and space (for children) for the public realm where initiated actions could be enacted with consideration for others.

The downside of pursuing play as a political space that makes civic action possible is that civic action possibilities may be limited to just that time and space, rather than interwoven throughout the day in many different types of situations. In settings where there is a limited allocation of time to play freely, these may be the only times that children can act for the collective, and thus there is a limit placed on when shared care, concern and action may be initiated and pursued. When children were responsible for more actions on their own or when they were able to have time and space to lead their own actions, they could better pursue civic action. Play outside or during work time was the main time and space in which children could act for the collective and think collectively. There are many more opportunities for children to initiate civic action. It should not be left only for 'play' time or 'free time'.

While play can be used as a signal for teachers to not intervene as much as usual and to give children more control and choice over what they do, it is also helpful to regard civic action as an important part of early childhood and make environmental, pedagogical and attitudinal changes that better accommodate children's capabilities to act civically, or collectively, to advocate for one another, work towards a shared interest, care for others as a group and make space for more people in activities.

Note

1. Native bees in Australia are stingless, and are culturally significant to Aboriginal Australians, with their honey valued as a prized gift and commodity.

Disclosure statement

No potential conflict of interest was reported by the authors.

Funding

This work was funded by the Spencer Foundation.

References

Adair, J. K. (2014). Agency and expanding capabilities in early grade classrooms: What it could mean for young children. *Harvard Educational Review, 84*(2), 217–241. doi:10.17763/haer.84.2.y46vh546h41l2144

Adair, J. K., & Colegrove, K. S. S. (2014). Communal agency and social development: Examples from first grade classrooms serving children of immigrants. *Asia-Pacific Journal of Research in Early Childhood Education, 8*(2), 69–91.

Adair, J. K., & Doucet, F. (2014). The impact of race and culture on play in early childhood classrooms. In L. Brooker, M. Blaise, & S. Edwards (Eds.), *SAGE handbook of play and learning in early childhood* (pp. 354–365). New York, NY: Russell Sage Foundation.

Arendt, H. (1958). *The human condition*. Chicago, IL: The University of Chicago Press.

Arendt, H. (1998). *The human condition* (2nd ed.). Chicago, IL: The University of Chicago Press.

Biesta, G. (2010). How to exist politically and learn from it: Hannah Arendt and the problem of democratic education. *Teachers College Record, 112*(10), 9–10. Retrieved from http://www.tcrecord.org/content.asp?contentid = 15744

Bingham, C., & Biesta, G. J. J. (2010). *Jacques Rancière: Education, truth, emancipation*. London: Continuum.

Blaise, M., & Taylor, A. (2012). Using queer theory to rethink gender equity in early childhood education. *YC: Young Children, 67*(1), 88–98.

Bock, J., Gaskins, S., & Lancy, D. F. (2008). A four-field anthropology of childhood. *Anthropology News, 4*, 391–420.

Brown, C. P. (2009). Confronting the contradictions: A case study of early childhood teacher development in neoliberal times. *Contemporary Issues in Early Childhood, 10*(3), 240–259. doi:10.2304/ciec.2009.10.3.240

Brown, C. P. (2010). Children of reform: The impact of high-stakes education reform on preservice teachers. *Journal of Teacher Education, 61*(5), 477–491. doi:10.1177/0022487109352905

Copeland, S. N., Sherman, S., Kendeigh, C., Kalkwarf, H., & Saelens, B. (2012). Societal values and policies may curtail preschool children's physical activity in child care centers. *Pediatrics, 129*(2), 265–274. doi:10.1542/peds.2011-2102

Corsaro, W. A. (2005). Collective action and agency in young children's peer cultures. In J. Qvortrup (Ed.), *Studies in modern childhood: Society, agency and culture* (pp. 231–247). Basingstok: Palgrave Macmillan.

Delanty, G. (2002). Communitarianism and citizenship. In E. F. Isin & B. Turner (Eds.), *Handbook of citizenship studies* (pp. 161–174). London: Sage.

Delpit, L. D. (2006). *Other people's children: Cultural conflict in the classroom*. New York, NY: The New Press.

Department of Education, Employment and Workplace Relations (DEEWR). (2009). *Belonging, being, becoming: The early years learning framework for Australia*. Canberra: Commonwealth of Australia.

Duncan, J., & Dalli, C. (2006). *Under-3-year-olds in kindergarten: Children's experiences and teachers' practices: Summary report*. Wellington: Teaching and Learning Research Initiative.

Etzioni, A. (1993). *The spirit of community: Rights, responsibilities, and the communitarian agenda*. New York, NY: Crown.

Fasoli, L., Wunungmurra, A., Ecenarro, V., & Fleet, A. (2010). Playing as becoming: Sharing Australian aboriginal voices on play. In M. Ebbeck & M. Waniganayake (Eds.), *Play in early childhood education: Learning in diverse contexts* (pp. 215–232). South Melbourne: Oxford.

Frost, J. L., Wortham, S. C., & Reifel, R. S. (2008). *Play and child development*. Newark, NJ: Pearson/Merrill Prentice Hall.

Gaskins, S. (2014). Children's play as cultural activity. In L. Brooker, M. Glaise, & S. Edwards (Eds.), *The Sage handbook of play and learning in early childhood* (pp. 31–42). London: Sage.

Goldstein, L. S. (2008). Teaching the standards is developmentally appropriate practice: Strategies for incorporating the sociopolitical dimension of DAP in early childhood teaching. *Early Childhood Education Journal, 36*(3), 253–260. doi:10.1007/s10643-008-0268-x

Gupta, A. (2009). Vygotskian perspectives on using dramatic play to enhance children's development and balance creativity with structure in the early childhood classroom. *Early Child Development and Care, 179*(8), 1041–1054. doi:10.1080/03004430701731654

Hayashi, A., & Tobin, J. (2011). The Japanese preschool's pedagogy of peripheral participation. *Ethos, 39*(2), 139–164. doi:10.1111/j.1548-1352.2011.01182.x

Howard, G. R. (2006). *We can't teach what we don't know: White teachers, multiracial schools* (2nd ed.). New York, NY: Teachers College Press.

Kane, N. (2015). The play-learning binary: US parents' perceptions on preschool play in a neoliberal age. *Children & Society, 30*(4), 290–301. doi:10.1111/chso.12140

Kessler, S., & Hauser, M. (2000). Critical pedagogy and the politics of play. In L. D. Soto. (Ed.), *The politics of early childhood education* (pp. 59–71). New York, NY: Peter Lang.

Kreutz, A. (2014). *Children and the environment in an Australian indigenous community*. Abingdon, OX: Routledge.

MacNaughton, G. (2007). Trials and transitions to citizenship: What really matters in early childhood education? Paper presented at the Dean's lecture series, Faculty of Education, University of Melbourne.

Maddison, S. (2009). *Black politics: Inside the complexity of Aboriginal political culture*. Crows Nest, NSW: Allen & Unwin.

May, H. (2009). *Politics in the playground: The world of early childhood in New Zealand* (2nd ed.). Dunedin: Otago University Press.

May, H. (2013). *The discovery of early childhood* (2nd ed.). Wellington: NZCER Press.

Meier, E., Engle, B., & Taylor, B. (2010). *Playing for keeps: Life and learning on a public school playground.* New York, NY: Teachers College Press.

Miller, E., & Almon, J. (2009). Crisis in the Kindergarten: Why children need to play in school. *Education digest: Essential Readings Condensed for Quick Review, 75* (1), 42–45.

Monro, S. (2005). *Gender politics: Citizenship, activism, and sexual diversity.* London: Pluto.

New Zealand Ministry of Education. (1996). *Te Whāriki. He whāriki mātauranga mō ngā mokopuna o Aotearoa: Early childhood curriculum.* Wellington: Learning Media. Retrieved from http://www.education.govt.nz/early-childhood/teaching-and-learning/ece-curriculum/te-whariki/

Nicholson, J., Shimpi, P. M., Kurnik, J., Carducci, C., & Jevgjovikj, M. (2014). Listening to children's perspectives on play across the lifespan: Children's right to inform adults' discussions of contemporary play. *International Journal of Play, 3*(2), 136–156. doi:10.1080/21594937.2014.937963

Nicholson, J., Shimpi, P. M., & Rabin, C. (2014). 'If I am not doing my own playing then I am not able to truly share the gift of play with children': Using poststructuralism and care ethics to examine future early childhood educators' relationships with play in adulthood. *Early Child Development and Care, 184*(8), 1192–1210. doi:10.1080/03004430.2013.856894

Pacini-Ketchabaw, V., & Nxumalo, F. (2015). Unruly raccoons and troubled educators: Nature/culture divides in a childcare centre. *Environmental Humanities, 7*(1), 151–168. doi:10.1215/22011919-3616380

Paley, V. G. (2004). *A child's work: The importance of fantasy play.* Chicago, IL: University of Chicago Press.

Queensland Government Department of Education and Training and Griffith University. (2015). *Age-appropriate pedagogies for the early years of schooling: Foundation paper.* Brisbane: Queensland Government Department of Education and Training. Retrieved from http://deta.qld.gov.au/earlychildhood/pdfs/foundation-paper.pdf

Rancière, J. (1991). *The ignorant schoolmaster: Five lessons in intellectual emancipation* (K. Ross, Trans.). Stanford, CA: Stanford University Press.

Rancière, J. (2010a). *Dissensus.* London: Continuum.

Rancière, J. (2010b). On ignorant schoolmasters. In C. Bingham & G. Biesta (Eds.), *Jacques Rancière: Education, truth, empacipation* (pp. 1–24). London: Continuum.

Somerset, G. (1976). *Vital play in early childhood.* Auckland: Playcentre Association.

Stipek, D. (2006). No child left behind comes to preschool. *The Elementary School Journal, 106*(5), 455–466. doi:10.1086/505440

Subramanian, M. (2015). Rethinking play: A postcolonial feminist critique of international early childhood education policy. *International Journal of Educational Development, 45*, 161–168. doi:10.1016/j.ijedudev.2015.10.001

Tobin, J. J. (Ed.). (2008). *Making a place for pleasure in early childhood education.* New Haven: Yale University Press.

Whānau Manaaki. (2016). Kindergarten. Education and care. Whānau Manaaki. Our vision. Wellington: Whānau Manaaki. Retrieved from http://www.wmkindergartens.org.nz/About-Us/Our-vision-__I.928

Wisneski, D. B. (2011). Complicating the role of play in building classroom community. In C. Lobman & B. E. O'Neill (Eds.), *Play and performance: Play & culture studies volume 11* (pp. 33–58). New York, NY: University Press of America.

Rethinking young children's digital game play outside of the home as a means of coping with modern life[†]

Youn Jung Huh

ABSTRACT

This study explores young children's digital game play outside of the home as a means of surviving and thriving in modern spaces that limit young children's participation by looking at four digital game-playing three-year-old children. In this ethnographic study, critical theory is used to examine how modern public spaces (e.g., a grocery market, a beauty salon, a kid's club in a gym) function to control young children's participation. This study sheds light on the way we view young children's digital game-playing spaces and argues that young children's digital game play in public spaces serves as a useful tactic for them to negotiate with public regulations, constraints, and their daily schedules.

Introduction

With the development of mobile technology, the sight of young children playing digital games in public spaces has become familiar in modern society. However, young children's digital game play in public spaces has been overlooked in many studies of young children, play, and digital games. This lack of research may be due to its momentary and ubiquitous features (Ito, Okabe, & Matsuda, 2006; Rowsell, 2014; Tobin, 2013). Educators often dismiss digital game play as children's play (Ailwood, 2003; Sefton-Green, 2004; Sutton-Smith, 1997). Also, very little attention has been paid to young children's participation in public spaces (Elsley, 2004; Harden, 2000; O'brien, Jones, Sloan, & Rustin, 2000).

Contemporary sociologists and early childhood education scholars have argued that even very young children derive power from their play, and they are able to tactically use this power in order to survive within existing social structures (Buckingham, 2007; Tobin, 2000). With this awareness, research has shown that young children transform public spaces into their own play spaces by navigating boundaries and rules imposed by adults in these spaces (Elsley, 2004; Ito et al., 2006; Tobin, 2000). These studies clearly show the power of young children as active social actors, but they also point to the ways that children are marginalised and excluded from public spaces. Elsley (2004) argues that children should be understood as 'human beings rather than human becomings' and that it is important to 'promote their rights and capacity to contribute to the decisions that impact their lives,' in public spaces (p. 155).

Recently, digital media studies and studies of children and digital technology have focused on the role of digital technology as a means of resisting modern spaces. In their study of teenagers using mobile phones as an everyday practice, Thompson and Cupples (2008) reveal that young people use digital technology 'to manage and rework social space and escape oppressive forms of

---

[†]Portions of this work were presented and published in dissertation form in fulfilment of the requirements for the Ph.D. for me from Arizona State University.

surveillance from adults' (p. 102). Ito (2008) argues that mobile technology supports and enriches children's play within public spaces as they are able to shape and reshape the public spaces while playing mobile games. This allows them to cope with immediate situations and negotiate with public regulations and constraints as an everyday practice.

Richardson (2007) argues that mobile devices penetrate existing spaces, effectively transforming people's perspectives against the idea that digital is a separate space from reality. For example, mobile games like location-based games (LBGs) such as Pokémon GO that 'integrate virtual objects into the camera view of the actual environment, and require teams of players to 'capture' them at leisure, or whenever a player happens to be walking past a particular location in the city' can blur boundaries between virtual and real spaces as the game players engage with the spaces simultaneously (Richardson, 2007, p. 209). This suggests that digital technology may cause people to create new practices within the physical spaces that they occupy.

Also, Hjorth and Richardson (2009) found that digital gaming in public spaces allows young women to deal with waiting times and loneliness while also allowing them to remain aware of their surroundings. In their study, young women reported that they played mobile games in public simply to pass the time 'when there's nothing else to do' (Hjorth & Richardson, 2009, p. 29). Although the focus of the studies was primarily older children or young adults, the argument that digital games are used to cope with immediate situations in modern spaces may apply to young children. Young children may also use digital game play to survive and thrive in public spaces that limit their participation.

Few empirical studies have focused on young children's digital game playing in public spaces. Because of this, young children's digital game play in public spaces is not yet well understood by parents, early childhood educators, and policy-makers. In order to promote young children's right to participate in public spaces and to develop public spaces for young children's play, it is important to explore young children's digital game play in public spaces within the context of their everyday lives.

What happens when young children play digital games outside of their homes? How does their game play function as a means of participation in these spaces? Using four case studies of three-year-old children and their digital game play within public spaces, this study attempts to answer the preceding questions in an attempt to move toward an understanding of the meaning of young children's digital game play as a way of participating in modern spaces.

Theoretical framework

Quotidian studies

Quotidian studies attempt to understand everyday life and culture through immediate social and historical settings by analysing the patterns of behaviour and speeches found in ordinary people's lives. Tobin (2013) argues that quotidian studies are meaningful for understanding mobile game practices because this approach draws our attention to the ordinariness and mundane quality of our everyday lives that is overlooked in most research. His study shows that many people play games while on public transportation, in doctors' waiting rooms, and even in the restroom. Despite its ubiquity, many people tend to give little attention or significance to this play because of its feeling of triviality and mundaneness.

Tobin (2013) views game play as a way to deal with boredom in modern life. He argues that modern quotidian life is so inherently alienating and boring that it brings about new types of play. These new types of play have paralleled advances in modern life. Just as the rise of train travel produced the pulp novel and subway commuting led to the tabloid newspaper, riding in the backseats of family cars is spurring the development of handheld video games for young children.

In Japan, Ito, Okabe, and Matsuda (2006) have described the mundaneness of new technologies in our everyday life with the three terms *personal, portable,* and *pedestrian*. They argue, it is 'not so much about a new technical capability or freedom of motion but about a snug and intimate techno-social tethering, a personal device supporting communications that are a constant, lightweight, and mundane presence in everyday life' (p.1).

Another researcher, e Silva (2006), focused his work on the digital spaces created in public spaces in modern society. With the development of mobile technology, mobile digital game spaces have become hybrid spaces, blurring the boundaries between physical and digital spaces. While people are moving and spending time in public spaces, their mobile devices are always on, waiting for the next interactive play session. In seeking to understand mobile game practices, it is essential to look at the social space, this hybrid space of digital space and virtual space, around the mobile game players.

A chronotope of game play

According to Bakhtin (1981), a chronotope is literally a 'time space,' meaning 'the intrinsic connectedness of temporal and spatial relationships that are artistically expressed in literature' (p. 84). Like a novel, the reader must consider both the space and the time narratively. Young children's game play in public spaces only makes sense when considering the variables of time and space and their changes during the process. Using Bakhtin's concept (1981), the connectedness between the time and the space in game players' narratives forms a mental map that leads players to make decisions and respond to the situations that they face while playing games.

Dormans (2011) pointed out that game-playing experiences might seem disorganised, but they were, in fact, highly controlled by a sequence of events. Similar to Bakhtin (1981), Dormans argues that the relationship between game space and game missions is not total chaos; within each series of events created by individual game players, the individual digital gaming experiences contributed to an interpretation of the game players' lives in modern spaces.

Children's game space as heterotopia

McNamee (2000) defined game spaces with the term 'heterotopia,' originally used by Foucault in 1986. Heterotopias represent utopias, ideal and unreal spaces, and yet, physical and real spaces. Game spaces are the perfect mix of spaces between utopias and heterotopias (McNamee, 2000). They are still located in and surrounded by reality, but the virtual spaces and the images from the spaces are unreal forming a duality of reality and unreality. According to McNamee (2000), these game spaces allow children to resist the way that modern spaces function as a means of controlling children's lives, where fewer spaces are designed exclusively for children. Without a physical space for play, children are instead turning to virtual spaces for play.

In order to understand young children's digital game play in public spaces, this paper critically examines these spaces in various ways; first, this paper analyses artefacts from within the game spaces to reveal how these objects function as controllers of young children and elicit game play. Second, this paper seeks to define children's game spaces, which are quickly created and disappeared. This paper also explores young children's daily routines often occurring before, after, and even between their game play. Finally, this paper explains the game spaces as a form of resistance against modern space by using Foucault's concept of heterotopias, Bakhtin's concept of a chronotope, and quotidian studies.

Methodology

Ethnographic case study

This study is part of a larger ethnographic case study exploring young children's digital game play in everyday life. Through case studies, four three-year-old children show the meaningful ways young children play digital games outside of their own homes.

All of the participants in this study lived in a suburban area, yet each came from unique sociocultural backgrounds. A brief description follows of the children and their families. All names are pseudonyms.

David is a Mexican American child from a low-socio-economic background. He is very interested in cars and loves police cars best. His mother thinks this love originates from seeing the police cars patrolling his neighbourhood every day. On Saturdays, David's mother's day off, she takes her children to a fast food restaurant for breakfast, followed by a trip to a shopping mall or park.

Mike and Amy are European Americans, coming from upper-middle-class families. They both have working parents and older siblings. Until his mom, Lisa, comes back from work, Mike spends his time with a babysitter and his older siblings, Kelly and Kevin. Mike often calls Kelly 'mom' when his mother is not home.

All the children in Amy's family have their own bedrooms with their own television sets. Although Amy's parents do not have much interest in digital game playing, the children all have their own Nintendo Dual Screen (DS) sets.

Chan is from a middle-class, Korean immigrant family. Chan's mother, Eunsook, is a house wife. He has one older sister. While Chan plays games or watches television, Eunsook cleans the house, prepares food, and writes in her diary. Chan's father likes to play digital games. When he was single, he was a member of a StarCraft game community. He still likes to play games and wants to buy games for his children, but Eunsook dislikes them.

To understand young children's natural digital game play occurring both inside and outside of the home, I visited each child's home six times over the course of six weeks and shadowed their daily activities for a total of 20–24 hours per each child. Children's digital game play was observed in various contexts (e.g., in the car, in a kids' club, at a shopping mall). Participant observations and informal interviews were data sources. In my first visit, parents were also interviewed to understand and to learn each child's daily schedule.

Cultural inventory

A cultural inventory was used to understand the children's game space. According to Collier and Collier (1986), the placement of items in a particular space can provide insights into people's lives and their culture. To apply this method in this study, pictures of the children's game spaces were taken. Analysis included the arrangement of the items and the types of possessions in the space. This paper focuses on three spaces: (1) the settings where the digital games were played, such as the backseats of cars, grocery carts, and dining room tables; (2) the bodily orientation of the player with the game as a related space – how the game was held, touched, and watched during play; and (3) the space within the game – the way that each child experienced and described the virtual game space.

Bakhtinian interpretative analysis

Data were collected through field notes, photography, and videotaping; these were each then documented, coded, and analysed using Bakhtinian interpretative analysis developed by Tobin (2000). Tobin identified four key Bakhtinian principles for interpretation of utterances, which will be described. These principles provided insights that helped answer the research questions of this study.

Principle 1: The meaning of an utterance is always contextual

This principle indicates the importance of understanding the social context where the utterance is made. I approached the task of interpreting the meaning of utterances by including the external situation around speakers (e.g., different public spaces, various gaming devices, daily routines) as well as the identity of the speakers (e.g., ages, sociocultural backgrounds) to understand the meaning of a single utterance.

Principle 2: The word is only half ours

Instead of focusing on the dictionary definition of the words that were spoken, I looked at how the words were combined and recreated by speakers to understand what they really want to say. For example, Mike's sister, Kelly, often directly and indirectly cited her mother's words to control Mike's game play. She often told him 'good boy' when she thought he did a good job, behaved well, or showed good manners. Kelly said the words, but the words represent the voice of another (Mike's mother, in this case). This is what Bakhtin calls double-voiced or hybrid discourse and shows how words are only 'half ours.'

Principle 3: The content of psychic life is thoroughly ideological

By looking at conflicts and tensions experienced and expressed by individuals, we can gain insight into the conflicts and tensions of our greater society. I looked for the conflicts and tensions experienced and expressed by the young children by attending not only to what was said but also to what was left unsaid, what French literary theorists (Macherey, 1978) refer to as the *non-dit*. For example, the children in this paper were silent (and maybe silenced) about public spaces that limited their freedom to play. They did not complain about the spaces or the social norms that restricted their participation. However, as I focused on how their mobile game play occurred, when it was stopped in those space, and how they used their strategies to play digital games, questions arose about how young children's participation in public spaces had been regulated and limited.

Principle 4: We have an ethical imperative to answer (or answerability)

According to Bakhtin (1990), we can see ourselves only through how we are reflected in others' reactions to us. To help others see themselves, we have an obligation to answer. Although the words or gestures one may use to answer the utterance of another can never be completely adequate, the meaning of their utterance is double-voiced, and contradictory and unfixed, my attempt to understand and then answer is nevertheless meaningful if I am deeply engaged in the conversation. This is what Bakhtin (1990) calls *answerability*. For example, I found that the four children actively sought out opportunities for playing digital games, but at the same time they quickly became bored and gave up on their game play. Their behaviours seemed contradictory and inconsistent, but I could find them meaningful that help our understanding of young children living in modern spaces as I seriously attempted to understand them.

This study sought to answer how young children participate in public spaces by understanding the experiences of the four individual children playing digital games in public spaces.

Results

To more effectively explain individual children's digital gaming contexts generated in the intersection of their daily schedules, I categorised their game-playing spaces into three spaces: a moving space, a public open space, and a commercial space. Within each category, I described how the three-year-old children created and recreated their game time and space in public spaces, and analysed their game playing by using Bakthininan interpretative analysis and critical theories. This study revealed that the four three-year-old children used digital games as a means of participating in modern spaces.

Game play within a moving space

The first space, a moving space, included the backseat of a car or riding in a shopping cart. In this study, a typical Saturday morning in David's family followed this pattern:

> David just left his home with his mother, his younger brother, and older sister to eat breakfast at the local McDonald's within a five minute driving distance from his house. David brings his PSP with him, as usual, and gets in his

> mother's car. As soon as David has a seat belt on, David starts to play a racing game called *Cars 2* (Sony Computer Entertainment, 2011). As his mother starts the car, David stops the game and looks out the window. Then, David looks out the back window to see a car approaching behind them. (Field note description of David in his mother's car)

Here is another description of David in his mother's car on the same day:

> David looks out the window to see vehicles on the road. Then, David plays *Cars 2* for a little while, and then he checks out the window again as he pauses it. Looking out the window happens for a very short moment – it is more like a distracted stare. David restarts the game. After a few minutes, he stops it and looks back to see another car behind his car. (Field note description of David in his mother's car)

In these two episodes, David kept checking on multiple spaces at a time. The time that David was being in the car was not very long, less than 10 minutes, but he, started, paused, restarted, and stopped the game multiples times. In the first episode, when the car started to move, David stopped playing the game and looked out the window, which is a sign that he noticed the movement of the car while he was playing the game. He was aware of both the virtual space in the game and the physical space of the car on the road. However, he did not give his full attention to either one of the spaces. While he was playing the game, other vehicles next to and behind his car easily distracted him.

None of the cars, including the virtual cars in the game, shared the same space, and their locations were in constant flux. David was the only one showing this behaviour in the car; but, by applying Bakhtin's concept of answerability, this situation 'answers' for young children who spend their time in a car backseat in their everyday lives.

According to Tobin (2013), developments of modern transportation systems enable us to create new types of play. In modern society, children have more transition time and more waiting when they are in cars, trains, and elevators. Due to this situation, cars have become a significant place for children to play, be relaxed, do their homework, form relationships with others, and enjoy family life (Barker, 2009). Although the children do not move within this space, their space is perpetually in motion (Tobin, 2013). This enables children to play games although they are still moving in reality.

However, many studies show that there are complex and contingent power relations and conflicts generated between car drivers and passengers or between children and adults in the car space (Barker, 2009; Hoffman, Gal-Oz, David, & Zuckerman, 2013). Within the space, parents often control and regulate technology, thus limiting their children's freedom, but the children often challenge their parents' authority and claim their autonomy as they create various activities and find their ways to 'influence and transform the spaces of cars' (Barker, 2009, p. 74).

The car backseat, in which David was seated, was designed for young children's safety. However, it also functions to limit their freedom as it ties their body and constrains their movements. The car is moving, but David cannot control the car. Instead, David continuously checked and looked at the vehicles around his car.

What was left unsaid, the *non*-dit (Macherey, 1978) is that the situation seems very frustrating for David. Although he could play with the racing game, which is his favourite, he seemed to have more interest in the real cars on the road. He mentioned the car approaching behind them several times to his mother, but it did not help him get her attention or invite the others into his conversation. He is relatively powerless and weak while sitting in the car seat. However, when it comes to his game space, he is in complete control. He is able to operate his virtual car and decide to stop or start the car. Following the notion of Foucault's heterotoplas, David's game play is his means of resisting constraints on space and time. During the game play, David remains in the car back seat and aware of the reality, but the contradiction of control offered by the game allows him to contest and resist his reality.

I found that a shopping cart is another common space where young children may play games at the same time that their physical space is moving. To understand why young children play games in a shopping cart, it is important to understand the function of a shopping cart as a way of restricting children's movement. Shopping carts are easy to find in most shopping malls and grocery stores, and some of them are specifically designed for young children's tastes – they look like toy cars with steering wheels. However, like a child sitting in the back seat of a car, a child sitting in a shopping cart has no control over the movement of the cart. They can turn the pretend steering wheel; however, it does not affect the movement of the cart.

While grocery shopping with his mother, Mike sat in the shopping cart and engaged in the following dialogue:

Mike:	Look at, Mama. Look at. [His mother, Lisa, and his sister, Kelly, discuss what to buy. He looks down and draws something with his mother's phone as he is sitting in a shopping cart. Even while the cart is moving, his eyes are stuck to the screen. Lisa and his sister check their shopping list.]
Mike:	Look at. [showing me his drawing] poo-poo! [As his cart approaches to a dessert section, Mike looks at the products in a shelf] Mama! I want strawberry ice cream.
Lisa:	Mike! That's what we asked you.
Mike:	Can we have the strawberry ice cream? [Lisa and his sister look for it in a refrigerator. He is drawing something on his mother's iPhone with his thumbs.]
Mike:	I made a spider web again. [No response from Lisa or his sister] Look at! I made a spider web. Look at! [He lifts the phone higher and shows it to me.] You can watch that.
Researcher:	Ok. [The cart begins to move again and he looks around at the shelves.]
Mike:	It looks yummy. [showing his drawing to me and then stretching his arm to touch my camera]
Lisa:	Alright! We're moving.
Mike:	[passing by the vegetable section of the grocery store] What are those, Mama?
Lisa:	[looking off at something else] Mike! Draw another one.
Mike:	What's that mommy?
Lisa:	I'm carrying in the back. Try another one. [looks at her daughter] Stay there. I will get it.
Kelly:	Ok.
Mike:	What's this?
Mike's sister:	This one's mine. You play your game. [Mike presses the home button] Oh. No, no, no … Mike! Not that one. Not that one. Not that one Mike!
Mike:	I just want to.
Kelly:	No, no, no … Mike! Not this one.
Mike:	Please …
Kelly:	No, Mom said no. Only M's one …
Mike:	[clicking his siblings' game folder] I don't wanna do that one. Those ones are not hard.
Kelly:	You want me to do it?
Mike:	No.
Researcher:	Is it your game?
Mike:	Yea … [clicking on his own game folder]
Researcher:	There are a lot.
Kelly:	Mike! No, no, no … Don't leave it right there. You have to hold it. [grabbing game] Alright, I will hold it. You want me to hold it?
Mike:	No …
Kelly:	You wanna hold it?
Mike:	Yea. Watch this. [takes the game back from her]
Kelly:	Try this one. (Field notes from a conversation at a grocery market)

Mike was the only one sitting in the shopping cart while his 12-year-old sister was walking around the grocery market with her mother during their grocery shopping. They were able to occupy different spaces and take on different roles in the grocery store. There also appears to be much that is left unsaid.

In his study of parents and children shopping together, Rust (1993) revealed that there are big differences between parents' expectations and the shopping behaviours of younger children (ages 2–3) and older children (ages 10–13). The study showed that parents were more likely to tolerate older children's shopping behaviours and accept their requests. According to Rust, 'this may have been a function either of altered power relationships or of more educated children who knew ahead of time what mom would accept' (p. 7). In other words, older children were more likely to behave as their parents would expect them to while they were shopping together.

Mike is constrained to this specific space during their time in the grocery store, and he is usually strapped in with the seatbelt. The children's seat in the shopping cart might be designed to prevent young children from hidden dangers such as falling products from a shelf. However, it is also used as a means of controlling unpredictable children, for the sake of the adults in the store.

However, regardless of his physical limitations, Mike kept trying to find ways to create his own space for play and engage others in his space. When he could not participate in the shopping or when his requests were denied or overlooked by his mother and sister, he instead tried to play with his mother's phone, using it as a medium to attract the attention of others. He said, 'Look at! I made a spider web. Look at!' to me to call my attention toward his play. He also said, 'You can watch that,' which was an invitation to his play with the caveat that he is still the host of the play. In this short conversation, we can see how he used the mobile device to participate in the space and to have power within the space, although it was temporal and he was not successful in involving his mother in the play.

Mike also attempted to open his sister's game folder and searched the phone screen. According to Lisa, she has three different game folders on her iPhone for her three children's games, and she does not allow Mike to open his siblings' game folders because the games were not 'age appropriate.' Mike knew the rules, just like his sister. However, he chose to break the rules, and spent time playing his sister's games. When his mother was away from him, he asked his sister, 'What's this?' It was not really a question, but rather a strategy for showing off that he was playing new games. This exchange was a double-voiced discourse; multiple voices were involved in one individual discourse. Kelly directly and indirectly cited her mother's words to control Mike's game play as she said, 'No, Mom said no. Only M's one ... ' or, 'Don't leave it right there. You have to hold it.' Kelly spoke the words, but the words were only half hers. In the moment, Kelly took the role of Lisa and reminded Mike of the game play rules to stop his behaviour and to control his participation in the space.

Mike failed to play the new games because his sister stopped him. However, it was meaningful that he used the mobile device to invite people around him to his play as a play host. He was never physically free from the public space (the shopping cart) or from the game rules and boundaries created by his mother; nevertheless, his behaviour proves that he was an active social participant in this space.

Children's game play in public open spaces

Eunsook often visits a local McDonald's restaurant to allow her children to have playtime with their friends. There is a playroom separated from the main dining area where people can order and eat their meals, and the playroom consists of two different spaces: one is a small dining area with tables and chairs, and the other is a play area surrounded by a safety fence. The play area is double protected and separated by two different walls; one is the wall placed between the main area and the playroom, and the other is the safety wall placed between the small dining area and the play area.

Young children and their parents or caregivers go in and out of the playroom using the outside area of the indoor playground, which I will call the 'intermediate space.' However, the direction of movement in and out of this space is opposite for parents and children; the children go in and out of the space from the indoor playground, but their parents go in and out of it from the main dining area. While the children play in the indoor playground, their parents order their food in the main dining area. After they pick up their food and enter the intermediate space, the children typically leave the playground and meet their parents in this intermediate space. With these opposing movements, a double-voiced space is formed, suggesting that the physical space functions to control the children's movement, keeping their bodies within the playroom. The children's space is distinct from the adults' space.

There are three video game cabinets located next to the wall of the playroom. They have low-end graphics, and the games have simple rules, allowing children to play the games without needing additional help from adults or older siblings. The game cabinets have vivid colours and child-friendly features, making them very appealing for children as they are waiting for their parents. The game cabinets located near the playroom are effective enough to make children stay in the area but do not require an extended period of time or involvement. In his study, Guins (2004) discussed the quotidian game space, including video game cabinets where digital games were played, and he questioned what individuals should do as they looked out from the game screen. The video game cabinets located near the playroom in the McDonald's do not just make a statement about the games that children play; they also show how their existence or their spatial location affects young children's play culture in their everyday lives.

It is possible to see how these machines function to distract children and keep them within the play area in the restaurant. After Chan's family went outside of the playroom and while his mother was cleaning up their trash, he was holding the controller and pressing its buttons. The game cabinets, the location of the space, and the various play structures were orchestrated to control children's bodies by sending them a hidden message: 'You need to play in either the indoor playground or the gaming area if you want to stay here.' Game devices located in public open spaces enabled young children to play in these public spaces, but their primary purpose was not to support young children's play but rather to limit or control their participation in and out of the space, just like the shopping cart.

There are many public places like the McDonald's playroom where children are separated from adults. A kids' club serves as another example of a children's space within a public area. The main purpose of this space is to keep the children safely in place until their parents come to pick them up. Many commercial spaces, such as IKEA, contain a kids' area, e.g., Småles, for children's play. It is a space for waiting; the children wait for their parents to call their name like patients waiting for a nurse to call.

These spaces often contain mobile games. These mobile games do not serve a purpose by themselves, but they are able to serve as a sort of medium, connecting split and scattered time from space to space as children move about in their daily lives. In this study, Amy played mobile games in a kids' club located within a local gym, but she was not fully immersed in the game. As Amy was waiting for her mother to pick her up, she was prepared to stop her game with little notice. The physical and mental spaces created during this type of mobile play are more like a bubble – they can be popped at any time and recreated easily – rather than like a sacred place for children's play. The mobile game perfectly functioned in the kids' club. Amy could have played with the toys or any other children in the room, but she decided to play with her mother's iPhone. Tobin (2013) described this function of mobile game play in quotidian life. For him, mobile game play was opportunistic, and depended on the situation. 'It fits in a purse, a pocket, a train ride, a waiting room attended to without dominating the attention' (p. 4).

Amy's mobile game play was never complete, and it did not require her to be fully immersed or unaware of her physical surroundings. The mobile game player could be turned on and off anytime. This temporal game play allowed Amy to fill up her waiting time, challenging boredom as she played throughout the day. Her use of game play appears to be far removed from the type of meaningful play discussed by many educators, but as we consider the situation in which her mother comes to pick her up at any moment, we can say that she was actively searching for the right tool and ways to fill her time (Tobin, 2013). Like choosing what to wear on a rainy day or a snowy day, young children occasionally choose to play mobile games even in a room with children's toys when they face the challenges of negotiating time and space in modern life.

Young children's digital game play in commercial spaces

Commercial structures such as electronic shops, toy stores, department stores, and discount stores have become sites of family time, where families hang out, shop, and eat. David's mother described her family's schedule, 'I go to a mall with my kids every Saturday afternoon.' Like many other mothers, going to the mall or a shopping center had become a ritual in everyday family life, similar to other families who go to church on Sunday mornings.

In this study, children were observed in several commercial spaces, such as the 99¢ Store, Target, and shops in a shopping mall. In these settings, children's game play seemed to not only kill time while their parents shopped, but was also used for testing new games and game players that were displayed in the commercial areas. The displays and arrangements of the game products beckon the children to come and play with them. In these areas, the children were not just game players, but also future consumers. They were practising how to buy and consume the commodities while they were testing the games and game players. This practice became habitual as they repeatedly visited these spaces.

Consumption is not the only practice that occurs within commercial spaces. Young children also used the gaming space within these spaces to escape from their reality – a child who must wait for their parents to finish their task. Whenever Chan found a game testing device, he asked his father for his permission to stay in the area, or Chan invited him to play the game together. It was Chan's tactic to lead the family toward his personal goal. The repetition of his actions gave him power to create a rule for play in the space. According to Chan's mother, playing and testing new games in commercial areas was a habitual family practice. Together they visited Best Buy, not to purchase products, but to check out new games. For example, Chan and his father played tennis on the Wii and also drove a virtual race together. This moment was not very long, but for the father and the children, this place became a version of a video arcade where they could play games and watch others play. In the moment, for Chan, Best Buy became a heterotopia – he could experience utopia while he was still in reality. Chan playing digital games in the commercial space illustrates how young children can transform commercial spaces into contexts for play by tactically using displayed digital game players in these spaces.

Game space as a threshold within public areas

Games may also play an important role in establishing 'thresholds' within public spaces. The following interaction between Mike, Lisa, and Kevin occurred on their way to a local hair salon:

Lisa: You're gonna get your hair cut first, Mike!
Kevin: I know. I just want a hair cut, too.
Lisa: Woo ... What about Mike? You want Kevin to go first?
Mike: Yea ...
Lisa: Ok ... Let's see when we get there. Who is easier? Maybe Kevin should get to go first this time. Should Mommy go first?
Mike: Yea. I am gonna watch you.
Lisa: You are?
Mike: I can play ... on your ... I can see your phone.
Lisa: Ok ... But Mike! You have to sit very quietly, and if you won't sit quietly, you have to come outside and no phone.
Mike: Why?
Lisa: Why? Because you have to behave if you want to play with the phone. Do you understand?
Mike: Mmmhmm ... (Transcription of conversation in the car)

The space within the hair salon required different behaviours and approaches than the car space if Mike wanted to remain inside that space. As soon as Mike crossed the threshold of the hair salon, he needed to behave and be quiet, as his mother suggested. This set of behavioural changes, followed by the changes in their space (from the car to the hair salon) as well as the change in time (from when they left to the time that they arrived) can be explained by the term, 'the chronotope of the threshold' (Bakhtin, 1981, p. 248).

In a novel, a hero may encounter many events that affect his path. When he crosses the threshold of an event, it becomes a breaking point, changing his life. When Mike crossed the threshold of the hair salon, which is not typically a children's place, he was expected to practice different social rules. As he experienced this type of space, the social norms expected him to leave his childhood behaviours and enter a type of adulthood.

In another encounter inside the hair salon, Mike was allowed to be free from the social expectations as he played digital games:

Mike: [while playing *Angry Birds* on his mother's phone] Oh! That's a big angry bird. [speaking loudly]
Lisa: M!
Mike: Yeah!
Lisa: Oh! Mike! Please be quiet.
Mike: Haha! [laughing loudly] Oh yea! [making the birds fly and looking at Youn] (Transcribed conversation at the local hair salon)

In the hair salon, Mike was supposed to be quiet; however, as soon as he started the *Angry Birds* game on his mother's phone, he forgot, reverting to his typical behaviour, and became absorbed in the game. The temporal game space created a brief moment of crisis between Mike and his mother, but it also allowed him to feel as though he was more in control of his body and mind in the unfamiliar space. Also, the conflict created between Mike and Lisa showed how young children resist the space created or experienced by adults by using their own tactics. In this scenario, the digital gaming space within the larger public space was a threshold, a breaking point within young Chan's life that allowed him to escape from the social norms and rules expected by adults while he was playing digital games.

Conclusion

This study showed how young children experienced and worked to control modern public spaces where social norms often limited young children's participation. Like other studies (Elsley, 2004; Ito et al., 2006; Tobin, 2000), these participants used digital games to resist the controls they were subjected to in modern spaces. Young children's digital game play in public spaces does not help the children escape from their reality; rather, it serves as a useful tactic for them to negotiate with public regulations, constraints, and their imposed daily schedules Young children also use digital game play as a means of escaping from adults' surveillance (Thompson & Cupples, 2008).

Clearly, young children are able to reshape spaces, which were designed for adults' usage (e.g., a hair salon) into play spaces by playing digital games. These digital game spaces served as 'heterotopias,' which allowed the children to resist the external conditions around them as they experienced both virtual and physical spaces (Foucault, 1986).

While many would argue that digital games are not ideal for young children, digital games should be understood as one of the many activities that young children use to cope with modern life. As Tobin (2013) argued, digital games, especially mobile games, are personal, situational, and opportunistic, and young children utilise them for their own purposes. Also, the development of location-based game such as Pokémon GO allows players to blur boundaries between physical and virtual spaces.

In this study, young children touch, test, and play their games to create a playful experience within public spaces. They also became distracted, gave up on playing games, or refused to play games in certain ways as they were aware of the environments surrounding them. The experiences of the individual children cannot be generalised, but their experiences point to the need to rethink young game players who are marginalised and excluded from public participation. In many ways, they are actively searching for ways to play and negotiate their experiences in a variety of public spaces.

Young children's digital game play in public spaces may seem trivial, and consequently it has been overlooked by educators, policy-makers, and caregivers who make important decisions on young children's participation in public spaces. As seen in this study, young children's play with digital games within the public spaces can also be valued as they offer a tactic for resisting the controls imposed on them in spaces that are designed primarily for adult usage.

Disclosure statement

No potential conflict of interest was reported by the author.

References

Ailwood, J. (2003). Governing early childhood education through play. *Contemporary Issues in Early Childhood, 4*(3), 286–299.

Angry Birds [Mobile application software]. (2009). Retrieved from https://www.angrybirds.com/

Bakhtin, M. M. (1981). *The dialogic imagination four essays.* (M. Holquist, Ed., C. Emerson & M. Holquist, Trans.). Austin, TX: University of Texas Press (original work published 1975).

Bakhtin, M. M. (1990). *Art and answerability: Early philosophical essays* (M. Holquist & V. Liapunov, Eds., V. Liapunov & K. Brostrom, Trans). Austin, TX: University of Texas Press.

Barker, J. (2009). 'Driven to distraction?': Children's experiences of car travel. *Mobilities, 4*(1), 59–76.

Buckingham, D. (2007). *Beyond technology.* Cambridge, MA: Polity Press.

Cars 2 [Mobile application software]. (2011). Retrieved from https://www.playstation.com/en-us/games/cars-2-the-video-game-psp/

Collier, J., & Collier, M. (1986). *Visual anthropology: Photography as a research method.* Albuquerque, NM: University of New Mexico Press.

Dormans, J. (2011, September 14–17). *Integrating emergence and progression.* Paper presented at the DiGRA 2011 conference: Think design play. Hilversum the Netherlands, DiGRA.

Elsley, S. (2004). Children's experience of public space. *Children & Society, 18*(2), 155–164.

e Silva, A. D. S. (2006). From cyber to hybrid mobile technologies as interfaces of hybrid spaces. *Space and culture, 9*(3), 261–278.

Foucault, M. (1986). Of other spaces. (J. Miskowiec, Trans.) *Diacritics, 16*(1), 22–27.

Guins, R. (2004). 'Intruder alert! intruder alert!' video games in space. *Journal of Visual Culture, 3*(2), 195–211.

Harden, J. (2000). There's no place like home the public/private distinction in children's theorizing of risk and safety. *Childhood, 7*(1), 43–59.

Hjorth, L., & Richardson, I. (2009). The waiting game: Complicating notions of (tele) presence and gendered distraction in casual mobile gaming. *Australian Journal of Communication, 36*(1), 23–35.

Hoffman, G., Gal-Oz, A., David, S., & Zuckerman, O. (2013, June). *In-car game design for children: child vs. parent perspective.* Paper presented at proceedings of the 12th international conference on interaction design and children (pp. 112–119). New York, ACM.

Ito, M. (2008). Education vs. entertainment: A cultural history of children's software. In K. Salen (Ed.), *The ecology of games: Connecting youth, games, and learning* (pp. 89–116). Cambridge, MA: The MIT Press.

Ito, M., Okabe, D., & Matsuda, M. (2006). *Personal, portable, pedestrian: Mobile phones in Japanese life.* Cambridge, MA: MIT Press.

Macherey, P. (1978). *A theory of literary production* (G. Wall, Trans.) London: Routledge & K. Paul (original work published 1966).

McNamee, S. (2000). Foucault's heterotopia and children's everyday lives. *Childhood, 7*(4), 479–492.

O'brien, M., Jones, D., Sloan, D., & Rustin, M. (2000). Children's independent spatial mobility in the urban public realm. *Childhood, 7*(3), 257–277.

Richardson, I. (2007). Pocket technospaces: the bodily incorporation of mobile media. *Continuum: Journal of Media & Cultural Studies, 21*(2), 205–215.

Rowsell, J. (2014). Toward a phenomenology of contemporary reading. *Australian Journal of Language and Literacy, 37*(2), 117–127.

Rust, L. (1993). Parents and children shopping together: A new approach to the qualitative analysis of observational data. *Journal of Advertising Research, 33*(4), 65–70.

Sefton-Green, J. (2004). Initiation rites: Small boy in a poke-world. In J. Tobin (Ed.), *Pikachu's global adventure: The rise and fall of Pokémon* (pp. 141–164). Durham, NC: Duke University Press.

Sutton-Smith, B. (1997). *The ambiguity of play.* Cambridge, MA: Harvard University Press.

Thompson, L., & Cupples, J. (2008). Seen and not heard? Text messaging and digital sociality. *Social & Cultural Geography, 9*(1), 95–108.

Tobin, J. (2000). *Good guys don't' wear hats.* New York, NY: Teachers College Press.

Tobin, S. (2013). *Portable play in everyday life: The Nintendo DS.* New York, NY: Palgrave Macmillan.

Playing with power: an outdoor classroom exploration*

Eden Haywood-Bird

ABSTRACT
In this ethnographic research, discovery of how preschool-aged children use play to wield their individual power in the outdoors is documented in a single classroom. Embedded as a participant-researcher and working from constructivist and critical theory orientations, the researcher seeks to understand how children use their play to construct the shared classroom cultural understanding of what it means to hold and wield power. Children age two and a half through five years old engage in a number of activities to experiment with what it means to be powerful. Imaginative play, physically risky play, as well as solo play are all explored. In light of the findings, various theories of power as expressed through the lens of critical theory will be used to analyse student and teacher voices.

Introduction and problem

In past generations, children were allowed to explore and play in their environments in ways that allowed children to express themselves. Children climbed trees, threw rocks, and often played out of the now ever-present gaze of adults, even as preschoolers. Not more than two years old, I distinctly remember being in my hot and dry, Tucson backyard, climbing up a very large hill of dirt. Why the pile of dirt? I cannot recall, but I do remember the glee I felt at feeling the soil in my fingers and toes, and how powerful it felt to get to the top and roll down the other side, pretending to be a monkey. I reflected on this memory, being present again in my two-year-old body, if only for a moment in my mind, that my experience was so markedly different than my own child's, always supervised, hands below her, to cushion any fall, in all her activities.

I again return on myself, this time with my hat as teacher firmly in place. After 13 years scaffolding children through their first 5 years in the classroom, I know that I personally have become part of the problem, even though I know that risk and outdoor play often do, and as some argue should, go hand in hand. Learning how to navigate situations that are risky and make proper choices in safety is a common theme in the early childhood empirical literature. Rivkin (1997) is echoed a decade later by Maller (2009) in finding that children who are given an opportunity to play in a natural area are more flexible. Just as interesting, Berger and Lahad (2009) found that children in nature were better at appropriate risk-taking. Basically, these children are allowed to take appropriate risks in nature and because of this, they are more resilient and flexible in other aspects of their lives. Flexibility in thinking and the ability to discriminate an activity as overly risky are developed throughout childhood and are both important skills for adults (Berger & Lahad, 2009)

Children today are not being allowed to play out of doors nearly as much as children in the past (Louv, 2008; O'Brien, 2009). Lack of physical play, in particular unscripted play out of doors in nature,

*This article is adapted from the author's dissertation research completed at Colorado State University.

has become restricted in the last 25–30 years. The large scale Tort reform in the 1980s allowed for more personal injury lawsuits (Moore & Wong, 1997). These reforms make it possible for angry or hurt parents to sue municipalities, schools, other parents, and manufacturers of play equipment if their child was injured on their property or toy, even if there was no negligence on the other party's part. Our culture now seems to be guided by fear and now fear has become a common reason for not allowing children to play out of doors (Louv, 2008). It is possible that these reforms have led our culture to the current status as risk-adverse.

I find the empirical body to lack the child's perspective and experiences. Where is the voice of the child? What do the children think and feel about outdoor play? How do the children express themselves while in the outdoors? I wonder what their experiences are in this sort of environment. There seems to be a great deal of research that looks at what the teacher or parent feels the child 'gets' out of being outdoors but nothing from the child her- or himself. I am most interested in documenting the experience of the child as directly as possible. This paper seeks to address these two identified gaps in the current research about outdoor play, and the young child's development of self-reflecting power in that outdoor environment.

Method of inquiry

The purpose of this ethnography is to discover how preschool-aged children use play to develop powerful agency in the outdoors, specifically to answer the question, what is the experience of a young child out of doors? I spent 5 months as a participant-observer within a preschool classroom where the 25 children age 2½–5 years are given extensive time outdoors every day. All the children in the programme were of European-American decent and all were from middle-class, professional families. The school was a private, non-profit childcare that considered themselves to be Waldorf-inspired. Since I was originally interested in how the children interacted within the outdoor environment, I chose to only join the classroom during this daily outdoor time. The outdoor time took place outside the school's boundaries and included a walk up the street to a natural area owned by the city, affectionately referred to as the Forest by the children. After careful deliberation with the teachers and parents, the decision was made I should join the group at the school, walk to the Forest, stay for their entire play, and walk back to the school with the group. All involved felt this would help me become part of the school culture.

I used an ethnographic approach for data collection, capturing my observations in a handwritten field notebook. The inquiry was conducted in a constructivist, emergent method where I was also a co-constructor of the culture and experiences in the classroom. Being a member and co-constructor of the experiences in this classroom of 25 children in real time, the field notes were not a passive reconstruction of the memories of play, but took place in real time (Hesse-Biber & Leavy, 2011).

As defined by Hesse-Biber and Leavy (2011), I sought to '… get a holistic understanding of how individuals in different cultures and subcultures make sense of their lived realities' (p. 193), in this case, within the context of the preschool class. As I embarked on this research, I also felt that a constructivist viewpoint would be most beneficial. As a participant-observer, I knew that I would be co-constructing the culture and reality of the classroom along with the children and that as an adult myself, I would influence the dynamic of what it means to be powerful in the classroom culture. I also knew that through ethnography, this co-construction would be helpful for me to understand the internal social structure and what it means to be part of this culture of risk and play in a way I would not be party to as a singular observer. However, I also knew that I needed more than just a co-construction for this work to be an authentic representation of the children's experience; I needed to be an active participant who interacted directly with the teachers.

Post-Marxist critical theory was chosen as the theoretical perspective because young children are considered a culture that is dominated by another group – adults. Not allowed to speak with a collective voice, young children are caught in a power dynamic where their feelings and experiences are discounted to what the adults around them deem they 'should' be instead of how the child relates to the natural world through their own experience. These adults interpret how they believe the children should believe and feel, instead of acknowledging children relate to the world through their own, unique experiences. As Soto and Swadener (2002) argue, early childhood should be looked at as currently colonized by adult minds. I am cognizant of how far I can take this interpretation of how I think the children should be instead of how the children actually relate to powerful agency through their own experiences. The implicit dynamic of 'adult vs. child' should not be overlooked.

However, a distinction should be made between an ethnographic study that uses a critical lens and a critical ethnography. A critical ethnography is expressly focused on working towards change for the marginalized group being studied. What I did here was use the critical lens to ground my thinking about the children as whole, human beings. While these children do live in a marginalized paradigm, my ultimate goal in this study is to learn about their experiences in the outdoors instead of work towards their broader social justice. While I make a marked attempt to provide the voice of the child in this work, the majority of the analysis was completed using the children's perspective as interpreted through both actions and dialogue, and not through direct interviews.

I was constrained by the wishes of the children's families to not directly engage children in questioning beyond inquiry into their play actions, so the vignettes found here are representative of play dynamics seen multiple times in the field. This constraint was challenging for me because it meant I was not able to directly engage the children in conversations about their concepts of power, agency, and play. I attempted to instead learn about the children featured in the vignettes through interviews with the families, and thus use my understanding of their individuality and personality in my analysis of their play. This process also included detailed narratives of each child, which after feedback from the families with multiple additions and revisions, I was better able to ground my understanding of my influences on the culture and power dynamics and help me deconstruct what I was seeing and participating in in the field. By understanding the children from multiple perspectives, I endeavoured to carve out a little of the unknowable – how my presence changed the children's play.

I used Wolcott's (1994) method described as transformational process as a touchstone in my analysis of my expanded field notes by developing themes through a process of coding. The three-step process in Wolcott (1994) for data transformation is: (1) Description: where I asked myself, 'what's going here?': (2) Analysis: where I began sorting data in charts and action themes, asking myself, 'what does it say?'; (3) Interpretation: where I looked back over my sorted data, asking myself, 'what does it all mean?' I then took these initial codes and created a frequency table of actions. Using the table, I chose to exclude any action that was recorded less than five times.

Within these first codes, I recoded the notes for sub-themes, using a basic thematic approach. It was during this second coding the themes around powerful agency began to emerge. I used thick, rich descriptions and details throughout to describe to readers the complexity of both the setting and the interactions. I did not see any that I would consider overtly dangerous activities from any children during my observations. However, since I made a choice to only focus on single actions and games that were seen more than once, I know that I have only a very slim section of time captured in my observation in regard to the children's experience in the cultural environment. The titles in the table indicate whether the actions where physical choices from the child or children, or if the actions were emotional choices being made. For example, in the physical actions column, if children made the choice to hold hands, I saw this as a powerful choice as hand holding was not required on the walk to and from the school. Examples of the action codes are found in Table 1.

Trustworthiness

A strong danger to trustworthiness in ethnography is that the researcher is unable to see herself as part of the experience of the group's culture in study and therefore downplays her personal impact

Table 1. Sub-themes matrix-power.

Physical actions	Emotional actions
Sitting alone – 14	Choosing friends – 35
Choosing who to walk with – 19	Vocally stating needs – 47
Climbing trees – 27	Organizing play – 32
Walking on rocks – 7	Negotiating pretend drama – 45
Creating tools – 6	Leaving play – 17
Helping friend out of tree – 15	Directing conflict – 26
Holding hands with friend – 12	

on change in that culture (Gubrium & Holstein, 2008). Interpersonal relationships with the children will in all likelihood develop in such a close and physical research orientation (Josselson, 2007) which was certainly the case with me in this study. I became friends with many of the children, engaging is intimate and complex play. I acknowledge that there is a potential that the children when they grow could be jarred by what was written about them as young children by another person and while it is nearly impossible to negate all possibilities of this (Josselson, 2007) there are actions I can take to minimize the risk (Gubrium & Holstein, 2008; Josselson, 2007). The names of the participants are changed, as is the school and city names, to negate the impacts of this possibility.

Doing ethnography with preliterate children is challenging from a best practice stand point. Taking a cue from Rossholt's (2009) ethnographic work with young children and body awareness, I followed her suggestions for noninvasive field work with young preschoolers by allowing the children to take the lead. Because children this young sometimes lack the skills to always vocally articulate what they may want from me in the field, I made a concerted effort to notice and read each child's body language for any sort of distress or discomfort (Rossholt, 2009). I did not pressure anyone to engage. I was also always cognizant that not all dynamics of power and privilege between me and the children could not be erased (Rossholt, 2009; Walcott, 1994). My position both as an adult and as a parent innately created a sort of permission-based power structure that can never be dispelled. I am an adult and they are small children and the cultural norm of the adult as the being in charge will be seen as evident in my experiences in the field in the findings section (Walcott, 1994).

However, I always attempted absolute assent. I asked the children if I could play with them before joining their group or walking along the road next to them. Through in-field reflexive notes in my notebook, I was able to capture my thoughts in the moment about my researcher role whenever I was with the children, acknowledging that my presence may be changing their play and questioning what I was seeing or experiencing as authentic representations of the classroom culture. I acknowledge that my presence alone likely created an entirely new cultural norm (Rossholt, 2009). I also attempted to clarify with the children what I think I understood as the meaning of their actions or words by asking each of them about their play. I did not always get an answer and the answers I did get could very easily have been influenced by the power dynamic that is implicate between child and adult. This is one of the main reasons I engaged with the families of the children as well, to try to mitigate the developmental impulse from the children to tell me what they thought I might want to hear.

To solve both these queries, I engaged in reflexive memo-ing in the moment when I was in the outdoor classroom. I engaged in personal thoughts about what I thought I was seeing and what I perceive the children are doing in my presence. Reflexive practice is often defined as a reflection in the moment where the researcher changes their actions or way of questioning to better support the subjects and not cause any harm (Josselson, 2007). In my case, I memo-ed in the field so I was better able to bring forth that intersubjectivity in the final work without also dehumanizing the participants' stories through over generalization of the analysis (Josselson, 2007, Tillman-Healy, 2001). After the final paper was completed, the manuscript was sent via email to all participant families to read before publication. Comments were encouraged but none were received.

Findings and discussion

The nest bush

Children in the forest were often engaged in tree-climbing play, both as independent play and in group. Children could be found hanging, climbing, and sometimes falling during this play. There were several trees and bushes that were used for climbing by the children, the first being called by the class, 'the nest bush'. The nest bush is four feet tall and around six feet wide. It has the look of a weeping willow, with branches that fold over upon themselves, creating a sort of branch waterfall effect. At the time of my observations, the net bush was without its leaves, so looked like a thicket of thin, messily woven branches from top to bottom. The backside of the bush was flat, and the thick trunk was able to be seen and accessed, while the front showed only the cascade of shiny branches. The nest bush sits right at the front of the Forest.

The first time I was part of an interaction with the nest bush, three children engaged me in their play. Ryan (m, age 4), Sarah (f, age 4), and Ronny (m, age 3) were all climbing up what is the backside of the nest bush. Each was climbing to the top of what seemed to me a very unstable climbing surface. Taking a cue from the teacher standing nearby who, while watching, did not interfere, I walked nearer and asked if I could watch their play. After getting a positive response, I stood near the top of the highest part of the nest bush.

Climbing this bush seemed to be a challenge for Ryan as he slowly made his way to the top. Ryan was very slowly and meticulously having to look down at his feet before deciding where to place it next. As he rounded the top, I read the look upon his face as fear and asked him if I could help him down. Answering a strained yes, I moved to his area, and told him I was going to help him down. He responded, 'No, fly me!' Never having heard this term before, I asked Ryan to help me understand. He coached me with where to put my hands on his body. I grasped Ryan under each arm and gently pulled him down to the ground, over the top of the bush. He ran back around to the other side of it to climb it again.

Sarah, a confident climber, who did not seem to be fearful at all, rounded the top and I asked her if she would like to fly. Her answer, 'No, I'm jumping.' I took a couple steps back, out of the way. Instead of jumping from the top as I expected, Sarah moved herself down the front of the bush, sliding very carefully on her bottom with her legs bent in front of her. When she had reached her destination around the front, about two feet from the ground, she sprang off the bush with a strong push of her legs, landing with what I saw as a practised manoeuvre. The entire bush shook as she pushed off, but her jump to the ground was sound. She stuck the landing, both feet flat on the ground. Sarah ran back to the bush swiftly and again began to quickly climb.

Ronny, who had been climbing along with Sarah, reached the top of the bush at the same time. Sarah's jumping exit left Ronny at the crest, looking down. I waited for a moment, assessing the situation and perceived Ronny's hesitance as him being conflicted about if he wanted to jump or not, so I asked him if he wanted to fly. Without taking a moment to mull it over, he answered fly. Using the same method as I had to hold Ryan, I flew Ronny down to the ground as well and he ran for the back of the bush again to climb again.

This interaction examines how taking the risk to climb the nest bush was at different levels for each of these three individual children. It seemed that by the space allowed to take this risk outdoors, the children were able to determine what level of risk each could tolerate. Feeling powerful to choose this risk seemed to lead to a strong sense of personal accountability in how the individual child wanted to leave the nest bush, either through their own physical power as Sarah did, or through my physical power as Ronny and Ryan chose to do. It is, of course, entirely possible that Ronny and/or Ryan would not have chosen to climb the bush at all had I not been near it and already interacting with Sarah, thus never exploring this feat of powerful agency in the first place.

The children of different physical abilities and risk tolerance were all able to use the same area of the forest to practice what it means to be powerful. Because each child had differing physical abilities, the choice to be flown down by me from the nest bush, or to jump without aid, allowed for that personal tolerance of risk to go un-judged. Being powerful in that moment was about ascertaining and then having respected his or her own ability to tolerate the risk involved with leaving the nest bush. As I reflect on my own role in this interaction, I wonder if my presence alone created this powerful moment for the children. This interaction is just a snapshot of the multiple interactions I had with the three children at the bush, and I wonder, as this was the first, if my being there facilitated this exploration of powerful activity.

This is my house

I was often drawn in to participate in the drama of the pretend play by the children. I made a point of only following directions from the children instead of adding in my own imagined ideas because I wanted to record the children's participation experience more than I wanted to record my own. That said, I fully understood that my presence alone was not benign and even as I was purposefully putting myself in the hand of the children, my presence alone created a dynamic that did not occur when I was not in the mix.

One game that I was part of quite a bit was what I called The House Game. This game predated my time in the classroom and was played in some form by many of the children. Each time the House Game was played, it was slightly different in format and approach with the only constant being the placement inside the Forest. The House Game always took place under a mass of bushes on the Forest's southern treed area. In order to be part of The House Game, I was required to crawl under these bushes on my hands and knees and then be seated in a small, cleared area on the frozen ground. I never engaged in the House Game without being invited by a child but I was fortunate to be invited into the house often.

On a sunny and cold day in early December, I stepped off the road and into the Forest. Nearby me are Jake (m, age 5) and Trevor (m, age 3).

Jake: Do you want me to show you mine in Trevor's house?
Researcher: Sure.

I walk with both Trevor and Jake through the whole woods area, going to the back bushes. Eve and Omar follow us through the forest. We make a line, snaking back through the wooded area as we make our way to the back. Together, we come to the back clump of bushes and Omar, Eve, and Jake begin to climb through the bushes while I couch down to crawl through to the place where the house game is always played. Being much smaller than I am, the children can take different paths to the place under the bushes known as the House. I sit in the only place tall enough under the bushes for me to sit upright. Near me is Eve, making her way to another section under the bushes.

Eve, seeing me sitting: I have a different house. The house is over here. I just like it, it's nice and warm. There is also a sunny place that can make you warm.

I attempt to move to her spot, about six feet away from where I am currently seated. I am not very successful as the canopy of branches is rather low on my head, so Eve moves closer to me, while remaining under a different bush than I am. Another child, Mary (f, age 4), comes over to where Eve is. Mary sits down next to where I am sitting.

Eve: This is my house.
Eve says this very matter-of-factly like she is stating something that everybody should already know. It has the feel of being informative and there is no meanness or exclusivity I can detect in her tone.
Mary: Can I come in?
Eve: Yes.

Mary scoots to the other side of the bushes and sits next to where Juliet is sitting. I am still sitting rather close to them but under a different bush. At this point Jen (f, age 5) and Monica (f, age 3) come climbing under the bushes to where we are.

Eve:	This is my house.
Jen:	But we need shelter for little kitty.
Researcher:	Jen, are you little kitty?
Jen, flabbergasted:	No! Monica! I'm little puppy! Jen says this in a tone that suggests I should know that she is a puppy and Monica is a kitty.

Jen, Monica, and Mary run out of the forest at this point, leaving me and Eve underneath the bushes alone. Eve comes from *her* house into *my* house and asks me about my notebook. I explained that I am taking notes on what the children are doing and how they are playing. Eve asks me if she can write in my notebook so I give her pen and she draws a picture in my notebook. It is a big, round-shaped figure with two arms. I asked her about the picture to describe it to me.

Eve: He's big and he's not nice.

Before I have a chance to ask more, Omar comes into the house. As he is walking up to where I am sitting, he finds a half branch sticking out of the ground. He begins to kick it back and forth. As he does this, the branch makes a crazy, strange vibration.

Omar:	It's a tornado.
Eve:	Omar, can I try it?
Omar:	Yep.

Eve and Omar essentially change places, with Eve going to my right side and Omar going to my left.

Eve, pushing the branch back and forth with her hands: I'm making a fire for us. This is my house.

Again, it is to be understood that Eve is not trying to be exclusive when she says this is my house. Eve sounds so much like she is just being informative, stating a fact rather than attempting to enforce her will. Omar says nothing but continues on and out of Eve's 'house'.

Marcus then appears behind the stick that Omar called a tornado and Eve called a fire.

Eve, to Marcus:	Do you want to come in?
Marcus:	Yes, what are you doing?

I get the impression that Marcus is talking to me and not to Eve because he is looking at me when he speaks. After a moment, Eve does not answer so I do.

Researcher:	Omar was exploring the branch, the way it moves and then Eve explored it and that's about it.
Eve:	Do you want to come in?

Marcus does not answer but he comes through under the brush to where we are sitting. Monica and Jen reappear on the left side, being cats and dogs complete with cat and dog sounds of meows and barks.

Eve, to Monica and Jen:	Do you want to rest your paws?
Jen, in a doggie sounding voice:	Yes please.
Marcus, exploring the stick:	This stick is magic. It has candy.

We hear the call from the teachers to resemble as a class for the walk back to the school at the same time that Omar has come through and begun climbing the bush.

Omar:	Look at me!
Researcher:	I need help getting out of this house.
Eve:	No, you have to stay in here all day.
Researcher:	Oh, I hear Miss Star singing follow and I follow the rules so I'm going.

I make my way out of the Forest and Marcus and Eve follow me out.

The drama above unfolded over the course of the entire time the children play in the Forest, about 40 minutes. The way that the children moved in and out of the house area, co-constructing the reality of the house, what the house represented to each child, and the way that Eve felt the demonstrated confidence to state to each friend that it was 'her house' gives the impression that these children feel completely empowered by the environment to facilitate their own choices of where to be in the Forest, how to play in the Forest, and who to play with in the Forest. Children who played the house game often seemed to have very different concepts of what this pretend game represented by way of powerfulness, and as the experience above presents. These ideas of the house game often overlapped and intersected, leading to a sort of shared power between the children. In the story, Eve starts out as the one who holds the power in the play; she indicates the game with me and directs me on what to do, but as we interact, other children come into the house and either express they are equally powerful in their play, as with Jen and Monica who choose not to stay at first but come back to play and Omar and Marcus who both are playing their own version of the game in a complex intersection with Eve's version.

Dragons, soldiers, and wizards: choose your own drama

The children spent a great deal of their time in the forest engaging in pretend play drama. Since there were no props as there are inside the indoor classroom to give the children inspiration, the games rose organically from their imaginations and often collided with each other. I regularly saw one group who were pretending one drama intersect for a time with another group playing a completely different drama and for a moment, a third, co-constructed drama would emerge before the groups would separate again by mutual choice. These pretend games were the only games I did not actively participate in. At the start of my time in the Forest with the children, I attempted to participate, but the children either would stop playing or run fast and far from me. I took this to mean I was not welcome to join. Instead I was relegated to an observer. The children seemed to feel equally empowered by the space afforded by the Forest as well as by the opportunity to switch groups, combine groups, and reform new groups in this outdoor classroom.

Jamie (m, age 4), a sweet-faced little boy with glasses, is standing under one of the big trees that is on the edge of the Forest and the grassy area, organizing a group of four boys into two equal groups of two. Jamie is pointing that one group should stand on the north side of the tree and the other group should stand on the south side of the tree, not looking at each other. The tree is a very large elm and has a trunk that can easily hide one group from the other. As Jamie is continuing to tell the four boys what they are to be doing in this drama, another group of children, Marcus (m, age 4), Riley (m, age 3), and Jake (m, age 4), comes running around another large elm tree, just to the east of the tree Jamie is directing his drama. For a moment, the two groups negotiate but I am not able to hear what is being said as I am not close enough to catch it. After a short moment, Jamie opens his arms wide and begins to run, pretending to fly. The other four boys of Jamie's original group follow his lead, also spreading their arms out to use pretend wings. Marcus, Riley, and Jake watch for a moment and take off running into the Forest, away from the other group.

Jamie and his group spend some time running around the amply spaced trees in the grassy area. Another group of children, this one seemingly led by Eve (f, age 4), has entered the space where Jamie's group is flying. Jamie and Eve meet first and I am finally able to hear their conversation.

Jamie yells: 'We are all dragons!' He demonstrates how to be a dragon to the new group by growling and flapping his arms.
Eve, looking incredulous says-'No, no, I don't hear the roar.'
Jamie tried the roar again but Eve still seems unconvinced. She takes the stick she is holding and instead casts a spell on Jamie, using a sound that sounds like air quickly escaping from her mouth. Jamie runs away from her in a large arc, making his roar dragon sound.

At this point, Marcus's group re-emerges from the forest and they began to beat and kick at a large tree with their hands and feet, kung fu style. They then join up with the other two groups. For a moment, a large group comprising all the three separate groups has emerged and there is some negotiating going on about how the play will continue. It does not last long. Eve watches for a moment while Jamie and his group break away continuing their dragon play, not interested in having Marcus' group of soldiers become part of the play. Eve yells after Jamie, reminding him that her group is wizards.

As the group of soldiers headed by Marcus leaves the area, one of the children from Eve's group leaves with them. Eve looks after them for a moment and then turns back to her remaining member, Ryan. She turns her stick turned wand upon him and he slowly crumples to the ground. As Ryan is on the ground, Eve continues to pretend to cast her spell, becoming louder and louder and Ryan stands back up. Jaime's group runs by again, still flying dragons and Eve takes the time to cast a spell upon this group again. One of the members of Jamie's group stops and says something to Eve I cannot hear. She answers and her group follows him to Jaime's group on the others side of the grassy area, creating a new, larger group of wizards and dragons.

This reconstruction of a single dramatic episode illustrates how the children used powerful agency to make choices in their pretend play. While it can be argued, and I agree, that pretend play choices as a powerful activity for the young child in not exclusive to the outdoor classroom, I believe what I saw illustrated in this drama is importantly free of the conflicts often seen in pretend play in the classroom. Since the children have a far larger space and because the teachers do not have a hand in the direction of the play through prop choice and placement, the children have a wide open canvas of creation.

Additionally, I believe the lack of fighting I experience in these pretend play situations increased the children's constructing agency and practising methods of social engagement. Conflict did exist, and resolution is important to learn but what I discovered is that in the large open space, the children had the freedom of choice to move to another group, create a new group, or leave the play all together. The children were not right on top of each other in a small, confined space. It was a fluid construction, deconstruction, and reconstruction process with children moving in out of the position of the creative power, in the construction of their play. Interestingly, just as the first three stories illustrate, the teachers were completely uninvolved in the play. In fact, all the times I observed these pretend games, the teachers where not in sight.

Being alone by choice

One sunny and cold winter morning, I found myself standing alone on the western side of the Forest. All the children except for Sally were climbing through the treed area in quite a noisy fashion. Over my left shoulder, I was aware of Sally singing Old McDonald softly to herself so I turned and slowly began to walk near her. As I closed the gap to about six feet away, her singing stopped and in response, I stop walking closer to her . I stood there a moment, facing away from Sally. After about a minute, when her singing did not begin again, I took a few steps away from the table, back in the direction I had come. Sally began to sing again and I took this to say I had not been what she considered a suitable distance way, about 10 feet from her.

From the north side of the treed area, Jasmine and Eve burst forth into the grassy area, making their presence known through their loud giggling, running and quickly closing in on

Sally's table; I heard Sally stop singing again. I turned to watch the trio. Jasmine is sticking her head between the table top and the table seat, asking Sally if they could play with her. Sally remained silent but looked up at Jasmine with an expression I read as wonder and curiosity. Eve took a seat at the table, took off a glove, and began to use her right index finger to draw on the table's frosty top.

Not receiving any sort of answer from Sally, Jasmine joins Eve to draw on the table but instead of using her fingers, she uses a stick she has found on the ground. Jasmine seems to quickly tire of the drawing because she begins to use the stick to drum on the table top. The drumming makes a dull thudding noise and Sally begins to peek out from under the table to see what the noise is. Jasmine throws the stick away from her and takes up running to the other side of the treed area of the forest. After a moment, Eve follows her, Sally watching them leave. When alone again, Sally crawled out from under the table and procured the stick Jasmine has been using and brings it back to her spot under the table. I hear her soft voice begin Old McDonald again, this time using the stick to lightly bang the table seat in front of her face.

Sally seems to be playing with others in her own way. She is mostly alone by choice in this episode but what I understand about this action is that it is indeed a choice. She could have easily entered Jasmine's and Eve's play. Jasmine and Eve gave Sally three very clear opportunities to join them. When they entered her space and talked to her, when they sat at the table playing in the frost, and in the space where Jasmine left and Eve stayed with her. Instead, Sally decided she would stay under her table, using her power to make choices for herself.

Reflecting on my role in this drama, I am left to wonder if Sally would have joined the girls if I had not been nearby. While being alone by choice was a method of powerful agency observed many times over the 20 weeks from multiple children, Sally was the child who most often engaged in this action. There were times I observed Sally in the same place, seated under the table, from the other side of the Forest. Children would always come to and go from her table, and she never joined.

Conclusion and reflections

For the 20 weeks I spent as a participant-observer in the Forest, I was able to be part of an incredibly complex cultural web of co-constructed norms. Originally, my goal for this research was to provide a voice for young children and what it was like to be in a school where a great deal of the day was spent out of doors in free-play but over the course of my time in the field, this shifted. Instead, I found children with a complex culture around what it was to be in charge of one's own 'destiny' in this classroom. Indeed, what I believe I saw was something as innate and human as free-will being fulfilled by the children through their play.

The critical gaze was most beneficial for my analysis of the activity themes that emerged from my field notes, as well as revisiting my in-the-moment memos of my own thoughts and feelings. I defined my critical gaze as a way of looking at my own actions in feelings at the time of the field notes and by taking notice of my influences and feelings, attempting to think of myself as a child in the moment. By this, I felt better able to make the necessary assertions and analyses without assigning a top-down type of adult meaning to the actions. Engagement with the children, at their own level, was enhanced by my critical viewpoint. Hence, my use of the critical gaze was not specifically for defining academically for myself what was happening, but instead to formulate the specific emerging questions to help define and redefine my shared experiences with the children using the Wolcott method of transformation of my field notes.

While my mere presence in the classroom culture created a new and unique culture, different than the one that would have emerged had I not been present, using the idealist model of the critical gaze in a third-person style framed what I was seeing and experiencing with the children. Given that I already accepted the notion that children were not submissive, empty vessels waiting for those in power to shape their being (Kicheloe & McLaren, 2002), I believe that my notions of the children's power are as accurate a representation as any adult in a child's world can describe. I came to understand that power for this group of children was a place of agency, a place where choice was allowed.

Upon reflection, I have come to understand and agree with Willis (1977) and Warming (2011) that what it means to have 'powerful agency' is not a concept that adults should be endeavouring to answer for children. Instead, all I could do was take what I saw and experienced and attempt to draw out meaning through cues, repletion of actions, and direct experiences with the children. In this classroom culture, power did not mean 'power in oneself' but instead is linked to actions that demonstrated the children concepts of powerfulness. Power need not be at the expense of others, it is not the action of dominance over another, as is the case for many works using a critical theory thread. Children should be given the space in the culture, in these typically marginalized environments for children, to define power for themselves. All I, as an adult and the researcher, could try and do is try to piece out what I saw and experienced within my own contexts, that of my adult understanding. However, it is fully acknowledged that through this methodology approach, my interactions with these children is coloured fully by my own experiences.

Waller and Bitou (2011) attacked challenges they believe exist in engaging young children in participator and critical-framed research. The main concern of the authors is that the researcher may not understand how, as an adult, his or her own agenda influences child behaviour and if participatory research is actually empowering to children. The article discovered that many children just 'opted out' of the research by not being near the researcher doing the fieldwork while others instead 'played it up.' The authors argue that the only true way to empower children in the research process is to make a leap from 'listening' to the children to giving the children a 'voice' by acting on their concerns. With that leap comes a separation of the researcher from the children, where observation instead of participation takes the lead in the field.

Warming (2011) conducted an ethnographic study within a childcare setting that broached the sticky topic of what it means to 'give voice to children's own perspectives' (p. 49). Contrary to Waller and Bitou (2011), who feel the researchers should be outside the child's play, Warming argues that the only way a researcher can authentically represent the children's experience is through actual participation in the child's activities, at the child's level. This is what I attempted to do in this work. Through my experiences in the field as an ethnographer, I soon discovered that whatever my original research intention, I was learning more about the children's use of power through my experiences alongside the children than anything else.

I was most surprised to find that it was not physical choices of power that showed up the most in the classroom with the children. Even those times where the physical seemed on the forefront of the activity, the emotional choices being made were just under the surface, sometimes seemingly hidden from my adult eye by some sort of physical actions (Martin, 2004). This is evident in The Nest Bush vignette, where the children were completing physical actions, but ultimately were wielding power through challenging themselves in their individual risk tolerance. Humans are emotional beings and children, being at an early stage of emotional development, are still trying to puzzle out what they need to know about themselves (Johansson, 2009). I did see children who were receptive to developmentally appropriate social cues within the developing social structure between children and were able to model power in a productive way for their peers, just as I found in the literature (Crain, 1997; Wilson, 1995). This came out in a sort of power sharing, what I came to experience and view as a power give and take. The children who most often coordinated play for a group, represented in the stories of Eve and Ronny, were also most adept at reading the other children. By giving up what I perceived as their power, these coordinators would openly take in the other child's comments on the current direction of play, and make adjustments to plot and character development. I feel as if I was actually watching agency in these children develop as each made choices and wielded power within both the cultural and physical environment (Martin, 2004).

What I came to view as the children's ideas of what is powerful seemed to shift, depending on the social cues. Because the layers of power in the play was so complex, I found that the child's perceptions of what it meant to be powerful were very fluid in nature. For example, I came to understand that Sally wanted to control her play as being distant from the other children. While this could easily have been considered by me as anti-social had I not used a critical gaze to deconstruct my own perceptions, by standing aside and allowing the drama with the other two girls to unfold I understood that Sally was making a purposeful, powerful choice. Equally, the other two girls' acceptance of her choice appeared to me to be an example of how the cultural understanding of power as fluid could be represented in the classroom. Just as Warming (2011) advocates for researchers to always keep in mind when doing ethnographic work with young children, the children are still constructing what they believe to be their individual truths.

Study should be made into how the concept of 'powerful play' can be used to influence Developmentally Appropriate Practice construction in an early schooling classroom. There has been some research looking at the teacher's role in pretend play and how that influences the power dynamic between teacher and student, but much less has been discovered about the child's understanding of what it means to be powerful. As there is very little in the empirical body specifically investigating how play, risk, power, and the outdoors intersect; a more complete understanding of how these topics weave together will help create a paradigm shift where teachers, administrators, and policy-makers can better understand and modify current best practices in the classroom to reflect a more holistic understanding of the developing young child.

Disclosure statement

No potential conflict of interest was reported by the author.

References

Berger, R., & Lahad, M. (2009). A safe place: Ways in which nature, play and creativity can help children cope with stress and crisis-establishing the kindergarten as a safe haven where children can develop resiliency. *Early Child Development and Care, 180*(7), 889–900.

Crain, W. (1997). How nature helps children develop. *Montessori Life, 9* (2), 41–45.

Gubrium, J. F. and Holstein, J. A. (2008). Narrative Ethnography in *Handbook of Emergent Methods.* In J. Hesse-Biber & P. Leavy (Eds.) New York: Guilford.

Hesse-Biber, S. N., & Leavy, P. (2011). *The practice of qualitative research* (2nd ed.). Thousand Oaks, CA: Sage.

Johansson, E. (2009). 'Doing the right thing' – a moral concern from the perspectives of young preschool children. In D. Berthelsen, J. Brownlee, & E. Johansson (Eds.), *Participatory learning and the early years* (pp. 44–60). New York, NY: Routledge.

Josselson, R. (2007). The Ethical Attitude in Narrative Research. In Clandinin, D. J (Eds.), *Handbook of Narrative Inquiry: Mapping a Methodology* (pp. 537–552). Thousand Oaks, CA: Sage Publishing.

Kicheloe, J. L., & McLaren, P. (2002). Rethinking critical theory and qualitative research. In Y. Zou & E. T. Trueba (Eds.), *Ethnography and schools: Qualitative approaches to the study of education* (pp. 87–138). Lanham, MD: Rowman and Littlefield.

Louv, R. (2008). *Last child in the woods: Saving our children from nature-deficit disorder.* Chapel Hill, NC: Algonquin Books of Chapel Hill.

Maller, C. J. (2009). Promoting children's mental, emotional and social health through contact with nature: A model. *Health Education, 109*(6), 522–543.

Martin, J. (2004). Self-regulated learning, social cognitive theory, and agency. *Educational Psychologist, 39*(2), 135–145.

Moore, R. C., & Wong, H. H. (1997). *Natural learning: Creating environments for rediscovering nature's way of teaching.* Berkeley, CA: MIG Communications.

O'Brien, L. (2009). Learning outdoors: The forest school approach. *Education 3-1, 37*(1), 45–60.

Rivkin, M. (1997). The schoolyard habitat movement: What it is and why children need it. *Early Childhood Education Journal, 25*(1), 61–66.

Rossholt, N. (2009). The complexity of bodily events through an ethnographer's gaze: focusing on the youngest children in preschool. *Contemporary Issues in Early Childhood, 10*(1), 55–65.

Soto, L. D., & Swadener, E. B. (2002). Toward a liberating early childhood praxis. *Contemporary Issues in Early Childhood, 3* (1), 38–66.

Tillman-Healy, L. M. (2001). *Between Gay and Straight: Understanding Friendship Across Sexual Orientation.* New York, NY: AltaMira.

Waller, T. & Bitou, A. (2011). Research with children: three challenges for participatory research in early childhood. *European Early Childhood Education Research Journal. 19*(1), 5–20.

Walcott, H. F. (1994). *Transforming Qualitative Data: Description, Analysis, and Interpretation.* Thousand Oaks, CA: Sage Publishing.

Warming, H. (2011). Getting under their skins? Accessing young children's perspectives through ethnographic fieldwork. *Childhood, 18*(1), 39–53.

Willis, P. (1977). *Learning to labor: How working class kids get working class jobs.* New York, NY: Columbia University Press.

Wilson, R. (1995). Nature and the young child: A natural connection. *Young Children, 50*(6), 4–11.

Wolcott, H. F. (1994). *Transforming qualitative data: Description, analysis, and interpretation.* Thousand Oaks, CA: Sage.

Where do the children play?: An investigation of the intersection of nature, early childhood education and play

Jeanne M. Brown and Candace Kaye

ABSTRACT

What is the role of early education and care in advocating and providing for nature play in an era when children's exposure to nature play and risk is threatened? This review deconstructs the word 'nature,' as well as discusses nature's role in centuries of theorists and early childhood care pioneers. The article concludes with some hopeful current directions in early childhood education, advocating for the role of teachers and institutions as powerful activists in providing intentionally risky affordances for nature play in early childhood settings.

Introduction

In 2015, a generous gift from a private donor to the school where the first author teaches on the grounds of a university campus in New Mexico provided her with an unprecedented opportunity – to design a nature playground in the backyard of our preschool classroom. The design architect, whose prior experience was with US public schools, presented her original drawings to the first author. An amphitheatre-like area, with concrete benches arrayed in rows facing a platform, dominated the plan. 'That's where the teacher will give the nature lessons,' she explained. The author responded that open areas for running, hills for rolling and rocks for hiding would be better. 'Hiding? You couldn't see the children?'. The architect paled. We had come from two entirely worlds of thinking about nature.

The design architect and the 'natural playground' she designed represent one strain in the long and complicated history of the interaction between children, their desire to play and the provision – and prevention – of that very play by early childhood educators and care providers. From the first philosophers and pedagogues who thought consciously about what it meant to educate and provide care for children, tension around what defines a good relationship of children to nature has been a point of contention.

In this paper, we will examine the history of the social construction of childhood and how children's play has been changed through historical conceptions of what are appropriate locations for children to play. We will examine the history of the provision of early childhood care and education in Europe and the United States, with particular attention on the question of how early philosophers and educational pioneers grappled with the role of nature in this provision, and how they imagined children as 'players' in nature. The term nature itself will be de-constructed, with an examination of what is meant by terms such as 'nature' and 'wilderness.' Finally, we will explore the current state of nature play, with attention both to how early childhood education and care facilitate and constrain such play, as well as promising directions forward.

Children's places

A helpful guide to thinking through the history of childhood, nature and play is the idea of children's spaces. According to Rasmussen (2004), when thinking through space as it relates to children, there are two primary phenomena. The first is 'places *for* children' (p. 157), which are adult defined rather than child defined as spaces that were planned for children. The second is 'children's places' (p. 157). Rasmussen states the distinction between these two descriptions is that 'a place, including "places for children", becomes a "children's place" after a child connects with it physically' (p. 157). He posits that physical sensation allows a place to be encoded with meaning 'as special emotions arise, [and] knowledge of place is generated' (p. 165). The notion of children's places also includes the idea that there are both overlaps and discontinuities between places that are designed for children and places in which children have a stake. This notion also makes clear the notion that children, as actors and protagonists of their own lives, can make these choices. Adults who understand this distinction also acknowledge the power of children to define and make meaning of specific sites.

However, the ability for children to make their own children's spaces has not been constant within the history of early childhood. We will spotlight several situations that speak to the threatened nature of children's play in nature.

Spotlight: the Commons and the enclosures in England and Wales

The Commons

In the feudal, agricultural system that dominated Europe in the Middle Ages, the raising of children was an afterthought. Until they were old enough to be productive, working members of society, peasant children were disciplined but largely ignored. About the age of 4 or 5, children were considered of an age to begin work, at which time they would be assigned unsupervised chores (Aries, 1962). The notion of childhood as a separate time in which vulnerable beings needing special care or education was not part of this system. This socially constructed notion did not arise until the mid-1700s, when there began to arise beliefs around childhood as a distinct stage, and children in that stage as in need of protection (Postman, 1985).

Within this system, throughout Europe and Asia, many societies were dominated by a social and physical system that was characterized by local villages surrounded by a Commons, wild and semi-wild land held in common by village residents. This communal property was key to both the social and economic life of the village. In forested areas, often filled with streams, villagers would hunt and fish, collect wood for building and fires, clay for pots and plants and herbs for cooking and dyeing. In the pastures immediately adjacent to the villages, residents would graze horses, cattle, pigs, sheep and goats, as well as celebrate communal festivals (Griffiths, 2013; Neeson, 1996; Snyder, 2010).

This system of the Commons provided rich opportunities for creating 'children's spaces' for the children of that time. In these spaces, unfettered by boundaries of any kind, children could roam, forage, gather and create their own special wild spaces. Children could and did establish rich sub-societies of play, unsupervised and child-governed. Here, children's lives, enriched not only by community festivals on the Commons, but also unbounded exploration, was rife with children's spaces.

The enclosures

The Age of the Commons conflicted with the elites' desires for private wealth and land ownership. The first encroachments upon the Commons came with the Statue of Merton (1235), which granted land grants to former knights and overlords (Snyder, 2010). Early movements to fence in the land with ditches and walls, however, were met with fierce local resistance, the walls torn down, the ditches filled. Although this resistance continued, the inexorable forces of government and military power moved against the local villagers. The Enclosures Acts, in a series of movements initiated by the gentry and formalized by Parliament between the years of 1604 and 1914, forced privatization of what had been the Commons, fencing off forests and pastureland (Thompson, 2010).

From this time forward, it was a punishable offence to trespass upon, much less hunt, fish or gather wood in these now privately owned lands (Griffiths, 2013). The results were predictable: devastating effects on the economic and social lives of villagers, with now landless peasants forced to move to urban centres to find work. In fact, it was this population of rural homeless who became the first industrial working class, according to Polanyi (1977, in Snyder, 2010). In addition, Neeson (1996) suggests that the severe social consequences run deep. Not only did the former village dwellers continue to resist the enclosures through widespread poaching, these residents' sense of the injustice done to them and the disrespect by which their lands were taken continue to inform social divisions that plague England to this day. The citizens' relationship to the state was changed; whereas prior to the Enclosure movement the state could have been seen as invisible or benign, now the state became dangerous, unpredictable and an ally to the rich and powerful (Linebaugh, 2010).

The consequences were just as severe for the land itself and the children who had made it their own. While previously the Commons had represented at least one quarter of total of the available land in England and Wales (Linebaugh, 2010), England became the country with the least forest and wildlife of all the nations in Europe (Snyder, 2010). The forest and meadows, which had been the 'children's space' for so many children's lives, were now forbidden to them. Griffiths (2013) writes: 'For those habituated to the Vast, enclosure is deadly' (p. 346).

Spotlight: Roger Hart's geography of children

Researcher Roger Hart, as his doctoral research, mapped the lives of 86 children in a rural New England town, to create a 'geography of children' (Hart, 1979, p. 3). Setting up headquarters at the local elementary school, Hart literally followed these otherwise unsupervised children around to their children's spaces. Rosin (2014) writes about Hart's study, 'Children were comfortable with him and loved to share their moments of pride, their secrets. Often they took him to places adults had never seen before – playhouses or forts the kids had made just for themselves.' The children had created an intricate, complex social world of their own, on which they had spent enormous time, creating what Rosin calls 'imaginary landscapes.'

In 2004, Hart returned to the same town in an attempt to do a follow-up study. Even when he managed to track down adults he had known as children – 'Roger Hart! Oh my God, my childhood existed!' one participant, Sylvia, shouted to him on the phone when they first made contact (Rosin, 2014, p. 9) – the moment when a kind-hearted stranger could access the inner lives of children had passed. In a 2014 interview Hart said, 'There's a fear among parents, an exaggeration of the dangers, a lost of trust that isn't totally clearly explainable' (Rosin, p. 8). Parents stated that they could not let Hart follow their child to a place where they played unsupervised, and that no such place existed – their children did *not* play unsupervised. Furthermore, even a private interview was perceived as a threat – Hart was forced to interview children in the presence of their parents, even though he had a prior relationship with them from the parents' childhood.

Spotlight: Frog-hole, with Foucault commentary

Returning to England, Giddings and Yarwood's research (2005) details interviews with children in rural England about their favourite places. According to the children, what made a place a 'children's place' was its lack of adult surveillance, and they went to great lengths to achieve this. The places cited as conducive to avoiding surveillance were borderland natural spaces within the village, for example, streams, woods and 'areas of undergrowth that were colonised by children for dens and play' (p. 106). One special place was the 'Frog-hole' (p. 1066), desired for its lack of visibility, allowing secret, imaginative play. Many children self-reported that parents had forbidden access to the Frog-hole, but that they could not enforce their regulation because they could not see them. However, children were, technically, trespassing whenever they used those spaces. 'The sense of "open space" around the village is contradicted by its restricted access. It is formally off limits to young people and represents a constraint in a supposed "golden land" of play opportunity' (p. 109).

A Note á la Foucault

Bowdridge and Blenkinsop (2011) note that just because an activity takes place outside, that activity is not exempted from societal power dynamics. Although their research is on outdoor and experiential education programmes, their analysis applies here. The three signs of power creating 'docile bodies' (p. 151) described by Foucault (1975) are (a) hierarchical observation; (b) normalizing judgments; and (c) the examination. Children in the Giddings and Yarwood study (2005) reported great effort in resisting hierarchical observation, situations in which constant adult observation leads to docility. Their rationale for this resistance was the judgment that adults had placed upon children themselves in the past, and in particular children's play. This judgment is what Foucault refers to as normalizing judgments, the action of adults prescribing acceptable behaviour. Foucault's third category, the examination, is defined as a definitive occasion that combines observation and judgment, often accompanied by documentation of that judgment. By resisting the chance to be observed at Frog-hole, children not only resisted the opportunity to be judged, but also to be examined. Such unexamined play for children is becoming increasingly rare. Hart's follow-up research failure was directly connected to the fact that in the 2004 US setting, children experienced no play that was not under adult surveillance. This begs the question whether children who cannot play unsupervised can create children's spaces.

Early education philosophers and pioneers

The end of the Age of the Commons also ushered in a time of systematic philosophies of early childhood education. These early philosophers and the children whose lives were the objects of their work were white, male, wealthy Europeans. Philosophers of the time, influenced by the Enlightenment, were concerned with questions concerning the nature of the relationships between idealism and reason, the empirical to the rational and humans to nature (Strauch-Nelson, 2012). Another influence was Romanticism and its poets, who would transform an entire society's views of nature from a feared wilderness to a pristine idyll, an escape from the urban blight that was part of the transition to the Industrial Revolution (McDonald, Wearing, & Ponting, 2009).

Boy and man: first steps

The first publications to prescribe methods for raising children were addressed to noble households raising their courtly sons in the 1500s. Carrying on in this tradition is the writing of John Locke.

Locke

John Locke, in *Some thoughts concerning education* (1693), imagined a noble tutor and a noble son. According to Gregoriou and Papastephanou (2013), Locke's philosophy contained a curious mixture of envisioning the child as both imprintable and contaminable. The theme of a child's impressionable nature persists in Locke's writing, the *tabula rasa*, the blank slate of childhood, is one of Locke's enduring images. Locke also warns that children should be surrounded by appropriate models of behaviour and language. Locke suggests that servants and bad peer examples are the foremost of dangers for children, and that contact with them must be avoided. Locke, who in other works suggested the mass deportation of the unemployed and criminals to the colonies, and literally drew up the laws for English slavery in the Americas (Ball, 2014) suggests strict segregation of gentry to only be with other similar gentry to minimize the risk of exposure to undesirable models. After all, according to Locke, 'the privilege or duty of governing belongs to the gentry' (Gregoriou & Papastephanou, 2013, p. 19).

The strict segregation proposed by Locke, and others begs the question: how did children interact with nature, given that nature was filled with undesirable characters? In addition, what are the separating effects of the adult surveillance required to ensure that children would not unduly be influenced by peers or servants?

Rousseau: patron philosopher of nature

Jean-Jacques Rousseau (1712–1778) famously articulated contrasting views about children's free interaction with nature in *Emile, or on education* (1762), in which Rousseau advocated 'the difficult art of ruling without a mandate and of doing everything by doing nothing' (Koops, 2012). Rousseau's biography provides an interesting backdrop to his philosophy. Rousseau's birth to high society in Geneva was followed two days later by the death of his aristocratic mother (Cranston, 1991). Rousseau was raised by his father following Locke: he was neither allowed to play outdoors in the street nor sent to school, but taught at home. When Rousseau was 10, his father was caught poaching on patrician land and found guilty in court. Fleeing the country, he abandoned Rousseau. A wealthy uncle then sent Rousseau and his cousin, the uncle's son, to be educated by a country parish pastor in the hills outside of Geneva. Here Rousseau experienced a blissful, idyllic time playing in mountains, valleys, orchards and fields. His *Emile* offers this pastoral setting as a guide. According to Rousseau, the first two stages of life are infancy, 0–2, and the age of nature, 2–12, in which children should be allowed to explore naturally, without any systematic schooling or books – these are left until age 12.

A feminine turn: the next generations

In the 1700s, a new class arose across Europe: landed and politically influential elites, which included a class of literate women (Davis, 2010). Scholarship specifically addressed to women and mothers began to appear about this time. Early scholars, such as Comenius and Pestalozzi (1746–1827) focused on the home as the site for education for the very young, and specifically the mother–child relationship. Two general themes emerge from this early research: the vulnerability and impressionability of the young child, and the necessity of mother-facilitated experiences to implant correct values in the child (Platz & Arellano, 2011). These early writers published guides for mothers, and began to introduce books for children. Comenius proclaimed that schooling before the age of six would be dangerous; instead, naturalistic learning was recommended, with children learning from experiences with life and nature.

Fröbel: 'professionalizing femininity'

Friedrich Fröbel (1782–1852), although maintaining the ideal image of education as that of mother and child, took a new step in early childhood education. The youngest of six children, Fröbel was raised in the Thuringian Forest of eastern Germany. His mother's death when he was one, his father's immediate remarriage and his stepmother's rejection of him when he was a toddler for her first own biological child, left Fröbel until the age of 11 to wander the verdant fields unsupervised (Bruce, 2011). Fröbel became a self-professed nature lover, which infused his influential childhood philosophies and practices. Fröbel declared that the very characteristics that made mothers so ideal in the raising of their children: their caring nature, their patient observation skills, their receptiveness to letting the child become who s/he might be, their intuitive connection with nature, their ability to foster play, were the very skills needed by teachers in the schools for young children he initiated, and that he would name 'kinder-gartens,' or children's gardens (Davis, 2010). The centrepieces of these schools were individual garden plots for each child in a central courtyard, surrounded by communal gardens. Significantly, these schools were staffed by women, whose 'professionalized femininity' (Davis, 2010, p. 292) sparked a renegotiation of the relationship between home and school across Europe.

Sir Robert Owen: benefactor of the working class?

Far from Fröbel's gardens lay the grimy streets of the industrial urban centres. Beginning with Pestalozzi, who raised this issue in his work, the question was asked: how about education for the children of the working classes? The Industrial Revolution of the 1800s had sprung up an entire class of urban, working poor. Their children, denied the rights of the Commons, spent their days either working themselves or on the street (Davis, 2010; Read, 2013). What of them? Sir Robert Owen (1771–1858), owner of a mill in New Lanark, Scotland, came up with an innovative solution: he sponsored a school for the children of his workers. He made plain his motivation in his own writing: 'The child will be removed so far as it is at present practicable from erroneous treatment of the yet untrained and untaught parent.' (Owen, 1814, p. 14; quoted in Davis, 2010, p. 289).

Thus began the idea of compulsory education for children of lower classes. The impetus to provide these classes was formalized by the government of England in 1870 with the passage of the School Board Act, which introduced compulsory education for the ages of 5–10 and the possibility of local school boards creating 'infant school' classes for ages of 3–5 (Davis, 2010). But what was the nature of these classes? Formal, punitive classes were introduced, with solely male teachers supervising stepped classes of up to 100 students. Rote lessons, accompanied by severe discipline, were the norm. Nature as a curricular experience disappeared.

Fröbel's descendants arise

Fröbel's ideas spread across the continent of Europe, into England, as well as to the United States, but were adopted chiefly by the middle class and used in privatized settings. However, in both England and the United States, strong female advocates, with whom the idea of a professionalized place in education had resonated deeply, began to push for the adoption of Fröbel's ideas.

Fröbel comes to England

Read (2013) notes that a group of Fröbel advocates, the 'Froebel Society Witnesses,' visited 'infant school' classrooms in 1886 and were appalled at what they found. They presented these demands to the government:

- Classrooms that were spacious and appropriate
- Equal bench and floor space
- Opportunities for games and exercise
- Manual occupations (Fröbel's 'gifts and occupations')
- Training for teachers government certificate
- Inspection by Fröbelian trained experts vs. the traditional exams given to students as the appropriate judge of a program's progress (Read, 2013, p. 746)

These advocates were initially successful, according to Read, because their aims coincided with the government's broader imperialist aims for a manually skilled workforce. However, this method proved too radical for a sustained adoption. The antipathy of male-dominated government and teaching structures revolted against these progressive methods, and education, in most public schools, reverted to the formal, rote and punitive methods (Davis, 2010).

Rachel and Margaret McMillan and the Deptford School

Fröbel's influence, however, continued to flourish in some progressive and private circles. One exemplar of such a school was that of the Deptford School of Rachel (1859–1917) and Margaret (1860–1931) McMillan. The McMillan Sisters, influenced by socialism as well as Fröbel, founded the school on the grounds of a local health clinic for the poor in 1914 (Lascarides & Hinitz, 2013). They founded an open-air school in which play and nature study would be the curriculum, a school whose clientele would be those whom the sisters imagined needed it most, the poor children of Deptford. Their school featured classrooms that had panels that could be added for inclement weather, but for the most part were open to the elements (McMillan, 1921). The school was situated among gardens as well as a natural forest glade, which the students were encouraged to explore. In fact, much of the curriculum involved students mindfully observing their surroundings, incorporating art and physical activities along with nature study. This curriculum stemmed from both the sisters' philosophical beliefs and a practical belief that open air was a curative for the 80% rate of rickets among the students in their school (Lascarides & Hinitz, 2013).

Elizabeth Shaw and London schools

Another woman advocate was Fröbel-trained Elizabeth Shaw. Shaw, herself a member of the urban poor who rose from student teacher to school director, was a fierce advocate for children's involvement in nature in her role as teacher and later administrator of several schools in the London area. She promoted a curriculum for children that included nature activities, such as caring for goldfish and doves, planting seeds and bulbs, and tending flowers. Although she advocated for an outdoor garden to her tarmac schoolyards, she was resisted by school caretakers and the School Board Work Department, who argued that no one would be there to maintain the outdoor areas during school holidays and that it would place an undue burden of extra work on caretakers cleaning up mess and dirt (Read, 2013). As a substitute for on-site outdoor experiences, Shaw was famous for leading entire schools on all-day weekend outdoor expeditions to nature sites including Epping Forest and Oxshott Woods.

Fröbel comes to the United States

The ideas of Fröbel met an enthusiastic reception in the United States when they were popularized in the late 1800s, particularly by those associated with the Transcendentalist movement. Ralph Waldo Emerson, Henry David Thoreau and Bronson Alcott, father of the author Lousia May Alcott, were eager and early adopters of this nature-loving approach. For Transcendentalists, the universal value of spirituality was central. They believed that spirituality, or a person's soul, was born with a desire to connect with that beyond itself, including nature. Their beliefs are a forerunner of the twentieth-century notion of biophilia, which esteemed biologist E.O. Wilson describes what sees as an innate, programmed positive response to intertwining nature as experienced by all human beings. His definition is, simply, 'the urge to affiliate with other forms of life' (Wilson, 1984, p. 5). For Transcendentalists in particular, this desire to experience connection was in contrast to, and even hindered by education or custom (Ingman, 2011).

Thoreau (1817–1862), already famous for writings such as *Walden* (1854), went further than Fröbel in his rejection of formal schooling. Writing in his journal on 5 October 1859, Thoreau says, 'It is only when we forget all our learning that we begin to know' (Thoreau, in Ingman, 2011, pp. 149–150). Two weeks later, on 15 October, Thoreau followed up with this: 'We boast of our system of education, but why stop at schoolmasters and schoolhouses. We are all schoolmasters, and our schoolhouse is the universe. To attend chiefly to the desk or the schoolhouse while we reject the scenery in which is placed is absurd' (www.walden.org). Thoreau emphatically prioritized experience over knowledge. He also tried his hand at education, with mixed results at Concord Elementary, and more successfully in a private school he founded with his brother that focused on nature (Ingman, 2011).

Widespread adoption

The influence of the Transcendentalist movement, as well as fierce women advocates such as Elizabeth Peabody, cemented a place for Fröbel-influenced practice in early childhood education in the United States throughout the nineteenth and twentieth centuries. Davis (2010) writes, 'In the hands of its Americans supporters especially, the Fröbelian method became integral for many years to the conception of kindergarten as a unique synthesis of private flourishing and public good' (p. 293). While Fröbel-based foci such as a professional class of women educators, hands-on experiences, the importance of play, art and child-friendly educational materials were key components in most of these educational settings, nature as a site for learning and play was not consistently as valued as a focal point.

Nature: an inherently risky endeavour

Sobel (2012) posits that one of the barriers to adopting outdoor play as part of the educational experience is the inherently risky nature of that play. Schools, along with many societies, have grown risk-adverse, and experiences in nature have been a victim of this aversion. Connecting to that idea, Maynard and Waters (2007) write,

> the justification for monitoring and regulating children's lives is based on a philosophy of protectiveness. That is, in order to protect the innocent of childhood, to shield children and the very essence of childhood from the potential evils of the world then special places and inevitably different codes of behavior (and inevitably laws) need to be constructed specially for children. (p. 515)

This results, according to Maynard, in a 'bubble-wrap generation' of children who have been denied the opportunity to develop their own psychological, social, cultural, physical and environmental competencies.

Risk avoidance: home consequences

Evidence documenting Maynard's thesis abound. US children are six times more likely, on any given day, to spend screen time than to ride a bicycle (Strife & Downey, 2009). Children from the US spend, on average, 52 hours on any given week engaged with electronic media and less than 40 minutes outside built environments (Kellert, 2012). In the United States, the area in which children were allowed to roam by their parents freely from their house shrank by 90% between 1970 (Griffiths, 2013). In one US study, 'few children identified play places they walked to with family members, in part because of the absence of sidewalks on certain streets, or because the width of sidewalks cannot accommodate ... large families' (Wridt, 2010, p. 137). Many of the families which took part in the study reported that McDonald's playgrounds were the sole venue to which they had access. Additionally, children, when asked to map out their local worlds, easily pointed out 'bad places' in their immediate neighbourhood, including drug dealing and gang locations (p. 140).

Risk avoidance: school consequences

Sandseter (2009) reports on the mediating role of adults' beliefs about risk that lead to the provision or denial of risky opportunities for children. 'Handling risk and children's risk-taking in play is one of the challenges that ECED practitioners face during their daily life' (p. 96). Because unwritten rules and knowledge of individual situations and children guide these decisions, the teachers' role is key in allowing risky play to occur.

In a comparison study between Norway and Australia on risky play provision, Little, Sandseter, and Wyver (2012) note that a key difference between the two is the regulatory environment. Specifically, childcare standards in Australia governing outdoor play circumscribe play and demote risk, while their parallel standards in Norway promote not only risky play but also promote the outdoors as the ideal environment to promote that play. In a move reminiscent of Rasmussen's 'children's places' definition, Wyver et al. (2010) contend that children, not adults, are the best judges of risk and are in the best position to manage risk-taking.

Many researchers have focused on the benefits of risk-taking. Little and Wyver (2008) write about the development of a 'risk-taking disposition,' which is seen in some contexts as a positive attribute associated with persistence (p. 36). People who hold this disposition would not be devastated by a mistake, but prepared to move on. Barker (2004) also holds positive views of risk, claiming that experience with risk actually allows children to develop decision-making skills that allow them to appropriately evaluate risk and make accurate risk judgments. Stephenson (2003) similarly notes that young children's physical risk-taking outdoors holds the potential for children to evaluate risk effectively, as well as having the additional benefit of increasing children's self-confidence.

A case study of teachers' role in risk provision occurs in research by Maynard and Waters (2007) in Wales. Teachers, even when they went outside, which they did only in good weather, were observed as using teacher-directed tasks focusing on basic skill building. They neither promoted interaction with the natural environment nor promoted children's risk-taking behaviour. The authors note the cultural feature of 'protectionism' which places children in a position of helplessness rather than strength, was apparent in the teachers' stated need to see the children at all times. This was commonly quoted by the teachers as a reason for not making more use of their outdoor environments although they also informally referred to their concerns about a growing culture among the parent body of blame and litigation. In other words, they were concerned about risk not only to children, but also to themselves.

What constitutes a nature experience?

Sobel (2012) indicates that the last 20 years have seen a resurgence of interest in nature as a complementary site for early childhood education and care, both as a site for play and for learning. Despite a plethora of articles in the popular and scholarly press on the benefits of nature, a careful reading of these works demonstrates a gaping hole in them – the lack of a consistent definition of 'nature.' While authors describe sites of nature experiences – gardens (Fröbel), ponds (Thoreau) or mountains (Wordsworth), or the activities undertaken there, there is seldom a systematic attempt to define nature. In addition, many researchers leave open the question of whether how their unspoken definition of nature interacts with childhood care settings.

Practical definitions: nature defined by what it does

When the rare writer attempts to directly define nature, those definitions have something in common: they have the practical component that nature is defined by what it does.

For the Romantic poets, nature had a very practical effect: it brought one closer to God. For these writers such as Wordsworth, Keats and Coleridge, an encounter with the divine was an important goal and deliberately seeking out encounters with nature a means to achieve that goal.

Cronon (1996) explains

> Romantics had a clear notion of where one could be most sure of having this experience ... Although God might, of course, choose to show Himself anywhere, He could most often be found in those vast, powerful landscapes where one could not help feeling insignificant and reminded of one's mortality ... Among the best proofs that one had entered a sublime landscape was the emotion it invoked. (p. 10)

Louv (2005), who popularized the term 'nature deficit disorder,' used a twenty-first century practical definition for nature in *Last child in the woods*. Louv's writing reflected a society for whom physical, social and emotional goals meant more than spiritual ones. Nature produced results. Nature reduced attention deficity with hyperactivity symptoms, feelings of depression, stress and loneliness. Nature reduced obesity, improved school grades and the ability to focus. Louv's emphasis on practicality continued to his next book, *The nature principle* (2012), which contains this definition of nature:

> Human beings exist in nature anywhere they experience meaningful kinship with other species. By this description, a natural environment may be found in wilderness or in a city; while not required to be pristine, this nature is influenced at least as much by a modicum of wildness and weather as by developers, scientists, beer drinkers, or debutantes. We know this nature when we see it. (pp. 52–53)

Stephen and Rachel Kaplan (1989), pioneers in social science research on the effects of nature-based experiences, offer a similar practical definition:

> The discussion of nature here is not limited to those faraway, vast and pristine places designated as 'natural areas' by some government authority. Nature includes parks and open spaces, meadows and abandoned fields, street trees and backyard gardens. We are referring to places near and far, common and unusual, managed and unkempt, big, small and in-between, where plants grow by human design or even despite it. (p. 2)

Wilderness

Contrast these definitions with those of wilderness, which has a legal definition, at least in the United States. The Wilderness Act of 1964 defines wilderness as 'untrammeled by man' (Watson, Cordell, Manning, & Martin, 2016, p. 329). It also adds that wilderness should provide 'outstanding opportunities for solitude' (p. 330).

Garden

'Kindergarten,' that German word first offered by Froebel that continues to define a common entry point for many US children to early education, gives a clue to the important role of gardens throughout the history of early childhood education. Fröbel's recommendation that a garden be part of early educational experiences has been taken seriously by generations of early childhood educators, who found in gardens a manageable way to approach nature (Read, 2013).

The idea of the use of 'garden' in early childhood programmes is a nuanced one. Gardens are certainly filled with species we associate with nature – plants, birds and insects. However, nature is circumscribed by its relationship to the garden. In fact, the very idea of the garden implies an interaction between humans and the natural world. Gardens are nature tamed and rule-bound, filled with weedless, planned symmetry. Gardeners plant, tend and harvest, interacting with nature – but the plants are there on humans' terms.

What do early educators and care-givers wish to provide in their setting – a garden, a nature experience, a wilderness experience? Teacher education programmes addressing risk, child advocates working within a regulatory environment that is pro-exploration and administrators who support outdoor experiential education are all part of this equation. Thoughtful early educators continue to consciously claim a definition of nature and work to provide it.

Early childhood care and education: the appropriate site for nature play

Malone (2007) argues that if a 'bubble-wrap generation' of parents, either due to their own parenting beliefs or to their fear of others' judgments of their lax parenting, cannot provide appropriately independent and risky outdoor play experiences for youth, that schools and teachers must take on that role. She further argues that teachers must challenge themselves to provide the outdoor environmental experiences, outside the walls of the classroom that are not being provided in other settings. She and her colleague also assert that, because of parental limiting of neighbourhood experience, the schoolyard becomes one of the very few places that children can interact with peers in a natural, outdoor setting with minimal adult restrictions (Malone & Tranter, 2003). Greenfield (2003) contends similarly that early childhood centres are well-positioned to provide children with positive risk-taking experiences that are not available to them elsewhere.

Using what you have: backyards, indoors and traditional playgrounds

For some schools, the beginning point may simply be providing a 'backyard' experience. The University of Hawaii, Manoa Children's Center, for example, has invested in a diverse, and rich backyard space in which children spend half of each day, in addition to regularly scheduled neighbourhood walking trips. The backyard includes a child-tended garden, water and sand experiences, wild areas and a multitude of flora and fauna. Staff of the centre write, 'we realize that for many families who live in apartments and have busy lives, we are providing them a backyard' (Au, 2013, p. 97).

Generally, other schools, though they may not have the infrastructure to provide outdoor nature experiences, ensure that children have a chance to have first-hand experience with nature through creative teachers who bring nature indoors through animals in the classroom, child-centred inquiry and school-sponsored field trips (Gostev & Weiss, 2007). As Griffin (1992) describes, typical built playground can also be the site of natural inquiry and first-hand experience to the extent that teachers take advantage of 'teachable moments' to connect with trees in playgrounds, roots in the sandbox, the cycle of leaf growth on a particular tree or planting seeds.

Forest schools of northern Europe: exemplars of risk in early childhood care

Forest kindergartens, a common practice in Germany, Scandinavia and other European countries, feature year-round early childhood care in an outdoor environment, regardless of the weather. These forest kindergartens typically have no indoor facility at all, simply a three-sided shelter and meeting place, though most of their activity takes place in unstructured activities in a natural environment. Children are free to build, to climb, to use fantasy play, to interact with the flora and fauna of the forest, all day, every day. Sobel (2015), environmental educator, quotes a father who sent his daughter to one such kindergarten:

> For two years my little girl went to kindergarten in the forest. Not a school in the forest, just the forest. No walls, no roof, no heating, only the forest, a few tools, and incredibly dedicated teachers. One day she came home from a day of particularly vicious downpours, her feet inevitably soaked, her eyelashes caked in mud, her cheeks ruddy with the cold and her eyes sparkling with fire, and I said to her it must have been tough being outside all morning in such weather. She looked at me in genuine incomprehension, looked out the window: 'What weather?' she asked. (p. 2)

North American forest kindergartens

The Educating Children Outside preschool programme on Vancouver Island, which models itself on the Forest Schools of Europe, provides 'an exclusively outdoor experiential and immersive model' (Filler, 2015, p. 1). Three- and four-year-old children are regularly offered a chance for first-hand experiences in nature. Filler explains that 'These are self-regulated, resilient, physically fit and capable preschool-aged children, who are also learning to navigate risks and make decisions which impact both themselves and their group' (p. 1). Programmes such as this and others, like the Wilderness Youth Project in Santa Barbara, CA, translate their capable image of the child into deeply challenging encounters with nature. David Sobel, returning from a trip with the Wilderness Youth Project, overheard a child say, 'Three hours isn't enough for these trips. We should do five hours. We should do all day! We should build forts and live out here' (Sobel, 2012, p. 7).

Signs of hope in the regulatory environment

One sign that the movement to engage children in nature has made an impact on the mainstream are 2015 playground guidelines that emerge from the US Head Start programme. These guidelines have the potential to directly impact 1.2 million children (datacenter.kidscount.org) enrolled in Head Start. Added to this are the children who share the playground space with Head Start programmes or use their policies to guide their own practice. The guidelines specifically call for nature features such as trees, stumps, boulders, long grass water and pebbles; and explicitly call for inclusion of risky play elements (Head Start Play Space Assessment, 2014).

Commenting on the guidelines, Spencer and Wright (2014) note, 'Children need opportunities to do things that are exciting and adventurous,' if provided opportunities, they will '... engage in increasingly more difficult and complex activities' (p. 30). Because Head Start is a federal office, the authors wonder whether these guidelines will be utilized by urban planners in the next generation of city-provided playgrounds, in addition to affecting school playgrounds.

Conclusion: New Mexico evening

As the sun goes down over the Organ Mountains, the shadows of the mountains fall on a group of over 100 children and families who have gathered for a school-sponsored cookout and campout, the result of months of conscious planning. The teacher watches as Elijah loops wildflowers in his mother's hair, while a gang of shrieking preschoolers climb and slide down boulders. Other children are poking the campfire with sticks; big brothers and sisters are out of sight, exploring somewhere. Contented adults exchange stories and occasional glances at their children. Owls call, bats fly, while children's arcs of play swing closer to their parents' laps.

Early childhood's intersection with nature has and continues to be uneven and often contentious. Today's early childhood and education leaders are encountered with stark choices. Voices that call for tougher standards and more readiness skills conflict with voices that call for respect for the autonomy and wisdom of children. Part of that wisdom is to follow children's lead, their intuitive connection with nature, as we seek to provide not only spaces for children, but also for children to create 'children's spaces.'

Disclosure statement

No potential conflict of interest was reported by the authors.

References

Aries, P. (1962). *Centuries of childhood: A social history of family life.* (R. Baldick, Trans., from French). New York, NY: Knopf [1970].

Au, L. (2013). Reflection: Providing a backyard. *Exchange: The Early Childhood Leaders' Magazine, 214*, 97.

Ball, E. (2014). *Slaves in the family.* New York, NY: Macmillan.

Barker, M. (2004). *Outdoor education: An actual reality experience.* Paper presented at the Outdoor Education Conference, Bendigo, Victoria. Retrieved April 22, 2015, from http://www.latrobe.edu.au/education/downloads/2004_conference_barker.pdf

Bowdridge, M., & Blenkinsop, S. (2011). Michel Foucault goes outside: Discipline and control in the practice of outdoor education. *Journal of Experiential Education, 34*(2), 149–163.

Bruce, T. (2011). All about ... Friedrich Froebel. *Nursery World, 111*(4263), 15–19.

Cranston, M. (1991). *Jean-Jacques: The early life and work of Jean-Jacques Rousseau, 1712–1754.* Chicago, IL: University of Chicago Press.

Cronon, W. (1996). The trouble with wilderness: Or, getting back to the wrong nature. *Environmental History, 1*(1), 7–28.

Davis, R.A. (2010). Government intervention in child rearing: Governing infancy. *Educational Theory, 60*(3), 285–298.

Filler, C. (2015). Physical activity in nature: Lessons learned from a preschool program. *Wellspring, 26*(2), 1–4.

Foucault, M. (1975). *Discipline & punish: The birth of the prison.* (A. Sheridan, Trans.). New York, NY: Vintage Books.

Giddings, R., & Yarwood, R. (2005). Growing up, going out and growing out of the countryside: Childhood experiences in rural England. *Children's Geographies, 3*(1), 101–114.

Gostev, M., & Weiss, F.M. (2007). Firsthand nature. *Science and Children, 44*(8), 48–51.

Greenfield, C. (2003). Outdoor play: The case for risks and challenges in children's learning and development. *Safekids News, 21*(5).

Gregoriou, Z., & Papastephanou, M. (2013). The utopianism of John Locke's natural learning. *Ethics and Education, 8*(1), 18–30.

Griffin, S. (1992). Wondering about trees: Playground discoveries can lead to new learning. *Dimensions of Early Childhood, 20*(4), 31–34.

Griffiths, J. (2013). *Kith: The riddle of the childscape.* London: Penguin.

Hart, R. (1979). *Children's experience of place.* New York, NY: Irvington.

Head Start Play Space Assessment. (2014). Retrieved from https://eclkc.ohs.acf.hhs.gov/hslc/tta-system/teaching/eecd/nature-based-learning/Create%20and%20Naturalize%20a%20Play%20Space/play-space-assessment-preschool.pdf

Ingman, B.C. (2011). Henry David Thoreau: Spirituality and experiential education. *Curriculum and Teaching Dialogue, 13* (1/2), 143–158.

Kaplan, R., & Kaplan, S. (1989). *The experience of nature: A psychological perspective.* Ann Arbor, MI: Ulrichs Books.

Kellert, S.R. (2012). *Building for life: Designing and understanding the human-nature connection.* Washington, DC: Island Press.

Kids Count Data Center. (2015). Retrieved April 25, 2015, from http://datacenter.kidscount.org/data/tables/5938-head-start-enrollment-by-age-group#detailed/1/any/false/36,868,867,133,38/1830,558,559,1831,122/12570

Koops, W. (2012). Jean Jacques Rousseau, modern developmental psychology, and education. *European Journal of Developmental Psychology, 9,* 46–56.

Lascarides, V.C., & Hinitz, B.F. (2013). *History of early childhood education* (Vol. 982). Routledge. [In S. Lester & M. Maudsley (Eds.) (2007). *Play, Naturally: A Review of Children's Natural Play.* London: Play England, NCB].

Linebaugh, P. (2010). Enclosures from the bottom up. *Radical History Review, 2010*(108), 11–27.

Little, H., Sandseter, E.B.H., & Wyver, S. (2012). Early childhood teachers' beliefs about children's risky play in Australia and Norway. *Contemporary Issues in Early Childhood, 13*(4), 300–316.

Little, H., & Wyver, S. (2008). Outdoor play: Does avoiding the risk reduce the benefits? *Australian Journal of Early Childhood, 33*(2), 33–40.

Louv, R. (2005). *Last child in the woods: Saving our children from nature-deficit disorder.* New York, NY: Algonquin Books.

Louv, R. (2012). *The nature principle: Human restoration and the end of nature-deficit disorder.* Chapel Hill, NC: Algonquin Books.

Malone, K. (2007). The bubble-wrap generation: children growing up in walled gardens. *Environmental Education Research, 13*(4), 513–527.

Malone, K., & Tranter, P.J. (2003). School grounds as sites for learning: Making the most of environmental opportunities. *Environmental Education Research, 9*(3), 283–303.

Maynard, T., & Waters, J. (2007). Learning in the outdoor environment: A missed opportunity? *Early Years, 27*(3), 255–265.

McDonald, M.G., Wearing, S., & Ponting, J. (2009). The nature of peak experience in wilderness. *The Humanistic Psychologist, 37*(4), 370–385.

McMillan, M. (1921). *The nursery school.* London: Dutton.

Neeson, J.M. (1996). *Commoners: Common right, enclosure and social change in England, 1700–1820.* Cambridge: Cambridge University Press.

Owen, R. (1814). *A new view of society: Or, essays on the principle of formation of the human character, and the application of the principle to practice* (Vol. 4). London: Cadell & Davies.

Platz, D., & Arellano, J. (2011). Time tested early childhood theories and practices. *Education, 132*(1), 54–63.

Polanyi, K. (1977). In H.W. Pearson (Ed.), *The livelihood of man.* New York, NY: Academic Press.

Postman, N. (1985). The disappearance of childhood. *Childhood Education, 61*(4), 286–293.

Rasmussen, K. (2004). Places for children–children's places. *Childhood, 11*(2), 155–173.

Read, J. (2013). Bringing Froebel into London's infant schools: The reforming practice of two head teachers, Elizabeth Shaw and Frances Roe, from the 1890s to the 1930s. *History of Education, 42*(6), 745–764.

Rosin, H. (2014). The overprotected kid. *The Atlantic,* electronic version retrieved April 22, 2015, from http://www.theatlantic.com/features/archive/2014/03/hey-parents-leave-those-kids-alone/358631/

Sandseter, E.B.H. (2009). Affordances for risky play in preschool: The importance of features in the play environment. *Early Childhood Education Journal, 36*(5), 439–446.

Snyder, G. (2010). *The practice of the wild.* Berkeley, CA: Counterpoint Press.

Sobel, D. (2012). Look, don't touch: The problem with environmental education. *Orion,* electronic version retrieved April 15, 2015, from https://orionmagazine.org/article/look-dont-touch1/

Sobel, D. (2015). You can't bounce off the walls if there are no walls: Outdoor schools make kids happier – and smarter. *Yes Magazine,* electronic version retrieved April 15, 2015, from http://www.yesmagazine.org/issues/education-uprising/the-original-kindergarten

Spencer, K.H., & Wright, P.M. (2014). Quality outdoor spaces for young children. *Young Children, 69*(5), 28–34.

Stephenson, A. (2003). Physical risk-taking: Dangerous or endangered? *Early Years: An International Journal of Research and Development, 23*(1), 35–43.

Strauch-Nelson, W. (2012). Transplanting Froebel into the present. *International Journal of Education Through Art, 8*(1), 59–72.

Strife, S., & Downey, L. (2009). Childhood development and access to nature: A new direction for environmental inequality research. *Organization & Environment, 22*(1), 99–122.

Thompson, W.I. (2010). Thinking otherwise. *Annals of Earth, 28*(3), 19–20.

Thoreau diary. Retrieved July 16, 2016, from https://www.walden.org/Library/Quotations/Education

Watson, A.E., Cordell, H.K., Manning, R., & Martin, S. (2016). The evolution of wilderness social science and future research to protect experiences, resources, and societal benefits. *Journal of Forestry, 114*(3), 329–338.

Wilson, E.O. (1984). *Biophilia.* Cambridge, MA: Harvard University Press.

Wridt, P. (2010). A qualitative GIS approach to mapping urban neighborhoods with children to promote physical activity and child-friendly community planning. *Environment and Planning. B, Planning & Design, 37*(1), 129–147.

Wyver, S., Tranter, P., Naughton, G., Little, H., Sandseter, E.B.H., & Bundy, A. (2010). Ten ways to restrict children's freedom to play: The problem of surplus safety. *Contemporary Issues in Early Childhood, 11*(3), 263–277.

Sandboxes, loose parts, and playground equipment: a descriptive exploration of outdoor play environments

Heather Olsen and Brandy Smith

ABSTRACT
The purpose of the study was to examine outdoor environments to understand whether or not young children had access to play materials and loose parts to enhance their playful experiences. This study sought to gather the availability of SAFE and quality play opportunities in early childhood outdoor environments. The study took place in one state of the United States. The study found 75% of outdoor spaces had a playground structure that including a place for children to climb and slide down. The study found 83% of programs had appropriate surfacing materials provided in the outdoor play environment. Loose parts, such as toys, balls, and action figures were also included in the outdoor play and learning environment. The significance of play that this study shows is outdoor environments have an abundant opportunities to support the developmental characteristics of children.

Introduction

As more and more children are enrolled in early childhood settings for a significant part of their day, the relationship of play and the outdoor environment in early childhood programmes is a mandatory element of discussion. Unfortunately, child-initiated play opportunities for young children are altering due in part to increasing accountability to pre-kindergarten readiness (Miller & Almond, 2009). Early childhood educators are being faced with continual pressures to strengthen the rigour of their curriculum (Wohlwend & Peppler, 2015). Educators must balance developmentally appropriate practice with assurance that the curriculum is being delivered thoroughly while meeting diverse learning needs. Educators would also agree that play-based hands-on learning for young children is important in today's society (Bergen, 2007; Cutter-Mackenzie & Edwards, 2013; Lawson, 1996).

The continued pressure for increased academic rigour in the early childhood field call for an ecological approach to change, which are strategies put forth in order to improve communities or other environmental factors (Mandell & Schram, 2008). Early childhood standards and developmentally appropriate best practices adhere to child-initiated learning opportunities and the basis for an ecological approach to change. An ecological approach to change examines how environmental factors, such as neighbourhoods, early child care programmes, schools, and social service agencies, need to change in order to help people (Bronfenbrenner, 1979). The National Association for the Education of Young Children (NAEYC) and National Health and Safety Performance Standards (NHSPS)' Caring for Our Children (CFOC) have in place best practices for attempts to promote children's access to healthy and safe outdoor environments. In particular, NAEYC (2012) state a variety of age- and developmentally appropriate materials and equipment should be available for children to play inside and outside (p. 11). Also, NHSPS give recommendations to not only how the indoor environment is designed, but specific mandates and expectations for the outdoor environment. These governing agencies provide an ecological perspective to developmentally appropriate practice for outdoor time by educating and training programmes to make environmental changes so all children have access and opportunity of safe and quality outdoor play experiences. An ecological approach to inclusion can potentially influence local, state, and national organizations to develop social policy that is directed towards outdoor developmentally appropriate play.

Research shows children who are engaged and given time to be in outdoors have a variety of opportunities to develop physically, socially, emotionally, and intellectually (Acar, 2014; Czalczynska-Podolska, 2014) have a chance to make sense of the world (Elkind, 2007). Small exposure to playing in nature have had positive effects on (1) children's attention (Grahn, Martensson, Lindblad, Nilsson, & Ekman, 1997), (2) reduction of stress levels (Well & Evans, 2003), and (3) reducing childhood obesity (Liu, Qi, & Ying, 2007).

In light of pressures of kindergarten readiness and academic success in the early years (Stipek, 2003; Stipek & Byler, 2001; Vecchiotti, 2003), it is challenging and often overlooked by early childhood educational leaders to utilize the outdoor play environment (Loukaitou-Sideris & Sideris, 2009; Rivkin, 2014). Even though best practice demonstrates that outdoor play time is important to children's developmental milestones, the amount of planning that occurs to provide a safe and quality space is often ignored (Olsen, 2013; White, 2014). Outdoor play environments in early childhood programmes need to be more than a cluster of playground equipment and toys scattered throughout the space. White (2014) indicates that optimal learning and play in the outdoor environment requires careful thought, preparation, and planning.

An ecological approach to equitable outdoor play opportunities can potentially influence early childhood profession to develop social policies that are directed towards inclusive, developmentally appropriate play. Social policy is a plan of action adopted by a government, non-government organization, or business enterprise to remedy or prevent a social problem or make society better (Hall & Midgley, 2004) to create, maintain, or improve living conditions (Dawson, 2010; Segal, 2007; Smith, Stebbins, & Dover, 2006). Adopting a social policy at the local or state level that mandates inclusive, safe, and developmentally appropriate outdoor environments which offers authentic play opportunities for all children and their families can foster social interactions and create opportunities for healthy children and families. The National Program for Playground Safety (NPPS) established a S.A.F.E. playground framework for early childhood programmes to use at the local, state, and national level. The S.A.F.E. model for playgrounds represents variables in outdoor environments, which indicate the possible relationships and interactions of those variables in producing safe play areas (Thompson, Hudson, & Olsen, 2007). The purpose of this study was to investigate early childhood outdoor environments to determine the availability of SAFE™ and quality play environments that may enhance or eliminate playful childhood experiences. The SAFE™ framework provides a foundation for developing a social policy to support quality and inclusive outdoor play environments. Furthermore, the aim of this paper will discuss outdoor environments in early childhood in order to elevate children's play opportunities while supporting children's interest and developmental characteristics.

The value of outdoor play in the early years

Today more than ever children's access to outdoor play has lessened (Loukaitou-Sideris & Sideris, 2009; Rivkin, 2014) and is under attack by many conditions in today's society (Miller & Almond, 2009). A presentation before the American Academy of Pediatrics, Dr Kristen Copeland reported the concern for children stating that children were supposed to stay inside because caregivers did not provide appropriate clothing for weather conditions (Copeland, Sherman, Kendeigh, Saelens, & Kalkwar, 2009). The researchers found staff reported parents intentionally sent children to their programmes without coats so their children would have to stay inside. 'Nature deficient disorder' has been termed by Louv (2008), in which he discusses the growing decrease in today's children's outside time.

While the research illustrates a concern with children's experience outdoors, there has been a call to restoring the great outdoors (Rivkin, 2014). The American Academy of Pediatrics (2011) issued a report stating unstructured play time is more valuable for children than passive entertainment. Furthermore, they stressed 'recess is crucial and necessary component of a child's development and, as such, it should not be withheld for punitive or academic reasons' (AAP, 2013). In addition, Ginsbeurg (2007) encourages the importance of free and unstructured play in young children. He states 'free and unstructured play is healthy and – in fact – essential for helping children reach important social, emotional, and cognitive developmental milestones as well as helping them manage stress and become resilient' (p. 183).

The development of outdoor spaces does not just happen. It should involve a process where decisions are made concerning multiple factors such as the users (children, educators, and families), outdoor play regulations, early childhood best practices, financial resources available, and agency standards and requirements. The process should be dynamic, with involvement from diverse individuals who have a concern for the welfare of the children who will be using the site. Thus, in planning an outdoor space, one of the first requirements is to understand early childhood outdoor play regulations and best practices.

United States safety standards and guidelines

Since the 1980s, two of the most influential groups leading the way in playground safety in the United States have been the Consumer Product Safety Commission (CPSC) and the American Society for Standards and Materials (ASTM International). Although these guidelines and standards are voluntary (neither group has the ability to send out playground inspectors or enforce them directly), they have been adopted by many professional organizations and various state governments. They have been recognized in the United State's courts as the standard of care. The influence of the CPSC has provided the public with technical safety information for designing, constructing, operating, and maintaining public playgrounds. CPSC offers a handbook, *Handbook for Public Playground Safety,* to guide the public against unreasonable risk of injury and death from consumer products and assist in evaluating the safety of products (2010).

ASTM International is a national non-profit organization with a long history of creating manufacturing standards for a range of industries. ASTM International standards are used by manufacturing companies, installers, and architects and designers. Governmental and other agencies may adopt the ASTM International standards for regulations, codes, or reference them for guidance. The ASTM International has developed 16 standards related to children's play, playground surfacing, or playground equipment as issues and needs have emerged. The ASTM International playground standards are topics around the design playground equipment, playground surface materials, accessibility, and fencing.

SAFE™ model

Using injury data from the Centers for Disease Control and Injury Prevention and the safety guidelines from CPSC and ASTM, the *National Program for Playground Safety* identified four risk factors (SAFE™) that interpret the playground safety standards and guidelines: Supervision of children in playground, Age-appropriate design of materials and equipment used in outdoor spaces, Fall surfacing under and around the equipment, and Equipment and surface maintenance (NPPS, 1996). Since the identification of the risk factor, the SAFE™ model has been a foundation for assessing the safety of playgrounds in other environments (Thompson et al., 2007; Xethali, Christoforidis, Kambas, Aggelousis, & Fatouros, 2009) and has been a guide for planners on playground design (Burris & Boyd, 2005;

Frost, 2001; Hudson & Thompson, 2013; Olsen, Hudson, & Thompson, 2010). Addressing only one of the SAFE™ elements within the model alone, such as fall surfacing, cannot ensure children's safety, and a quality learning experience.

Each outdoor space will have specific needs and challenges related to the placement of equipment and support structures, which facilitate the first category in the SAFE™ model, supervision. It is imperative that all agencies have discussion on creating the area for supervision so adults are able to see and move throughout the area. Morrongiello and Schell (2010) specified three critical supervision dimensions to consider: attention (extent of watching and listening), proximity (within versus beyond arms reach), and continuity of attention and proximity (constant/intermittent/not at all). Supervision considerations also include signage, open sight lines, and zones for play (Olsen, Hudson, & Thompson, 2016).

Outdoor play environments for children should be designed according to the age and developmental ability of the child, which considers the next category in the SAFE™ model, age appropriateness of the equipment and materials. The CPSC recommends play areas be designed for and separated by age categories 6–24 months, 2–5 years, and 5–12 years (CPSC, 2010). For instance, young children do not have the strength or agility to use upper body equipment such as horizontal ladders (CPSC, 2010). Younger children could get injured if they play on equipment not developmentally appropriate for them. Likewise older children can be injured if they inappropriately use equipment meant for younger children.

The third category in the SAFE™ model is fall surfacing. Falls are the number one factor cited of nonfatal unintentional injuries suffered by children interacting with playground equipment (National Center for Injury and Prevention, 2009). Selecting and maintaining proper fall surfacing under and around the playground equipment is a crucial element in providing a safe play environment (ASTM, 2013; Laforest, Robitaille, Lesage, & Dorval, 2001). Outdoor environments for young children should install and maintain an acceptable shock-absorbing surface under and around playground equipment that will sustain the fall heights (ASTM, 2013; CPSC, 2010).

The fourth category in the SAFE™ model is equipment and surface maintenance. The standard of care and best practice for equipment maintenance involves a playground maintenance policy (Philpott & Serluco, 2010). According to CPSC (2010), routine inspection and maintenance issues include identifying broken equipment, cracks, dangerous debris, vandalism, missing parts, and rot.

Accessibility requirements

Along with safety guidelines, there is also a regulation in the United States, the Americans with Disabilities Act (ADA). As Frost, Brown, Sutterby, and Thornton (2004) indicate a decade ago 'accessibility is one of the critical issues of playground design for the future' (p. 221). Many playgrounds are not accessible to children with disabilities (Burkhour & Almon, 2010; Olsen & Dieser, 2012). ADA became mandatory regulations in 2013 by the United States federal government (USDOJ, 2010). Failure to do so is deemed a violation.

The standards apply to play areas designed and constructed at community parks, neighbourhoods, schools, and childcare facilities. The document provides technical provisions for ground-level and elevated play components, accessible routes, transfer systems, ground surfaces, and soft contained play structures. It also provides requirements for inclusive play by enabling children to get to and from playgrounds, providing opportunities for them to play, and by enhancing possibilities for interaction with other children (USDOJ, 2010).

Early childhood outdoor spaces best practices

The profession of early childhood in the United States has several agencies that support best practices in young children education.

Caring for our Children: National Health and Safety Performance Standards addresses health and safety in the United State outdoor environment. Information presented in these standards includes size and location of space, types of play and playground equipment, water play areas, toys, maintenance, appropriate surfacing materials, and inspection processes (American Academy of Pediatrics, et al., 2011).

The *Early Childhood Environment Rating Scale (ECERS)* is designed to assess the quality of early childhood environments with specific suggestions on amount of uninterrupted free play, protection from sun and wind, adequate supervision, access to gross motor equipment, and semi-private space in the outdoor environment. The *Infant/Toddler Environment Rating Scale* is designed to assess outdoor environments designed for children aged 0–30 months, addressing similar elements to the ECERS and also includes suggestions on science and nature elements and dramatic play materials in the outdoor environment (Garnsm, Cryer, & Clifford, 2006).

The National Association for the Education of Young Children *Standard 9: Physical Environment (NAEYC)* Physical Environment standard highlights several social, emotional, and intellectual domains in the outdoor environment, specifically referencing dramatic play, expressive arts, math, science and nature, literacy, and social studies (National Association for the Education of Young Children, 2005). The *Head Start Program Performance Standards* expectations for Head Start agencies addressing the maintenance, repair, safety, and security of all facilities (US Department of Health and Human Services, 2005).

Methods

This study sought to gather the availability of SAFE™ and quality play opportunities in early childhood outdoor environments. The intent was to examine outdoor environments to understand whether or not young children had access to play materials and loose parts to enhance their playful experiences and to understand whether or not they complied with safety requirements.

Child care environments

The study took place in the United States throughout one state (name to be released after the blind review process). The researchers utilized a random sample selection in order to maintain the ability to generalize findings throughout the state of (release of state after blind review). The researchers identified six quadrants in the state using the state's Early Childhood Areas. The Early Childhood Areas was founded by the state's Department of Human Services on the premise that communities and state government can work together to improve the well-being of the youngest children (Early Childhood, 2016). The areas receive state funding in six quadrants. The quadrants were Northwest, Southwest, North Central, South Central, North East, and South East. The researchers used the six quadrants as the method for selecting the child care programmes.

Within each quadrant, the researchers then identified three cities in each of the population categories. The population categories were determined by the researchers (a) cities under 5000, (b) cities between 5,001–24,999, and (c) cities who have over 25,000 population. Once the cities were determined in each population category, a child care list from the selected city was then generated from the state's Department of Human Services database. The researchers identified all of the licenced childcare facilities in that city.

Once the list was obtained from the state's Department of Human Service database, there was a randomized selection between the numbers of child care programmes in each city to the number of programmes visited in the selected city. During a four-month period, the researchers visited 61 early childhood programmes. Forty-two early childhood outdoor areas were visited with a population over 25,000. Twelve early childhood outdoor areas were visited with a population between 5001 and 24,999. Seven early childhood outdoor areas were visited with a population under 5000. In addition,

23% locations visited were from South East, 20% were from Northwest, 16% were from North Central, 16% were from South West, 15% were from North East, and 10% were from South Central.

Survey instrument

Using the NPPS's inspection programme handbook (Olsen, Hudson, & Thompson, 2015) and the playground safety checklist found in the *Handbook for Public Playground Safety* (CPSC, 2010), researchers evaluated the randomly selected early childhood programmes outdoor play environments. Researchers piloted the survey in a neighbouring community with an estimated inter-rater reliability ($r = 0.89$). The survey instrument was a checklist composed of 108 questions. The survey was composed of four parts: (1) basic description of the outdoor environment, (2) physical layout of the outdoor environment, (3) SAFE™ factors of outdoor environment, and (4) specific pieces of materials, equipment, and toys.

Results

Description and physical layout of outdoor play environments

A summary of the data found 51% of the outdoor environments had playground equipment that was relatively new, installed after 2011. Thirty-one per cent of the playground equipment was installed between 2005 and 2010, 2% prior to 2005, and 15% was undetermined. United State's guidelines regarding playgrounds were first published by CPSC in 1981 and have been revised five times since, with the latest revisions published in 2010. Ninety-eight per cent of outdoor environments were buffered by a fence, natural element, or distance from cars or other motorized hazards. In addition, 83% had a buffer between playground equipment and play zones.

Many of the outdoor play areas had nature elements (71%) and materials for gross motor skill development (59%). Only 59% had an open grass area for children to run freely in an open space. The American Academy of Public Health Association (2013) encourages nature access for children as nature exposure has been related to lower mortality and illness, higher levels of physical activity, lower stress, and a greater sense of well-being. Natural environments have found to improve children's attention, self-regulation, and motor abilities (Flouri, Midoushas, & Joshi, 2014).

Whole child development is critical in early childhood environments (Bergen, 2007; Lawson, 1996). Hands-on experiences, especially through play opportunities, for young children is natural in most early childhood settings (Cutter-Mackenzie & Edwards, 2013). This study found only 40% of the outdoor environments had dramatic play materials. However, the majority of outdoor play areas have some type of loose parts or toys (90%), slides (89%), climbing structures (82%), sandboxes (64%), and storage units (62%).

A study conducted in 2004 by the NPPS reported a variety of equipment in child care programmes (NPPS, 2004). Table 1 identifies the percentage of play materials and playground equipment pieces

Table 1. Comparison of outdoor equipment in child care in 2004 and 2016.

Equipment	2015 (%)	2004 (%)	Change % 2004–2015
Slide	89	83	+6
Swings	3	48	−45
Climbing structures	82	NA	
Merry-go-rounds	5	9	−4
Balance beam	11	4	+7
Steering wheels	44	13	+31
Play panels	41	4	+37
Storage units	62	NA	
Sand boxes	64	17	+47

found in outdoor play areas compared to 2004. There has been a 45% decrease in the percentage of swinging opportunities for children to play. In addition, a 47% increase in sandboxes and 27% increase in play panels (such as tic-tac-toe boards, spin the shapes, mirrors, etc.) has occurred since 2004.

Another component examined was inclusiveness and accessibility. The 2010 United States' ADA Standards for Accessible Design became law in 2012. The reviewers found 58% had an accessible path from the programme's building to the outdoor play area. In addition, 43% included a path from the edge of the play area was connected to the play equipment. Only 31% of the outdoor environment was inclusively designed for children of all abilities to play with others and have access to the outdoor materials and equipment.

SAFE™ factors of outdoor environment

Part of a high-quality outdoor space involves some key safety concepts that should be considered during the planning process. At least four factors are contributing factors regarding injuries to children on playgrounds: Supervision, Age appropriate design, Falls surfacing, and Equipment maintenance (Thompson & Hudson, 2001).

Supervision

The presence and ability to supervise properly is crucial in outdoor environments. Most surveys (97%) were administrated at times when children were not present in the outdoor environment. Supervision is more than viewing children (Schwebel, 2006) and has been cited as a contributing factor in practically all expert witness cases (Frost & Sweeney, 1996), supervision questions related to the layout, organization of space, and blind spots. It was found only 9% of the programmes had signs posted indicating the need for supervision. In addition, 66% allowed supervisors to see inside closed spaces and 68% the area is free of blind spots, where children may not be easily seen or heard.

Age-appropriate design

Playground guidelines published by the CPSC indicate that equipment should be manufactured and installed for ages 6 months–23 months, 2–5 years of age, and 5–12 years of age (CPSC, 2010). Fifteen of the programmes (25%) visited had a designated space outside for children aged 6–23 months. Sixty-three per cent of the early childhood outdoor environments had one play area for all the children they serve. Twenty-nine per cent of the outdoor environments had two play areas. Seventy-five per cent of programmes provided toys, manipulative objects, and playground equipment that was age-appropriate for 2- to 5-year-olds.

Based on the review of literature, early childhood programmes are encouraged to provide semi-private spaces where children can play alone or with small groups of friends (American Academy of Pediatrics, et al., 2001). In this study, 54% of the programmes had some type of semi-private space. These spaces may have included a semi-enclosed reading nook, miniature willow tree, and dramatic play area. ASTM standards state playgrounds should post signs illustrating age appropriateness of the area (2011). Ten per cent of programmes had posted age appropriateness signs.

Fall surfacing

Falls to the surface are cited as a contributing factor in 70% of the playground injury data (O'Brien, 2009). Thus, proper surfacing under and around the playground equipment is a crucial element in providing a proper surface. According to CPSC guidelines, acceptable playground surface materials include unitary or loose-fill material (CPSC, 2010). Unitary materials include rubber mats, rubber tiles, or a synthetic grass. Some examples of loose-fill material include wood

Table 2. Type of surfacing material underneath playground equipment.

Type of surfacing materials	Percentages (%)
Programmes using some type of wood product	51
Programmes using pea gravel	15
Programmes using rubber tiles	10
Programmes using poured-in-place rubber	3
Programmes using sand	2
Programmes using crumb rubber	2
Programmes mixing loose-fill surfacing material	23

products (engineered wood fibre, wood chips), shredded/recycled rubber mulch, sand, and pea gravel. CPSC recommends that unitary and loose-fill materials must be tested and comply with ASTM F1292 (CPSC, 2010). The study found that 83% of programmes had appropriate surfacing materials provided in the outdoor play environment and 77% of the surface area was free of foreign objects and evidence of poor drainage. Table 2 illustrates the types of surfacing material underneath the playground equipment.

Skin cancer is the most common form of cancer in the United States (Balk, O'Conner, & Saraiya, 2004). Intense exposure to high solar rays in childhood increases the risk for developing skin cancer later in life. The United States CPSC warns adults the risk of thermal burns from playground equipment and surfacing material (2016). In this study, it was found 90% of surfaces are protected by some type of shade structure to prevent from blistering feet or hands.

Equipment maintenance

Maintenance of toys, manipulative objects, and playground equipment is critical in order for children to have quality experiences during play outdoors. Equipment maintenance is an important element because without routine inspection and repair any equipment will fall into disrepair and thus pose a hazard to children using the equipment. In addition, the lack of maintenance could void a manufacturer's warranty, put children in physical danger, and waste dollars on unusable equipment. In the study, overall the composite playground structures were recorded to be in good condition (92%). However, only 43% of play toys, materials, and loose parts were reported to be in good condition. Table 3 highlights maintenance components with playground equipment and other toys and materials children engage with during outdoor play experiences.

Sand play, loose parts, and other play materials

Children love to engage with their physical environment and the manipulative equipment that are present in these spaces (Nicholson, 1971). Manipulative objects are materials that children can pick up, sort, arrange, and collect. Examples of these objects include holding containers, sand toys, building toys such as blocks, boxes, dolls and action figures, wheeled toys, art supplies such as brushes, paint, cups, water tables, sponges, and dramatic play toys such as kitchen materials/cooking utensils, dress-up, dolls, and action figures, and materials found in nature such as pine cones, rocks, sticks, and smooth stones. Brown (2009) indicated play is an essential

Table 3. Maintenance check of playground equipment and play toys/materials

Equipment maintenance check	Playground equipment (%)	Play toys and materials (%)
Free of missing parts	89	49
Free of protruding bolts	83	56
Free of head entrapments	69	54
Free of splinters	62	51
Free of cracks and holes	85	48

way that humans learn to socialize and play provides a platform for exploration (Colton & Gore, 1991). Therefore, loose parts, toys, and manipulative objects are instrumental pieces of a child's play experience. Diverse types of play materials should be available so each child has the opportunity to manipulate and explore. Construction of loose parts enhances children's outdoor environments (Dempsey & Strickland, 1999). As was previously mentioned, the majority of outdoor play areas in this study had loose parts, play materials, and toys (90%) present. The study identified the types of loose parts, play materials, and toys that were located in the outdoor environment (Table 4).

The outdoor environment is filled with opportunities for pretend and constructive play. Sand and water are one of the most critical, yet controversial elements of the outdoor environment in early childhood. Sand and water play has the great value for children's social and cognitive development (Dodge, Colder, & Heroman, 2010; Frost et al., 2004). The ever-changing materials lead to creative thinking and provide rich tactile experiences, yet in many cases, teachers must navigate cross cultural discussions with families and manage the care of the maintenance of sand and water materials. This study found 64% of the outdoor play environment had evidence of sand and water play.

It is encouraging to know early childhood programmes are including loose parts to the outdoor environment for children to play. Children are born with natural curiosity about the world. Outdoor environments are ideal for children when they include dramatic play props, playhouses, stages, gazebos, decks, and amphitheatres to name a few. If these types of play opportunities are provided in early childhood environments, then storage becomes a critical component of the outdoor environment. Storage space is a necessity in the environment and is one of the most overlooked features (U.S. General Services Administration, 2003). Storage compartments should include a

Table 4. Identification of loose parts, manipulative play materials.

Loose parts, Play materials, and Toys	61 Total play areas visited
Tricycle path	27 locations
Picnic table	26 locations
Buckets and shovels	22 locations
Kitchen playset	21 locations
Painting	19 locations
Balls	16 locations
Nature elements (trees, rocks, woods)	15 locations
Chalk board	12 locations
Riding equipment	8 locations
Children chairs	8 locations
Rocking equipment	7 locations
Balance beams	7 locations
Play house	7 locations
Balance beams	7 locations
Reading and writing materials	7 locations
Basketball hoops	6 locations
Action figures	5 locations
Bubbles	5 locations
Standing-alone equipment with a slide	4 locations
Jump ropes	3 locations
Musical instruments	3 locations
Bench	2 locations
Talk tubes	2 locations
Stepping pods	2 locations
Standing-alone equipment without a slide	1 location
Wagon	1 location
Sand digger	1 location
Stage	1 location
Lego table	1 location
Push/Pull toys	1 location
Blocks	0 location
Miniature cars/Trucks	0 location
Riding slide toys	0 location

combination of large storage units for tricycles, balls, and large blocks and smaller child accessible shelves for art supplies, dramatic play elements, building supplies, cars, marbles, and other loose materials. This study found 62% of the early childhood programmes had some type of storage unit placed in the outdoor play environment.

Discussion and implications

The purpose of this study was to investigate early childhood outdoor environments to determine the availability of SAFE™ and quality play environments that may enhance or eliminate playful childhood experiences. Examining quality outdoor play environments is a relatively new and emerging area of interest within early education as there is no clear definition of quality outdoor play environments. This study produced an initial description of outdoor play environments in early childhood. Although the study was conducted in one state in the United States and is not generalizable, it does provide a useful a snapshot of play environments outdoors.

This study has provided a starting discussion on quality, engaging, and SAFE™ outdoor playful children experiences in early childhood. Despite the research findings highlighted in this study, outdoor environments in early child care programmes should be at the forefront of discussion by educators, researchers, and influential political agencies to support an ecological approach to change. The findings conclude that the traditional model with a playground equipment structure continues to be the staple of play outdoor spaces for children, as 85% of the outdoor play environments had playground structure that was designed for children to climb up and slide down. Early childhood outdoor environments are filled with possibilities for meaningful and playful experiences.

Creating an outdoor play environment that is safe and of high quality and that encourages opportunities for children to learn and develop physically, emotionally, socially, and intellectually should be the intent (Mustapa, Maliki, & Hamzah, 2015). Richardson (2007) indicates whole, body multi-sensory experiences are critical for children. If social policy improves living conditions, betters opportunities, and prevents social injustices, the suggestion is to make a commitment to create social policies that value developmentally appropriate, inclusive outdoor environments for all children to meet developmental needs and to experience the joys of childhood.

To ensure quality (whole, body multi-sensory experience) and SAFE™ outdoor play experiences, a thoughtful plan must be developed to characterize the purpose and meaning of the outdoor space. Developing a purpose of the outdoor space provides a framework within which the programme can plan a quality experience for all children. Similar to developing and establishing indoor curriculum, a quality outdoor space should allow all children to progress in their development through the provisions of challenging and appropriate equipment, furnishing, and materials. Through a planning process, all children can be exposed to a play environment where some, if not all, of the developmental milestones are present.

The first consideration is for educators to allow plenty of time for inclusive child-centred outdoor play exploration. Kuh (2014) highlights the first step for early childhood educators is to go outside and make outside time a priority. Specifically, she recognizes classroom time is precious, 'the outdoors can open the possibilities for projects, investigations, and increased social opportunities that positively impact development' (p. 85).

The second consideration to support high quality through multi-sensory experience is by providing children play materials, toys, and loose parts. Dowda et al. (2009) concluded that the environment and the type of materials can increase physical movement. Research has also consistently shown that during outdoor time, gross motor activity is more likely to happen (Baranowski, Thompson, DuRant, Baranowski, & Puhl, 1993; Burdette, Whitaker, & Daniels, 2004). Therefore, play environments that support and encourage movement supports high quality.

The third consideration to support high quality through multi-sensory experience is by providing play environments that support emotional development. Denham (1998) describes emotions are at the centre of children's relationships, well-being, and sense of self allowing these characteristics to foster children's understanding of how the world works. Flouri et al. (2014) found when children had access to quality natural environments, children's attention, self-regulation, and motor skills were improved.

The fourth consideration to support high quality through multi-sensory experience is by providing play environments that support social development. Bourke and Sargisson (2014) found that the outdoor space allows for more peer interactions than the indoor space. The time outside is a place when children can have opportunities to make friends, learn about being accepted by peers, resolving conflicts, and expressing feelings (Trawick-Smith, 2010). In addition, Czalczynska-Podolska (2014) reported traditional playgrounds promote competitive and solitary play rather than cooperative and social interaction.

The fifth consideration to support high quality through multi-sensory experience is by providing play environments that support intellectual development. Cognitive learning, which could include math and science, happens naturally when children have access and time in the outdoor space (Wellhousen, 2002). In order to have a naturalistic and intelligences, Nilsen (2014) suggests designing specific spaces for play only. The space should not be 'overly designed or filled with construction or play equipment restricting children's creativity' (p. 2).

The final consideration to support high quality through multi-sensory experience is by providing play environments that follow health and safety standards and guidelines. Outdoor environments for young children need to be more than a cluster of equipment scattered throughout the space. It is apparent that creating an enriching and safe outdoor play environment is not a haphazard process, but rather should be based upon the literature and best practices for children. Outdoor play environments should be purposeful, with high quality through multi-sensory experience. Outdoor play environments should be planned for inclusive use, while complying with regulations and standards.

In conclusion, while we all agree getting children playing outdoors is important, it is the responsibility of the early childhood programmes and educators to provide safe and quality outdoor play environments that support the developmental appropriate practice. It should be more than going to a catalogue to purchase equipment. Children deserve to have outdoor play environments that are designed with intention of them learning, discovering, and enjoying. Outdoor play environments in early childhood programmes need to be more than a cluster of playground equipment and toys scattered throughout the outdoor space. Outdoor play environments have abundant opportunities to support the whole body experience of children.

Disclosure statement

No potential conflict of interest was reported by the authors.

References

Acar, H. (2014). Learning environments for children in outdoor spaces. *Procedia – Social and Behavioral Sciences, 141*, 846–853.

American Academy of Pediatrics, American Public Health Association, National Resource Center for Health and Safety in Child Care and Early Education. (2011). *Caring for our children: National health and safety performance standards guidelines for early care and education programs* (3rd ed.). Elk Grove Village, IL: Author.

American Academy of Pediatrics. (2013). *The crucial role of recess in schools.* Policy statement. Retrieved from http://pediatrics.aappublications.org/content/pediatrics/131/1/183.full.pdf

American Public Health Association. (2013). *Improving health and wellness through access to nature.* Policy statement. Retrieved from http://apha.org/policies-and-advocacy/public-health-policy-statements/policy-database/2014/07/08/09/18/improving-health-and-wellness-through-access-to-nature

American Society for Testing and Materials. (2011). *F1487: Standard consumer safety performance specification for playground equipment for public use.* Philadelphia, PA: Author.

American Society for Testing and Materials. (2013). *F1292: Impact attenuation of surfacing materials within the use zone of playground equipment.* Philadelphia, PA: Author.

Balk, S. J., O'Conner, K. G., & Saraiya, M. (2004). Counseling parents and children on sun protection: A national survey of pediatricians. *Pediatrics, 114*(4), 1056–1064.

Baranowski, T., Thompson, W. O., DuRant, R. H., Baranowski, J., & Puhl, J. (1993). Observations on physical activity in physical locations: Age, gender, ethnicity, and month effects. *Research Exercise and Sport Quarterly, 64*(2), 127–133.

Bergen, D. (2007). Play and the brain. In C. J. Ferguson & E. Dettore (Eds.), *To play or not to play is it really a question?* (pp. 11–22). Olney, MD: Association for Childhood Education International.

Bourke, M. T., & Sargisson, R. J. (2014). A behavioral investigation of preference in a newly designed New Zealand playground. *American Journal of Play, 6*(3), 370–391.

Bronfenbrenner, U. (1979). *The ecology of human development: Experiments by nature and design.* Cambridge, MA: Harvard University Press.

Brown, S. (2009). *Play: How it shapes the brain, opens the imagination, and invigorates the soul.* New York, NY: Avery.

Burdette, H. L., Whitaker, R. C., & Daniels, S. R. (2004). Parental report of outdoor playtime as a measure of physical activity in preschool-aged children. *Archive of Pediatrics & Adolescent Medicine, 158*, 353–357.

Burris, K. G., & Boyd, F. B. (2005). *Outdoor learning and play, ages 8–12.* Portland, OR: Association for Childhood Education International.

Colton, M. E., & Gore, S. (1991). *Adolescent stress cause and consequences.* New York, NY: Aldine De Gruyter.

Consumer Product Safety Commission. (2010). *Handbook for public playground safety.* Washington, DC: U.S. Government Printing Office

Consumer Product Safety Commission. (2016). *CPSC fact sheet: Burn safety awareness on playgrounds.* Retrieved from https://www.cpsc.gov/PageFiles/122121/3200.pdf

Copeland, K. A., Sherman, S. N., Kendeigh, C. A., Saelens, B. E., & Kalkwar, H. J. (2009). Flip flops, dress codes, and no coats: Clothing barriers to children's physical activity in child-care centers identified from a qualitative study. *International Journal of Behavioral Nutrition and Physical Activity, 6*, 74–89.

Cutter-Mackenzie, A., & Edwards, S. (2013). Toward a model for early childhood environmental education: Foregrounding, developing and connecting knowledge through play-based learning. *The Journal of Environmental Education, 44*(3), 195–213.

Czalczynska-Podolska, M. (2014). The impact of playground spatial features on children's play and activity forms: An evaluation of contemporary playgrounds' play and social value. *Journal of Environmental Psychology, 38*, 132–142.

Dawson, D. (2010). Leisure and social policy. In H. Mair, S. M. Arai, & D. G. Reid (Eds.), *Decentering work: Critical perspectives on leisure, social policy, and human development* (pp. 9–34). Calgary, AB: University of Calgary Press.

Dempsey, J., & Strickland, E. (1999). Staff workshop teacher handout: The whys have it! Why to include loose parts on the playground. *Early Childhood Today, 14*(1), 24–25.

Denham, S. (1998). *Emotional development in young children.* New York: Guilford Press.

Dodge, D. T., Colder, L. J., & Heroman, C. (2010). *The creative curriculum for preschool: Interest areas.* Washington, DC: Teaching Strategies.

Dowda, M., Brown, W. H., McIver, K. L., Pfeiffer, K. A., O'Neill, J. R., Addy, C. L., & Pate, R. R. (2009). Policies and characteristics of the preschool environment and physical activity of young children. *Pediatrics, 123*(2), e261–e266.

Early Childhood. (2010). *ECI initiative.* Retrieved from http://www.state.ia.us/earlychildhood/ECI_initiative/index.html

Elkind, D. (2007). *The power of play: How spontaneous, imaginative activities lead to happier, healthier children.* Cambridge, MA: Da Capo Press.

Flouri, E., Midoushas, E., & Joshi, H. (2014). The role of urban neighborhood green space in children's emotional and behavioral resilience. *Journal of Environmental Psychology, 40*, 179–186.

Frost, J. L. (Ed.). (2001). *Children and injuries.* Tucson, AZ: Lawwyers & Judges.

Frost, J., Brown, P., Sutterby, J. A., & Thornton, C. D. (2004). *The developmental benefits of playgrounds.* Olney, MD: Association for Childhood Education International.

Frost, J. L., & Sweeney, T. B. (1996). *Cause and prevention of playground injuries and litigation: Case studies.* Wheaton, MD: Association for Childhood Education International.

Garnsm , T., Cryer, D., & Clifford, R. M. (2006). *Early childhood environment rating scale: Revised edition.* New York: Teachers College, Columbia University.

Ginsbeurg, K. R. (2007). The importance of play in promoting healthy child development and maintaining strong parent-child bonds. *American Academy of Pediatrics, 119,* 182–190.

Grahn, P., Martensson, F., Lindblad, B., Nilsson, P., & Ekman, A. (1997). Ute pa Dagis (Out in the preschools). Stad and Land, 145.

Hall, A., & Midgley, J. (2004). *Social policy for development.* Thousand Oaks, CA: Sage.

Hudson, S., & Thompson, D. (2013). Playgrounds. In T. Sawyer (Ed.), *Facility planning and design for health, physical activity, recreation, and sport.* Urbana, IL: Sagamore.

Burkhour, C., & Almon, J. (2010). Play and playgrounds. In Human Kinetics (Ed.), *Inclusive recreation: Programs and services for diverse populations* (pp. 177–191). Champaign, IL: Human Kinetics.

Kuh, L. (2014). *Thinking critically about environments for young children: Bridging theory and practice.* New York: Teachers College Press.

Laforest, S., Robitaille, Y., Lesage, D., & Dorval, D. (2001). Surface characteristics, equipment height and the occurrence and severity of playground injuries. *Injury Prevention, 7,* 35–40.

Lawson, C. (1996). *The power of play.* West Chester, PA: Chrysalis Reader.

Liu, G. W., Qi, R., & Ying, J. (2007). Green neighborhoods, food retail, and childhood overweight: Differences by population density. *American Journal of Health Promotion, 21*(4), 317–325.

Loukaitou-Sideris, A., & Sideris, A. (2009). What brings children to the park? Analysis and measurement of the variables affecting children's use of parks. *Journal of the American Planning Association, 76*(1), 89–107. doi:10.1080/01944360903418338

Louv, R. (2008). *Last child in the woods.* New York, NY: Workman.

Mandell, B. R., & Schram, B. (2008). *Introduction to human services: Policy and practice* (7th ed.). Salt Lake City, UT: Allyn & Bacon.

Miller, E., & Almond, J. (2009). *Crisis in the kindergarten: Why children need to play in school.* College Park, MD: Alliance for Childhood.

Morrongiello, B. A., & Schell, S. L. (2010). Child injury: The role of supervision in prevention. *American Journal of Lifestyle Medicine, 4*(1), 65–74.

Mustapa, N. D., Maliki, N. Z., & Hamzah, A. (2015). *Repositioning children's developmental needs in space planning: A review of connection to nature.* Procedia – social and behavioral sciences, 170(AcE-Bs 2014 Seoul (Asian Conference on Environment-Behaviour Studies), Chung-Ang University, Seoul, S. Korea, 25–27 August 2014), 330–339. doi:10.1016/j.sbspro.2015.01.043

National Association for the Education of Young Children. (2005). *Physical environment: A guide to the NAEYC early childhood program standard and related accrediation criteria.* Washington, DC: NAEYC.

National Association for the Education of Young Children. (2012). *References to play in NAEYC position statements: Developmentally appropriate practice guidelines* Retrieved fromhttps://www.naeyc.org/files/naeyc/files/Play%20references%20in%20NAEYC%20position%20statements%2011-12.pdf

National Center for Injury and Prevention. (2009). *Falls.* Retrieved from http://www.cdc.gov/SafeChild/Falls/default.htm

National Program for Playground Safety. (1996). *National action plan for the prevention of playground injuries.* Cedar Falls, IA: Author.

National Program for Playground Safety. (2004). *Iowa's child care grade.* Retrieved from http://www.playgroundsafety.org/sites/default/files/reports/childcare/ia_childcare.pdf

Nicholson, S. (1971). How not to cheat children: The theory of loose parts. *Landscape Architecture, 62*(1), 30–35.

Nilsen, A. H. (2014). Available outdoor space and competing needs in public kindergartens in Oslo. *FORMakademisk, 7*(2), 1–13.

O'Brien, C. (2009). *Injuries and investigated deaths associated with playground equipment, 2001–2008.* Washington, DC: U.S. Consumer Product Safety Commission.

Olsen, H. (2013). Creating and enriching quality and safe outdoor environments. *Dimensions of Early Childhood, 41*(3), 11–17.

Olsen, H. M., & Dieser, R. B. (2012). I am hoping you can point me in the right direction regarding playground accessibility: A case study of a community that lacked social policy toward playground accessibility. *World Leisure, 54*(3), 269–279.

Olsen, H., Hudson, S., & Thompson, D. (2010). Building engaging science labs outdoors. *Texas Child Care Quarterly, 33*(3), 30–37.

Olsen, H., Hudson, S., & Thompson, D. (2015). *Early childhood assessment manual.* Cedar Falls, IA: University of Northern Iowa.

Olsen, H., Hudson, S., & Thompson, D. (2016). *SAFE and fun playgrounds: A handbook.* St. Paul, MN: Redleaf Press.

Philpott, D., & Serluco, P. (2010). *Public school emergency preparedness & crisis management plan.* Toronto: The Scarecrow Press.

Richardson, G. R. (2007). The great outdoors. *Education Review, 20*(1), 92–99.

Rivkin, M. (2014). *The great outdoors: Advocating for natural spaces for young children*. Washington, DC: National Association for the Education of Young Children.

Schwebel, D. C. (2006). Safety on the playground: Mechanisms through which adult supervision might prevent child playground injury. *Journal of Clinical Psychology in Medical Settings, 13*(2), 135–143.

Segal, E. A. (2007). *Social welfare policy and social programs: A value perspective*. Belmont, CA: Thomson Brooks/Cole.

Smith, D. H., Stebbins, R. A., & Dover, M. A. (2006). *A dictionary of nonprofit terms and concepts*. Bloomington, IL: Indiana University Press.

Stipek, D., & Byler, P. (2001). Academic achievement and social behaviors associated with age of entry into kindergarten. *Journal of Applied Developmental Psychology, 22*, 175–189.

Stipek, D. (2003). School entry age. In R. Trembley & R. Barr (Eds.), *Encyclopedia on early childhood development* (pp. 1–5). Montreal, Quebec: Centre of Excellence for Early Childhood Development. Retrieved from http://www.child-encyclopedia.com/documents/StipekANGxp.pdf

Stypek, D. J. (2003). School entry age. In: R. E. Tremblay, R. G. Barr, & Peters RDeV, (Eds.), *Encyclopedia on early childhood development* [online] (pp. 1–5). Montreal, Quebec: Centre of Excellence for Early Childhood Development. Retrieved from http://www.child-encyclopedia.com/documents/StipekANGxp.pdf

Thompson, D., & Hudson, S. (2001). Children and playground injuries. In J. Frost (Ed.), *Children and injuries* (pp. 249–312). Tucson, AZ: Lawyers & Judges.

Thompson, D., Hudson, S., & Olsen, H. (2007). *S.A.F.E. Play areas: Creation, maintenance, and renovation*. Champaign, IL: Human Kinetics.

Trawick-Smith, J. (2010). *From playpen to playground – the importance of physical play for the motor development of young children*. Retrieved from http://www.playscotland.org/wp-content/uploads/assets/Playpen-to-Playground.pdf

U.S. Department of Justice. (2010). *ADA standards for accessible design: Play areas*. Washington, DC: Author.

U.S. General Services Administration . (2003). *2003 facilities standards (P100)*. Retrieved fromhttps://www.gsa.gov/portal/category/21049.

US Department of Health and Human Services. (2005). *Head start design guide: A guide for building a head start facility*. Arlington, VA: National Head Start Training and Technical Assistance Resource Center.

Vecchiotti, S. (2003). Kindergarten: An overlooked educational policy priority. *Social Policy Report, 17*, 3–19.

Well, N. A., & Evans, G. W. (2003). *Nearby nature: A buffer of life stress among rural children*. Retrieved from http://www.mparks.org/Portals/0/Resource-Center/Justifying20Parks20and20Recreation/Health20and20Wellness/Nearby20Nature20-20A20Buffer20of20Life20Stress20Among20Rural20Children20-20Wells20and%20Evans.pdf

Wellhousen, K. (2002). *Outdoor play every day: Innovative play concepts for early childhood*. Canada, CA: Thomson Learning.

White, J. (2014). *Playing and learning outdoors: Making provisions for high quality experiences in the outdoor environment with children 3–7*. New York, NY: Routledge.

Wohlwend, K., & Peppler, K. (2015). All rigor and no play is no way to improve learning: The common core's higher academic standards are forcing schools into a false dichotomy of reducing playtime in favor of more time to learn math and literacy. But play can deepen learning even in core content areas. *Phi Delta Kappen, 96*, 22–26.

Xethali, V., Christoforidis, C., Kambas, A., Aggelousis, N., & Fatouros, I. (2009). Test-retest reliability of the National Program for Playground Safety report card. *International Journal of Injury Control and Safety Promotion, 16*(4), 249–251.

'They get enough of play at home': a Bakhtinian interpretation of the dialogic space of public school preschool

Jamie Huff Sisson and Janice Kroeger

ABSTRACT
This dialogic analysis, on the professional identities of five public preschool teachers from a major metropolitan school district in the United States, examines the dialogic space of participants in a context where discourses of play-based pedagogies and academic readiness were in competition. In discussing the pedagogical tensions that ensued for these preschool teachers, we explore how each engaged in dialogue with official discourses that best aligned with their values and beliefs as informed by their personal histories. The findings, part of a larger narrative inquiry focused on life histories and teacher practice, demonstrate the importance of understanding the connection between personal histories, competing discourses within personal narratives and teaching practice as each relates to teachers' construction of their professional identities and the role of play in their work.

Introduction

Within the context of the state of Ohio, USA, there have been an increasing number of preschools being included in public school campuses. This trend has also become visible in countries like Australia where government-managed preschools are being amalgamated with schools (the Australian Bureau of Statistics, 2014) and in the United Kingdom where the Child Care Minister announced the government has committed to assisting schools in providing high-quality nursery school provisions to make early education more accessible (Gyimah, 2014). Historically, preschool has been characterized by informal play-based and 'child-centred approaches' to curriculum (Bloch, Seward, & Seidlinger, 2001, p. 17), whereas primary schools have traditionally been characterized by standardized academic curriculum and assessments (Devaney & Sykes, 1988). As preschools become more associated with public schools they 'seem to gradually adopt more formal academic curricula' at the cost of play-based pedagogies (Bloch et al., 2001, p. 18).

The literature suggests play is beneficial for young children's learning and development. Researchers demonstrate the importance of play for social, emotional, cognitive and academic development (i.e. Elias & Berk, 2002; Galda, Pellegrini, & Cox, 1989; Göncu, 1993; Singer & Singer, 1990; Smilansky & Shefatya, 1990). Literature also focuses on assisting early childhood educators in including play into their curriculum (i.e. Bredekamp & Copple, 1997; Brown & Marchant, 2002; Chalufour & Worth, 2004; Curtis & Carter, 2008; Ebbeck & Waniganayake, 2010; Epstein, 2007; Heidemann & Hewitt, 2010; Jones & Reynolds, 1992). Furthermore, Article 31 of the United Nations Convention on the Rights of the Child promotes children's right to play (United Nations, 1989). While much attention has been given to the importance of play in children's learning and development, play is not widely considered important to education beyond early childhood. Early childhood educators are thus faced with the tension between discourses of play and academic readiness.

Researchers who draw on Bakhtin recognize conflicts or tensions as an important or even necessary part of dialogue about education. Fecho, Falter, and Hong (2016) suggests, 'We should recognise the tensions that exist, try to understand how we are transacting with those tensions, and then do what we can to seek equilibrium across them' (p. 12). Such research in early childhood has focused on the dialogical space within play to understand the struggle between an authoritative voice and internally persuasive voices in play (Cohen, 2009), dialogic properties of play where children negotiate tensions (Stetsenko & Ho, 2015), such as tensions between notions about child development and violently themed play (Rosen, 2015) and have found that players engage dialogically with each other (Marjanovic-Shane & White, 2014), through various types of play such as block play (Cohen, 2015). Dialogic engagements provide opportunities to balance power tensions as White, Redder, and Peter (2015) found as teachers engage as dialogic partners with infants rather than experts. In teacher education, researchers have explored the tensions between theory and practices and have found that dialogic practice was instrumental in impacting pedagogical change in field placements (Kroeger, Pech, & Cope, 2009; Naughton, 2016) and have suggested that Bakhtin's dialogic approach promotes more complex understandings of teaching perspectives to impact children (de Vocht, 2015). As more preschools are incorporated into primary school sites, research must focus on understanding what is lost and/or gained from such affiliations (Bloch et al., 2001). There are unintended consequences of translating the priorities of preschool education across contexts without special attention to pedagogic intent of teachers. For example, in a recent study in the United States, we learned including preschools in the primary schooling context compromised the use of play-based pedagogical practices that are often viewed as being paramount to the field of early childhood education (Sisson, 2011). Similarly, in Australia, we learned that primary teachers' lack of understanding about the role of play served as one of the challenges to their collaboration with preschool teachers (Sisson, Johnson, Harris, & Webb-Williams 2014). In another, we noted that the focus on the link between future academic success and preschool curriculum often compromises the responsiveness of teachers as they struggle to score, deliver and 'keep up with' the administrative tasks associated with state and federal assessments common in publicly funded settings (Kroeger et al., 2009). Drawing on Bakhtin's notion of dialogism Kroeger et al. (2009) demonstrated how dialogue allowed mentors and teacher candidates to create a helpful climate despite assessment pressures. While these examples remind us of the complexities that exist concerning preschool teaching and learning, and of the uniqueness of the young child, the analysis we share here contributes to the literature by offering a dialogic reading of these teachers' personal narratives about play and academic work in school that affect practice. Ultimately striking *tensions* and compromises that ensue within teachers' internal dialogues when preschool merges with primary school in public school settings in the United States are central to understanding the loss of play in early childhood classrooms.

Bakhtin is significant as his work provides a theoretical lens for understanding how public preschool teachers struggled in making sense of competing discourses about play in this present day, where we believe school settings can be interpreted as 'polyphonic' because of the multiple voices which inhabit the inner-lives of teachers' work (Bakhtin, 1934/1981; Connelly & Clandinin, 1999). We show how the teacher 'as author' of self (Bakhtin, 1973) incorporates her own priorities for play against the local and state conversations about the purposes of early childhood education. Bakhtin's theories provided a useful lens to illuminate these findings as teachers' talk was at times contradictory and filled with the powerful lines of discussions taking place in various ways and places throughout these women's working environments in tandem to their personal histories.

While many early childhood educational scholars have applied Bakhtin's work to early education (Cohen, 2009; White et al. 2015), often using carnival and double-voicedness as key features of theoretical analysis, we start with Bakhtin's original use of polyphony, a term closely related to heteroglossia to describe how discourses animate these women's justifications for actions in their everyday teaching, which may or may not suit young children in a way which the field of early childhood education anticipates. First, we describe and define original translations of Bakhtin's ideas as theoretical frames; then we show how the concepts worked in our methodological analysis.

Theoretical framework

Bakhtin (1973) uses the term 'polyphony' to describe the multiple circulating voices of characters that exist in the novel at any given time against the voice of the novel author himself (Bakhtin, 1929/1973). Bakhtin's work in literary scholarship opened up conversations in social sciences about how 'thinking human consciousness and the dialogic sphere of man's existence' cannot be mastered from a 'monologic' position (1929/1973, p. 228) but is always being constructed in dialogic encounters. To that end, human actors *as thinking beings* both respond to and incorporate the 'dialogues' that are common to the times and places in which they exist. Humans are also powerful to reject these dialogues, alter them or reappropriate them in new ways.

Bakhtin's notion of dialogism helps us to discuss in this article how participants used their own *inner dialogue*, animated within polyphonic environment in their district. Sisson's original analysis using narrative history uncovered that for these preschool teachers each was influenced sharply by two competing discourses about curriculum. Moreover, these teachers made sense of their classroom practices in relation to the discourses that were circulating in their positioning in primary schools.

Bakhtin argues in his original writing (and therefore translations of his work) that dialogues can never be solitary endeavours, but are 'juxtaposed to one another, and mutually supplement one another, contradict one another and are interrelated' (1934/1981, p. 292). Bakhtin holds that polyglossia refers to multiple perspectives or languages within one utterance; and such qualities of language inner-animate any perspective that a person or group might hold (nationalistic, societal, personal) (Morris, 1994, pp. 248–249). Bakhtin (1934/1981) often described the terms centripetal (official) and centrifugal (unofficial) forces that work to centralize and decentralize meaning within dialogues, extending the nature of how strong forces in public discussion (or the text within novels) produce official discourses (or unofficial discourses), depending upon the popularity or strength of any spoken utterance. Bakhtin's (1929/1973) idea of polyphony – which was sometimes conveyed by heteroglossia (Morris, 1994) – provides a useful theoretical lens for understanding how participants made sense of their own internal thoughts as the authoritative discourse(s) of either play or academic readiness promoted by national, state or district priorities came into their working consciousness and shaped their teaching.

A central underpinning of polyphony and hetteroglossia is dialogic tension. In other words, each teacher described her understanding of play and its importance in her preschool classroom, while also articulating the role of play in her own work with children, but play as a pedagogic strategy was always in deep tension with other aspects of preschool teachers' work. Similar findings have populated the literature on tensions in schools and tensions about play in particular (Cohen, 2009; Kroeger, 2006; Kroeger et al., 2009).

As we explore further how personal histories of teachers are brought into tension with official discourse in schools, and understood by individual teachers to inform how they understand the role of play in young children's learning, we argue that the more powerful centripetal forces of the district department, Head Start (HS) and Universal Pre-kindergarten (UPK) focus on readiness and academics were problematic insofar as they promoted the competition of play (as a discourse) versus academic skills or readiness (as a discourse) and while both are important, these discourses influenced teachers' thinking in highly unequal ways. We illustrate the discourses that existed in the minds of teachers, informing participants' views of curriculum. Teachers' examples shared here illuminate the way teachers used internally persuasive discourses to either contest or reject the official discourses of play in preschool. Overall, discourses shaped teachers' actions in complex ways and teachers made sense of their professional identities within the primary school context. Each of these women 'authored' her professional identity and embodied the position of classroom 'play' uniquely.

Methodology

The Bakhtinian analysis presented here was completed after the primary data from a narrative history research study. One finding which emerged was treated with dialogic analysis (Connelly & Clandinin, 1999). The primary data are from a larger research project focused on understanding how five public preschool teachers understood and negotiated their professional identities within a major metropolitan school district (Sisson, 2011). Cultural Models (Holland, Lachicotte, Skinner, & Cain, 1998), a Bakhtinian informed theory, was used for the larger narrative inquiry (Connelly & Clandinin, 1999) to explore the lived stories of teachers' experiences. In drawing on Bakhtin (1934/1981), the authors of cultural models theory provide an understanding of how professional identities are socially constructed, individually understood and negotiated in social spaces. Holland et al. (1998) suggest the 'development of identities and agency specific to practices and activities are situated in historically contingent, socially enacted' ... 'frames of social life' (p. 7). Data helped us understand how individual participants' multiple 'frames of social life' come together to inform individuals' understanding of their professional identities. During this second round of analysis we returned to the emerging theme and used categorical aggregation (Stake, 1995) to organize and analyse the common thread between participants and across interviews. Dialogic theorization of data helped us understand how individual participants' multiple and polyphonic frames of social life come together to inform individuals' understanding of their professional identities and shape preschool practice.

Participants' understandings were explored through their life experiences including those throughout their personal and work life, paying particular attention to how they understood those experiences as contributing to their professional identities using Connelly and Clandinin's (1999) dimensions of backwards/forwards, inwards/outwards and situated in place. Data were collected through four semi-structured interviews; one, two-hour life history interview, one, one-hour context interview, and two, one-hour follow-up interview that occurred after classroom observations. Observations were selected by participants and nominated as instances each identified as important challenges and supports to their professional identities. In keeping with the nature of narrative inquiry these observations were used to inform interview questions concerning how participants negotiate their professional identities during the follow-up interviews.

Findings suggest that teachers operated with great power, yet all but one seemed unquestioning of the official discourse of academic readiness they subscribed to (Sisson, 2011). In theorizing the strength of academic readiness, we turned to Bakhtin's (1934/1981) 'dialogic processes' as a second round of analysis to understand the power of official discourses and the risk of taking these discourses for granted as unidirectional and at times used without recognition of other competing discourses. We argue that, used as a persuasive discourse over the teacher, the official discursive position of academic readiness is at risk of being taken on by the field as a singular truth (Bakhtin, 1934/1981) and disregarding multiple discourses that exist, namely discourse of play-based pedagogies. Moss (2013) argues that at risk is the domination by mostly unequal politics of compulsory education with a 'creeping advance of "readiness for school" relationship, with an accompanying "schoolification" of the ECE system' (p. 32).

Study context and participants

Participants were solicited from the Midwestern Metropolitan School District (MMSD), a large urban school district with 52 preschool classrooms across 45 schools led by a district CEO. In using convenience sampling (Creswell, 2007), all five volunteers that answered the call for participants were included. Two participants, Sam and Nanci, were public preschool teachers from Watson Public School (pseudonyms). Watson was a traditional public school with an instructional programme focused on state standards. The preschool classrooms at Watson were managed in collaboration with the local HS Agency. The remaining three participants, Jill, CeCe and Sophia, were public preschool teachers from Blake Montessori Public School (pseudonyms). Blake Montessori was a specialty

Table 1. Participants and their backgrounds.

School site	Preschool teacher/age	Teaching experience	Qualifications
Watson	Sam, 29	8 years preschool – 5th grade	Bachelor: moderate-intensive special education k-12, Master: Early Intervention
Watson	Nanci, 52	27 years childcare – 2nd grade	Associate: child development, bachelor in Kindergarten – Third Education, Master: Elementary Education
Blake Montessori	Jill, 40	17 year preschool – 1st grade	Master: Education, Montessori training
Blake Montessori	CeCe, 58	11 years child care – 1st grade	Bachelor: Elementary Education, Master: Education, Montessori training
Blake Montessori	Sophia, 40	12 years childcare – 2nd grade	Bachelor: Social Science, minor in English, Master: Elementary Education, minor in Early Childhood

school where parents district wide were able to choose to send their children rather than their traditional neighbourhood schools. The preschool classrooms at Blake Montessori were managed in collaboration with the UPK pilot project. Both Watson and Blake Montessori were situated in urban neighbourhoods where 99% and 76% of the population of students were African-American, respectively (Table 1).

Here, we illuminate some of the ways that competing discourses were present in teachers' talk, while examining the personal histories participants brought into internal *dialogic* encounter with official discourses. This analysis reveals how teachers *responded* to play and academic readiness, by authoring their identities as teachers. We shed light on how individuals made sense of the discourses of play and how they at times reappropriated the nature of the discourses about play in their classrooms to make practices of teaching their own.

Competing discourses about the role of play

The data below illustrate the complexity of socially and historically positioned contexts for preschool teachers. We describe the complexities for preschool teachers in a public school context where two circulating official discourses send competing messages about the role of play in education. In what follows we describe the official discourses of academic readiness and play-based pedagogies and the official and unofficial forces that perpetuate them.

Official discourses of play-based pedagogies

The discourse of play-based pedagogies was promoted by the district head of the department of early childhood education and their partners HS and UPK (Sisson, 2011). The department of early childhood education was situated within MMSD and served the purpose of managing and maintaining the preschool classrooms, licensing requirements, partnerships and professional development. HS and UPK are both U.S.-funded programmes designed to make quality preschool education accessible to all children. Jill describes the UPK pilot project,

> So we have a grant that like the state has said ... we feel that you are the best of the best (preschool programs). We had to meet certain criteria that said that we were above and beyond other preschools so they're usings us as a pilot.

At the time of the study only two classrooms from Blake Montessori were participating in the UPK pilot project. MMSD preschool classrooms participating in partnerships with HS or UPK were held accountable to comply with regulations set by each agency. The priority for each of these agencies was accountability of teachers to provide a play-based learning environment.

Participants' narratives described how the discourse of play was perpetuated and sustained through mandated professional development. Teachers were held accountable to use play-based practices through 'monitoring visits' by the department of education, HS and UPK. Nanci said, 'You know, like [Head Start] is coming … just like in daycare licensing comes [to evaluate play environments and practice]' Each of these monitoring mechanisms created centripetal (official) forces requiring a play-based learning environment to include dramatic play and block play areas; nonetheless, only one of the participants honoured this officially while the others aligned themselves and their practice more with the discourse of academic readiness.

Official discourse of academic readiness

The official discourse of academic readiness was enforced upon preschool and school teachers by the school district CEO and individual school principals. When asked about the discourse of academic school readiness participants shared a section of the district website that provided the district plan for academic transformation. This information was reviewed to understand the discourse of academic school readiness. This official district document described the purpose of preschool education as building core academic skills for school. The discourse of academic readiness was perpetuated through mandated standardized curricula and standardized assessments where teachers were held accountable for student scores. The focus on academic achievement placed emphasis on educational outcomes while the mandated curricula were valued as significant in meeting these educational outcomes.

Play-based pedagogies and academic readiness as competing discourses

These official discourses of play-based pedagogies and academic readiness were unique because they were not necessarily spoken about in tandem or as compliments within the district overall; however, both held sway within the accountability systems of teachers. Rather, the absence of play-based pedagogies within the discourse of academic readiness sent the message that such pedagogies were not viewed as significant in meeting academic outcomes; thus the prevailing centrifugal/centripetal force of academic readiness is present in the United States much like across the globe (Moss, 2013). Although preschool teachers were informed by the discourses of play *and* academic readiness their primary school-based colleagues were only consistently informed by the latter.

Participants' description of their school colleagues' perspectives on play demonstrated how the overall lack of prevailing discourses of play can serve to marginalize it, despite its centrality for preschool professionals. For instance, Nanci said, 'A lot of teachers think, especially middle school teachers, [that] preschool is not a grade; you're just babysitting in there.' Sam explained that school colleagues had the perception, 'preschool, it's easy, it's little kids, oh you get nap time, oh how easy. We get that all the time and we get very defensive over [it]'. CeCe said, 'They still looked at preschool as just playing.' These accounts from preschool teachers demonstrate how the discourses of play-based pedagogies and academic readiness were co-existing yet not complimentary to each other. This non-complimentary co-existence of dialogic patterns within this context served as a double bind that not only marginalized the discourse of play but also preschool teachers as their work is often associated with play-based practices.

Authoring identities

Although preschool teachers existed in a context where the discourses of academic readiness and play were enforced by school leaders and other stakeholders' centripetal (official) forces, the centrifugal (unofficial) nature of their primary school colleagues and their personal narratives were also powerful in informing how these preschool teachers chose to uptake, improvise or reject these discourses. Exploring the personal narratives participants bring into dialogue with official discourses of play and academic readiness is important in understanding how each teacher responded or authored her identities within the classroom. When teachers reappropriated the nature of the discourses about play or academic readiness in their classrooms, they were doing what Bakhtin

Table 2. Participant dialogues.

Personal histories brought into dialogue with the discourses of play and academic readiness			Response to official discourses
Preschool Teacher	Teacher education and training	Significant childhood experiences	Dialogic encounter with official discourses
Sam, 29	special education k-12 and early intervention	Mother's learning difficulties Grandmother and mother emphasized academics	Academics readiness-Rejects discourse of play-based pedagogy
Nanci, 52	Child development, General elementary education k-3	Desired approval from mother. Struggled with her fine motor development	Academics readiness-Rejects discourse of play-based pedagogy
Jill, 40	General prek- 3 Education, Montessori training	Importance of teamwork coming from a large family	Academics readiness-Rejects discourse of play-based pedagogy
CeCe, 58	Elementary Education, Montessori training	Muslim background and marginalized African-American child	Academics readiness-Rejects discourse of play-based pedagogy
Sophia, 40	Social Science, English, Elementary Education and Early Childhood	Family of educators and experiences with University laboratory school.	Play and academic readiness-elevates play discourse in practice

might have called 'double-voiced' discourse. The encounter became a dynamic, 'vari-directional' force, and at times was stronger or weaker as the teachers' own agency transformed the intention of the discourses (Bakhtin, 1984, p. 199). In this way, the discourses of play and academic readiness were reappropriated as these teachers' own. The following excerpts from each teacher's personal narrative demonstrate how they brought their life experiences into dialogic encounter with the official discourses that existed within this public school context (see also Table 2).

Sam's internal dialogue with academic readiness

Sam always wanted to be a teacher as she loved school as a child. Sam was raised by her mother and her grandmother who highly valued academics and grades. Sam said,

> It was you better get an A or you're going to get it, kind of deal. If I had bad grades I had to do extra homework. Bad grades being A-, B+ or less so if I got a B+ it was like 10 hours of extra homework.

Sam suggests this emphasis on academic success was because her mom suffered from an unidentified learning disability and thus wanted her to have a different life than she did. Sam said, 'I really think too that's why my mom pushed me so much to do extra because she was so afraid that I would be like her.' These past experiences inform how Sam viewed her role as an educator and the purpose of preschool. Sam said, 'I feel that every kid needs to be given a chance ... even if their disabilities are severe, as long as they are exposed to it.'

Sam brought her personal values of the importance of academic success cultivated from childhood as well as her background in special education into dialogue with the discourse of academic readiness. Sam said,

> Everyone can't learn the same way and as a special education teacher I think you really kind of get that drilled into your head and that's what my thing is ... if I have to teach something six different ways to get each [child] to know what they need to know; I'll do it.

While Sam suggests she is willing to draw on different approaches to support children's learning she does not recognize play as being one of them. This was particularly interesting given her position as a preschool teacher and the official discourse of play circulating at MMSD. Sam rather subscribed to the discourse of academic readiness as this more aligned with her values as informed by her past experiences and that of her primary school colleagues. Sam felt most validated as a professional when test scores show children's improvement. Sam said as part of her background she has 'always taken data ... I do like to see the results'.

Although Sam was a preschool teacher play did not have an important role in her classroom. Sam rejected the official discourse of play as a useful pedagogy as she believed play was used as a break from learning and work. Sam said, 'You see our fun little centers [points to dramatic play and block play areas], they only get in those maybe once a week if that.' In asserting her professional identity as a teacher Sam restricted children's opportunities for play and categorized play as a break from 'working' and learning. Sam's rejection of the discourse of play aligns with her conception of the role of the teacher in 'teaching' children particular concepts.

Sam's narrative demonstrates how teachers' past histories can serve to further dichotomize official discourses and lead to the alignment with the discourse that is representative of their own experiences while rejecting others. By enacting agency in limiting children's opportunities for play Sam also restricts children's opportunity to have their personal histories that include play-based pedagogies. Such practices serve to perpetuate the marginalization of the discourse of play.

Nanci's internal dialogue with academic readiness

As a child Nanci struggled with her fine motor development and was particularly subconscious about her writing. Nanci said, 'I made [my parents] get me a tutor to learn how to write smaller. I think maybe I missed that part of [development] – the fine motor part.'

Nanci brought her background in child development, particularly the importance of fine motor development, to the discourse of academic readiness. While she rejected the push down of academics in preschool, she believed that providing children with support in developing their fine motor skills was foundational for further academic success. Nanci said, 'their babies ... I just think fine motor ... it's so important. I mean everything revolves around your hands. You can't do anything without them'. Nanci continued, 'This is the most important age to learn how to grip the pencil and do all that.' Nanci spent most of her time involving children in creating craft projects to help support their fine motor development. This emphasis, to an extent, denied play as she placed value on what children learned by creating an exact 'product' over the learning that happens during the 'process'.

In describing her childhood Nanci talked about how her mother and influential teachers were hard on her. In looking back on these experiences she suggests that these were acts of care in wanting her to try harder and do better with her life. Nanci took a similar attitude with her students and suggested that being 'strict' and 'hard' on them was important to prepare them for later school. Nanci had strict rules for her classroom; one of these rules being no playing in the block or dramatic play areas. Rejecting the discourse of play, Nanci said, 'I know play is educational but not the way they do it [in the dramatic play and block play area].' As such Nanci put the 'closed' sign on these areas, limiting children's time for dramatic and block play to only during times of inspection.

Although Nanci knew the children enjoyed playing in those restricted areas she believed that being tough on the children and providing them with activities to develop their fine motor skills was important in preparing them for future academic learning. Nanci said, 'We can all play the game. You know like HS is coming, Okay, I can put on a show; I can do what I need to do. I know what needs to be done.' Ironically while Nanci did not indicate that play was important to children, she used the colloquial notion of play in her own role as 'player' in the evaluation processes. She recognized that evaluations from federal sources would look for indications of evidence that she valued play and used it in her room, and she provided markers of play even when she did not subscribe to it pedagogically.

Nancy's narrative raises concern about personalized views of child development. As a child Nanci struggled with her own fine motor development and thus made this the main focus of her own work with young children as she believed this was important for all children. A narrow focus on one aspect of child development is not adequate in meeting the needs of the whole child. While Nanci felt that this part of development was missing from her own education she potentially contributed not only to other developmental gaps for the children within her classroom but also disenfranchised their right to experience a play-based pedagogy in covert ways.

Jill's internal dialogue with academic readiness

As the second youngest in a large family Jill learned of the importance of working as a team where everyone pitched in and cared for each other. Jill said, 'Just knowing we all have each other ... its nice.' In explaining the significance of Montessori to her philosophy of education Jill said,

> Montessori said that you have a window of opportunity for every skill ... and if you miss it, then it's that much harder. There's a lot of things that they learn at three and four that are so important if you don't get them, then when they go to kindergarten and they've never been to school, it's not too late, but it's much more difficult.

Jill explained the role of the teacher as a 'directress' who teaches children through pre-written lessons that are incrementally stepped. Jill said, before a child can learn to add they must first learn 'how to count, so there's a lesson on counting, there's lessons on learning numbers, and there's lessons on number/numeral matching ... you know, and they all start from easier to harder'.

Jill brings her background in Montessori as well as her understanding of the importance of being a team into dialogue with the discourse of academic readiness. For Jill, the mastery of particular skills during the appropriate stages for optimal development is critical in preparing children for later stages of academic learning. Because the Montessori approach does not recognize play as a useful pedagogy, Jill rejected the official discourse of play circulating in her sphere. Jill said,

> I make the executive decision that [play is] not going to be in here because it's not the Montessori classroom. So we just take our marks for it. Get marked down and say we're trying to stay as true to Montessori as we can. They get enough of that [play] outside of school. [Play] doesn't fit here [in school].

In bringing her background in Montessori into dialogue with the discourse of academic readiness Jill improvised the mandated curriculum. Jill recognized her classroom might be down-marked for play's absence in her room, but she used its counter discourse school readiness to justify its absence. Jill said, 'I use the district's curriculum as supplemental to my Montessori. I've got all those belter, Montessori materials that teach the same and more.'

As being a team member was important to Jill having a shared philosophy informed by Montessori was significant to her professional identity. In rejecting the discourse of play Jill's philosophy more aligned with her elementary colleagues whom she works with on a daily basis.

Jill's narrative contributes to an understanding of the complexities that exist when professional development introduces additional discourses that are counter to official discourses. While such professional development opportunities provide an opportunity to critically reflect upon how these discourses come into dialogic form with other discourses it is not known to what extent these opportunities are taken. Presenting additional discourse without reflection of their implications for particular contexts with competing circulating discourses runs the risk of perpetuating practices that are not critically reflective.

Cece's internal dialogue with academic readiness

As an African-American CeCe spoke about how she was marginalized in school during the 1960s. CeCe suggested racial tensions in school left her with feelings of low self-esteem because many of her Caucasian teachers did not 'care to know' her or help her succeed. As a response, CeCe did not put forth effort in her school work and was labelled as a low achieving student. CeCe's struggle in school continued through community college until the encouragement of one teacher served as a critical incident in dismantling her subject position as a low achieving student and provided her with the opportunity to re-author her identity as a high achieving student (Sisson, 2016).

CeCe brought her background in Montessori and her experiences as a marginalized student into dialogue with the force of academic readiness. CeCe 'double-voiced' the readiness discourse, stressing the importance of helping every child be successful in school and to develop confidence in their academic abilities within her internal sense of fairness and having been a marginalized student racially. In stressing the importance of realizing children's potentials CeCe said,

> there's so much they can do and people just don't [know]. Okay, they can make the first initial of their name. They can write a paragraph when they leave [preschool]. If they can write their name they can write the other letters you know, come on let go, chop, chop.

Like Jill, CeCe believed that making sure children mastered particular skills at particular stages of development was important to her work as a teacher. Because play was not a part of Montessorian philosophy CeCe in return rejected the official discourse of play. In bringing her experience as a marginalized student into dialogue with the discourse of academic readiness CeCe inner-animated the mandated curriculum with both her perspective(s) and that of her Montessori materials and philosophy to support the State standards. CeCe said,

> We have to like balance it so we have to find a way like to incorporate both things, all things like what the district wants you to do and how to support it with the Montessori materials. So you have State standards and you have district materials and you have Montessori materials so blending it together. I think with anything you take what you need out of it and then add what you can and delete what you have to.

CeCe did not, however, include the requirements of a play-based environment or play-based pedagogy. In justifying the importance of preschool CeCe said, 'A while back they still looked at preschool as just playing … Things are changing.' While CeCe rejected the discourse of play-based pedagogies she brought her past experiences as a marginalized student and her background in Montessori into dialogic encounter with academic readiness. Through her use of Montessori, children were valued as high achievers and were thus meeting standards beyond what was required by the district. CeCe said,

> When they leave preschool they're only supposed to know some of the alphabet and they're only supposed to recognize numbers one through ten. Our children (those of the Montessori classrooms) we want them to recognize numbers one through a hundred. You know, be able to count to a hundred when they leave preschool.

In bringing her personal history into dialogue with the official discourses CeCe made decisions about her practice based on her own needs (to have teachers care to know her and to academically succeed) rather than confirming children's needs with them. While personal histories are important in informing teachers' professional identities and the discourses they align with, it is also important for teachers to consider the (confirmed) needs of the children when making decisions about circulating discourses that impact their lives. Similar to Nanci, CeCe's narrow view of children's needs leads to her limiting opportunities for them to play.

Sophia's internal dialogue with play-based pedagogies and academic readiness

Sophia grew up on the university campus where her father was a professor and went to school where her mother was a science teacher. Sophia decided she wanted to become a teacher while working at the university laboratory school while she was receiving her bachelor's degree. In describing her experience at the university laboratory school Sophia said, '[Play] was very big and I learned it so much in working in the [Laboratory school]; my director was MG who happens to be very big. She's written a lot of books for High Scope.'

Sophia began her career teaching preschool at a university Lab school where she later became the director. Afterwards, she became a director of a local day care centre before becoming a teacher at MMSD. Of all the participants, Sophia with her background in Elementary/Early Childhood Education as well as her knowledge of play-based pedagogies brought the discourses of academic readiness *and* play together in order to activate her current curriculum and pedagogy within her classroom. In doing so, her work became more than a sum of two competing discourses. Sophia explained how she brought play and academic learning together in her room,

> Usually how it works is that I pull a couple of kids to work with me, [the assistant] pulls one or two and then one or two are playing and then we kind of switch. Then we get done with this and we pull somebody else to maybe go write their name and that seems to be working so that they get a nice balance of, yes I'm working but I'm also getting to play.

Sophia, in her own unique description of the value of play, in particular 'pretend play' was able to re-appropriate both of the official discourses in the district in a way that brought forth the value of play to children's development and her classroom environment. Sophia said,

> They love the blocks and housekeeping. I know, you'd think, man they're going to get bored but they love it! I mean, I try to add new things and keep it, like I just added the shark hat and the dinosaur tail and dinosaur hat, they love that. Um, and it's actually great like I love it that they want to do that because a lot of times they need practice on pretend play and I've really seen it kind of evolve over this year where they actually will make a dinner and say here's your dinner, sit down.

For Sophia, play was an essential element in providing pre-schoolers with experiences that were important and appropriate for their development. Sophia however felt alone in her beliefs and struggled with the messages that play was not a part of her professional work. Sophia was able to articulate the contradictory nature of the discourse (s) of academic achievement (and that of play) brought about by her classroom being incorporated into the elementary school setting. She said,

> For me it's still a struggle. I just feel like there's so much pressure on these little kids, that by the time they get to kindergarten they're supposed to be reading sight words. They're supposed to be writing complete sentences, they're supposed to know all of their letters and letter sounds.

Sophie captured how other preschool teachers felt the pressure of 'academic achievement' and yet they also celebrated their adherence to and ability to meet the mandates of 'readiness'.

> It's like some kids are just not ready for that and that's okay, but nobody ever says that. I feel like they [other public preschool teachers] are okay with that because what I get is 'yeah, no this is great look what my four-year-old can do'. It's like, ugh!

In striving to pull from both discourses Sophia 'deployed a pedagogy of care' (Noddings, 2006), appropriating her powerful position as a preschool teacher. She both resisted and felt the pressure from her colleagues to achieve the academic readiness mandates. Yet, Sophia also did not allow herself to reject the discourse of play, but instead animated the discourses of play with her own notions of readiness, balance and choice. She did not decrease the amount of play in her classroom to resemble their classrooms, but rather built a case for play within a caring, joyful and supportive atmosphere.

In being the only public preschool teacher at her school who did not reject play, Sophia felt the pressure to compromise her beliefs. Concerned for the competing discourses of play and academic achievement Sophia said,

> You just get sucked into the public school – it's so different than your child care background. It's so different from what's developmentally appropriate. They just want you cramming [academics] down their throats. 12 years later, I'm still struggling with what's developmentally appropriate and best practice and ... [academics] ... how do you meld it all together? I think sometimes I might have lost track of some of the developmentally appropriate things because you just are so into school mode and testing mode.

These findings demonstrate how participants brought their own personal narratives into dialogue with official discourses in different ways (Table 2). In particular Sam, Nanci, Jill and CeCe brought their personal narratives into dialogue with the discourse of academic readiness, thus consequently rejecting the discourse of play-based pedagogies, while Sophia brought her personal narrative into dialogue with both official discourses elevating her stance on nurturing and care to inform her practice. As participants' personal narratives played an important role as each made sense of official discourses, they also informed how these women authored their identities as teachers.

Discussion and implication

Tensions, particularly those of a philosophical nature, are inevitable in a diverse world. Bakhtin provides us with a tool to reconceptualize tensions in early childhood as opportunities to learn about diverse perspectives and offers dialogical practice as a means to establish 'equilibrium' (Fecho et al., 2016). This dialogic analysis of the internal dialogic space of public preschool teachers provides a deeper understanding of how teachers take up the discourses of the time and place in which they teach and contributes to our understanding of how certain discourses and related practices become codified. We have shared the internal and pedagogic tensions that ensue for teachers when official discourses (play-based pedagogies and academic readiness) are in competition with each other, showing in this context that play is often short-circuited for academic readiness. The field has grappled with this problem almost universally (Bennett, 2013; Cohen, 2009; Dyson, 2013; Kroeger et al., 2009; Moss, 2013; Sisson, 2011) as playful, child-centric approaches are supplanted with escalating academic approaches in preschool settings. What is special about our theoretical interpretation of the findings here is evidence to show the micro-emergence of the dominance of one official discourse over another within teachers' language, thought and practice.

The polyphonic atmosphere (Bakhtin, 1934/1981) for preschool teachers is complicated with multiple competing discourses. CeCe and Jill's engagement with additional professional development demonstrates how dialogues do not exist within a vacuum separate from other dialogues. As highlighted through Jill's narrative, the discourse of Montessori-based pedagogy aligned more comfortably with the official discourse of academic readiness and served to contradict the discourse of play (Bakhtin, 1934/1981). Teachers are active agents and have the power to take on, reject or alter dialogues in different ways (Bakhtin, 1934/1981). Teachers within this study engaged in an internal dialogue with the official discourses that best aligned with their values, beliefs and histories.

Sam, Nanci and CeCe focused their work on aspects they believed were beneficial or lacking from their own experiences in schools as children. These personal histories did not include experiences with play-based pedagogies as children. Although the discourse of play-based pedagogies was an official discourse circulating within the district that was promoted through professional development and assessed through official observations, these four teachers did not align their identities or their practice with the discourse of play. Instead, they engaged in covert forms of agency to reject this discourse. Conversely, they engaged in dialogue with the official discourse of academic readiness in ways that aligned with their own understandings informed by their experiences as children.

Through Sam's narrative we highlight how limiting children's opportunities to play can serve to perpetuate the marginalization of play-based pedagogies. Children from classrooms that limit or omit play will in the future be drawing on these personal histories that do not include experiences in play-based pedagogies. As these children become future teachers, parents and leaders they will be making important decisions about education and the role of play. Without personal histories of experiences in play-based pedagogies we run the risk of play no longer being a circulating discourse and being further diminished in schools for the centripetal power of academics, skills and school readiness taking hold more fully.

These findings shed light on the power of personal histories, particularly those which have not been critically reflected upon, in perpetuating persuasive official discourse as singular truths (Bakhtin, 1934/1981). By uncritically drawing on their own personal histories teachers did not consider how those histories might be different from those of the children in their classrooms nor did they engage in dialogue with the discourse that was different from their own experience, namely play-based pedagogies. These findings suggest further research is needed to understand how we might promote teacher engagement in dialogic practice with circulating discourses that are not in alignment only with personal histories. Such research will be important in deepening our understandings of the tensions between play and academic readiness in teacher education as we discuss democracies in continuities of education and care (Lazzari & Balduzzi, 2013, p. 151). Programmes of education need to consider the co-construction, a shared understanding of how to reach equilibrium between the academic and play approaches (Kroeger et al., 2009). This work will be important within teacher education and primary education, and Bennet reasserts that 'primary education could benefit from the knowledge and expertise of young children accumulated in the early childhood sector' (2013, p. 53). We should look at teachers like Sophie, CeCe, Nanci, Sam and Jill as our resources within organizations; to learn from and to celebrate, especially when Sophie's work holds fast to the expertise within the field that celebrates the uniqueness of the young child.

Teacher educators and educational leaders are significant to this discussion as they have the opportunity to engage staff in dialogue that explores competing official discourses in co-constructing understandings that acknowledge academic readiness without abandoning play. In literacy, this might mean furthering children's playful, 'unofficial' cultural centric writing (Dyson, 2010). In preschools, this means understanding how play is situated 'dialogically' as a contested, perhaps even vulnerable anchor (Bloch et al., 2001; Cohen, 2009). We argue further that an exploration of ways of critical reflection of personal histories, critical appraisal of circulating discourses and authentically engaging children's perspectives in dialogic encounters can be used to inform practice and would be particularly useful in informing teacher education, professional learning and primary as well as preschool practice (Kroeger et al., 2009; Kuby, 2013).

Sophia's narrative provides further insight into the potential of teacher education in strengthening teachers' understanding of engagement with play-based pedagogies. Sophia's experiences in a university laboratory school during her teacher education programme were far more powerful in informing her understanding of addressing children as learners beyond either of the official discourse of play or readiness. Sophie's experiences provided the basis for a solid understanding of how theories of play-based pedagogies applied to practice. Having taught within a laboratory school served to further solidify her ability to defend and negotiate play-based pedagogies in the face of the official discourse of academic readiness. As demonstrated by the remaining teachers and our analysis, the lack of such experiences may result in less informed teachers rejecting the discourse of play and limiting children's opportunities to engage in play, and turning back to their own 'lived experience' rather than pedagogic options. This finding is significant as quality field placements are often difficult for universities to secure, but for teacher candidates, such inspiring pre-service experiences often set the stage for life-long philosophical pedagogic underpinnings, anchoring the field in its history and uniqueness.

Conclusion

This paper highlights the importance of understanding the connection between personal histories, competing discourses of play and academic skills and a practical effort to help teachers understand how their professional identities and particularly their alignment/engagement with or rejection of the discourse of play-based pedagogies interacts. As preschools and early childhood programmes are incorporated into the formal school setting, it is important that educational leaders and policy makers work together in a dialogic manner to either dismantle the dichotomy between academic readiness and play-based pedagogies for preschool teachers and primary teachers alike; or recognize that the value of play must continue to be elevated not only as a mechanism of learning for young children but also for the benefits it provides beyond learning. Doing so would not only provide a shared understanding of both pedagogic priorities but would also provide a model for teachers faced with the tension of competing official discourses (of which academic readiness is likely to prevail as a dominant centripetal force). Ongoing support to assist teachers in drawing from both readiness and play in ways that are meaningful for the learning and development of the children in their professional lives is necessary.

Disclosure statement

No potential conflict of interest was reported by the authors.

References

Australian Bureau of Statistics. (2013). Preschool education Australia, 2013 (cat. no. 4240.0). Retrieved from http://www.abs.gov.au

Bakhtin M. M. (1929/1973). *Problems of Dostoevsky's poetics.* (R. W. Rotsel, Trans.). Ann Arbor, MI: Ardis.

Bakhtin, M. M. (1934/1981). *The dialogic imagination: Four essays by M.M. Bakhtin* (C. Emerson & M. Holquist, Trans.). Austin: University of Texas Press.

Bakhtin, M. M. (1984). *Problems of Dostoevsky's poetics.* (C. Emerson, Trans.). Minneapolis: University of Minnesota Press.

Bennett, J. (2013). A response from the co-author of 'a strong and equal partnership'. In P. Moss (Ed.), *Early childhood and compulsory education: Reconceptualizing the relationship* (pp. 52–71). London: Routledge and Taylor & Francis Group.

Bloch, M. N., Seward, D., & Seidlinger, P. (2001). What history tells us about public schools for 4-year-olds. *Theory into Practice, 28*(1), 11–18.

Bredekamp, S., & Copple, C. (1997). *Developmentally appropriate practice in early childhood programs.* Washington, DC: National Association for the Education of Young Children.

Brown, C. R., & Marchant, C. (2002). *Play in practice: Case studies in young children's play.* St. Paul, MD: Redleaf Press.

Chalufour, I., & Worth, K. (2004). *Building structures with young children.* Washington, DC: National Association for the Education of Young Children.

Cohen, L. E. (2009). The heteroglossic world of preschoolers' pretend play. *Contemporary Issues in Early Childhood, 10*(4), 331–342.

Cohen, L. E. (2015). Layers of discourse in preschool block play: An examination of children's social interactions. *International Journal of Early Childhood, 47*(2), 267–281. doi:10.1007/s13158–015-0138-9

Connelly, M. F., & Clandinin, J. D. (1999). *Shaping a professional identity: Stories of educational practice.* New York, NY: Teachers College Press.

Creswell, J. W. (2007). *Qualitative inquiry and research design: Choosing among five approaches* (2nd ed.). Thousand Oaks, CA: Sage.

Curtis, D., & Carter, M. (2008). *Learning together with young children: A curriculum framework for reflective teachers.* St. Paul, MN: Redleaf Press.

Devaney, K., & Sykes, G. (1988). Making the case for professionalism. In A. Lieberman (Ed.), *Building a professional culture in school* (pp. 3–22). New York, NY: Teachers College Press.

Dyson, A. H. (2010). Childhoods left behind? Official and unofficial basics of child writing. In N. Yelland (Ed.), *Contemporary perspectives on early childhood education* (pp. 159–176). Berkshire: McGraw-Hill and Open University Press.

Dyson, A. H. (2013). The case of the missing childhoods. *Written Communication, 30*(4), 399–427.

Ebbeck, M., & Waniganayake, M. (2010). *Play in early childhood education: Learning in diverse contexts.* South Melbourne: Oxford University Press.

Elias, C. L., & Berk, L. E. (2002). Self-regulation in young children: Is there a role for sociodramatic play? *Early Childhood Research Quarterly, 17*(2), 216–238.

Epstein, A. S. (2007). *The intentional teacher: Choosing the best strategies for young children's learning.* Washington, DC: National Association for the Education of Young Children.

Fecho, B., Falter, M., & Hong, X. (2016). *Teaching outside the Box but inside the standards: Making room for dialogue.* New York, NY: Teachers College Press.

Galda, L., Pellegrini, A. D., & Cox, S. (1989). A short-term longitudinal study of preschoolers' emergent literacy. *Research in the Teaching of English, 23*, 292–309.

Göncu, A., (1993). Development of intersubjectivity in the dyadic play of pre-schoolers. *Early Childhood Research Quarterly, 8*(1), 99–116.

Gyimah, S. (2014). Sam Gyimah's speech at Policy Exchange on giving the most disadvantaged children the best start in life. Retrieved from https://www.gov.uk/government/speeches/childcare-minister-speaks-about-more-pre-schools-in-schools

Heidemann, S. & Hewitt, D. (2010). *Play: The pathway from theory to practice.* St. Paul, MN: Redleaf Press.

Holland, D., Lachicotte, W., Skinner, D., & Cain, C. (1998). *Identity and agency in cultural worlds.* Cambridge, MA: Harvard University Press.

Jones, E., & Reynolds, G. (1992). *The play's the thing: Teachers' roles in children's play.* New York, NY: Teachers College Press.

Kroeger, J. (2006). Social heteroglossia; The contentious practice or potential place of middle-class parents in home-school relations. *The Urban Review, 37*(1), 1–30.

Kroeger, J., Pech, S., & Cope, J. (2009). Investigating change in field sites through mentor and candidate dialogues. *Journal of Early Childhood Teacher Education, 30*, 328–345.

Kuby, C. (2013). *Critical literacy in the early childhood classroom.* New York, NY: Teachers College Press.

Lazzari, A., & Balduzzi, L. (2013). Bruno Ciari and 'educational continuity': The relationship from an Italian perspective. In P. Moss (Ed.), *Early childhood and compulsory education: Reconceptualizing the relationship* (pp. 149–173). New York, NY: Routledge.

Marjanovic-Shane, A., & White, E. J. (2014). When the footlights are off: A Bakhtinian interrogation of play as postupok. *International Journal of Play, 3*(2), 119–135.

Morris, P. (1994). *The Bakhtin reader: Selected writings of Bakhtin.* Medvedev: Arnold.

Moss, P. (2013). The relationship between early childhood education and compulsory education: A properly political question. In P. Moss (Ed.), *Early childhood and compulsory education: Reconceptualizing the relationship* (pp. 1–50). London: Routledge.

Naughton, C. (2016). A reflection on Bakhtin's 'Epic and Novel' in the context of early childhood student teachers' practicum. *Studies in Philosophy and Education, 35*(1), 93–101.

Noddings, N. (2006). Educational leaders as caring teachers. *School Leadership and Management, 26*(4), 339–345.

Rosen, R. (2015). Children's violently themed play and adult imaginaries of childhood: A Bakhtinian analysis. *International Journal of Early Childhood, 47*(2), 235–250.

Singer, D. G., & Singer, J. L. (1990). *The house of make believe.* Cambridge, MA: Harvard University Press.

Sisson, J. H. (2011). *Professional identities: A narrative inquiry of public preschool teachers* (Doctoral dissertation). Ann Arbor, MI: ProQuest.

Sisson, J. H., Johnson, T., Harris, P., & Webb-Williams, J. (2014, September). *Collaboration, is proximity enough? A narrative inquiry of preschool and Jr. primary teachers.* Paper presented at the Early Childhood Australia conference, Melbourne, AU.

Sisson, J. H. (2016). The significance of critical incidents and voice to identity and agency. *Teachers and Teaching: Theory and Practice, 22*(6), 670–682.

Smilansky, S., & Shefatya, L. (1990). *Facilitating play: A medium for promoting cognitive, socio-emotional and academic development in young children.* Gaithersburd, MD: Psychosocial & Educational.

Stake, R. E. (1995). *The art of case study research.* Thousand Oaks, CA: Sage.

Stetsenko, A., & Ho, P. (2015). The serious Joy and the joyful work of play: Children becoming agentive actors in co-authoring themselves and their world through play. *International Journal of Early Childhood, 47*(2), 221–234.

United Nations. (1989). *Convention on the rights of the child.* Retrieved from http://www.unicef.org/crc/

de Vocht, L. (2015). Reconceptualising teacher-child dialogue in early years education as a moral answerability. *International Journal of Early Childhood, 47*(2), 317–330. doi:10.1007/s13158-015-0140-2

White, E., Redder, B., & Peter, M. (2015). The work of the Eye in infant pedagogy: A dialogic encounter of 'Seeing' in an education and care setting. *International Journal of Early Childhood, 47*(2), 283–299.

REVIEW ARTICLE

Rooms with gender: physical environment and play culture in kindergarten

Hege Eggen Børve and Elin Børve

ABSTRACT
This article focuses on the impact of the physical environment and construction of play culture in kindergartens. Based on a case study, we explore employees' perception of indoor physical environment and children's play. The findings revealed that gender is interwoven in the physical environments and materials. Children's play practices are associated with gender and perceived as setting different requirements for physical design. These play practices are anchored to different rooms and create a connection between rooms, zones, and gender. In additional, play practices produce and reproduce the employees' ideas of gender. The physical environment has a structural power on children's play practices. The impact of the environment on the construction of play practices makes visible the importance of reflecting on the construction of the indoor environment and gender meaning in order to contribute to using the kindergarten in an equal manner.

Introduction

A kindergarten's physical environment and material constitute important conditions for play and action (Nordin-Hultman, 2004). By providing children with experiences such as arousal, excitement, fun, merriment and light-heartedness (Sutton-Smith, 1997), play is an important part in children's childhood (Pellegrini, 2009; Pellegrini & Bjorklund, 2004; Wisneski & Reifel, 2012). Play also has an impact on learning (Alvestad, 2013), health in terms of physical activity, and cognitive and social outcomes (Broekhuizen, Scholten, & de Vries, 2014; Corsaro, 2002). The construction of the environment constitutes kindergartens' pedagogical space as to whether it is facilitated for every child (Gulbrandsen & Eliassen, 2012). This implies that a kindergarten's environment is significant for whether one can use the kindergarten in an equal manner and support gender diversity, or not. This article examines employees' perceptions of indoor physical environments and the construction of children's play culture.

There is a growing interest in studying the significance of kindergartens' environments (Björklid, 2005; Kampmann, 2006). A central topic for this is the impact on children's play (Moser & Martinsen, 2010) such as physical activities (Broekhuizen et al., 2014; Sørensen, 2013; Storli & Sandseter, 2015), while others have emphasized the impact of environments on pedagogic quality, creativity and children's learning (Clark, 2010; Fjørtoft, 2001; Følnnebø & Rolfsen, 2014; Kyttä, 2003; Spencer & Blades, 2006). These studies revealed that both indoor and outdoor environments constitute important settings for children's play, learning, growth and development. Findings also revealed that kindergarten teachers perceive children's play as gendered in their choice of friends, use of play areas and games (e.g. Hardardottir & Petursdottir, 2014; Månsson, 2000; Østrem, 2008). According to Gulbrandsen, Johansson, and Nilsen (2002), kindergarten studies often do not locate play practice in a physical environmental context. Adults' physical presence can be seen as a backdrop for children's play (Röthle, 2005) in the sense that if there are no adults in the room, children will not be there (Østrem et al., 2009). Employees as role models for children's play practices illustrate that they are part of the construction of children's play culture. However, playgrounds are usually cast as being gender-neutral (Ärlemalm-Hagsér, 2010). In kindergarten studies, the perceptions of employees in day-care settings on possible gendered meanings of indoor physical environments, and the impact on the construction of children's play culture, have been less prevalent.

In this article, we explore indoor physical environments and children's play culture by analysing the understanding of employees in day-care settings of physical environments and children's play practices. The aims are to gain an insight into how gender is interwoven into the construction of physical environment and the impact on children's play culture. We use a case study from one kindergarten in Norway to analyse the employees' experiences and practices. With equality ambitions and well-developed gender equality policies towards kindergartens, combined with the highest proportion of males working in kindergartens in Europe (SSB, 2015), Norway provides an interesting context when studying the impact of the physical environment on the construction of children's play culture. By adding a gender perspective on physical environment, our intention is to contribute to the ongoing discussion on physical environment and children's play culture, especially as it is linked to gender equality. In the next section, we outline previous research and theoretical approaches adapted to this study. We then describe the Norwegian kindergarten context followed by a description of the method and design. Next, we focus on the empirical data by presenting a case study outlining the employees' understandings and experiences of their physical environment and children's play culture. Lastly, we discuss findings in light of theory and previous research and their implications for gender equality.

Physical environment in kindergarten

We base our understanding of physical environment within a cultural social construction perspective (Berger & Luckman, 1966). This means that the construction of rooms is viewed as a part of the local culture, knowledge and identity, which function as the rules and norms of social action (Birkeland, 2012). Environments are constructed for specific social patterns and have an impact on social actions. Growing up in a culture implies developing knowledge of how to act in various rooms and in different social contexts (Larsen, 2005).

A physical environment consists of structures that can be divided into three distinct elements: physical localization, such as buildings and placing them, a room's physical layout and a room's physical conditions, including furniture, equipment, design and decoration (Jacobsen & Thorsvik, 2007). In kindergartens, as in other organizations, indoor physical environments are usually divided into different social zones that give signals and normative guidelines to what tends to take place there and what is inappropriate to do there (Frønes, 2001; Gulløv & Højlund, 2005). Some rooms may have strong or weak cultural codes in the sense that they can have a strong normative meaning of what is expected to be done in the rooms, or opposite to this, weakly coded rooms that provide few indications of action (Kirkeby, Gitz-Johansen, & Kampmann, 2005). For instance, when children's opportunity to participate within the planned intention rooms is strongly coded, they are vaguely coded if children have a great opportunity to decide for themselves how to use the room (Kirkeby et al., 2005). Depending on the strength of the rooms' cultural codes, they may contribute to the discipline of individual behaviour.

Foucault (1977) uses the term panoptical to describe how individuals are monitored and controlled within prisons, hospitals, military and other institutions. In a panoptic society, prison-like devices are always present and contribute to help discipline the body and its reaction pattern. Panoptical discipline refers to the internal of a building as space and inventory, and is connected to the body through space and time. Power is embedded in the construction of the rooms, and affects the individual freedom of action. This implies focusing on the practices and processes of organizing, rather than on entities as individuals and organizations only (Foucault, 2005). As Bengtsson (2011) illustrates in a study of school buildings, physical environments contribute to help discipline children, even if they are alone in a room. This stems from just knowing that someone can see you, which gives you less freedom to choose how to use the room.

At the same time as environments are physical, they are also symbols that provide signals to the users or who the users are (Frønes, 2001). In her analysis, Lie (2004) shows how the meaning of chains related to technology is linked to gender symbolism. She argues that to understand materials, and how they are embedded in the culture, requires studying materials as symbols. As technology symbols, physical inventions such as furniture, toys or materials are integrated and linked to knowledge and practice. Nordin-Hultman (2004) illustrates this in her study of how materials contained in kindergartens convey notions of how children should do gender. Materials have a symbolic meaning, which reflects that boys are portrayed as strong and active, while girls are portrayed as passive and proper. The symbolic meaning can hence contribute to reinforcing the child's perception of traditional gender roles through given signals of traditional ways of doing gender. Toys and materials are symbolic elements, as their shape, colour and function are connected to different users, and are reminiscent of the contexts they are embedded in.

Gender is constructed through action and is understood as being socially constructed (Gherardi, 1994), and varies in different contexts (Acker, 1997). Construction of gender refers to both social relations between men and women, and that gender can attribute to abstract notions. A symbolic approach of gender implies that gender is considered as a system of ideas and understanding that produce and reproduce through social practice (West & Zimmerman, 1987). This means that gender is a symbolic category in which phenomena are viewed as having gendered features. Materials associated with the gender distinction imply that gender appears as a metaphor. However, the symbolic meanings of materials are not a one-sided reflection of culture, but instead are products that through interactions are embedded within the construction of culture (Lie, 2004). Social actions as play practices are embedded in the room through the impact of the relationship among the symbolic, social and physical environments.

Physical environment and play culture in kindergarten

The concern of this article is the impact of indoor physical environments in kindergartens for the construction of children's play culture. The physical surroundings constitute the framework for the construction of children's play culture. This is based on an understanding that play culture is understood as being socially constructed and a result of the interaction between children and between adults and children within the physical space. Studies show that kindergarten staff perceive that boys' and girls' play practices are different due to behaviour, bodily use, organization of play activities and the choice of play areas and toys (e.g. Kvalheim, 2002; Østrem et al., 2009; Rithander, 2005). This can be illustrated with Rithander's (2005) survey of girls' and boys' play behaviour and staff practices. The study showed that staff shared an understanding that boys demanded a lot of attention from the staff, and used large areas of kindergarten space. Boys' play was noisy, either muted or stopped by staff. Girls' play was described as being quieter, requiring little attention from the staff, playing in restricted areas indoors and playing more indoors. In a comparison of children's practices in the 1970s and 1990s, Kvalheim (2002) found that boys' and girls' play practices in kindergarten have moved towards one another; boys and girls play more together. She also concluded that the employees have different perceptions of girls' and boys' play practices, and choose different toys for girls and boys depending on what they deem to be appropriate.

Nicholsen, Kurnik, Jevgjovikj, and Ufoegbune's (2015) analysis of children's play showed that adult discourse regarding children's play differed significantly from children's descriptions of their own play. They suggested the importance of including children's perspectives in research on children's play.

According to Francis (1998), young children do not initially understand toys as being gendered, but they learn that certain toys are for boys and others are for girls. However, Francis' (2010) findings in a study of parents of 3- to 5-year-old children revealed that toy preferences were highly gendered, with boys' toys and resources concentrated on technology and action, while those for girls concentrated on care and stereotypical feminine interests. These findings are in harmony with Logue and Harvey's (2009) study of pre-kindergarten teachers. In this survey, teachers reported gender differences in children's engagement in play. Girls engaged more in house/family and care play, whereas boys were more engaged in superhero play and play-fighting. Nonetheless, as other studies have shown that there is a strong tendency among preschool teachers to classify children into categories of boys/masculine and girls/feminine, specific norms direct the children into the dominant feminine and masculine categories (Hardardottir & Petursdottir, 2014), thus maintaining and reinforcing their stereotypes.

The construction of rooms and the inventory and materials reflect the staff's pedagogical understanding of childcare (Cameron, Moss, & Owen, 1999), as well as their social mandate as a kindergarten (Gulløv & Højlund, 2005). To understand the construction of rooms and children's play culture may, therefore, include the institutional environment, the historical context and traditional circumstances (Markström, 2005; Nordin-Hultman, 2004).

The Norwegian kindergarten's context

Since the mid-2000s, the Norwegian kindergarten sector has been subject to various changes. Since 2009, all children older than one year have a formal right to attend kindergarten. This has contributed to a tremendous growth in kindergartens, either by building new kindergartens or by using existing buildings originally not built to house kindergartens. Along with these changes, the understanding of children's development has also changed (The Norwegian Ministry of Education and Research, 2013).

Kindergartens as a physical environment are regulated through national law and various political documents.[1] In accordance with these regulations, kindergartens should adapt and design the environment so that all children have the opportunity to use the kindergarten in an equal manner. This implies constructing the physical environment and outdoor playground in ways that give children opportunities for play, self-expression and meaningful experiences and activities (The Norwegian Ministry of Education and Research, 2011). The planning, location and construction of new kindergartens should be based on principles of universal design. This means that products, buildings and outdoor areas should be designed in such a way that everyone should have an equal opportunity to use them without special adaptations (The Norwegian Ministry of Education and Research, 2011).

In Norway and other Nordic countries, the growing influence of the Italian Reggio Emilia pedagogy has contributed to more of a focus on space and architecture in early childhood education (Moser & Martinsen, 2010). In general, more attention seems to be given to outdoor environments for children's physical play and learning (e.g. Fjørtoft, 2001; Martinsen, 2015; Moser & Martinsen, 2010; Sandseter, 2009; Vassenden, Thyesen, Brosvik, Alvestad, & Abrahamsen, 2011). Previous studies show that kindergarten employees largely perceive a physical environment as accessible for all children (Gulbrandsen & Eliassen, 2012). Others point out that an institution's design reflects the employee's taste, while educational facilitation is given less attention (Thorbergsen, 2007).

Modern organizational forms, as theme- or base-organized kindergartens, have contributed to different ways of organizing children, space, materials and time (Martinsen, 2015). These new forms of organizing imply constructing rooms more fluidly so that they can be used by different groups of varying sizes. It has been claimed that base-organized kindergartens allow less educational time for children (Seland, 2009), and are less suitable for young children (Amundsen et al., 2007; Vassenden et al., 2011). However, approximately 79% of institutions have a traditional departmental organization (Gulbrandsen & Eliassen, 2012), which implies that children are divided into permanent groups with a defined area within the building. The size of the kindergarten and the organizing forms seem to have a significant impact on the quality of the kindergartens (Vassenden et al., 2011) by providing varying structural conditions for children's play, which may promote the quality of children's play (Martinsen, 2015).

The main research questions in this article centre on what impact physical environments have on the construction of play culture. First, we explore the staff's understanding of the indoor physical environment, and how this is interwoven with notions of gender. Second, we analyse how the physical environment and materials are embedded in the staff's perception of children's play practices.

Method and data

This article is based on a case study collected in connection with a research and development project called 'Gender equality in kindergartens'. The research project's purpose was to obtain insight on a kindergarten's work-organization, environment, practices, working conditions and gender equality works. The data material originally consisted of two case studies of kindergartens located in Norway. Selection criteria were strategically justified, having both female and male staff members and having both a traditional organizational structure and a traditional departmental organization. For this article, we use data from one of the kindergartens.

The kindergarten was privately run and had 73 children and 18 employees, including 3 men and 15 women. The staff composition was in accordance with the Kindergarten Act Law, which stipulates that a minimum of one-third of the staff are required to be qualified kindergarten teachers (The Norwegian Ministry of Education and Research, 2005), which reflected the national picture (Johannesen & Hoel, 2010), with male workers more likely to be assistants. Most of the employees worked full-time, while a minority worked part-time. The kindergarten had a traditional departmental organization, which is the most common organizational form in Norway. The data consist of eight in-depth interviews, with two men and six women. The women were either kindergarten teachers (four) or assistants (two), while both of the men worked as assistants.

During the interviews, employees were asked several questions. An important part of the questions was that the employees should describe their environment, which was a question posed to all of the informants. The answers led to follow-up and clarifying questions, such as 'Who designed the rooms?' and 'How do children use the rooms?' The employees were encouraged to develop their answers, with each interview taking roughly 90 minutes. To ensure the credibility and reliability of the data material (Repstad, 2007), an interview guide was used to make sure all the informants were asked questions about the same topics. The interviews were all recorded and later transcribed.

The quotes we used are direct reproductions of what the informants stated during the interviews. We increased the reliability by double-checking quotations and by using caution in our interpretation of the data. The main point of the analysis was the understandings that emerged, rather than how many people said what and had experienced what.

Gendered physical environment

The kindergarten was organized into four departments based on the children's age: two departments had children aged one to three years, while two departments were for children above three years of age. The departmental organization implied that children were divided into permanent groups with their own defined area in the building. The kindergarten was located in a building originally built to house a primary school. Before the kindergarten took occupancy, the building was renovated to a small degree. Each department had a wardrobe, a large play- and living room, a smaller playroom and a gender-neutral restroom. The departments shared a large common room, a kitchen, a gym and a staffroom. One of the assistants described the physical environment in this manner:

> There are lots of rooms (...). We are divided into different departments so we have the ability to be by ourselves, only one department. It is worth gold (...). That means that there are not people everywhere all the time. In addition, we have a gym we can use. We are really lucky. (Female kindergarten teacher)

As this assistant indicated, several others pointed out that they were lucky to have a function-based room as the gym. To have many rooms was perceived to contribute to children and adults having good conditions for bodily movement, moving between different places, activities and relationships, all of which implied good conditions for interactions.

In policy documents, the size of the play and recreational area per child is considered to be a measure of structural quality (The Norwegian Ministry of Education and Research, 2013). In general, employees were concerned with the significance of the large common room, which was divided through the use of partitioned walls by the employees into different zones with specific functions/activities. This was explained by the size of the room and the necessity to organize the children into smaller groups. For example, the zones were named the dolls corner, the paint corner and the car corner. The common room was perceived to provide opportunities for children and adults to move and flow between different departments. The large size of the common room created flexibility in the sense that it could easily be reshaped and redefined as needed. Both the rooms and zones were strongly coded by the employees, with a clear message for the expectations and intention of the space. The employees were asked about who had designed and decorated the indoor environment. One of the kindergarten teachers' reflection was:

> The kindergarten is constructed in a woman's head many times. No men have constructed kindergartens (...). We [referring to herself and her female colleagues] like to have it cosy with tidy shelves, arrangements and some flowerpots, but maybe men do not give these things the same attention. (Female kindergarten teacher)

This kindergarten teacher expressed that in general, the female staff had constructed the kindergarten. According to her, women were more interested in the indoor environment and interior design in relation to making it organized and cozy.

During the interviews, employees expressed that although all of the staff took part in discussions regarding the kindergarten's physical environment, female employees were both more interested and had stronger opinions about changes, how they should be done and how to improve things. This can be illustrated by a story one of the kindergarten teachers told during the interviews. Shortly before the interview process, the staffroom was changed. Ahead of this change, the staff had long discussions about what kind of sofa they should choose, including the colour, shape, size and location. Employees were involved in the discussion, although according to both the women and men the male employees did not articulate their views – as one said: 'He did not care very much about which sofa we should choose'. The women made the decision, but when the sofa arrived, the male employees were entrusted with the responsibility of installing it.

The employees were responsible for the room's structures, design and materials, whereas the children never participated in the design process of the rooms. Women were positioned as the architects behind the construction of the physical environment, which was explained to be as a result of women constituting the majority of the staff. As one put it: 'Still, there is a lot embedded in the walls. The environment is marked by women because there are only women who supposedly who work here'. The term 'embedded in the walls' is a metaphorical expression that has a figurative meaning. In this context, the expression was used to characterize the culture, a work culture in which women predominating in positions of modes of behaviour and opinions is taken as the norm (Nordberg, 2002). Interestingly, although men were part of the staff, they were not mentioned as having positions in the construction of the environment. One of the female kindergarten teachers used the term 'female culture' in her talk about the kindergarten's physical environment, while one of the male assistants used 'dolls corners' in his description of the physical environment. According to him, 'There are dolls corners everywhere. I think that is because there are a lot of women here'. Dolls corners were used as symbols to substantiate how female dominance among the staff was reflected in the physical layout. Linking environment to gender and being associated with women is a reflection of a traditional understanding of a connection between family, childcare and women. The employees' descriptions illustrate that a physical environment is not only perceived as physical, but also has symbolic markers that give signals and refer to gender.

Embedded in the construction of the environment are the norms and expectations of practices such as play practices, what should be played and how. This means that the norms and rules of play practices are defined in relation to the construction of rooms, while at the same time play practices are developed in relation to space and the availability of toys and materials. In the next section, we explore the staff's perception of the significance of physical conditions and materials in children's play practices.

Gendered rooms: physical environment and play practices

The kindergarten's daily life was characterized as following up on open plans and fixed routines, including making sure that activities were done at a certain time. Yearly, monthly and weekly plans functioned as action guidelines for the staff's organization of the daily life, thereby making workdays predictable and standardized. Like other educational establishments, meals, as well as indoor and outdoor activities and play, were regulated and scheduled in a certain space and time.

In Norway, free play is an important part of children's daily life in kindergartens (The Norwegian Ministry of Education and Research, 2011; Seland, 2009). The employees used the terms 'fine' and 'good' play practices when children were included without interference from the staff. The description coincides with 'self-organization' and 'free play', that is, play planned by the children themselves (Hewes, 2014). Adults provide the space and resources, and might get involved and respond to cues from the children, while children take the lead (Santer, Griffiths, & Goodall, 2007).

Employees' descriptions of children's 'good' play included notions about the use of body and the level of sound. One of the kindergarten teachers elaborated on this by saying that: 'They are not despoiling and running, throwing toys everywhere and anywhere, but children are sitting and doing an activity and talking together'. According to this female kindergarten teacher, 'good' play refers to children sitting and doing table activities. This practice entailed rooms prepared for non-bodily movements and requires little space. Others had a more nuanced description of the 'good play' by mentioning both quiet and loud play as 'good play'. One of the female kindergarten teachers said:

> Even though boys have a different way of playing, their play practice can be as good and fine as girls'. They are equally engaged as the girls. Maybe they are more vociferous, more physical, but that's not the same as saying that the play is not good. Their play practices can be just fine, regardless of them being quite or loud.

In line with previous research on children's play practices, boys and girls were perceived as traditional in the sense of being each other's opposites. Unlike girls, play practices associated with boys were attributed to requiring qualities such as using their voice and body, both of which are markers of masculine rules (Eidevald, 2009). Compared to the boys, girls were described as calmer and quieter in their play. In terms of bodily movement and noise, norms and rules connected to the various play practices required different physical environments.

Employees also told stories about children crossing gender boundaries; for example, boys playing in zones constructed for activities linked to girls, or girls using areas associated with boys. Interestingly, children crossing gender boundaries were generally expressed in positive terms by saying it is wonderful. This can be illustrated by the following quotes:

> In the dolls corner, we have both girls and boys. It is so wonderful to see boys putting an apron on. They put on an apron, and they stand and move the saucepan talking with the girls and saying: 'Dinner is soon.' It is so wonderful. (Female assistant)

> We have two girls who are really into cars. There is lots of sound, and they push the cars across the floor. (...). It is a lot of action as the boys involve the girls and they send cars between them. We heard various sound effects. It is wonderful, but it is noisy; when they talk together, their voices are much higher than in the doll corner. (Female assistant)

Boys and girls crossing stereotypical gender boundaries were perceived as following the rules related to play activities. This shows that children adapt to and meet the requirements and standards embedded in the rooms. This established a form of equality between boys' and girls' play practices, although when boys were playing in the same room and with the same play activities as the girls, the girls' practices were marked as masculine and associated with the stereotypical boys' practices. Some pointed that a significant difference was the use of space. As one of the female kindergarten teachers said: 'I see little princesses playing, you know, in small corners they play gently. The boys can also play with the same carriages and the same play material, but they use the whole space of the room and there is speed when they have dolls in the carriages'. Play practices associated with boys implied more use of space, while play practices related to girls entailed a limited use of space.

According to the staff, boys more frequently preferred to play in rooms containing materials associated with boys, whereas girls tended to occupy rooms with activities related to girls. The consequence of boys and girls doing different activities was that they occupied different rooms and zones in the kindergarten, hence indicating that rooms are gender-coded through the symbol of the materials in the rooms. In addition, rooms were also gendered through the meaning of children's play practices. As one of the female assistants said during the interview: 'The boys like to spend time there [pointing to a room], because then they are allowed to use their voices in their play'. Boys' preferences to play in rooms where they could use their bodies and voices contributed to having boys and girls in different rooms and zones in the kindergarten. A female assistant illustrated this by saying: 'The boys run between rooms. They are also involved in other activities, and even seem satisfied sitting at the table. Boys also like construction play such as Legos, or being in a room where they can jump and bounce and use their voices'. The employees observed children's play practices and their use of rooms and zones. One of the female assistants said:

> When we observed the physical environment, we saw that girls occupied some activities while the boys occupied some activities. The consequences were that they were not crossing space in the sense that where the female activity was located there were fewer boys in those rooms, and vice versa.

Attention to children's play action visibly contributed to girls and boys using different rooms depending on the type of activities they were prepared for and what kind of materials the rooms contained. Linking girls' and boys' play practices to different rooms indicates that rooms also provide signals as to what should take place there and how the toys should be used, thereby giving signals about the user's gender.

For some of the employees, the observations of children's play practices had led to a reflection of children's opportunity to use the environment in an equal manner. One of the female assistants pointed out that 'availability does not necessarily mean equal opportunities'. She continued to say:

> When the play material is available for everybody, we think that children have the same opportunities. However, when the boys occupy the so-called typical 'boyish' material and girls occupy 'girlish' material, they may not have the same opportunities in practice. I think we need to facilitate to some degree, so that every child should have the opportunity to play with the same materials and activities.

This assistant reflected that as long as girls or boys occupy certain zones or rooms, this may contribute to limiting children's opportunities to use the kindergarten in an equal manner. In the following, she said that the observation of children's play made, 'It clear that the space and rooms were not available for all of the children'.

Although the employees said they were happy to have a gym, especially the women, it was seldom used for physical activities with the children. The gym was a large room located in the cellar, which some labelled as a room with a 'cold atmosphere' that contained few materials. One of the male assistants expressed that he did not mind spending time with the children in the gym. He continued by saying: 'I like to be more physical and I tolerate the noise. It does not bother me. I would rather use the gym instead of sitting and making Easter chickens, as they [women] do now'. The employees mentioned that the staff's use of the rooms had significance for the use of the room and the materials for play. In this kindergarten, employees emphasized the significance of both the employees' presence and gender. Adults' physical presence can be seen as a backdrop for children's play (Röthle, 2005) in the sense that if there are no adults in the room, children will not be there (Østrem et al., 2009). As one said: 'I see significant differences. The girls go to puppets, drawing and stuff like that, while the boys like to play with Legos. But it might have to do with the male employees sitting right next to them'. According to this employee, boys doing different activities and using different rooms may be a consequence of employees as role models, rather than a reflection of the gender symbolic materials. Like the children, employees selecting different rooms and play activities, which are dependent on gender, indicate that through their practices the adults supported and legitimized gendered play practices. Others mention that men and women employees were doing things differently: 'They [men] ravage more with the children, they use more of the space and do things different compared to when we [women] are caring for the children. We take them on our lap while they do completely different things'. This illustrates how through both their understanding and practices the employees were part of the construction of gendered play practices located in different rooms in the kindergarten.

Employees had to sometimes interrupt or stop children's play, particularly play activities related to boys. The reason was either because of a loud sound or because the play was considered as being too rough. The underlying cause was that the physical environment was not perceived as suitable and adapted to all types of play practices:

> I see them running around. The boys are busy playing with cars. It gets a little wild, and sometime they bump into each other. It is clear that it has to do with the physical environment, and that perhaps it is cramped. They do not have the opportunities to express themselves enough. (Female assistant)

Employees sometimes sanctioned play practices that violated the expectations of plays in certain rooms. Another option was to use partition walls.

During the interviews, staff members were asked how they would prefer to form the physical environment. Male employees consistently expressed that they would like to have a room that was adapted for 'chaos', meaning a room constructed for physical activity and loud noise. This may indicate that rooms designed for physical activity are not given the same amount of attention, and that rooms are more suitable for play activities related to girls' practice. If boys' play practices are not seen as suitable for the design of the kindergarten's indoor physical environment, or viewed as appropriate to the same degree as practices related to girls, this may indicate that the kindergarten is not constructed as an arena that gives children equal opportunities regardless of gender.

Discussion and conclusion

The beginning of this article was about the indoor physical environment and the construction of children's play culture. In addition to being a context for children's play, a kindergarten's physical environment is for learning and development, an actor and team player in important processes that can contribute to increasing the quality of Norwegian kindergartens (Birkeland, 2012). The construction of an indoor and outdoor environment constitutes a pedagogical space for whether children can use the kindergarten in an equal manner or not. By using a case study from a kindergarten in Norway, we explored employees' perceptions of the impact of indoor physical environments on children's play practices.

The findings are that female employees had the responsibility of forming the physical environment. According to the employees, the environment was marked as feminine and associated with women, with the consequence being that the environment was seen as symbolizing femininity. This indicates that the environment is not cast as gender-neutral.

Rooms and zones were constructed for activities and contained different materials and the rooms and zones were also strongly coded with a message of expectations and intention for the space. In this way, the physical environment has a structural power on children's play practices in regard to what to do there and vice versa. The employees' responsibilities of the construction of the rooms imply that their understandings of environment have had a significant impact on children's play conditions in the kindergarten.

The body speed, noise and use of space created different stories about children playing in the kindergarten. Play practices associated with boys demanded masculine qualities such as toughness and roughness and the use of the body and voice. In turn, play practices connected to girls required feminine qualities such as being gentle and using an 'indoor' voice. Moreover, it implies using a limited space. Although the children occasionally crossed gender lines by taking part in play practices that were not associated with their gender, girls and boys were perceived to use rooms differently. Even so, play practices seen as gendered are in accordance with previous findings. Play practices produced and reproduced the adults' ideas of gender. Likewise, through play, children define and redefine their understandings of gender (Taguchi, 2004). How children play can provide different terms for what girls and boys learn through free play (Rossholt, 2009).

Rooms and zones give signals as to what should take place there, how materials as toys should be used and the user's gender. Play practices associated with boys and girls were perceived to occupy different rooms and zones. The link between rooms and play practices indicates that rooms, beyond providing signals of activities, also symbolize gender. Employees' observation of children's play practices made it clear that girls and boys played in different zones and rooms. Rooms and zones occupied by either girls or boys may imply that the environment is not available for every child.

The employees emphasized the significance of the employee's presence and gender for children's play practices. Children learn practices and understanding through watching both adults and other children's actions. Like the children, adults selecting different rooms and play activities dependent on gender indicate that through their practices adults supported and legitimized gendered play practices. This illustrates that through both their understanding and practices, the employees were part of the construction of gendered play practices located in different rooms within the kindergarten. Adults' choice on the construction of rooms, the availability of materials and employees' practices are all important for both children's practices and the use of the kindergarten in an equal manner.

Employees' understanding of the physical environment can be seen as institutionalized arguments. This means that some understandings of the physical environment and its impact on play practice are perceived as obvious or natural, while others are considered inappropriate. For instance, perceptions of play practices as gendered may be an understanding that is taken for granted among the employees. The result is that it is expected that boys and girls use different materials, involve in different activities and occupy different rooms and zones. 'Kindergartens shall promote democracy and equality, and counteract all forms of discrimination' (The Norwegian Ministry of Education and Research, 2011). This implies that boys and girls should have equal opportunities to be seen, heard and encouraged to participate jointly in all activities of the institution. Article 2 from The United Nations Convention on the Rights of the Child (1989): 'The Rights of the Child to be Heard' (p. 31) points out that regardless of their background and circumstances, children have equal value. This means that every child has the right to play, create a play world, ask others to participate and participate in someone else's play. However, employees' perceptions of gendered play practices may not be interpreted as an expression of the kindergarten not working as an equal arena accessible for all children, although, if play practices associated with girls form the basis and serve as models for the design of the physical environment, it may appear reasonable to draw such a conclusion. The play practices' strong link to the physical environment and materials illustrates the impact of the physical environment on the construction of play culture. Children occupying different rooms and zones may indicate that some of the space is not available for all the children.

The physical environment's importance for the construction of children's gendered play culture indicates the importance of the discussion on environment and gender meaning. A precondition for breaking with performances that have gained a natural status is to open up for other understandings.

An important part of this may be employees' reflection on pedagogical issues related to the construction of the indoor environment and gender meaning. Studies show that children in kindergarten are competent to both reflect and construct rooms (Hansson, Jansen, & Aasen, 2005; Moser, Melvold, Jørgensen, & Hagheim, 2008). This indicates that to involve the children might be a solution to construct the indoor environment as gender-neutral.

Note

1. 'The Kindergarten Act' (The Norwegian Ministry of Education, 2005), 'Framework Plan for Content and Tasks for Kindergartens' (The Norwegian Ministry of Education and Research, 2011), governmental action plans to promote gender equality, propositions related to gender equality such as Parliamentary White Paper no. 24, 'The Kindergarten of the Future' (The Norwegian Ministry of Education and Research, 2013).

Disclosure statement

No potential conflict of interest was reported by the authors.

References

Acker, J. (1997). Rewriting class, race and gender problems in feminist rethinking. *Sosiologisk Tidsskrift, 5*(2), 93–103.

Alvestad, T. (2013). Relasjonsbygging i barns lek [Building relationships in children's play]. In E. Foss & O. F. Lillemyr (Eds.), *Til barnas beste. Veier til omsorg og lek, læring og danning* (pp. 56–76). Oslo: Gyldendal akademisk.

Amundsen, H. M., Blakstad, S. H., Krogstad, A., Knutsen, W., Manum, B., Sve, L., & Wågø, S. (2007). *Barn og rom- refleksjoner over barns opplevelser av rom* [Children and room – reflections of children's experiences of room]. Trondheim: Trondheim kommune, Sintef, DMMH.

Ärlemalm- Hagsér, E. (2010). Gender choreography and microstructures: Early childhood professionals' understanding of gender roles and gender patterns in outplay and learning. *European Early Childhood Education Research Journal, 8*(4), 515–525.

Bengtsson, J. (2011). Educational significations in school buildings. In J. Bengtsson (Ed.), *Educational dimension of school buildings* (pp. 11–33). Frankfurt am Main: Peter Lang.

Berger, P. L., & Luckman, T. (1966). *The social construction of reality: A treatise in the sociology of knowledge*. Garden City, NY: Anchor Books.

Birkeland, I. (2012). Rom, sted og kjønn. Begrepsavklaringer og bruksanvisninger [Room, place and gender. Clarification of concepts and manuals]. In A. Krogstad, K. G. Hansen, K. Høyland, & T. Moser (Eds.), *Rom for barnehage. Flerfaglig perspektiver på barnehagens fysiske miljø* (pp. 47–63). Bergen: Fagbokforlaget.

Björklid, P. (2005). *Lärande och fysisk miljö: en kunskapsöversikt om samspelet mellan lärande och fysisk miljö i förskola och skola* [Learning and physical environment in pre-school and school]. Stockholm: Myndigheten för skolutveckling.

Broekhuizen, K., Scholten, A.-M., & de Vries, S. I. (2014). The value of (pre) school playgrounds for children's physical activity level: A systematic review. *International Journal of Behavioral Nutrition and Physical Activity, 11*, 59. doi:10.1186/1479-5868-11-59

Cameron, C., Moss, P., & Owen, C. (1999). *Men in the nursery: Gender and caring work*. London: Paul Chapman.

Clark, A. (2010). *Transforming children's spaces: Children's and adult's participation in designing learning environment*. London: Routledge.

Corsaro, W. A. (2002). *Barndommens sociologi* [Sociology of childhood]. Kobenhagen: Gyldendal Uddannelse.

Eidevald, C. (2009). *Det fins inga tjejbestämmare: att förstä kön som position i förskolans vardagsrutiner och lek* [There are no female determiners: Understanding gender as a position in the preschool daily routines and play]. Ph.d. Högskolan i Jönköping, Göteborg.

Fjørtoft, I. (2001). The natural environment as a playground for children: The impact of outdoor play activities in pre-primary school children. *Early Childhood Education Journal, 29*(2), 111–117.

Fønnebø, B., & Rolfsen, C. N. (2014). Areal til skapende lek, læring og utforskning i barnehagen [Area used to creative play, learning and exploration in the kindergarten]. *Journal of Nordic Early Childhood Education Research, 7*(1), 1–11.

Foucault, M. (1977). *Discipline and Punish: The birth of the prison.* London: Allen Lane.

Foucault, M. (2005). *The Hermeneutics of the subject: Lectures at the Collège de France 1981-1982.* New York (NY): Macmillan.

Francis, B. (1998). *Power plays: Primary school children's constructions of gender, power, and adult work.* London: Trentham Books.

Francis, B. (2010). Gender, toys and learning. *Oxford Review of Education, 36*(3), 325–344.

Frønes, I. (2001). *Handling, kultur og mening* [Action, culture and meaning]. Bergen: Fagbokforlaget.

Gherardi, S. (1994). *Gender, symbolism, organizational cultures.* Sage: London.

Gulbrandsen, L., & Eliassen, E. (2012). *Kvalitet i barnehagen* [Quality in kindergarten] (NOVA rapport 1/3). Oslo: NOVA.

Gulbrandsen, L., Johansson, J. E., & Nilsen, R. D. (2002). *Forskning om barnehager: en Kunnskapsstatus* [Research on kindergarten: A knowledge status]. Oslo: Forskningsrådet.

Gulløv, E., & Højlund, S. (2005). Materialitetens pædagogiske kraft [Materiality educational force]. In K. Larsen (Ed.), *Arkitektur, krop og læring* (pp. 21–43). København: Hans Reitzels Forlag.

Hansson, H., Jansen, S. K., & Aasen, G. (2005). *Rommet som intensjonal tekst: et utviklingsprosjekt ved Høgskolen i Vestfold, førskolelærerutdanningen* [The room as intentional text: A development project at Vestfold University College, pre-school education] (Rapport 5). Tønsberg: Høgskolen i Vestfold.

Hardardottir, G. A., & Petursdottir, G. M. (2014). Gendering in one Icelandic preschool. *Nordisk barnehageforskning, 7*(9), 1–14.

Hewes, J. (2014). Seeking balance in motion: The role of spontaneous free play in promoting social and emotional health in early childhood care and education. *Children, 1*(3), 280–301. doi:10.3390/children1030280

Jacobsen, D. I., & Thorsvik, J. (2007). *Hvordan organisasjoner fungerer* [How organizations function]. 3. utgave. Bergen: Fagbokforlaget.

Johannesen, N., & Hoel, A. (2010). *Status of gender equality work in Norwegian Kindergartens - New kindergartens in old tracks.* Paper presented at the 20th ECECERA annual conference, Birmingham: England. Retrieved from http://www.koordination-maennerinkitas.de/uploads/media/EECERA__2010__Johannesen_Hoel_01.pdf

Kampmann, J. (2006). Børn, rum og rummelighed [Children, room and spaciousness]. In K. Rasmussen (Ed.), *Børns steder. Om børns egne steder og voksnes steder til børn* (pp. 106–120). København: Billesø and Baltzer.

Kirkeby, I. M., Gitz-Johansen, T., & Kampmann, J. (2005). Samspil mellem fysisk rum og hverdagsliv i skolen [Interaction between physical room and daily life in the school]. In K. Larsen (Ed.), *Arkitektur, krop og læring* (pp. 43–67). København: Hans Reitzels Forlag.

Kvalheim, I. L. (2002). *Leken var annerledes* [The play was different]. Fiin gammel, 3, 5. Bergen: Bergen Kommune.

Kyttä, M. (2003). *Children in outdoor contexts. Affordances and independent mobility in the assessment of environment child friendliness* (Doctoral dissertation). Helsinki University of technology, Helsinki.

Larsen, K. (red.). (2005). *Arkitektur, krop og læring* [Architecture, body and learning]. København: Hans Reitzels Forlag.

Lie, M. (2004). Tingenes kjønnssymbolikk. Om teknologi som kulturens modeller [Things gender symbolism. About technology as culture models]. *Kulturstudier, 38,* 71–90.

Logue, M. E., & Harvey, H. (2009). Preschool teachers' views of active play. *Journal of Research in Childhood Education, 24* (1), 32–49.

Markström, A.-M. (2005). *Förskolan som normaliseringspraktik: en etnografisk studie* [Pre-school as normalization-practice; an ethnographic study] (PhD-thesis). Institutionen för utbildningsvetenskap, Linköping University, Linköping.

Martinsen, M. T. (2015). Structural conditions for children's play in kindergarten. *Nordic Early Childhood Education Research, 10*(1), 1–18.

Moser, T., & Martinsen, M. T. (2010). The outdoor environment in Norwegian kindergartens as pedagogical space for toddlers' play, learning and development. *European Early Childhood Education Research Journal, 18*(4), 457–471.

Moser, T., Melvold, L. B., Jørgensen, K. A., & Hagheim, A. K. (2008). Om kropp og barnas rom, om kaos og ro, kjedsomhet og utfordringer. Kropp, bevegelse og helse [About body and children's room, about chaos and calmness, boringness and challenges]. In T. Moser & M. Pettersvold (Eds.), *En verden av muligheter. Fagområdene i barnehagen* (pp. 60–79). Oslo: Universitetsforlaget.

Månsson, A. (2000). *Möten som formar: interaktionsmönster på förskola mellan pedagoger och de yngsta barnen i ett genusperspektiv* [Meetings that shapes: Patterns of interaction between preschool teachers and the youngest child in a gender perspective] (Phd-avhandling). Malmö University, Malmö.

Nicholsen, J., Kurnik, J., Jevgjovikj, M., & Ufoegbune, V. (2015). Deconstructing adult's and children's discourses on children's play: Listening to children's voices to destabilize deficit narrative. *Early Child Development and Care, 185*(10), 1569–1586.

Nordberg, M. (2002). Constructing masculinity in woman`s world: Men working as pre-school teachers and hairdressers. *NORA - Nordic Journal of Feminist and Gender Research, 10*(1), 26–37.

Nordin-Hultman, E. (2004). *Pedagogiske miljøer og barns subjektskapning* [Educational environment and children's subject constructing]. Stockholm: Liber.

Østrem, S. (2008). *Barns subjektivitet og likeverd. Et bidrag til en diskusjon om barnehagens pedagogiske innhold og etiske forankring* [Child's subjectivity and equality. A contribution to a discussion about kindergartens pedagogical content and ethical anchor] (Ph.d.). Universitetet i Oslo, Oslo.

Østrem, S., Bjar, H., Føsker, L. R., Hognes, H. D., Jansen, T. T., Nordtømme, S., & Tholin, K. R. (2009). *Alle teller mer. En evaluering av hvordan Rammeplan for barnehagens innhold og oppgaver blir innført, brukt og erfart* [Everybody count more: An evaluation of how the Framework Plan for the kindergarten's content and tasks in introduced, applied and experienced] (Report 1/2009). Tønsberg: Høgskolen i Vestfold.

Pellegrini, A. (2009). *The role and play in human development*. New York, NY: Oxford University Press.

Pellegrini, A., & Bjorklund, D. F. (2004). The ontogeny and phylogeny of children's object and fantasy play. *Human Nature, 15*, 23–43.

Repstad, P. (2007). *Mellom nærhet og distanse. Kvalitative metoder i samfunnsfag* [Between closeness and distance: Qualitative methods in social science]. Oslo: Universitetsforlaget.

Rithander, S. (2005). *Snille piker og rabagaster? Jenter og gutter i barnehagen* [Kind girls and rabagaster? Girls and boys in kindergarten]. Oslo: Universitetsforlaget.

Rossholt, N. (2009). Begrepene omsorg, læring og lek [The concepts care, learning and play]. In L. Askeland & N. Roosholt (Eds.), *Kjønnsdiskurser i barnehagen. Mening, makt og medvirkning* (pp. 71–80). Bergen: Fagbokforlaget.

Röthle, M. (2005). Rom for lærende småbarn [Rooms for learning toddlers]. *Barnehagefolk, 3*, 42–53.

Sandseter, E. B. (2009). Affordances for risky play in pre-school. The importance of features in the play environment. *Early Childhood Education Journal, 36*, 439–446.

Santer, J., Griffiths, C., & Goodall, D. L. (2007). *Free play in early childhood. A literaturereview*. London: National Children`s Bureau.

Seland, M. (2009). *Det moderne barn og den fleksible barnehagen. En etnografisk studie av barnehagens hverdagsliv i lys av nyere diskurser og kommunal virksomhet* [The Modern Child and the flexible kindergarten] (Phd.). NTNU/Norsk senter for barneforskning, Trondheim.

Sørensen, H. V. (2013). *Børns fysiske aktiviteter i børnehaver. En analyse av 5-6 årige børns muligheder og betingelser for fysisk aktivitet i forskellige børnehaver og den fysiske aktivitets betydning for barns udvikling* [Children's physical activities in kindergartens. An analysis of 5-6 years old children possibilities and conditions for physical activities of physic activities in different kindergartens and the physical activities significance for children's development] (Ph.d.-afhandling). Syddansk Universitet, Danmark.

Spencer, C., & Blades, M. (2006). *Children and their environments. Learning, using and designing spaces*. Cambridge: Cambridge University Press.

SSB. (2015). *Statistics Norway Barnehager. Endelige tall 2015 (Kindergartens<preliminary numbers, 2015)*. Retrieved from http://www.ssb.no/barnehager/

Storli, R., & Sandseter, E. B. H. (2015). Preschool teachers' perception of children's rough-and-tumble play (R & T) in indoor and outdoor environments. *Early Child Development and Care, 185*(11–12), 1995–2009. doi:10-1080/03004430.2015.1028394

Sutton-Smith, B. (1997). *The ambiguity of play*. Cambridge, MA: Harvard University Press.

Taguchi, H. L. (2004). *In på bara benet. En introduksjon til feministisk poststrukturalisme* [Down to the bone. An introduction to feminist post-structuralism]. Stockholm: HLS förlag.

The Norwegian Ministry of Education and Research. (2005). *The kindergarten act*. Oslo: Author.

The Norwegian Ministry of Education and Research. (2011). *The framework plan for the content and task for kindergartens*. Oslo: Author.

The Norwegian Ministry of Education and Research. (2013). *The kindergarten of the future, parliamentary* (White Paper No. 24). Oslo: Author.

The United Nations Convention on the Rights of the Child. (1989). Retrieved from http://www.ohchr.org/EN/ProfessinalInterest/Pages/CRC.aspx

Thorbergsen, E. (2007). *Barnehagens rom: - nye muligheter* [The kindergarten's space: – new opportunities]. Oslo: Pedagogisk Forum.

Vassenden, A., Thyesen, J., Brosvik, S. B., Alvestad, M., & Abrahamsen, G. (2011). *Barnehagers organisering og strukturelle faktorers betydning for kvalitet* [Kindergarten organization and structural factors influence on quality] (Rapport IRIS). Stavanger: IRIS, International Research Institute of Stavanger.

West, C., & Zimmerman, D. (1987). Doing gender. *Gender and Society, 1*, 125–151.

Wisneski, D. B., & Reifel, S. (2012). The place of play in early childhood curriculum. In N. File, J. J., Mueller, & D. B. Wisneski (Eds.), *Curriculum in early childhood education: Reexamined, rediscovered, renewed* (pp. 175–188). New York, NY: Routledge.

Children's engagement in play at home: a parent's role in supporting play opportunities during early childhood

Doré R. LaForett and Julia L. Mendez

ABSTRACT
This study examined parents' developmentally appropriate beliefs about young children's play and parents' views on their child's play skills. This exploratory secondary data analysis was drawn from data on low-income African-American and Latino parents and their children ($n = 109$) participating in Head Start programmes in the USA. Compared with African-American parents, Latino parents were more likely to endorse play as valuable (Play Support) for promoting preschool children's social skills and school readiness, yet were also more likely to see play as not as important as academic readiness activities (Academic Focus). Parental endorsement of Play Support beliefs positively related to children's interactive play skills; Academic Focus beliefs negatively related to interactive play. These relations emerged for African American, but not Latino, children. Implications for understanding how culture may intersect with parents' play beliefs, opportunities to promote children's play competence, and alignment with play-based pedagogies are discussed.

Play is a naturally occurring context for development during the early childhood period. Through play with others, children are exposed to a language and experience of social interaction that is novel, exciting, frivolous, and magical. However, the value of play for children's development has been much debated and dissected within the empirical and theoretical literature. Research has established specific contributions of play to social and cognitive development via meta-analysis (Fisher, 1992) as well as documented the nature of skills required to sustain high-quality play interactions (Eggum-Wilkens et al., 2014; Mendez, McDermott, & Fantuzzo, 2002). For example, children come to understand turn-taking and encounter opportunities for expressing and regulating powerful emotions (Fantuzzo, Coolahan, Mendez, McDermott, & Sutton-Smith, 1998; Pelligrini, 1992). Adults in the child's life often serve as a valuable guide in this process, as they are equipped to scaffold emerging play skills of the child during the early developmental years (Bulotsky-Shearer, McWayne, Mendez, & Manz, 2016).

To advance the knowledge base, for several decades a group of researchers has been studying and describing the play behaviours of low income, ethnic minority children in the USA who attend Head Start programmes (Bulotsky-Shearer, McWayne, et al., 2016; Fantuzzo et al., 1995). Head Start is an early intervention programme that seeks to strengthen children's developmental outcomes for a population of children at risk for academic and social difficulties due to negative consequences of poverty. The conceptualization and empirical examination of children's play within this early intervention programme has focused on the necessary conditions or contexts under which children's successful play experiences with peers emerge, despite threats to development associated with poverty (Fantuzzo et al., 1995). For example, children's interactive peer play is enhanced through attainment of optimal levels of emotion regulation and language during play (Cohen & Mendez, 2009) as well as having an adaptable temperament (Mendez, Fantuzzo, & Cicchetti, 2002). Classroom features, such as teachers who create organized and predictable learning environments, have been associated with more favourable academic outcomes for children who are disengaged from peer play during early childhood (Bulotsky-Shearer, Bell, & Domínguez, 2012). Therefore, play opportunities with adults and children have been conceptualized as occasions for fostering growth and development for children (Jiang & Han, 2015), as well as strategies for ensuring that negative impact of poverty is mitigated by ensuring low-income at-risk children are offered high quality, stimulating play interactions (Bulotsky-Shearer, McWayne, et al., 2016).

However, classroom play opportunities with peers that are available via participation in early care and education (ECE) programmes such as Head Start may be less effective in promoting development if low-income children enter these environments ill-equipped to take advantage of the play. There is a need to gain a better understanding of adults' beliefs about young children's play, how these beliefs may be shaped by culture, and together how these factors may facilitate or perhaps even limit children's play opportunities and subsequent play competence. Thus, the purpose of this study is to better understand what play looks like for low-income children from the view of their parent. To do this, we examine parent beliefs about the importance of play or value of play for children's development and reports of children's actual play experiences, in terms of engaged, interactive peer play, or disruptive or disengaged peer play with others in the home and neighbourhood setting as reported on by parents themselves. By understanding more precisely those types of play experiences children are having outside of their ECE programmes, we can obtain a more complete picture of their development. We focus on low-income families, specifically African-American and Latino parents, to expand the field's cultural lens on how adults contribute children's play skills

Background and conceptual framework

A leading child care expert recently underscored the importance of acknowledging the 'dispositions and communicative skills, practices developed within their [children's] home cultural community, their relationships with caregivers at home' (Howes, 2016, p. 5) which impact children's development and eventually their experiences within early intervention programmes. For low-income, ethnic minority children, such routines and behaviours may be disconnected from those practices that are common within ECE settings, including standards and approaches used by teachers to foster interactive peer play (Fantuzzo, Mendez, & Tighe, 1998). Thus, to better conceptualize the experience of play, we need a wider lens to describe the play experiences of young children in multiple cultural contexts, especially those outside of ECE settings which have been overlooked in contemporary play research. Several scholars have underscored similar concerns for the study of play among children, noting the critical importance of the child's immediate cultural context as establishing parameters for the types of activities and formative influences that will shape their development (Gaskins, 1994; Rogoff, 2003). Therefore, recent conceptualizations of children's play during early childhood explicitly consider the role of the context (e.g. home, community or ECE setting), as well as the adults and peers within these settings, and how the parent's perspective on these interactions and opportunities may facilitate or hinder play (LaForett & Mendez, 2016).

Parents as a cultural influence on children's play experiences

Cultural context influences the types of experiences and opportunities children have for engaging in play, serving to determine the outcomes that members of a culture value and nurture (Fogle & Mendez, 2006; Ogbu, 1999). Therefore, an essential understanding of play and the emergence of quality play experiences for low-income ethnic minority children in particular should consider parents as key influences on children's play. Although relatively understudied in the literature, a small body of work has examined how parental beliefs about play may relate to the degree to which children both experience positive play experiences in the home or community, as well as whether these experiences would facilitate their entry in peer play experiences in an early intervention programme. Parents who were exposed to play themselves as children, or somehow have also acquired favourable views about the value of play in promoting children's development should be more disposed to access and support play experiences, across all cultures. The nature of the play may vary; however, the common element across cultures would be that play somehow is enjoyable and also may facilitate future development (Fogle & Mendez, 2006). Parents who are disconnected from these ideas, or whose ideas about play differ, would have a different influence potentially on children's ability to enjoy, access, and benefit from play with adults and also subsequently with peers.

Bulotsky-Shearer, McWayne, et al. (2016) report on mothers who changed from a view of play as insignificant and wasteful relative to time spent in academic develop to an endorsement of play as meaningful for education and development of their Head Start child. This research showed that parent play beliefs were an important determinant of the types of learning experiences that children access, particularly those involving play with other children. Moreover, immigrant families could bring their existing views about play to an American context of early intervention for low-income children; therefore, the examination of parent beliefs about play and parent reports of children's play behaviour would be essential data for a deeper understanding of the play experiences of all children. In the present study, we are able to draw contrasts between two of the largest groups served by Head Start programmes in the USA – African-American families, and Latino immigrant families (Child Trends, 2014).

Prior study of parent beliefs

Two foundational studies have been conducted on parent play beliefs with parents of low-income children attending Head Start programmes in the USA. First, Fogle and Mendez (2006) developed a measure of parent play beliefs (Parent Play Beliefs Scale; PPBS) and validated two key constructs, Play Support and Academic Focus. This measure asks parents to rate how strongly they agree or disagree with statements about play for their child. The Play Support subscale assesses beliefs of parents that play is enjoyable and meaningful for children to acquire a range of developmental benefits during early childhood. The Academic Focus subscale reflects beliefs that play tends to be irrelevant to children's social and cognitive development, and parents view other academic readiness experiences such as teaching and reading as more critical for supporting child development. This study also showed that Play Support beliefs were positively associated with parent and teacher reports of African-American children, as well as an adaptable child temperament. Recommended future directions were to replicate these findings, and to further explore the contributions of children's skills in contributing to their own play abilities. In a second study involving a different sample of Head Start children, LaForett and Mendez (2016) reported associations between Play Support and responsive parenting, which was defined as high levels of warmth and responsiveness, and low levels of hostility. Additionally, this study found that parents with higher scores for Play Support beliefs had higher parent efficacy and lower levels of depression. Taken together, these results suggest that Play Support beliefs may be related to a positive parenting approach that is more likely to facilitate the development of children's play abilities.

Parental reports of children's play: the Penn Interactive Peer Play Scale

A rating system that captures parent and teacher views of play experiences of Head Start children was developed and validated through a series of empirical studies (see Bulotsky-Shearer, Manz, et al., 2012 for review). First, children's play was observed by research teams, parents, and teachers. Items for the rating scale were derived from play behaviours that differentiate successful play episodes with engagement in play by children from disengaged play. The resulting rating system has a teacher and parent form that asks that the informant provide information about 32 different play behaviours. Three reliable and valid dimensions of children's peer play with others are derived from this instrument. In the present study, we utilize the parent report of three scales. *Play interaction* captures the positive, prosocial behaviours that are evident among children who play well with others. *Play disruption* consists of items regarding aggressive or negative actions that interfere with ongoing play with others. *Play disconnection* captures behaviours such as watching play, hovering, or having trouble entering play with other children that reflect disengagement from the play experience. Prior research using the parent PIPPS has shown this measure is predictive of children's expressive and receptive language abilities over an 8-month period (Mendez & Fogle, 2002). Another study showed that children's play in the home and community context predicted observed emotion regulation in the classroom setting and teacher reported academic motivation and attention skills (McWayne, Fantuzzo, & McDermott, 2004). Therefore, this research shows that capturing parental reports of children's play in the home and community is essential to obtaining a more complete picture of a given child's play repertoire or capacity.

Gaps in the literature on play beliefs and children's play

To date, the study of play beliefs using the PPBS has been primarily limited to low-income children in the USA, with outcomes only examined for African-American child samples (for an exception involving Chinese American children, see Jiang & Han, 2015). Therefore, we need to more closely examine the utility of measures of play beliefs with more ethnically diverse samples of low-income preschool age children. Additionally, we need a deeper understanding of how play beliefs and academic readiness views might predict child play outcomes, particularly as we acknowledge that children's prior experiences with play may engage or serve to disconnect children from play within the ECE settings they attend in the USA. Lastly, as recommended by Howes (2016) and Bulotsky-Shearer, McWayne, et al. (2016), we need a rich understanding of the home and community influences on the child's peer group, and how these contexts are navigated by children and their families upon entry into preschool.

Overview of the study and research questions

This study contributes to this special issue on Reconsidering Play in the Early Years by focusing a cultural lens on the parent perspective of play. We seek to accomplish this goal by examining the relation between parent beliefs about play and parental reports of children's peer play within their homes and neighbourhood for using a diverse sample of low-income children, both African American, U.S. born children and Latino, U.S. born children living within recently arriving immigrant families. Specifically, we examined differences in play beliefs according to the cultural background of the parents. Next, we report on the relations between beliefs and play skills of the children in terms of engaged, interactive peer play or less adaptive peer play that is disruptive or disconnected. Our research questions add to the literature on parental beliefs and views of children's play to inform a more complete picture of the development of low income, at-risk children. Our research questions were:

1. Are there group differences in beliefs about the value of young children's play and perceptions of children's play for African-American and Latino parents of pre-schoolers participating in Head Start in the USA?
2. What are the associations among play beliefs, children's play skills, and key child characteristics (i.e. child age and gender)? Are these associations different between cultural groups?
3. Do parent play beliefs predict children's play skills, after accounting for child age and gender? Are there different patterns of prediction for African-American and Latino families?

Methods

Participants

The data for this exploratory study were drawn from two larger studies examining parent involvement and children's school readiness among young children participating in Head Start programmes in the USA. Children who were identified as either African American or Latino, and whose parents had completed ratings of parent beliefs, were selected for the present analyses ($n = 109$). Demographic information was obtained via phone interviews with the child's parent, 91% of which were with the child's biological mother, stepmother, foster mother, or the female partner of the child's father. The sample was relatively equally split between African-American (46%) and Latino (54%) children, with the African-American sample drawn from the Southeastern USA and the Latino sample obtained in the Northeastern USA. On average, children were just under 4.5 years of age ($M_{age} = 53.1$ months; SD = 7.2), and half of the children were boys (50%). Over two-thirds of parents were employed (36% full-time and 31% part-time), and 41% of parents were married. Just over half of parents reported that they were educated in the USA (51%); most parents of Latino children were not educated in the USA (85%), though the majority of the children were born in the USA. When education was reported, the most commonly reported educational attainment was some college (18% across the full sample).

Measures

Parent play beliefs

The PPBS (Fogle & Mendez, 2006) was used to assess parents' views about the function of play in their child's development. Developed with a sample of African-American children in Head Start, the PPBS contains thirty 5-point Likert-type items (1 = disagree, 5 = very much agree) that yield two subscales: Play Support and Academic Focus. The Play Support subscale reflects beliefs that play is an enjoyable activity with the potential to offer a range of developmental benefits to children. A representative item from the Play Support subscale is: 'Play can help my child develop better thinking abilities.' The Academic Focus subscale reflects beliefs that play tends to be irrelevant to children's social and cognitive development, thereby suggesting parents may implicitly value more academically oriented activities. A representative Academic Focus item is: 'I do not think my child learns important skills by playing.' The range of scores of the Play Support subscale is 16–80, whereas the range is 8–40 for the Academic Focus subscale. Internal consistency for both subscales ranges from high to moderate (validation study with African-American children: $\alpha = .90$ and .73, original study of culturally diverse immigrant families [$n = 70$] from which the Latino sample was drawn: $\alpha = .88$ and .68, respectively).

Peer play

The Penn Interactive Peer Play Scale – Parent Version (PIPPS; Fantuzzo, Mendez, et al., 1998) was used to capture parent ratings of children's engagement and disengagement in play at home or in the neighbourhood. This parent measure uses 32 items to capture children's play behaviours that facilitate and promote positive play experiences, or serve to hinder or interfere with play with other children. Multiple factor analytic studies of both the parent and teacher version of the PIPPS (Coolahan, Fantuzzo, Mendez, & McDermott, 2000; Fantuzzo, Coolahan, et al., 1998) have shown support for three underlying dimensions of peer play, Play Interaction, Play Disruption, and Play Disconnection. In the present study, we use Play Interaction, a subscale that contains items measuring children's creative, cooperative, and adaptive behaviours that facilitate play. We also use Play Disruption, a subscale that consists of negative and aggressive behaviours children display during play, and Play Disconnection, a subscale that contains items measuring children's avoidance behaviours that impede play, including hovering near play, watching or having trouble engaging in play. Psychometric properties of the PIPPS show Cronbach's alpha with acceptable internal consistency and this measure was predictive of children's school readiness over an 8-month period of time (Mendez & Fogle, 2002). The PIPPS has been used to study Spanish and English speaking Latino children enrolled in Head Start (Bulotsky-Shearer, López, & Mendez, 2016), and the parent and teacher PIPPS have been validated and are comparable measures (Coolahan et al., 2000). Scores are calculated on a t distribution with a range spanning two standard deviations from the mean (mean = 50, SD = 10). For this sample, there were 24 children whose scores did not reach a high enough threshold to generate a t-score for the Play Disconnection variable, and therefore those cases were not included in analyses examining this variable.

Procedures

The original studies from which the data were drawn were conducted in accordance with university IRB approvals. Procedures included the following: permissions from Head Start programme administrators; approvals from the Head Start programme parent policy council; and review of measures by the parent leadership of the programme. Data from parents including family demographic information, parents' play beliefs, and parents' ratings of their child's play were collected via phone interviews conducted with parents by trained data collectors. Latino parents were given the option of having the interview conducted in Spanish by a bilingual interviewer, with the majority of Latino parents completing the interview in Spanish. The data for the present study were collected during the second half of the school year.

Analytic approach

Our primary research question was to better understand the influence of parents' play beliefs on their perceptions of their child's play skills. Descriptive statistics (i.e. means and standard deviations for continuous variables; frequency counts for categorical variables) were conducted for the full sample and for the African-American and Latino samples separately. For continuous variables, group differences were tested for significance using a series of one-way Analysis of Variance (ANOVA), where African Americans were the reference group. Chi-square tests were used to examine differences between categorical variables. Pearson product–moment correlations were calculated separately for each group. When significant correlations emerged for either group, this was followed by Fisher's z-test to examine whether the correlation for the African-American sample was statistically significant from the correlation for the Latino sample following procedures outlined by Knight and Hill (1998). Finally, separate hierarchical regression models for each group were used to examine whether parents' play beliefs (i.e. Play Support factor, Academic Focus factor) predicted children's play (i.e. Play Interaction, Play Disruption, Play Disconnection). Predictor variables were entered in the following steps: (1) child covariates (i.e. age in months, gender) and (2) play belief indicator (i.e. Play Support, Academic Focus). Due to the large proportion of parents who had not completed their education in the USA, parent education was not included as a covariate in the regression analyses.

Results

Descriptive statistics and group differences

Table 1 presents descriptive statistics for the variables used in the analyses. Children in the African-American sample were approximately 5 months older than children in the Latino sample, which was a significant difference as tested with ANOVA, $F(1, 106) = 13.51$, $p < .001$, $d = 0.71$. There were about 8% more boys in the Latino sample relative to the African-American sample; however, a Chi-square test did not reveal a significant difference. For the play beliefs variables, overall parents endorsed higher

Table 1. Descriptive statistics and group comparisons for regression variables.

					African American ($n = 50$)			Latino ($n = 59$)			Full ($n = 109$)		
Variable	Source	Scale mean	Min	Max	Mean/freq.	SD	Range	Mean/freq.	SD	Range	Mean/Freq.	SD	Range
Child age (months)***	Parent	–	36	71	55.72	7.04	42–65	50.88	6.64	38–63	53.12	7.21	38–65
Child gender (% male)	Parent	–	–	–	46%	–	–	54%	–	–	50%	–	–
PPBS academic Focus***	Parent	24.0	8	40	14.18	5.04	8–33	23.32	5.46	13–34	19.13	6.96	8–34
PPBS Play Support*	Parent	48.0	16	80	67.68	6.76	52–80	71.39	8.05	40–80	69.69	7.68	40–80
PIPPS-P Play Interaction	Parent	50.0	30	70	48.80	10.89	23–72	47.22	12.05	10–70	47.95	11.51	10–72
PIPPS-P Play Disruption	Parent	50.0	30	70	48.51	10.57	27–66	47.31	7.85	29–64	47.84	9.11	27–66
PIPPS-P Play Disconnection[a]	Parent	50.0	30	70	47.15	9.16	37–63	46.10	8.17	33–61	46.51	3.53	33–63

PIPPS-P, Penn Peer Interactive Peer Play Scale – Parent; PPBS, Parent Play Belief Scale.
*$p < .05$; **$p < .01$; ***$p < .001$.
[a]$n = 84$, due to cases with scores too low to generate a t-score.

levels of Play Support and lower levels of Academic Focus relative to the scale means. Compared with African-American parents, Latino parents reported higher endorsement of beliefs indicating that play is important for children's learning (Play Support), as well as greater endorsement that play is less valuable for children's learning (Academic Focus), $F(1, 107) = 6.65$, $p = .011$, $d = 0.50$ and $F(1, 107) = 81.32$, $p < .001$, $d = 1.77$, respectively. For the child peer play skills outcome variables (i.e. Play Interaction, Play Disruption, Play Disconnection), on average parents reported their children to be within one standard deviation of the scale mean. There were no ethnic group differences on the peer play skills variables.

Associations among variables and group equivalence

Table 2 reports Pearson correlations among the study variables. The top of the diagonal displays correlations for the Latino sample, whereas the bottom of the diagonal shows correlations for the African-American sample. For both African-American and Latino parents, beliefs that play is not important for children's development (Academic Focus) were positively related to child age. However, these correlations were not significantly different from one another, suggesting that this association is not stronger for a particular group ($z = 0.13$, $p = .896$). In addition, Play Support beliefs were positively associated with child gender in Latino families, where increased endorsement of these beliefs was stronger for parents when the child was female versus male. This correlation, although also negative but not significant for African-American families, was not significantly different between the two groups ($z = 0.88$, $p = .379$).

For associations between parents' play beliefs and children's play skills, endorsement of Academic Focus beliefs was associated with lower ratings of children's play interaction skills, whereas Play Support beliefs were associated with higher ratings of children's play interaction skills. These associations only emerged for the African-American sample, and were not significantly different from the associations for the Latino sample ($z = -1.21$, $p = .226$ and $z = 1.17$, $p = .246$, respectively).

Finally, there were significant correlations between some of the indicators of child play skills for each cultural group. There was a negative association between interactive and disruptive play for African-American families, which was not observed for Latino families. These correlations were significantly different between the two groups, $z = -2.44$, $p = .015$. In addition, for Latino families, disruptive play behaviours were positively correlated with disconnected play behaviours; a positive correlation for African-American families was also observed but was not significant. Still, the correlations between the two groups were significant ($z = -2.47$, $p = .014$).

Hierarchical regression analyses: play beliefs predict peer play interaction

A series of hierarchical regression analyses was conducted to examine whether parents' play beliefs predicted parents' perceptions of their child's play skills. For each separate regression model, one of

Table 2. Correlations among regression variables for African-American and Latino samples.

1	2	3	4	5	6	7	_
1. Child age	–	−0.05	0.27*	−0.04	−0.07	0.17	0.23
2. Child gender	0.09	–	0.05	−0.34**	−0.02	−0.14	−0.19
3. Academic Focus	0.30*	−0.03	–	−0.10	−0.07	0.13	0.22
4. Play Support	−0.09	−0.17	0.06	–	0.09	0.08	−0.21
5. Play Interaction	0.11	−0.04	−0.30*	0.31*	–	0.06	−0.09
6. Play Disruption	−0.13	0.01	−0.18	−0.18	−0.40**	–	−0.57**
7. Play Disconnection[a]	0.01	−0.03	0.20	0.13	−0.30	0.16	–

Note: Correlations for the African-American sample in the bottom diagonal ($n = 50$); correlations for the Latino sample in the top diagonal ($n = 59$). *$p < .05$; **$p < .01$

[a]$n = 84$, due to cases with scores too low to generate a t-score

the subscales from the Parent PIPPS was the designated outcome. No regressions involving Latino parents were significant, and are not presented further.

Overall, parent play beliefs were a significant predictor for models using Play Interaction as the dependent variable. Play Disruption and Disconnection are not discussed further, as these models were not significant. African-American parents who endorsed play as important for their children's learning (Play Support) rated their child as having stronger play interaction skills after accounting for child age and gender. Table 3 displays the unstandardized predictor beta weights, parameter estimates, standard errors, and ΔR^2 for the individual predictor variables at each step of the equation. Together, this constellation of variables did not significantly account for the variance in Play Interaction $F(3, 46) = 1.96$, $p = .134$, adj. $R^2 = 0.06$. Further, African-American parents who did not think that play was important for children's learning (Academic Focus) tended to rate their children as less skilled in engaging in interactive play with peers. Similar to the Play Support model, the constellation of variables that included Academic Focus did not significantly account for the variance in Play Interaction $F(3, 46) = 2.38$, $p = .082$, adj. $R^2 = 0.08$.

Discussion

Young children's play is shaped by the experiences they live, which includes the influence of cultural context. This exploratory secondary data analysis sought to further our understanding of how parents' beliefs about young children's play relate to parents' perceptions of their child's play skills. By studying this issue in African-American and immigrant Latino low-income families, these findings suggest that there may be variability in how parents from different cultural backgrounds conceptualize play as a learning context for young children and how they judge their child's play competence.

Adding to the small body of literature on parents' play beliefs, among African-American parents, greater endorsement of academic readiness beliefs were related to lower ratings of their child's play skills. Conversely, parents who rated their child as showing high levels of interactive peer play also saw play as important for children's learning. These findings replicate the pattern found in Fogle and Mendez's (2006) original study of the PPBS conducted with another low-income sample of African-American families participating in Head Start in the same region of the USA as those African-American families in the present analyses. Moreover, hierarchical regression analyses showed that the correlations between the two play beliefs with interactive play remained significant after accounting for child age and gender. Although not significant, negative associations between Play Support and disruptive play and positive associations between Academic Focus and disconnected play mirrored those found in Fogle and Mendez (2006).

Table 3. Hierarchical regression of parent beliefs about play predicting African-American children's play interaction skills.

	Play beliefs indicator					
	Play Support[a]			Academic Focus[b]		
Predictor	*B*	SE *B*	*β*	*B*	SE *B*	*β*
Step 1						
Constant	39.80	12.60		39.80	12.60	
Child age	0.17	0.23	0.11	0.17	0.23	0.11
Child gender	−0.97	3.15	−0.05	−0.97	3.15	−0.05
Step 2						
Constant	2.22	20.44		41.74	11.96	
Child age	0.20	0.22	0.13	0.34	0.22	0.22
Child gender	0.19	3.06	0.01	−1.44	2.99	−0.07
Play beliefs indicator	0.52	0.23	0.32*	−0.79	0.31	−0.37*

*$p < .05$.
[a]$R^2 = 0.01$ for Step 1; $\Delta R^2 = 0.10$* for Step 2.
[b]$R^2 = 0.01$ for Step 1; $\Delta R^2 = 0.12$* for Step 2.

Associations between parents' play beliefs and children's play skills were not replicated for the Latino families in our sample. There were cultural differences between the two groups on the different play beliefs variables and on some of the play skills variables. Specifically, Latino parents in our study were more likely than African-American parents to endorse play as important for children's learning (Play Support factor). Yet at the same time, Latino parents also more often endorsed beliefs suggesting that play is irrelevant to young children's learning and that they are better served by more formalized and structured activities that promote learning (Academic Focus factor). That Latino parents seem to be endorsing both types of play beliefs may be a departure from and also a confirmation of Farver and Howes's (1993) study comparing Mexican and U.S. born mothers on their values regarding adult-directed play; in that study, the majority of Mexican parents viewed play as primarily an amusement activity for children whereas White, American mothers reported that play was important for providing educational benefits to their children. Further, African-American parents' endorsements of Play Support and Academic Focus were significantly positively and negatively related to ratings of Play Interaction, respectively, and no such significant associations were observed for Latino parents. However, the magnitude of these differences between the two groups was stronger for the association between Academic Focus and Play Interaction than that between Play Support and Play Interaction. That is, there seems to be more discrepant views on Academic Focus between the two cultural groups than for Play Support as it related to children's play skills.

Despite our emergent evidence of cultural differences on the parent play beliefs factors, lack of associations between beliefs and parents' perceptions of their child's play skills for Latino families may tap into cultural differences in how parents view their child's play. Although there were no significant group differences between African-American and Latino parents on the three play skills outcomes, there were differences between the groups in how they saw the play skills as related to one another. Examining the inter-factor correlations suggests that African-American parents make clear distinctions between interactive and disruptive play, and that a child showing interactive play looks very different from a child that is displaying disruptive play behaviours. This distinction was not made among the Latino families, who instead saw strong similarities in disruptive and disconnected play behaviours. Nonetheless, for both groups of parents, academic readiness beliefs were positively related to child age, indicating that the older the child was the more likely the parent was to endorse readiness beliefs. This finding makes sense developmentally, and may reflect parents' awareness that pending entry into kindergarten might signal a switch in parental expectations for children's learning. Latino parents also endorsed more Play Support beliefs when their children were girls, whereas no relation with gender was found for African-American families.

Findings from this underpowered, exploratory secondary data analysis must be interpreted with caution. We acknowledge that the size of our African-American and Latino groups makes these findings susceptible to the challenges associated with small sample studies, such as having enough power to detect statistically meaningful effects and vulnerability to outliers. Further, the generalizability of the findings is limited to mothers, who were the primary participants in the study. This area of inquiry can be enhanced by additional study of these and other cultural groups using larger samples. In addition, our study was not able to model the effects of parents' education, given the large number of parents who were not educated within the USA. Measuring family-level covariates, such as parents' own educational experiences, in a way that is meaningful across cultural groups would be beneficial for better understanding influences on family processes. Nonetheless, we believe that this study sheds light on the need for understanding play itself, play opportunities, and adults as facilitators of play experiences within a cultural context.

Conclusions

This study advances our understanding about parent play beliefs by raising important questions about how different cultural groups think about children's play – both in terms of its importance and in their perceptions of their own child's play behaviours. This exploration can help us broaden our understanding of how children's play opportunities and skills may be situated within culturally constrained parental influences. Such information is needed to maximize parents' own contributions, as well as those by family engagement initiatives and ECE settings, in efforts to use play strategies to promote children's growth and development. Strengths of this study include targeting low-income parents from two cultural groups with the goal of uncovering heterogeneity in parents' play beliefs. This is important for three reasons: (1) low-income families are often portrayed from a deficit perspective suggesting less parent engagement in their children's education; (2) low-income families are at heterogeneous group, with much of this heterogeneity stemming from cultural factors including country of origin, ethnicity, and languages spoken; and (3) ECE programmes targeting low-income children, such as Head Start in the USA, serve a broad range of culturally diverse children and families. Other strengths were using empirically derived tools, the PIPPS – Parent Version (Fantuzzo, Mendez, et al., 1998) and the PPBS (Fogle & Mendez, 2006) that were developed with samples of low-income African-American families participating in Head Start; thus, we are at the beginning stages of understanding how these constructs are best measured with culturally diverse families.

Further, this study contributes to needed research illustrating normative development and family life among low-income families who are from diverse cultural groups, especially African-American and immigrant Latino families. As we begin to understand how parents develop beliefs about play and how they view their own child's play skills, it is important to consider how culture play may a role in shaping parents' perspectives on a range of play-related topics including how they feel about early childhood care and education settings valuing play-based learning. This intersection between culturally influenced perspectives on play has important implications for understanding the degree of continuity between children's experiences and home and at school. Among the theories used to describe racial and ethnic gaps in achievement among older children, the cultural capital mismatch theory (e.g. Swidler, 1986) may be relevant for considering issues of continuity of experiences with respect to play. Children who have fewer opportunities to engage in play before entering ECE settings may have less experience to draw from as they learn to negotiate interactions with peers during play (e.g. sharing, taking turns, considering peers' preferences) and how to meet classroom expectations for play in school-based settings (e.g. degree of rough-and-tumble play, voice volume, cleaning up and caring for play items). As suggested by Barbarin, Downer, Odom, and Head (2010), the experience of discontinuities between home and school is likely to begin when children enter early childhood settings, which may have implications for children's trajectories as they advance to the early elementary grades.

Further, some parents themselves may experience a 'mismatch' between their own expectations for what strategies are most effective for promoting their child's learning and development, and the strategies being used in ECE settings that employ play-based learning approaches. Parents who do not endorse play as a learning vehicle for young children may be concerned about how ECE settings are preparing their child to be successful upon transitioning to more 'formal' educational experiences with higher expectations for academic competence as children get older. In addition, parents who may see school readiness as important, but within the domain of educators and not parents, may be less likely to conceptualize play as a learning context for children and one in which adults can play an important role. In LaForett and Mendez's (2016) sample of African-American parents, those who endorsed play as developmentally important (Play Support) also felt more efficacious in contributing to their child's education; the reverse pattern was found when parents endorsed academic readiness beliefs (Academic Focus). Other research has previously documented that parents who feel efficacious in their ability to contribute to their child's education reported engaging in more learning activities with their child at home (Downer & Mendez, 2005; Waanders, Mendez, & Downer, 2007).

To the extent that parents' beliefs and other perspectives about play are influenced by culture, this has bearing for how parents receive and ultimately respond to parent-focused efforts that incorporate parents' use of play-based interactions with their child. Indeed, low-income families are often the target of large-scale early intervention and school readiness programmes, such as Head Start and some state-level pre-kindergarten programmes, as well as family engagement initiatives (e.g. Head Start Parent, Family, and Community Engagement Framework; Administration for Children and Families, 2011) or other family-focused interventions (Nurse Family Partnership; Olds, Kitzman, Cole, & Robinson, 1997; Parents as Teachers; see Castro, Mendez, Garcia, & Westerberg, 2012) that may or may not be linked to families' participation in ECE programmes. Indeed, parents' use of play-based learning approaches with their child is a key component of parent engagement activities, particularly for preschool-aged children, according to the National Center for Children in Poverty (Smith, Robbins, Stagman, & Mahur, 2013). In summary, ECE programmes, family engagement initiatives, and family-focused interventions would benefit from considering how parents' cultural experiences may shape their perspectives on play. Efforts to intentionally explore how to explicitly honour and incorporate parents' beliefs and cultural values in the development and delivery of such programmes may prove useful for developing strategies on how to talk about play in early childhood with culturally diverse parents of young children.

Disclosure statement

No potential conflict of interest was reported by the authors.

Funding

This work was supported in part by grants 90YF0069 and 90YF0069/01 awarded to the second author by the U.S. Department of Health and Human Services. Portions of this work were completed at the University of South Carolina, Columbia, SC, USA and Temple University, Philadelphia, PA, USA.

References

Administration on Children and Families. (2011). *The head start parent, family, and community engagement framework. Promoting family engagement and school readiness, from prenatal to age 8*. Retrieved from http://eclkc.ohs.acf.hhs.gov/hslc/standards/im/2011/pfce-framework.pdf.

Barbarin, O. A., Downer, J., Odom, E., & Head, D. (2010). Home–school differences in beliefs, support, and control during public pre-kindergarten and their link to children's kindergarten readiness. *Early Childhood Research Quarterly*, *25*(3), 358–372. doi:10.1016/j.ecresq.2010.02.003

Bulotsky-Shearer, R. J., Bell, E. R., & Domínguez, X. (2012). Latent profiles of problem behavior within learning, peer, and teacher contexts: Identifying subgroups of children at academic risk across the preschool year. *Journal of School Psychology*, *50*(6), 775–798. doi:10.1016/j.jsp.2012.08.001

Bulotsky-Shearer, R. J., López, L. M., & Mendez, J. L. (2016). The validity of interactive peer play competencies for Latino preschool children from low-income households. *Early Childhood Research Quarterly*, *34*, 78–91. doi:10.1016/j.ecresq.2015.09.002

Bulotsky-Shearer, R. J., Manz, P. H., Mendez, J. L., McWayne, C. M., Sekino, Y., & Fantuzzo, J. W. (2012). Peer play interactions and readiness to learn: A protective influence for African American preschool children from low-income households. *Child Development Perspectives, 6*(3), 225–231. doi:10.1111/j.1750-8606.2011.00221.x

Bulotsky-Shearer, R. J., McWayne, C. M., Mendez, J. L., & Manz, P. H. (2016). Preschool peer play interactions – a developmental context for learning for ALL children: Rethinking issues of equity and opportunity. In K. Sanders & A. Wishard Guerra (Eds.), *The culture of child care: Attachment, peers, and quality in diverse communities* (pp. 179–202). New York, NY: Oxford University Press.

Castro, D., Mendez, J. L., Garcia, S., & Westerberg, D. (2012). Family literacy programs for Latino families in the United States. In B. Wasik (Ed.), *Handbook on Family Literacy* (pp. 270–288, 2nd ed.). New York, NY: Routledge.

Child Trends Databank. (2014). *Head Start*. Retrieved from: http://www.childtrends.org/?indicators=head-start/

Cohen, J. S., & Mendez, J. L. (2009). Emotion regulation, language ability, and the stability of preschool children's peer play behavior. *Early Education and Development, 20*(6), 1016–1037. doi:10.1080/10409280903430745

Coolahan, K., Fantuzzo, J., Mendez, J., & McDermott, P. (2000). Preschool peer interactions and readiness to learn: Relationships between classroom peer play and learning behaviors and conduct. *Journal of Educational Psychology, 92*, 458–465. doi:10.1037/0022-0663.92.3.458

Downer, J. T., & Mendez, J. L. (2005). African American father involvement and preschool children's school readiness. *Early Education and Development, 16*(3), 317–340. doi:10.1207/s15566935eed1603_2

Eggum-Wilkens, N. D., Fabes, R. A., Castle, S., Zhang, L., Hanish, L. D., & Martin, C. L. (2014). Playing with others: Head Start children's peer play and relations with kindergarten school competence. *Early Childhood Research Quarterly, 29*, 345–356. http://dx.doi.org/10.1016/j.ecresq.2014.04.008

Fantuzzo, J., Coolahan, K., Mendez, J., McDermott, P., & Sutton-Smith, B. (1998). Contextually-relevant validation of peer play constructs with African American Head Start children: Penn Interactive Peer Play Scale. *Early Childhood Research Quarterly, 13*, 411–431. doi:10.1016/S0885-2006(99)80048-9

Fantuzzo, J., Mendez, J., & Tighe, E. (1998). Parental assessment of peer play: Development and validation of the parent version of the Penn Interactive Peer Play Scale. *Early Childhood Research Quarterly, 13*, 659–676. doi:10.1016/S0885-2006(99)80066-0

Fantuzzo, J. W., Sutton-Smith, B., Coolahan, K. C., Manz, P., Canning, S., & Debnam, D. (1995). Assessment of preschool play interaction behaviors in young low-income children: Penn interactive peer play scale. *Early Childhood Research Quarterly, 10*, 105–120. doi:10.1016/0885-2006(95)90028-4

Farver, J. M., & Howes, C. (1993). Cultural differences in American and Mexican mother–child pretend play. *Merrill-Palmer Quarterly, 39*, 344–358.

Fisher, E. P. (1992). The impact of play on development: A meta-analysis. *Play & Culture, 5*(2), 159–181.

Fogle, L. M., & Mendez, J. L. (2006). Assessing the play beliefs of African American mothers with preschool children. *Early Childhood Research Quarterly, 21*, 507–518. doi:10.1016/j.ecresq.2006.08.002

Gaskins, S. (1994). Integrating interpretive and quantitative methods in socialization research. *Merrill-Palmer Quarterly, 40*, 313–333.

Howes, C. (2016). Children and child care: A theory of relationships within cultural communities. In K. Sanders & A. Wishard Guerra (Eds.), *The culture of child care: Attachment, peers, and quality in diverse communities* (pp. 3–24). New York, NY: Oxford University Press.

Jiang, S., & Han, M. (2015). Parental beliefs on children's play: Comparison among mainland Chinese, Chinese immigrants in the USA, and European Americans. *Early Child Development and Care*, 1–12. doi:10.1080/03004430.2015.1030633

Knight, G. P., & Hill, N. E. (1998). Measurement equivalence in research involving minority adolescents. In V. C. McLoyd & L. Steinberg (Eds.), *Studying minority adolescents: Conceptual, methodological, and theoretical issues* (pp. 183–210). Mahwah, NJ: Lawrence Erlbaum.

LaForett, D. R., & Mendez, J. L. (2016). Play beliefs and responsive parenting among low-income mothers of preschoolers in the United States. *Early Child Development and Care*, 1–13. doi:10.1080/03004430.2016.1169180

McWayne, C. M., Fantuzzo, J. W., & McDermott, P. A. (2004). Preschool competency in context: An investigation of the unique contribution of child competencies to early academic success. *Developmental Psychology, 40*, 633–645. doi:10.1037/0012-1649.40.4.633

Mendez, J., & Fogle, L. (2002). Parental reports of children's social behavior: Relations among peer play, language competence, and problem behavior. *Journal of Psychoeducational Assessment, 20*, 370–385. doi:10.1177/073428290202000405

Mendez, J. L., Fantuzzo, J., & Cicchetti, D. (2002). Profiles in social competence among low-income African American preschool children. *Child Development, 73*, 1085–1100.

Mendez, J. L., McDermott, P. A., & Fantuzzo, J. (2002). Identifying and promoting social competence with African American preschool children: Developmental and contextual considerations. *Psychology in the Schools, 39*, 111–123. doi:10.1002/pits.10039

Ogbu, J. U. (1999). Cultural context of children's development. In H. E. Fitzgerald, B. M. Lester, & B. Zuckerman (Eds.), *Children of color: Research, health, and policy issues* (pp. 73–92). New York, NY: Garland.

Olds, D., Kitzman, H., Cole, R., & Robinson, J. (1997). Theoretical foundations of a program of home visitation for pregnant women and parents of young children. *Journal of Community Psychology, 25*(1), 9–25. doi:10.1002/(SICI)1520-6629

Pelligrini, A. (1992). Ethological studies of the categorization of children's social behavior in preschool: A review. *Early Education and Development, 3,* 284–297. doi:10.1207/s15566935eed0304_2

Rogoff, B. (2003). *The cultural nature of human development.* New York, NY: Oxford University Press.

Smith, S., Robbins, T., Stagman, S., & Mahur, D. (2013). *Parent engagement from preschool through grade 3: A guide for policymakers.* Report. New York, NY: National Center for Children in Poverty.

Swidler, A. (1986). Culture in action: Symbols and strategies. *American Sociological Review, 51*(2), 273–286.

Waanders, C., Mendez, J. L., & Downer, J. T. (2007). Parent characteristics, economic stress and neighborhood context as predictors of parent involvement in preschool children's education. *Journal of School Psychology, 45*(6), 619–636.

Parents' perceptions of play: a comparative study of spousal perspectives

Barbara G. Warash, Amy E. Root and Meghan Devito Doris

ABSTRACT
Play is essential for growth and learning during early childhood. However, the current focus on academics in preschool education has resulted in less emphasis placed on play as a learning tool. In the current study, parents' value of play was investigated. Parent gender, child gender, and child age were examined as potential influences on parents' value of play. Participants included 38 mothers and 38 fathers of preschool-aged children. Parents completed surveys about the value of play (play support) and the value of academic activities (academic focus). Results indicated that mothers rated play support higher than fathers. In addition, child age was negatively associated with parents' ratings of play support, and the relation between child age and academic focus differed by child gender. The findings suggest that parents in this study perceive play as valuable, but these perceptions change as children approach formal schooling.

Play is a fundamental component of learning and development among young children (Fisher, Hirsh-Pasek, Golinkoff, & Gryfe, 2008; Fisher, Hirsh-Pasek, Golinkoff, Singer, & Berk, 2011; Hanline, Milton, & Phelps, 2010; NAEYC, 2009; Van Hoorn, Nourot, Scales, & Alward, 2011). Froebel (1887), the founder of kindergarten, provided one of the first definitions of play stating that, 'Play is the highest expression of human development in childhood for it alone is the free expression of what is in a child's soul' (Froebel, 1887 as quoted by Sluss, 2005, p. 7). This definition is consistent with a constructivist point of view: that development during childhood is facilitated through the exploration of the social and physical environment that occurs when children play (Van Hoorn et al., 2011). Numerous theorists have stated the significance of play in child development. For instance, Piaget (1962) argued that play helps children to move beyond egocentrism through interaction with peers, and that pretense play helps children to understand others' perspectives. This allows children to incorporate new information about the world around them (i.e. learn about their environment). In addition, Vygotsky (1967) asserted that pretend play was a primary avenue for child development, including the development of children's language, cognitive, and social skills. He believed that development occurs when children engage in play (i.e. play is a critical mechanism for learning), especially play with others.

School readiness is not solely based on academics; rather, it is a compilation of children's physical, social–emotional, language, and cognitive development (The NAEYC, 2009; National Education Goal Panels, 1997). The National Association for the Education of Young Children (NAEYC) has advocated the need for teachers to engage young children in developmentally appropriate activities (NAEYC, 2009). There is a 'play-learning' conceptualisation in which 'play, in its many forms, represents a natural, age-appropriate method for children to explore and learn about themselves and the world around them' (Fisher et al., 2008, p. 306). Thus, play is a vehicle for learning and growth in multiple areas early childhood development.

Given that play provides children with opportunities to explore and interact with the world around them, it is not surprising that playtime during early childhood is linked with later school success (e.g. E. Bodrova (personal communication, October 3, 2012); Fisher et al., 2011; Hanline et al., 2010). In a review of the literature examining the impact of pretend play on children's development, Lillard et al. (2013) concluded that causal links are possible between pretend play and the development of skills related to academic readiness, including emotion regulation, linguistic skills, and reasoning. But, they did not conclude that causal links for other school-readiness skills, including the development of problem-solving and executive function; they suggested that the associations between pretend play and these may be indirect. However, the authors argued that this does not mean that early childhood educators should abandon or decrease play-based learning. Indeed, they stated that child-centred classrooms are optimal learning environments for young children as they provide opportunities for '... free choice, interesting hands-on activities of which the child is intrinsically motivated, and peer interactions' (Lillard et al., 2013, p. 26).

Regardless of the evidence of the importance of play, play has been overshadowed in schools. There is an increased emphasis placed on academic readiness during early childhood (Christakis, 2016; Hirsh-Pasek, Golinkoff, Berk, & Singer, 2009; Miller & Almon, 2009a, 2009b; Nicolopoulou, 2010; Stipek, 2006). Early learning standards for preschoolers have been established in most states despite evidence linking teacher-centred approaches (i.e. not play-based) to decreased academic motivation in the early childhood years (Stipek, Feiler, Daniels, & Milburn, 1995). As a result, experts in early childhood education are concerned that this may translate into young children spending more time in structured activities and less time engaged in developmentally appropriate activities, such as play (Katz, 2015). Unfortunately, there is evidence indicating that this may be the case (Carlsson-Paige, Almon, & McLaughlin, 2015; Miller & Almon, 2009a, 2009b).

Moreover, growing misconceptions that the early onset of basic reading skills is an indicator of school success have drastically altered children's play (Miller & Almon, 2009a, 2009b). Several studies have shown that play in school and home environments has transformed from being child-initiated, unstructured play to structured, educationally based activities (Fisher et al., 2008; Sluss, 2005). Moreover, one study indicated that kindergarten-aged children in New York and Los Angeles spend more time on reading and mathematics instruction than in choice play in the classroom (Miller & Almon, 2009b). These changes have been made despite the experts urging for more playtime in early childhood classrooms, including preschool and kindergarten (Carlsson-Paige et al., 2015; Katz, 2015).

Despite these warnings, play opportunities for young children are increasingly sacrificed due to the push for academic excellence in the school settings. Rather than providing optimal learning experiences through play, young children are expected to learn through methods of memorisation to meet academic standards (Miller & Almon, 2009b). These techniques are contrary to research indicating that play fosters learning in early childhood, including the development of language skills, social skills, self-regulation, and higher level thinking (Becker, McClelland, Loprinzi, & Trost, 2014; Fisher et al., 2011; Hanline et al., 2010). There is some evidence suggesting that parents view academics as more beneficial to school readiness than play. For instance, Haight, Parke, and Black (1997) reported that middle-class parents rated reading as making a more significant contribution to children's development compared to pretend play and rough-and-tumble play. Shine and Acosta (2000) reported complementary findings. Specifically, in an observational study of middle-class parents and children, they found that parents spent more time teaching than playing with children at museum exhibits, even though these exhibits encouraged pretend play. More recently, Belfield and Garcia (2014) conducted a study of parents' opinions about school readiness from 1993 to 2007. They reported that parents' expectations for the types of skills their child should have by kindergarten increased significantly from 1993 to 2007 (Belfield & Garcia, 2014).

Moreover, there is likely variability in how parents view play; and parents may differ in their perspectives about the value of play, as well as the types of play that promote academic readiness. Gonzalez-Mena (2008) explains:

> One adult may see play as an opportunity for individual involvement with the physical environment, as in self-motivated, solitary play. Another adult my regard play as an opportunity for learning to get along with others. If solitary play is valued, interruptions by others will be discouraged ... If play is regarded primarily as socialization, the adult will encourage children to interact. (p. 104)

Thus, parents may vary in what they view as what constitutes meaningful play; and this may differ between parents within the same family. In research comparing mothers' and fathers' perceptions of the value of play, Warash, Pelliccioni, and Yoon (2000) compared middle-class parents' views about developmentally appropriate practices during the preschool years. Parents, who were predominantly Caucasian, reported that mothers support formal teaching methods for their children, whereas fathers value more developmentally appropriate approaches to learning. They hypothesised that this finding was due to the fact that the mothers in this setting were the primary parent picking their children up from school, and were more likely to see their children, as well as other children, engaged in activities. This may have triggered a sense of competition where mothers were motivated to push their children to achieve academically. However, in another study, Gleason (2005) reported that middle-class Caucasian mothers perceived their child's pretend play more favourable than fathers. The differing value placed on play was thought to be that fathers view play as fun, whereas mothers focus on the educational benefits of their preschoolers' pretend play. Thus, it seems that mothers and fathers may differ in their perceptions of play; however, the literature is mixed about the quality of these differences.

Differences in mothers' and fathers' perceptions of play is not surprising given the extensive literature indicating that mothers and fathers prefer and engage in different types of play with their children. Middle-class, Caucasian fathers report preferring to engage in rough-and-tumble play over pretend play and book reading, while mothers report prefer pretend play and book reading over rough-and-tumble play (Haight et al., 1997; Power & Parke, 1986). Similarly, Aesha, Halliburton, and Humphrey (2012) compared spouses' perceptions of play; mothers reported engaging in structured play with their preschoolers that incorporated academic skills and guiding the child through setting limits. However, fathers reported that they were more involved in physical play, such as rough-and-tumble play, with their children.

Parents' perceptions and involvement in play may also vary depending on certain characteristics of their child. For instance, Elkind (2010) found that mothers have more play interactions and conversations with their daughters than with their sons; and they are less likely than fathers to engage in physical play with their children. However, when mothers engage in physical play with their children, it tends to be with their sons or later-born children (Schoppe-Sullivan, Kotila, Jia, Lang, & Bower, 2013). Furthermore, mothers and fathers of daughters tend to view pretend play more positively and are more involved in play than those with sons (Aesha et al., 2012).

Thus, from the literature reviewed, it is clear that parents' perceptions of play vary. Importantly, parents' perceptions of play are related to children's frequency and quality of play, which has implications for their school readiness. For instance, in a study by Fisher et al. (2008), mothers were asked to rate different types of activities as whether or not they could be classified as play. The list of activities included both traditional play activities (e.g. dress-up) and more structured play activities (e.g. puzzles). Mothers who rated both traditional and structured activities as play had children who were reported to engage in more unstructured play activities (e.g. freeplay) than mothers who made clear distinctions between play and non-play activities. Moreover, mothers and fathers differ in their views of play and ways that they play with their own children. These differences between mothers and fathers appear to be influenced by child characteristics (e.g. child gender). However, to our knowledge, no studies have examined how parents differ in their perceptions of the value of play compared to the value of academic skills; and how their perceptions may differ by child gender and child age. This area of inquiry seems significant, as when parents 'buy in' to the push down of academics, they will be less likely to advocate for developmentally appropriate practices in classrooms (e.g. play focused). This moves early childhood education away from child-centred practices, which disregards evidence underscoring the importance of play to academic readiness. Therefore, the following research questions were examined: 1. Is there a difference in mothers' and fathers' value of play?; 2. Is there a difference in mothers' and fathers' value of early academic skills?; and 3. Do child age and child gender influence these differences?

Method

Participants

Sixty-eight mothers and fathers were recruited from a university laboratory school and reported their beliefs about play and academic readiness. The school serves as a laboratory school for students completing field placements in child development. The laboratory school is a teaching facility within a college of education and is designed to provide observational, practicum, and student teaching experiences. The school supports the philosophy that the early years are formative years and the most important in children's development. Young children between the ages of three and five attend a part-day session, which means working parents adjust their schedules or make arrangements for children to be dropped and picked up. Young children are in a learning environment that assists them to strengthen their ability to focus, plan, self-monitor, and self-evaluate their own progress through long-term projects. The Reggio Emilia approach has influenced the school's philosophy with the use of child-initiated projects. Play is a major element of the day where teachers prepare an environment rich in pretend play and various centres. There are also teacher-directed learning experiences that teachers and student teachers prepare.

At the time of data collection, all participants were co-parenting their preschool-aged child with their participating spouse. A total of 68 parents (34 mothers, 34 fathers) voluntarily participated in this study. Mothers' age ranged from 31 to 40 years. Fathers' age ranged from 36 to 40 years. The director of the school reported that the majority of participants were of a middle-class socio-economic status; 98% of the participants were White/Caucasian. Approximately 71% of parents obtained a standard college or university bachelor's degree or higher. The estimated 29% of parents without a degree had some type of specialised training or partially completed college (at least one year). The distribution of the children parents reported on was as follows: 29 females and 39 males. The average child's age was 51.82 months ($SD = 8.29$).

Measures

An adapted version of the Parent Play Belief Scale (PPBS) developed by Fogle and Mendez (2006) was distributed to measure parents' beliefs about their preschool children's play. The questionnaire consisted of 29 items rated on a 5-point Likert Scale ranging from 1 (*Strongly Disagree*) to 5 (*Strongly Agree*). The PPBS was designed as a measurement tool to examine the multidimensional avenues of African-American parents' play beliefs including 'developmental significance of play, participation in play, enjoyment of play' as well as 'perspectives on play and pre-academic activities' (Fogle & Mendez, 2006, p. 509). The PPBS has also been used reliably with Caucasian samples in unpublished studies conducted by the first author. The 30-item pilot version of the measure had an alpha coefficient of .86, indicating good internal consistency. All items from the piloted questionnaire were included in Fogle and Mendez's (2006) study which determined 2 significant factor loadings: *play support* consisted of 17 items (e.g. 'playing at home will help my child get ready for kindergarten') and *academic focus* contained 8 items (e.g. 'I do not think my child learns important skills by play'). Fogle and Mendez (2006) reported that the play support subscale yielded a Cronbach's alpha of .90 and academic focus subscale had a Cronbach's alpha of .73. The measure has also been reliably adapted for use in Turkey (Ivrendi & Isikoglu, 2010) and Taiwan (Lin & Yawkey, 2014).

In the current study, 25 items under the 2 subscales, play support and academic focus, were retained for use; an additional four questions that were structured by two experts in the field of child development were also administered. These items included statements regarding outdoor play ('I encourage my child to go outside to play.'); parents' history of play ('My parents encouraged me to go outside and play.'; 'I feel like my parents valued play.'), and the use of technology for educational purposes ('I think my letting my child play computer games or other electronic games is helpful to their educational future.'). These four items were not included in the analyses.

In the current study, the play support subscale had a Cronbach's alpha of .90 and the academic focus subscale had a Cronbach's alpha coefficient of .71. In order to improve the alpha for academic focus, two items ('Reading to my child is more worthwhile than playing with him or her.' and 'I would rather read to my child than play together.') about reading were removed resulting in a Cronbach's alpha coefficient of .80.

Procedures

One packet consisting of two surveys and a covering letter providing general information about the study was hand delivered to participants. Mothers and fathers completed the survey independently at home. Upon completion, one of the parents returned the completed surveys to the school. The return rate was approximately 80%. The procedure was approved by the university's Institutional Review Board as a part of a larger study.

Results

Descriptive statistics (means, standard deviations, and correlations) were computed for all variables and are displayed in Table 1. Since parents rated their beliefs about the same child, a paired samples t-test was conducted to compare play support and academic focus, and indicated that they were significantly different from one another, $t(67) = 42.94, p = .001$. The mean for play support was 4.60 (SD = 0.38) and for academic focus was 1.31 ($SD = 0.36$), thereby indicating that parents rated the value of play as higher than academic focus.

Next, a paired samples t-test was conducted to examine the differences between mothers' and fathers' value of play. This procedure was selected given that there was a significant correlation between mothers' and fathers' ratings of their values of children's play (rs ranged from .47 to .48) and both parents rated their beliefs about the same child. Results indicated that fathers placed a higher value on academic focus ($M = 1.42$, $SD = .06$) than mothers ($M = 1.20$, $SD = .06$), $t(33) = 3.92$, $p < .004$. In addition, mothers placed a higher value on play support ($M = 4.67$, $SE = .05$) than fathers ($M = 4.53$, $SD = .07$), $t(33) = -2.23$, $p < .005$.

Pearson r correlations were also computed to examine how child age may affect parents' ratings of play support and academic focus. First, correlations were run for the whole sample, and a trend-level finding emerged ($r = -.20$, $p = .10$) between child age and play support, but there was no significant relation between child age and academic focus, $r = .13$, *ns*. Next, Pearson r correlations were examined separately for boys and girls. The results indicated that for boys, there were no significant relations between child age and parents' ratings of play support, $r = -.19$, *ns*, and academic focus,

Table 1. Descriptive statistics for mean and standard deviation for PPBS.

	Total		Fathers		Mothers	
Variable	*M*	*SD*	*M*	*SD*	*M*	*SD*
Play support	4.60	0.38	4.53	0.42	4.67	0.32
Academic focus	1.31	0.36	1.42	0.35	1.20	0.34

$r = -.007$, *ns*. However, for girls, there was a significant, positive relation between child age and academic focus, $r = .48$, $p = .007$, but there was no significant relation between child age and play support, $r = -.19$, *ns*. When parent gender was considered in these relations, the relation between child age and academic focus was positive and significant for the ratings of mothers of girls, $r = .57$, $p = .03$, but not fathers of girls, $r = .45$, $p = .11$. There were no significant correlations between age and play support for mothers, $r = -.25$, *ns*, or fathers, $r = -.17$, *ns*.

Discussion

This study investigated parents' beliefs regarding their preschool children's play. The perspectives of mothers and fathers were compared, as well as how those perspectives differed by child gender and change with child age. Overall, the data indicated that parents in this study value play and do not prioritise academics with their preschool-aged children. These findings are encouraging given the links between play and academic readiness in preschoolers (e.g. Fisher et al., 2011), as well as the links between parents' perceptions of play and children's play behaviours (Roopnarine & Jin, 2012). The parents included in the current sample actively chose a preschool that values play, as stated in the school's website and other promotional materials. It is likely that parents who want their children to attend this type of preschool would value the philosophical undertone that play has in the curriculum. Thus, these parents are likely aware of developmentally appropriate practices and support these types of learning environments. These findings support work by Miller (1989) who found that parents from middle-class and/or professional backgrounds seek child-directed centres where the focus in on creativity. Importantly, the findings presented are also similar to those reported by Fogle and Mendez (2006) with a sample of African-American mothers who were attending Head Start. Specifically, mothers in this study reported similar levels of value for play ($M = 4.13$) as found herein, but slightly higher levels for academic focus ($M = 2.18$).

However, with the emphasis on academics in preschool programmes and the national importance placed on universal pre-K, it cannot be assumed that all parents of preschool-aged children focus on play. Indeed, the success of expensive, early educational videos suggests that some parents may feel pressured to push academics at an early age, even though many of these programmes have no research basis (e.g. Lipka, 2014). Furthermore, in research conducted by Belfield and Garcia (2014), a national data set was used to analyse data from a 14-year period; the findings indicated that parents reported higher expectations for children to know their letters and count in 2007 compared to 1993 (Belfield & Garcia, 2014). Based on previous research, these expectations may lead to changes in overall children's playtime and quality of play at home and school.

While it can be generally stated that parents in this study value play, when mothers and fathers were compared, mothers in this study placed a higher value on play support than fathers. Furthermore, fathers in this study placed a higher value on academic focus than mothers. These differences may be the result of school selection falling into the purview of mothers' responsibilities in the family, as women still tend to be responsible for the majority of household and childcare tasks (e.g. Rubin & Wooten, 2007). More specifically, if mothers are responsible for the selection of their child's pre-K, they may have done more research regarding the importance of play. Thus, they may have more knowledge about its importance, which is reflected in their ratings of the value play.

Importantly, fathers in the current study still valued play support, but at significantly lower levels than mothers did. This is consistent with previous research. For instance, Gleason (2005) found that mothers were more involved during play, and that mothers placed greater value on pretend play when compared to fathers. Thus, mothers may be more attuned to the significance of play.

It is also important to note that child age appeared to play an important role in parents' value of play in the current study, with play support decreasing as children get older (at the trend level). This finding suggests that parents alter their views of play as their children approach entry into formal schooling (e.g. kindergarten). While it is logical that parents' beliefs would change as children age, this finding underscores the power of the demarcation of formal schooling as well as the prevalent view that kindergarten should focus on academics. To our knowledge, this finding is the first to examine, albeit cross-sectionally, how parents' perceptions of play may change as children develop.

While we did not examine how parents' values affect the quality and quantity of time parents spend in play with their children, it may be that as parents' value of play decreases, the frequency, type, and quality of play also change, and likely decrease. This line of conjecture is speculative and requires empirical testing; however, if parents are not valuing play, it may have a significant, negative impact on children given that play should be encouraged through the kindergarten years (e.g. Lynch, 2015). The amount of playtime during kindergarten has decreased over the past two decades (Frost, Wortham, & Reifel, 2008). Thus, if children have fewer opportunities to play at school and they have parents who do not value play highly, children may be provided with even fewer opportunities to engage in play, a developmentally appropriate best practice for children in kindergarten (Lynch, 2015). This is an important and critical consideration for the children in the American school system. It is likely that when parents' value of play decreases, they will be less likely to advocate for this developmentally appropriate practice in schools. This, in turn, may lead to less child-centred educational practices (e.g. play; active learning) through the kindergarten years (and beyond). It has been argued by educational and developmental experts that this type of practice is necessary and beneficial for children through the early elementary years (e.g. Katz, 2015); yet, the prevailing practice in the schools is academic-focused (Miller & Almon, 2009b). Thus, if parents are made aware of the importance of play, they may advocate for more play-focused educational practices in the public school system. This type of change could potentially promote practices that are child-centred, which could provide all children with the best environment to develop. Importantly, previous research indicates that these types of child-centred practices are linked to better increases in mathematics and reading through the third grade for children with and without special needs (Hanline et al., 2010).

Interestingly, mothers and fathers in this study differed in their endorsement of academic focus when child gender was considered. Specifically, parents of daughters in this study placed an increased importance on academics as girls got older, and this was especially true for mothers of daughters. Importantly, there were no significant associations between child age and valuing play or academic focus for boys. These findings are consistent with previous work on gender differences in play (Aesha et al., 2012; Gleason, 2005). However, the findings herein indicated that parents were focused on girls' academics over boys', which is a novel finding. It may be that parents of girls are aware of some of the difficulties that can arise from gender in formal schooling (e.g. differences in achievement motivation; differential treatment by teachers; see Simpkins, Fredricks, & Eccles, 2015 for review). It may also be that parents view their sons as less mature or ready for formal schooling, which is suggested by the current trend to 'redshirt' boys (i.e. delay the start of formal schooling) a year prior to starting kindergarten (Bassok & Reardon, 2013).

While the current study provided new information about parents' value of play, there were several limitations that must be noted. The sample size was considerably small and analyses were underpowered; in addition, the sample was homogenous. Therefore, these results are not generalisable beyond a middle-income, predominantly Caucasian, highly educated sample. In addition, parents completed questionnaires at home, which may have given spouses the opportunity to compare answers with one another and may have resulted in their answers converging. Finally, the measures used were parent report and could have been influenced by social desirability.

In light of these limitations, future research should replicate this study in more socio-economically diverse samples, as well as with larger samples and multiple methods (e.g. observations and teacher-report questionnaires). In addition, the findings suggest that middle-class parents value play, but it would be interesting to investigate if these beliefs decrease as children enter kindergarten, an age when children should still be taught through play-based/active learning (Clark, 2001; Lynch, 2015). It was also found that mothers and fathers differ in their value of play support and value of academic focus, which dovetails with the literature indicating that mothers and fathers differ in the type and quality of parent–child play (Aesha et al., 2012). As such, future research should extend the focus of this study by examining how parents' play beliefs are linked to their children's play behaviour and academic readiness.

In conclusion, with a national movement towards universal pre-K, it seems prudent to further understand how parents contribute to play in young children. At present, the ramifications of the push for academic instruction in early childhood education remain unknown. However, when considering the numerous studies that have indicated that play is a vital part of children's development (e.g. Katz, 2015; Lillard et al., 2013; Miller & Almon, 2009b), it seems plausible that the reduction in playtime will be detrimental to children's academic motivation and achievement over time. What is more, the ramifications of schools that preclude opportunities for play may be exacerbated (or ameliorated) by parents' value of play. Thus, additional research is required to fully understand the nature of parents' beliefs about play and the consequences of those beliefs.

Disclosure statement

No potential conflict of interest was reported by the authors.

References

Aesha, J., Halliburton, A., & Humphrey, J. (2012). Child-mother and child-father play interaction patterns with preschoolers. *Early Child Development and Care, 183*(3–4), 483–497.

Bassok, D., & Reardon, S. F. (2013). Academic redshirting in kindergarten: Prevalence, patterns, and implications. *Educational Evaluation and Policy Analysis, 35*, 283–297. doi:10.3102/0162373713482764

Becker, D. R., McClelland, M. M., Loprinzi, P., & Trost, S. G. (2014). Physical activity, self-regulation, and early academic achievement in preschool children. *Early Education and Development, 25*, 56–70. doi:10.1080/10409289.2013.780505

Belfield, C., & Garcia, E. (2014). Parental notions of school readiness: How have they changed and has preschool made a difference? *The Journal of Educational Research, 107*, 138–151.

Carlsson-Paige, N., Almon, J., & McLaughlin, G. (2015). *Reading instruction in kindergarten: Little to gain and much to lose.* Boston, MA: Defending the Early Years; New York, NY: Alliance for Childhood.

Christakis, E. (2016). *The importance of being little: What preschoolers really need from grownups.* New York, NY: Viking.

Clark, P. (2001). *Recent research on all day kindergarten.* Champaign, IL: ERIC Clearinghouse on Elementary and Early Childhood Education.

Elkind, D. (2010). Play. In V. Washington & J. D. Andrews (Eds.), *Children of 2020: Creating a better tomorrow* (pp. 85–89). Washington, DC: The Council for Professional Recognition.

Fisher, K., Hirsh-Pasek, K., Golinkoff, R. M., Singer, D. G., & Berk, L. (2011). Playing around in school: Implications for learning and educational policy. In A. Pellegrini (Eds.), *The Oxford handbook of play* (pp. 341–362). New York, NY: Oxford University Press.

Fisher, K. R., Hirsh-Pasek, K., Golinkoff, R. M., & Gryfe, S. G. (2008). Conceptual split? Parents' and experts' perceptions of play in the 21st century. *Journal of Applied Developmental Psychology, 29*, 305–316.

Fogle, L. M., & Mendez, J. L. (2006). Assessing the play beliefs of African American mothers with preschool children. *Early Childhood Research Quarterly, 21*, 507–518.

Froebel, F. (1887). *The education of man.* (W.N. Hailmann, Trans.). New York, NY: Appleton.

Frost, J. L., Wortham, S., & Reifel, R. S. (2008). *Play and child development* (3rd ed.). Pearson: Boston.

Gleason, T. R. (2005). Mothers' and fathers' attitudes regarding pretend play in the context of imaginary companions and of child gender. *Merrill-Palmer Quarterly, 51*(4), 412–436.

Gonzalez-Mena, J. (2008). *Diversity in early care and education: Honoring differences* (5th ed.). Washington, DC: McGraw-Hill.

Haight, W. L., Parke, R. D., & Black, J. E. (1997). Mothers' and fathers' beliefs about and spontaneous participation in their toddlers' pretend play. *Merrill-Palmer Quarterly, 43*(2), 271–290.

Hanline, M. F., Milton, S., & Phelps, P. C. (2010). The relationship between preschool block play and reading and math abilities in early elementary school: A longitudinal study of children with and without disabilities. *Early Child Development and Care, 180,* 1005–1017.

Hirsh-Pasek, K., Golinkoff, R. M., Berk, L. E., & Singer, D. G. (2009). *A mandate for playful learning in preschool: Presenting the evidence.* New York: Oxford University Press.

Ivrendi, A., & Isikoglu, N. (2010). A Turkish view on fathers' involvement in children's play. *Early Childhood Education Journal, 37,* 519–526.

Katz, L. G. (2015). Lively minds: Distinctions between academic versus intellectual goals for young children. In *Defending the Early Years* (2015). Retrieved from https://deyproject.files.wordpress.com/2015/04/dey-lively-minds-4-8-15.pdf

Lillard, A. S., Lerner, M. D., Hopkins, E. J., Dore, R. A., Smith, E. D., & Palmquist, C. M. (2013). The impact of pretend play on children's development: A review of the evidence. *Psychological Bulletin, 139*(1), 1–34.

Lin, Y.-C., & Yawkey, T. D. (2014). Parents' play beliefs and the relationship to children's social competence. *Education, 135,* 107–114.

Lipka, M. (2014, August). Feds: Your baby can't read. *CBS Money Watch.* Retrieved from: http://www.cbsnews.com/news/my-baby-cant-read-company-penalized-for-reading-claims/

Lynch, M. (2015). More play, please: The perspective of kindergarten teachers on play in the classroom. *Americal Journal of Play, 7,* 347–370.

Miller, D. F. (1989). *First steps towards cultural difference: Socialization in infant/toddler daycare.* Washington, DC: Child Welfare League of America.

Miller, E., & Almon, J. (2009a). *Crisis in the kindergarten: Why children need to play in school.* College Park, MD: Alliance for Childhood.

Miller, E., & Almon, J. (2009b). The transformation of kindergarten. *ENCOUNTER: Education for Meaning and Social Justice, 22*(2), 6–11.

National Association for the Education of Young Children. (2009). *Position statement: Developmentally appropriate practice in early childhood programs serving children from birth through age 8.* Washington, DC: National Association for the Education of Young Children.

National Education Goals Panel. (1997). *The national education goals report: Building a nation of learners.* Washington, DC: U.S. Government Printing Office.

Nicolopolou, A. (2010). The alarming disappearance of play from early childhood education. *Human Development, 53,* 1–4. doi:10.1159/000268135

Piaget, J. (1962). *Play, dreams, and imitation in childhood.* New York, NY: Garland.

Power, T. G., & Parke, R. D. (1986). Patterns of early socialization: Mother-and father-infant interaction in the home. *International Journal of Behavioural Development, 9,* 331–341.

Roopnarine, J. L., & Jin, B. (2012). Indo carribbean immigrant beliefs about play and its impact on early academic performance. *American Journal of Play, 4,* 441–463.

Rubin, S. E., & Wooten, H. R. (2007). Highly educated stay-at-home mothers: A study of commitment and conflict. *The Family Journal, 15,* 336–345.

Schoppe-Sullivan, S. J., Kotila, L. E., Jia, R., Lang, S. N., & Bower, D. J. (2013). Comparison levels and predictors of mothers' and fathers' engagement with their preschool-aged children. *Early Child Development and Care, 183*(3–4), 498–514.

Shine, S., & Acosta, T. Y. (2000). Parent-child social play in a children's museum. *Family Relations, 49*(1), 45–52.

Simpkins, S. D., Fredricks, J. A., & Eccles, J. S. (2015). Families, schools, and developing achievement-related motivations and engagement. In J. E. Grusec & P. D. Hastings (Eds.), *Handbook of socialization: Theory and practice* (pp. 614–636). New York, NY: Guilford.

Sluss, D. J. (2005). *Supporting play: Birth through eight.* Clifton Park, NY: Thomson/Delmar Learning.

Stipek, D. (2006). No child left behind comes to preschool. *The Elementary School Journal, 106,* 455–466.

Stipek, D., Feiler, R., Daniels, D., & Milburn, S. (1995). Effects of different instructional approaches on young children's achievement and motivation. *Child Development, 66*(1), 209–223.

Van Hoorn, J., Nourot, P. M., Scales, B., & Alward, K. R. (2011). *Play at the center of the curriculum* (5th ed.). Upper Saddle River, NJ: Pearson Education.

Vygotsky, L. S. (1967). Play and its role in the mental development of the child. *Soviet Psychology, 5,* 6–18.

Warash, B. G., Pelliccioni, M. W., & Yoon, D. P. (2000). The views of middle-class parents on developmentally appropriate practice. *Journal of Leadership Quest, 4*(2), 8–11.

The social kindergartener: comparing children's perspectives of full- and half-day kindergarten

Kaitlyn Heagle, Kristy Timmons, Fabienne Hargreaves and Janette Pelletier

ABSTRACT

The objective of the present study is to capture children's voices to compare traditional half-day and play-based full-day kindergarten children's perspectives on two research questions: What is important about kindergarten, and what is your favourite thing about school? Children's responses were compared for emerging academic and social themes. Half-day kindergarten children reported academic activities significantly more often as being important compared with their full-day counterparts. No significant differences were found in children's reports of their favourite thing about school, demonstrating that regardless of programme, children most enjoy play and social activities. These findings reinforce the importance of play-based full-day kindergarten programmes.

Introduction

The modern day kindergarten classroom is moving away from the constraints of traditional education and towards a more play-based learning environment. Play-based learning is a child-centred approach in which students interact with the learning environment at their own developmental pace (FDELK, 2010). This is in contrast to traditional half-day kindergarten programmes which aim to educate students through teacher-directed group exercises designed to accustom students to the regulatory rigours of grade one. Play-based full-day kindergarten provides opportunities for the whole child to learn academic concepts and social skills through play and exploration (FDELK, 2010; Frost, Wortham, & Reifel, 2008). The province of Ontario took a bold initiative in implementing a new full-day, play-based early learning kindergarten programme co-taught by a kindergarten teacher and a registered early childhood educator. Since the programme was unrolled over five years, it provided an opportunity for a natural experiment to compare half-day and full-day programmes (Pelletier, 2014b). This study seeks to uncover and compare kindergarten children's perceptions of their school experiences in Ontario's traditional half-day and play-based full-day programmes.

Policy and framework of full-day kindergarten

The academic, social, and cognitive benefits of full-day kindergarten programmes are reflected in research and policy documents worldwide (Cannon, Jacknowitz, & Painter, 2011; Miller & Almon, 2009). In recent years, many school districts have implemented extended day kindergarten programmes as a way to increase student achievement (Cannon, Jacknowitz, & Painter, 2006) through the education of the whole child, including curriculum guidelines that promote academic, social-emotional, and cognitive development (Kauerz, 2005). Full-day programmes seek to promote early development through integration of curriculum areas and inquiry-based learning, and are associated with improved social and academic outcomes (Ray & Smith, 2010). Research in education suggests that student achievement is cumulative, and high-quality education in kindergarten is associated with future success (Pianta, Cox, & Snow, 2007).

Children enter kindergarten with diverse cognitive, social, and learning experiences. Lee and Burkam (2002) found an association between lower socioeconomic statuses, for example, and lower test scores upon entry to kindergarten. The full-day kindergarten programme in Ontario offers a play-based curriculum that seeks to close this gap by providing more time for development, interaction, and instruction. Students following a play-based full-day kindergarten programme enjoy a more balanced and integrated school day than those in half-day programmes (FDELK, 2010). Within the play-based programme, teachers incorporate a combination of group lessons and child-directed activities designed to individualize the learning experience. By allowing students to learn independently through play, teachers create more opportunities for simultaneous learning, resulting in greater skill development and more advanced instruction (Graue, 2009; Walston & West, 2004). Further, the longer day allows educators to provide more small-group and child-led play interactions. Interestingly, kindergarten children are more engaged in these small-group and child-led play interactions than they are when interacting in whole-group contexts (Timmons, Pelletier, & Corter, 2016).

Kindergarten students are at a critical period for development, and success in future schooling is largely determined by one's ability to transition into the full-day school environment (Ray & Smith, 2010). When asked to describe their pre-conceptions about starting kindergarten, Di Santo and Berman found that most children expected a play-based, child-centred environment, similar to how learning occurs in the preschool environment (2012). More specifically, researchers asked small groups of preschoolers to discuss kindergarten, and found that children most frequently mentioned play as being central to their role as future kindergarteners. Those children who did mention academics expected learning activities to be child-driven and play-based, not teacher-directed as in traditional kindergarten classrooms. Similar results on children's perceptions of school were found in the Toronto First Duty project in which children were interviewed about their experiences in integrated full-day care and education programmes (Corter, Janmohamed, & Pelletier, 2012) and in earlier research on exemplary kindergarten practice (Corter & Park, 1993). For many children, the kindergarten years form a bridge from the free-play settings of early childhood education to the academic rigours of the grade one classroom; the play-based full-day programme in Ontario aims to create a natural transition across these contexts.

Social and academic outcomes of full-day kindergarten

A central feature of kindergarten is to equip children with the knowledge and skills to be successful learners as they continue their education (Kauerz, 2005). Students who follow a full-day kindergarten programme have shown to be better prepared both academically and socially upon entry to grade one than students in half-day programmes (Cooper, Allen, Patall, & Dent, 2010; Ray & Smith, 2010). Play-based full-day programmes promote the development of social-emotional skills, such as healthy peer interaction and self-regulation, which in turn promotes academic knowledge (FDELK, 2010). Extended child-directed play periods create integrated opportunities for students to explore social and academic learning, contributing to the education of the whole child. The social and academic benefits of the play-based full-day kindergarten programme are well represented in past research.

Social development

The ideal kindergarten curriculum needs to focus on children's cognitive and social-emotional development (Ray & Smith, 2010). Full-day kindergarten programmes promote young children's natural association between play and peer interaction through increased opportunities for social learning (Cooper et al., 2010; Howard, Jenvey, & Hill, 2006).

Research that observes kindergarten children in classroom contexts found that children are most engaged when they are at play or working in small groups (Timmons et al., 2016). Child-directed play, rather than teacher-directed learning, is most strongly associated with cognitive and affective development in kindergarten students (Gmitrova & Gmitrova, 2004). However, teachers play an important role in creating an environment that supports a positive social culture among peers, which enhances children's quality of experience in all-day programmes (Stephen, 2003). Students in full-day kindergarten programmes enjoy increased opportunities for child-directed play, and are more independent and self-directed in their learning than students in half-day programmes (Carnes & Albrecht, 2007; Plucker et al., 2004). Children in full-day kindergarten spend a greater proportion of their school day engaged in active free play, while children in traditional programmes spend more time in teacher-directed large groups (Cryan, Sheehan, Wiechel, & Bandy-Hedden, 1992; Elicker & Mathur, 1997). Through extended periods of child-directed play, the play-based full-day curriculum provides more frequent opportunities for children to interact with each other (FDELK, 2010). It is during this type of child-directed play that children have uninterrupted time to engage in conversation with peers, and learn to cooperate within a group (Leseman, Rollenberg, & Rispens, 2001).

The play-based full-day kindergarten programme supports social development through increased opportunities for peer interaction and socialization during extended active play periods (FDELK, 2010). Children who follow a full-day curriculum are less aggressive than students in traditional programmes, and make greater gains in overall social-emotional development, including important skills such as waiting their turn during group games, and gaining peer attention in appropriate ways (Carnes & Albrecht, 2007). Additionally, students who attend full-day programmes score higher on measures of self-esteem and self-confidence, which are positively associated with their ability to play with others (Cooper et al., 2010). While students in full-day programmes are more likely to exhibit positive social behaviours, students in half-day kindergarten are more likely to be withdrawn, shy, and anxious (Cryan et al., 1992).

Regardless of kindergarten programme, young children naturally view play and social experiences as connected (Howard et al., 2006). When asked to draw a picture of themselves at school, children depict themselves at play or engaged socially with peers more often than any other activity, including academics (Pelletier, 2012a). While 'play' is often mentioned as their favourite activity in kindergarten (Pelletier, 1998), students also understand that play is a form of learning. A study by Karrby (1990) revealed that kindergarten students appreciate that one might learn social skills during play situations, such as learning to make decisions as a group. In fact, the children in this study described learning that occurred during active free-play periods more accurately and in greater detail than learning that happened during adult-directed activities. This supports the theory that children not only prefer play to other activities, but also are retaining more knowledge while at play than during teacher-directed group lessons.

Academic outcomes

Compared with those implementing a traditional half-day curriculum, teachers of full-day programmes consistently rate a greater number of students as reading at grade level and being ready for grade one (Hall-Kenyon, Bingham, & Korth, 2009). Overall, students who enjoy a full-day programme spend more time successfully developing academic skills, and score higher on measures of literacy and mathematics, including greater achievement in the areas of reading, printing, phonics, vocabulary, number knowledge, measurement, and problem solving (Chang & Singh, 2008; Lee, Burkam, Ready, Honigman, & Meisels, 2006; Walston & West, 2004).

Children enter kindergarten with a wide range of developmental skills and experiences (Lee & Burkam, 2002). By enabling students to be independent learners, the full-day play-based curriculum allows for more time for remediation and support for students who may be at risk. In fact, children who attend full-day kindergarten have greater achievement in literacy and mathematics than half-day students, regardless of social and academic background (Lee et al., 2006). Kindergarten students who are English-language learners make greater gains in language when in full-day programmes, and students from low socioeconomic households score higher on measures of academic achievement in full-day classrooms (Cooper et al., 2010; Hall-Kenyon et al., 2009). Full-day kindergarten is also associated with a reduced need for student grade retention, remediation, and special education referrals in subsequent grades (Cannon et al., 2011; Housden & Kam, 1992; Plucker et al., 2004)

Students who follow a play-based full-day curriculum enjoy a more balanced and integrated school day. Teachers of half-day programmes are rarely afforded the time to cover each curriculum area more than two times per week. Conversely, students in full-day programmes are more likely to spend time each day on a range of curriculum areas, and teachers report higher levels of satisfaction as the extra time allows them to 'go deeper' in planning and implementing a more integrated curriculum (Carnes & Albrecht, 2007; Hall-Kenyon et al., 2009). Many teachers also note that the full-day programme affords more opportunities for observational assessment and one-to-one interactions with all students (Elicker & Mathur, 1997). Research from the National Center for Education Statistics found that full-day classes focused on a greater number of literacy and mathematics skills, many of which are considered 'too advanced' in the half-day programme, including reading fluency, reading multisyllabic words, and alphabetizing (Walston & West, 2004).

The benefits of increased achievement in full-day programmes extend beyond the early years; full-day kindergarten has been associated with lasting gains in achievement (Plucker et al., 2004; Raskin, Mankato, & Haar, 2009; Villegas, 2005). One longitudinal study conducted in Indiana found that students who attended full-day kindergarten scored higher on basic skills tests in the 3rd, 5th, and 7th grades than their half-day counterparts (Plucker et al., 2004). Similar results have been produced in Canada, where students who attended full-day kindergarten attained greater linguistic and academic development in reading and math in grades two and five than students in traditional programmes (Maltais, Herry, Emond, & Mougeot, 2011).

While the majority of research studies support the social and academic outcomes of a play-based programme, there are some concerns associated with extending the kindergarten day. Opponents of full-day kindergarten argue that the programme is costly, and point out that the resources required to implement the curriculum may take resources away from other programmes, such as after-school activities and reading programmes (Levin, 2002). This research has examined the potential negative impacts associated with long-term cost benefit (DeCicca, 2007; Reynolds & Temple, 2008). While introducing a new kindergarten programme may lead to initial cost increases, most research suggests that the overall benefits for students are valuable, and school boards maintain the power to allocate funds in the way that best serves each institution (Lee et al., 2006). Opponents of full-day kindergarten also emphasize that the initial short-term benefits of the programme may fade in subsequent grades (Cooper et al., 2010). Despite mixed results concerning the long-term academic benefits of full-day kindergarten, it is important to consider that the kindergarten programme described in this study is a play-based curriculum co-taught by a kindergarten teacher and an early childhood educator, not simply an extended school day (FDELK, 2010). Furthermore, previous research has failed to take into account the opinions of the key stakeholders in describing full-day programmes. To fully understand the impact of play-based full-day kindergarten, this study seeks to understand the programme from the perspective of the most important stakeholders, the students themselves.

Capturing children's voices

Despite an abundance of research surrounding education and development in early childhood, few studies seek to examine children's perspectives in describing the kindergarten experience (Di Santo & Berman, 2012; Janzen, 2008). This reflects the dominant paradigm in the social sciences to conduct research on, rather than with children. However, it has been determined that children are in fact capable, competent, and effective in communicating their own perspectives when the research context is appropriate and sensitive to their developmental needs (Corter & Park, 1993; Dockett & Perry, 2007; Smith, Duncan, & Marshall, 2005).

When implemented appropriately, interviews are an especially effective way to elicit truthful information from young children (Clark, 2005). It is important to create an environment in which the child feels comfortable to share openly, and the interview context should align with the child's developmental level (Langstead, 1994). Research suggests a range of strategies that aim to enhance comfort, including the use of props, drawing, and role-playing (Irwin & Johnson, 2005). For example, the use of puppets helps to reduce the power of authority between adult and child, creating a play-based interview where the child feels at ease sharing his or her experiences and ideas (Di Santo & Berman, 2012; Pelletier, 1998, 1999). Research has also found that asking children to revisit past actions by talking about photographs or videotapes of themselves results in rich descriptions of perspective because it lessens the pressures on working memory, and provides a shared experience for the researcher and child to reflect together (Makin & Whiteman, 2006). Children feel comfortable sharing their ideas in an environment where their ideas are valued (Clark, 2005), and the researcher should aim to create an interview context in which children can communicate with adults who can interpret or 'read' their voices (Smith et al., 2005). The use of open-ended questions permits a more diverse range of opinions, allowing children to express their own interpretations and ideas (Di Santo & Berman, 2012). Moving forward, researchers should seek to create contexts in which kindergarten students are able to contribute valuable knowledge and perspectives to the evaluation of early years' education programmes.

It has been determined that experience, not age, is becoming increasingly important in the description of children's development and learning (Smith et al., 2005). As policy documents worldwide are becoming more play-based (Miller & Almon, 2009), it is important to consider children's perspectives on their experiences in such programmes. Effective early childhood educators use a multitude of ways to assess children's voices, collecting information through conversation and studying children's drawings, constructions, and interactions (Makin & Whiteman, 2006). The use of children's voices to inform decisions about curriculum requires an adult who has an understanding of children's perspectives in learning and incorporates this into the setting's pedagogical approach (Coleyshaw, Whitmarsh, Jopling, & Hadfield, 2010). This includes ensuring children have the language to express their views, and allowing children to co-construct their environment and make decisions about their own learning. While the presence of familiar adults and peers can add to the construction of a child's view, speaking directly with the child is the best way to elicit his or her perspective (Makin & Whiteman, 2006; Smith et al., 2005).

In research that explored children's beliefs and ideas, findings indicate that kindergarten students consistently report 'play' to be activities that are voluntary, self-chosen, and student-centred (Ceglowski, 1997; Robson, 1993). When asked to elaborate, children often described play as a self-chosen activity that takes place after the completion of teacher-directed work (Howard et al., 2002). Through experience, play has been perceived as a reward for working, as opposed to a vehicle for learning. Children consider play and work to be mutually exclusive; more specifically, 'play' occurs when children initiate a task by choice, and 'work' is defined as undertaking a task required by an adult (Robson, 1993). This supports the idea that the more control a child has over a specific activity, the more likely he or she will be to classify it as play (King, 1979).

Children's perceptions of play at school reflect their teachers' approaches to instruction within the classroom (Dickinson & Smith, 1991), and in traditional half-day kindergarten classrooms, teachers are rarely seen as play partners (Robson, 1993). Educators in half-day programmes report that the pressure to complete curriculum expectations within a restricted timeline inhibits both the time available for play and adult involvement in play (Keating, Fabian, Jordan, Mavers, & Roberts, 2000). Research into other all-day programmes reveals a tension between practice and theory where children are often removed from a free-play setting to participate in a teacher-directed group activity to satisfy a curriculum requirement (Stephen, 2003). If all-day provision is going to be successful, the curriculum needs to reflect student preference. The play-based full-day kindergarten programme seeks to create integrated whole-group, small-group, and independent learning opportunities, where students interact with teachers in a range of adult-directed and child-initiated activities throughout each day (FDELK, 2010). In this way, teachers have time to provide individual support to students on specific subject areas, while other students learn simultaneously through independent or group play activities. The play-based programme not only allows teachers more time to effectively deliver curriculum guidelines, but also provides students with more time to do what they love, play.

Our study

While the positive impacts of play-based learning are widely supported in research, most studies rely on adult reports or observations to describe children's experiences. Relatively little is known regarding children's perceptions of the modern play-based kindergarten curriculum. As kindergarten programmes worldwide continue to shift towards a play-based learning curriculum, it is essential that research consider the perceptions of the key stakeholders, in this case the children themselves. This study seeks to determine whether children in play-based full-day kindergarten classrooms perceive play and learning differently from children enrolled in half-day kindergarten programmes. The purpose of this study was to compare kindergarten children's responses to two questions: (1) What is important about kindergarten and (2) What is your favourite thing about school?

Methods

This research is part of an ongoing longitudinal study examining the implementation and impact of school-based integrated early childhood services including full-day kindergarten and childcare programmes. The purpose of the larger study is to examine the impact of the full-day kindergarten programme in Ontario with kindergarten children, parents, and staff teams of early childhood educators and kindergarten teachers. The research is being carried out over time with children participating each year from junior or senior kindergarten until grade six. The play-based full-day kindergarten programme in Ontario began in the 2010/2011 school year. This first cohort participated in data collection each year; Grade 2 data collection was completed in the spring of 2014. In the 2012/2013 school year, a new cohort of full and half-day junior and senior kindergarten students were recruited to participate (children in this cohort completed the first round of data collection in the spring of 2013). For more information about the larger study please see (Pelletier, 2012a, 2012b, 2014a). For the purpose of this paper, analyses were conducted during the first round of data collection, therefore, with children in junior or senior kindergarten in both cohorts. The objective of the current paper was to compare half-day and play-based full-day kindergarten children's perspectives on two research questions:

Question 1: What is important about kindergarten?
Question 2: What is your favourite thing about school?

Setting and participants

Five hundred and fifty-seven participants (48% girls, 52% boys) from half-day and full-day kindergartens were included. The sample was composed of 306 full-day kindergarten children (mean age = 63 months) and 251 half-day kindergarten children (mean age = 61 months) from elementary schools in the western part of the Greater Toronto Area in Ontario, Canada. During the first round of data collection, 55% of the children were in junior kindergarten and the remaining 45% in senior kindergarten. Fifty-seven per cent of the participants were English-language learners, with the more predominant home languages of these children including Cantonese, Punjabi, and Urdu. Both mothers' and fathers' education levels were significantly higher in the half-day control group sites than in the full-day kindergarten group; this was controlled for in the analyses.

Procedure

As part of the larger study, finger puppet interviews were completed with the kindergarten children in both half- and full-day kindergarten classrooms. Children were withdrawn from the kindergarten class to take part in a series of research tasks including the interview. Children selected a finger puppet for themselves and one for the researcher to use. The researcher and child would then go through the interview using their puppets to communicate. The children were asked a series of questions aimed at understanding their perspectives and experiences of kindergarten.

Measures

Finger puppets were used to engage children in a playful way during the interview process. Finger puppets were used by both the participant and the researcher and answers were transcribed by the researcher. Data were coded by trained Master's and Ph.D. graduate students. Qualitative data from the child interviews were coded thematically and scored for the presence or absence of the themes. More specifically, the scripts from the interview questions reported in this paper were coded based on two emerging themes: social and academic responses. Social activities included responses that related to play and peer interactions. Academic responses included discussion about learning, work, and specific academic curriculum areas. Inter-rater reliability of 95% was obtained for the coding of children's interviews.

Results

Children's perspectives: what is important about kindergarten?

Two one-way ANOVAs were conducted to evaluate the relationship between kindergarten programmes (half-day and full-day), and what children perceive as important about kindergarten.

Descriptive statistics were carried out in order to understand the distribution of children's responses to the question, 'What is important about kindergarten?' by programme. In reviewing the findings, differences were seen particularly in the area of social and academic development. Based on the social nature of play interactions and the frequency of student responses, a new variable for social development was computed, which collapsed responses related to play and social development.

The first ANOVA analysed children's responses in relation to social development. The independent variable, kindergarten programme, included two levels: half-day kindergarten and full-day kindergarten. The dependent variable was children's responses related to social development. The ANOVA was significant, F (1556) = 8.42, $p = .004$. The strength of the relationship between kindergarten programme and children's responses related to social development, η^2, was moderate, with the kindergarten programme accounting for 14% of the variance of the dependent variable. The results demonstrate that children in full-day kindergarten programmes report social development significantly more often as being what is important about kindergarten ($M = .26$), than do children in half-day kindergarten programmes ($M = .17$).

A second ANOVA was conducted to understand children's responses in relation to academic development. The independent variable was the kindergarten programme, and the dependent variable was children's responses related to academic development. The ANOVA was significant, F (1556), = 8.30, $p = .004$. The strength of the relationship between the kindergarten programme and children's responses related to academic development, η^2, was moderate, with the kindergarten programme accounting for 15% of the variance of the dependent variable. The results demonstrate that children in full-day kindergarten programmes report academic development significantly less often as being what is important about kindergarten ($M = .07$) than do children in half-day kindergarten ($M = .15$). To better understand the findings from the interview question, 'what is important about kindergarten?' direct quotes from the children are provided. Please note that pseudonyms have been used in all examples.

Sample of responses from full-day kindergarten children:

'To play' (Jasmine)
'To share' (Blake)
'Kindergarten, I like friends' (Joshua)
'It's about we can have fun and learn stuff and have fun' (Elizabeth)
'Um, playing with your friends' (Paulina)
'We get to play and we get to play outside' (Corey)

Sample of responses from half-day kindergarten children:

'You learn for grade 1, and the important thing in grade 1 is to learn more about grade 2, then 2 to 3, 3 to 4, 4 to 5 – the last grade ... grade 5 learns about teenagers and then they learn about almost grown-ups' (Carolina)
'Kindergarten is important to learn how to write' (Joey)
'To work' (Luke)
'Doing work ... ' (Connie)
'For you to study' (Nick)
'Kids come to school and they work hard' (Sebastian)
'Kids come to school and they work hard' (Patricia)

Children's perspectives: favourite thing about school

Two one-way ANOVAs were conducted to understand children's responses to the question, 'What is your favourite thing about school?'

To better understand children's responses, descriptive statistics were run. We hypothesized that children's responses to this question would be distributed similarly to the previous question regarding what children think is important about kindergarten, that is that students in full-day programmes would mention play and social development more often than children in half-day kindergarten. However, in reviewing the findings, it appeared as if children in both programmes were responding similarly. In order to better understand children's responses, two one-way ANOVAs were conducted.

The first ANOVA analysed children's responses in relation to social development. The variable was computed in the same way as the previous example to include responses about play and social development. The ANOVA was not significant, demonstrating that there is no significant difference between full-day kindergarten and half-day kindergarten children's responses in relation to social development as being their favourite thing about school. Next, a second ANOVA was conducted to understand children's responses in relation to academic development. Again, no significant differences were found. This indicates that children in full-day kindergarten and half-day kindergarten do not differ in reporting academic development as being their favourite thing about school. To better understand this finding, samples of children's responses are included:

Sample of responses from full-day kindergarten children:

'Play at the creative centre' (Celia)
'Play at the play-dough and the house centre. And the water table and the sand' (Donota)
'Playing with my friends. And I like to play on the computer' (David)
'I like to play outside, go on the field, play with my friends, and go inside and play with my friends' (Franklin)
'Play with the puppets and do something a lot of the days and play and play and play and my friends do that with me' (Stephanie)

Sample of responses from half-day kindergarten children:

'Play with my friends' (Michael)
'I like to play, to play with my friends, go to cut and paste and try to make things with my friends'. (Stacy)
'I like to play with toys' (Charlie)
'I get to play with everything I get to play with my friends' (Liam)
'Play with my friends, and play time' (Isabella)

Interestingly, when comparing the sample of children's responses on the two questions, we found that some of the children in half-day kindergarten, who reported academic development as being important about kindergarten, later reported social aspects as being their favourite thing about school as demonstrated by Luke, Nick, and Patricia *'playing.'* Similarly, Connie responded, *'to play.'*

Discussion

The findings from this study show that reports about what is important about school differs based on the type of kindergarten programme students attend. Kindergarten children who follow a play-based full-day programme report social activities significantly more often as what is important about school than do students attending traditional half-day kindergarten. Conversely, students enrolled in half-day kindergarten cite academic activities as most important. However, regardless of programme type, kindergarten students overwhelmingly choose play as their favourite activity at school.

These results support the idea that kindergarten children are reliable, competent responders who are capable of providing diverse and informative reports of their experiences (Dockett & Perry, 2007; Smith et al., 2005). The diversity of the students' responses shows that participants are not simply answering questions randomly, but are communicating their opinions and preferences based on the type of programme in which they are enrolled. Previous research demonstrated that teachers' perspectives affect the ways students perceive learning (Dickinson & Smith, 1991); the findings from this study suggest that children's perspectives are influenced by programme type as well.

How students define a presented task at school affects their enjoyment of learning. Academic learning occurs within both half-day and play-based full-day kindergarten classrooms (Pelletier 2012a, 2012b, 2014a). However, students across programmes define these activities differently, which changes how they experience learning. Students in half-day programmes perceive academic activities or 'work' to be of the utmost importance in kindergarten, despite their overwhelming preference of 'play' activities. In this way, learning and play become mutually exclusive. Students in the play-based full-day kindergarten programme view 'play' as a central feature of their learning, citing it as an important component of their role as students. While doing academic 'work' is not necessarily a negative experience, play-based learning provides a more positive and expansive learning framework for students to concurrently develop social, emotional, cognitive, and academic skills (FDELK, 2010; Frost et al., 2008; Pascal, 2009). These findings suggest that play-based full-day kindergarten programmes are more aligned with what young children value and enjoy.

Policy changes in early childhood affect the way children perceive learning. As play-based learning becomes more prominent in policy documents (Miller & Almon, 2009), educators should be purposefully aware of how they interact with students. How an adult presents learning activities and their role within play in the classroom affects how students understand the learning experience. According to young children, 'play' activities are self-chosen, whereas any type of activity required by the teacher cannot be play (Ceglowski, 1997; Howard et al., 2002; Robson, 1993). Keeping in mind that child-directed play is most strongly associated with cognitive and affective development (Gmitrova & Gmitrova, 2004), teachers should be conscious of allowing students choices and control within the learning experience.

Students are the key stakeholders in kindergarten programmes, and future research should seek to capture their perspectives as a way to inform and evaluate programme policy. Moving forward, it would be beneficial to employ additional research strategies within the interview context that would allow for a deeper understanding of the kindergarten perspective. The use of open-ended interview questions would encourage students to provide more diverse and creative responses, allowing for a more complete interpretation of their ideas or opinions (Di Santo & Berman, 2012). Creating an interview context where the child feels comfortable sharing with the researcher is essential, and strategies such as role-playing, drawing, revisiting photographs or videos, and the use of developmentally appropriate props make for a more playful, child-friendly setting (Clark, 2005; Irwin & Johnson, 2005; Makin & Whiteman, 2006). Following from this, it would be useful to build on the findings from the current study by asking kindergarten students to expand on their definitions of 'play' and 'work' within the classroom. To fully understand the long-term effects of the play-based full-day programme, it would also be worthwhile to revisit student perception and achievement as they complete subsequent grades.

The use of children's perspectives in describing teaching and learning at the kindergarten level is uncommon, and there is a need within research to create more opportunities for children to be heard (Smith et al., 2005). Moving forward, future studies should strive to build from this research to construct a greater understanding of the kindergarten perspective. This study confirms that kindergarten students are reliable responders and it is important to consider their perspectives in education as they provide valid information on matters that affect them.

Disclosure statement

No potential conflict of interest was reported by the authors.

ORCiD

Kaitlyn Heagle http://orcid.org/0000-0003-0680-7182

References

Cannon, J. S., Jacknowitz, A., & Painter, G. (2006). Is full better than half? Examining the longitudinal effects of full-day kindergarten attendance. *Journal of Policy Analysis and Management, 25*(2), 299–321.

Cannon, J. S., Jacknowitz, A., & Painter, G. (2011). The effect of attending full-day kindergarten on English learner students. *Journal of Policy Analysis and Management, 30*(2), 287–309.

Carnes, G., & Albrecht, N. (2007). Academic and social-emotional effects of full-day kindergarten: The benefits of time. *Emporia State Research Studies, 43*(2), 64–72.

Ceglowski, D. (1997). Understanding and building upon children's perceptions of play activities in early childhood programs. *Early Childhood Education Journal, 25*(2), 107–112.

Chang, M., & Singh, K. (2008). Is all-day kindergarten better for children's academic performance? Evidence from the early childhood longitudinal study. *Australian Journal of Early Childhood, 33*(4), 35–42.

Clark, A. (2005). Listening to and involving young children: A review of research and practice. *Early Child Development and Care, 175*(6), 489–505.

Coleyshaw, L., Whitmarsh, J., Jopling, M., & Hadfield, M. (2010). Listening to children's perspectives: Improving the quality of provision in early years settings. *Department for Education, 5*, 33–46.

Cooper, H., Allen, A. B., Patall, E. A., & Dent, A. L. (2010). Effects of full-day kindergarten on academic achievement and social development. *Review of Educational Research, 80*(1), 34–70.

Corter, C., Janmohamed, Z., & Pelletier, J. (Eds.). (2012). *Toronto First Duty Phase 3 Report*. Toronto, ON: Atkinson Centre for Society and Child Development, OISE/University of Toronto.

Corter, C., & Park, N. W. (1993). *What makes exemplary kindergarten programs effective? Les programmes exemplaires de jardins d'enfants*. Toronto: Ministry of Education of Ontario.

Cryan, J., Sheehan, R., Wiechel, J., & Bandy-Hedden, I. G. (1992). Success outcomes of full-day kindergarten: More positive behavior and increased achievement in the years after. *Early Childhood Research Quarterly, 7*(2), 187–203.

DeCicca, P. (2007). Does full-day kindergarten matter? Evidence from the first two years of schooling. *Economics of Education Review, 26*(1), 67–82.

Dickinson, D. K., & Smith, M. W. (1991). Preschool talk: Patterns of teacher–child interaction in early childhood classrooms. *Journal of Research in Childhood Education, 6*(1), 20–29.

Di Santo, A., & Berman, R. (2012). Beyond the preschool years: Children's perceptions about starting kindergarten. *Children & Society, 26*, 469–479.

Dockett, S., & Perry, B. (2007). Trusting children's accounts in research. *Journal of Early Childhood Research, 5*(1), 47–63.

Elicker, J., & Mathur, S. (1997). What do they do all day? Comprehensive evaluation of a full-day kindergarten. *Early Childhood Research Quarterly, 12*, 459–480.

FDELK. (2010). *Full-day early learning kindergarten program draft version*. Toronto: Ministry of Education.

Frost, J. L., Wortham, S. C., & Reifel, R. S. (2008). *Play and child development*. Upper Saddle River, NJ: Pearson/Merrill Prentice Hall.

Gmitrova, V., & Gmitrova, J. (2004). The primacy of child-directed pretend play on cognitive competence in a mixed-age environment: Possible interpretations. *Early Child Development and Care, 174*(3), 267–279.

Graue, E. (2009). Reimagining kindergarten. *Education Digest*, March 2010.

Hall-Kenyon, K. M., Bingham, G. E., & Korth, B. B. (2009). How do linguistically diverse students fare in full-and half-day kindergarten? Examining academic achievement, instructional quality, and attendance. *Early Education and Development, 20*(1), 25–52.

Housden, R., & Kam, R. (1992). *Full-day kindergarten: A summary of research* (ERIC Document Reproduction Service No. ED 345 868). Carmichael, CA: San Juan Unified School District.

Howard, J. (2002). Eliciting young children's perceptions of play, work and learning using the activity apperception story procedure. *Early Child Development and Care, 172*(5), 489–502.

Howard, J., Jenvey, V., & Hill, C. (2006). Children's categorisation of play and learning based on social context. *Early Child Development and Care, 176*(3–4), 379–393.

Irwin, L. G., & Johnson, J. (2005). Interviewing young children: Explicating our practices and dilemmas. *Qualitative Health Research, 15*(6), 821–831.

Janzen, M. D. (2008). Where is the (postmodern) child in early childhood education research? *Early Years: An International Journal of Research and Development, 28*(3), 287–298.

Karrby, G. (1990). Children's conceptions of their own play. *Early Child Development and Care, 58*, 81–85.

Kauerz, K. (2005). *Full-day kindergarten: A study of state policies in the United States*. Denver, CO: Education Commission of the States.

Keating, I., Fabian, H., Jordan, P., Mavers, D., & Roberts, J. (2000). 'Well, I've not done any work today. I don't know why I came to school'. Perceptions of play in the reception class. *Educational Studies, 26*(4), 437–454.

King, N. (1979). Play: The Kindergartener's perspective. *The Elementary School Journal, 80*(2), 81–87.

Langstead, O. (1994). Looking at quality from a child's perspective. In P. Moss & A. Pence (Eds.), *Valuing quality in early childhood services* (pp. 28–42). Thousand Oaks, CA: Sage.

Lee, V. E., & Burkam, D. T. (2002). *Inequality at the starting gate: Social background differences in achievement as children begin school*. Washington, DC: Economic Policy Institute.

Lee, V. E., Burkam, D. T., Ready, D. D., Honigman, J., & Meisels, S. J. (2006). Full-day versus half-day kindergarten: In which program do children learn more? *American Journal of Education, 112*(2), 163–208.

Leseman, P., Rollenberg, L., & Rispens, J. (2001). Playing and working in kindergarten: Cognitive co-construction in two educational situations. *Early Childhood Research Quarterly, 16*, 363–384.

Levin, H. (2002). *The cost effectiveness of whole school reforms*. New York, NY: Eric Clearinghouse on Urban Education. (Urban Diversity Series, #114).

Makin, L., & Whiteman, P. (2006). Young children as active participants in the investigation of teaching and learning. *European Early Childhood Education Research Journal, 14*(1), 33–41.

Maltais, C., Herry, Y., Emond, I., & Mougeot, C. (2011). Les effects d'un programma de maternelle 4 ans A temps plein. *International Journal of Early Childhood, 43*(1), 67–85.

Miller, E., & Almon, J. (2009). *Crisis in the kindergarten: Why children need to play in school.* College Park, MD: Alliance for Childhood.

Pascal, C. E. (2009). *With our best future in mind: Implementing early learning in Ontario.* Toronto: Government of Ontario.

Pelletier, J. (1998). A comparison of children's understanding of school in regular English language and French immersion kindergartens. *Canadian Modern Language Review, 55*(2), 239–259.

Pelletier, J. (1999). "Tell me what you do at school" … A comparison of children's school scripts in English first language and French immersion second language kindergarten programmes. *Language and Education, 13*(3), 207–222.

Pelletier, J. (2012a). *Key findings from year 1 of Full-Day Early Learning Kindergarten in Peel.* Toronto: Dr. Eric Jackman Institute of Child Study, Ontario Institute for Studies in Education.

Pelletier, J. (2012b). *Key findings from year 2 of Full-Day Early Learning Kindergarten in Peel.* Toronto: Dr. Eric Jackman Institute of Child Study, Ontario Institute for Studies in Education.

Pelletier, J. (2014a). *Key findings from year 3 of Full-Day Early Learning Kindergarten in Peel.* Toronto: Ontario Institute for Studies in Education.

Pelletier, J. (2014b). Ontarios full-day kindergarten: A bold public policy initiative. *Public Sector Digest*, June Issue: Education, 41–49.

Pianta, R. C., Cox , M. J., & Snow, K. L. (2007). *School readiness and the transition to kindergarten in the era of accountability.* Baltimore, MD: Paul H Brookes Publishing.

Plucker, J. A., Eaton, J. J., Rapp, K. E., Lim, W., Nowak, J., Hansen, J. A., & Bartleson, A. (2004). The effects of full day versus half day kindergarten: Review and analysis of national and Indiana data. *The Center for Evaluation and Education Policy, 21*, 21–26.

Raskin, C. F., Mankato, M. N., & Haar, J. M. (2009). Full-day kindergarten results in significant achievement gains. *Research and Best Practices That Advance the Profession of Education Administration, 21*, 21–27.

Ray, K., & Smith, M. C. (2010). The kindergarten child: What teachers and administrators need to know to promote academic success in all children. *Early Childhood Education Journal, 38*(1), 5–18.

Reynolds, A. J., & Temple, J. A. (2008). Cost-effective early childhood development programs from preschool to third grade. *Annual Review of Clinical Psychology, 4*, 109–139.

Robson, S. (1993). "Best of all I like choosing time" Talking with children about play and work. *Early Child Development and Care, 92*(1), 37–51.

Smith, A., Duncan, J., & Marshall, K. (2005). Children's perspectives on their learning: Exploring methods. *Early Child Development and Care, 175*(6), 473–487.

Stephen, C. (2003). What makes all-day provision satisfactory for three and four year olds? *Early Child Development and Care, 173*(6), 577–588.

Timmons, K., Pelletier, J., & Corter, C. (2016). Understanding children's self-regulation within different classroom contexts. *Early Child Development and Care, 186*(2), 249–267.

Villegas, M. (2005). *Full-day kindergarten: Expanding learning opportunities.* San Fransisco, CA: WestEd.

Walston, J., & West, J. (2004). *Full-day and half-day kindergarten in the United States: Findings from the early childhood longitudinal study, kindergarten class of 1998–99.* NCES 2004-078. National Center for Education Statistics.

Interpersonal fields of play

Sophie Jane Alcock

ABSTRACT
Ethnographic methods are used to investigate infant–toddlers relationships in an early childhood setting. The metaphorical and emotionally based concepts of holding [Winnicott, D. W. (1960). The theory of the parent–infant relationship. *International Journal of Psychoanalysis*, 41, 585–595.] and container: contained [Bion, W. R. (1962). *Learning from experience*. London: William Heinemann.] provide complementary angles for interpreting pre-verbal, pre-symbolic, conscious and unconscious processes in the play of young children feeling and thinking, connecting and communicating with and in their bodies, sensually within interpersonal fields [Lewin, K. (1935). *A dynamic theory of personality*. New York, NY: McGraw-Hill]. Vitality affects [Stern, D. (2010). *Forms of vitality: Exploring dynamic experience in psychology, the arts, psychotherapy, and development*. Oxford: Oxford University Press] add the felt-tone of moving bodies to these interpretations. The complex relational ways in which these young toddlers played, co-creating interpersonal fields of play are the focus of this paper.

Introduction

Concepts associated with interpersonal field theory (Ferro, 2009; Lewin, 1935; D. B. Stern, 2013a, 2013b) and relational psychoanalytic theory (Benjamin, 2004; Mitchell, 1991; Mitchell & Aron, 1999) expand understandings and interpretations of the matrix-like interconnecting layers in young children's play and in fields of play. This paper presents case-study data from a research project that focussed on infant–toddlers relationships in one early childhood care and education (ECCE) setting. The complexly interconnecting relational ways in which these young toddlers played are the focus of this paper.

Teachers at Puriri ECCE centre wanted to better understand the relational attachment experiences of their youngest pre-verbal children. I became involved as an interested academic, teacher, and researcher who had recently moved to Auckland and wanted to make connections and build some grass roots early childhood relationships. The research project that developed out of our conversations focused very broadly on infant–toddlers emotional experiences of belonging and attachment, with the main research question addressed in this paper becoming: 'What is the role of the conceptual frameworks of holding, containment, and interpersonal fields in babies and one-year-old children's relational engagement with their environment?'

Emotions are understood as 'relational experiences lived through bodies; bodies that co-regulate their movements with the movements of others' (Garvey & Fogel, 2008, p. 62). The emphasis on bodies relating fits with infant–toddlers' pre-verbal ways of feeling, thinking, and coming to know themselves and the world, in and with their physical bodies.

This paper explores several interconnecting thematic and metaphorical concepts that emerged out of the research process and readings around attachment and belonging. Concepts of *holding*, (Ogden, 2004; Winnicott, 1960, 1974) *container-contained*, (Bion, 1962; Ogden, 2004), *vitality affect* felt in bodies (D. Stern, 2010), and the relational *interpersonal field* (Lewin, 1935; D. B. Stern, 2013a, 2013b) all expand understandings of the experiences of pre-verbal toddlers who lived in this home-like setting most week days. I suggest that these relational concepts may be more widely used to expand teacher understandings of infant–toddlers' emotional experiences in early childhood settings, with further implications for teachers' self-other awareness.

Conceptual framework

Continuous movement and emotion are integral to the concepts addressed in this paper and to play. The word *e-motion* conveys movement and as Sheets-Johnstone (2009) eloquently points out, movement is fundamental in the interconnectedness of all life; every living thing moves.

> When we strip the lexical band-aid '*embodiment*' off the more than 350 year old wound inflicted by the Cartesian split of mind and body, we find *animation*, the foundational dimension of living. Everything living is animated. Flowers turn towards the sun; pill bugs curl into spheres; lambs rise on untried legs, finding their way into patterned coordinations. (Sheets-Johnstone, 2009, p. 375, italics in original)

The *interpersonal field* (Ferro, 2009; Lewin, 1935; D. B. Stern, 2013a, 2013b) includes the emotions, feelings and thoughts, conscious and unconscious (out of awareness) that pervade the group space between and in people, which in this case study was Puriri centre's infant–toddler area. As part of this relational field and as a participant researcher, my conscious and unconsciously felt thoughts also sit within the observations and the research process. My body–mind is integral to the field as figure and ground blend, interconnecting across space and time (Merleau-Ponty, 1968). This conscious inclusion of unconscious and invisible feelings makes the concept of interpersonal field profound in a way that distinguishes it from context and physical environment and prioritizes a focus on feelings and emotions.

The metaphorical and emotionally based concepts of *holding* (Winnicott, 1960) and *container: contained* (Bion, 1962), as used here, flow into interpersonal field. They provide different, yet complementary angles for appreciating and interpreting the pre-verbal, pre-symbolic, conscious and unconscious processes at play when observing very young children feeling and thinking, connecting and communicating with and in their bodies, relating sensually within interpersonal fields. Awareness of *vitality affects* (D. Stern, 2010) adds the energy of emotion to interpretations of infant–toddler bodies playing interactively – energetically – within interpersonal fields.

Holding, as described by Winnicott (1960, 1974), refers to the security of both being and feeling held. More than the physical maternal holding of an infant, holding also involves feeling safely securely at ease, being internally and externally held. It includes feelings of being in and with time, so able to just carry on being, (in the moment) not overtaken by time. A holding environment includes these body-based feelings of being held internally, feeling secure in and with the wider interpersonal field and the world. This security extends beyond physical bodies to include *third* spaces in-between participants (Benjamin, 2004). Securely held young children feel able to move away from the secure base of their caregivers, to explore, to play, and to simply be. Thus, holding environments may expand to become interpersonal fields of play.

In playing, as in dreaming, feelings and thoughts, conscious and unconscious, may be turned upside-down, flipped about, played with and processed. Bion's (1962) container-contained metaphor refers to unconscious sense-making and fitting together processes that emerge, sometimes symbolically in young children's play and in dreams.

Feeling held enables the unconscious meaning and sense-making processes of containing, of processing thoughts that may be half-felt but not yet recognized, understood, or known. As Ogden points out:

> The container is a process ... It is the capacity for the unconscious psychological work of dreaming, ... The contained, like the container, is not a static thing, but a living process that in health is continuously expanding and changing. The term refers to thoughts (in the broadest sense of the word) that are in the process of being derived from one's lived emotional experience. (2004, p. 1356)

Thoughts are felt; the feeling of feelings and thinking about feelings involves emotional processing: container-contained processing.

While the actual words *holding* and *container: contained* can sound and feel rather statically dry, they refer to dynamically shifting processes observed in and amongst children playing within interpersonal – relational – fields.

The concept of vitality adds the tone of energy to the mix of children playing. Vitality affects allude to the subjective feeling tone of and in experience; the felt body-based feelings that are so fundamentally obvious that we can easily overlook them. D. Stern (2010, p. 5) has described vitality as: 'a whole ... It is a Gestalt that emerges from the theoretically separate experiences of movement, force, time, space and intention'. Young children playing exude vitality in feeling and expressing emotions such as joy, sadness, love, hate, envy, anger, and frustration. And it is children's moving bodies, their motion, that interconnects and is core to play and to emotions.

These concepts: vitality, holding, container-contained and interpersonal field, applied relationally, expand ways of viewing, interpreting and understanding interconnectedness in the emotional experiences of pre-verbal children, and their teachers. These same concepts reflexively expanded my researcher ways of interpreting the observed experience of pre-verbal children relating with and in play. I was implicitly interconnected with the observations.

Centre philosophy and background

Puriri ECCE centre is a private community-based centre located in the city of Auckland, in Aotearoa-New Zealand. I was new to Auckland, teaching prospective early childhood teachers at a tertiary institution and missing the early childhood centre contacts of my home city, Wellington. When the owner-manager of Puriri centre suggested we might research how their youngest children fared, with no formal primary caregiving system, I jumped at the opportunity. I was looking for the world of ECCE in Auckland.

Puriri early childhood centre's philosophy emphasized principles of sustainability and interconnectedness which did not sit easily with the perceived dyadic and individualistic nature of primary caregiving. Their written philosophy states:

> At Puriri centre we (teachers, children, families) work together to address the environmental issues, which face Aotearoa and the rest of the world.
>
> *The principles of this community are*:
> Care for the self
> Care for others
> Care for our immediate and global environment that sustains us
> A commitment to Aotearoa's bicultural heritage, particularly our responsibility to exercise kaitiakitanga (guardianship of the environment)

These sustainability principles provided a rationale supporting teachers' views of primary caregiving as an unsustainable and inappropriate model (at least in this centre), with children and adults viewed as interconnected parts of the collective centre. Primary caregiving systems, as these teachers understood them, overemphasized individualistic one-on-one relationships between children and teachers.

Furthermore, sustainability fits with indigenous Maori worldviews in emphasizing the interconnectedness of all phenomena and Puriri centre also wanted to prioritize bicultural Maori values. Ideas of the interconnectedness of all phenomena are implicit in Maori beliefs, expressed in proverbs (whakatoiki) such as: 'Manaaki whenua, manaaki tangata, haere whakamua', roughly translated as: 'care for the land – care for the people – go forward bringing together old and new knowledges'.

Manaaki means to cherish, conserve, and sustain. Whenua encompasses the soil, rocks plants, animals, and the people inhabiting the land – the tangata whenua. People are linked physically and spiritually to the land – it is the earth through which we are connected to our ancestors and all the generations that will come after us. Whenua is the place where we stand; it is also the placenta.

This centre philosophy was integral to the felt ethos of Puriri; it was also visible in the fair trade coffee and bananas, the edible gardens, cloth nappies and recycling toy systems, as well as in the shared caregiving practices.

The under-twos' area functioned as a secure holding environment for up to 10 infants and toddlers who lived there, before later transitioning into the larger, noisier, and more populated adjoining area when they were two years old. Actual numbers of children and teachers fluctuated flexibly with several three-year-olds regularly choosing to be with the babies and wanting to help care for the babies and several teachers floating between the under and over two's areas accordingly. Upwards of two teachers were usually present. In New Zealand, Aotearoa government funding subsidies and early childhood regulations are tied to children being either under or over two years old and this was reflected in teacher:child ratios as well as the group size. Puriri teachers prioritized family and community connections and several of the children also had siblings at the centre.

Ethics and methods

Staff at Puriri centre were familiar with research protocols having been part of several centre-based national research projects. They had developed a research policy addressing ethical issues of protection, rights, and responsibilities for all participants. In this project, Mary, the centre owner-manager, informed all the families with children in the under two's area about the proposed research and their rights to choose not to participate. She had obtained consent from all but one family before I even met with families to further explain the research process and answer questions and request written consent from the parents of children in the under two-year-olds' area. The complicated consent process around the use of video for data gathering including reassuring parents that video was primarily for data gathering and photos would not be put on the web. Informed consent for all data gathering was obtained from the parents of all the under two's children and their teachers.

The ethics committee of the tertiary institution where I worked approved the ethics application five months after submitting the initial application. The summer break had interrupted the process and the committee was very cautious about video usage with young children. This waiting period became a familiarization time, during which I visited and developed relationships with children, parents, and teachers in the centre. The time spent hanging out in Puriri centre enabled the emergence of a third space, an in-between phase within the research process, where relaxed familiarity became our shared priority rather than inquisitive observational research. When the in-depth observational part of the study began, I had become a familiar friendly visitor to Puriri and was no longer a stranger to the toddlers. This was important; infant–toddlers who were fearful of strangers could so easily confuse and confound this research. As part of the centre policy, the teachers had also asked me to spend time getting to know them, and the children, before beginning the video data-gathering process.

The concept of thirdness was implicit throughout the research process, including in my attempts to focus on the intersubjective relational spaces between children, adults, and things. As a researcher, I explicitly tried to hone my awareness towards whatever might be happening or emerging between these very young children, the environment and myself. Thus, at times, I simply surrendered to the research process of feeling and listening, while watching and ruminating.

The research followed ethnographic methods and as a participant observer, an inside-outsider, I aimed for minimal disruption to the everyday practices and routines at Puriri. As well as eyes, ears, voice, and heart, I used a small hand-held video camera as an invaluable aid for observing preverbal children, who predominantly used body language to relate and communicate feelings and desires. Video enabled me to revisit and reflect deeply on what I saw and felt, with the video images as memory prompts. I made notes while visiting and tried to write notes immediately following visits, while my memory was fresh. That worked well when I did not need to rush away to teach. I selectively and purposely focused on five regularly attending children whose ages at the start of the project were 7–20 months. The following examples are focused on these children's interactions. Observations were focused on the children's relationships generally, so who and what they connected with in this interpersonal relational field of Puriri centre.

Over a year, I visited Puriri centre approximately every fortnight for between one and three hours (apart from during semester breaks when the composition of children attending Puriri also changed). I came to enjoy catching up with staff as well as children and parents. I did not always use the video camera or take photos, the comfort of the children, parents, and teachers being a priority. My pre-service teaching work included visiting students in ECCE centres all around the city. Coming back to Puriri began to feel like returning to an oasis of sanity – a secure community and secure base for me in a place where commercial for-profit ECCE chains have proliferated, popping up like wild mushrooms across the urban landscape.

Data with interpretive analyses are presented here in the form of two examples of toddlers playing in different ways with interpretations grounded in observed experience and informed by concepts associated with relational psychoanalytic literature. These two examples illuminate layers of complexity in young children's play activity within interpersonal fields in quite different ways. The first example is longer: it includes detailed focus initially on one child, Nina, relating, containing, connecting and holding things, in the form of a baby doll and fabric wrapping materials. The second example focuses initially on one material thing, in the form of a large cane picnic basket that serves to mediate children relating, containing, feeling held, and connecting. The wider interpersonal field of Puriri centre becomes a dominant feature in both examples.

Example 1: Baby-doll wrapping play: covering and smothering; holding and containing

Background

For several weeks, 18-month Nina had been spending hours every day intensely playing with wrapping baby dolls in fabric. The teachers and I all commented on her 'obsession'. The dolls were realistic life-size rubber babies, about half Nina's own size. The wrapping fabrics included old cloth nappies, baby shawls, scarves, and bed covers. Nina's wrapping activity was incredibly physical. She exuded vitality (D. Stern, 2010) with force, sometimes lying over the doll and on the floor, squashing and trying to fit fabric, baby doll and her own body together.

The inside–outside in-between space where Nina played was a covered and enclosed deck area, slightly apart from both the out and inside areas, yet connected to them. This holding environment also served as a pathway to and from the back entrance to the house. A group of three one-year-old children and a teacher played in the covered sandpit on the same deck, only a few metres away, on the edge of Nina's space.

Repetition in wrapping play

Nina's play intrigued me and I visited Puriri more frequently simply to observe, ponder and wonder at her activity. On this occasion, I observed her intensely engaged with containing by wrapping the baby doll for over 20 absorbing minutes. She seemed to appreciate my sitting nearby, occasionally glancing towards me and, on one occasion, passing the baby doll for me to hold while she wrestled with spreading the shawl on the floor.

Trusting and feeling securely held enabled Nina to play so freely. Her body exuded energetic vitality and concentration as she half-wrapped first herself, then the baby doll, connecting and attempting to contain everything in one big chaotic bundle. After repeatedly shaking the shawl, Nina spread the shawl on the floor in front of her, placed the baby doll on it, and proceeded to tightly wrap the shawl over the doll and over herself. In reality, she could have smothered a baby with both her body and the shawl as she struggled with wrapping the baby doll. Nina groaned and moaned while moving continuously, stretching her body-self out, around, over and under cloth and baby doll. She sounded like a frustrated weightlifter, her groans accompanying strenuous exercise and frustration when baby doll and shawl would not fit together as intended. Muffled words blended with her groans: 'my babeee, meeee, babeee meee, myyy, oooooh … .'

Watching Nina, I wondered

Was she re-playing dressing herself? Nina did want to be in charge of dressing her own body. Without a body, we are nobody. We have no self.

She had half-wrapped her body before trying to wrap the baby doll. Nina had recently begun to dress herself with huge perseverance strongly resisting offers of assistance. Finding the places for arms and legs, and fitting through soft fabric holes was challenging. Fitting the baby doll into the shawl – a material and metaphorical container – was similarly challenging. For Nina, the shawl possibly shared the feeling of clothes. The shawl, like clothes, folded into another body-containing layer, like another skin. Nina drapes a see-through cloth over her own body, also like a translucent layer of skin. She then fetches an old cloth nappy with which she continues her baby wrapping–squashing–smothering process.

I wondered why Nina began each episode of doll wrapping by covering her own face and head, as if hiding and practising on herself before covering the baby doll. Her actions reminded me of young children thinking that if they cannot see us, we cannot see them. Or perhaps the cloth connected her to the doll and to herself somehow, like another layer of translucent skin? (Bick, 1968).

Life in this baby-doll wrapping play looked and felt like a struggle. Was doll control a way of being agentic and feeling feelings of being in control? Perhaps Nina was playing at smothering the new baby Sam, that her favourite teacher Jan now held (instead of holding Nina). Whatever the interpretations, this holding environment enabled Nina to repetitively wrap and rewrap the baby doll, and herself, processing dressing, fitting together, squashing and smothering, mastering processes. Repetition in play supports learning as meanings and feelings are internalized in the meaning-making containing process of repetitive play activity (Bion, 1962; Vygotsky, 1978, 2004).

Nina thinks and speaks her feelings symbolically, and with her body, in this physically challenging, and absorbing baby-doll wrapping play. Perhaps she was simply expressing struggles and frustrations around everyday experiences, like dressing herself. Communicating without words is challenging and frustrating for young children who are learning to speak with words. Nina understands far more than she can say.

Nina brings layers of complexity to this layered wrapping activity. What motivates her baby-doll wrapping obsession? Is it in the wrapping, or the baby doll, the fabric, the caring, the hiding, covering, smothering, the holding and protecting, or the creation of a fabric skin-like container for the baby? Who or what might the doll represent? Perhaps the doll functions as a material container for Nina's aggressive projections? Or is the doll Sam or Nina? She does seem to be playing her feelings around being dressed and dressing herself, being clothed, smothered, protected, and frustrated. Whatever the theoretical explanations are, Nina does put a great deal of vitality, feeling and time into this repetitive doll-wrapping play. I watch fascinated, intrigued by the complexity.-

Layers of wrapping: Interconnecting interpersonal fields

Teacher Jan comes into the field, seating herself on a step close to Nina, holding new baby Sam (seven months old) in her lap. Another toddler, Ben, follows. He seats himself beside Jan, snuggling as close as he can get without pushing baby Sam off Jan's lap. Ben proceeds to carefully and clumsily place a pair of long woollen socks over baby Sam's head covering, containing and hiding Sam's head. While speaking 'duh duh, ba ba ba' sounds, Ben sits back a little and points towards Sam, before rearranging the sock-hat more tightly over her head. I wonder if he is consciously imitating Nina's baby wrapping schema, and think not.

Perhaps this baby-doll wrapping, and sock-hat dressing is a play on covering and smothering baby Sam? Are Nina and Ben both envious of baby Sam's favoured place in Jan's lap? Sam has supplanted both Ben and Nina's place with Jan. Sam cannot even crawl; she is now the baby that Jan holds most. But when Jan is seated, as now, Ben can almost squeeze into her lap alongside Sam. He tries.

Ben and Nina regularly follow and encircle Jan as their favourite teachers. She is the one they follow most despite Puriri centre having no formal primary caregiver system. Teacher Jan's body does exude a calm caregiver presence and she is usually in the infant–toddler area for three–four full days every week.

As the area surrounding Nina's doll-wrapping play becomes busier, I become increasingly aware of the layers of wrapping activity connecting players across interpersonal field of relations. Wrapping play seems to spread outwards from Nina's individual baby-doll wrapping beginnings.

Ema (three years old) strolls into the space, looking fixedly at Nina's wrapping cloth nappy; Ema wants this nappy to wrap her baby doll. Picking up on Ema's body signals, teacher Jan calmly suggests to Ema that she find another 'blanket' to offer Nina as a 'swap', in exchange for the desired nappy. Ema goes away and quickly returns with a doll-size quilt which she holds out to Nina who generously gives Ema the nappy and takes the offering. Teacher Jan talks the children's negotiating actions in friendly tone. 'Ema has another blanket for you Nina ... can you give her the nappy.' It is a padded quilt, slightly smaller than the nappy, so possibly more manageable for Nina and possibly more attractive. Nina continues wrapping, squashing containing and holding her baby doll, wrestling with fitting doll, covering and herself together with the quilt.

Holding environments expanding into interpersonal fields

Over this 20-minute observation, not only Nina, but Ben, Ema and teacher Jan were all involved with holding and wrapping babies in different ways. Teacher Jan, holding new baby Sam, seemed to be both central and peripheral to the wrapping play. Certainly, these children did encircle her on this, and other occasions. Jan mediated the negotiated blanket swap. And in carrying Sam, she modelled physically holding babies. Teacher Jan's larger adult size and her physical presence ensured that she felt central to the wrapping play, even when she was not physically in the middle. When Nina, Ben and Ema played off to one side and in another room, Jan still felt central. The children gravitated towards her. Teacher Jan exuded holding. She held them psychically, safely, securely apart, yet connected in a holding environment, which also fed into ever-changing interpersonal fields.

Holding together over time

On another occasion, I observed Jan picking up a distraught Nina and saying to her, while explaining to me: 'I'll just hold you back together again.' A few minutes later, a calm, emotionally contained Nina slipped out of Jan's arms, slid down her legs and resumed playing. In such actions, Jan implicitly expressed physical, spiritual and psychological dimensions of holding and belonging for these infant–toddlers and herself. These holding, containing, caring actions contributed to the centre ethos, the freedom to play and the co-creation of the interpersonal field of feelings that pervaded Puriri.

On visiting Puriri about 10 months later, I was intrigued to see baby Sam, now about 17 months old, playing intently with wrapping baby dolls. Instead of being wrapped, she was now wrapping, a part of this interpersonal field.

The layers of wrapping in example one show thinking with feeling-containing – as a physical struggle, between baby dolls, fabric and the toddlers' own bodies. The physicality of bodies fitting into spaces is also a theme in this second example, though the containing by fitting together process does not look so much like a struggle; at times, it is quite playful.

Example 2: basket play: containing and fitting together

Background

The room is the place where the one-year-old children and babies play, eat and generally spend most of their non-sleeping time when inside. A very large curved cane picnic basket with two flap-top door-like lids lies on its side, nestled against a set of wooden climbing-crawling steps on one side of the infant–toddler room. The basket has been recycled to Puriri centre by a family who no longer want it. In keeping with their sustainability philosophy, most of the 'toys' in this place are recycled from family homes.

This oversized basket has been sitting here on its side, avoided and ignored, since Monday, which is surprising given its size. Today is Thursday and no children have played with it. Nell and Quentin (both about 18 months old) have been absorbed in repetitively practising climbing up and down the steps that sit beside the basket. How can they have not seen the basket? Perhaps, like adults, children see what they want or need to see, and this basket was a huge invisible intrusion for the three days that it was ignored. It did not fit with the children's preconceived impressions of their room, so was not noticed.

Familiarity and noticing anew: whole-body sensory play with an object

Today, these two toddlers almost simultaneously notice the basket. Nell pushes it around so it slides, glides, and spins around in one spot, on the wooden floor; she opens the flap-lid and proceeds to crawl inside it. Quentin leans against the basket and swings shut the flap-lid door behind Nell's feet. Nell continues crawling, coming out the other open flap-lid door. The basket is too narrow inside for bodies to turn around. Its curved tunnel shape fits, enveloping and containing Nell's body like a cocoon, a snail shell, a womb, or a birth canal.

The children play with the basket, just as they play with other objects, by using their bodies and sometimes turn-taking. They explore it in relation to their bodies, just as they had done with the climbing steps. The steps offered another way of moving their toddling bodies, legs first, alongside each other and apart. The basket demands individual whole-body wriggling as Nell moulds her body into and inside the curved basket. Venturing inside the basket, one after the other, the children explore their feeling bodies from the inside out.

I wonder

How does it feel to be so enclosed, held, contained, in a body-fitting shell? A thick outer-skin? A safe hiding place? The shutting and opening flaps at both ends seem important; they enclose the tunnel basket, shutting out and enclosing Nell inside, apart from others, not seen, invisible, but we know she is there in the tunnel, shell, womb, birth-canal basket.

The ways in which children adapted this large woven cane basket object to fit their bodies in fields of play are fascinating and interpretations are many. Over the next weeks, the basket moved between the under and the over two-year-olds' areas in the wider Puriri centre. Children put objects into the basket, as well as themselves, when bodies were small enough. Carol, three years old, understood that her body was almost too large to squeeze into the basket, so she removed her jacket and like an explorer on an adventure, opened a flap and crawled into and through the basket. Pushing open the shut flap at the other end, she emerged triumphant. The basket held things and people. It functioned as a container for feelings felt in bodies as well as for holding toys and other things.

Perhaps most significantly, this free exploratory basket play required space, time, materials, and an open ethos that supported children to play freely with objects co-creating their interpersonal fields. It is significant that the teachers let the basket sit ignored for three days before the children saw and began incorporating it into their play as a major play stimulus. In simply letting the basket lie, the teachers empowered the children to decide when to notice and begin using the basket in their play.

The basket play provoked imaginative and creative ways of being and thinking in bodies and with feelings, dreamlike. In such wild ways, play is like dreaming and in play, children can dream unconscious thoughts that are not yet thought (Bion, 1962). Thus, through imaginative playing, emotions may be felt and contained.

Discussion

Vitality affects connecting children

Both the baby-doll wrapping and the basket play proceeded at child's pace, extending over days and weeks as children revisited, repeated, and replayed themes that mattered for them, using processes of holding, feeling and being held, fitting together and containing. Their play exuded bodily felt energy, described by D. Stern as 'vitality affect' (2010). Though difficult to define concisely, vitality was an obvious quality in the play. Vitality empowered children with confidence and agency expressed in their body-based actions of wrapping, holding, containing, with dolls, fabric, the basket, themselves and each other, within the interpersonal field of Puriri. D. Stern (2010) has identified five components of vitality affect as 'movement, force, time, space and intention' (p. 4), explaining that these components operate together as an emotion-based gestalt. It is likely that the activity and movement, – the vitality affect – in these children's bodies also created interconnecting patterns of connectedness between these children playing loosely together. Mirror neurones within individual children's bodies fire empathically and responsively in tune with the activities of other moving bodies (Ammaniti & Ferrari, 2013).

Attachment themes at play in the interpersonal field

Attachment theory emphasizes the critical importance for infant toddlers of having deeply loving relationships with a few other people and has important implications for later psychological well-being (Cassidy & Shaver, 2008; Fonagy & Target, 2005). Emotional attachment patterns are learnt and internalized relationally, in early childhood. These toddlers played relationally, symbolically, unconsciously, and implicitly with themes of attachment.

Thus, themes of covering, hiding and finding, coming and going, enclosure and freedom, container: contained, security and feeling held pervade these two play examples, and many other examples of young children's play (Alcock, 2016). The play of infant–toddlers is particularly interesting because it is almost without words, yet so rich and brimming with feelings.

At times, this play looked and felt surreal and dreamlike, when watching Quentin shut the basket lid on Nell and Nina struggle with fitting her baby doll inside a fabric shawl.

Themes of belonging, attachment and fitting together address the relational environment, which was the focus of this project. The original research question asked about 'the nature of the relational environment for the infant–toddlers in this ECCE centre where eco-sustainability is an overarching philosophical principle.'

Despite the lack of a formal primary caregiving system in Puriri centre, the small numbers of toddlers and the same few consistent and caring teachers ensured that these children did form reciprocally loving relationships with those teachers, such as Jan, in example 1, who spent most time with them. Despite no formal key caregiver system, teacher Jan provided a secure base; she was a 'good enough' caregiver from whom these toddlers ventured out to play with wrapping baby dolls and selves. The basket, the teachers and children, the time, place and space, also contributed to co-creating secure interpersonal and relational fields of play in example 2.

Good enough caregiving

Though Puriri centre did not implement a formal primary caregiving system, caring relationships did develop between children, their caregivers and the parents. I frequently observed parents and teachers taking, talking and connecting when children were dropped off and picked up. The staffing rosters did ensure that the same few teachers were regularly rostered to the under-twos' area, which did ensure some consistency in caregiving for the infant–toddlers and their parents. Half way through the project, the owner-manager decided to trial moving staff around between the over and under twos area. The resultant chaos ensured that the trial was aborted within a week. During that time, I observed teachers trying to physically hold too many babies while working in the over-twos area. Young toddlers seem to encircle teacher Jan's body, an island of security amidst the noisier, bigger, busier worlds of the three four-year-old children in the over two's area at Puriri.

Sustainability and the capacity to care

Principles of sustainability as care, as articulated in Puriri's written philosophy, implicitly underpinned the play in these two examples. With a focus on feelings, care includes the capacity to feel (Hollway, 2006). These examples include children being supported and allowed to feel and express a wide range of feelings including, envy, anger, jealousy, and hatred as well as more acceptable feelings of love, kindness, and happiness, within secure holding environments. Thus, Nina could aggressively smother the baby doll, Ben could disappear baby Sam under a sock-hat, and Nell could collapse in tearful pieces and be held together again. Quentin could also shut the flap basket door on Nell, getting rid of her. Care is complex and includes feeling.

Conclusion

Children played with the basket, the blankets, and the dolls, with feeling, in ways that connected them as objects and subjects, almost intersubjectively. I wondered about the feelings these child subjects projected into the wrapping dolls and the containing basket, as objects. Feelings as interconnecting threads of emotion link children, subjects and objects. Interconnectionism too is also complex.

From a pragmatic perspective, the freedom for toddlers to simply choose to play with these and other material objects feels fundamental. However, this freedom depends on conditions including the feeling of being securely held, in a holding environment. Feeling held enabled these children to play with feeling and to contain feelings, with vitality, within ever-evolving interpersonal relational fields of being. In practising the centre philosophy of shared care as sustainability, the teachers at Puriri centre provided a caring holding environment. The small number of children and the consistency in caregivers contributed to the shared care at Puriri centre looking like primary caregiving, though without the formal structure, or the potentially individualistic language of primary caregiving. The centre's philosophy prioritized an interconnected understanding of care and of all phenomena. This sort of interconnectedness has implications too for how we as teachers and researchers view ourselves in relation to and with children, families and communities where we interact and which we are part of.

Disclosure statement

No potential conflict of interest was reported by the authors.

References

Alcock, S. J. (2016). *Young children playing: Relational approaches to emotional learning in early childhood*. Singapore: Springer.

Ammaniti, M., & Ferrari, P. (2013). Vitality affects in Daniel Stern's thinking – a psychological and neurobiological perspective. *Infant Mental Health Journal, 34*(5), 367–375. doi:10.1002/imhj.21405

Benjamin, J. (2004). Beyond doer and done to: An intersubjective view of thirdness. *The Psychoanalytic Quarterly, LXXIII*(1), 5–46. doi:10.1002/j.2167-4086.2004.tb00151.x

Bick, E. (1968). The experience of the skin in early object relations. *International Journal of Psychoanalysis, 49*, 484–486.

Bion, W. R. (1962). *Learning from experience*. London: William Heinemann.

Cassidy, J., & Shaver, P. (2008). *Handbook of attachment, second edition: Theory, research, and clinical applications*. Retrieved from http://VUW.eblib.com/patron/FullRecord.aspx?p=360938

Ferro, A. (2009). Transformations in dreaming and characters in the psychoanalytic field. *International Journal of Psychoanalysis, 90*, 209–230.

Fonagy, P., & Target, M. (2005). Bridging the transmission gap: An end to an important mystery of attachment research? *Attachment and Human Development, 7*(3), 333–343. doi:10.1080/14616730500269278

Garvey, A., & Fogel, A. (2008). Emotions and communication as a dynamic developmental system. *Espaciotiempo*, 2, 62–73.

Hollway, W. (2006). *The capacity to care: Gender and ethical subjectivity*. London: Routledge.

Lewin, K. (1935). *A dynamic theory of personality*. New York, NY: McGraw-Hill.

Merleau-Ponty, M. (1968). *The visible and the invisible*. Evanston, IL: Northwestern University Press.

Mitchell, S. A. (1991). Contemporary perspectives on self: Toward an integration. *Psychoanalytic Dialogues, 1*(2), 121–147. doi:10.1080/10481889109538889

Mitchell, S. A., & Aron, L. (1999). *Relational psychoanalysis: The emergence of a tradition*. Hillsdale, NJ: Analytic Press.

Ogden, T. (2004). On holding and containing, being and dreaming. *The International Journal of Psychoanalysis, 85*(6), 1349–1364. doi:10.1516/T41H-DGUX-9JY4-GQC7

Sheets-Johnstone, M. (2009). Animation: The fundamental, essential, and properly descriptive concept. *Continental Philosophy Review, 42*(3), 375–400. doi:10.1007/s11007-009-9109-x

Stern, D. (2010). *Forms of vitality: Exploring dynamic experience in psychology, the arts, psychotherapy, and development*. Oxford: Oxford University Press.

Stern, D. B. (2013a). Field theory in psychoanalysis, part 1: Harry Stack Sullivan and Madeleine and Willy Baranger. *Psychoanalytic Dialogues, 23*(5), 487–501. doi:10.1080/10481885.2013.832607

Stern, D. B. (2013b). Field theory in psychoanalysis, part 2: Bionian Field Theory and Contemporary Interpersonal/ Relational Psychoanalysis. *Psychoanalytic Dialogues*, 23, 630–645. doi:10.1080/10481885.2013.851548

Vygotsky, L. S. (1978). *Mind in society: The development of higher psychological processes*. In: M. Cole, V. John-Steiner, S. Scribner, & E. Souberman (Eds.), Cambridge, MA: Harvard University Press.

Vygotsky, L. S. (2004). Imagination and creativity in childhood. *Journal of Russian and East European Psychology, 42*(1), 7–97.

Winnicott, D. W. (1960). The theory of the parent–infant relationship. *International Journal of Psychoanalysis, 41*, 585–595.

Winnicott, D. W. (1974). *Playing and reality*. Harmondsworth: Penguin.

The Black baby doll doesn't fit the disconnect between early childhood diversity policy, early childhood educator practice, and children's play

Maggie MacNevin and Rachel Berman

ABSTRACT

This article explores how multicultural policy approaches, which mandate the inclusion of culturally and ethnically 'diverse' play materials in early childhood classrooms influence the pedagogical practice of educators and, in turn, children's play and social interactions. Using data collected through participant observation of children's play in a preschool/kindergarten classroom, interviews with early childhood professionals, and document analysis of a particular early years policy, we highlight the shortcomings of the focus on physical materials as the primary strategy for addressing 'race' and other forms of difference in early childhood education. Assumptions about children's play are examined and critiqued, with examples of children's play episodes provided to emphasize how play reproduces systems of power and oppression present in the broader social context. A number of recommendations are offered for both professional practice and the reconceptualization of early childhood policy.

Introduction

In the city of Toronto, Ontario, Canada declared in May 2016 as the most multicultural city in the world by the BBC, licensed childcare centres are expected to stock their classrooms with a variety of 'culturally diverse' artefacts, including art materials, dolls, play food, dress-up clothing, musical instruments, display photos, recorded music, and books (City of Toronto, 2016). However, the same policy documents that mandate the inclusion of racially and culturally diverse play materials are virtually silent on the topic of how race, ethnicity, culture, and other dimensions of difference should inform teacher–child interactions or the development of curriculum. In this paper, we look at how 'race' and racial identity are (or is not) taken up in early childhood policy documents in Ontario, examine and critique a number of assumptions that underlie these policies, particularly regarding beliefs about play and development. We discuss observations of children's play in an early learning centre in order to provide some examples of social interactions and the use of play materials in a classroom containing the legislated diverse artefacts. We also consider statements made by early childhood educators (ECEs) that demonstrate a disconnect between what teachers believe children understand about 'race' and what children are demonstrating in their play. Finally, we provide some recommendations for early childhood policy and practice to move beyond the current focus on physical environments and towards a deeper engagement with issues of 'race' and difference in the social life of the early childhood classroom.

Background

The larger study

The *Can We Talk About Race?* (CWTAR) study is an ongoing research project based in Toronto, Ontario, Canada. The project includes the following research questions: What strategies or materials do ECEs use to discuss (or not discuss) race with children? What discourses about race and racial identities are employed by ECEs and by children? How does race factor into children's play? Who benefits from the use of certain discourses, and who is disadvantaged? Some of our project goals include: How can we best foster conversations about 'race' in early childhood settings? How can we support early childhood teachers in fostering these conversations? How can we best support children's positive identification with 'race'? Data collection included interviews with 17 professionals in the field of early childhood education and care, including ECEs, centre managers, and administrators at a variety of sites; interviews with 21 children aged 2.5–5 years who attended one particular childcare centre; participant observation with 12 children in a combined preschool/kindergarten class from that same child care centre. On the parental consent form, parents were asked "how would you identify your child's ethnic identity(ies) and/or race(s)? Answers included: East Asian and Caucasian; Caucasian; Goan & Punjabi/South Asian/Brown/Person of Colour; Egyptian, Coptic, Orthodox, Visible minority; White; Scottish/Chinese; Caucasian, he is not aware of his ethnic identity, maybe Irish; White, Jewish; ½ European and ½ Afro-Trinidadian Canadian; White; Canadian Serbian; Chinese; White; We usually don't think in those terms about our children; White with a bi-racial mother; Latin; Caucasian, Italian-Brazilian; Taiwanese; Chinese; Asian; A mix of Armenian, Koptic, Lebanese, Jordanian. Early childhood professionals filled out a demographic form prior to the start of the interview. They were asked to answer eleven questions including their race. Of those who responded, one person identified as Black, one as Brown, one as Filipino, Eight as White or Caucasian, two as South Asian, one as Italian, one as mixed, and one as Hispanic. One melting pot, one Canadian, one Caucasian, one former Yugoslavian/Bosian, one Fillipino, one Sri Lankan, two Italians, one of African Descent, one English, one English/Italian/Native Canadian/Scot, one Caribbean. A content analysis of 12 policy documents was also undertaken. These documents include provincial and municipal legislation, as well as centre-based policies specific to the sites in our study.

Theoretical framework(s)

The theoretical frameworks that undergird our study are Critical Race Theory (CRT) and Post-Structural theory.

Critical race theory

CRT originated in legal studies and is based on the premise that race is a social construct, race-based belief systems make up all parts of our social life, and that the approach to race by (the dominant) society is colour blindness, or the idea that race does not matter (Delgado & Stefancic, 2012). When used in education, CRT scholars examine the ways in which racism is practised across institutions by looking at the power structures embedded in educational policies and practices. According to CRT, these power structures are based on white privilege and further marginalize people of colour (Milner, 2013). Generally, CRT has not been employed by researchers in the field of ECE (see MacNaughton & Davis, 2009 for a notable exception), although attention to issues of 'race' has been taken up in anti-bias, anti-racist and postcolonial approaches to ECE curriculum (see Pacini-Ketchabaw, 2014 for a review and discussion of these approaches as they connect to children's play).

Post-structural theory

We draw on the work of MacNaughton, Davis, and Smith (2010), who in turn draw on Foucault (1972), and assert

> Discourses of 'race' like all discourses, are inherently linked with power/knowledge relationships. Knowledge is constructed within and through privileged powerful dominant positions, and those enacting and embodying these dominant knowledges are accorded power and privilege ... We contend that young children enact, produce, and perform their subjectivities from the shadow of 'race' discourses that circulate within and around them .... (pp. 136–137)

In short, children are active agents who draw on the discourses available to them in the historical, social and political context in which they live. The discourses they draw upon may be observed in their play.

A note about the term diversity

The term 'diversity' appears frequently in early years policy documents and in various forms in discourses on 'race' and difference. Children's author and illustrator Maclear (2016) has noted how often the term 'diversity' is used in the world of children's literature world without agreement about its meaning. Maclear describes a number of ways the term is employed, including 'backdrop diversity' in which 'difference is portrayed as non-threatening and universal' (para. 9); and 'encyclopedic diversity' which depicts 'a glorious array of costume, décor, landscape, homes, to represent worldliness and/or cosmopolitanism' (para. 10). We argue that there is a common unsaid discourse connecting the many nuanced employments of the term 'diversity': things or people that are 'diverse' are non-white. We believe that this common meaning is generally understood by ECEs and administrators, who are well aware of what needs to be on the bookshelf or in the dramatic play centre in order to comply with regulations requiring these areas to include diverse materials. Because we will be discussing the impact of these same policy regulations, our use of the term 'diversity' in this article can also be understood to mean 'non-white.' However, our goal in critiquing these (supposedly apolitical) multicultural policies is to push for the field of early childhood education to move towards a model of critical diversity, a model that 'does not only work at the level of representational inclusion, rather critical diversity asks some difficult questions about inclusion and what inclusion signals and or means in each context' (Walcott, 2011, p. 3).

Analysis

The analyses in this article include a focus on (1) the city of Toronto's *Early Learning and Care Assessment for Quality Improvement* document, hereafter referred to as the AQI, (2) Observations of children's play (3) Excerpts from interviews with ECEs.

Analysis of the early learning and care assessment for quality improvement

The AQI

> prescribes clear expectations, service standards and guidelines for all child care providers who have a service contract with the City. It also serves as a self-evaluation and planning tool for child care operators, and educators ... The assessment measure uses the program, environment and interactions collaboratively to advance quality in child care. (City of Toronto, 2016)

Childcare operators in Toronto, where the CWTAR study took place, must meet the expectations set out in the AQI in order to secure municipal childcare funding. Because the results of annual inspections are published and made available to parents (i.e. potential clients), operators are additionally motivated to obtain a score in the 'exceeds expectations' range.

In the analysis of the AQI document, as with all documents analysed in the larger study, the frequency and context of use of the following terms were noted: *culture, gender, race, ethnicity, diversity, gender, disability*. Truncated search terms were used in order to capture variations of each term, for example, *rac** for *race, racial, racism, racist* and so forth. Analysis of the AQI found that all uses of the terms *cultur**, *rac**, and *ethnic** are in keeping with multicultural approaches in early childhood education and refer to physical objects in the room, or to music. These guidelines are quite specific and often include precise quantities of 'diverse' objects that should be present in the classroom. For example, 'Two or more books which include diverse people/cultures are accessible' (p. 15) and 'There are at least three dramatic play accessories that are culturally diverse' (p. 21). Other guidelines such as 'Educational play materials may include dolls with different skin tones, *ethnic foods*, wooden dolls reflecting diverse people' (p. 7, emphasis added) and 'Two or more displays include cultures/races. May include people from different races or cultures, international flags, language displays' (p. 8) imply the existence of neutral play materials that are free from any ethnic, racial, or cultural association. This finding aligns well with the perspective of Critical Race Theorists who have argued that Whiteness is normalized to the point of invisibility (Delgado & Stefancic, 1997). Furthermore, the terms *cultur**, *rac**, and *ethnic** were entirely absent from all AQI guidelines addressing teacher–child interactions. Taken together, results of the analysis of the AQI reflect a belief that an appropriately 'diverse' and inclusive early learning environment can be achieved solely through the addition of culturally, racially, and ethnically diverse (i.e. non-White) play materials to a neutral, culture-free space that is presumed to exist.

Notably, this emphasis on physical objects as a means to achieving a 'culturally diverse' environment was also reflected by ECEs who participated in interviews as part of the CWTAR study. When asked how 'cultural diversity' was reflected in their classrooms, participants frequently and eagerly described play materials such as skin-tone markers and paints, racially diverse dolls, dramatic play props from a variety of cultures, and books depicting diverse people. These adult participants rarely discussed ways in which race/ethnicity/culture influenced social interactions or programme planning in the classroom, which given the focus of the AQI is perhaps not surprising. More will be said about this shortly.

This emphasis on 'multicultural' artefacts, found in the AQI (and many of the other policy documents we analysed), and reproduced in practice by ECEs in the CWTAR study, coupled with the near-absence of race/ethnicity/culture in guidelines around social interactions, programme planning and curriculum, creates a context in which children may find themselves surrounded by 'diverse' artefacts without being given any opportunities to talk about 'race' and difference with teachers and peers. Park (2011) observed a similar disconnect in her study in an American preschool classroom, and noted, 'It was unclear ... what the mere presence of difference in the perceptual realm, unaccompanied by explanation and dialogue, was teaching students about the politics or *meaning* of difference in the larger society' (p. 406, emphasis in original). Park (2011) goes on to ask, 'Is it sufficiently beneficial for multicultural images to simply be absorbed by children?' (p. 406).

As we consider this question, we also need to consider what processes are assumed to be at work when children play. Grieshaber and McArdle (2010) note that the field of early childhood education has long accepted the taken-for-granted idea that play leads inevitably and predictably to positive development. These authors describe how, for example, children are assumed to automatically gain communication and negotiation skills through dramatic play with peers. They assert, 'There is no consideration of the type or appropriateness of the skills that are gained as a result of engaging in play. Instead a blanket assumption gives the impression that whatever the skills, they will be advantageous' (p. 7). We suggest that a similar assumption underlies the emphasis on 'multicultural' artefacts in early years policy; that is, the belief that playing with these materials will necessarily result in an appreciation of difference and a preservation of the non-biased worldview children are often simply assumed to innately possess.

Grieshaber and McArdle (2010) are critical of the discourse that play is natural and always beneficial to all children. They argue instead, 'Much play in early childhood settings reproduces the status quo. That is, it reproduces what exists in terms of relations of power about "race"; gender; social, economic and cultural capital; ethnicity; heteronormativity, and proficiency with English' (p. 75). These power relations are continually at work during interactions in the early learning environment and exert a strong influence on children's play: who gets what roles, who has access to preferred materials and spaces, and how conflicts are resolved.

Barron (2009) has also pointed out that the broader structures and practices of the classroom can exclude children who are racialized or members of non-dominant cultural groups. For example, a dramatic play centre that is set up as a type of store or cultural institution that is familiar only to White children serves to marginalize children from other social groups, who may lack the insider cultural knowledge required to know what is 'supposed to happen' in such a setting. The presence of standalone objects in the play space (e.g. an 'ethnic food' on the shelf or a costume in the dress-up box) does little to mitigate this exclusion. Educators may further contribute to this marginalization by expecting and promoting particular roles and types of play in the space, whether intentionally or not.

We also know that young children *do* notice race and other forms of difference, and that without explanations from adults, children form their own conclusions (often biased and inaccurate) about observable social groups (Farago, Sanders, & Gaias, 2015). We can expect that in an environment in which 'diverse' images and artefacts abound while planned and spontaneous discussion about these materials is absent, children will construct their own meanings about both the materials and the social groups to whom these materials 'belong.' We can also expect that these meanings will reflect the dynamics of power and oppression at work in classroom social interactions, and in the larger society (Grieshaber & McArdle, 2010). In the next section, we share some examples of children's play with 'diverse' materials that seem to support this view.

Observations of children's play

After approval from the University's Research Ethics Board, participant observation was conducted by three research assistants in a combined preschool/kindergarten classroom at an urban childcare centre that identifies itself as following a play-based curriculum. The centre has obtained AQI scores in the 'meets expectations to exceeds expectations' range for the previous two years, indicating that the classroom in which observations took place contained all the required 'diverse' materials. Each of the research assistants had worked in the field and they were registered with the College of ECEs, as is required in the province of Ontario. One of the researcher assistants was employed as an ECE at the observation site, but did not work in the classroom where participant observation took place. Observation sessions lasted two to three hours each for a total of 29 hours and took place several times per week over the course of two months. The goal of the observations was to locate and map the dynamics of 'race' across a group of children (MacNaughton & Davis, 2009, p. 44). We looked at patterns of play, peer interactions, and social relationships. We paid attention to characters specific children played/took up, areas where children were playing, who directed the play, who led and who followed, who had an active role, and the props or physical objects used in the play and how they were used.Information about the children's age and the descriptions of racial identity were provided by parents during the consent process (the latter was noted previously). The observations are analyzed in keeping with ideas drawn from CRT and Post-Structuralism.The researcher ('MM') in all episodes is the first author.

Episode one

Sarah (age 4, Egyptian) and Ruby (age 3.5, half European and half Afro-Trinidadian) were playing in the dramatic play centre. Ruby was holding a White baby doll while Sarah was holding a Black baby and rummaging through a basket of clothes. She uncovered a White baby in the clothes basket, picked it up and dropped the Black doll on the floor. Sarah told Ruby the babies were hungry and needed to be fed. The two girls laid their babies on the table and pretended to feed them carrots; they did not pretend to feed another Black baby that was also lying on the table. Ruby and Sarah then brought all three dolls from the table to an empty bookshelf adjacent to the dramatic play centre, and said they were putting the babies to bed because they were sick. They placed the two White dolls together on one shelf and the Black doll on another shelf. I pointed to the Black doll and asked why that baby was sleeping by herself; Ruby responded, 'She didn't fit.' Sarah soon announced that the babies were awake. Both children picked up a White doll and left the Black doll on the shelf. While the children selected some new clothes and began dressing their dolls, I pointed to the Black doll that was still lying on the floor, where Sarah had dropped it earlier. I asked, 'Whose baby is this?' Sarah replied, 'I dunno. I'm not having that one.

In this episode, the two children seemed to be exhibiting a clear preference for White dolls over Black dolls, particularly Sara who appears to be the leader in this play episode. This preference echoes the finding from the classic doll study conducted by Clark and Clark (1939) over 75 years ago where children when presented with the choice of White or Black dolls, and regardless of their own 'race,' overwhelmingly selected White dolls. As Grieshaber and McArdle (2010) suggest, both children, including Ruby who has Black family members but who seems to be picking up on messages Sara is communicating of the desirableness of White skin, are reproducing discourses of race and power relations in their play.

Episode two

Sarah was playing independently at the dollhouse. She had three White female dolls, two of which were blonde and very fair-skinned while one had brown hair and a slightly darker skin tone. Sarah put all three dolls on to a bed in the dollhouse and brought another doll into the room. This doll was a male with dark brown skin, wearing a long white robe and a red and white keffiyeh head scarf. I asked Sarah who all the dolls were. She told me the two blonde dolls were the mom and the baby, and the brown-haired doll was the sister. She then told me the brown-skinned male doll was the witch, and that 'She is mean to them.' She told me, 'The witch made them all dead because she kicked their heart.' We then had the following interaction:

MM: How can you tell that she's a witch?
S: She's mean.
MM: What about how she looks? Is there any way we can know she's a witch?
S: She's brown.
MM: What does that mean?
S: My mom says brown in Spanish is lo-kee. Lokee lokee lokee. Like Goldilocks.
MM: Oh. Is Goldilocks brown?
S: No, she's White.

In this episode, Sarah chose a brown-skinned doll to play the role of a scary antagonist who harms the White dolls. Sarah herself identified the character's brownness as a way of knowing he is a witch. Interestingly, Sarah consistently used female pronouns when talking about this doll, perhaps because she interpreted its long robe as a woman's dress. Sarah's response, 'My mom says brown in Spanish is lo-kee. Lokee lokee lokee. Like Goldilocks' is quite intriguing. It is possible that at home, Sarah heard something about Brown people that she did not fully understand, hence her use of the nonsense word 'lokee.' She seems also to be aware of a connection between brown skin and the Spanish language. In her final statement, she demonstrates awareness of racial categories and a confident knowledge of the Whiteness of a fictional character, Goldilocks. This play episode provides compelling evidence that children do indeed attach their own meaning and form inaccurate conclusions about racialized groups (Farago et al., 2015) and reproduce these biases in their play (Grieshaber & McArdle, 2010).

Episode three

Marko (age 3, Serbian Canadian) was playing at a table with two other children. There was a large quantity of Lego on the table, as well as a few mini skateboards. Some of the Lego appeared to belong to a set and had accessories that looked to be inspired by Chinese dragon boats. I noticed one of the Lego figurines had a highly stereotyped Chinese appearance: conical hat, slanted eyebrows and a long moustache, and a shirt with what appeared to be Chinese characters on it. Marko picked up another figurine, which also had many stereotypically Asian markers. This one had a red hat with horns, traditional Japanese wooden sandals, a sword in its hand and nunchucks in its belt. Marko told me, 'This guy's a ninja.' I asked him, 'How do you know he's a ninja?' Marko responded, 'I just know. He's the best ninja in the whole world'.

The first author was surprised to observe the presence of what she judged to be stereotypical and racist toys in the classroom. She later learned that this Lego is part of a product line called Lego Ninjago, which is also connected to a children's television show of the same name. Marko was likely familiar with this product line, hence his response 'I just know. He's the best ninja in the whole world.' There is a mythology created around this product and its characters that seems to borrow elements from Japanese and Chinese history and culture (e.g. ninjas, samurais, names such as 'Master Wu' and 'Chen'). It is arguably quite problematic for children to have access to these play materials, which depict stereotypical representations of Asian people and culture, without any critical discussion initiated by teachers. Of course, we cannot be certain that no such discussion ever took place; however, as we discuss shortly, ECEs working at this site who participated in interviews indicated that very few intentional discussions about race ever occurred with the children.

Social exclusion episodes

During participant observation sessions, several instances of social exclusion during which racial dynamics could have been at play were observed. Because some of the children involved in these episodes did not have parental consent to participate in the research, these incidents cannot be discussed. During participant observation research in an American preschool class, Park (2011) noted that initially, 'It was difficult to assess whether there was a racial or ethnic component to specific exclusionary behaviours ... No child ever explained a conflict in racialized terms or used racial epithets.' (p. 408). However, when Park (2011) analysed children's friendship networks and overall patterns of social interaction, she found clear evidence of children racially segregating themselves, as well as disproportionately high rates of social exclusion experienced by children of colour. Such an in-depth analysis of children's social behaviour was not possible in the CWTAR study due to time limitations on participant observation and because only about half of the children in the classroom had consent to participate in the research. Nevertheless, as the three brief episodes selected for discussion in this paper demonstrate, there is evidence that children in this setting were actively constructing meanings around 'race' and difference as they played; we would not be surprised to discover racialized patterns to friendship networks and social exclusion in this or any classroom.

Excerpts from interviews with ECEs

ECEs in our study often described potentially racialized behaviour and provided alternative explanations and motivations for this behaviour as is apparent in the following quotes. As with our observational data, our analysis of the interview data drew on the tenets of CRT and Post-Structuralist ideas. Adherence to a colourblind discourse is apparent in each of the following interview excerpts. When asked if she noticed any patterns in the formation of children's friendship groups, one participant responded

> So it may look like those groups have formed, but I don't know that they've done that intentionally or if it's just the demographics of the area ... Um I wouldn't say that they're particularly picking out somebody of the same race as them, it's just something, who has something similar to them. (P36, White female, age 43)

Another participant suggested that friendship groups that appear racialized in fact form due to language preferences: 'Right, but it's just the comfort of the language that sometimes we see, I won't even call it segregation but they're in their small groups and the children are comfortable playing with each other' (P39, South Asian female, age 54). A third participant noted, 'I noticed I had some children [at the childcare centre] that wouldn't play with other children because their parents didn't want them playing together. Now, was it race? I don't know' (P37, White female, age 53). When asked how children respond to the required 'diverse' materials in the classroom, one participant stated,

> So I think the children respond to them, I mean they play with it and I don't know that they're necessarily picking out their own cultures and stuff. In books I've seen them point to pictures of things that they have in their home and stuff like that, but I don't think they like fight over a specific doll of their ethnic background or anything like that. I think they just, they just use them. (P36, White female, age 43)

Discussion and recommendations

A growing body of research lends support to the idea that young children are aware of 'race' and reproduce existing power dynamics in their play and social interactions. Researchers from the United Kingdom, Australia, the United States, Canada, and elsewhere have written about ways to work with issues of racism in early childhood settings, particularly through anti-racist approaches (e.g. see the work of Janmohamed, 2005; MacNaughton & Davis, 2009; Pacini-Ketchabaw & Berikoff, 2008). Yet, many ECEs persistently adhere to a 'colourblind' ideology (Boutte, Lopez-Robertson, & Powers-Costello, 2011), avoiding any discussion about race due to a belief that their students are too young to understand bias. Very few ECEs interviewed for the CWTAR study indicated that any race-related incidents ever occurred in their classrooms, or that children used racially or culturally 'diverse' play materials in any problematic ways. Yet, within just seven sessions of participant observation, significant evidence that the children have a clear understanding of racial categories, exhibit a preference for White play materials, and consistently reproduce the power dynamics of the larger society in their play was witnessed.

Two conclusions seem warranted. First, simply providing children with racially and culturally diverse materials in the classroom is not sufficient to nurture positive racial identity development or to challenge biased and stereotyped beliefs and prepare children to confront racism and other forms of oppression when they encounter it. Thus, we agree with Lane (2008) who argues that such play resources need to be accompanied by discussions with teachers. Second, ECEs are not always aware of their students' knowledge about race and the ways in which children use this knowledge in their play and social interactions. Following are some recommendations for policy and practice. Although they are specifically geared towards ECEs working in an Ontario context, we assert that they are relevant for those working in other contexts as the discourse of colourblindness continues to dominate the field of early learning and care throughout North America (Boutte et al., 2011) and elsewhere. Additionally, while the need to address 'race' and racism in a highly multicultural city like Toronto may be obvious, Derman-Sparks, Ramsey, and Edwards (2006) note that it is no less important to do so in more racially homogenous contexts. The following recommendations are geared towards ECEs already working in the field, although certainly many of these recommendations are valid for pre-service programmes at Colleges and Universities as well.

Self-reflection

ECEs may avoid discussing race and bias with young children for a variety of reasons. They often report a lack of confidence in their abilities to appropriately engage children in these discussions, and may fear offending parents or creating and instilling biases in their students (Farago et al., 2015). These authors also note that White teachers, who have the privilege of maintaining a colourblind ideology, may not believe that racism and discrimination are particularly salient or contemporary topics. For these reasons, an important starting point for engaging meaningfully with these issues in early childhood education is ongoing self-reflection by educators. This may be particularly important for White teachers who may seldom have had occasion to think about the ways in which their Whiteness influences their beliefs and practices in the classroom. This is a recommendation that can easily be incorporated into existing policy documents that govern early childhood education. In Ontario, the provincial document *How Does Learning Happen?* (Government of Ontario, 2014) already focuses significant attention on self-reflection by concluding each of four sections on learning foundations with a series of reflective questions for educators. These questions often invite teachers to examine their beliefs and biases: 'Which policies and practices may be barriers to establishing relationships and ensuring the meaningful participation of all children? Of all families?' (p. 28); 'What environmental factors may be causing stress for children? What changes can be made to reduce stress for *all* who use the space?' (p. 34). However, without explicitly naming and interrogating race and racialized beliefs, these questions are not sufficient to interrupt the colourblind ideology held by many ECEs.

Observing children's play

Pacini-Ketchabaw (2014) asserts that '[e]ducators need to become vigilant to how racist and gendered discourses might creep into children's conversations in play encounters' (p. 73). As discussed earlier, it can be difficult or impossible to categorize individual episodes of play or social interaction as incidents of racism (Park, 2011). However, by observing and analysing children's behaviour over time, patterns may emerge that suggest that children are actively constructing their own understanding of race, and that these understandings play a role in organizing children's social interactions and their preferences for and use of play materials. As discussed previously, in interviews conducted as part of the CWTAR study, most ECEs reported that children's play and social interactions were seldom if ever influenced by 'race' or racism. We suggest that without intentionally and systematically observing and analysing children's behaviour over time, it is easy to overlook 'race' as an influencing factor in the classroom, particularly for White teachers who do not feel the impact of racism on their daily lives.

We propose that ECEs would benefit from taking on the role of close observer of children's play, in order to examine more intentionally how children are using materials in the classroom and to consider racialized patterns in friendships and social exclusion. This focused observation and analysis of children's behaviour could produce greater awareness of children's understanding of 'race,' and enable ECEs to develop intentional plans to address issues of 'race,' difference and bias in the classroom. In Ontario, this recommendation aligns well with the goals of the College of Early Childhood Educators' (CECE, a professional regulatory body) Continuous Professional Learning programme. Participation in this programme is currently voluntary for registered ECEs; it 'supports RECEs in meeting the expectations outlined in government legislation and College by-laws, policies, practices and programs' (CECE, 2015a). Participants in the programme complete a reflective self-assessment in order to create professional development goals based on the CECE's Code of Ethics and Standards of Practice (CECE, 2011), and then develop a plan of action to meet their learning goals. One suggested course of action is for ECEs to undertake 'professional inquiry/action research' (CECE, 2015a). Assuming a researcher's stance in the classroom may enable ECEs to question their own taken-for-granted beliefs about children's play and to consider alternative interpretations of behaviour. This professional learning would strengthen educators' competence in the following standards of practice: 'Observe and monitor the learning environment' (CECE, 2015b, p. 10) and 'Support children in culturally, linguistically and developmentally sensitive ways' (CECE, 2015b, p. 8).

Of course, ECEs do engage in observation of children's play on a daily basis, but this is typically done from a developmentalist perspective with the intention of assessing individual and group learning. Campbell and Smith (2001) highlight the importance of using alternative theoretical perspectives to produce multiple readings of children's play, in order to uncover themes of power and inequity that otherwise go unnoticed. These authors also recommend working with another teacher to simultaneously record and observe a play episode and then compare and critically analyse each other's description and analysis of the play. They suggest teachers ask, 'What personal and professional knowledge has enabled each person to record, see, and understand the play in a particular way? What personal and professional investment does each person have in the different ways of seeing and understanding play?' (pp. 99–100). By viewing children's play through a lens informed by CRT and working collaboratively with colleagues, ECEs can better see and understand the ways 'race and racism' operate in children's play.

Getting inside children's play

In addition to observing children's play, Fleer (2015) makes the case that although the dominant approach to children's play is that adults position themselves outside children's play for it to be considered 'legitimate,' adults need not be passive observers of children's play, but can instead be partners. Through her research, where she examines the role adults take in children's play within play-based early childhood settings, she developed a typology of play pedagogy that shows the range of teacher pedagogical positioning in play: teacher proximity to children's play; teacher intent is in parallel with the children's play; teaching is following the children's play; teachers are engaged in sustained collective play with groups of children; teacher is inside the children's imaginary play. She asserts that

> [w]hen the teacher is part of the imaginary play, she/he has an opportunity from inside of the play, to develop the play further, introducing complexity and I would suggest genuinely using learning goals that are detailed in curriculum to help solve the tensions in imaginary situations. (p. 1812)

We suggest that teachers purposefully engage with children in their play in order to extend and challenge their understandings and use of particular play materials that are linked to 'race' gender, and other differences.

Fostering positive identifications with race

A fourth recommendation for practice is for ECEs to develop and implement strategies to foster children's positive identifications with race. Here, clearly, authentic diversity of classroom materials is important: all children should see themselves represented and reflected in many positive ways throughout the classroom environment. However, as we have argued, the diverse classroom environment must be thoughtfully constructed and accompanied by ongoing discussions and interventions if it is to be effective. Children's author and illustrator Myers (2014) has argued that books should function as mirrors, reflecting children's lived experiences, but also as maps that offer expansive imaginative possibilities for the future. Myers draws attention to the scarcity of books that fulfil this need for children of colour; he notes that characters of colour, when they appear at all, are most often found in historical tales of slavery and civil rights, or as background characters in someone else's story. We suggest that this idea can apply not only to books but also more broadly to the entire classroom environment. It is critical that the early learning environment be one in which children of colour see myriad possibilities for their place in the world, currently and in the future, rather than seeing themselves as colourful additions to a predominantly white world. Dramatic play props, wall displays, art materials, puzzles and cognitive materials: everything in the room should be thoughtfully chosen and employed not only to meet policy requirements for representation, but also to provide a landscape of positive identities for children.

Explicit teaching about 'race' and racism

A final recommendation for practice is for ECEs to engage in teaching and dialogue regarding 'race' and racism. ECEs in the CWTAR study most often identified books and discussion about fairness, sameness and kindness as their primary or sole strategy for addressing difference in the classroom. For example, 'I would make it a general thing … reading books … and making ideas or games that we can play together showing that everyone's the same and we can be all, be all friends' (P34, Italian female, age 37); and

> [The book] just talks about differences but it's all the same … Like it's a funny book that I have big ears for example, and I can move them around, or I have big eyebrows I can put up and down. Right, so it doesn't specifically talk about particular race, it just talks about differences, and teaching children we are different but we are still the same. (P31, White female, age 42)

This is likely a confounding lesson for children whose own experiences in the classroom and the larger world tell them that racial differences in fact matter very much. We also question the effectiveness of books that employ what Maclear (2016) refers to as 'allegorical/parable diversity.' She notes, 'These books tend to tackle "prejudice" by taking a disarmingly whimsical and/or symbolic approach' (para. 6). There is little research to support the effectiveness of these types of interventions. Farago et al. (2015) note that the available literature on bias reduction interventions in early childhood suggests the need for lessons to explicitly address racism; 'positive talk focusing on treating others kindly and fairly is not enough' (p. 51).

Boutte et al. (2011), Husband (2012), and others who take an anti-racist approach to early education advocate using books and other media to provoke discussion about race; they also emphasize the importance of explicitly naming and interrogating incidents of racism in order to counter the development of stereotypical beliefs and bias, and to provide young children with tools to challenge discrimination and inequity when they encounter it.

For this teaching to be effective, it is critical that educators engage in a continuous cycle of self-reflection and focused, thoughtful observation of children's play and social interactions, and make use of opportunities to be inside children's play. Farago et al. (2015) caution, 'Teachers have to be vigilant that the messages they intend to send children are what children take away' (p. 51). Observation of children's play can provide educators with useful information about the social climate of the classroom and the children's current understanding of 'race,' and enable them to plan appropriate interventions, and moving inside children's play can enable such intervention or understand of children's understandings to occur spontaneously. Ongoing self-reflection is needed to evaluate the effectiveness of one's teaching, strengthen one's awareness of how race and other forms of difference influence classroom dynamics, and continually improve intentional teaching strategies.

Summary and conclusions

In the preceding analysis, we began by examining how one policy document addresses (or does not address) 'race' and difference in early learning and care environments by critiquing the multicultural approach taken by the AQI (City of Toronto, 2016), in which stocking the classroom with a prescribed number and type of diverse artefacts is positioned as sufficient. Our thoughts about the inclusion of diverse materials in the classroom align with those of one adult participant in the CWTAR study who stated, 'I think that they're good but they're a place to start, they're not the place to end. And I think the other thing is you can have a very toxic environment systemically and you could have those [diverse materials]' (P35, Black female, age 51). Evidence from the children's play episodes and interviews with early childhood professionals discussed earlier support this idea. We have seen how children exhibit preferences for White play materials, demonstrate understanding of racial categories, and engage in the ongoing construction of meaning around 'race' and difference as they play. We have also seen how ECEs often fail to consider the influence that 'race' exerts on children's play and the social life of the classroom. In addition to the recommendations for pedagogical practice outlined above, we offer a final and essential proposal: the reconsideration and revision of early years policies. We assert that a new policy approach is necessary to better support practitioners to create environments that foster the development of positive racial identities and to confidently engage children in meaningful dialogue about 'race' and other forms of difference.

Just as general messages of fairness and kindness are not adequate to teach anti-racism to young children, vague guidelines about inclusion and cultural sensitivity are not adequate to counter racism at the institutional level. The policy approach currently taken by the City of Toronto is built upon an assumption that status quo early learning environments are culture-free, and can be made inclusive by the addition of 'ethnic' materials. This multicultural approach serves to validate and preserve Whiteness as the dominant and invisible cultural force, and does little to support ECEs and children to recognize and challenge bias and exclusion (Pacini-Ketchabaw, 2014). We further suggest that this approach is perceived by many ECEs as 'one more thing' to be added to an already overwhelming workload. ECEs and childcare managers face considerable pressure to meet increasingly stringent provincial and municipal guidelines in the name of accountability. They are also required to complete significant amounts of daily documentation of individual children's experiences and group programming, while also attending to the hands-on care and education of young children. It is also important to acknowledge ECEs' ongoing struggle for professional status and recognition; at present, many

ECEs do not have the benefit of institutional support that is required to engage in meaningful professional development. It is therefore imperative that policies be reconstructed to make this work clearer, easier, and more meaningful, not harder.

Rather than simply adding more guidelines to existing policies to address race in the classroom, these policies should be reconstructed to authentically incorporate multiple perspectives and practices, and informed throughout by the central tenets of CRT. A thorough discussion of this considerable task lies beyond the scope of this article. However, we will conclude by offering some thoughts about the connections among policy, pedagogy, and children's play.

Our interviews with ECEs in the Toronto area provided evidence of the influence that policy has on practice. Most participants described a similar approach to incorporating ethnic and cultural diversity in the classroom, and this approach mirrored the requirements of the AQI: the addition of non-white dolls, art materials, books, wall photos, music, costumes, and play food to the existing environment. Of course, educators are free to take up a deeper engagement with issues of 'race' and difference, and some do. However, while policies continue to send the message that providing children with the required number of diverse play materials is a sufficient response to the question of difference, it is unlikely that we will see the majority of ECEs take on the challenging recommendations for practice we propose in this article. The policy focus on diverse materials reinforces the false assumption that children's play is naturally free from bias and stereotyping and is always beneficial to all children (Grieshaber & McArdle, 2010). Current policies thus fail to consider the complexity of children's play and do not support ECEs to consider the ways in which children's play reproduces larger social systems of power and oppression. In such a climate, we would not expect most ECEs to have the pedagogical tools to intervene and respond appropriately to children's racialized play and social behaviour; in fact, data from interviews with ECEs in the CWTAR study supported this expectation. We acknowledge the efforts made by ECEs to provide optimal care and education to young children in often challenging working conditions, while we call attention to the urgent need for action at the level of professional practice and, crucially, in the realm of policy. As Walcott (2011) argues,

> multicultural policies produce a kind of diversity that reproduces the historical legitimacy of the institutions in question without having to address the deeper structures of their orientation. Representational inclusion, both numeric and otherwise is valued at the expense of more thorough institutional questioning and rethinking. (p. 2)

Disclosure statement

No potential conflict of interest was reported by the authors.

Funding

This work was supported by the Social Sciences and Humanities Research Council of Canada's Insight Development Program [grant number #430-2014-00889].

References

Barron, I. (2009). Illegitimate participation? A group of young minority ethnic children's experiences of early childhood education. *Pedagogy, Culture & Society, 17*(3), 341–354.

Boutte, G. S., Lopez-Robertson, J., & Powers-Costello, E. (2011). Moving beyond colorblindness in early childhood classrooms. *Early Childhood Education Journal, 39*(5), 335–342.

Campbell, S., & Smith, K. (2001). Equity observation and images of fairness in childhood. In G. S. Cannella & S. Grieshaber (Eds.), *Embracing identities in early childhood education: Diversity and possibilities* (pp. 89–102). New York, NY: Teachers College Press.

City of Toronto. (2016). *Preschool early learning and care assessment for quality improvement: Guidelines.* Retrieved from http://www1.toronto.ca/City20Of20Toronto/Children's20Services/Files/pdf/O/Operating20criteria/oc_guidelines_preschool.pdf

Clark, K. B. & Clark, M. K. (1939). The development of consciousness of self and the emergence of racial identification in Negro preschool children. *The Journal of Social Psychology, 10*, 591–599.

College of Early Childhood Educators. (2011). *Code of ethics and standards of practice: Recognizing and honouring our profession.* Retrieved from https://www.college-ece.ca/en/Public/Pages/professionalstandards.aspx

College of Early Childhood Educators. (2015a). *Continuous professional learning program: Portfolio handbook.* Retrieved from https://www.college-ece.ca/en/Members/Pages/CPL-Program.aspx

College of Early Childhood Educators. (2015b). *Self-assessment tool.* Retrieved from https://www.college-ece.ca/en/Members/Pages/CPL-Program.aspx

Delgado, R., & Stefancic, J. (1997). *Critical White studies: Looking behind the mirror.* Philadelphia: Temple University Press.

Delgado, R., & Stefancic, J. (2012). Introduction. *Critical race theory: An introduction* (2nd ed., pp. 1–14). New York, NY: NYU Press.

Derman-Sparks, L., Ramsey, P. G., & Edwards, J. O. (2006). *What if all the kids are White? Anti-bias multicultural education with young children and families.* New York, NY: Teachers College Press.

Farago, F., Sanders, K., & Gaias, L. (2015). Addressing race and racism in early childhood: challenges and opportunities. *Advances in Early Education and Day Care, 19*, 29–66.

Fleer, M. (2015). Pedagogical positioning in play – teachers being inside and outside of children's imaginary play. *Early Child Development and Care, 185*(11–12), 1801–1814.

Foucault, M. (1972). *The archaeology of knowledge.* London: Tavistock.

Government of Ontario. (2014). *How does learning happen? Ontario's pedagogy for the early years.* Retrieved from: http://www.edu.gov.on.ca/childcare/HowLearningHappens.pdf

Grieshaber, S., & McArdle, F. (2010). *The trouble with play* [ebook version]. Berkshire: Open University Press.

Husband, T. (2012). "I Don't See color": challenging assumptions about discussing race with young children. *Early Childhood Education Journal*, 39(6), 365–371.

Janmohamed, Z. (2005). Rethinking anti-bias approaches in early childhood education; A shift toward anti-racism education. In G. J. Sefa Dei & G. Singh Johal (Eds.), *Critical issues in anti-racist research methodologies* (pp. 163–182). New York, NY: Peter Lang.

Lane, J. (2008). *Young children and racial justice: Taking action for racial equality in the early years: understanding the past, thinking about the present, planning for the future.* London: National Children's Bureau.

Maclear, K. (2016, March 1). *What we talk about when we talk about diversity.* Retrieved from http://kyomaclearkids.com/what-we-talk-about-when-we-talk-about-diversity/

MacNaughton, G. & Davis, K. (2009). *"Race" and early childhood education-An international approach to identity, politics and pedagogy.* New York, NY: Palgrave Macmillan.

MacNaughton, G., Davis, K. & Smith, K. (2010). Working and reworking children's performance of 'whiteness' in early childhood education. In M. O'Loughlin & R. T. Johnson (Eds.), *Imagining children otherwise: theoretical and critical perspectives on childhood subjectivity* (pp. 135–155). New York, NY: Peter Lang.

Milner, H. R. (2013). Analyzing poverty, learning, and teaching through a critical race theory lens. *Review of Research in Education*, 37(1), 1–53.

Myers, C. (2014, March 15). The apartheid of children's literature. *The New York Times.* Retrieved from http://www.nytimes.com/2014/03/16/opinion/sunday/the-apartheid-of-childrens-literature.html?_r=0

Pacini-Ketchabaw, V. (2014). Postcolonial and anti-racist approaches to understanding play. In L. Brooker, M. Blaise & S. Edwards (Eds.), *The Sage handbook of play and learning in early childhood* (pp. 67–78). Thousand Oaks, CA: Sage.

Pacini-Ketchabaw, V. & Berikoff, A. (2008). The politics of difference and diversity: From young children's violence to creative power expressions. *Contemporary Issues in Early Childhood, 9*(3), 256–264.

Park, C. C. (2011). Young children making sense of racial and ethnic differences: A sociocultural approach. *American Educational Research Journal, 48*(2), 387–420.

Walcott, R. (2011, June). *What's art good for: Critical diversity, social justice and future of art and culture in Canada.* Speech presented at the Canadian Public Arts Funders Strategic Development Meeting on Equity, Edmonton, AB. Retrieved from http://www.cpaf-opsac.org/en/themes/documents/WhatsArtGoodFor-RinaldoWalcott-June2011.pdf

Using cross-cultural conversations to contextualize understandings of play: a multinational study

Zoyah Kinkead-Clark and Charlotte Hardacre

ABSTRACT

The following study examines two researchers' perspectives on play in the lives of children from diverse cultural contexts. Two questions guided this study: (1) how do researchers conceptualize children's play and (2) what shapes their understanding of play. In order to answer these questions, a critical discourse was established between two researchers who had each completed ethnographic studies of play in the UK and Jamaica. The initial research studies comprised of observations, semi-structured interviews, field notes and collection of artefacts relating to play. Through discourse, new understandings were unearthed by examining the different contexts of play. The aim of this study is to contextualize our understanding of play and to expand our notions of play beyond researcher positionalities. This discursive method allows concepts of play to be grounded, but not restricted by national contexts through juxtaposition with multinational policies, programmes and practices.

Introduction

Children's engagement and use of play have long been explored within the research sphere. Multidisciplinary, interdisciplinary and transdisciplinary attempts at interrogating this area have been grounded in the goal of achieving greater breadth and depth of knowledge of the factors shaping children's play, while simultaneously removing professional boundaries, which often serve as limitations and hindrances in the research process (Choi & Pak, 2007). Diversity on the focus of studies on children's play has added greater clarity about this natural childhood past time. For instance, Parten (1933), a psychologist, focussed on children's social play at home and in the wider community, Veitch, Bagley, Ball, and Salmon (2006), researchers in health and nutrition, examined the spaces in which children's played and how parents perceived it, while Rubin (1977), a human development expert, focussed on describing the behaviours children exhibit during play.

While such studies have added great richness to the field and have contributed significantly to the body of literature guiding our understanding of play as an activity, not merely for pleasure, but more so because of its benefits in supporting children's cognitive, socio-emotional and affective development, it has also been recognized that such studies have been narrowly focussed.

Though the literature substantiating the importance and value of play has gained steady global acceptance, it has been overwhelmingly evident that the majority of these studies have emerged from researchers from dominant-hegemonic perspectives (Europe, North America and Australasia). As two researchers from different professional backgrounds (one from Jamaica and the other from the UK) who have also conducted ethnographic research on children's play, we were very interested in how we have been shaped by our positionalities and how these influence our perspectives and our interpretation of children's play within our own research and professional contexts.

In the following study, we draw on data derived from our engagement in critical discourse to 'unplug' how we have been influenced by our individual positionalities and to assess how these have guided our interpretation and conceptualization of children's play. Our primary aim is to contextualize our understanding of play and to expand our notions of play beyond researcher positionalities.

Researchers' positionalities

The nature of our discourse is grounded in reflexivity. Our aim is simple. As suggested by England (1994) and Watt (2007), we want to engage in introspection and examine how our personal and professional experiences, interests and beliefs have influenced the way we look at our research and understand our researched work. We see this as opening ourselves, our lives and our experiences to unveil the factors we believe have shaped our positionalities and that have formed the lens through which we look at our research, our research contexts and our research participants, who we refer to throughout this study as our co-constructors.

Bearing in mind the aforementioned, as researchers, from different disciplines, engaged in this reflexive process, it was important that we examine our positionalities because we recognize that the positions from which we come are powerful and cloud the lens through which we look at the world (England, 1994; Merriam et al., 2001; Skelton, 2001; Watt, 2007). As Skelton (2001) explains, our experiences

> ... have a bearing upon who we are, how our identities are formed and how we do our research; we are not neutral, scientific observers, untouched by the emotional and political contexts of places where we do our research. (p. 89)

For mere expediency, we have found it quite useful to outline our positionalities in tabular format (Table 1).

A brief review of cross-cultural studies on play

For this article, we have found it important to review cross-cultural studies conducted about children's play to highlight some of the studies examining the nature, similarities and differences of the play in diverse contexts.

Understanding children's play from a cross-cultural perspective

Several studies have sought to present cross-cultural perspectives of children's play and to understand how adults, more specifically parents, support children in this activity. Throughout all of this,

Table 1. Researchers' positionalities.

Zoyah	Charlotte
Wife, mother, lecturer, researcher	Lecturer, practitioner, aunt, researcher
Former kindergarten teacher, now an early childhood teacher educator and researcher	Family learning tutor
Middle income background	Middle income background
Jamaican of African descent	English of European descent
From a country labelled as developing with minimal visibility in research studies on early childhood education (ECE)	From a country labelled as developed and highly visible in research studies on ECE
Most research conducted in communities labelled as disadvantaged/inner-city overwhelmingly populated by families of lower socio-economic means	Most research conducted in communities labelled as disadvantaged/inner-city. Notable segregation of ethnic minority groups in north-west meaning that some settings have high numbers of children from Pakistan and Bangladesh and others are almost exclusively white British

research has been fairly balanced in outlining the impact of culture or lack thereof, on shaping children's play. For instance, Farver and Lee-Shin's (2000) study of Korean American mothers highlighted the role of acculturation in changing dominant parent practices and beliefs in supporting children's play, while, Göncü, Mistry, and Mosier's (2000) study (conducted in the United States, Turkey, Guatemala and India) described how toddlers' play vary across cultures. Their findings suggest that though all children engage in social play, the frequency of this play differs.

Perhaps one of the most ground-breaking studies which initially sought to explore this issue from a cross-cultural perspective was Whiting's (1963) Six Cultures Study, conducted in six countries: Kenya, India, Japan, Mexico, the United States and the Philippines. Though the primary aim of this study was to describe how child rearing practices across different cultures had an impact on 'subsequent differences in children's personalities', one of the findings that was unearthed was how parents' engagement in play activities with their children differed across cultural lines. Subsequent studies have also affirmed these different parental approaches. Carvalho, Magalhães, Pontes, and Bichara's (2003) exploration of children's play in Brazil outline that for Brazilian children, play differs along gender, geographical and socio-economic lines. Bornstein, Haynes, Pascual, Painter, and Galperín's (1999) study, in a similar vein, also explored this issue. In their research, which compared how mothers from the United States and Argentina engaged in various forms of play with their toddler children, the authors concluded that Argentinean mothers were far more expressive in their praise and engaged in more social play with their children. Similar to Carvalho et al. (2003), Bornstein et al. (1999) suggest that differences emerge along cultural and gender lines. They too highlight that Argentine mothers had more frequent play experiences with their children than their American counterpart. Interestingly enough, both sets of mothers played with their sons differently from how they played with their daughters.

Another study which explored cultural differences in play was that of Edwards (2000) who drew on Whiting's (1963) Six Cultures Study. According to Edwards, at the more visible level, culture shapes play because it influences whether or not adults support and encourage children's play, whether or not they design the environment in ways conducive to play and whether or not they supply the resources to facilitate children's engagement in various types of play. Hyun and Dong (2004) examination of 'gender doing and gender-bending' in children's play also highlights similar practices among South Korean parents. In their comparative study of American and South Korean children, the authors suggest that children from South Korea, unlike their North American counterpart, are 'uncomfortable' with play that require them to usurp perceived gender norms. This discomfort stems from the differences in dominant cultural norms in both countries. In South Korea, as with many other countries, including Jamaica, cultural norms dictate girl behaviours and boy behaviours. Activities which require children to usurp or dismiss these social boundaries are not readily accepted. These findings highlight that children learn very quickly the dominant social and cultural norms of their contexts and are mindful of them as they play (Hyun & Dong, 2004; Kinkead-Clark, 2016).

Another study which also compares South Korean and North American children highlights that little difference exists in their play. Farver, Kim, and Lee-Shin's (2000) study, specifically focussing on pretend play in Korean American and European American children, concludes that minimal difference can be seen in the play of the two groups of children from distinct cultural backgrounds. Several factors may account for this. For instance, these findings support Farver and Lee-Shin's (2000) study about the role of acculturation in guiding parents' practices about play. In extension, the authors outline that other behaviours supported by parents facilitate the minimal differences in children's behaviour.

Parents' beliefs shaping children's play: a multicultural perspective

The authenticity of children's play is affected by multiple factors. Parental beliefs are particularly important because parents, as their child's first teacher, serve as powerful influencers of what, where and how children play. Literature has documented much about parental beliefs about play and how these shape children's play. Interest in this aspect is also crucial because social mores, values and attitudes are primarily transmitted within homes and communities and it is within these environments that children learn how to respond to, and fit in with the prevailing cultures. The aforementioned studies of Hyun and Dong (2004) and Bornstein et al. (1999) serve as examples of how parents can influence how children play, the types of play they engage in and children's willingness or not to push dominant cultural and social norms in play. Gaskins, Haight, and Lancy (2007) refer to these as the three cultural variations on parents' acceptance of play and the value of it to children. These are 'Culturally curtailed play', 'Culturally accepted play' and 'Culturally cultivated play':

1. 'Culturally curtailed play' refers to the practice of discouraging children from playing. Within the Caribbean, especially in poorer communities, parents curtail children's play because they see little value in the activity.
2. 'Culturally cultivated play', as the name suggests, refers to cultures that support and encourage children's play. In such cultures, parents engage in play with their children because they are cognisant of the significant benefits of it. This typically occurs in wealthier and more educated families in the Caribbean. This is also typical in more developed countries such as North America and some European countries.
3. 'Culturally accepted play' refers to cultures where play is tolerated but not supported. In such cultures, parents do not recognize the value of play but accept children play for fun or to pass time. Parents in this context refrain from engaging in play with their children.

Carvalho et al. (2003), Göncü et al. (2000) and Gosso and Carvalhlo's (2013) studies all serve as examples of three cultural variations on parents' acceptance of play. For instance, Göncü et al.'s (2000) study concluded that American and Turkish parents think of themselves as play partners with their children and encouraged frequent moments where they played with their children. Parmar, Harkness, and Super's (2004) study also confirms this as it relates to European American parents. In their study of Asian and European American parents' beliefs about play and how this shapes children's behaviours at home and school, their findings suggest that Asian parents saw very little value of play in supporting their child's development and as such did not encourage their engagement in this activity. This has also been a similar practice within most Caribbean communities.

Findings from Roopnarine and Jin (2012), Leo-Rhynie (1997), Grantham-McGregor, Landman, and Desai (1983), Barrow and Ince (2008) and Kinkead-Clark (2016) outline that within the English-speaking Caribbean, there is great reluctance to accept play as a valuable activity which supports children's development: intellectually, cognitively, socially and physically. This is particularly the case for families from lower income communities.

Similar to Asian families, as highlighted by Parmar et al.'s (2004) study, Caribbean parents predominantly encourage their children to develop robust academic skills rather than play. According to Roopnarine and Jin (2012), this is because parents see moments of play as time which could otherwise have been used for meaningful, intellectually stimulating activities. As Barrow and Ince (2008) and Roopnarine and Jin (2012) explain, in Caribbean communities, play is considered to be wasteful, unproductive and a 'distraction and a potential problem ... making children and their homes dirty and untidy' (Barrow & Ince, 2008, p. 14).

Further to this, as is the case in many other cultures, data suggest that there is a strong correlation between parents' socio-economic and educational backgrounds and their perspectives about play. According to Roopnarine and Davidson (2015), Tamis-Lemonda, Baumwell, and Cristofaro (2012) and Veitch et al. (2006), parents from homes with less capital are less likely to engage in play with their children. Undoubtedly factors such as high levels of stress, other home and parenting responsibilities and job obligations among other factors account for this.

Methodology

Data collection

To gather the data for this qualitative study, we engaged in four cross-cultural conversations (one face to face and three via Skype) about our individual ethnographic studies on play. The nature of our conversations necessitated the need for both of us to thoroughly examine our role, beliefs and practices as researchers. By doing this, it allowed us to have rich discussions about how we viewed play and the factors which shaped our understanding of children's play.

Our conversations were guided by our two research questions:

1. How do we conceptualize children's play?
2. What shapes our understanding of play?

The unique nature of our study and time constraints warranted the need for us to be creative in how we collected our data. We decided to use the App, Google Docs, to document our data because it facilitated our audio recording of our conversations and allowed us to simultaneously make jottings of salient points which we individually thought were significant to our study and which illuminated critical issues surrounding our perception and understanding of play.

Upon completion of each of our conversations, summaries were also written to provide a detailed overview of what took place in our discussion and provide an overview of what different parts of our conversations were about.

As stated before, each conversation sessions lasted for approximately 30 minutes. During these sessions we discussed several issues germane to our understanding of how we perceive play, factors shaping play within our research contexts and how these influenced us. In order to achieve this, we drew on; our previous research, our research methodology, how we accessed our data, how we analysed our data, the contexts of our research and how our positionalities (both life experiences and the contexts in which we were situated) influenced our conceptualization and understanding of play.

Data analysis

Because of time constraints and the need to ensure the reliability of the coding, coding was done throughout the period of data collection. After each conversation, we briefly discussed the codes which were starkly apparent. Focus throughout these coding sessions revolved around similarities and differences in terms and jargons used.

To analyse the data for this study, inductive qualitative content analysis was used. This multi-tiered coding method as defined by Downe-Wamboldt (1992) is 'to provide knowledge and understanding of the phenomenon under study' (p. 314). The initial stage of our data analysis was what Elo and Kyngäs (2008) refer to as the preparation stage. In this stage, our transcribed interview and notes/ jotting taken during our conversations were scanned to highlight information which was starkly 'interesting, important or relevant' to the study. In this context, note was specifically made of examples shared by each of us, quotes which richly captured the focus of our study and information which added great substance to our research. This step was especially important because it allowed us to sift through the data and gain some sense of what it was 'saying to us'. For example, Charlotte's comment ' ... you [*Zoyah*] *have to look at (literature on play) from a best fits approach. For me* [*Charlotte*] *it's familiar*'. A comment such as this connoted a great deal about our perception of the nature of research on children's play. During the coding process, it was both coded as perceptions of play and reflections of cultural identity in play.

The next step of the coding process was open coding. Somewhat similar to our initial step, the data were more thoroughly examined to determine broad categories, heading and descriptions to indicate the nature and importance of the information presented. These broad terms and categories were then transcribed to our code book where we sought to condense the number of headings and categories. To do this, terms similar in meaning, phrases and comments which indicated our perceptions and feelings about play were then placed in similar groups. The process of condensing the data into more succinct categories was particularly lengthy. In this context, it was done in three stages because continuous examination of the data revealed further similarities in the meanings and concepts which lent itself to further condensing.

The final step of the coding process, abstraction, illuminated the broad themes or topics of our conversations. Packer (2011) defines abstraction as the process '... of dividing a whole into elements that are distinct from one another and from their original context' (p. 59). In the context of this study, abstraction gave us the opportunity to highlight the dominant issues at the nexus of the study. In this sense, this stage allowed us to answer the following questions, at the end of our conversations:

1. What conclusions did we arrive at?
2. What was/were really the focus of our discussion?

To answer these questions we assessed the issues that were central to our discussions. Some of these issues include the nature and context of children's play in our individual research, our ability to relate to previous studies on children's play, parents' perceptions of play and how this influenced children's play. Abstraction of the data revealed four dominant themes emerged as being at the nexus of our conversations.

Findings

Our conversations revealed several underlying factors which influenced our understandings of play and how we conceptualized play. Four dominant themes emerged from our conversations:

1. Changing lives, changing perspectives
2. Dominant positions
3. The gap; play interrupted by policy, practice and cultural norms?
4. Complexity in its simplicity

Changing lives, changing perspectives

Throughout our conversations, a dominant construct we frequently referred to was how we approached our research. It was quite evident that our perspectives of our research about children's play evolved as we experienced significant change in our lives. These changes in our positionalities were significant because they transformed the lens through which we examined our research settings, how we understood our co-constructors (participants) behaviours and actions, and how we made meaning of their play. Changing lives came through a range of new experiences. Whether through increased experience as researchers, opportunities to conduct research in other countries, contexts and cultures dissimilar to ours, or even changes in our personal lives, all these shifts modified how we looked at and approached our research.

For instance, in one of our conversations we spoke of the changes in our approach to our research when we reflected on our lives as parents and aunts. These changes were great and had a significant impact on how we viewed our co-constructors. In one such case, Zoyah shared:

> ... when I became a parent my interpretation of children's play changed. Through new eyes I was able to truly understand or perhaps justify why children reacted to situations in the way they do. I was also able to look at my co-constructors and see similarities in my children's behaviours ... before I became a mother I never once thought of these things ...

Dominant positions

Though we understood prior to commencing our conversations that we came from different positions and had diverse experiences in our individual research studies, as we became more engaged in our discourse, we recognized that, while dissimilar, we also had much in common. In one sense, we recognized that we had a commonality as two female researchers exploring an issue which has been historically dominated by male researchers; however, we also recognized we were dissimilar in that we came from dominant and non-dominant research cultures and this significantly impacted on how we approached and understood the value of our research.

As female researchers, we recognized that our positionalities as mother and aunt undergirded our feminist approach to our research. As Zoyah explained, in one of our conversations, there was the recognition that her role of mother influenced how she understood the behaviours and actions of her co-constructors.

Through reflexive practice, as we sought to situate our research, and interrogate our identities and our understanding of our play, we recognized the significance of our gender and the impact it had on how she approached her research. For instances in Zoyah's case, as 'a female outsider, invading the protected spaces' of her co-constructors commonsense had to be used. It is well known that Jamaica's inner-city communities can be some of the most dangerous spaces for women. As Zoyah explained,

> ... as a woman, I had to take into consideration my safety. I had to look at the physical risk I was putting myself in ... in some instances, I entered spaces that I knew I had to leave before the sun went down ... commonsense had to be used ... not because of the risks from my co-constructors but because of the communities in which they lived. There were a couple occasions when I had to ask my husband to be my chauffer and if needed my body guard ... In some way, this served as a lesson for the struggles of my co-constructors ... of the risks they faced as they played. In some sense my experienced helped me as a researcher. Frequently conducting research in some of Jamaica's most volatile inner-city communities served as a reminder of what my co-constructors' lives are like on a daily basis.

Another issue that emerged throughout our discussions was our frequent reference to the different contexts and cultures from which we came and how these broadly influenced our research, the issues we explored and the lens through which we viewed our co-constructors. We understood that we were representatives of dominant (Charlotte) and non-dominant (Zoyah) research voices. Dominant in the sense that much of the research about children's play comes from a European perspective and non-dominant in the sense that very little research about play has emerged from a Jamaican perspective.

This occurrence had implications for how we approached our research. For one of us (Charlotte, from the UK) the research is relatable. In our conversation about extant research on play, Charlotte shared: 'literature about play is very familiar to me ... I can relate to it more ... it makes sense'. In direct contradiction to this, Zoyah (from Jamaica) shared:

> I come from a context where there really is a dearth of literature germane to the Jamaican context ... most times literature is unreflective and in some instances irrelevant to my context. When I read about children's play and issues about play being at risk ... I can't relate to it ... Jamaican children still play. In authentic settings at home and in their communities, they play with sticks, they play in the streets ... my experience is very different from what [dominant) research alludes to.

The gap; play interrupted by policy, practice and cultural norms?

An interesting finding that was evident through our discussions was the gap that existed between policy and practice/rhetoric and reality in our individual contexts. We addressed how play, especially at school, the home and in the wider community, had become influenced by 'political correctness' and notions of good play, appropriate play, constructive play and safe play. As explained by Charlotte, in the UK, ' ... adults feel the need to dictate what children's play should look like'.

We discussed how adult ideas of what children's play should look like have begun to affect the authenticity of this natural childhood activity. We discussed how play is viewed from a Jamaican perspective and focussed on how prevailing cultural notions of play as being unconstructive, 'romping' contradicted the dominant British perspective of play as a valuable activity all children were encouraged to participate in. As Charlotte explained,

> We [The Government] have done a good job of selling to parents (in England) the value of play. They understand its importance, however, it is frequently the case where adults; teachers and parents, feel the need to dictate what children's play should look like.

From a Jamaican point of view, adult interruptions of play frequently hinge on gender appropriateness. Within the Jamaican context, there still remains rigid adherence to 'boy play' and 'girl play'. Boys are often reprimanded and forbidden from engaging in play experiences that replicate or closely resemble stereotypical girl behaviours. In such situations, boys may be punished, scolded or even have toys taken away. One such example of the gendered nature of children's play was evidenced in Zoyah's observation of children at play; she witnessed how boys refused to play a game called Chinese Skip, because they considered it a 'girl game' and more so because the elastic bands used to create the circular rope were pink and lavender coloured.

Girls also face similar condemnation. Historically, it was often the case where rough and tumble play was considered only for boys. It was frequently the case where boys were the ones who were allowed to play, while girls had to remain indoors and help with housekeeping chores. In many Jamaican families, it still exists where girls are forbidden from engaging in play which could result in their clothes getting dirty, their skin being bruised or, sadly, their skin would be tanned by playing in the sun.

In Jamaica, in direct contradiction to what predominantly is observed in the UK is that play is not necessarily seen as a valuable childhood pastime; for this reason, we see play as being interrupted by cultural and historical perceptions of rightness and appropriateness and acceptability.

Complexity in its simplicity

Our discussions revealed that as researchers, we had a common understanding of play and that we recognized quite clearly that, for children, it served as a means for expressing themselves, a means of participating in family and community events and, perhaps more importantly, a powerful tool for learning. Our conceptualization of play was grounded in our awareness that despite the differences in the types of play children engaged in, the spaces they played in or the tools and/or persons they played with, play was unique and not easily understood. In other words, we recognized that even in the simplicity of children's play, underlining meanings behind the play were far more complex. One example of this complexity could be seen in Zoyah's research of children's play in an inner-city community in Jamaica. Kevin, the child being observed, along with his friends, often played a game called police against gunman. The nature of the play was not only about imitating the policeman and a criminal, but it was also very clear that the children also shared their feelings about the characters. For Kevin, his bitterness towards the policeman came out in the words he used and in the expressions he showed.

As two researchers, who had conducted much research about children's play, our primary aims were to make meaning of the plurality of these play experiences. Our research affirmed to both of us that it was important to value the uniqueness of children's play, to recognize the authenticity of its value and the need for research to assess the underlying meanings of this 'natural childhood pastime'.

As two researchers, who had the opportunity to interrogate play, our conceptualization of play was dynamic. The more opportunities we had to observe children's play also brought about a shift in our conceptualization of what play meant and how play was used. For both of us, we understood and conceptualized play to be an activity that children engaged in both for enjoyment, but also as a means of taking part and sharing in home, family and community experiences.

Discussion and implications

The primary aim of this study was to examine researcher perspectives on play in the lives of children from diverse cultural contexts. Through use of cross-cultural discourse, we were able to acquire some understanding of each other's approach, interpretation and conceptualization of play. As researchers, this discursive method draws attention to the need for concepts of play to be grounded, but not restricted by national contexts, social policies, school programmes and family practices.

Four themes: changing lives, changing perspectives, dominant positions, the gap; play interrupted by policy, practice and cultural norms? and complexity in its simplicity, were found to be central to our conversations. Our findings confirm those of other studies which highlight the influence of researcher positionalities on their interpretation and contextualization, and of their research (England, 1994; Merriam et al., 2001; Skelton, 2001). Our rich discourse about extant literature on play elicited substantive responses on researcher hegemony and how non-dominant communities, such as Jamaica, and dare we say many of the other developing countries, struggle with a 'best fits approach'. Tantamount to a Cinderella approach, in many instances researchers, from such non-dominant contexts, have to siphon through the research from more prolific and dominant voices on children's play to find literature that fits or closely resembles what relates to their context.

Our findings also highlight the risk factors of childrens play. Similar to the findings of multicultural studies from Farver et al. (2000), Parmar et al. (2004), Roopnarine and Jin (2012), Leo-Rhynie (1997), Hyun and Dong (2004), Grantham-McGregor et al. (1983), Barrow and Ince (2008) and Kinkead-Clark (2016), we were able to highlight how adult notions of what play should look like have interrupted the authentic nature of children's play. This, essentially puts children's play at risk. For instance, from a Jamaican standpoint, gender stereotyping (i.e. perceptions of boy play and girl play) has the potential to curtail children's creativity and stifle their curiosity. In line with this, as is the case in the UK, adult fears have begun to impact nature of children's play.

Undoubtedly, as both our societies become 'less safe' for children, there is growing need for adults to dictate when and how children ought to play. From Charlotte's British perceptive, fear of accidents, increased use of technology and other social dangers have significantly limited the time children play outside. Interestingly, this also obtains in Zoyah's context. In Jamaica however, there is also the additional issue of crime and violence which has weaselled its way into many of Jamaica's communities and has interrupted the spaces and time of when and where children play.

Our findings highlight that play is a multifaceted phenomenon. As researchers, an awareness of this dynamic nature of play and the factors influencing play have shaped how we conceptualize and understand play, and perhaps more importantly, make meaning of its impact in children's lives. Our understanding of play aligns well with the findings of Kibele (2006), Rogers (2010) and Slade and Wolf (1994) who outline that 'play is play is not "just" about imagination, but about the possibility or the defeat of intimacy' (p. v1). As was also affirmed by our discussions, play also serves as a connector for children. Through play, they are able to demonstrate and, in large and small ways, connect with home and community cultural activities.

Conclusion

This article highlights the findings of four grassroots conversations between two researchers who have conducted research about children's play. Our overarching aim was to highlight the gap between policy and practice/rhetoric and reality and to find ways to encourage children's authentic play while being true to our values as educators and researchers. As two researchers, who have conducted research about children's play, we sought to contextualize our understanding of play and to expand our notions of play beyond researcher positionalities and to embrace cross-cultural conversations.

Similar to England (1994) and Ortlipp (2008), our findings reaffirm the need for researchers to interrogate their own identities and to examine the 'baggage' they take with them into their research settings. As individual researchers, we had to consider how our gender, our cultural and national identities, and our life experiences shaped the lens through which we interpreted play. Though the findings of this study are not generalizable they provide fodder for other researchers to consider how they make meaning of their studies and to consider how concepts of play can be grounded, but not restricted by national contexts.

Disclosure statement

No potential conflict of interest was reported by the authors.

References

Barrow, C., & Ince, M. (2008). *Early childhood in the Caribbean* (Working papers in Early Childhood Development, No. 47). The Hague, The Netherlands: Bernard van Leer Foundation.

Bornstein, M., Haynes, O., Pascual, L., Painter, K., & Galperín, C. (1999). Play in two societies: Pervasiveness of process, specificity of structure. *Child Development, 70*(2), 317–331.

Carvalho, A. M. A., Magalhães, C. M. C., Pontes, F. A. R., & Bichara, I. D. (Eds.). (2003). *Brincadeira e cultura: Viajando pelo Brazil que brinca* [Play and culture: A travel through Brazil at play]. São Paulo, SP: Casa do Psicólogo.

Choi, B. C., & Pak, A. W. (2007). Multidisciplinarity, interdisciplinarity, and transdisciplinarity in health research, services, education and policy: 2. Promotors, barriers, and strategies of enhancement. *Clinical & Investigative Medicine, 30*(6), 224–232.

Downe-Wamboldt, B. (1992). Content analysis: Method, applications, and issues. *Health Care for Women International, 13*, 313–321.

Edwards, C. P. (2000). Children's play in cross-cultural perspective: A new look at the Six Cultures Study. *Cross-Cultural Research, 34*, 318–338.

Elo, S., & Kyngäs, H. (2008). The qualitative content analysis process. *Journal of Advanced Nursing, 62*(1), 107–115.

England, K. V. L. (1994). Getting personal: Reflexivity, positionality, and feminist research. *The Professional Geographer, 46* (1), 80–89.

Farver, J. A. M., Kim, Y. K., & Lee-Shin, Y. (2000). Within cultural differences examining individual differences in Korean American and European American preschoolers' social pretend play. *Journal of Cross-Cultural Psychology, 31*(5), 583–602.

Farver, J. A. M., & Lee-Shin, Y. (2000). Acculturation and Korean-American children's social and play behavior. *Social Development, 9*(3), 316–336.

Gaskins, S., Haight, W., & Lancy, D. F. (2007). The cultural construction of play. In A. Göncü & S. Gaskins (Eds.), *Play and development: Evolutionary, sociocultural and functional perspectives* (pp. 179–202). New York: Lawrence Erlbaum.

Göncü, A., Mistry, J., & Mosier, C. (2000). Cultural variations in the play of toddlers. *International Journal of Behavioral Development, 24*(3), 321–329.

Gosso, Y., & Carvalho, A. M. A. (2013). Play and cultural context. *Play, 21*. Retrieved from http://www.child-encyclopedia.com/sites/default/files/textes-experts/en/774/play-and-cultural-context.pdf

Grantham-McGregor, S., Landman, J., & Desai, P. (1983). Child rearing in poor urban Jamaica. *Child: Care, Health and Development, 9*, 57–71.

Hyun, E., & Dong, H. C. (2004). Examination of young children's gender-doing and gender-bending in their play dynamics: A cross-cultural exploration. *International Journal of Early Childhood, 36*(1), 49–64.

Kibele, A. (2006). *At play with meaning: Toys and other favorite objects in the everyday lives of young children.* (Unpublished doctoral dissertation). University of Southern California, Los Angeles.

Kinkead-Clark, Z. (2016). *'... pass the ball ... and score the goal man!' An ethnographic perspective of play in the lives of three children.* Manuscript submitted for publication.

Leo-Rhynie, E. (1997). Class, race, and gender issues in child rearing in the Caribbean. In J. L. Roopnarine & J. Brown (Eds.), *Caribbean families: Diversity among ethnic groups* (pp. 25–55). Greenwich, CT: Ablex.

Merriam, S. B., Johnson-Bailey, J., Lee, M. Y., Kee, Y., Ntseane, G., & Muhamad, M. (2001). Power and positionality: Negotiating insider/outsider status within and across cultures. *International Journal of Lifelong Education, 20*(5), 405–416.

Ortlipp, M. (2008). Keeping and using reflective journals in the qualitative research process. *The Qualitative Report, 13*(4), 695–705.

Packer, M. J. (2011). *The science of qualitative research.* New York, NY: Cambridge University Press.

Parmar, P., Harkness, S., & Super, C. M. (2004). Asian and Euro-American parents' ethnotheories of play and learning: Effects on preschool children's home routines and school behaviour. *International Journal of Behavioral Development, 28*(2), 97–104.

Parten, M. B. (1933). Social play among preschool children. *The Journal of Abnormal and Social Psychology, 28*(2), 136–147.

Rogers, S. (2010). Play and pedagogy: A conflict of interests? In S. Rogers (Ed.), *Rethinking play and pedagogy: Concepts, contexts and cultures* (pp. 5–18). London: Routledge.

Roopnarine, J. L., & Davidson, K. L. (2015). Parent-child play across cultures: Advancing play research. *American Journal of Play* 7(2), 228–252. Retrieved from http://www.journalofplay.org/issues/7/2/article/4-parent-child-play-across-cultures-advancing-play-research

Roopnarine, J. L., & Jin, B. (2012). Indo Caribbean immigrant beliefs about play and its impact on early academic performance. *American Journal of Play, 4*(4), 441–463.

Rubin, K. H. (1977). Play behaviors of young children. *Young children, 32*(6), 16–24.

Skelton, T. (2001). Cross-cultural research: Issues of power, positionality and 'race'. In M. Limb & C. Dwyer (Eds.), *Qualitative methodologies for geographers* (pp. 87–100). London: Arnold.

Slade, A., & Wolf, D. P. (1994). *Children at play: Clinical and developmental approaches to meaning and representation.* Oxford: Oxford University Press.

Tamis-Lemonda, C. S., Baumwell, L., & Cristofaro, T. (2012). Parent–child conversations during play. *First Language, 32,* 413–438.

Veitch, J., Bagley, S., Ball, K., & Salmon, J. (2006). Where do children usually play? A qualitative study of parents' perceptions of influences on children's active free-play. *Health & Place, 12*(4), 383–393.

Watt, D. (2007). On becoming a qualitative researcher: The value of reflexivity. *The Qualitative Report, 12*(1), 82–101.

Whiting, B. B. (1963). Six cultures: Studies of child rearing. New York: John Wiley and Sons.

Index

9780367583798